HISTORICAL FOUNDATIONS OF THE COMMON LAW

SECOND EDITION

S. F. C. MILSON

This book has been printed digitally and produced in a standard specification in order to ensure its continuing availability

OXFORD
UNIVERSITY PRESS

Great Clarendon Street, Oxford OX2 6DP

Oxford University Press is a department of the University of Oxford.
It furthers the University's objective of excellence in research, scholarship,
and education by publishing worldwide in

Oxford New York

Auckland Cape Town Dar es Salaam Hong Kong Karachi
Kuala Lumpur Madrid Melbourne Mexico City Nairobi
New Delhi Shanghai Taipei Toronto
With offices in
Argentina Austria Brazil Chile Czech Republic France Greece
Guatemala Hungary Italy Japan South Korea Poland Portugal
Singapore Switzerland Thailand Turkey Ukraine Vietnam

Oxford is a registered trade mark of Oxford University Press
in the UK and in certain other countries

Published in the United States
by Oxford University Press Inc., New York

Reprinted 2009

ISBN 978-0-406-62503-8

Preface to the Second Edition

I hesitated when the publishers suggested a second edition of this book. The first edition had often been found difficult for the purpose which they had in mind, a short account of what seemed important about the growth of the common law. And if it had served its other purpose of suggesting a framework for the subject different from the established framework, then for better or worse its work was done.

But one's mind moves on; and though the force of freshness would be lost, it seemed worth attempting a description of the view as it appears ten years later. Much of that time has been spent on the early land law; and the discipline of standing back to retrace the outline of a detailed study has predictably taken me a little beyond the study itself. The parts of this book which deal with the early land law have in consequence been rewritten; and so, since there are implications for the nature of early law itself, has the introduction.

Other rewriting has been to accommodate changes of mind or substance, or in the hope of greater clarity. A single decision may have caused difficulty at various points in the first edition. The outline being propounded was altogether different from that assumed in all the literature; and it seemed to me that signalling of individual differences would only get in the way. It would obtrude upon one line of thought the premises of another. But, as I should have foreseen, serious readers then met the difficulty without warning, when they tried to reconcile this with the ubiquitous classical account. On many matters it cannot be done, in the sense that you cannot identify detailed questions which require different answers to fit into this account or that. As a childish analogy which remains at the end of the introduction tried to suggest, it is not the details that change: it is the way you put them together. In this edition I have pointed out the largest differences, but only by way of warning. One cannot follow two interpretations at once.

How can the same evidence be interpreted so differently, and is there a common factor in the differences? It is in the nature of law that what is done in the present must be congruous with the immediate past; and it is therefore in the nature of legal history that the evidence is systematically deceptive. The largest changes cannot be obvious to historians because they could not be obvious at the time. In the thirteenth century, for example, the changes most obvious on the surface of the law are legislative provisions dealing with scattered and seemingly unrelated points of irritation. These were small symptoms of a structural change too large to be knowingly borne, but too piecemeal to be seen; and in the legal records it is hidden behind the changed meaning of some words, the changed operation of some rules. What has really changed is not so much 'the law' as the context; and it is the earlier context that may be lost to historians, overlaid by the later. Perhaps more than in any other kind of history, the historian of law is enticed into carrying concepts and even social frameworks back into periods to which they do not belong.

One of the main things that we have carried back is our vision of the law as a system of substantive rules having some existence separate from society and requiring separate adjustment. The legal historian scans his sources looking for change as he would look for new or altered passages in a modern legal textbook, and the social historian is consequentially misled. In this misapprehension an accident played its part. The classical account has largely been built upon the foundations laid by Maitland in the incomparable *History of English Law* known as 'Pollock and Maitland' which ends with the accession of Edward I. Maitland came to it fresh from his first big task in legal history, his edition of *Bracton's Note Book*. For that he had immersed himself in the treatise known by Bracton's name, which displays familiarity with substantive rules and abstract concepts. Who could suspect that this intangible sophistication had got into the thirteenth-century source, like some of its tangible detail, from Roman learning and not because it was already characteristic of the English law of the time?

Near the end of his life Maitland turned to editing year books of the early fourteenth century. These unadulterated native discussions begin decades after *Bracton* in time, but are centuries earlier in spirit. 'A stage in the history of jurisprudence is here pictured for us, photographed for us, in minute detail. The parallel stage in the history of Roman law is represented, and can only be represented, by ingenious guesswork: acute and cautious it may be, but it is guesswork still.' Perhaps these words from Maitland's first year book introduction show a sudden sense that the common law began from something more primitive than he had supposed. But his first picture had taken its compelling hold; and its assumption of continuity was given substance by another accident. In a course of seven undergraduate lectures he had thrown a bridge between the law as he saw it in 'Pollock and Maitland' and the law as it was still remembered when he himself went to the bar. After his death, though he would have disapproved of the authority thereby lent to them, those lectures were published as *The Forms of Action at Common Law*. The classical account has been erected partly upon his thirteenth-century foundation and partly upon that single span across the centuries. Only lately has work begun on intermediate piers, and it will have to be a different bridge.

This book was an enterprise of the same nature, undertaken in the hope that a new framework would help to provide a new start. The theme which may be of most interest to lawyers is precisely the changing nature of the law itself; and perhaps I should explicitly refer, as possible sources of bias, to those differences in background of which I am conscious. This account grew from early work not on Bracton but on the kind of formulary which lies behind the year books, our earliest representation of a law-suit. And the kind of law which it sees as the starting-point is more accessible to the imagination now than it would have been when Maitland wrote. The legal realists for example have told us something about the relationship between rules and decisions. The complexity of our own society is turning law into something like a code of management, with procedural rather than substantive protection for the individual. And developments in public law are reducing abstract rights of property to visible dependence upon authority. But these last changes are still too large to be integrated into our books on property law, in parts of which the reader can sometimes wonder what century he is in. It illustrates another theme, this time for historians, the tricky nature of legal sources as evidence for social and economic facts. But for many medieval facts the legal sources form the largest body of surviving evidence; and in this edition I have tried to show what kinds of trick they play.

S.F.C.M

St. John's College, Cambridge
May, 1980

Table of Contents

Page

PREFACE TO THE SECOND EDITION v

INTRODUCTION: A GENERAL VIEW 1

I *Institutional Background*

1 THE CENTRALISATION OF JUSTICE 11

- Local and customary laws 11
- County courts 13
- Hundred and franchise courts 15
- Records of local courts 17
- Feudal jurisdictions 18
- Jurisdiction of the church 23
- The pattern of centralisation 25
- The eyre system 27
- Rise of the central courts 31
- The writ system 33

2 THE INSTITUTIONS OF THE COMMON LAW IN ITS FIRST FORMATIVE PERIOD 37

- Writs and their learning 37
- Ancient pattern of law-suit 38
- Counting 39
- Pleading 42
- The year books 44
- The trial 48
- Other business done on circuit 50
- The king's bench 52
- Jurisdiction in error 55
- The limit of early development 58

Page

3 THE INSTITUTIONS OF THE COMMON LAW IN ITS SECOND FORMATIVE PERIOD .. 60

The nature of the change .. 60
Fictions concerning jurisdiction .. 61
The increase of business .. 65
Replacement of old actions by new .. 67
Changing pattern of law-suit .. 70
The rise of written pleadings .. 70
Demurrer .. 72
Discussion after trial of facts alleged in the pleadings .. 73
Discussion of facts coming out at the trial .. 75
Substantive result of procedural changes .. 79

4 THE RISE OF EQUITY .. 82

Procedural bearings of early equity .. 82
Equity and uses .. 86
Theoretical relationship between law and equity .. 88
Conflict between law and equity .. 91
The regularisation of equity .. 93

II *Property in Land*

5 TENURES .. 99

Lordship and ownership .. 99
Tenure and ownership .. 100
Agricultural tenures .. 101
Military tenures .. 102
The living tenant: freehold and services .. 103
The dying tenant: fee and inheritance .. 105
The incidents of tenure .. 107
Alienability .. 110
Mortmain .. 113
Quia Emptores .. 113
Consequences of *Quia Emptores* and of the incidents 116

6 EARLY ACTIONS .. 119

Seisin and right .. 119
Nature of the early actions .. 122
The writ of right .. 124
The assize of mort d'ancestor .. 134

	Page
The assize of novel disseisin	137
Writs of entry	143
The nature of the change	149
7 LATER ACTIONS	152
Protection of the term of years	152
Novel disseisin and the trial of title	157
Use of ejectment by freeholders	161
Copyhold	163
8 SETTLEMENT OF LAND AT LAW	166
Estates in land	166
Dower and curtesy	167
Family gifts	169
Maritagium	171
Beginnings of the entail	172
De Donis Conditionalibus	175
Later history of entails	178
Entails and warranties	178
Fines and recoveries	181
Contemporary attitudes to entails and their barring	188
Settlement and resettlement	190
Remainders	192
Contingent remainders	194
9 USES AND TRUSTS OF LAND	200
The problem of origins	200
Situations in which one held land for another	202
Grant and regrant	205
Relationship with devise	206
The feudal incidents	208
Uses as an institution	211
The mischiefs of uses	216
The Statute of Uses	218
The Statute of Wills	221
Uses at law	222
Uses and conveyancing	223
Legal executory interests	225
Perpetuities	229
Rise of the trust	233

III *Obligations*

Page

10 OLD PERSONAL ACTIONS 243

Covenant 246
Debt on an obligation 250
Covenant and conditional bonds 251
Debt on a contract 253
The basis of obligation in debt 257
Debt and detinue 262
Detinue for goods bought 265
Detinue on a bailment 266
Detinue not based upon transactions 269
Account 275

11 THE RISE OF TRESPASS AND CASE 283

The early treatment of wrongs 285
Jurisdiction over trespass 286
Liability in trespass *vi et armis* 295
Actions on the case 300
The relationship between trespass and case 305

12 GROWTH OF THE MODERN LAW OF CONTRACT 314

Assumpsit for misfeasance 316
Actions on warranties 320
Assumpsit for nonfeasance 322
The early nonfeasance cases 323
Disablement and deceit 328
Pure nonfeasance 332
Assumpsit for money: the background 339
Assumpsit for money: the kinds of claim 346
Consequences of *Slade's Case* 353
Consideration 356

13 RISE OF MODERN LAW OF TORTS 361

Deceit 361
Conversion 366
Defamation 379
Negligence 392

IV *Crime*

Page

14 CRIMINAL ADMINISTRATION AND LAW 403

Pleas of the crown: felony and misdemeanour 403
Accusation and proof 406
Trial by jury 410
Organisation of criminal courts 413
Vehicles of change in criminal law 417
Substantive development of criminal law 421

TABLES OF CASES 429

Cases from court records 429
Year book cases 432
Cases from reports 438

TABLE OF STATUTES AND DOCUMENTS 443

INDEX 449

IV *Crime*

Page

14 CRIMINAL ADMINISTRATION AND LAW 403

Pleas of the crown: felony and misdemeanour 403
Accusation and proof 406
Trial by jury 410
Organisation of criminal courts 413
Vehicles of change in criminal law 417
Substantive development of criminal law 421

TABLES OF CASES 429

Cases from court records 429
Year book cases 432
Cases from reports 438

TABLE OF STATUTES AND DOCUMENTS 443

INDEX 449

Introduction: A General View

I

It has happened twice only that the customs of European peoples were worked up into intellectual systems of law; and much of the world today is governed by laws derived from the one or the other. The two developments may have passed through similar stages, but separated in time by something like a millennium and a half; and the early stages of the Roman development were earlier than surviving evidence. The English development lies almost entirely within the reach of records; and though large questions are unfashionable and large answers suspect, it would be mean to describe it without recognising that large questions arise. Why these two societies and no others? How does it happen? A series of accidents, of course, not really a human achievement: but still something was created.

II

The starting-point is in customs, not the customs of individuals but the customs of courts governing communities. Those courts, in England essentially community meetings, had to make all kinds of decision. What shall we do now? What do we usually do? Factually the human and sometimes supernatural pressures to do the same thing again may be strong. But if the body is sovereign in the matter and its decisions final, legal analysis can get no more out of this kind of customary law than those two questions. What matters is the present decision, the choice made now. That is guided or not by the past, but cannot be 'wrong' because of it. It is the past that must give way, and then the present will have refined or modified the custom. Explicit 'legislation' may indeed be embodied in a particular decision; and early records show this sometimes happening at all levels in England, even the king's courts being first seen as applying customs of the community of the realm.

Two kinds of decision were important for the legal future, those concerning the allocation of resources and those concerning the settlement of disputes. In any society the facts of land use and the needs of family provision make for complicated arrangements over resources; and in England the feudal structure of the economy was to complicate matters further. But to begin with 'legal' questions were simple, because cast in the present tense equally appropriate to management. This tenant is dead; tenements vacant by death customarily go to the dead tenant's eldest son; this eldest son is feeble-minded, so shall we let his brother have it? What we did last time is just a factor in our decision: we do not have to do the same thing again; nor, if we decide not to do the same thing again, do we thereby reopen last time's decision. And, looking to the future of this tenement, we do not contemplate that the present decision will be in any way relevant when our present beneficiary in turn dies. He has become the tenant to whose eldest son we shall by custom look; and it will not then occur to us to consider the son of the present loser. Of course we may project arrangements for the future. We might, for example, resolve our present difficulty with a compromise, arranging now that the younger son should have the tenement for his life, but that after his death it should go to the son of the incapable elder son. That would be a declaration of intention; and when the younger son came to die, the son of the incapable elder son would get the tenement only because we should carry out our intention and give it to him. There is just the present decision, just the water flowing under the bridge.

It is easy to see how such customs can become more 'binding'. They must be formed by economic needs: when people generally die young, eldest sons are most likely to be fit to take over. But equally it is the economic need that makes for flexibility: the feeble-minded eldest son will never be fit. If the managerial requirement recedes, the custom is more likely to be seen as a somehow binding rule. In England this may have happened as the superior tenures ceased to be seen as having much to do with the provision of fighting men, so that except at the lowest levels the feudal structure lost touch with the economic reality that had once shaped it. But more is needed before abstract rights of property could come into being. So long as the allocations made by authority cannot be questioned, the customs can only be criteria for a present decision. However confident he can be, the eldest son can have no property right until he is given the property. And however certain it is that today's arrangement will be carried out, it cannot make a gift tomorrow. The agreement that the land should go to one person for his life, then to another, cannot give anything to the second person: like the eldest son, he can just be confident that he will be given it.

It is a simple starting-point; but the English law did not move from it by a process of evolution. A structural change had magical effects. Largely meaning only to enforce regularisation of these customs, the king's court brought to an end the feudal jurisdictions which had applied them, and had to apply the customs itself. But the change of habitat changed their nature. The king's court looking from outside the unit could not think in terms of management, only of rules and some abstract right. And what is more, since its first interference had been on the basis that the management might have done wrong, the rules had to reach back into the past. It is not only that the eldest son must now never be passed over, however incapable. It is that a choice made generations ago may be tested against the inflexible rule, and undone as wrong; and it follows that the person then passed over must have had a sort of ownership which has been transmitted in some abstract world to the present heir of that line. Similarly the arrangement made for the future can no longer be just a matter of intention which in due course will be carried out: there will be no management to carry it out, and it must somehow work now by conferring a property right to take future effect. Even more obviously managerial arrangements like the allocation of pasture were astonishingly absorbed as abstract rights of property. And the entire change was in a sense invisible. The canons of inheritance, for example, could be stated in the same words after as before. It is just that they did quite different things.

The change of jurisdiction therefore produced instant law, a system of substantive rules and abstract concepts. For the concepts, perhaps partly because Latin words were used, Roman analogies were seen; and this has confused historians, and may have affected the law itself. As for the substantive statement, it is worth observing that Littleton could write his *Tenures*, which can properly be regarded as a text-book of land law, nearly four centuries before text-books were written on other branches of the law. It is not meaningful to wonder what 'natural' evolution might have done: but Littleton's title reminds us of the nature of the arrangements which that jurisdictional happening fixed in conceptualisation. The bizarre qualities of the law of future interests in particular stem from an initial confusion between the proprietary rights of an owner and the governmental powers of a lord.

These events pose a difficulty in arrangement which this book does not tidily meet. The institutional and the substantive changes are so intimately connected that it seemed better to discuss them together in the second section on Property in Land. Feudal courts are no more than mentioned in the first section on Institutional Background, which, as a matter of comprehension, is therefore largely introductory to the third section on Obligations. To transpose the section on Land seemed historically too perverse; but it is almost self-contained, and the reader interested mainly in the intellectual development may prefer to transpose it for himself.

III

The other early customs important for the future were those governing the settlement of disputes; and with these the sequence of events followed a pattern perhaps less peculiar to England. In any community there would be a canon of acceptable claims, which might come to be written down in a formulary. And that canon comprised what substantive law there was about transactions and wrongs. You must not beat your neighbour, must pay your debts and so on, because there are claims for these things. But there is nothing beyond the claims except customs about procedure and, most important, about proof. Proof was not a matter of establishing the facts so that rules could be applied. The claim is made and denied in equally formal terms, and the unanalysed dispute is put to supernatural decision by ordeal or the like. A blank result settles the dispute but can make no law. What if the beating was accidental or the debt forgiven? The questions cannot be asked as legal questions until the supernatural is replaced by a rational deciding mechanism.

We may never know whether the Roman *judex* first replaced some reference to the gods; but English records begin some twenty years before the prohibition of ordeals, and probably only some thirty years after the earliest regular use of jury procedures in any kind of dispute. To the extent that legal development is a matter of dealing with facts as they emerge in disputes, we can trace it from a beginning.

It was a long and untidy process. The jury was first used as a new ordeal, giving an equally blank result. Of course it reached that result by considering detailed facts. But the facts did not get onto the record, so that the historian can misinterpret as a crude dispute about the commission of an obvious wrong what was really a delicate dispute about the details of an undisputed event. The lawyers at the time generally knew at least what the dispute was about. But only slowly and deviously were they able to raise individual facts for discussion, and so make law of them. Even slower and more devious was the process by which law-suits were turned round, so that all the facts of a dispute came out before their legal effect was decided. Not until that happened, not until a court was sat down to a problem like an examination candidate today, did we have a substantive system of law. Text-books of contract and tort were not written until the nineteenth century; and nothing in the subject is so hard to reckon with as the implications of that fact.

These procedural developments are the main concern of the first section of this book on Institutions. Even the rise of the chancellor's equitable jurisdiction is a part of the process, a result of the transfer of decisions from God to man. Otherwise these developments, unlike the development of the land law, were in principle independent of jurisdictional changes, which are therefore discussed only so far as they are relevant to what may be called the intellectual development. Centralisation played an obvious part in bringing professional men together to talk shop, the English counterpart of Roman juristic thought, and a less obvious part in creating new complications over proof. Large changes came about because it was not practicable to bring local people to Westminster. And the accident which produced not one central court but three had some influence not so much on the growth of the law to maturity as on the ways in which it changed.

IV

The more explicitly law is stated, the less readily can it respond to changing circumstances; and the mechanisms of change are another theme of this book. The largest changes have never been deliberate. Even when large consequences follow from a legislative act, one can be sure that they were not intended. The legislator addresses a problem small enough to be identified: what may happen is that the current of events catches on his remedy and produces a larger diversion. The current may catch on anything. Its force is that of clients coming to lawyers with what seems to common sense like a case, although the law is against them. All the lawyer can do for one hit by a rule is to look for a way round it, make a distinction, bring some new idea to bear. If he succeeds, the rule is formally unimpaired. If the route that the special facts of his client's case enabled him to take can be used by others, the result may be reversed, but the rule remains. Even when it is abolished or forgotten, its shape will be seen in the twisting route by which it was circumvented. And the ideas he has imported will prove their own strength. The first resort to them may have been artificial; but their natural properties will assert themselves, and consequences may follow as far-reaching as the ecological disturbances produced by alien animals or plants.

The life of the common law has been in the abuse of its elementary ideas. If the rules of property give what now seems an unjust answer, try obligation; and equity has proved that from the materials of obligation you can counterfeit the phenomena of property. If the rules of contract give what now seems an unjust answer, try tort. Your counterfeit will look odd to one brought up on categories of Roman origin; but it will work. If the rules of one tort, say deceit, give what now seems an unjust answer, try another, try negligence. And so the legal world goes round.

But it goes round slowly, too slowly for the changes to be seen. Only when rapid adjustment is essential, as in the sixteenth century, does the artifice become so obvious that one thinks in terms of tricks. In the twentieth century, with varying success, we use legislation; and our familiarity with deliberate change makes it easy for us to misread history. How could our ancestors be so perverse in doing deviously what could be done directly? How could they descend to tricks to reach desirable results? Certainly if we view the common law on the eve of reform as a piece of social engineering, we see the spirit of Heath Robinson at his most extravagant. But the viewpoint is anachronistic and the question unreal. It is a real question why nobody before Bentham was provoked, and a part of the answer is that nobody before Blackstone described the system as a whole. Lawyers have always been preoccupied with today's details, and have worked with their eyes down. The historian, if he is lucky, can see why a rule came into existence, what change left it working injustice, how it came to be evaded, how the evasion produced a new rule, and sometimes how that new rule in its turn came to be overtaken by change. But he misunderstands it all if he endows the lawyers who took part with vision on any comparable scale, or attributes to them any intention beyond getting today's client out of his difficulty.

V

If change is largely brought about by re-classification, by transferring a matter from, say, contract to tort, it follows that the legal historian can avoid anachronism only by writing about a short period at a time. In the hope of giving a single picture of the growth of the common law, however flawed, this book commits the fundamental anachronism of a single classification to cover its whole life: Property; Obligations; and Crime. In a general way this can be applied to any developed system and in detail it has never been applicable in England, so the pervasive anachronism is at least obvious. But the reader must remember that these labels are a modern expository device, which tell him nothing about what was in the minds of the lawyers he is thinking about. If there was a 'true' starting-point it was probably a simple division into rights and wrongs. Our concept of crime separated from tort for procedural reasons; and for that reason the criminal law and its institutions will be discussed together. Our concept of property appears to have grown from factual possession, and the right to get possession may have been indistinguishable from what we should call an obligation: the lender of a chattel started from the same legal position as the lender of money; and the heir's right to his ancestor's land began as an obligation on the lord to admit him as tenant. 'We must not', wrote Maitland, 'be wise above what is written or more precise than the lawyers of the age.' We shall inevitably do these things: but something will be gained if we are conscious of the danger.

That the three divisions are of unequal size reflects the density of the learning generated in each field. Large though the Property section is, it still does not reflect how much of lawyers' lives was devoted to proprietary matters: it has here been kept down by the omission of whole topics, because there seemed no point in a degree of compression which would leave only unconnected assertions of fact. And small though the Crime section is, it still does not reflect how little lawyers thought about crime until modern times: since criminal trials with their blank Not guilty have never departed from the ancient pattern of litigation, there was little opportunity for legal thought until such things as the direction of a jury could formally be questioned.

VI

The attempt to give a single picture poses a problem more fundamental than that of arrangement. Legal history is not unlike that children's game in which you draw lines between numbered dots, and suddenly from the jumble a picture emerges: but our dots are not numbered. We have unrivalled sources from an early period, but they are business documents, made by and for men who knew the business. They give us detail with certainty and precision. They do not show us the framework into which the detail fitted, the assumptions upon which it rested. No major proposition in legal history is ever likely to be final, and any single picture must be a personal one.

I

INSTITUTIONAL BACKGROUND

1 *The Centralisation of Justice*

LOCAL AND CUSTOMARY LAWS

The common law is the by-product of an administrative triumph, the way in which the government of England came to be centralised and specialised during the centuries after the Conquest. Our starting-point will therefore be a sketch of the local and unspecialised institutions from which that process began, and of their own development we shall say nothing; but of course we thereby miss the beginnings. The Conqueror took over a going concern, one to which he claimed lawful title; and he expressly confirmed the laws of his predecessors. Those laws had first come with earlier conquerors, not rulers seeking control of an existing society, but peoples seeking land and livelihood, largely destroying what was there before, and bringing with them their own ways. Those ways, refined and modified by Christian influence, by administrative needs, and by accident, had become the laws by which Englishmen were governed when the Normans came.

They were, however, by no means the same all over England. Laws as well as institutions were local, and the differences between one district and another sometimes reflected not different answers to the same problem but different ways of life; and these in turn may sometimes go back to the piecemeal nature of those earlier conquests and settlements. As recently as 1925, for example, when the rule of intestate succession assigning land to the eldest son was abolished, itself long an anomaly, there was abolished with it an anomalous exception: in Kent the sons shared equally. But this began as something integral to the social arrangements of a people whose agrarian structure, whose whole civilisation indeed, differed from those obtaining in the central districts of England; and how much of all this they had brought with them from their first home we shall never know. To the north and east there were other ways again, the ways of more recent arrivals; and the Danelaw was to be a reality long after the conquest, and perhaps to be the source of important institutions in the common law[1]. But the common law, the acceptance for all England of a single rule on any matter, the suppression of contrary customs, leaving as something special those like the Kentish rule of inheritance deep-rooted enough to survive, all this lay in the future, the slow result of institutional centralisation.

The materials of the common law, therefore, were the customs of true communities whose geographical boundaries had in some cases divided peoples and cultures, and not just areas of governmental authority. But within each body of custom, what we think of as the law was not marked off from other aspects of society. Courts were the governing bodies of their communities, dealing with all their public business; and to us they would look more like public meetings than courts of law. But the way in which they performed their functions, even those which we should class as administrative, was largely judicial. The needs of society were diverse but unchanging, and they were for the most part supplied by customary obligations resting upon ordinary people. Thieves were caught because it was the duty of everybody to catch them. Bridges were mended, and stretches of highway kept clear, because each was the customary responsibility of a particular landowner or the inhabitants of a particular township. Such duties were enforced *ex post facto* by penalty; but we mean more than that when we say that most of government had a judicial aspect. It appeared largely as the application of pre-existing rules. There were few overt decisions to be made. Custom decided what should be done, and generally who should do it. And even when, as was often the case in the smaller local units, people had to be chosen for particular duties, to mind hedges, for example, or to check on brewers or bakers, still the duties themselves were fixed. Early law does not have to cater much for choice. In the private sphere we shall find this reflected in the small part played by contract, and the large part played by enduring relationships of a proprietary nature. In public affairs, to use

1. Kent: J. E. A. Jolliffe, *Pre-Feudal England: The Jutes* (1933). Danelaw: F. M. Stenton, *The Danes in England* (British Academy lecture, 1928). See generally, F. M. Stenton, *Anglo-Saxon England* (2nd edn., 1947).

modern terms, there was no separation of powers but a strict and general rule of law.

The kingdom, then, may be pictured as a two-tier structure. It was to courts of this kind that ordinary people looked up and the king looked down; and neither would often look beyond them. To the king what mattered was the effectiveness of his control; and the methods used made the common law. But the courts themselves may in a sense be classified according to the king's relationship with the men actually in charge. Were they merely agents, or were they seen as grantees having some proprietary right in the government of their territory?[1] Our modern terminology imposes a distinction to which many of the facts do not respond: government as well as property could be farmed out; and some kinds of property were not at first heritable, and some kinds of office became so. But it is central to English institutional history, and a necessary condition for the making of the common law, that the proprietary or feudal element in government took second place.

COUNTY COURTS

After the Conquest, as before it, the primary government of England was through counties and hundreds. The beginnings of the county courts raise questions our starting-point enables us to avoid. But if some were administrative creations, some look like the governing bodies of once independent kingdoms. And what mattered for the future was that their control, with partial exceptions in the great palatinates like Chester, remained in the hands of royal ministers. The earl's place may once have been that of under-king; but now he was at most entitled to a share of the profits of justice. Actual power was in the hands of one still called in Latin the earl's deputy, *vicecomes*; but in English the sheriff was understood as the king's reeve in the shire, and was accountable to the king. The county boundaries long remained important in our law, but it was as the limits of an agent's authority and not an owner's rights. The sheriff, though not always without difficulty, was kept in his place as a servant of the king; and that is what made

1. Of course an over-simplification: see H. M. Cam, 'The Evolution of the Medieval English Franchise' (1957) 32 Speculum, p. 427; reprinted in *Law-Finders and Law-Makers* (1962), p. 22.

possible his own decline and that of his court[1]. From presiding over what was, for all ordinary purposes, the most important kind of court in the land, he slowly became the executive addressee of commands from higher central bodies.

That the sheriff was always convener is almost the only general statement we can make about county courts, because the customs peculiar to each included the rules governing their own meetings. In the absence of communications, an invariable routine of times and places was essential. Even an unaccustomed adjournment could appear as a denial of justice; and, though some courts alternated by turns between one town and another, there was an outcry in Surrey when the appointed place was changed from the central Leatherhead to Guildford, which lies at one end of the county[2]. The period was generally monthly, in some counties every six weeks, and in this matter a rule was imposed: the Great Charter prohibited meetings more frequent than from month to month[3]. Attendance was evidently a burden. And although custom seems generally to have provided for a meeting of the great men of the county and representatives of the lesser, the great man would not often want to come, and if he held land in several counties he could not. He might make permanent provision by granting land to a tenant for the feudal service of performing the suit that he owed to the court, or he might each time send a representative, such as his steward. Stewards in particular, the businessmen of the countryside, to whose competence in affairs was added the weight of their masters' authority, seem often to have played a leading part: one writer likens them to bell-wethers of the flock[4]. And similar influence might no doubt be gained by any suitor with the personal qualities

1. County court: W. A. Morris, *The Early English County Court* (1926); G. T. Lapsley, 'The Court, Record and Roll of the County in the Thirteenth Century' (1935) 51 LQR, p. 299, and literature there cited. Sheriff: W. A. Morris, *The Medieval English Sheriff to 1300* (1927).
2. Regularity generally: W. A. Morris, *The Early English County Court* (1926), pp. 90 ff; H. M. Cam, *The Hundred and the Hundred Rolls* (1930), pp. 107 ff; G. O. Sayles, *Select Cases in the Court of King's Bench*, vol. III (Selden Society, vol. 58), p. xcv. Protests at the change in Surrey: H. G. Richardson and G. O. Sayles, *Select Cases of Procedure without Writ* (Selden Society, vol. 60), pp. 87, 90.
3. *Magna Carta* (1225), c. 35.
4. *Fleta*, II, 66 (ed. H. G. Richardson and G. O. Sayles (Selden Society, vol. 72), p. 225).

to master both the business and his fellows. In some counties, indeed, it seems that there was more to it than this, and that the suitors were of two classes, the ascendancy of a few being somehow institutionalised[1]. And it is even possible that these few were at one time held specially responsible to the king; but any such responsibility was probably not for judgment in the ancient internal affairs of the community, but for answering questions about royal rights, part of the rise of the jury and of the process by which the king came to govern people directly and not through the agency of local institutions. By the thirteenth century, when this process was already well advanced and when concomitantly our evidence is fuller, the responsibility for judgment clearly rested upon the court, the community as a whole.

HUNDRED AND FRANCHISE COURTS

The geographical sub-divisions of counties, most often known as hundreds and obscure in origin, also had their courts. The hundred court was of the same nature as the county: a meeting, generally at intervals of three weeks, of the more important persons holding land in the area or their representatives, and of representatives of the communities of lesser persons; and it was presided over by a bailiff. But unlike the sheriff, the hundred bailiff often served two masters. By royal grant, by usage and usurpation, or by the continuance of a state of affairs sometimes older than the counties and hundreds themselves, many hundreds – at the accession of Edward I it was more than half of all those in England – were in private hands[2]. The actual meaning of this in practice varied greatly. The lord of the hundred might be entitled merely to a share in the profits of justice, or he might exercise a substantial measure of control. But the bailiff, whether appointed by the sheriff in a royal hundred or by the lord

1. H. G. Richardson and G. O. Sayles, *The Governance of Medieval England* (1963), esp. at p. 182; G. T. Lapsley, 'Buzones' (1932) 47 English Historical Review, pp. 177, 545.
2. H. M. Cam, *The Hundred and the Hundred Rolls* (1930), pp. 137, 260 and map at end. On hundreds and franchises generally see also papers collected in *Liberties and Communities in Medieval England* (1944), and *Law-Finders and Law-Makers* (1962).

in a private one, was a royal officer and sworn in as such, in many respects the everyday embodiment of government for ordinary people.

Just as a hundred might be in private hands, and yet be part of the king's machinery of government, so all over England there were all kinds of liberties and franchises, in which some or all of the jurisdiction of counties and hundreds, or in later days of the jurisdiction which had in principle been withdrawn from them into central institutions, was exercised in courts of the feudal pattern. Here to a greater or lesser extent government was indeed in the hands of persons seen as the king's grantees rather than his agents. But many of these, at any rate, went back to a time when this distinction was by no means so clear as it is to us. If order was to be kept, the co-operation of the man with actual local power had to be enlisted. This could best be done by allowing him a financial interest; and if personal arrangements seem to have grown into heritable proprietary rights, the same thing happened with interests in land itself. To the institutional historian anxious to understand and evaluate the ways in which a medieval kingdom could be effectively governed, these franchises are important. But for those who want to understand the framework out of which the common law grew, what matters is that, numerous as they were, each was seen as something special and in some degree precarious. The right and duty to perform some governmental act might rest upon the officials of the liberty; but if they did not do it, the sheriff's men would.

In England, then, proprietary justice and feudal government were in general harnessed by the royal power rather than opposed to it, and we simplify social and political facts but do not distort the pattern of events if we think of law and order as fundamentally residing in the courts of counties and hundreds, and under the control of officials. It follows from what has already been said about the nature of these courts that to begin with they were in principle omnicompetent and had, in our language, jurisdiction over all kinds of legal dispute; and the making of the common law was largely a process of transfer to new central institutions. What happened in county and hundred courts is therefore of the first importance to us; and our means of knowledge are sadly inadequate.

RECORDS OF LOCAL COURTS

Accounts of law-suits may be written for various purposes. There is first the interest of the journalist or chronicler who will immortalise the exceptional. In the middle ages, when a large proportion of all writing was done in ecclesiastical houses, the interest of the chronicler might merge into that of the diarist, the litigant who wished for his own purposes to record suits in which his house had been involved[1]. Such unilateral accounts are our chief source of information about actual law-suits in the period before the Conquest and for a century and more after it; and what they tell us is mostly about great territorial disputes. The commonplace is recorded only when courts themselves come to keep records, minutes of their proceedings. But the earliest motive for doing this is financial, to ensure that the proper penalties are collected from the wrongdoer, from the unsuccessful litigant who claimed or denied unjustly, from the litigant or the man owing suit of court who did not come, and from all the others to whom the profits of justice were almost an inevitable tax. In the case of the county court, the state of the records reflects the two-tier structure of government. On the rolls of the king's exchequer, kept in the preservative air of officialdom, would be entered the mute totals for which the sheriff had accounted. Such records as were kept of county court proceedings were for his use and remained in his private keeping; and they have perished except for a few fragments from the fourteenth century, and one, probably untypical, from the thirteenth[2]. Some owners of private hundreds, especially religious houses, preserved the rolls of their courts, and of these a few do survive from the later thirteenth century[3]. And some accounts of

1. D. M. Stenton, *English Justice between the Norman Conquest and the Great Charter* (1964), ch. 1.
2. W. A. Morris, *The Early English County Court* (1926); T. F. T. Plucknett, 'New Light on the Old County Court' (1929) 42 Harvard Law Review, p. 639 and ibid. (1929) 43, p. 1111; G. H. Fowler, *Rolls from the Office of the Sheriff of Beds and Bucks, 1332–1334* (Bedfordshire Historical Record Society, Quarto Series, vol. III, 1929); H. Jenkinson, 'Plea Rolls of the Medieval County Court' (1923) 1 Cambridge Historical Journal, p. 103. Untypical rolls from Chester: R. Stewart-Brown, *Calendar of County Court, City Court and Eyre Rolls of Chester* (Chetham Society, NS vol. 84).
3. See e.g. B. Farr, *Rolls of Highworth Hundred, 1275–1287* (Wilts. Archaeological Society, vols. XXI and XXII).

the doings of all kinds of local courts, often in effect extracts from their records, are also preserved at second-hand in the rolls of the king's central courts, brought there by procedures which we should classify as supervisory or appellate; and they give irregular glimpses of regular institutions[1].

Literature produced by lawyers for their own purposes also fails us. A few precedent books survive, giving the formulae for making and denying various kinds of claim in local courts[2]. But it was centralisation that created a legal profession, and the king's central courts which left us a professional literature as well as systematic records. The description known by the name of *Glanvill* was written before 1190. The earliest records to survive are only a few years later. It is hard to remember that what we have is a spotlight trained on the special. What has sunk into the dark is the business of the principal instruments of government and judicature for a century and more after the Conquest. And for most ordinary men and many ordinary causes, the county court was the highest regular forum for long after that, and therefore a principal source of things that will strike us as novelties when we first see them transacted on the lighted stage of the royal courts.

FEUDAL JURISDICTIONS

For the sake of putting first things first, feudal jurisdiction has so far been spoken of only as modifying what may be described as the national system of government and judicature. Special or franchise jurisdictions have been mentioned, but not the regular jurisdiction incident to lordship; and this constitutes a large exception to the principle that the courts of county and hundred were at the beginning the primary bodies for all kinds of governmental business and all kinds of dispute. What chiefly matters about feudal jurisdiction in England, however, is precisely that its regular scope

1. Examples in *Bracton's Note Book* (ed. F. W. Maitland, 1887), and in the printed *Curia Regis Rolls*.
2. See F. W. Maitland, *The Court Baron* (Selden Society, vol. 4). Fictional discussion of common possibilities is sometimes included. When year book reporting had begun in central courts (pp. 44 ff, below), actual notes may occasionally have been made in county courts; R. C. Palmer, 'County Year Book Reports' (1976) 91 English Historical Review, p. 776.

was limited. This need not have been so. Feudalism was not a system, or even an ideal, having fixed properties. Such definite ideas as the word connotes are the creation of lawyers and historians seeking to systematise certain features which the facts of power might produce in medieval society. Of these facts, the most elementary is the coincidence that effective government was necessarily local, and wealth, since land was the only form of income-bearing capital, was territorial. Lordship and ownership, government and property, were not therefore clearly distinct as they seem to us; and whether we start at the bottom and think of the small man anxious to hold what he had in peace, or at the top and think of the king or great lord anxious to provide for his governmental and economic needs, there was a tendency toward the organisation of society by dependent tenures. From top to bottom one can imagine a series of bargains in which each superior allowed a measure of immediate control to his inferior, whose holding he undertook to protect in return for a tribute in food or money or services or fighting men. At the top fighting men were commonly demanded. At the bottom agrarian facts tended to produce their own uniformity. The plough drawn by more oxen than most peasants could own, the need to fallow and to rotate crops, these and many other factors produced co-operative units of one kind or another, notably the nucleated village community with its great open fields in which each peasant had his scattered strips. If we add a lord, with his own demesne land worked by the peasants in return for their holdings, we have the typical manor, the natural unit taken over, as it were, to be the base of the feudal pyramid.

These forces, operating together in a society without structure, could have pushed its entire organisation up into the pyramid, devolution of all aspects of government being by the simplest territorial division and sub-division. In England, many of the phenomena existed before the Normans came. Agrarian facts had produced many manors of the typical pattern, and many other kinds of unit to which the Norman administrators were to give the name of manor. Governmental facts had produced jurisdictional lordships. The desire for security was still producing the free man claiming to be able to betake himself and his land to what lord he chose. But, whatever pattern may have been latent in all this, its development was interrupted by the Conquest, which produced all at once the pyramid. It was, however, a pyramid in the economic dimension and not the governmental. The entrenched order of the counties and hundreds remained as the governmental framework; and when the Conqueror's men produced their great description of England, listing the fees of the tenants-in-chief and the holdings of the king himself, the information was arranged county by county, and had been collected through the county machinery. Domesday is a register of property and proprietors before and after the Norman takeover. But it assumes that the bearings of society are as they were in the time of King Edward the Confessor[1].

The new proprietors, of course, were mainly Frenchmen, participants in the gains of the adventure, who had either displaced one or more English owners or had been intruded over their heads to become their lords. The tenures of those who held in chief of the king, and some tenures at a lower level, were thus created instantly. More came into being as the king laid on his tenants-in-chief the obligation to furnish fighting men, and as the tenants-in-chief came to meet this obligation by means of the enfeoffed knight, not kept and paid like the household retainer but granted a living in land. The military tenures, of uncertain value as a provision for warfare, brought with them a logic which was to generate anachronisms throughout our history. These will be considered in connection with the development of property law; and what has mattered for the system as a whole is precisely that the feudal forces were so largely confined to the economic sphere. Had lordship regularly carried most of government with it, jurisdiction would have been defended as property against centralisation, customary law would not have been transformed by professional handling, and Roman law would perhaps have no rival in the western world today.

The regular scope of feudal jurisdiction is hard to discover, and clarity will be served by distinguishing between manorial courts and courts at higher levels of tenure. About the latter we know the less, though it is clear that in the century after the Conquest the courts of honours, the greater fees whose tenants might style themselves barons, were doing much important work[2]. Franchise jurisdiction apart, and setting it apart is not always easy, their proper field was

1. V. H. Galbraith, *The Making of Domesday Book* (1961).
2. F. M. Stenton, *The First Century of English Feudalism* (2nd edn., 1961). Cf. W. O. Ault, *Private Jurisdiction in England* (1923).

the business of the fee as such: the ownership, if that word is appropriate, of the various holdings; the dues proper to each; and, perhaps most important of all, inheritance, or rather those decisions about whose homage to accept out of which grew together both heritability and the canons of descent. The courts of these communities of tenants, including of course the king's as the highest such court, created the customs of English feudalism, and so imposed on English property law a logic as indestructible as it soon became irrelevant.

At the lower level, the courts of manors governed communities, not just of tenants of the same lord, but of neighbours whose lives touched each other every day and at every point, and whose subjection to their lord was different in kind from that of the merely feudal compact. The manor was often also a village, and the village was often also an economic unit which needed, like a modern factory, to be managed. Three elements thus merged in the work of these courts. There was the determination of property rights in the land of the manor; and here very ancient customary rules may have been enforced, free at first both of the uniformity and of the peculiar logic inherent in the newer and higher military tenures. Some of this law was to perish, some to live to a sad old age as what came to be called copyhold, and some, most notably the intricate regulation of pasture, to survive as chapters in today's books on real property. But at the time the matter of pasture would perhaps have been classified – if anybody had attempted classification – as part of the function of the manor court in managing an economic unit. That the plough-oxen should live and that the arable should be manured in the appropriate seasons was no less important than that growing crops should be protected; and the punishment of those who defaulted in such arrangements, which was the most ordinary business of manor courts, was the equivalent of our modern managerial function. Then lastly if a peasant injured another, or slandered him, or did not pay for the eggs he had bought, or cheated him over the cloth he had sold, the victim was more likely than not a neighbour[1]. And although the institutional theory, if there was any, is far from clear, it seems that litigation in such matters between tenants of the same manor would generally take

1. See e.g. F. W. Maitland, *Select Pleas in Manorial and other Seignorial Courts* (Selden Society, vol. 2).

place in the manor court rather than in that of the hundred or county.

The wider ambit of manorial courts, reaching into more areas of life than courts at higher feudal levels, would alone have kept them longer in being. But there was another reason for their long survival. The higher feudal courts perished when their proprietary jurisdiction, their prime business, passed to royal courts; and at the manorial level this never wholly happened. To later eyes there was a clear distinction between free and unfree holdings. The free tenants were protected by the king's law. They could get a royal writ directing the lord to do right to them; and it would be done in a court in which, as at the higher levels, the free tenants themselves were the judges. This kind of court came to be called the court baron; and like the higher feudal courts it ceased to exist when such claims came to be heard directly in royal courts. But royal courts would not help the unfree, and rationalised the matter by saying that in their law unfree land belonged to the lord, at whose will the unfree tenants held. Seen from above, therefore, there were no rights in such land, no courts, and no judges: there was a gathering at which the lord's will was declared and recorded. This came to be known as the court customary; and since there could be no other title to unfree land, it continued to exist although increasingly controlled by royal courts. The matter is one of many in which the king's courts rejected a class of business as not their concern at a time when many things were not their concern; and their exclusive rules posed great difficulties as other jurisdictions decayed. The reality underlying the rejection in this case was the need for managerial discretion: the unfree peasant's tenement was not so much his property as the pay he received for service which could not be exactly specified. But the indicia of free and unfree were never wholly clear, and mattered less in fact than common law theory would suggest. It is unlikely at any period that there were often two separate courts in any one manor; and we must not suppose that the customs of a court customary were not law just because the king's courts took no notice of them.

We have then the ancient public courts of shire and hundred, the feudal courts, and the franchises in which feudal courts might exercise a public jurisdiction. In the compass of this book no consideration at all will be given to the courts of cities and boroughs, the urban equivalents of county and hundred and sometimes also of private courts. And the courts merchant, which depended upon the concentration of trade in fairs and markets, and where merchants applied their own customs to their own transactions, can only be mentioned[1]. Their needs and therefore their customs were different from those of a society in which true contract otherwise played a small part; and here again difficulties resulted when these matters were forced into the common law courts.

JURISDICTION OF THE CHURCH

Of one other jurisdiction, however, something must be said, namely that of the church. The courts Christian in England were part of a European system subject to the papal *curia*, administering a sophisticated and in principle uniform law based upon the Roman. This law was not, of course, confined as is modern English ecclesiastical law to questions about doctrine, clergy discipline, pulling down churches and the like. All lawful men were Christian, and important areas of their lives were subject to the law of the church and to no other. There was a jurisdictional frontier guarded on the one side by the writ of prohibition and on the other by a weapon too powerful for common use, the withdrawal of spiritual sanction from the lay power itself. But many difficulties arose. Testamentary jurisdiction was clearly for the church; but was the church's nominee or some other to represent the dead man in the lay courts if he died owing or being owed an enforceable debt? Questions about the fact and validity of marriage were clearly for the church, and therefore questions of legitimacy; but were its determinations to bind the lay courts in deciding upon inheritance? Ordinary contracts were plainly for lay courts, but to break a promise, at least if it had been supported by some form of oath, was also a sin. To speak ill of one's neighbour might at first be matter either for a lay court as an ordinary wrong, or for court Christian as a sin, particularly if the ill spoken was itself an allegation of sin

1. For urban and mercantile courts see *Calendar of Early Mayor's Court Rolls of the City of London, 1298–1307; Calendar of Plea & Memoranda Rolls of the City of London* (a series now running from 1323 to 1482); and *Select Cases Concerning the Law Merchant*, vol. I (Selden Society, vol. 23).

which might lead to a spiritual charge. How could the frontier be defined?[1].

So far as possible, kinds of question were allocated to the one side or to the other, and formally at least the other accepted the consequences. The lay courts followed the church as to testamentary representation; and if they did not always follow it on legitimacy, they avoided direct contradiction. Sometimes the line had to be drawn arbitrarily as a matter of degree. Questions about tithes, for example, were for ecclesiastical decision; but the right to present a parson to a church was, after a bitter struggle, admitted to be lay property. Since the value of that property depended upon the tithes due to the church, a rule emerged that a sufficiently large dispute over tithes between neighbouring parsons would have to await the results of a lay suit between their patrons[2]. But although lay courts could and did leave some matters wholly to the church, the church could not so easily relinquish cognisance of those sins which happened to be unlawful. A second principle was therefore brought into play: crudely stated it was that only lay courts could impose lay sanctions, for example order the payment of money. But moral issues are not so easily segregated. Suppose for example that one who owed a lay debt promised by his faith to pay it, and broke his promise: if the church courts could impose a penance for the sin, could they not equally impose an excommunication to take effect if the sinner would not do right? At any rate they did.

As will be seen later, this was also how the equitable jurisdiction of the court of Chancery worked, except that prison rather than excommunication was the threat that made a defendant himself do

1. Working of church courts: B. L. Woodcock, *Medieval Ecclesiastical Courts in the Diocese of Canterbury* (1952); J. E. Sayers, *Papal Judges Delegate in the Province of Canterbury, 1198–1254* (1971); a forthcoming volume edited for the Selden Society by N. Adams and C. Donahue will print many documents, some early. Prohibitions: N. Adams, 'The Writ of Prohibition to Court Christian' (1935–36) 20 Minnesota Law Review, p. 272, and 'The Judicial Conflict over Tithes' (1937) 52 English Historical Review, p. 1; G. B. Flahiff, 'The Use of Prohibitions by Clerics', (1941) 3 Medieval Studies (Pontifical Institute of Toronto), p. 101, and 'The Writ of Prohibition to Court Christian in the Thirteenth Century', (1944) 6, op. cit., p. 261; (1945) 7, p. 229; S. F. C. Milsom, *Novae Narrationes* (Selden Society, vol. 80), p. cxcviii; R. H. Helmholz, 'Writs of Prohibition and Ecclesiastical Sanctions in the English Courts Christian' (1976) 60 Minnesota Law Review, p. 1011.
2. *Novae Narrationes*, p. cxcix. For a general view, see C. Donahue, 'Roman Canon Law in the Medieval English Church' (1974) 72 Michigan Law Review, p. 647.

right. And although we have long ago ceased to look for the origin of that jurisdiction in some identification of the chancellor as the king's confessor, we shall also do wrong to assume that the whole truth lies in administrative details. The rise of equity is intelligible only if we remember the medieval familiarity with earthly institutions of conscience, and the medieval belief in an absolute right. Our own age is the first which has felt able to relegate the relationship between law and morals to the class-room.

The courts Christian are important in a different way. They were the earliest in England that would have looked to us like courts of law. Documents survive from actual litigation very nearly as old as the earliest rolls of the king's courts; and what we see is a single judge trying to find out what had happened by considering and comparing the evidence of witnesses, and applying to the facts so found rules of law which could be looked up in books[1]. Although the king's courts early lost the appearance of public meetings and became the sessions of specially authorised justices, centuries were to pass before they could be seen as ascertaining facts and applying known rules, before there were indeed systematic rules of substantive law that could be written down in books. Such a system is the final product of a development which the English secular law was only just beginning, and even the king's justices at the end of the twelfth century were presiding over a process which was, as will appear, deeply primitive by comparison.

But it is not just that the two kinds of process were going on in the same society and ordering the affairs of the same litigants. They were conducted by the same people. Until the process of centralisation was complete at the end of the thirteenth century, the royal justices who brought it about were largely clerics with knowledge and often experience of the canon law. It is one of the odder contradictions of intellectual history.

THE PATTERN OF CENTRALISATION

The pattern of centralisation from local institutions is clear to hindsight. People were at first governed by the courts of county and

1. For documents showing detailed consideration of evidence, see the forthcoming Selden Society volume edited by N. Adams and C. Donahue.

hundred, those courts by the king. Government in the upper tier was largely a matter of accounting for what had become due to the king from the lower. Certain wrongs, for example, entailed a forfeiture to the king of the wrongdoer's goods; local institutions must therefore produce what was in effect a balance-sheet of wrongs and goods, and would be penalised for any failure. The earliest method of control appears to have been a system of local agents, local justiciars, who were to take part in the determination of any matter involving royal rights[1]. This gave way to a system of periodic audit by commissioners sent out from the centre, the justices in eyre, supplemented by a permanent local accountant, the coroner, whose records provided a check on the accounts given by the local institutions themselves. Seen from another angle, the system of eyres, journeys by the king's commissioners and the king himself, represents a system of governing the kingdom bit by bit, checking on one county after another; and within each county the sheriff would similarly make periodic tours of the hundreds. But there was an inevitable tendency for matters to be drawn up from the lower tier of the old structure, for the king to govern people directly and for people to seek justice from the king directly. As this happened in more and more matters, the realm became the important community. Instead of the king coming to the counties one after another, the counties sent representatives to treat together with the king and to become the house of commons. And as more and more kinds of dispute were brought to royal judges, visitations at a frequency suitable for the old audit were less and less appropriate. Litigants sought royal justice wherever they could find royal power, which was most often in the exchequer; there a permanent central court was established. Centralisation and specialisation proceeded together.

But the pattern which hindsight can see was not being consciously drawn at the time. Institutions begin in expedients. An immediate problem arises: an immediate solution is found. Nobody can know that the solution will later be seen as the origin of something, or the problem as the effective end of something else. There was never a time at which the county was consciously reduced from its position as the most important court for ordinary

1. H. A. Cronne, 'The Office of Local Justiciar in England under the Norman Kings' (1957–58) 6 University of Birmingham Historical Journal, p. 18.

people. Indeed, attempts were made to stem or reverse the tide of centralisation and send some matters back there. Nor were eyres consciously abolished, or the central courts adjusted to their new function. With legal institutions as with the law itself, change was until the nineteenth century an almost sedimentary deposit of expedients.

THE EYRE SYSTEM

Of the earliest eyres the only official traces are entries of the proceeds in the pipe rolls, the great central accounts, from which the personnel and the circuits of some commissions can be reconstructed. But from the late twelfth century we have records made for the commissioners themselves, eyre rolls; and for some fourteenth-century eyres these are supplemented by year book reports, made for the technical purposes of lawyers[1]. In all this we can see not judges on circuit but a whole system of government. The coming of the justices in eyre was the coming of royal power, and before them would appear the fullest assembly of the county. The ordinary governmental authorities stopped working, and they themselves came to judgment. The catastrophic nature of the visitation can be seen in events at the opening of the eyre. For example machinery had to be set up to regulate more minutely than in ordinary times the prices of food, and special arrangements had to be made about accommodation for the crowds who were to come. And the sheriff surrendered to the justices his wand of office and received it back at their hands: they were the king and he was to act at their command and to hold office at their will.

The conduct of business at an eyre epitomised its historical role. The work was divided into two parts, and sometimes at least the

1. Printed eyre rolls include: three volumes covering various counties, 1218–22, edited by D. M. Stenton (Selden Society, vols. 53, 56, 59); M. T. Clanchy, *Roll and Writ File of the Berkshire Eyre, 1248* (Selden Society, vol. 90); two volumes covering Wiltshire Eyre of 1249, respectively edited by C. A. F. Meekings and M. T. Clanchy (Wilts. Archaeological and Record Society, vols. XVI, XXVI for 1960 and 1970). Printed eyre year books include: W. C. Bolland, *The Eyre of Kent, 1313–1314* (Selden Society, vols. 24, 27, 29); H. M. Cam, *The Eyre of London, 1321* (Selden Society, vols. 85, 86); others are being edited for the Selden Society by D. W. Sutherland and J. S. Beckerman.

commissioners formed themselves into two groups to deal with them. The first part, the pleas of the crown, represents the system of itinerant government, the first stage in institutional centralisation. At its core was a list of questions, the articles of the eyre, about all matters of possible profit to the king. Some of these were about the feudal rights of the crown, wardships and the like, which will later be discussed for their own sake. Some were about such arbitrary oddities as wreck and treasure trove; and the coroner's inquest into treasure trove survives today to remind us that the enforcement of rules, and not the refinement of their content, was the first achievement. The coroner's inquest into unexplained deaths reminds us even more clearly that law and order on the national scale were first expressed in terms of revenue. When in 1221 a Worcestershire hundred jury, answering the articles of the eyre, said that Roger's wife Emma had been drowned in the Avon, it turned out that she had really been killed by Roger. Roger had already been hanged for it, and he had no chattels to be forfeited to the king; but if the untruth had passed unchecked, two other communal imposts would have been saved. Roger had not been in a tithing, one of the groups into which the population of each area was required to be divided, and upon which was cast the responsibility of producing such of their members as should be called to justice. And upon Emma's death Englishry had not been presented, a requirement dating from the time when the Normans were in the position of an occupying army, protected by a fine levied upon any community in which one of their number, or anyone not proved to be English, was found dead[1]. But of course we misunderstand the eyre if we imagine some distinction between the financial motive and the aims of government; this was how government was conducted. And other articles of the eyre asked questions more obviously governmental in character, for example concerning franchises, the controlled market in cloth and wine, or the misdeeds of sheriffs and other royal officers.

The other part of the eyre's business was the common pleas, ordinary litigation between ordinary people. And since almost all our evidence comes from a time when there existed also the central court which came to be known as the court of common pleas, and

1. D. M. Stenton, *Rolls of the Justices in Eyre for Lincolnshire and Worcestershire* (Selden Society, vol. 53), no. 1071.

since that court became the ordinary forum for such litigation, it is important to emphasise that it was in the eyre that such pleas could first come to royal justice as a matter of routine. It was the central court that was at first the exceptional thing, in that cases were begun there for special reason, sometimes for special payment by a litigant unwilling to wait for the next eyre; and it always needed the special authorisation of a writ.

Particularly in connection with the personal actions, this exchange between the ordinary and the exceptional is a source of misunderstanding. Seemingly avoidable difficulties arose, for example, because modes of proof which depended upon a litigant's standing with his neighbours were transplanted from local courts to Westminster Hall. But it was not in Westminster that they were first accepted by the king's judges: it was in the county town with the neighbours present.

Misunderstanding has gone deeper than that. The first scholar to investigate the eyre, assuming that what the court of common pleas did was and always had been the essence of the common law, was surprised to find personal actions begun without writ, and even more surprised to find complaints of kinds of wrong which never appeared in the court of common pleas at all. These last were in fact cases so humdrum that normally they would be settled at an ordinary session of the county and never reach royal justice. But they and the procedure by mere bill of complaint were taken as evidence of a power to override the rules of the common law, and the eyre was identified as the first home of English equity[1]. What matters is not the particular misapprehension about the eyre, or even the larger misapprehension about the nature of early equity: it is an underlying misconception of the early common law itself, to be considered at the end of this chapter and from time to time throughout this book.

More numerous than personal actions on the common pleas section of an eyre roll are actions concerning land; and in any court these required a writ for a reason which was not purely administrative, and which will be explained together with the actions

1. W. C. Bolland, *Select Bills in Eyre* (Selden Society, vol. 30). For the procedural ordinariness of bills see H. G. Richardson and G. O. Sayles, *Select Cases of Procedure without Writ under Henry III* (Selden Society, vol. 60); and G. O. Sayles, *Select Cases in the Court of King's Bench*, vol. IV (Selden Society, vol. 74), pp. lxvii ff.

themselves. It seems to flow from a feature of the actions which is relevant to their place in the overall pattern of centralisation. The two most frequently brought were legislative creations of the late twelfth century, the 'possessory assizes' of novel disseisin and mort d'ancestor. And these have been seen by historians as alternatives to remedies in feudal courts, so that their part in centralisation was just to expand the demand for royal justice by competitive attraction. But their original function turns out to have been more integral to that of the eyre. They began as measures for the control of feudal jurisdictions themselves; and it is even possible that novel disseisin was first a matter for the presentment of the countryside like the pleas of the crown[1].

The judicial functions of the eyre may be seen as having ultimately been inherited partly by the court of common pleas and partly by itinerant justices commissioned more frequently but with restricted rather than general powers. Both of course were in use long before the eyre began to decline from being the regular arm of central government to its last state in the fourteenth century as an occasional means of extortion. Visitations at intervals of seven years or so, which became accepted as the minimum, were appropriate for an auditing function, for checking what local men had done; but for the actual conduct of business, for the dispensation of royal justice when that was in common demand, other machinery had to be found. The two matters in which this first happened both followed from changes made under Henry II. The introduction of the possessory assizes brought great numbers of small disputes about property to be settled by royal inquest. And the elaboration of the indictment system, which we see as the beginning of crime as a separate branch of the law, replaced royal supervision by royal action in the case of most serious wrongs. Local communities were increasingly concerned not merely to account for what had happened about wrongs from which profit might come to the king, but to accuse the wrongdoers before royal justices[2].

For both these purposes frequent local sessions of royal justices were needed. But the business was trivial in comparison with that of the eyre, and did not require great men for its settlement. The

1. See pp. 134 ff, below.
2. Possessory assizes to be taken at regular intervals at day and place of county court: *Magna Carta* (1215), c.18; (1225), c.12. Indictments: see pp. 406 ff, below.

commissioners to whom it was entrusted might therefore be persons of no more than local importance; and in the case of pleas of the crown this feature came to be accepted by the establishment in the fourteenth century of permanent commissioners for each county, the justices of the peace, who were to act at regular intervals without further instruction. But the regular dispatch from the centre of royal officers never ceased, and the name and business of those assizes which lasted until our own day went back to a time when their usual commission was to hear possessory assizes and to deliver the jails. To these there came to be added a new class of what we should call civil business, the taking from local juries of verdicts in cases depending before the central courts; and it was partly for this reason that the commissioners sent on circuit nearly always included professional judges from those courts[1]. But when we speak of professional judges, we are speaking of a time at which the law has become distinct from government in general, something to which a man can devote his life; and this was by far the most important result of the rise of the central courts themselves.

RISE OF THE CENTRAL COURTS

The process had its beginnings in itinerant government, which had two centres. There was first the king himself, constantly on the move within his kingdom and in his other possessions, having with him a court in all the institutional senses of that word. From this court *coram rege* there slowly developed the king's bench, a regular court of law separate from the king's person and separate from his council, which was in time to engross much ordinary civil litigation. But it could not be a regular channel for royal justice so long as it was in constant motion, and in the thirteenth century to commence an action there seems to have been one way of harassing an enemy[2].

The second centre of itinerant government was the exchequer, brought to rest by the weight of its financial apparatus, but playing a much larger part in the kingdom than that of a modern financial

1. *Nisi prius*: p. 49, below.
2. G. O. Sayles, *Select Cases in the Court of King's Bench*, vol. II (Selden Society, vol. 57), p. lxxv; introductions to these volumes (others are Selden Society, vols. 55, 58, 74, 76, 82, 88) contain much information relevant to this chapter.

department of state. We have seen that central government took the form of accountancy, and consisted in the enforcement by financial sanctions of the financial rights of the crown. The eyres can be seen as local audits by officers sent out from the centre; and that centre was the exchequer. If the will of government was with the king, this was its mind; and the frequent absences of the king assured it the control of all necessary routines and the services of those who made government their profession. At the head of this machine, the embodiment of all these factors, was the chief justiciar, the regent in the king's absence and the centre around which royal justice first grew[1].

By a process of specialisation of which the details may be beyond recovery, not one but two regular courts of law grew from this centre. There was the court of exchequer itself, which had for its special business the legal disputes arising out of revenue. This court was later to justify a large concern with purely private causes by colour of a fictitious revenue interest; but in fact it seems never to have quite given up the wide jurisdiction of the old undifferentiated body from which it grew. The other offspring of that body was the common bench or court of common pleas, whose name, happily preserved in many American jurisdictions, was allowed to disappear from the English legal system in 1880. Here the common law was made.

The common bench had to establish an identity distinct not only from the exchequer, but also from the court *coram rege*. A single body of justices served the common and the king's bench, and they merged when the king was out of the country or was an infant. And that is why, although the Great Charter of 1215 was only confirming the practice of many years when it required that possessory assizes should be heard locally at frequent intervals and that other common pleas should be held in some fixed place, the court emerges as a distinct and permanent institution only after the majority of Henry III, who had succeeded John as a child in the year after the Charter was issued[2].

Ninety years later, when Henry III's son died, the three central courts of common pleas, exchequer and king's bench were settled institutions. Eyres would occasionally be commissioned for a few

1. F. West, *The Justiciarship in England* (1966).
2. *Magna Carta* (1215), cc.17, 18; (1225), cc. 11, 12.

decades longer, but they were no longer integral to either government or judicature. What were integral were lesser commissions by which justices on circuit took the possessory assizes and took also verdicts in cases in which jury issues had been reached in the central courts. And many disputes, especially in what we should call contract and tort, were still heard in local courts. The system was to make some sense until the sixteenth century, to last until the nineteenth, and to leave its imprint in every common law jurisdiction today. But it was not devised as a national system of civil judicature. It was an accumulation of expedients as more and more kinds of dispute were drawn first to a jurisdictional and then also to a geographical centre. One result was to invest the machinery which controlled jurisdiction with an importance that was to outlive and to overshadow its reason.

THE WRIT SYSTEM

That machinery was the system of writs, and in principle it was no more than a part of the administrative routine made necessary by centralisation. In the ancient jurisdiction of the county court, for example, a law-suit was started by simple complaint, and the only preliminary required was that the plaintiff should give security to pursue it before the defendant would be summoned to answer. But when matters arose which it was convenient to refer to the county but which were not within its accepted jurisdiction, the sheriff was given royal authority to act by what is called a viscontiel writ[1]. This probably came to happen most often when the royal courts themselves began to hear private disputes as a regular thing. Lines of demarcation emerged between local and royal jurisdictions, depending upon the amount at stake or upon some royal interest; and if a plaintiff preferred to sue in the county on a matter lying on the royal side of the boundary, the sheriff could not act without the authority of a viscontiel writ. But the earliest writs seem to have dealt with matters properly within the jurisdiction not of the king but of some lord, but in which the lord was unable to act. His

1. G. J. Turner and T. F. T. Plucknett, *Brevia Placitata* (Selden Society, vol. 66); for the part played by writs in the development of a jurisdictional boundary, see p. 245, below.

inability was itself sometimes a result of royal control; and royal writs interfered with feudal jurisdiction, originally as self-sufficient as that of the county, in fundamental ways to be considered later in this book[1].

More important for the later development of the common law was the part played by writs in the king's courts themselves[2]. The plaintiff makes his first complaint to a secretariat, the chancery. The writ is in form just an order telling the sheriff – again only if the plaintiff gives security to prosecute his claim – to bring the defendant to answer. But since it has to specify the court to which the defendant is to come it operates also as that court's warrant to proceed. In some situations, however, the plaintiff could be heard without going through the secretariat at all[3]. Take first the eyre. Like the county court, the eyre was older than the writ system. The commission under which the judges went out gave them almost unlimited jurisdiction in the county concerned; and as for the other function of writs, that of securing the presence of defendants, the sheriff attended on the judges and was directly under their orders. Direct complaint to the eyre was then a normal routine for seeking royal justice, and it was the later development of the writ system that was to make it look exceptional. Much the same is true of the king's bench. The king's own court needed no warrant to give it jurisdiction, and if it would entertain a dispute at all, it could do so directly at the instance of the plaintiff as well as on a formal reference by writ. But the court in fact came to restrict the cases it would hear by plaint to those arising in the county in which it was sitting; and this is probably because the sheriff of that county was in attendance upon the court, so that there was no difficulty about securing the presence of the defendant. The result was like that reached in the eyre, but reflected the practical function performed by writs in getting the defendant, rather than a theoretical limit on jurisdiction. In the sixteenth century, as will appear, this procedure by bill in the king's bench, under the name of the Bill of Middlesex

1. Chapter 6, esp. p. 127, below.
2. E. de Haas and G. D. G. Hall, *Early Registers of Writs* (Selden Society, vol. 87); R. C. Van Caenegem, *Royal Writs in England from the Conquest to Glanvill* (Selden Society, vol. 77).
3. H. G. Richardson and G. O. Sayles, *Select Cases of Procedure without Writ* (Selden Society, vol. 60); G. O. Sayles, *Select Cases in the Court of King's Bench*, vol. IV (Selden Society, vol. 74), p. lxvii.

since that was the county in which the court then always sat, was used to subvert the jurisdictional order whose establishment is now being described.

That order hinged upon the position of the common bench. This court had come into being to provide royal justice in ordinary disputes between subject and subject, and its emergence had been compelled by a demand for this on a scale beyond the capacity of the eyre system. But the demand was, to begin with, for a luxury. The plaintiff seeking to begin a case there was asking not just for royal rather than local justice, but also for royal justice at once: his right, if such it can be called, was to have it in the eyre. The most regular institution of the middle ages therefore started, not as a part of the regular routine of government, but as a provision for exceptional cases. One could not apply directly to the court for justice, because the court had no inherent power to act. Its nature was that of a committee to which cases were individually referred by writ; and, except for matters involving the court's own staff and practitioners, bills came to play no part in its jurisdiction.

The need for a writ in the common pleas as the court's warrant to act, an accidental result of its earliest business being outside the ordinary course of things, was to have many consequences. It explains a great deal of what looks like captiousness in the early common law: a plaintiff who brought a writ for £20 and claimed £19 was not making the claim the court was authorised to hear. And it explains a great deal of inflexibility in the scope of the law, the kinds of matters with which it could deal at all. However much royal and central justice had started as something exceptional, as it became more and more the regular thing, the court slowly established a monopoly. It was not merely the body to which private disputes could conveniently be sent; they could not normally be sent to any other central court, for example the king's bench. Partly this was the familiar hardening of practice into right, but partly it was a matter of 'due process'. When the Great Charter required common pleas to be held in some fixed place, it was perhaps mainly concerned with the need of the plaintiff to have access to justice[1]. But there was also the defendant to consider. Litigation in a travelling court could be intolerable; and even when the king's bench came increasingly to rest, great men and great corporations,

1. *Magna Carta* (1215), c.17; (1225), c.11.

who retained standing attorneys in the common pleas, could argue that they should not be forced elsewhere. The paradoxical result was that the regular court to which ordinary disputes had to go was a court which could not act without special authority in each case, namely a writ from the chancery.

This jurisdictional accident was to be of growing consequence. In the middle ages it hampered the expansion of the common law by restricting the kinds of claim that could be brought before the court. If ordinary private disputes had continued to come before a jurisdiction like that of the eyre, to which plaintiffs had direct access, the common law could have reacted directly to changing needs; and in particular it could have continued to admit kinds of claim familiar in local courts but at first regarded as inappropriate for royal judges. But plaintiffs could not get to the court without a chancery writ, and the formulae of the writs, most of which were highly practical responses to the needs of thirteenth-century litigants, became an authoritative canon which could not easily be altered or added to. Important areas, some new but many older than the king's courts themselves, were in this way cut off from legal regulation; and they could later be reached only by devious ingenuity in the common law courts, or by resorting to the chancellor's equitable jurisdiction, to which once more the litigant could directly complain.

All this was no more than the constriction of red tape. But so complete did it become that in the eighteenth century it engendered a purely formalistic view of the law and of its development which has lasted until our own day. The common law writs came to be seen as somehow basic, almost like the Ten Commandments or the Twelve Tables, the data from which the law itself was derived. And since the mechanism of change within the common law had been to allow one writ to do the work formerly done by another, the whole process came to be seen as an irrational interplay between 'the forms of action'[1]. It was not. It was the product of men thinking.

1. F. W. Maitland, *The Forms of Action at Common Law* (posthumously published with another course of lectures on *Equity*, 1909; published separately, 1936).

2 The Institutions of the Common Law in its First Formative Period

The institutions in which the common law grew to maturity between the thirteenth century and the sixteenth revolved around the court of common pleas. And the clearest view of them may be had, not by a chronological account of each, but by considering their functions in relation to an action in that court.

WRITS AND THEIR LEARNING

The first step was the purchase of the writ, and some knowledge of writs was therefore necessary to all concerned. It is no accident that the earliest item in the literature of the common law, the book known by the name of *Glanvill*, which dates from a time before the common pleas had separated from the exchequer and before central justice was at all the normal thing, should take the form of an exposition of the writs which controlled such cases as were then brought before the court[1]. As central justice became the normal thing, formularies began to appear. These have become compendiously known as the *Register of Writs*; but the definite article, implying that there were many copies of a single book having that as its title, misrepresents the original Latin[2]. A lawyer, or a frequent litigant such as a religious house with great possessions, would have a *registrum*, a collection of forms. In the nature of the case the forms themselves would vary little. But there are also some recurring patterns of arrangement; and if we do wrong to think of 'a' book, we do right to think of a body of learning in constant

1. *Glanvill* (ed. G. D. G. Hall, 1965).
2. E. de Haas and G. D. G. Hall, *Early Registers of Writs* (Selden Society, vol. 87); *Registrum Omnium Brevium*, first printed 1531; F. W. Maitland, 'The History of the Register of Original Writs', in *Collected Papers*, vol. II, p. 110.

professional use by clerks and lawyers, admitting of few doubts at any one time, and subject to traditions which may or may not reflect some physical album or file actually kept in the chancery, but probably do reflect, as it were, a juridical alphabet.

Besides the bare forms, the registers contain all sorts of notes and rules; and the need for instruction about writs later produced commentaries giving only those forms in daily use but with a great deal of explanatory matter more or less systematically arranged. Two of these achieved wide circulation, and came to be printed under the names of the old and Fitzherbert's new *Natura Brevium*; and the latter, last reprinted at the end of the eighteenth century, remains an essential tool for those who want to understand the medieval common law. It seems, moreover, that when the common law came in some sense to be taught, and not just learnt, instruction about the writs came to be the special business of those lesser inns which became attached as preparatory schools to the four great inns of court, and that this function is reflected in their name, the inns of chancery.

But before we transfer our attention, as those apprentice lawyers did, from the chancery to the court, we must understand that in the thirteenth century the common law itself underwent a similar change of emphasis. Its first achievement, that of having come into existence at all, was an exploit not of juristic thought but of administration. Most of the important justices in eyre in the twelfth century, the chief justiciars including Henry II's justiciar Glanvill himself, no doubt the shadowy figure who wrote the book we know by Glanvill's name, most of those who figure in thirteenth-century records mainly as judges, the mysterious Bracton – all these were what we should call civil servants. Professional lawyers, in our sense, did not at first exist.

ANCIENT PATTERN OF LAW-SUIT

This implies that what happened actually in court did not call for much specialist expertise; and we cannot understand the development of the common law without some picture of the procedure from which it started, a procedure which has the appearance of great antiquity. The plaintiff put his claim in settled formal terms.

The defendant made an equally formal denial, recapitulating and denying the claim point by point. One of them swore to the justice of his cause, and that oath was tested, put to proof. The nature of proof as the test of an oath in a believing age, so that the loser lost more than the law-suit, is relevant to many things, for example the frequency of settlements.

Although the underlying assumption is to us irrational, there was more reason to the modes of proof than historians have allowed. A plaintiff could not put his defendant to answer by his simple word: and the kinds of proof that he must offer were themselves fixed by custom and had fixed customary consequences. What battle tested, for example, was the affirmative oath of a witness; and if there was nobody who could swear to what he had seen there could be no battle. If all that could be produced in support of the claim were neighbours who believed the plaintiff, his *secta*, or who suspected the defendant, then the oath to be tested must be one of denial. The defendant would then wage and make 'his law' by the manifestation of an ordeal or by the lesser and longer-lasting test of compurgation, in which a set number of neighbours must swear to their belief in his credibility and get through their oaths without slip.

All this was legal knowledge, but it was the settled knowledge which all lawful men had of their customs. There was not much discretion over proof, still less anything like our own assessment of evidence: the test was conclusive. Nor was there any law to state in a judgment: right was now known to be with the one side or the other, and there was no more for the court to do except make an automatic order. In the whole process the only substantive rules visibly at work are those implicit in the canon of acceptable claims.

COUNTING

But even in such a law-suit the litigant needed skill, his own or somebody else's, because the formal statement of claim, which might be long and complicated, had to be composed and spoken correctly. Since its terms were exactly followed by the denial, they became the terms of the oath whose testing would determine the action; and the making of the count, in Latin the *narratio*, was the very centre of the legal process. We do not know how it came about that the litigant was allowed to speak through the mouth of another, though it has been suggested that it was not to prevent mistakes being made but to prevent them being fatal[1]. Certainly the litigant could disavow what was said on his behalf; and perhaps it was only 'said' by him when he formally adopted it. If this is right, our modern barrister began as one who could harmlessly blunder.

But we are at several removes from the barrister yet. We are envisaging men in each community known among their neighbours to have the necessary precision of mind and tongue, and becoming professionals only when litigation became a sufficiently concentrated business. This may first have happened in, for example, the city of London; but it must surely have been the emergence of the fixed bench, the court of common pleas, which brought into being a cohesive profession of *narratores* or counters. By the end of the thirteenth century it had in the court of common pleas become a closed profession. Only those in some way licensed, the serjeant-counters, might practise there; and for reasons to which we shall return the 'counter' became dropped from their title and these men became the serjeants-at-law, the monopolists of all ordinary civil litigation.

Although counting had been the heart of a law-suit long before there were royal courts or royal writs, it has no early literature; and this is because it was not generally the concern of literate men. But in the thirteenth and early fourteenth centuries formularies appear, many of them, like 'the' *Register of Writs*, becoming thought of as 'a' book eventually printed under the title *Novae Narrationes*. Others, of more restricted scope, became known as *Placita Coronae* and the *Court Baron*. In one respect the most illuminating of these formularies was that which acquired the title *Brevia Placitata*[2]. Dating from soon after the middle of the thirteenth century, it is a conflated formulary giving both writs and counts. But the writs, which in real life were always in Latin, are here translated into French, the language in which counts, at any rate in the king's

1. F. Pollock and F. W. Maitland, *History of English Law* (2nd edn., 1898; reissued 1968), vol. I, p. 211.
2. *Novae Narrationes*, edited by E. Shanks and S. F. C. Milsom (Selden Society, vol. 80). *Placita Corone*, edited by J. M. Kaye (Selden Society, Supp. Series, vol. IV). *Court Baron*, edited by F. W. Maitland (Selden Society, vol. 4). *Brevia Placitata*, edited by G. J. Turner and T. F. T. Plucknett (Selden Society, vol. 66).

courts, were actually spoken, the ordinary language of the upper classes. This collection was for the use, or more probably the instruction, of professional men, literate men, but men not at home in the Latin tongue and not interested in the riches to which it gave access. The common law had started its career as an alternative learning, cut off from even the legal learning of the universities which until the eighteenth century taught only Roman and canon law.

Almost at the same time as the counters' modest *Brevia Placitata* Bracton gave final shape to a much larger and more ambitious book; and it is one of the important facts in the history of western thought that the former was to prove fruitful, the latter sterile. Bracton himself, and probably whoever wrote the earlier material which he seems to have adapted, were administrator-judges of the tradition which had brought the common law into being. But, just as the writs in *Brevia Placitata* show counters looking upward to learn the administrative and jurisdictional elements, so Bracton's book shows the administrator looking downward at what was happening in court. Many actual cases cited are taken from the plea rolls, mostly of the earlier thirteenth century. But the attempt is to make more than just administrative sense: it is to systematise in a substantive and not just a practical and procedural way[1]. This is, as it were, a university law-book.

When, in the half century after Bracton's death, his kind ceased to play any part in the common law and the bench came to be filled from below by counters, two qualities were lost. One was the administrative habit of seeing problems as a whole and making solutions work: the kind of man who had brought the common law into being would not have let it get into the state in which so many cases required the special treatment of the chancellor's equitable jurisdiction. The other was a more specific quality. The ecclesiastical background of the clerical judges ensured that they had some experience of canon law; and many of them read what there was to read about Roman law too. This was a part of their world; and, though scholars will argue for ever about the depth of the Roman learning in Bracton's book, it is Roman in conception and partly in

1. *Bracton* (ed. G. E. Woodbine, 1915–42), 4 vols.; new edition with translation by S. E. Thorne (Harvard UP and Selden Society, 1968–); *Bracton's Note Book* (ed. F. W. Maitland, 1887), 3 vols.

content. Had the development of the common law remained in such hands, Roman law would surely have had a larger, and possibly a preponderant influence. But it was no part of the counters' world. What centuries of development had made so clear centuries earlier was to them alien learning in closed books; and they were starting again from the beginning.

PLEADING

The beginning was in court, in changes which broke up the ancient pattern of law-suit. Some variations had always been possible on the standard sequence of claim and denial, oath and test. In law-suits concerning property and wrongs, for example, a defendant might sometimes rely upon the right or authority of a third party: he vouches a warrant. Mainly in law-suits arising out of transactions discussion might arise about the mode of proof; and this is partly because transactions were largely made enforceable by providing proof which would be effective if the matter came to a law-suit. But the discussion generated by such possibilities had been limited. The fertile changes were those by which the old modes of proof came to be replaced by jury processes. These will be described in connection with the various kinds of action concerned; but the important result can be stated quite shortly. If the general question of right between the parties is to be settled, not by putting an oath to divine test, but by demanding an answer from rational and fallible human beings, two kinds of problem arise. Because they are fallible, there will be many situations in which it seems unsafe to leave the general question to them. Suppose for example that land is claimed by one whose formal statement of claim is entirely true: his grandfather held it, his father was his grandfather's heir, and he his father's. God would not be misled: but who could be sure about the neighbours if in fact the plaintiff's father had granted the land to the defendant's, and the defendant can only make the ancient word-for-word denial of that misleadingly truthful count? The court, no longer just presiding over the ritual formulation of a question to be put to an oracle beyond the need of human guidance, but now in some way responsible for the answer, may be inclined to let the defendant depart from the ancient general denial, and to specify his own facts.

This was a larger change than it sounds. The example just given assumed that the 'right' answer would be clear to the court. But, and this is where the rational nature of the new form of trial comes in, consideration of the actual facts requires the expression, for the first time, of rules of law. Suppose, in the same example, that all the facts are somehow put to the neighbours: the plaintiff makes his misleadingly truthful count; the defendant tells of the grant to his father; and then it emerges that the plaintiff's father had been mad when he made that grant. What is the effect of a grant made by a lunatic? The question may not have been difficult. What matters is that it was new. Law, like fact, had hitherto been comfortably wrapped in the judgment of God[1].

Such new questions would suggest one kind of answer to the older clerical judges with their Roman learning, and a quite different kind to the up and coming counters. In Bracton's book, for example, written in Latin and unable to avoid technical terms of Roman law, a clear-headed English answer may sometimes look to Romanists like a muddled Roman answer. But sometimes an undoubtedly Roman answer is given and Roman concepts applied: a striking example is the analysis of a bailment, considered later in this book. The important fact, however, is that to Bracton and his kind, such answers were possible. They would not have been dismayed by the emergence of facts which required legal analysis and legal decision. They were accustomed to think in terms of substantive law. But this was the last English law-book for centuries to be written with such terms in mind.

Those centuries lay unseen between Bracton and the counters who practised before him; and they are a measure of what was lost when his kind were displaced from the bench. There was to be no short cut through history. What was gained was the common law as an entirely independent system. It is not just that the counters, being unfamiliar with the Roman system, could not adopt ready-made Roman rules. They did not see the law as a system of substantive rules at all. They saw that their ancient pattern of claim and denial had been disturbed because jurymen were fallible, and

1. S. F. C. Milsom, 'Law and Fact in Legal Development' (1967) 17 University of Toronto Law Journal, p. 1. For the particular example, see below, pp. 131 (tenant's special mise), 147 (demandant's proffer to have special issue), 143 (fact asserted in writ of entry).

that in some circumstances the defendant must be allowed a new kind of answer. Upon the infinite details of this problem they concentrated their great abilities; and they never looked up to consider as a whole the substantive system they did not know they were making.

The change in court is reflected in the literature. The count still has to be made, and formularies are still produced. But early attempts show the impossibility of dealing with the defendant's answer in the same kind of way, listing the answers available against each claim. The variety is too great, development is too rapid, and above all the logic of the thing cuts across the different kinds of claim. Take for example just one aspect, though a pervasive one, of the fallibility of jurymen. Their knowledge stopped at the county boundary. If an obligation was incurred in one county, and discharged in another, there were endless problems about whether the defendant had to make the ancient general denial, which would go to a jury of the first county, or could specifically plead the discharge and have a jury from the second. And these problems arose in all kinds of actions, and the reasoning of one might or might not apply to another. There was suddenly a flood of such learning; and no literary form could deal with it except the reporter's note book.

THE YEAR BOOKS

And so the year books grew out of such works as *Brevia Placitata*. First short notes of actual cases are written into the formularies, and then the reporting of cases becomes an end in itself. The question which historians have asked most about the year books concerns their authorship[1]. They seem to begin as the common-place books

1. Beginnings: W. H. Dunham, *Casus Placitorum* (Selden Society, vol. 69); T. F. T. Plucknett, *Early English Legal Literature*, chs. V and VI; introductions to *Year Books of Edward II*, by F. W. Maitland (Selden Society, vols. 17, 20) and G. J. Turner (Selden Society, vols. 26, 42). Change of character: T. F. T. Plucknett, *Year Books of 13 Richard II* (Ames Foundation). Later year books: A. W. B. Simpson, 'Keilwey's Reports' and 'The Circulation of Year Books in the Fifteenth Century' (1957) 73 LQR, pp. 89, 492, and 'The Source and Function of the later Year Books' (1971) 87 LQR, p. 94; E. W. Ives, 'The Purpose and Making of the later Year Books' (1973) 89 LQR, p. 64; J. H. Baker, *Spelman's Reports*, vol. II (Selden Society, vol. 94), p. *164*; L. W. Abbott, *Law Reporting in England, 1485–1585* (1973).

of students. Indeed, we find persons describing themselves as 'apprentices' petitioning the king for enlargement of the space reserved for them in the common bench[1], and these apprentices are evidently learning the serjeants' art by watching them at work. But in the course of the fourteenth century some organisation seems to take hold: instead of many reports being made of each case there is generally one, and that a more earnest affair less often noting the happy phrase or the anecdote. That organisation may have been a business or an association of practitioners. But there is some reason to think that both the year books and the abridgments of them were somehow creatures of the inns of court: that as apprentice lawyers banded together in their inns, as did university students in their colleges, and evolved an educational routine which included lectures significantly confined to statute law, they also formalised a method of learning about the core of their art. And if the year books, which went on being made after the reign of Henry VIII, seem to have long outlived the interest which first produced them, that too sounds like an educational routine.

A more important question is what legal process is reported in the year books. In the earliest of them the count itself is often set out in whole or in part, and this, until recently the only skill of the counters, still engages some of the learner's attention. But usually it is the next step that interests the reporter, and he gives only such summary of the count as is necessary to understand what happens next, which is argument about the defendant's answer, about the plea. The matter can most easily be understood from an example. Suppose an action for battery. So long as there is only ordeal or the like, the defendant can only deny liability at large. The natural reaction to the introduction of the rational jury would be to let him plead whatever facts seemed to tell in his favour, for example that he slipped and hurt the plaintiff by accident, or that he was only defending himself from an attack by the plaintiff, or that he did it deliberately because the plaintiff was having a fit and this was the recognised treatment[2]. In fact his freedom was confined by rules which at first sight seem artificial. But the last of these pleas was open to him, and we will assume that it has been made. It is now the

1. G. J. Turner, YB 3 & 4 Ed. II (Selden Society, vol. 22), pp. xli ff.
2. YB 22 Lib. Ass., pl. 56, f. 98. See generally S. F. C. Milsom, 'Trespass from Henry III to Edward III' (1958) 74 LQR, pp. 195, 407, 561, esp. at p. 578.

turn of the plaintiff's serjeant, and two courses are open to him. He can deny that the facts justified what the defendant did: the plaintiff was not having a fit at all, or the beating was continued after the last devil had been driven out. Or he can challenge the legal assumption on which the plea is based, that it is lawful to beat those suffering from fits. If he takes the latter course, which is called a demurrer, all the facts are taken as admitted, and the year book will show, even more clearly than a modern law report, the decision of a question of substantive law. But if he takes the former course, he is for the purpose of the action accepting that the law is against him, that it is lawful to beat one having a fit. The year book writer will still report the case so far; but he will have no interest in the outcome, and will not note it. He is a lawyer and will not care whether a jury says the plaintiff was or was not in truth having a fit. The point of law will not now be expressed in any judgment; it has not been 'decided' at all; but the course of the pleading tells a year book reader the professional opinion.

Often, however, the reported discussion will not reflect the actual pleading at all. To take the same example a step further, the defendant's serjeant would not make the plea in the first place if he thought there might be a demurrer which would go against him. It therefore often happens that a year book discussion is about a plea which is proposed but not made. In the end the defendant's serjeant betakes himself to the general denial. The verdict and judgment will now be even less interesting to the reporter. And the plea roll entry will give no hint that the point ever came up: it will record the writ, the formal count, the plea of Not guilty, and verdict and judgment thereon[1]. This might be the common case of a defendant denying that he was the culprit. But the year book reader still had guidance about the validity of the abandoned plea; and the scholar today can translate that guidance into a proposition about the substantive law of the time.

If that was all there was to it, if defendants had been free to plead whatever facts seemed to tell in their favour, and if the only motive for abandoning a plea had been fear that those facts would be held insufficient in law, then the year books would be immediately intelligible to modern minds. They would show us the evolution of

1. In year book editions of the Selden Society and the Ames Foundation the record, when found, is printed after the report.

a system of substantive rules; and that process might have occupied decades instead of centuries. During the last years of control by the clerical judges, there are signs that such a degree of freedom might have developed. But any such possibility depended upon lawyers to whom the terms of substantive thought were not alien. The year books are the inbred descendants of *Brevia Placitata*, and the serjeants' world was dominated by the ancient pattern of law-suit. For them the ancient denial, now called the general issue, was paramount; and it must always be made unless there was good reason for departing from it. Consider again the imaginary action for battery. Of the three pleas proposed, only one was discussed, namely that the beating was by way of medical treatment. Here the defendant confesses the fact complained of, and seeks to avoid liability by alleging a further fact in justification of what he did. Some such pleas, for example the peace officer justifying his arrest, may have existed before jury processes as a kind of voucher to warranty. But they seem to become common because a jury might not do justice if a true statement of fact was merely denied; and they serve the further purpose of withdrawing from the jury questions inappropriate for them to answer. Here is an unmistakable question of law, and one that must not be dodged.

A second possible plea to battery was self-defence. The wording of this plea suggests that it was first seen as a special form of denial: any harm that came to the plaintiff came from his own assault. But again it would have been unjust to insist upon a plain Not guilty. This, however, was apparently what happened with the third of the imaginary pleas, that the harm had been done accidentally. Such a plea was expressly made (in an action for burning the plaintiff's house down rather than for battery) in the year 1290. But nothing like it is found in the whole of the year books, and the reason seems to be that it was pushed back into the ancient denial, Not guilty[1].

It follows that year book discussions are not generally about the legal sufficiency of the defendant's facts. They are about the propriety of allowing him to plead them at all, and about the form in which he may do it: is he to add a preamble or rider to the general issue, or to depart from it altogether? To take again the example of a debt incurred in one county and paid in another, the utmost

1. G. O. Sayles, *Select Cases in the Court of King's Bench*, vol. I (Selden Society, vol. 55), p. 181. See further pp. 295 ff, below.

concession normally allowed to a defendant was to add a preamble to the general issue. Instead of 'I owe nothing' he could say 'I paid, and so I owe nothing'. But because this was only a variant of the general issue, it had to go to a jury from the county in which the debt was incurred; and they could have no direct knowledge of the payment. This, however, was thought no hardship to him because he need not have a jury at all. He could have the ancient mode of trial, swearing blankly that he owed nothing and waging his law; and his own knowledge was not confined by the county boundary. There were however a few ways of incurring debts, such as leasing land for a rent, to which wager of law was not applicable; and in such cases the defendant was allowed to depart altogether from the general issue and simply plead 'paid in such a county'; and then he got a jury from the county of payment[1].

The year books, then, and the legal process which they record, lie in the shadow of that ancient unvarying denial. The modern reader can hear real arguments by lawyers who would shine in any age; but often he finds the point of the argument elusive. The difficulty is in his own mind. The terms into which he is trying to translate the argument, the terms of substantive law, were not much in the minds of those arguing. For them the essence of a law-suit was still the formulation of a question to be put to some deciding mechanism, whether wager of law or jury. Practical considerations compelled departures from the old general question. To hindsight, the important result of these departures was the creation of substantive law. But this was not a focus of attention at the time. The year books astonishingly preserve the true infancy of a modern legal system; but they will not often answer legal questions asked in modern terms.

THE TRIAL

To go back once more into court, the pleadings are now over and the question has been formulated. If it is one of pure law, one side or the other having demurred, then it will be answered by the court itself; and, unless the reporter misses it after adjournments, the

1. S. F. C. Milsom, 'Sale of Goods in the Fifteenth Century' (1961) 77 LQR, p. 257 at p. 269.

answer is likely to be in a year book. If there is wager of law, the reporter is not normally interested beyond that point: judgment will follow mechanically. But it will still all take place at Westminster and if there is a problem, for example about how husband and wife should swear, the reporter can find out what happens. In the case of jury trial, however, this is not so. Getting juries to Westminster from all over England was not practicable; and by the early fourteenth century an expedient had been perfected which avoided the necessity. When issue had been joined, it was entrusted to a judge on circuit. The order to the sheriff to empanel a jury tells him to send it to Westminster on such a day unless before then (*nisi prius*) a judge has taken its verdict in the country[1]. It is in the country, therefore, that the trial actually takes place; and all that has to come to Westminster is a note to be added to the record of the pleadings: afterwards (*postea*, which word became its name) the jurors came and said that the defendant was or was not guilty. That was all that the court in Westminster needed to give its judgment, and it is all that the historian is normally going to know of what happened at the trial. The reporter is not there for the same reason that the serjeants are not there: they are interested in the pleadings, not in the result or even the facts.

But it is not just our picture that is affected, and not just details about the rules of evidence – if there were any – that we have lost. Suppose again an action for battery in which the defendant's true case is that the harm was accidental: if the proper plea for him was indeed the general issue, Not guilty, then it was at the jury stage that his liability was decided. At first the matter was presumably left each time to their unguided discretion: a teacher, speaking of an analogous problem toward the end of the thirteenth century, says that the defendant should take the general issue *e mettre sey en la grace du pays*[2]. Even when rules came to be formulated it was in the arguments of advocates or at best in the directions of a judge; and it happened out of our sight. More important still, it happened outside the area of contemporary legal learning. There are in fact two late year book discussions of liability for accident, both arising

1. Regulated by Stats. 13 Ed. I (Statute of Westminster II), c. 30; 27 Ed. I, stat. 1 (*De Finibus Levatis*), c. 4; 12 Ed. II, stat. 1, cc. 3, 4; 2 Ed. III (Statute of Northampton), c. 16; 14 Ed. III, stat. 1, c. 16.
2. *Brevia Placitata* (Selden Society, vol. 66), p. 209.

indirectly out of pleas of a different nature; and they both seem almost childish[1]. Probably they reflect some general understanding about what a jury would do, or ought to do, or perhaps ought to be told to do; but even this last is a very different thing from the disciplined learning generated by special pleas.

This, of course, is only an example. In every kind of action questions of law were latent within the general issue, and were brought more or less distinctly to the surface as facts which could not be pleaded emerged later at the trial. Perhaps argument arose when the party proposed to give them in evidence to the jury; perhaps the jury returned a special verdict or had to be directed on a general verdict; perhaps even a party proposing to wage his law would seek direction lest his oath should imperil his soul. But however deviously such questions came up and however imprecisely and irregularly they were answered, to us they are questions of substantive law.

OTHER BUSINESS DONE ON CIRCUIT

Besides taking verdicts as delegates of the court in Westminster, justices on circuit were doing other work in their own right. On the civil side this consisted of novel disseisin and the other possessory assizes, in which there was only the fixed question which the writ itself required to be put to the local people: did the defendant wrongfully disseise the plaintiff within such a time? Formally there was no room for pleading. But on the one side an explanatory plaint came to be required which was almost as formal as a count, and for which precedents found their way into the counters' formularies. And on the other side the pre-ordained question, like the general issue, proved too simple for the facts of daily life; and it was the possessory assizes which first produced great numbers of *exceptiones*, reasons why the fixed question must not be put to the men of the countryside. It was also in these assizes that the men of the countryside might first refuse to answer the fixed question: they could state the facts in a special verdict, and leave the judges to say whether or not there had been a disseisin. This is probably because, as will appear later, the assize of novel disseisin was now being used

1. YBB Mich. 6 Ed. IV, pl. 18, f. 7; Trin. 21 Hy. VII, pl. 5, f. 27.

in disputes for which other actions had long been available; and the fixed question often required the men of the countryside to answer what could be seen to be questions of law. It was in these county sessions, therefore, that the future first obtruded upon the year book pattern of litigation. The serjeants and their pleading were responsible for the initial creation of the common law. But the serjeants were not on circuit, unless as commissioners. Both in assizes and at *nisi prius* trials, the parties would be represented, if at all, by apprentices, who had begun as students aspiring to be pleaders and came in the later fourteenth century to be substantial practitioners in courts and procedures beneath the serjeants' notice. The next chapter will trace the steps by which theirs became the important kind of practice.

Glimpses of these happenings in the country can be had from two kinds of year book, which for that reason have struck historians as rich in apparent curiosities. The serjeants did of course go on eyre; and reporters, mainly there to note pleadings and also no doubt because the eyre itself had become an oddity, naturally noted interesting assizes and juries taken in their presence. These eyre year books did not become part of the canon, and it is only in modern times that they have been printed, a process still not complete[1]. Our other source of information is the *Liber Assisarum*, an exceptional collection of reports from judges on circuit to take possessory assizes and the like under Edward III. This was printed in the sixteenth century, and its very compilation shows that these matters were early regarded as important to somebody.

The *Liber Assisarum* tells us also something about what we should call criminal work on circuit: like the year books reporting eyres, but unlike other year books, it contains many pleas of the crown. Something will later be said of the two principal ways in which criminals were brought to trial, the indictment and the appeal. But though the appeal is generally supposed to have been obsolescent in the fourteenth century, the *Liber Assisarum* reports more appeals than indictments. At least one of the reasons for this is that counsel were allowed to take part in appeals, but not in indictments for felony. And indeed in the latter there would have been little to do, since special pleading was excluded. The pattern of a criminal case today, with its invariable plea of Not guilty,

1. See p. 27, n.1, above.

preserves in the twentieth century that general denial which was ancient in the twelfth. And although in all ages most accused have wished to deny only that they were the persons involved, the absence of special pleas must have contributed to the poverty of this branch of the common law.

THE KING'S BENCH

More obviously important for the future was civil work done in central courts other than the common pleas, and again by apprentices rather than serjeants. The exchequer will not be discussed: although not without interest in itself, the doings of that court seem to have had no important influence on the development of the common law, which is the theme of this book. But it is otherwise with the king's bench. The steps by which this became a regular channel of justice are the steps by which the law and legal institutions of the year book period were transformed. Its original nature appears from the language by which it was identified: it was the court *coram rege*, before the king; and when writs summoned persons before it, they directed them to come 'wherever we shall then be in England'. When the Great Charter required provision 'in some known place' for the disposition of common pleas, it was of course not seeking to limit the powers of the court with the king, but demanding a facility for litigants[1]. But the grievance of those sued 'wherever we shall then be in England' slowly built up a principle, accepted by the justices with the king as well as by the chancery clerks, that ordinary pleas between subjects must be directed to the court provided for them; and so it came about that the lower of the two great royal courts, the one which could not act at all without royal writ, secured a monopoly as against its autonomous superior. This monopoly came to appear as an abuse to be circumvented; but it first grew from ideas of due process.

By an irony which chronology has repeatedly devised for the common law, the rule became established only as its reason was fading. Although the court did not become finally fixed at Westminster until the fifteenth century, its movements in the fourteenth were less frequent and more predictable than was once supposed; and a less cumbersome body was serving as the king's

1. *Magna Carta* (1215), c. 17; (1225), c. 11.

travelling court. The king's bench was now doing a considerable volume of judicial work, though mostly in cases which did not, as did so many common pleas, drag on from term to term and year to year and for which any movement would have been disruptive.

Of its criminal jurisdiction nothing needs to be said here, except to observe that crime was not at first a conceptual entity distinct from what we should call tort. Most wrongs might be visited by two kinds of legal consequence, compensation for the injured party, and a penalty exacted by the authority whose law had been broken. Proceedings might be instituted by either; and the appropriate jurisdiction was that of the authority concerned. The seller of bad fish in the city of London might be sued by a deceived buyer, or (in our language) prosecuted by the city authorities; and in either case it was matter for the city courts. The man who beat another might similarly be sued or prosecuted; and it might be in the king's courts or some other, depending upon whether or not the battery had broken the king's law, the king's peace. If therefore the victim of such a battery sued for compensation to himself, and if he alleged that it had been in breach of the king's peace, then his success would make the defendant liable for a penalty to the king. Two things followed: the action must come before a royal court; and since it is a plea of the crown as much as a common plea, it can come to the king's bench as well as to the common pleas.

This scheme became infected by unreality. First, the plaintiff in a case like battery could choose whether he would allege breach of the king's peace and sue in a royal court, or omit the allegation and go to his county or other local jurisdiction. Then he could make the allegation for the purpose of coming to a royal court even when there was no sort of violence, and lend colour to his allegation by speaking of swords and bows and arrows. But if these weapons had no existence but on paper, the king's interest in the matter was no more than a formality: so why should not, say, the buyer of bad fish bring his equally wrong-doing seller before a royal court? By the end of the fourteenth century this was in fact happening, and the king's courts were hearing actions for private wrongs although there was no royal interest and no pretence of one.

But which of the king's courts were to hear such cases? The logic which had first brought actions for wrongs in from local jurisdictions would have assigned the last comers to the common pleas.

There was no royal interest, and no reason why they should not go with all other private disputes to the fixed tribunal specially provided; and it was probably these considerations that in 1372 prompted a petition to parliament complaining of cases going to the king's bench[1]. But this logic, if nothing else, had been wounded by those paper swords and bows and arrows. Though it could still be stated early in the sixteenth century, it seems never to have been followed in practice. The king's bench retained a concurrent jurisdiction over wrongs of all kinds, and this was important for the future. In the sixteenth century the common law and the judicial system were both to be transformed as claims ceased to be made by writs within the exclusive jurisdiction of the common pleas, and were expressed instead as wrongs which could equally go to the king's bench. But none of this could have been foreseen at the time. Even in the fifteenth century not many sales of bad fish were large enough to bring to a royal court, and the plea rolls of king's bench and common pleas alike show a tiny proportion of wrongs not alleging a breach of the king's peace.

A warning about such quantitative estimates is, however, necessary. The rolls of the common pleas faithfully reflect the doings of that court because every action was started by writ, and every step taken in pursuance of that royal order was recorded. Every case which reached the court at all is therefore to be found in the plea rolls; and the entry of the pleadings, verdict, and judgment in a case which actually finished is generally preceded by a long series of shorter and more formal entries. The same is true of actions begun by writ in the king's bench. But the king's bench could also hear cases begun by direct complaint, and it regularly did so when the complaint was of a wrong done in the county in which it was sitting. And it is a peculiarity of all proceedings by bill, in eyre as well as in the king's bench, that nothing generally went down on the plea roll until the case was at or near its end. There are no formal entries of appearance and the like[2].

The reason for this peculiarity is no doubt that the court was acting under its inherent power and not on a specific reference from

1. *Rotuli Parliamentorum,* vol. ii, p. 311.
2. H. G. Richardson and G. O. Sayles, *Select Cases of Procedure without Writ* (Selden Society, vol. 60); G. O. Sayles, *Select Cases in the Court of King's Bench,* vol. IV (Selden Society, vol. 74), pp. lxvii ff.

above, and so did not need to keep routine progress checks. The result for the modern investigator is that he must reckon with another area, like proceedings in county courts and proceedings before juries, which is largely screened from his vision. For example, any attempt to calculate from their respective plea rolls the relative volumes of business done by the common pleas and king's bench would be hazardous. Throughout the year book period the rolls of the common pleas are physically between four and ten times the size of those of the king's bench; and though a disproportion would remain if formal entries were discounted, it would not be so striking. For those chiefly interested in the history of the law, a more serious doubt concerns the kinds of matter brought to the king's bench. For example a mid-fourteenth century case, that of the *Humber Ferryman*, has given trouble to historians because it seems out of place[1]. It was first known from the *Liber Assisarum*, that year book volume already mentioned as rich in apparent curiosities; and the reason for that richness is precisely that it reports processes we do not otherwise see, on circuit, before juries, and in the king's bench. That case has also been found on the plea roll; but what we can never see are all the cases which were withdrawn or settled before they reached a stage at which they would be entered on the roll.

JURISDICTION IN ERROR

This, then, is what we know and what we do not know about the king's bench jurisdiction over wrongs, its only important civil work at first instance in the year book period. The increase of this work in the middle of the sixteenth century, to be considered in the next chapter, was signalled first by a dramatic swelling of the plea rolls and then by an institutional change which will serve to introduce the other important medieval jurisdiction of the king's bench. It was at the apex of the routine judicial hierarchy, and decisions of the court nominally held before the king himself could be questioned only before the king in parliament, that is to say the house of lords.

1. YB 22 Lib. Ass., pl. 41, f. 94; (1935–36) 13 Bulletin of Institute of Historical Research, p. 35; G. O. Sayles, *Select Cases in the Court of King's Bench*, vol. VI (Selden Society, vol. 82), p. 66.

This became impracticable as the increase in first instance jurisdiction began to turn the court into an alternative forum for common pleas, and in 1585 a special appellate tribunal was set up called the exchequer chamber[1].

This was the name of a meeting-place rather than of an institution, and it was confusingly the place where two earlier institutions also met. One of these was more meeting than institution. Courts had long referred difficult problems more or less formally to a meeting of all the judges and the serjeants. Such a meeting was without formal power, and could only advise the body which had referred the question to it. But it did something to supply the deficiencies of the appellate mechanisms, and much to regulate the anarchy which followed when in the sixteenth century the old division of work between common pleas and king's bench broke down.

The other body which had met in the exchequer chamber brings us to the routine appellate jurisdictions. It was before the king's bench that the decisions of all other royal courts might be questioned, with the sole exception of the exchequer. This court, perhaps partly because of the specialised nature of its main revenue business and partly with memories of its ancient institutional parity, resisted the claims of the king's bench; and in 1357 a special committee was set up, the earliest known to us as a court of exchequer chamber[2].

Otherwise any review of royal justice was the business of the king's bench; and in the year book period this probably seemed its most important work. In the thirteenth century, with the growing organisation of government, the king used writs of *certiorari* to demand further information about all sorts of matters from his officials, generally of course because somebody had complained of official action. It was the medieval equivalent of sending for the file. In judicial matters, what would come would be a transcript of the record, those entries on the plea rolls dealing with the case. There might be various reasons for thus evoking a case, for example that some royal interest was affected. But if the reason was a complaint of judicial error, then the complainant was required to 'assign

1. Stat. 27 Eliz., c. 8, amended by 31 Eliz., c. 1.
2. Stat. 31 Ed. III, stat. 1, c. 12; see L. O. Pike, *Year Books of 14 Edward III* (Rolls Series), pp. xvii ff.

errors', to point to those places in the record at which he alleged that the court below had gone wrong. This was a sensible arrangement, and its eventual abandonment in England is one of many examples of the common law jettisoning an appropriate principle instead of curing its defects in detail.

These defects may be introduced by comparing a forerunner of the *certiorari* process, the writ of false judgment. This was the remedy provided for a litigant who thought himself wronged by a decision in a county, hundred, or private court; and it took the only form possible in an age when the whole of government bore a judicial aspect. It was an action against the court for having judged unjustly, or rather against the community which that court governed. The principle was established that this action must be heard in a royal and not a superior local or private court; but the defendant community was a subject like the plaintiff, and so it came to be heard by the common pleas rather than by the king's bench[1]. To the common pleas the defendant community must send representatives to bear record, to say what had happened in their court. The plaintiff could accept their account and, as in the later *certiorari* process, point out where the court had gone wrong. But another course was open to him: he could deny the truth of the account and take issue on that.

In *certiorari*, considerations of seemliness early excluded the possibility of saying that a royal court's account of its action was untrue. And, though in the thirteenth century royal judges were sometimes asked for supplementary information, administrative convenience came generally to exclude also the possibility of saying that their account was incomplete. But even at that date there was a common situation in which, without any fault on the part of the clerk, the record might indeed be incomplete. If in a possessory assize the defendant put forward some exception, some reason why the pre-ordained question should not go to the men of the countryside, and if this exception was overruled, the record might well note only the taking of the assize and its result. To enable the validity of the exception in such a case to be reopened by *certiorari*, statute in 1285 provided the 'bill of exceptions': the defendant could

1. Stat. 52 Hy. III (Statute of Marlborough), c. 20; W. S. Holdsworth, *History of English Law*, vol. I, p. 201; G. O. Sayles, *Select Cases in the Court of King's Bench*, vol. II (Selden Society, vol. 57), p. xlix.

at the original hearing make his own private supplement to the record, which the court was required to authenticate by sealing it[1].

In the fourteenth century *certiorari* writs issued for this reason came to be differentiated by a clause saying that error was alleged; and it was that writ which came to be known as the 'writ of error' and which, with the bill of exceptions, remained the appellate mechanism at common law until the nineteenth century. Although a little capricious, it worked well enough in the year book period; and it continued to do so for questions arising out of the pleadings in an action. To take the most obvious case, if the pleadings ended in a demurrer, so that a point of pure law was left to the decision of the court, the losing party would have no difficulty in challenging that decision by a writ of error: everything relevant would be there on the plea roll. But more and more questions that we should identify as questions of law came to be raised off the record. To take the most obvious case, the entire proceedings before a jury would be represented by two lines saying that afterwards, *postea,* the jurors came and said that the defendant was or was not guilty. Suppose that the plaintiff had been run down by the defendant on his horse, and that at *nisi prius* the defendant produces a child witness who says that the horse bolted because of a flash of lightning. The plaintiff may make the objection, which we should regard as depending upon the rules of evidence, that a child is not a proper witness. Or he may make what we should regard as a substantive argument, namely that even if true the facts did not exonerate the defendant. But if he is overruled there will be nothing in the *postea* clause of the record to enable either matter to be raised on a writ of error. For the former he came to be allowed to use a bill of exceptions. For the latter, he came to be allowed a step which would appear in the *postea* clause itself, namely a demurrer to the evidence. This admitted its factual truth, and staked the case on the point of substantive law which would be decided by the court in Westminster.

THE LIMIT OF EARLY DEVELOPMENT

This last seems to be a late development, and at first confined to documents tendered at the trial; and it is not just to say something

1. Stat. 13 Ed. I (Statute of Westminster II), c. 31.

about the writ of error that this chapter reaches so far forward from the period with which it is concerned. The demurrer to the evidence is one of the clearest examples of the common law having to go back and deal with a matter once deliberately shut out from consideration. What had been shut out was any legal question latent within the general issue. The process of pleading made the common law: but it was not a happy juristic invention designed to that end. It was an uncomfortable necessity imposed by the jury, whose fallibility had broken up the comfortable old pattern of a general question to be put to an infallible test. But the necessity did not go beyond configurations of fact particularly likely to mislead, so that the old pattern, now known as the general issue, remained the normal thing; and so long as the general question was asked, even of a jury, lawyers had no occasion to ask all the particular questions of which it was composed. The potential area of legal discussion was divided by an almost arbitrary frontier, formally opened up in later days by the demurrer to the evidence, which carried the language and concepts of pleading into the zone previously shut off.

But this in turn is only an illustration, though a striking one, of the need to consider these institutions of the early common law in their own terms, and not in ours. When it is said, for example, that the writ of error was defective because questions could not be raised about the propriety of evidence given to the jury, we must remember that the excluded questions might be more serious than what we think of as matters of evidence. And when it is said, as it too often is, that the year books were inferior to modern law reports because they often did not give the facts or the judgment, it must be remembered that neither was generally important. The facts and the law are both reflected in the pleadings; and the equivalent of today's lawyer seeking a *ratio decidendi* was a year book reader trying to make out whether a particular plea would or would not be upheld on demurrer, or why it should be in this form rather than in that. There was no substantive law to which pleading was adjective. These were the terms in which the law existed and in which lawyers thought.

3 *The Institutions of the Common Law in its Second Formative Period*

THE NATURE OF THE CHANGE

The system described in the last chapter broke up, in substance though not in form, because centralisation had overreached itself. The administrative achievement was not matched in dealing with its consequences. The monetary limit on local jurisdictions, fixed at forty shillings at a time when that was of the order of a year's income for ordinary people, fell in real value to bring smaller and smaller and therefore more and more claims within the ambit of royal justice[1]. Royal justice was represented mainly by a single court, the common pleas, sitting only in the law terms. The reaching of issues by oral pleading must have been extravagant of time; and for the litigant, who had already had to buy a writ and who must now retain a serjeant, it was expensive in money too. And the issues reached were often decided by means which were ineffective outside their original neighbourhood setting.

The changes to be described in this chapter were therefore inevitable. Other courts and other lawyers had to take business from the common pleas and the serjeants. Law-suits had to work in a way more appropriate to large numbers. And they had to be decided by means not obviously open to abuse. But the inevitability was that of statistics, of market forces operating over many decades on the small everyday choices of lawyers and their clients. If we allow ourselves to think of the end result as in some way a response to perceived needs, we commit the historian's deadly sin of contempt for those about whom he is writing. People were generally doing their honest best with what immediately concerned them; and the dishonest appearance of a change considered as a

1. The original limitation applied to debts and was extended to other kinds of claims by confusion; see p. 245, below.

whole reflects the character not of lawyers but of law itself. This is how it serves a changing world. If the rule cannot be adjusted by direct legislation, it must be left on one side; and when, as in the sixteenth century, the world is changing quickly, the juxtaposition of the old and the new has a disingenuous look.

The system could not be altered, only transformed. Until the nineteenth century the serjeants kept their monopoly in the court of common pleas, the court kept its monopoly of many kinds of action, and some of these actions could still be decided by ancient modes of proof. But none of this mattered. The actions had long since ceased to be brought, and the part which the serjeants once played had ceased to be played by anyone. In a sense the court of common pleas had lost to the king's bench; and if we see that as an event like the murder in a detective story, we shall cleverly discern a motive for it and write our own variety of legal fiction. It is not courts that bring actions. The pressures are from litigants, from the changing world itself. And the lawyer who advised a litigant to take what we might see as the first small step, to proceed in one way rather than another, can never have been aiming at the rule, and often was not thinking about it at all but about some immediate point of convenience which may be too small and remote for the historian to see. Only in the late stages of such a change does it become a conscious process, so that one can realistically imagine a court considering the question as a legislator might.

FICTIONS CONCERNING JURISDICTION

All this needs particularly to be emphasised because about some of these changes we know little beyond the end result and the legal rationalisation by which it was accommodated. We can therefore give only an account which is too bad to be true. The jurisdictional monopoly of the court of common pleas was broken by two distinct processes. One was the disuse of the monopoly actions, in which much more than jurisdiction was at stake. The other was the adoption of what came to be mere devices by which an action within the monopoly could for particular reasons go elsewhere; and since the particular reasons became fictitious, this process has a particularly disreputable look.

The court of exchequer has been arbitrarily excluded from discussion on the ground that its doings had no particular influence on legal development; but the device by which it came to justify a jurisdiction over common pleas having no revenue interest deserves mention. Such an interest was simply surmised. The plaintiff was said to be indebted to the king, and to be so much the less able (*quo minus*) to pay because the defendant would not pay him[1]. By the time of its abolition in the nineteenth century, the plaintiff no doubt often was indebted to the king; but this was not the less a fiction for being sometimes true. It was an assertion made to keep the record straight; and with such assertions there is nothing except their regularity to distinguish them from the true statements from which they must have grown.

The device by which the king's bench came to hear actions within the common pleas monopoly was the more complicated Bill of Middlesex[2]. The desired result – and just who desired just what is the real question – was achieved by abusing two distinct features of medieval jurisdiction. The first was that the king's bench, like other medieval courts, had undoubted jurisdiction in nearly all matters over its own officials, and over anybody else in its own custody. What is more, since the court had both the jurisdiction and the defendant, there was no need for a chancery writ. If therefore Tom who owed a debt to Dick, happened to be in the king's bench prison at the suit of Harry, Dick could sue for the debt in the king's bench instead of in the common pleas, could do so without a writ, and could be sure that the case would be heard quickly because Tom was immediately available. So attractive did this become to the advisers of sixteenth-century creditors, that they arranged for Dick himself to play Harry's part, and begin a suit against Tom for the only purpose of getting him into the custody of the marshal, the king's bench jailer.

For this they employed another genuine feature of the court's medieval jurisdiction, one already mentioned. Because trespasses,

1. On the early history generally, see H. Jenkinson and B. Formoy, *Select Cases in the Exchequer of Pleas* (Selden Society, vol. 48); on *quo minus* see H. Wurzel, 'Origin and Development of Quo Minus' (1939) 49 Yale Law Journal, p. 39.
2. G. O. Sayles, *Select Cases in the Court of King's Bench*, vol. IV (Selden Society, vol. 74), pp. lxvii ff; M. Blatcher, *The Court of King's Bench, 1450–1550* (1978); C. A. F. Meekings, 'King's Bench Files', *Legal Records and the Historian* (1978), p. 97.

wrongs, first came before royal courts only when the king's rights were affected, the king's bench had jurisdiction in trespass concurrent with that of the common pleas. This jurisdiction they could always have exercised on their own authority without any reference of the matter to them by chancery writ. But chancery writs also set in motion the machinery for getting the defendant; and this was probably why the king's bench would accept direct complaints of trespass without writ only when the deed had been done in the county in which the court was sitting. Since the sheriff of that county was under the immediate orders of the court, it was easy for the court to get the defendant. But of course difficulties might emerge by the defendant fleeing to, or normally living in another county; and when the sheriff of the first county reported failure, the court would then issue judicial orders to the sheriff of the second.

The developed artefact therefore consisted of the following parts: a fictitious complaint of a trespass done in the county in which the court sat, now always Middlesex; a commonly abortive order to the sheriff of Middlesex to arrest the defendant and a formal report of failure; an effective order to the sheriff of the defendant's actual county; the defendant being held to bail and therefore placed in the nominal custody of the marshal; and lastly the true action. We do not know by what steps this became a recognised dodge. There was nothing fictitious about the opportunist creditor who took advantage of his debtor coming into custody at somebody else's suit. And when he is joined – and for a time the two appear in the rolls in roughly similar numbers – by the creditor who himself made the complaint which brought the debtor into custody, we cannot be sure that that complaint is entirely fictitious. Debtors have been known to answer roughly when pressed for payment. More important is the motive for these convolutions. To us and to the two courts the important result is that the true action is diverted from common pleas to king's bench; but this cannot have been very important to the plaintiff. He was, it is true, spared the risk of having to employ a serjeant; but for reasons to be discussed later in this chapter he would now not often need a serjeant even to sue in the common pleas. The diversion of jurisdiction was therefore not deliberately aimed at by anybody. The king's bench of course welcomed the end and connived at the means; but the force behind it was the plaintiff's desire for other qualities of the new procedure.

These were that he avoided the expense, delay and inconvenience of an original writ. The expense lay in the fees for its issue. The delay was in process: in a writ of debt, for example, it had been possible since the middle of the fourteenth century to arrest a defendant, but only after protracted attempts to make him come by the ancient processes of summons and attachment. The chief inconvenience arose from the part played by the writ as the court's warrant to act: if in this long interval reflection or new facts suggested to the plaintiff that he was claiming the wrong amount, or charging the defendant as executor when he should be liable in his own person, and if he counted accordingly, the variance from the writ would be fatal; he would be making a claim which the court was not authorised to hear. All this was avoided by the Bill of Middlesex. That is why we find the artificialities used even in actions of trespass and case, which were within the king's bench jurisdiction anyway. It is also why we find attempts to improve the service in the common pleas, by allowing a plaintiff in say debt to bring a fictitious action of trespass and use the swift process of the latter to accelerate his true action. This last is one of the points at which we can properly think in terms of 'competition' between the courts. But we must not allow such language to mislead us as to who at any one moment wanted to do what, or to blind us to the public benefit that resulted.

This is illustrated further by developments in the seventeenth century. The Bill of Middlesex was then found to offer opportunities to vexatious litigants, who could do much damage at small cost and no risk. This mischief was met after the Restoration by a statute which, in effect, prohibited the holding to bail of defendants except upon process stating the true cause of action[1]. This would have brought the Bill of Middlesex to an end, and the statute has therefore been attributed to machination by the common pleas; and no doubt that court and the clerks in chancery desired a return to the writ system. But success would not have rehabilitated the common pleas monopoly because the actions comprising that monopoly were by now almost out of use. Most litigation at

1. Stat. 13 Car. II, stat. 2, c. 2. Cf. 'Discourse' by Hale CJ in *Hargrave's Law Tracts* (1787), p. 359; Blackstone, *Commentaries* (5th edn., 1773), vol. III, p. 287; W. S. Holdsworth, *History of English Law*, vol. 1 (7th edn.), p. 200.

common law was being conducted under forms of action, trespass and case, which were equally within the king's bench proper jurisdiction. If therefore the statute was inspired by the common pleas, it was aimed only at competition on equal terms, with writs being generally necessary in both courts. It was in fact dodged by the *ac etiam* clause: the process continued to allege the fictitious trespass, 'and also' the true cause of action – a device of doubtful legality since until the defendant was in the custody of the marshal the court had no jurisdiction without writ over the true cause of action. But the device worked; the common pleas despondently allowed an *ac etiam* in their own fictitious trespass action; and with these last flourishes, the two courts moved into the age of reason.

Reason undertook some pruning. By the eighteenth century the whole business in both courts had become drill which attornies learnt to go through without worrying what it was all about; and they soon found that the earlier steps could be omitted without harm. Apart from colourful but meaningless phrases about the custody of the marshal and the like, the actual commencement of actions was therefore now sensible. But the losing defendant who brought a writ of error would set the ghosts walking: the plaintiff had then to complete his record by going through all the omitted steps, paying to have them ante-dated, and failing if his attorney had thoughtlessly left insufficient time in which they could have been taken. Such mishaps attracted critical notice of these procedural matters at a time when it would have been impious to question equally devious parts of the substantive law; and eighteenth-century critics went to the heart of the trouble, which was not the amelioration by fictions but the system of original writs itself[1].

THE INCREASE OF BUSINESS

The increase in king's bench work in the course of the sixteenth century is striking. A typical plea roll at the beginning of the century will have less than a hundred membranes, at the end ten times as many. Another indicator is the statute of 1585, already

1. See e.g. R. Boote, *An Historical Treatise of an Action or Suit at Law* (1st edn., 1766)..

mentioned, establishing a court of exchequer chamber which, until 1830, was to correct the errors of the king's bench[1]. The house of lords could not be the regular appellate body from a court operating on this scale. The statute speaks of actions 'first commenced' in the king's bench (Elizabeth I did not make it queen's bench); and the words 'first commenced' were taken to confine the statute to actions by bill, because an action begun by writ was begun in the chancery. The statute also specifies the kinds of action to which it is to apply. They are debt, detinue, covenant, account, action upon the case, *ejectio firmae* and trespass; and the unremarked enumeration of the first four, all within the common pleas monopoly, shows that the jurisdictional diversion produced by the Bill of Middlesex was part of the established order.

On the face of it, however, the increase in king's bench business does not reflect a diminution in the court of common pleas. A typical common pleas roll at the beginning of the sixteenth century will have something of the order of five hundred membranes, at the end something of the order of three thousand. The crude evidence of plea roll bulk therefore suggests a sharply expanding total of business, with the king's bench share increasing dramatically, but not to the point of reducing the absolute volume in the common pleas. But this evidence does not enable us to estimate the relative sizes of the two shares at any one time. At the end of the sixteenth century the rolls of the common pleas were still the more bulky. But – as will be remembered – the enrolment of formal steps had always caused that court to use more parchment for each case handled; and since it was in cases by writ that formal entries had to be made, the use of the Bill of Middlesex increased the disparity arising from this practice. There is, moreover, a more fundamental reason why plea roll bulk is an unreliable indicator, not only of the distribution of business between the two courts, but also of the increase of business in each one considered separately. Individual enrolments were growing longer. Except in actions of debt based on conditional bonds, in which a great deal of contractual detail was set out, the entry of a medieval action was generally quite short. The facts of cases, to our loss, were hidden behind common forms. But this was not so with actions on the case, in which the writ or bill and

1. Stat. 27 Eliz., c. 8.

therefore the whole entry was much more explicit; and in the sixteenth century, in both courts, actions on the case began to displace the older actions.

REPLACEMENT OF OLD ACTIONS BY NEW

This was the change, or rather the wave of roughly simultaneous changes, which enabled the common law to survive to our own time; and the pressure seems again to have been generated by the falling value of money leaving smaller and smaller cases outside the ambit of local justice. The tradesman's bill, for example, became tediously familiar in Westminster Hall. But the need was not for mechanical adjustment to large numbers. It was qualitative: Westminster Hall had never dealt well with the tradesman's bill.

However unsatisfactory to modern eyes looking at it out of its context, the ancient pattern of law-suit in local courts probably did as much justice between the parties to individual disputes as anything we know today. The plaintiff himself, the *secta* of neighbours who had in some way to authenticate his claim, the defendant, and those other neighbours who would have to swear that the defendant was a man to whose own oath credit should be given – all these had to live with each other afterwards, and with their parish priest. But the neighbours could not be dragged to Westminster; and there the *secta* became a word in the plea roll, and compurgators were hired on the spot. Now there was only the force of the defendant's own oath; and though a faithless age may underestimate the continuing effectiveness of that, the year books of the early fourteenth century show disquiet and even attempts to restrict the scope of compurgation. But the alternative was to force the defendant to a jury, and in contractual disputes in particular jury trial encountered a geographical difficulty already mentioned in connection with pleading: if the jury is itself supposed to consist of neighbours who know the facts, what is a court to do with a transaction alleged to have been made in one county, and performed or not in another? There were no such difficulties with compurgation, and it was left with a wide scope. But a quite different rule was adopted, again in the early fourteenth century, to reduce the difficulties of proof in contract litigation: in certain situations the plaintiff could not put the defendant to answer unless he could prove the agreement by a document under the defendant's seal; and unless the document itself was denied, that excluded altogether any question of proof.

It was these decisions of the early fourteenth century which had, as it were, to be reopened in the sixteenth. The requirement of a document under seal made no sense for the small transactions now brought within its scope by the fall in the value of money. And whether or not there had also been a fall in the value of oaths, more and more defendants were swearing them in metropolitan anonymity instead of among their neighbours. Jury trial, moreover, although it was to prove defective in many practical ways, was freed from the particular complication encountered in the fourteenth century: the jurors were now understood to decide upon the facts rather than to know them, and geography could therefore be disregarded.

But judges in the sixteenth century could not do what they had done in the fourteenth, and simply change the rules. They could not abandon the requirement of a document under seal in actions of covenant, or impose jury trial upon all defendants in actions of debt. Nor probably could they even have thought about the matter in such almost legislative terms. The old actions had, in effect, to disappear, and their work had to be taken over by others in which sealing-wax and compurgation could play no part. But except in their last stages the shifts were not made with that in mind.

The details belong to various later chapters of this book, especially that on the rise of the modern law of contract. But it may be helpful at this stage to attempt a statement in the largest terms. As a matter of social fact, what was going on was the last and greatest reception of business from other courts into the common law. Even the church courts will be seen to have played some part; but mainly, of course, the work was coming from local courts. And if we compare local records of the thirteenth and fourteenth centuries with common pleas and king's bench plea rolls of the sixteenth century, the process seems uncomplicated. Recognisably similar complaints have just moved from the one jurisdiction to the other.

But when we turn from records to year books and reports, we find that the transfer caused conceptual difficulty to lawyers at the time; and it is a difficulty of which historians have misunderstood the nature. The elementary ideas underlying the medieval covenant and debt were substantially narrower than our concept of contract, so that for example the contractor who caused harm by doing the job carelessly would be sued in what we should call tort rather than contract. And there was no difficulty about suing him in the king's courts, in an action of trespass on the case, once the king's courts were willing to entertain actions for wrongs in which no breach of the king's peace was alleged. What in our language was a tort action has been transferred from the one court to the other, and it is handled in the king's court as naturally as it had been in the local court. There was equally no difficulty about an action coming into the king's court which plainly was within the ideas of covenant and debt; but it must of course be subjected to the now unsuitable rules about sealed documents and compurgation. The unnatural part of the development is what happens at the very end, when plaintiffs whose true complaint is within the old ideas of contract are allowed to get their remedies in actions formally complaining of wrongs. Legal principle is more or less consciously surrendered to the times.

The difficult question is when the matter could be seen in those terms. Legal historians looking backwards from our own wide and woolly ideas of contract – themselves a product of the changes – have seen the whole development, from its very beginning with the careless contractor, as somehow directed towards its end. The relevant chapter in this book will try to tell the story forwards from the beginning; and it will appear that the natural analysis of situations as wrongs reaches a surprisingly long way towards the end – natural in the sense that the facts did disclose a genuine wrong distinct from the mere contractual failure. The realistic departure from principle begins out of sight like so much other development: juries award the damages appropriate to the contractual failure and not just those appropriate to the wrong. The world had all but imposed its changes by the time the lawyers accepted them.

The matter has been further confused for legal historians by what is essentially a coincidence. This is the circumstance already noted, that the old actions to be replaced were within the common pleas monopoly, whereas actions for wrongs were equally proper in the king's bench. The changes therefore had a jurisdictional effect like the Bill of Middlesex; and to the extent that they were intended this provides an apparent motive. It is true that some of the particular developments seem first to have happened in the king's bench, and that they gave rise to unseemly differences between the two courts. But we probably perpetuate a misunderstanding if we see this wholly or even mainly in terms of 'competition'. There seems to have been a genuine difference of approach. The king's bench did not have to accommodate their actions within the same framework as the old actions of covenant and debt; and they may have been the leaders not just in allowing remedies but in the new conceptualisation which was eventually to emerge as a new law of contract. Whatever its nature, the interplay between the two central courts is of small importance compared with the massive shift from local courts. The common law had now to deal with the simple questions and to reach the simple answers familiar in lesser jurisdictions; but it had cut itself off from the simple approach.

CHANGING PATTERN OF LAW-SUIT

The changes by which the year book pattern of litigation was replaced were less distinct and spread out over a longer period than the other changes considered in this chapter; and because the new pattern lasted until the Judicature Acts, they have been ignored as obsolete procedure not worth paper and ink. We do not know in detail what happened when, and still less why. But the largest practical result was to bring before the court itself, as distinct from the trial judge at *nisi prius*, only those cases in which a point of law ctually arose; and since in any age most law-suits are just about the facts, it seems likely that this segregation was ultimately a result of pressure on court time. But again the changes were piecemeal, and many began when the common pleas still carried most of the load by itself.

THE RISE OF WRITTEN PLEADINGS

Just as the formulation of the count had by the close of the thirteenth century been relegated from its position as the central skill of lawyers to become a formal preliminary to the pleadings, so in the fifteenth and sixteenth centuries the pleading slowly became a formal preliminary to court processes more sophisticated but less coherent.

The system of oral pleading collapsed under its own weight. In a simple case it was absurd, and for the poor man ruinous, to put serjeants through a ritual recitation of count and general issue. In a complex case, it was like setting grand masters to play lightning chess. What mattered was what went down on the plea roll; and by stages not precisely known, but not difficult to imagine, it became possible to make a plea by handing a draft to the clerk. The plea rolls themselves, as one would expect, do not signal this change except perhaps by an increasing tendency for each stage to be separated from the next by an 'imparlance', an adjournment for consultation. But it seems to have happened slowly. The handing in of papers probably began as something exceptional, to enable the poor man to manage without a serjeant or to give serjeants time to think; and even when it had become normal in the sixteenth century, serjeants may have been able to interrupt the written exchange in order to inaugurate a discussion in court about the propriety of a plea contemplated but not yet put in. To that extent the year book pattern of discussion seems to have overlapped with newer mechanisms.

Certainly the year books themselves, which had come into being with oral pleading, did not come to a distinct end. They merged into reports and notes no doubt more suitable for the new form of discussion, but all too often reporting the discussion in disembodied form so that we have no way of telling how it has been started. A less important but more distinctive literary reflection of the change is the appearance of the books of entries, formularies for the draftsmen. Here pleas are set out in Latin and in indirect speech, just like the clerk's record of something actually spoken in court; and they were indeed mostly taken from real records. But they were for the guidance, not of the clerks of the court, but of the parties' lawyers.

What kind of men drafted these written pleadings? We do not know; but probably it would not often be the serjeants. Their proper occupation had now gone. They had started as counters, having sole licence to perform the central act of the legal process in the court which had sole jurisdiction over ordinary law-suits. The shift of focus from counting to pleading had not undermined the logic of their position: the new art was an elaboration of the old and was dominated by the same pattern. But this further shift left them with the sole right of audience in the common pleas as a monopoly without reason and almost without explanation: though as late as the eighteenth century there was an occasional reminder of their beginnings, when certain antique actions were introduced by the ceremonial mumbling of a count in French.

But the end of oral pleading brought to an end more than the occupation of the serjeants and the subject-matter of the year books. If unaccompanied by other changes, it would have brought to an end all legal discussion in court. Indeed, in both king's bench and common pleas it is clear that many cases were completed without ever coming before the court at Westminster. The written pleadings would lead to an issue of fact, which would be decided at *nisi prius* or by wager of law; and judgment would be entered by the clerks. Only at *nisi prius* did such a case truly come before a judge; and legal argument there would rarely be reported until the eighteenth century. So what opportunities were there for legal discussion, and what were the courts *in banc* actually doing?

DEMURRER

The written pleadings might, of course, end in a demurrer. If one party claimed that the facts pleaded by the other, which had to be taken as true, were insufficient in law to sustain that other's case, then there was nothing but the matter of law to discuss; and it would be discussed *in banc* at Westminster. In the sixteenth century, at any rate, many reports from both common pleas and king's bench are of arguments on demurrer; and a clear picture is to be had from Plowden's reports. The pleadings are set out as though from the plea roll. Then comes the argument, which is introduced by a short statement of the case made by counsel on behalf of the party demurring. This statement is followed, by no means always all in one day, by a series of more or less set speeches by counsel giving their opinions; and in the common pleas a serjeant seems generally to have given his opinion whether he was retained in the case or not. Then come similar opinions by the individual judges;

and if there was a substantial difference of opinion between them, the case might be left unresolved. If judgment was given, it seems to have contained no further statements of principle. Plowden sets it out as though from the plea roll: on consideration it seemed to the court that the plea demurred to was or was not good.

At the beginning of the sixteenth century it looks as though the demurrer, and perhaps the old-style discussion of a case in which the pleadings were not yet finally formulated, were the principal vehicles of legal thought. But they were gradually to be replaced by new devices already coming into use.

DISCUSSION AFTER TRIAL OF FACTS ALLEGED IN THE PLEADINGS

In the year book pattern, law could be formally declared only upon a demurrer; but it rarely happened because of the risks involved. On the one side, nobody would wish to stake his case on a plea which might be held bad on demurrer. And on the other side, nobody would wish to stake his case on a demurrer, on his own view of a point of law, when he could do so only at the cost of admitting the facts pleaded by his opponent. The system was too tidy for life, which rarely generates law-suits in which only the law or only the facts are in dispute. That is why most law in year books is informally indicated rather than formally declared: after discussion, such a plea was or was not formally made.

The new possibility which emerges is that the case can go to trial on the facts, and then the loser can raise the propriety of the plea when the *postea* comes back to the court in Westminster for judgment[1]. In one situation the court *in banc* could actually enter judgment in favour of the party who had lost at the trial. Suppose for example a trespass action for pulling the plaintiff's house down, in which the defendant pleads what we should call necessity: he did

1. It is only since the first edition of this book that detailed study has begun of these changes and of the mechanisms which resulted: J. H. Baker, *Spelman's Reports*, vol. II (Selden Society, vol. 94), pp. *92* ff, *116* ff; *An Introduction to English Legal History* (1979), pp. 71 ff. Mr. N. le Poidevin is undertaking research on developments before the sixteenth century. An account of the developed system is R. Sutton, *Personal Actions at Common Law* (1929), esp. ch. 7; and there is relevant material in J. B. Thayer, *A Preliminary Treatise of Evidence at the Common Law* (1898).

it to stop a city fire spreading. Such a plea confesses the fact, and relies upon the justification to avoid liability. If the plaintiff makes the usual answer to a plea of justification, saying that the defendant did not do it for the reason stated but of his own wickedness and wrong (the replication *de son tort demesne*), the only issue for the jury is whether the destruction of the house, which in itself is admitted, was or was not done in the circumstances and for the reason stated. If not, the plaintiff is entitled to judgment without more. He would equally have been entitled to judgment without more if he had demurred to the plea and his demurrer had been upheld: the defendant has admitted pulling the house down, and the court has held as a matter of law that he was not justified in doing so even to stop a fire spreading. But on the year book pattern the plaintiff's two possible answers were strictly alternative. He could not say that the defendant had snatched the excuse of a distant fire to pull his house down maliciously, and that anyway it was not lawful to pull houses down to stop fires spreading. But this is just what the change allows. Having pleaded his replication and lost on the facts, the jury having found that the defendant did indeed do it to stop a fire spreading, the plaintiff can now move that judgment be entered in his favour *non obstante veredicto*. What the court has to decide on that motion is exactly the question that would have been raised if the plaintiff had demurred to the plea: as a matter of law does this compulsion of circumstances justify the defendant's act? If not, since the act itself is admitted, the plaintiff is entitled to judgment and damages.

More common and more important was the motion in arrest of judgment, in principle exactly similar except that instead of the plaintiff objecting to a defendant's plea it is the defendant who objects after the trial to the plaintiff's claim. But for the historian there is an important practical difference: if this motion is successful, no judgment is given, and there is no clear indication on the plea roll of what has happened. Law is being declared as definitively as if the defendant had demurred to the claim; but in a new sense it is being declared off the record. Motions in arrest became, however, common in the reports, and particularly in connection with actions on the case. The actual claim disclosed more of the facts in an action on the case than in any of the older actions, so that there was more for the defendant to catch hold of.

And actions on the case were doing many new things. Defamation actions, for example, were coming into royal courts for the first time: and the recurring question, whether these words were actionable, was normally settled by motion in arrest rather than on demurrer. Similarly *assumpsit,* though long put to more or less natural use in the king's courts, was in the sixteenth century being extended into the field of older actions; and the resulting difficulties, already mentioned in this chapter, were largely discussed on motions for arrest of judgment.

Neither of these motions was a direct alternative to demurrer. Statute had caused trivial errors in pleading to be 'cured' by verdict, so that a party who failed to demur could not always pick up the point by motion after trial[1]. But the converse proposition is always true: a party who succeeded on one of these motions could always have succeeded on demurrer without the case going to trial. The motions therefore did not allow any kind of point to be brought up for discussion that could not have been brought up within the old framework. There is no qualitative change in law-making capacity: there is a quantitative change. The year book freedom to put up pleas for discussion without actually making them was curtailed by written pleading, and is now more than restored by these motions. A party who has already lost on the facts has nothing more to lose, except perhaps some costs; and points of law will be not just discussed but definitively decided much more frequently.

DISCUSSION OF FACTS COMING OUT AT THE TRIAL

The year book pattern had divided the facts potentially relevant to any law-suit into two classes: those which could be specially pleaded and those which could not. What mattered was not juristic importance, but the danger that a jury would go wrong if left with a general issue which included the fact in question. It follows that to reach a general verdict on the general issue, a jury would often have to decide what we would today regard as a question of law. Unlike the motions in arrest and for judgment *non obstante*, therefore, the

1. Statutes of 'jeofails': Stats. 32 Hy. VIII, c. 30; 18 Eliz., c. 14; 27 Eliz., c. 5; 21 Jac. 1, c. 13.

mechanisms by which these questions could be formally put to the court for discussion caused law to be declared in entirely new areas.

One mechanism has been mentioned already. The demurrer to evidence did work which would have been done by the demurrer itself if pleading had not been distorted by the primacy of the general issue. The fact which could not be pleaded is now being tendered to the jury, usually upon the general issue; and the opposing party can dispute its legal relevance on the same terms as for a demurrer in pleading, namely that he admits its factual truth. No doubt for this reason it was never common; but it shows up the predicament of the law with the cruelty of a caricature.

Another device which did become common has also been mentioned before. The special verdict was known in the year book period and even earlier, but almost wholly in 'assizes' rather than juries, that is actions in which the question for the countryside was pre-ordained and not reached by pleading. The verdict of an assize could be challenged by attaint, essentially a charge of perjury against the recognitors; and severe penalties followed if a second and larger body found their verdict false. In the assize of novel disseisin in particular, a verdict that the defendant did or did not disseise the plaintiff might visibly involve the decision of difficult questions of property law; and as early as 1285 recognitors were given a statutory right to state the facts and leave it to the court to work out whether or not there had been a disseisin[1]. Special verdicts are not unknown in other kinds of action; but they are rare, and seem to be the last resort of kindly judges with bewildered juries. If the difficulty was foreseen, the parties would normally try to keep it from the jury by special pleading.

But in the course of the sixteenth century special verdicts become more common; and they are not the products of laymen confronted by an unexpected difficulty. A detailed statement of facts, sometimes long and probably settled between counsel and the trial judge, ends with a formula to this effect: 'And if it shall seem to the justices that (say) the entry of such a person was lawful, then the jurors say that the defendant is guilty; and if not, they say that he is not guilty.' The form represents a general verdict subject to alternative conditions, and makes explicit the thought processes

1. Stat. 13 Ed. I (Statute of Westminster II), c. 30. For a similar possibility in the grand assize see *Glanvill*, II, 18 (ed. G. D. G. Hall, p. 35).

which might be required to determine a general issue. But we must not suppose some sudden awakening to the juristic advantages of being explicit. The increase of special verdicts first came about in actions for trespass in which proprietary questions were raised, and in particular in the action of *ejectio firmae*. The details, as devious as the Bill of Middlesex, belong to a later chapter. In essence, as part of the movement whereby actions in trespass and case were made to do the work of older actions, this trespass action is doing work once done by the assize of novel disseisin in trying title; and these special verdicts are much the same as those long familiar in the assize. But in trespass, unlike the assize, there could in principle be special pleading; and it is not obvious why defendants took the general issue and so left complicated legal questions to come out in this way. An ancient principle of feudal origin had it that one could not act with force and arms within one's fee; and it is possible that failure to take the general issue at least to that allegation would constitute an admission about the point truly in issue, namely the defendant's title. Or perhaps factual complexity just made special pleading impracticable. For whatever reason, the special verdict became more generally acceptable; and it played its part in the great developments of the late sixteenth and early seventeenth centuries. For example the most controversial of the changes by which actions of trespass and case displaced the older actions was the displacement of debt by *assumpsit*, and it will be discussed for its own sake later in this book. The matter was brought to a head, perhaps deliberately, by the taking of a special verdict in *Slade's Case*. Like examination candidates today, the judges gave varying answers of varying coherence: but at least the facts of their problem were clear. The special verdict was unrivalled as a vehicle for legal development.

But practitioners and judges do not normally give a pin for legal development. Their duty is to these clients and the proper disposition of this case. Since an inherently difficult piece of drafting had to be agreed by both parties and accepted by the jurors, the special verdict required more cooperation than was often available; and it largely gave way to mechanisms which depended upon a general verdict. The judge at *nisi prius* would direct the jury on the questions of law raised by the facts, and any discussion would be about the propriety of his direction. The greater elasticity of this, however, had its own price. The demurrer to evidence and the special verdict both put the facts formally onto the record, so that the decision *in banc* could be followed by a writ of error and therefore by further consideration of the point of law. But the devices now to be described worked outside the record, so that the decision of the court *in banc* was final. On the other hand the court *in banc* had itself become essentially an appellate tribunal, reconsidering the actions of the trial judge; and it was indeed in this relationship, rather than in error proceedings, that the modern Court of Appeal largely had its origins.

There are three possible ways in which discussion might be raised on a general verdict. The trial judge might consult his fellows about the proper direction before giving it. Or, adapting the principle of the special verdict, he might in effect give alternative directions, have the doubtful point discussed afterwards, and then have the appropriate verdict entered accordingly. Or lastly, if the judge was sufficiently confident to give a straightforward direction, the losing party might be enabled to upset the resulting verdict on the ground that that direction was wrong. The reticence of most sixteenth-century reporters about the steps by which their discussion had been raised makes it difficult to distinguish between the first two. But a few reports seem clearly to be about a direction to be given in the future, and it is likely that this, the first of our possibilities, would happen only when the trial itself was at Westminster. In an ordinary *nisi prius* case, the resulting delay would make it impracticable.

The second possibility, which like the first would leave no trace on the record, is probably behind many sixteenth-century reports which open with some such phrase as 'The case upon the evidence was . . .'. It became common, being developed as an informal substitute for the special verdict; and like the special verdict it required, after the evidence had been heard, a measure of agreement between the parties about the facts. The trial judge would give a carefully formulated direction and take a general verdict; and this would be subject to an agreed statement of facts for the court *in banc*. If the court considered the direction wrong in law, the verdict, which had been taken conditionally, would be entered in accordance with the direction that ought to have been given.

In both these situations the difficulty had been recognised and provided for at the trial, and the second at least partly depended upon agreement. To allow one party to attack the direction and undo the verdict after it had been definitely taken was a larger step; and since there was no way of knowing whether the jury had based their verdict on the misdirection, it involved the inconvenience of a new trial. New trials were ordered in the sixteenth century, but apparently only when the jury had so misconducted themselves that the trial had to be held a nullity. It was in the seventeenth century that motions for a new trial became common, based upon misdirection; and apart from their impact on substantive law, such motions were of course also the medium in which much of the law of evidence was developed. Since the logic of the matter disappeared with the Judicature Acts, it is perhaps worth observing that the power to order a new trial was strictly a product of the *nisi prius* system. A commissioner of assize trying a criminal case entered the formal judgment on his own authority, and there was no court *in banc* to which to apply for a new trial on the grounds of misdirection or misreception of evidence. That is why the possibility of a new trial in criminal cases was limited to those formally prosecuted before the king's bench itself, and committed to trial at *nisi prius*.

SUBSTANTIVE RESULT OF PROCEDURAL CHANGES

Although these various mechanisms look as untidy as the pieces of jigsaw puzzle emptied from their box, they equally fit together to make a picture; and the picture is that of a modern legal system.

The most obvious gain is that facts which could be pleaded and facts which could emerge only at the trial were at last brought together. The logic of medieval pleading was directed to the possible misleading of juries. This was the consideration which had determined whether a fact could be lifted out and placed on the record, and therefore be thought about, or whether it had to be left within the general issue and so lost to legal analysis. But this was a procedural logic, and so far as substantive law was concerned it was arbitrary. In trespass to the person, for example, accident was lost within the general issue, justification brought to the surface; and we may still be paying the price of having left the former so long unconsidered.

Less tangible, but no less a gain, was that law-suits had been turned round to put ascertainment of the facts first. All the motions, those relating to facts which could be pleaded as well as those relating to facts emerging at the trial, were considered after the trial when the facts were known. A modern system is the product of thinking about facts taken as known. Early legal systems are not so presumptuous. Their aim is only to settle disputes, and the general issue in its most ancient form reflects this: the blank answer settles the dispute, and whether the winner has won on the facts or on the law is a question which itself does not arise. When facts could first be raised by special pleading it was in isolation and hypothetically; and the single rules that they generated were cast in procedural terms. The epileptic beaten by way of treatment and the house pulled down to halt the fire created particular pleas, not a general principle about necessity. And this turning round of law-suits could work together with another change outlined in this chapter, that by which older actions were replaced by trespass and case. When law is seen as a product of analysing the facts taken as a whole, the same facts can often be analysed in different ways, for example in tort rather than in contract; and procedure has lost control of substance.

But a legal system which matures can also decay; and it is possible to wonder whether English law today is not missing the self-discipline which procedure imposed. Consider pleading. The effective consequence of breaking down the distinction between facts which could and facts which could not be pleaded was that it became increasingly a matter of choice whether a defendant would plead specially or take the general issue. In 1834 an attempt was made to find a new and definite place for the general issue as a denial of the basic assertion in the plaintiff's case, the making of the contract, the commission of the tortious act, or whatever it might be[1]. But this still imposed an unacceptable technicality, and pleading was further relaxed to become little more than a means of saving costs by narrowing the area of dispute. A precise question is hardly ever identified, and it follows that the precise legal answers required by special pleading are hardly ever given.

1. The 'Hilary Rules' were made by the judges in pursuance of Stat. 3 & 4 Wm. IV, c. 42, s. 1.

Nor are statements any longer made with the clarity required in directing a jury on the general issue. Courts had then to declare law in fewer and simpler words than are found in today's reports. They were also more general words, stating principles in such terms as what the reasonable man should do, and leaving it to the jury to apply the principle to the details of the case. The virtual disappearance of the civil jury has removed any limit to the depth of detail which can be made legally relevant, and also any limit to the depth of technicality with which the law can be stated. Judgments in civil cases no longer state rules which juries could have understood, and which ordinary people could be expected to obey. Indeed the rules stated are often not about what people should do at all, but about what their insurance companies must pay for.

But this is associated with a deeper change. The largest impediment to the historian's vision, and one mentioned now because it is particularly relevant to the following chapter, is his own perception of law as conscious social regulation. This book has so far considered the changing framework which brought about development by raising more and more questions to be answered. But for most of the process judges thought of themselves as making law explicit rather than making it, as finding answers rather than choosing them on utilitarian grounds. Rights and wrongs were not made in the first place. They had been there within the ordeal, within the conscience of a defendant swearing with his compurgators, known in the same sense to jurors; and the judge who first directed them was focussing their own minds, not reading from a book which he knew and they did not. There was no book.

4 *The Rise of Equity*

PROCEDURAL BEARINGS OF EARLY EQUITY

Few beginnings are so elusive as that of the chancellor's equitable jurisdiction, and one reason is that the end is probably the most important and certainly the most astonishing of English contributions to legal thought: we search our documents for something too big. Nor are the documents themselves as copious or as well-ordered as a series of plea rolls. Not until the sixteenth century do we have the court's own records of action taken; and though some pleadings survive from the preceding century, the beginning must be reconstructed from petitions, bills of complaint, sometimes with the bonus of an endorsement ordering some action. Who was being petitioned to do what? Those are the questions for which we have expected answers on too grand a scale.

A bill was no more than a complaint addressed to whatever authority was thought able to handle it; and bills in eyre, mentioned earlier in this book, were a humdrum example. As authorities able to handle almost anything, the king and his council received many bills alleging all kinds of grievance, general and particular; and those complaining of individual wrongs were so regularly referred to the chancellor that by the fifteenth century they were often addressed directly to him, and decrees came to be expressed as made on his own authority. If we look at this sequence from a later framework in which 'equity' exists as something like a dispensing power from 'the law', we see a petition for specifically sovereign intervention which the sovereign delegates; and we find a utilitarian reason for his choosing the chancellor, namely that the appropriate response was often that the complainant should buy a writ and proceed in the usual way, and these cases could easily be disposed of by the chancellor's staff.

But there is both less and more to it than that. Of course the chancellor derived his power from the king. But this was not the delegation of some sovereign power to override the law, and a petitioner did not see himself as asking for the law to be overridden. The chancellor was in charge of the king's judicial machinery; and just as you bought a writ from one of his clerks in a routine case, so did you apply to him when for some particular reason the routine machinery was visibly not going to do justice. Many petitions of the fourteenth and fifteenth centuries complain of matters which in principle were remedied by the common law. Special treatment is sought because the petitioner is too poor to sue, or his adversary so powerful that sheriffs will not do their duty or jurors tell the truth. These the historian can set aside as having nothing to do with the later 'equity'; but he does so at his peril. They warn us to begin from institutions, not from ideas of substantive law.

In the fourteenth century there was no law of England, no body of rules complete in itself with known limits and visible defects; or if there was it was not the property of the common law courts or any others. There were justice and right, absolute values; but it was not yet the lawyer's business to comprehend them in the sense of knowing what was the just and right result upon these facts and those. His business was procedural, to see that disputes were properly submitted to the appropriate deciding mechanism. The mechanism would declare that justice lay with the one side rather than the other, but this was the inscrutable manifestation of a result. In time the jury system, by compelling the reasoned consideration of facts, would create substantive rules and the concept of substantive law. But the end of that was far in the future. In the present there were only situations in which the mechanism visibly would not work. One has been considered already, the true beginning of that compulsion to consider facts: unlike God, a jury could be misled by deceptive situations, and that is what started the fertile process of pleading. This was a mischief that could be dealt with by adapting the mechanism itself. But, also unlike God, a jury could be intimidated or corrupted. Here no adaptation was possible. The petitioner believed that his case was beyond the ordinary mechanism, and he sought another way. But he did not see himself as applying to a different system of rules, or even as applying outside an established set of rules to some superior having absolute authority at will. He wanted only the common justice[1].

The mechanisms themselves, the structure of courts and their procedures, were not part of the immutable order. They were matters for human decision, the business of lawyers and the whole content of what we should call positive law. And so far as all lay questions were concerned, they had come to be seen as matters which the king should order and for the ordering of which he was somehow answerable. Even to a lord who 'owned' his jurisdiction the king would say, in the great writ of right to be discussed in a later chapter, 'if you do not do right, the sheriff will'. And although local courts would normally act without his specific authorisation or order, the procedural and other propriety of their action could be questioned in the king's court. Propriety of jurisdiction at first instance as between the king's courts and the old local courts had come to depend largely upon the forty shilling barrier. But though the thirty shilling creditor and the fifty shilling creditor sued in different courts, they expected the same justice, probably manifested by compurgation; and if the fifty shilling creditor wished, he could have a *justicies* writ referring his claim to the sheriff instead of to the common pleas. Royal justices themselves were authorised as a matter of administrative convenience, either to hear classes of case like the justices in eyre or to hear individual cases like the common pleas; and these authorisations, whether commissions or writs, came from the chancery. This was the head office of the organisation; and it was here that application was made when the ordinary mechanisms appeared to be incapable of working. The approach to the chancellor has no more mysterious origin than that.

These then are the terms in which we must think. Not only was there no equity as a nascent body of rules different from those of the common law. There was no common law, no body of substantive rules from which equity could be different. And the idea that law could be unjust, if comprehensible at all, would have been abhorrent. Failures were mechanical. A jury would be intimidated,

1. Cf. F. W. Maitland, *Equity* (1909), Lecture 1, esp. p. 6: 'I do not think that in the fourteenth century the Chancellors considered that they had to administer any body of substantive rules that differed from the ordinary law of the land.' Cf. A. D. Hargreaves, 'Equity and the Latin Side of Chancery' (1952) 68 LQR, p. 481; G. O. Sayles, *Select Cases in the Court of King's Bench*, vol. V (Selden Society, vol. 76), pp. lxvii ff.

or documents of title would be suppressed, or the petitioner had by fraud been induced to seal a document which would be treated as conclusive proof. Only to hindsight is it clear that the first case is different from the other two. For gross interferences such as bribery and intimidation, it was not enough to accept their existence and prevent them achieving injustice in the individual case: they had to be stopped, and ironically it was the Star Chamber, an aspect of the king's council which was later abolished as an instrument of tyranny, that established this element of the rule of law. Perversion of the system itself was thus withdrawn, leaving as the general ground for seeking the chancellor's interference some private fraud or overreaching merely between the parties.

This common factor in so much of what the chancellor did coincides with an oddity in the common law; and together they seem to conjure up a picture of the law as set in some savage mould, able to understand force but not fraud, and leaving equity to cater for an emerging civilisation. It can colourably be said, for example, that the tort of deceit was not invented until the eighteenth century. But this is in the nature of an optical illusion. Fraud was a frequent cause of action in local courts from the earliest times of which we know. It was not frequent in royal courts because until the late fourteenth century no wrongs were meant to come there except those in which the king as well as the party had been injured. This is why the early records of the common law are filled with trespasses against the king's peace, but almost the only deceits of which they tell are those in which a royal court had been deceived. Fraud was beneath the notice of the king's judges rather than above their heads. This accident was followed by another. When in the late fourteenth century wrongs as such came within the avowed ambit of royal jurisdiction irrespective of any royal interest, actions alleging deceit duly appear in the records of the common law. But, by processes to be considered in a later chapter, they were denatured to provide new remedies in what we should call contract. The defendant formally charged as a cheat was really just a defaulting promisor; and against the true cheat there was no special remedy left. This did create something like a substantive gap, to be filled by chancery and by the later resurrection of a tort of deceit. But it was a gap in remedies and did not reflect some primitive incomprehension. Nobody had ever thought cheating was lawful[1].

1. See pp. 320 ff, 328 ff, 361 ff. below.

The procedural bearings of the chancellor's interference may best be seen in terms of a real situation. Suppose the borrower of money had provided his lender with a sealed acknowledgment of his indebtedness. If the lender has to sue, he will win on mere production of the document: the borrower can deny only its genuineness and that only at the cost of being imprisoned if it is found to be genuine. If he admits the document, he cannot deny the debt; and commercially this is a convenient result. But the convenience carries possible injustice with it: if the borrower pays the debt but omits to recover the document, he can be made to pay again. The chancellor could see as clearly as the judges that interference to prevent the individual injustice could impair the general convenience, and might prefer to leave the matter to the private conscience of the lender. And the judges could see as clearly as the chancellor that the mischief was procedural: because of the rules of proof a law-suit was going to be won unjustly, but of course a paid debt was not still owed. If there was no sealed acknowledgment, the debtor who had paid would simply deny that he owed and wage his law: and if there was any discussion about the propriety of his wager – as there may be in less straightforward cases – the judges would have no hesitation in declaring that he could 'safely in conscience' make his oath. There was only one justice.

EQUITY AND USES

Every proposition that can be made about the overall development of the common law requires a *caveat* about its application to property in land. In the areas that we know as contract and tort, it was only the changes described in the preceding chapter that enabled substantive rules to be declared on any large scale; and not until the nineteenth century can those rules be seen as self-sufficient systems existing independently of their procedural framework, and best expounded in text-books in the modern style. But for the law of property in land, Littleton's *Tenures* written in the fifteenth century can properly be described as a text-book; and substantive rules systematically related with each other and expressed in terms of highly abstract concepts were then already old. Explanation must await a later chapter: what matters in the present context is the result. There were clear rules about the dealings with land that were possible; but they did not accommodate all the things that a landowner might wish to do. If he died leaving a son and a daughter, for example, the son would inherit all his land; and the only way he could provide for his daughter was by an immediate grant which, like Lear, he might live to regret. The better course was to make his immediate grant to a group of friends to hold to his own use or benefit until he died, and then to convey the land according to his instructions. These instructions he could change as he liked; but if his last expressed wish was that the friends should convey the land to his daughter, they would naturally do so.

Arrangements of this nature were meant to be without legal sanction; and they were probably being made long before the chancellor would interfere. We do not even know in what kinds of circumstance his first interference was made. It may have been in cases of honest doubt on the part of the feoffees, for example, because the father had left no declaration or contradictory declarations in his will. If it was in cases of simple disloyalty, surely rare, it is conceivable that early interference was seen in procedural terms: the plaintiff might rest his case on the absence of proof that the grant to the friends had been conditional. But since even the existence of a common law condition would often not produce the result desired, as will appear when uses are discussed for their own sake, the enforcement of uses cannot long have been seen in terms of that sort of mechanical failure. It gave effect to the obligations of conscience in a situation in which the legal property rights were clear and had been deliberately created, and it was perhaps the first situation in which the chancellor could be seen as enforcing a separate body of rules. But even this may have been seen as the result of a different kind of mechanical failure, namely the incapacity of an appropriate tribunal. Testamentary jurisdiction belonged to the church; and it may be relevant that the church recognised rules of family provision: widow and children were entitled to fixed shares. Even with land a moral duty to make family provision may be reflected in the willingness of church courts to enforce a daughter's claim that her father and elder brother should maintain her marriage portion. But the testamentary jurisdiction was limited to chattel wealth; and the church courts could not interfere even in devises of urban tenements which were outside the feudal logic and therefore free of any special claim by the heir, and were devisable by custom. They had no jurisdiction to pass judgment about title to land. But they could always impose spiritual sanctions on persons who disobeyed their orders; and we now know that, at least in some dioceses, church courts were making orders against feoffees to testamentary uses of land until about the middle of the fifteenth century[1]. They presumably ceased to do so because the chancellor was then doing the same thing himself, only with lay instead of spiritual sanctions. And the chancellor had no doubt undertaken to do it because the church should not. The jurisdictional limitation could not alter right and wrong.

THEORETICAL RELATIONSHIP BETWEEN LAW AND EQUITY

Although in the case of uses the chancellor was probably developing and enforcing rules outside the common law, there was no possible conflict, just as there is not with trusts today. Nobody would think that the legal ought to carry the beneficial title with it, and from the beginning the explanation which uses called for was historical rather than intellectual; people wondered how they had come into being, but had little difficulty in accommodating their coexistence with legal titles. But intellectual explanation was required for cases in which one law-suit before the chancellor seemed to cancel out another at common law.

The explanation in theory, a commonplace by the late sixteenth century, was that any general rule must work injustice in particular cases, and therefore that the application of positive law must be subject to some dispensing power in the interest of a higher justice. This idea, established on the continent but dramatised in England by the jurisdictional separation of law and equity, became part of the world's legal currency; and equity in this sense may appear, not necessarily administered by separate courts, in any legal system. But in England, and perhaps generally, the true newcomer was not equity but positive law. Consider fraud playing what we see as the

1. R. H. Helmholz, 'The Early Enforcement of Uses' (1979) 79 Columbia Law Review, p. 1503. For an early view of jurisdiction over urban devises, see F. M. Nichols, *Britton*, vol. I, p. 174, n.f. For uses generally see ch. 9, below.

part of a defence. In the sixteenth century it will be seen as a rule of positive law that a promise made under seal is binding, and equitable relief will be sought on the ground that the promisor was tricked. Here in embryo are the mysteries of our voidable contract. But in the fourteenth century the seal was a matter of proof, not part of a substantive rule: there was only one justice, but the ordinary machine would not in this case produce it.

The appeal to a higher justice was of course further explained, most elaborately in the early sixteenth century by St Germain in his *Doctor and Student*[1]. St Germain was a barrister having extensive theological learning; and for him the higher justice was divine in origin, and its human manifestation was a matter of conscience. This was an important stage in English legal thought, not because it was new but because it linked the medieval world and the modern. There was nothing new in the appeal to conscience. The language is found in petitions from the earliest times; but it was not just designed to persuade chancellors who had nearly always been ecclesiastics; still less to persuade them to produce a different result from that reached by 'the law'. Justice was as single as truth, and conscience was man's knowledge of it. Positive law was about the means by which this single justice should be manifested; and the appeal to the chancellor was for the same justice, in circumstances in which the human machinery was going to fail. What was new in *Doctor and Student*, then, was not the idea of justice as divine: that was older than Christianity. The new element was a positive human law beginning to be conceived in substantive terms, in terms of a rule that on these facts this result ought to follow, and on those facts that result. And sometimes the result was visibly unjust. The achievement of St Germain was to reconcile this new concept of law with the medieval belief in divine justice.

For reasons that will appear, the actual terms of this reconciliation were important for the future; and it is worth considering how completely they may have been dictated by the past. Discussion has normally turned upon the fact that most medieval chancellors were clerics, and that canonist ideas may for that chance reason have

1. Edited by T. F. T. Plucknett and J. L. Barton (Selden Society, vol. 91): these vivid dialogues were printed many times between the sixteenth century and the nineteenth. Compare the rather later work by E. Hake, *Epieikeia* (edited with an introduction by D. E. C. Yale and a preface by S. E. Thorne, 1953).

played a large part in early equity. But there is probably more to it than that. How could divine justice manifest itself? There was no difficulty so long as all law-suits were settled by making a party swear to the justice of his cause, and submitting that oath to divine test. The true start of equity as well as of the common law was the replacement of the divine test by a fallible human result. This result might obviously fail to reflect a justice still seen as absolute; and it was apprehension of this that prompted application to the chancellor as head of the human system. But what was he to do about it? He had no special access either to absolute justice or to the minds of men; and he could not simply declare a result for himself. All he could do was to work upon the conscience of the party, where the rights of the matter were in some sense uniquely known.

This necessity, rather than the coincidence of clerical chancellors, seems to explain procedural resemblances between chancery and courts Christian, and makes it not unlikely that some matters dealt with in later equity had their first home in those courts. But most of all it seems to explain the nature of equitable decrees: results were not declared to be so; instead parties were told to make them so. When a seller of land refused to convey it, chancery did not declare that it belonged to the buyer notwithstanding this: it compelled the conveyance. Property in the land passed to the buyer because the seller after all conveyed it to him: the seller conveyed it because chancery told him to, and would punish disobedience. The equitable use of specific remedies has commonly been taken to reflect their absence from the common law. But they had not always been absent. They were well known in local jurisdictions, and in the early royal courts; and they disappeared only because they proved unenforceable in practice. It is not this accident that is reflected in equity, but the nature of equity itself. Equity acts *in personam* because conscience does.

On these terms, and probably on no others, can jurisdictions live together and yet ordain divergent results. In the medieval common law for example, no rule was so clear as that which prohibited spiritual courts from adjudicating upon temporal debts; and if, as seems to be the fact, they did this on a large scale, it may be because they did not technically infringe the rule[1]. They would not impose a

1. B. L. Woodcock, *Medieval Ecclesiastical Courts in the Diocese of Canterbury* (1952); R. H. Helmholz, 'Assumpsit and *Fidei Laesio*' (1975) 91 LQR, p. 406.

direct obligation to pay the debt, but make payment a condition of mitigating punishment for the sin of breaking faith. Conscience was quickened by its proper spiritual sanctions. The chancellor had to use earthly penalties: but it was his ability to make the party change his own position, and so to admit the common law rule while avoiding its result, that made possible the coexistence for centuries of separate systems giving different answers.

The durability of the arrangement is as astonishing and as English as the durability of the Reformation settlement itself. St Germain's legal cosmography had seen justice as divine, conscience as its human reflection. But the spirit which made the Reformation possible saw divine justice as belonging to another world than this; and in this world it was never again possible to believe wholeheartedly in the existence of a right answer to every dispute. If then we take our stand late in the sixteenth century we see the common law courts as the organs of the law of the land. The modern phrase describes the modern thing. The common law has largely taken on the aspect of a system of substantive rules. And it has also, by the fall in the real value of forty shillings, become the law which governs all but truly small cases: it has become the ordinary thing. It is against this background that we must imagine the court of chancery. A major court is hearing many cases according to a well-established procedural routine. It is a regular institution, but not applying rules; rather it is using its discretion to disturb their effect. The secularisation of conscience made conflict inevitable.

CONFLICT BETWEEN LAW AND EQUITY

At the political level this turned on the source of the court's authority. The king's divine duty to provide channels for an absolute justice turned into divine right; and the discretion of the chancery, like the other discretionary powers of government, was left seemingly dependent upon the royal prerogative. The court was therefore not untouched by the constitutional struggles of the seventeenth century, though it eventually emerged unharmed. Our concern, however, is with the growth and settlement of the conflict at the legal level.

Before the sixteenth century there was in general no conflict, for two reasons. The first is practical: so long as local jurisdictions did a large proportion of the country's judicial work, the failures complained of were often their failures, and the common law judges were aligned with rather than against the chancellor. But more important was the current concept of the legal process itself. Judges and chancellor both saw themselves as concerned to secure the application of the same absolute justice, rather than to do justice seen as a product of human thought about which men might differ. To consider again the promise under seal induced by fraud: so long as the deed was seen as a matter of proof, something like evidence of an abstract indebtedness, all would agree that justice was going to miscarry because of the fraud. It is only when the deed is seen as creating the debt that the question begins to look like one of substantial injustice: there is now a substantive rule of law to be defended and attacked.

But even when this had happened, and when the visibly substantive rules of the common law were being overridden at the discretion of the chancellor, the dialogue between the two sides often shows true perplexity rather than a true conflict between partisans committed to their causes. Medieval rules about proof and the like, sensible in their own day, had crystallised out as substantive rules of law which only the most bigoted common law judge could defend whole-heartedly. And since the chancellor operated by ordering the conduct of the party with regard to his admitted legal rights, and not by denial of those rights, there was generally no formal attack on the rule, and therefore no compulsion to defend it. Like many basic contradictions, the comfortable course was to ignore it.

In one case, however, it was difficult to ignore. To say that the chancellor ordered only the conduct of the party hardly glossed over the contradiction when the order was that a party who had actually won at common law should abstain from enforcing his judgment. Nor was this merely a case particularly provocative to pride. There were conceptual difficulties. The more obvious is that the proceedings in chancery look like an illegitimate form of appeal[1]. The less obvious, but the deeper, has a medieval and a

1. The argument was based upon Stat. 4 Hy. IV, c. 23, sometimes numbered 22 (1402). The discussion in *Doctor and Student*, Dialogue I, c. 18 (Selden Society, vol. 91, p. 107) is exactly followed in R. Crompton, *L'Authoritie et Iurisdiction des Courts* (1594), f. 67.

modern face. When the legal process is seen as procuring a result which reflects a single absolute justice, it is hard to admit that a result can be properly procured and yet be wrong. And when the legal process is seen as the application of substantive rules, it is equally hard to admit that the substantive rules, properly applied, are somehow wrong.

In this situation there was a long history of doubt and difficulty. It seems clear on the one hand that common law judges often welcomed applications to the chancery by litigants whom they were themselves unable to save from their own rules. On the other hand a certain unease in chancery may be seen in the wording of a late sixteenth-century note: 'this Court forbeareth directly to examine any judgment given at the common law'; and then, after mentioning cases in which such a direct examination seems to have been made, it finishes: 'but whether these and such other may seem rather to examine the manner, than the very matter and substance of the thing adjudged, it is worthy of consideration'[1]. These last words indicate the solution as well as the problem. In the second decade of the seventeenth century Coke forced the issue, characteristically in cases in which the judgment at law was in favour of parties without merit; and the matter had to be referred to the king. The king was advised that, as a matter of practice, injunctions after judgment had often been accepted; and that, as a matter of theory, they did not 'assume to reverse and undo the Judgment, as Error and Attaint doth, which the Chancery never doth, but leaves the Judgment in Peace, and only medleth with the corrupt Conscience of the Party'[2]. Equitable examination, in short, was always of the manner rather than the matter, and always external to the law. The order to the party after judgment was therefore no different from an order before judgment, or before action started, or in cases in which there could be no action at law. The two systems moved on different planes and could not collide.

THE REGULARISATION OF EQUITY

To the extent that there had been a serious attack upon the equitable jurisdiction, then, it was the foundation in conscience that enabled

1. *Anon*, Cary 3–4.
2. 1 Chan. Rep., Appendix. The words quoted are at p. 47. For an analysis of the dispute see J. H. Baker, 'The Common Lawyers and the Chancery: 1616' (1969) 4 Irish Jurist, New Series, p. 368.

the chancery to withstand it. But conscience itself raised a difficulty, and a more serious one. The discussion about the relative importance in a legal system of certainty and abstract justice is unending: but it begins at a definite stage of development, namely when the law is first seen as a system of substantive rules prescribing results upon given states of fact. In England this discussion was at once institutionalised: certainty resided in the common law courts, justice in the chancellor's equity. But there were calls for the regularisation of equity itself. Lambarde, writing about 1590, is clear-headed in his perplexity, and asks: 'whether it be meet that the *Chancellor* should appoint unto himselfe, and publish to others any certaine *Rules & Limits* of *Equity*, or no; about the which men both godly and learned doe varie in opinion: For on the one part it is thought as hard a thing to prescribe to *Equitie* any certaine bounds, as it is to make any one generall Law to be a meet measure of *Justice* in all particular cases. And on the other side it is said, that if it be not knowne beforehand in what cases the *Chancellour* will reach forth his helpe, and where not, then neither shall the Subject bee assured how, or when he may possesse his owne in peace, nor the Practizer in *Law* be able to informe his Client what may become of his Action'[1].

The answer is foreshadowed in a note by a chancery reporter: 'where a common inconvenience will follow, if the common law be broken, there the Chancery shall not help. For albeit the party cannot with a good conscience take the advantage of sundry things to which he comes, yet the Court of Conscience is not thereby bound to help the other, but must leave some things to the conscience of the party himself.' These utilitarian words were written in the late sixteenth century[2]. Some progress towards regularisation was made in the ensuing sixty years, largely by means of general orders issued by various holders of the great seal. But it was not until after the political upheavals of the seventeenth

1. Lambarde, *Archeion*, corrected 1635 edn., pp. 74–75 (ed. C. H. McIlwain and P. L. Ward, 1957, p. 46). For procedural regularity, see W. J. Jones, *The Elizabethan Court of Chancery* (1967).
2. Cary 12. The note is based upon *Doctor and Student*: the 'common inconvenience' may be compared with Dialogue I, c. 12 (Selden Society, vol. 91, p. 77) on the paid bond; the 'conscience of the party' with Dialogue I, c. 18 (ibid. at p. 109). The latter is followed in R. Crompton, *L'Authoritie et Iurisdiction des Courts* (1594), f. 67.

century, in which the very existence of the equitable jurisdiction was threatened, that equity took on its modern aspect as a coherent system of rules. The sixteenth-century distinction between compellable conscience and the conscience of the party became Lord Nottingham's distinction between his natural and his civil conscience[1]. What mattered now was the civil conscience of the court, which was nothing other than a new system of law; and the conscience of the party slowly passed out of consideration. The dialogue between certainty and justice, law and morals, had been acted out in real life; and the end of it was two systems of certainty, two systems of law.

The process of regularisation will not be traced; but it is worth remarking that the development of equity, more than of any other body of English doctrine, was the work of identifiable persons. The common law itself is to a surprising degree anonymous, largely because the intellectual initiative has come from the bar rather than the bench and has been directed to the single case rather than to the state of the law. In the single case the difficulty has always been to escape from the past, and there has been little opportunity to look to the future. Only where events or a bold hand had produced a clean slate, as with the mercantile work of Holt and Mansfield, could individuals in some sense mould the law. In equity the slate was largely clean, and Nottingham in the seventeenth century, Hardwicke in the eighteenth and Eldon in the nineteenth were in a real sense masters of the future, able to approach individual problems with a legislative mind.

But the intellectual coherence thereby achieved in the doctrines of equity was bought at a cost. The single mind, applying itself to problems in this kind of way, can do only so much. Although inquiries into the facts of cases were done by others, it was long thought that the actual decision must remain for the chancellor himself or for a deputy sitting when he was not. And even when it became settled that the master of the rolls might sit as a judge in equity in parallel with the chancellor, there was always an appeal from him to the chancellor himself; and indeed the chancellor

1. *Cook v Fountain* (1676) 3 Swanston 585 at 600; *Lord Nottingham's Chancery Cases*, vol. I (Selden Society, vol. 73), p. 362 at p. 371. Cf. *Lord Nottingham's . . . 'Prolegomena of Chancery and Equity'*, III, 27 (ed. D. E. C. Yale, 1965, p. 194).

himself might always be asked to reconsider his own decisions. Not until 1813 was the judicial staff of the court altered, and not until the middle of the century was it much improved[1]. In the common law, as has been seen, there were three courts each with about four judges. Since the only real hearing for most cases was that before the single judge at *nisi prius,* the effective judicial strength was of the order of a dozen; and even for cases taken by motion before a court *in banc,* there were the three separate courts. It was this feature, even more than the clerical abuses which the chancery shared with the common law courts, that accounted for the delays in the chancery and the sense of helplessness felt by those driven to litigate there. The fog which Dickens observed in the court obscured its vision of much human unhappiness, but not of juristic principle; and the great intellectual strength of equity even today, though partly and paradoxically due to the paramount claims of certainty in the field of property law, owes much to the singleness of the vision with which its foundations were laid.

1. The statute of 1813 created a single vice-chancellor: Stat. 53 Geo. III, c. 24. For a full account see W. S. Holdsworth, *History of English Law,* vol. I, esp. p. 442.

II

PROPERTY IN LAND

5 *Tenures*

LORDSHIP AND OWNERSHIP

From the earliest settlements until the industrial revolution the economic basis of society was agrarian. Land was wealth, livelihood, family provision, and the principal subject-matter of the law. To begin with, moreover, land was also government and the structure of society. Today we think of the ownership of a suburban garden, or even of a great agricultural estate, as being something like the ownership of a motor car. They are just forms of wealth, the objects of legal protection. Lordship, the Latin *dominium*, is to us an ambiguous word, because to us the concepts of ownership and jurisdiction are distinct: to understand this starting-point, we must think away that ambiguity, and not try to resolve it. The rights of a great landowner were not over empty land but over the people who worked the land, or over inferior lords with rights over those people. Lordship was property, the object of legal protection from above, just as it was jurisdiction, the source of legal protection for rights below.

A generation or so after the Conquest, a single plot of land may have been in some sense the property of several different people: a peasant, the lord of his manor, the lord's lord, the king. But only between the peasant and his lord in the manor court was it a question of rights in and jurisdiction over just that plot of land. To the lord's lord, the unit was the manor which included the peasant's land and jurisdiction over the peasant. To the king the unit might be some great honour, which included the manor and jurisdiction over its lord. The words 'jurisdiction' and 'rights', moreover, must not conjure up an idea of rights fixed by general rules, or of jurisdiction as being just a matter of who was to apply those rules. That this came to be the case, at every level except the lowest, was a major change; and it was followed by the virtual end of feudal jurisdiction. General rules came to be enforced, and the rights of tenants other than those holding immediately of the king himself came to be protected by the king's courts. But to begin with the relevant rules were those of each lord's court, and the rights which they protected might depend to a greater or lesser extent upon the will of the lord.

TENURE AND OWNERSHIP

Ownership belongs to a flat legal world in which rights in land or other forms of wealth are dependent upon no authority except the state. They are governed by general rules, which regulate transactions and resolve disputes between persons who are legally equal. Tenure belongs to a smaller world in which there is no need and no room for abstract ideas like ownership. Rights are dependent upon a lord seen as having total control of his lordship. A tenant is in by the lord's allocation. He can have no more by way of title, unless it is some obligation on the lord to keep him in, or to admit his successors. He cannot by his own transaction confer whatever title he has upon another: he can only surrender it to the lord who may then admit another. And he cannot by himself engage in dispute about the land: in principle, the lord must decide who is to be his tenant. And if, like the theatre management which has sold a numbered seat twice over, the lord has incurred obligations both to the tenant now in and to a third party, there are two valid 'titles', and the most that one 'owner' can hope for is compensation.

Analogies always make one point at the expense of another. The theatre management has at least incurred obligations which are enforceable according to rules having an external existence. In the prototype lordship regulation is undertaken by the lord's court, a meeting of all his tenants. This court acted in accordance with customs which were thought to have some independent existence, but there was no external enforcement. Any obligations resting upon the lord, upon the management of the lordship, were therefore determined by rules which were within the management's ultimate control. The subjection of that to control from outside by the king's court was to transform the jurisdictional situation. It was the first step towards making the tenant into an owner.

But of course the lord and his court are not just management, allocating tenements as a matter of government. The lord was in our language also the owner of wealth; and since there was no other form of wealth from which he could derive an income to pay for whatever services he desired, he paid directly in land. The obligations that were enforced by the lord's court arose out of what we should analyse as a contract rather than a grant. The tenant's right to his tenement was correlative to his duty to perform his services. But whereas we still think of contracts of service as individually made and infinitely variable, the arrangements between lord and tenant were more or less stereotyped. We can draw a rough distinction between lordships at the lowest level and all other lordships, and say that they applied different kinds of rule; and these two kinds of rule are the twin sources of the common law of property in land.

AGRICULTURAL TENURES

Lordships at the lowest level were the production units, the most typical being the midland manor. It was these units or groups of such units that changed hands as a result of the Conquest. But their new lords took them as units, not as areas of land; and the internal life of each unit probably continued to be governed by its own customs. Some of these customs would lay down agrarian routines, such as rights of pasture; and our modern rules about profits *à prendre* have very ancient roots. Others would regulate the terms of each man's holding, and in particular what was to happen if he failed to do the services by which he held his land, and what was to happen when he died. Performance of the services would be enforced by the manor court: he would be summoned to answer, then distrained by the taking of chattels, and ultimately the tenement itself might be sequestered or even in early times forfeited. This is a process which will be mentioned again in connection with the imposition of royal control[1]. But that control could be brought to bear only upon tenures for which the services due were capable of exact specification. If the lord could demand such return from the tenant as he or his bailiff thought proper, the whole

1. See p. 140, below.

arrangement including the tenant's tenure was in some sense at the will of the lord, or at least a matter for managerial discretion which could not be controlled from outside. Such tenures, said to be unfree, came within the ambit of royal justice only late and indirectly.

But they generally received very regular protection within the lord's own court, even in the matter of succession on death. Although lords could not allow the language of inheritance to be used, because it imperilled the unfree status of the tenure, tenements regularly descended, though often by partition rather than by descent to a single heir, according to customs which varied from place to place and were no doubt old when the conquerors came[1]. We may never know how much and how often the freedom of a tenement mattered in everyday life; but in the early rolls of the king's court it is common to find litigation concerning peasant tenements in which their freedom is plainly being questioned for the first time[2]. Partly this reflects the novelty of any royal interference, even on behalf of free tenants at this level. But it reflects also a social fact: even when a tenure was seen as much in terms of 'labour law' as in terms of 'property law', there were great pressures for regularity.

MILITARY TENURES

At higher levels the terms of the arrangement were of very different origin, and were not native English. They had grown up around the relationship of lord and fighting man in a warring world. Security lay only in the strength of a lord and his band; and even an allodial 'owner' might bring his land in and hold it of the lord on the same terms as the lord's other followers. Those terms revolved around an intense relationship of loyalty and protection, which was sealed by the almost sacramental homage and so subjected to sanctions which were not all of this world. As at the lower level, this world's sanctions were brought to bear in the lord's court of which his men were the judges. In an embattled situation, in which compassion for

1. For a discussion of the varying customs and their relationship to patterns of economic organisation see G. C. Homans, *English Villagers of the Thirteenth Century* (1941).
2. See p. 137 and 141, below.

a fellow's failures would be balanced against fear for the unit upon which all the holdings depended, it must have been an effective structure.

Customs which had grown from that starting point came to England with the Conqueror, and became the terms on which the king's tenants-in-chief and commonly their tenants were understood to hold. The original logic was appropriate to a single tier in which each tenant was himself the fighting man. But the obligation of a tenant-in-chief was to come with a contingent, for which he soon provided by subinfeudations, creating new tenures dependent upon himself in return for individual service. The sheer complication of the resulting network of dependent tenures was itself a force tending to conventionalise the relationship, so that holdings were thought of increasingly in proprietary terms. Another such force was economic artificiality. Except during the Anarchy following the death of Henry I, individual lords were not in the embattled situation; nor was the king himself in constant need of the full feudal army; nor was an army reliably composed of fighting men whose obligation might be limited both geographically and by the number of days they would serve in any one year. Service came to be a matter of money payments, and even those were not often demanded. Economically, the tenant became increasingly an owner as the return which could be demanded from him became unreal in relation to the value of the land. Legally, as this and the next chapter will show, he became an owner because the jurisdiction of the lord's court was first controlled and then replaced by the king's court: his rights ceased to be dependent upon customs internally enforced, and were fixed in an external set of rules.

THE LIVING TENANT: FREEHOLD AND SERVICES

There were two components in this nascent 'ownership'. One was the tenant's right to enjoy the tenement so long as he lived, for which the medieval word was 'freehold'. The other was a right arising on his death that the tenement should be given to his heir, for which the medieval word was 'fee'. Whether the present tenant entered as heir of an ancestor or as first grantee of a tenement formerly in the lord's own hand, his present right began only when he physically received the land from the lord by 'livery of seisin'; and it would end when he physically relinquished the land by surrender or by death, either of which in principle just brought the land back to the lord.

But of course his holding is in some sense conditional upon his performance of the services due. He has tenure in the same sense as a professor or a judge today. He is in and can be put out only for cause established by due process, namely the judgment of his fellow-tenants, his peers, in the lord's court. And the great change in this component of his 'ownership' comes when the lord's court loses its ultimate power to put him out. As with agricultural tenures, there were three stages of increasingly stringent process: summons, distraint by chattels, and sequestration or ultimately confiscation of the land itself. It was the last of these that royal control effectively brought to an end.

This was, however, partly compensated for by a curious shift in the thirteenth century concerning distraint by chattels. For reasons which will appear later in this chapter, there had come into being many lords of tenures who were not real lords and had no courts; and distraint by chattels ceased to be the process of a lord's court and became an independent extra-judicial remedy for the enforcement of services[1]. And this created an obvious problem in cases in which the tenant was genuinely disputing the lord's claim. So long as distraint had been truly process, a means of making the tenant answer in the lord's court, the usual routine would be that the tenant would replevy the chattels: that is, he would get them back upon giving other security that he would return them to the lord's officers if the lord's court found that the services claimed were indeed due. But now there was no court to make that decision, and the tenant must turn to public justice. No doubt because he often could not manage without the beasts or other chattels taken, any more than he could manage without the tenement itself, his right to replevy was itself an early object of royal protection. There had been a great process called *vee de nam* (refusal of security) by which the sheriff could coerce a recalcitrant lord; and from this rare application of royal power there grew a humdrum action called replevin which brought to the county court the simple question

1. S. F. C. Milsom, *The Legal Framework of English Feudalism* (1976), pp. 10 ff.

which had formerly gone to the lord's own court: did the tenant actually owe the services for which this distraint was made[1].

The new distraint of chattels, regulated by replevin in the county court, thus became an efficient way of enforcing tenurial obligations; and it was made even more efficient by another change, perhaps also a result of its ceasing to be seen as process of the lord's own court. The lord could take any chattels found in the tenement and keep them until his rightful claim was satisfied; and it did not matter that the chattels did not belong to his tenant. Suppose the tenant has subinfeudated, and it is the sub-tenant's beasts that are taken. Although the sub-tenant is not directly responsible to the lord for the services due from the lord's own tenant, he may be forced to pay them; and then he can recover from the 'mesne' by a royal action known by that name[2].

There was also an action by which the lord could sue directly in the king's court for the customs and services due to him; but for all ordinary cases distraint by chattels was effective except when the tenant went so far as to abandon his tenement, not working it and so not having on it any chattels which the lord could distrain. For this situation two statutes late in the thirteenth century provided an action called *cessavit*. The earlier protected only a very humble kind of 'lord', the medieval equivalent of our purchaser of an annuity, who granted away his capital in land for the 'service' of a guaranteed subsistence in food and the like. The later statute generalized this remedy, and even a real lord could now do by grace of the king's court what he would once have done in his own, namely take back the tenement from a tenant who was not doing his service[3].

THE DYING TENANT: FEE AND INHERITANCE

When the tenant died his seisin came to an end and the lord would, at any rate in principle, take the tenement into his own hand. He would then make livery of seisin to a new tenant, who would hold

1. F. Pollock and F. W. Maitland, *History of English Law* (2nd edn., 1898; reissued 1968), vol. II, pp. 577–8.
2. T. F. T. Plucknett, *Legislation of Edward I* (1949), pp. 93–4; S. F. C. Milsom, *Novae Narrationes* (Selden Society, vol. 80), pp. clxiii ff.
3. Stats. 6 Ed. I (Statute of Gloucester), c.4; 13 Ed. I (Statute of Westminster II), c. 21. Working discussed in T. F. T. Plucknett, op. cit., pp. 90 ff. S. F. C. Milsom, *Novae Narrationes*, pp. liv ff.

as the dead man had, and so the sequence would begin again. To the extent that seisin was a proprietary entity and tenure a proprietary relationship, the property right, the 'freehold', could not outlast the tenant's lifetime.

But there was a second component to the tenant's nascent 'ownership'. As well as 'freehold' he might have 'fee', essentially an obligation upon the lord to admit as his new tenant the dead tenant's heir. Before discussing the source of this obligation as a matter of feudal theory, it is necessary to recollect an obvious social fact: land had been regularly heritable in England before the Conqueror came. At the peasant level the old customs were probably little disturbed; and even at the higher levels there was a powerful sentiment adding its own force to the prescriptions of feudal custom. Within feudal custom, the force appears to have come from the homage which a lord took from his tenant. The original effect of that homage may have been first to oblige the lord's heir to honour the tenant's tenure, then to oblige the lord to admit the tenant's heir; and it seems that the force flowing from any particular act of homage was spent when both the parties to it were dead. But though homage was in fact done at every devolution on either side, the idea grew that one act of homage created a relationship which would extend to an indefinite series of heirs. The obligation was already beginning to have a proprietary look – to modern eyes still more so when the lord's livery of seisin is recorded in a charter which expresses the grant as made to the tenant 'and his heirs', though we should not assume that the plural at first envisaged an indefinite succession[1].

But the matter is strictly one of obligation. Until the lord makes livery to him the heir has no seisin, no freehold, no proprietary right at all; and if for example he dies before he is admitted, the person now entitled will not be his heir but the next heir of the dead tenant. Indeed, the obligation of the lord is not strictly correlative to a right in the heir. That the lord is obliged by his taking of homage to grant the tenement to an heir is clearly established long before custom has established in every case who the heir is. In

1. S. E. Thorne, 'English Feudalism and Estates in Land' [1959] Cambridge Law Journal, p. 193. See generally: F. L. Ganshof, *Feudalism* (English edition, 1952); and, especially for the control which honour courts felt able to exercise, F. M. Stenton, *The First Century of English Feudalism* (2nd edn., 1961), ch. II.

England it was not settled until the thirteenth century was well advanced that the son of a dead elder son was entitled as against the living younger son. For political reasons that particular doubt survived within the king's court[1]. But it arose because customs had differed, so that some lords' courts had preferred the nephew, others the uncle. The canons of inheritance did not grow up as rules about the devolution of property, but as customs about whom the lord should now admit; and so long as that question was for the sole decision of the lord's court, there was another sense in which the heir could have no right, nothing more than an expectation. There was nothing he could do about it if the 'wrong' decision was taken. Only when he could look outside the lord's court to the king's was there any external sanction for the lord's obligation.

Royal control came through the great writ of right and the assize of mort d'ancestor, to be discussed in the following chapter. The lord's jurisdiction ceased to be a power to decide and became a mechanical duty to follow the external rules of the king's court; and then it disappeared altogether, and the king's court applied its own rules directly, rules which were now indeed about the devolution of the fee seen as a property right.

THE INCIDENTS OF TENURE

This loss of any control over inheritance is one reflection of the underlying economic change. The personal element in the services has disappeared, and they have become a render, nearly always in money, which the lord can always recover by distraining upon whatever chattels are on the land itself. It no longer matters to him if his tenant is an imbecile or an enemy or even just a bad payer. Nor, we might think, would it matter if the heir was an infant. And in the inferior tenures indeed it did not matter: some relative would work the tenement on the infant's behalf and do whatever service was due to the lord; and so far as the lord was concerned the infancy made no difference, though the infant himself came to be entitled to an accounting from his guardian[2]. At the beginning of the twelfth

1. S. Painter, *The Reign of King John* (1949), p. 1; F. Pollock and F. W. Maitland, *History of English Law* (2nd edn., 1898; reissued 1968), vol. II, p. 285. A new study of the *casus regis* is expected.
2. Stat. 52 Hy. III (Statute of Marlborough), c. 17. See p. 279, below.

century, Henry I was content with a similar arrangement for infant tenants-in-chief; and at that time the lords of military tenures generally no doubt saw them as the provision for service which they needed. The lands of an infant heir might as well be committed to some relative so long as that relative made arrangements for the service to be done[1].

But that was a matter of choice. Because an infant could not himself be the lord's fighting man, it had always been understood that until he came of age the land was at the lord's disposal. And when a lord considers what disposition to make on the basis that military service is not often demanded, and is any way demanded in money which bears no relation to the real value of the land, he will either hold the land itself for the duration of the infancy, or will sell the right so to hold it, not for the service due but for the best price he can get. The feudal wardship was not fiduciary: the lord or his grantee kept the actual income for himself, though the law came to protect the infant against those capital depredations known as waste. And the wardship has become valuable precisely because the services have ceased to be in any way a real return for the land, because economically the land itself has become the tenant's property.

This changed reality worked upon the original logic of inheritance to produce other rights of value to the lord. When what he needed was the service of a man, he could permit a woman to inherit only on the basis that he would choose her husband; and this became a right to sell the heiress with her inheritance. That logic did not extend to male heirs; but the lord could in fact control the marriage of a boy in his wardship, and this too became a saleable commodity, though a less valuable one. This right to control marriages caused trouble when it became common for a tenant to hold lands of several lords. Though each could have the wardship of the land held of him, there was only one heir and only one marriage. In disputes about which lord should have these, often conducted like a modern interpleader, the law hesitated between the lord of the richest holding and the lord of the oldest. The eventual victory of the latter made good legal sense: the homage which the first lord took had priority over homage to later lords, and similarly

1. Coronation Charter of Henry I, c. 4 (*Stubbs' Select Charters*, 9th edn., 1913; reprinted 1946, at p. 118). An arrangement for the services must be assumed.

the tenant could not by later transactions derogate from the first lord's vested right to the wardship of heirs. But in economic terms the result might be surprising. If the earlier tenure were of a single poor holding, the later of a great and rich complex, the marriage which the lord of the first holding had for sale was that of the heir to the second; and its price would be fixed accordingly. Under Edward I one can imagine the purchaser of a wardship or of a seignory examining the tenurial position as a modern investor examines subsidiary corporate holdings[1].

The greatest gain of all would come to the lord if the tenant died without any heir. The obligation flowing from the homage is now ended, and the lord can take the land back as once again at his free disposal. For reasons to be considered in connection with crime, the same thing happened if the tenant was convicted of a felony, and the result was rationalised by the proposition that the felony so corrupted his blood that he could have no heirs. This right to recover the land itself was called an escheat, and the escheat for failure of heirs has a modern parallel in the death of a tenant protected by the Rent Acts. But in both cases the return which has become valueless had been what, at the time of the original transaction, the lord had desired.

Paradoxically the smallest gain that could come to the lord when his tenant died arose when the heir was a male of full age, able to perform the actual service which was no longer a reality. The lord had always been obliged to take his homage and deliver the land to him immediately; and his only entitlement was to the relief, a payment soon fixed which was no more than an acknowledgment of his formal control. Because fixed and in money the relief fell in with the services, both in importance to the lord and in the manner of its enforcement. But the other so-called 'incidents' of wardship, marriage and escheat came to be protected by a range of royal remedies. And though the details are beyond the scope of this book,

1. The image is taken from T. F. T. Plucknett, *Legislation of Edward I* (1949), p. 78. The incidents as they came to appear in the thirteenth century are discussed in ch. IV of that book and in F. Pollock and F. W. Maitland, *History of English Law* (2nd edn., 1898; reissued 1968), vol. I, esp. pp. 318 ff; and the royal remedies which came to be needed are described in S. F. C. Milsom, *Novae Narrationes* (Selden Society, vol. 80), pp. cxlviii ff (wardship and marriage), cxix ff (escheat). On the sixteenth-century working of wardship, see esp. J. Hurstfield, *The Queen's Wards* (1958).

the bare fact is important as showing yet again how the reality of a lord's control has dwindled to a bundle of purely economic rights. Even more striking is the reversal in what is desired. He had once needed service: now he looks for profit to precisely those happenings which would have imperilled that service.

But these happenings are not rare, and we must not be misled by the name 'incidents': they were as regular as death. A tenant might leave no heir or an infant or an adult heir, but he could not die in any other condition; and except in the case of the adult heir's relief the lord's right related to the land itself and was to be as valuable in the sixteenth century as in the thirteenth.

ALIENABILITY

The tenant who cannot be put out, and whose heirs will have a right protected by the external law of the king's court, is on the way to having something that we should call ownership. But it is not until he can give his land away, or sell it and keep the proceeds for himself, that the tenurial relationship finally becomes unreal; and the stages by which this happened are not altogether clear.

It is necessary to distinguish between substitution, a 'horizontal' transaction by which the grantee is substituted as the lord's tenant and the original tenant just drops out of the picture, and subinfeudation, a 'vertical' transaction by which the original tenant remains in place as the lord's tenant and creates a new tenure so that the grantee will hold of him. These were not just alternative forms of conveyance but different kinds of arrangement. The tenant-in-chief wishing to provide himself with a fighting man to satisfy his obligations to the king, for example, will make a subinfeudation. But the tenant who has acquired lands elsewhere, perhaps by marriage, may prefer to sell his present tenement outright for a capital sum rather than subinfeudate it for rent or other service[1].

1. S. F. C. Milsom, *The Legal Framework of English Feudalism* (1976), ch. 4; T. F. T. Plucknett, *Legislation of Edward I* (1949), ch. IV, esp. pp. 102 ff (discussing the problem in terms of the feudal incidents); F. Pollock and F. W. Maitland, *History of English Law* (2nd edn., 1898; reissued 1968), vol. I, pp. 329 ff; J. M. W. Bean, *The Decline of English Feudalism* (1968), ch. 2.

On feudal principle, substitution without the lord's consent was unthinkable. It is not really one 'horizontal' transaction but two 'vertical' ones: Tom who is now Harry's tenant must surrender the tenement to Harry, and Harry must make a new grant to Dick. Harry may naturally refuse if for example a tenement is to be divided, and his consent may anyway have to be paid for; but one would expect such arrangements to be common, and so they were with unfree tenures. With free tenures, however, they seem unnaturally rare in the thirteenth century; and this is probably a result of the royal jurisdiction to which the free tenures have been subjected, and particularly the royal protection so freely given to the heirs of persons who had once been seised. So long as any litigation must be in Harry's own court, there is no danger to Harry in accepting Tom's surrender and admitting Dick in his place. But when some heir of Tom's can make a prima facie claim in the king's court on the grounds that Tom had once been seised, it is not only Dick who is at risk. Dick has done homage as Harry's tenant; and if the king's court compels him to yield this tenement to Tom's heir, it may also, as will appear in the following chapter, compel Harry to compensate him with another. Perhaps the transaction itself had better be done by the authority not of Harry's court but of the king's, so that any possible claim by the grantor's heir will be barred in the court in which it would be made; and the rare early substitutions indeed seem generally to have been made by fine in the king's court[1].

A subinfeudation can obviously be made without the participation of the grantor's lord; but it does not follow that he never has any interest in the matter. For him the possible mischiefs are an impairment in either his services or his incidents. His services cannot be impaired if the subinfeudation entitles the grantor to services which cover the service owed to the lord for that parcel of land. In the case of military tenures, for example, it was common for a grantor by subinfeudation to make the grantee responsible for the lord's services as well as some extra service for his own benefit; and although that was a matter between themselves, so that the grantee's duty to do the lord's services was strictly owed to the grantor, still the lord's services were not imperilled.

On the face of it the lord's services were imperilled by any

1. F. Pollock and F. W. Maitland, op. cit., vol. I, p. 345.

subinfeudation which reserved less service than that owed to the lord for this parcel of land, by what was in effect a gift. Gifts were commonly made within the family and to the church; and since the grants were not buying military service, they were not sealed by homage and so created sub-tenures which the grantor and his heirs were not under the homage obligation to maintain. This precarious element was the safeguard of the grantor's lord. When the grantor himself died, his heir with his court would consider whether he could afford to continue this gratuitous allocation of part of his inheritance; and a later chapter will explain how the *maritagium*, the provision for a daughter which was the most distinctive family gift, had its origin in the customs governing that decision.

Although it is clear that the lord's original concern with subinfeudation by way of gift was for his services, this changed in the course of the thirteenth century to a concern with impairment of his incidents. Partly this reflects the general shift in economic reality: provision for service is no longer the desired object of a tenure. Partly it reflects also the change in the nature of distress. When distress was the process of a lord's court by which a tenant might be compelled to honour what was seen as his obligation, a lord would think in terms of the tenant's ability to honour it and would consider a subinfeudation as possibly diminishing the tenant's resources. But when distress by chattels became an independent remedy raising the services as it were from the land itself, no matter whose chattels were taken, then a lord's services were simply unaffected by a subinfeudation. They are no longer a general worry.

The impairment of incidents, however, provoked legislation as radical as any the common law has known; and the mischief needs explanation. When a tenant dies leaving, say, an infant heir, the lord will take a wardship, enjoying (or selling) the land itself for the duration of the infancy. But if the dead tenant had subinfeudated the land for service, the content of the lord's wardship would not be the land itself but the service due from the sub-tenant; and only if the sub-tenant himself dies leaving an infant heir will the lord get the land itself in 'wardship by reason of wardship'. As in the case of the lord's services, the danger is greatest when the subinfeudation is by way of gift; but the lord loses by any subinfeudation which reserves less service than the land is actually worth.

MORTMAIN

Piety and concern for salvation made grants to religious bodies common; and they were usually true gifts in frankalmoign reserving to the grantor no earthly service. The grantor had of course impoverished himself: he had parted with the land and got no services of money value in return; and what is more he would never become entitled to any of the incidents of tenure because his tenant would never die. But this was his own doing. The mischief was to his lord, and to begin with it is likely that such a grant would not be made unless the immediate and all other lords up to the king were willing to confirm it. But in the early thirteenth century tenants were making such grants on their own authority, and an ineffective provision of 1217 shows concern only for the lord's services. Since the lands of at least some religious bodies were immune from distraint, this mischief continued to be real; and it is still an expressed motive for the statute *De Viris Religiosis* in 1279 which gave lords power to take back lands granted to religious bodies without their consent – another probable example of statute restoring to lords a power which they would once have exercised on their own authority. But the greater mischief aimed at was the permanent nullification of the lord's incidents. The death of his tenant leaving an infant heir or no heir could bring him nothing of value, not even, since the religious house itself could never die, the outside chance of a 'wardship by reason of wardship' or a double escheat[1].

QUIA EMPTORES

Apart from these outside chances, the same damage to the lord would follow if his tenant made a subinfeudation to a mortal sub-tenant to hold for some nominal service like the traditional rose at midsummer: any escheat or wardship coming to the lord on the

1. *Magna Carta* (1217), c. 39; (1225), c. 32; Petition of the Barons (1258), c. 10; Provisions of Westminster (1259), c. 14; Stat. 7 Ed. I (*De Viris Religiosis*); S. F. C. Milsom, op. cit. (p. 110, n.1), pp. 114 ff; T. F. T. Plucknett, op. cit., pp. 94 ff; J. M. W. Bean, op. cit., p. 42; P. A. Brand, 'The Control of Mortmain Alienation in England, 1200–1300' in *Legal Records and the Historian* (1978).

death of his tenant would have no content beyond the annual rose. This mischief led in 1290 to the great statute *Quia Emptores* which ended grants in fee simple by subinfeudation. The grantor was in future to grant his land to be held directly of the lord, himself stepping out instead of remaining as tenant of the old tenure and lord of a new one. His death was then no longer relevant. The lord's incidents would accrue on the death of the grantee; and it was to the grantee that the lord must directly look for his services which, if only part of the holding was being alienated, had to be apportioned[1].

At first sight the remedy seems out of proportion to the likely mischief. Mortmain was a problem because there was always a motive to make gifts to religious bodies, though most people would so dispose only of a reasonable proportion of their lands. They might also make reasonable gifts within the family. But *Quia Emptores* is concerned with grants in general, which surely would not often be gifts. There is a great artificiality in the background. Its economic aspect goes back to the growing unreality of military service. A tenure has come to be seen as property in the tenant, not as a way of securing service which the lord desires. As property it will be sold for money; and though some vendors might choose to take a permanent income in return, to subinfeudate for an annual rent, many would prefer a once-for-all capital payment. For that the natural transaction would be a substitution; and the legal artificiality arises because for some reason the substitution is not being used.

Suppose the tenant who really wishes to sell his land for a capital sum: instead of the natural substitution he subinfeudates for a nominal service but still, of course, takes his capital payment. The new tenure so created is itself artificial, and the vendor will often be a lord in no other sense, and in particular will have no court; and he is probably responsible for the changing nature of distress by chattels and of replevin. He is thus a cause as well as a symptom of the disintegrating structure; and the artificial tenure he has created is clearly the mischief aimed at by *Quia Emptores*.

What is not yet clear is why sales were so often effected in this way. Substitutions seem unnaturally rare from the late twelfth century, when our systematic evidence begins; and it has already

1. Stat. 18 Ed. I; see references on p. 110, n. 1, above.

been suggested that this was because of a danger to the lord arising from royal jurisdiction. By taking homage he would become guarantor of the grantee's title, but would be at the mercy of the king's court in any claim brought by the grantor's heir based upon the grantor's former seisin. On that basis, the artificial subinfeudation was made because the lord dared not consent to a substitution. That it was often made because he would not consent, or asked too high a price, is unlikely because of the foreseeable danger to his incidents. But it is not impossible that deliberate evasion came to play some part. If the subinfeudation was for a tenure which did not itself carry wardship and marriage, the grantee would gain that measure of freedom from incidents at the direct expense of the grantor's lord; and this might be reflected in the grantor's price of which, since his consent was not needed, the lord could exact no share.

A separate factual doubt concerns the extent to which substitutions had in fact become common in the decades before *Quia Emptores*. A passage in Bracton was long taken as evidence that substitutions could already be made without the lord's consent; but it now appears that Bracton is describing a kind of trick: the grantor in effect put the grantee into seisin, and one effect of royal control in the shape of the assize of novel disseisin was that the lord could not get him out. But nor could he take service or the like without recognizing him as tenant, and so was saddled with him. This operation was certainly sometimes attempted; but it seems too hazardous to have become a regular form of conveyance, and *Quia Emptores* probably made rather than just accepted a change[1].

It was a great change. Tenants are expressly empowered to alienate at their own free will, so long as they do it by substituting their grantees for themselves. The lord has finally lost any control over who is to be his tenant, the most important thing of all when it was his services that mattered to him. The feudal relationship is recognized as dead, but his actual economic interests are saved.

Seen from the tenant's angle, the relationship between himself and his lord has no content beyond the lord's economic rights.

1. *Bracton*, f. 81 (ed. Woodbine-Thorne, vol. II, p. 235); F. Pollock and F. W. Maitland, *History of English Law* (2nd edn., 1898; reissued 1968), vol. I, p. 345; S. F. C. Milsom, *The Legal Framework of English Feudalism* (1976), pp. 146 ff (on *se demisit*), 152–3. For another view of the position in the thirteenth century, see D. W. Sutherland, *The Assize of Novel Disseisin* (1973), pp. 86 ff.

These rights have become a sort of servitude, and the tenant has become an owner. The tenurial reality of a grant to one 'and his heirs' is now wholly lost, as may be seen most vividly in connection with an escheat. Suppose that a lord originally granted to a tenant 'and his heirs', and that after *Quia Emptores* that tenant or one of his heirs alienates to a grantee 'and his heirs'. This alienation must be by way of substitution, and the failure of the original tenant's heirs is irrelevant. It is now the failure of the grantee's heirs that brings an escheat to the lord. But this is a property of the 'fee simple', and flows from a rule of law and not from the words of any grant. If the words still governed the matter, an escheat to the lord could follow only from a failure of heirs of the original tenant; and failure of heirs of the grantee should, if anything, bring what we would call a reversion to his grantor.

The fee simple has become an estate, 'and his heirs' magic words to create it, and this estate, this ownership, has become an article of commerce. The feudal services are income, the incidents are bonus gains, and land and lordship are being bought and sold for money. *Quia Emptores* epitomizes in a few lines the changes of a century and more. A social structure depending upon obligations in the vertical dimension between lord and tenant has been flattened out into technical rules about property.

CONSEQUENCES OF *QUIA EMPTORES* AND OF THE INCIDENTS

We have made much of *Quia Emptores* because hindsight can see it as acknowledging the end of an age. But the realities of that age had long been dead, and those who made the statute were not looking back to them. Still less were they looking forward to its consequences. Although reciting the mischief, it did not in terms prohibit subinfeudation, and investigation may show that it did not immediately stop it. But the doctrine that there cannot have been a subinfeudation since 1290 appears early in the year books, and its victims were persons who had certainly been innocent of any attempt to deprive a lord of his incidents. These were vendors who had sold their land not for a capital sum but for an annual rent, and who now found that they could not distrain for it because by the statute the land could not be held of them and so must be 'out of their fee'.[1] The particular muddle that resulted is too small and intricate to be examined here; but an important legal institution may have grown out of it, and that is the husbandry lease. The term of years had mostly been used for very specific purposes; and its increasing use as an arrangement between a landlord and a tenant farmer in the modern sense has commonly been attributed, like other unexplained phenomena, to the Black Death. But after *Quia Emptores* the lease was the simplest secure way of parting with the land in return for a fixed annual income. It was also the simplest way in which the lord of a manor or larger unit, to whom a holding had come by escheat or assart, could part with it again and yet keep his unit intact.

If the husbandry lease did develop partly to fill a gap left by *Quia Emptores*, the legal consequences are only the most striking example of a more general result of the statute and of the process which the statute completed and symbolised. The lease started as a matter of contract; and it grew into a counterfeit proprietary interest because the contractual protection was insufficient. Other needs had similarly to be provided for by what we should call the law of contract rather than the law of property. On the grantor's side, and as a direct result of the statute, obligations such as that of warranty could no longer rest upon tenure, and immediate technical difficulties were thereby raised. On the grantee's side there was the much slower process, in the case of superior tenures long complete at the date of the statute, by which land ceased to be used as the payment for services desired of the grantee by the grantor. In its early days the common law of contract was particularly scanty in the case of contracts for service, and this is one reflection of a society whose labour law took the form of manorial jurisdiction and of peasant holdings subject in some sense to the discretion of the lord. All this was beneath the attention of the king's courts and unaffected by *Quia Emptores*. But change, when it came, followed the same pattern as the events discussed in this chapter. As the unfree holding became a true property right, the lord's jurisdiction became unreal, being first subjected to royal control and then

1. The early year books show many problems arising from the reservation of freehold rents. On rent-service, rent-charge and rent-seck, see F. Pollock and F. W. Maitland, op. cit. (p. 115, n.1), vol. II, pp. 129 ff; cf. S. F. C. Milsom, *Novae Narrationes* (Selden Society, vol. 80), pp. clxix ff.

abandoned to royal courts. At the lower level as at the upper, land became just property, a thing to be bought and sold.

But tenure and its incidents were to have a long life yet, the subject-matter of a later chapter. After *Quia Emptores* tenures which disappeared by escheat could not be replaced, and the feudal chain could only contract. The tendency was therefore for lordship to be concentrated in the king, and for the king to become increasingly the one who gained from the feudal incidents and increasingly the loser from their evasion. A tenant could no longer drain off the economic value of his holding by a subinfeudation; he could only alienate it outright. But evasion would result if before dying he made an outright alienation to friends for them to deal with according to his instructions. This became a universal practice among landowners, not because they primarily sought to evade the feudal incidents, but because they could not otherwise dispose of their principal wealth by will. From this practice grew our modern law of trusts, and its development was gravely affected by the feudal interest of the king.

6 *Early Actions*

SEISIN AND RIGHT

The greatest difficulty in this subject exists in our own eyes, for ever dazzled by the Roman vision of possession and ownership to which, from the thirteenth century, the common law ideas of seisin and the right increasingly conformed. The right became something rather like *dominium,* abstract and ultimate. But whereas *dominium* was conceived of as absolute, a legal relationship between person and thing good against the world, the right of the common law was always relative: what could be determined for ever was only the better right as between the two parties to an action. And in the classical common law, this relativity was a matter of age. The better right was that generated by the older seisin; and any seisin generated a right which would be good, unless granted away, against all later comers.

Like *possessio* seisin became fundamentally a factual relationship between person and thing. Like *possessio* too, there is an element of contrast: the fact may be wrongfully so. A writ of right must be brought against one who is seised, and if it succeeds that seisin will have been proved wrongful. But seisin paradoxically contains larger elements of rightfulness than *possessio,* and has larger proprietary consequences. One who has the right but has never become seised, for example, cannot make a grant, and his descendants will not themselves establish a right merely by being his heirs: they must make themselves heirs of the ancestor from whom his right derived, the ancestor who was seised[1].

The traditional view of early English land law has supposed that these concepts were primeval, not fully intelligible in themselves but still the basic entities around which the system was arranged.

1. F. W. Maitland, 'The Mystery of Seisin', *Collected Papers* (1911), vol. I, p. 358.

For Bracton there is a 'pure right'[1]. But since legal ultimates are always mystical, little attempt has been made to analyse it: it was just a sort of ownership, but with the realistic strength of being relative. Attempts have been made to analyse seisin, in terms both of legal protection and of economic function, and almost inevitably they have proceeded from a Roman question: what is the difference from possession?

The truth seems to be, however, that these abstract concepts were not primeval: they are what is left when the vertical structure of society has been flattened out, when ideas which depended upon lordship survive into a world without true lords. Language has played tricks. 'To be in possession of' developed an illogical synonym 'to be possessed of'; and this probably came about by analogy with 'to be seised of' as synonymous with 'to be in seisin of'. To us all four phrases describe a condition like possession, a relationship betwen a person and a thing. But the verb 'to seise' is older than its noun. A lord seised a tenant of the tenement, and in the passive mood 'the tenant was seised' meant 'seised by the lord'. Seisin at first connoted not one person and a thing but two people; and the noun comes to denote a purely abstract concept as the lord is dissolved out, mainly as a result of the assize of novel disseisin to which this chapter will later turn. At first it was a lord who disseised a tenant as well as a lord who seised him. By seising him, making livery of seisin, he created the tenure and conferred freehold on the tenant; and properly he could disseise him only by process of his court for some failure in the tenant's obligations. Subject to that power of the lord and his court, the tenant's freehold and seisin lasted until he died, until the man who had done homage was no more.

Within the lord's court, it follows that there could be no larger proprietary idea than seisin: to be seised, to be in with the lord's authority, was to have the only title there could be. But although sovereign within the lordship, the lord's court made its decisions not at will, but according to its own understanding of the relevant

1. *Bracton*, ff. 283b, 434b (ed. Woodbine-Thorne, vol. III, pp. 324–5, vol. IV, p. 350). Cf. the references in both passages to *dreit dreit*; and G. J. Turner, *Brevia Placitata* (Selden Society, vol. 66), pp. lxix ff. Bracton's assertion that *possessio* has nothing in common with *proprietas* was taken from the Digest; *Bracton*, f. 113b (ed. Woodbine-Thorne, vol. II, p. 321); F. W. Maitland, op. cit. in preceding note, at p. 359.

feudal customs; and rival contenders for the allocation of a vacant tenement might therefore each claim 'right' in accordance with those customs. It would not be a claim to anything like 'ownership', but to the benefit of an obligation; and the obligation would be that the lord should seise this claimant, confer upon him freehold, something that would last not for ever but just for his life. Feudal custom prescribed, for example, that the heir of a dead tenant should grant some of his lands to his widow to hold of the heir for her life; and on this basis the widow might claim 'right' to her dower in the heir's court. In later terminology the widow's dower was of course a 'life estate': she did no homage, and had freehold but not fee. And this use of 'right', by warning us not to think in terms of an ownership which may last for ever, helps us to understand its more important use in the context of inheritance.

When the lord took homage from a tenant now dead, he placed himself under a customary obligation to admit that tenant's heir after him, to seise the heir and confer upon him a new freehold; and on this basis the heir might claim 'right' in the lord's court. But it is equally an immediate claim to be honoured or not upon this single occasion. If the heir is admitted, his right has been realized and is now spent, irrelevant to any later happening: he has freehold and does homage, and when he dies it will be his homage that confers a new right upon his heir. If the heir is passed over and someone else admitted, then the heir's 'right' is equally irrelevant: the lord takes homage from his new tenant, and when that new tenant dies it will similarly be his heir that has a new right.

Within the lord's court, then, 'the right' was no more than an expectation, a claim that a single decision would go in the claimant's favour, that he would be seised and granted freehold; but the decision actually taken was conclusive. Harry's tenant dies leaving Tom, the grandson by a dead elder son, and Dick, the living younger son. So long as the tenement is in Harry's hand, Tom and Dick can each claim right in Harry's court. But once Harry seises Dick and takes his homage, the question is concluded. And it does not matter whether this was because Harry's court decided that Dick was the nearer heir by custom, or did not know of Tom's existence, or believed him to be a bastard, or knew him to be incompetent, or believed both to be bastards so that Harry was granting Dick what he supposed to be an escheat at his free disposal.

The difference comes when Tom, passed over in Harry's court, can turn to the king's court. If the king will after all force Harry to accept Tom and put out Dick, Tom's right is now more than an expectation or claim. But it is still at first seen as an obligation enforceable against Harry; and by taking Dick's homage Harry has also placed himself under an obligation towards Dick. Tom and Dick both claim rights, and the question is which has the better right in a very concrete sense; and if Tom indeed has the better right to this tenement, Dick will still look to Harry for a tenement in return for his homage, and Harry must find him another one.

The change in what actually happened may not at first have been great: the customs were no doubt very generally followed. The important change was juristic. Because lords' courts now have no real part to play in inheritance, they drop out. Litigation goes to the king's court, which applies a common law of inheritance. Its rules are no longer just criteria for making a present choice, but can reach back to reverse a decision made yesterday or a century ago. Now indeed they are rules about the devolution of a sort of abstract ownership. To claim that ownership, one has only to make oneself out as heir to an ancestor who was seised. And that seisin has itself become abstract: a relationship between one person and land, with only vestigial mysteries to indicate that once a second person had been inherent in the very word. The lord still has his economic rights, a sort of servitude burdening what is clearly the tenant's property. But except for his right of wardship and the like, he has no part to play in the actual devolution of that property or in any law-suit it may generate, and no place in the legal concepts themselves.

NATURE OF THE EARLY ACTIONS

In forcing the elementary ideas into a Roman mould, we have made consequential assumptions about the relationship between the actions to be discussed in this chapter. In a flat world in which equals dispute about title to property, it is convenient to maintain both proprietary and possessory remedies. Since a proprietary remedy is in some sense conclusive, settling the 'ownership' in the disputed property, it is necessarily cumbersome. And since the person who is in possession and looks like owner is normally the person indeed entitled, it makes sense to give a remedy to him or his successor in title based upon that readily ascertainable fact, and for the sake of speed actually to exclude any consideration of the title itself. In the unusual case in which the immediate facts produce a result against the real 'owner' (for example because he has resorted to forcible self-help), then he must lose the possessory action and recover by means of his own proprietary remedy. Justice is generally served, and good order always.

It is into this pattern, Roman in origin, that the early English actions have been assumed to fit. The writ of right has been seen as proprietary, an action about 'the right' seen as a mystical ultimate of the nature of ownership, and therefore beyond analysis. Apart from trial by battle, itself thought to be beyond analysis, its only important property lay in the contrast with the 'possessory assizes' of novel disseisin and mort d'ancestor. And the writs of entry, the last of the actions to be discussed in this chapter, have been seen as bridging the gap between the two, possessory in nature to begin with but so extending their scope as to perform the proprietary function.

In this network of assumptions the most basic is that the legal world was flat, that disputes were always about abstract property rights and between equals as they were in ancient Rome and are in modern England. Lords had jurisdiction over the proprietary writs of right; but the possessory remedies were royal, and the effect and probably the purpose of their extension was to draw all litigation about land into the king's courts. The process of transfer was essentially competitive: litigants preferred the royal remedies. And what was transferred was just jurisdiction in the modern sense. Disputes were about abstract rights which could as well be determined in one court as in another, and lords had no more to lose than pride and the profits of justice[1].

1. See F. Pollock and F. W. Maitland, *History of English Law* (2nd edn., 1898; reissued 1968), vol. II, pp. 29 ff; F. W. Maitland, *The Forms of Action at Common Law* (with *Equity*, 1909; separately, 1936), esp. Lectures III and IV; and there is an even clearer and shorter statement of the traditional view, especially concerning the writs of entry, in his *Select Pleas in Manorial Courts* (Selden Society, vol. 2), pp. liv ff. The proprietary/possessory relationship has been assumed, and discussion has been about the motives for providing possessory protection and the extent to which the idea was consciously borrowed: e.g. R. C. Van Caenegem, *Royal Writs in England from the Conquest to Glanvill* (Selden Society, vol. 77), pp. 303, 386 ff and references there cited; F. Joüon des Longrais, *Henry II and his Justiciars had they a Political Plan in their Reforms about Seisin?* (1962); and for a study of seisin as such, see his *La conception anglaise de la saisine* (1924).

There are many respects in which these assumptions have turned out to be inconsistent with the early evidence; and the essential difference in the account that follows is that the world is three-dimensional. The actions came into being in a framework in which lords were still in control of their lordships, and in which therefore the king's court could seek only to control the doings of lords. The purpose of this control was not, and could not be, in any sense 'anti-feudal': it was to prevent and correct departures by lords' courts from the accepted body of feudal custom. The unintended effect was to deprive lordship of any legal reality. The power of lords' courts to make conclusive decisions was reduced to jurisdiction in the modern sense, to the power and duty to apply externally fixed rules. Then indeed litigants preferred to go directly to the king's court, and its rules became rules about abstract property rights in which lords played no part. Seisin becomes like possession, a relation between one person and a piece of land; and the lord, the second person in the original idea, vanishes. The heir of one seised no longer has just a claim that the lord will put him in seisin: the lord is irrelevant, and the heir is owner by operation of law. But to begin with the lord was as central to the actions as to the ideas.

THE WRIT OF RIGHT

In its earliest usage the phrase *breve de recto* denotes what is known as the writ patent. Most writs went to the sheriff and were sealed up closed; but royal orders to subjects, as opposed to officials, were sent open. The writ patent was directed to the lord of whom the demandant claimed to hold the land in question: 'do full right to the demandant concerning such-and-such land which he claims to hold of you by such-and-such service, and of which the tenant deforces him; and if you do not, the sheriff will'. Such a writ was appropriate for the demandant claiming fee; and that is the claim now to be discussed. But it was also appropriate for the widow claiming dower. The heir, as the person of whom she claimed to hold, would be ordered to do full right to her; and since this was equally called a *breve de recto* we have no warrant for confining 'the writ of right' to actions claiming fee[1].

Nor have we any early warrant for extending the phrase to include the closed *praecipe* writ directed to a sheriff: 'order the tenant to yield up such-and-such land to the demandant; and if he will not, summon him to answer before the king's justices'. Although not so called in the early sources, this has always been assumed to have been equally a 'writ of right'; and the older view was that its only proper use was for claiming land to be held in chief of the king so that even on the feudal principle the king's was the appropriate court. On this basis, a provision in *Magna Carta* prohibiting the issue of *praecipe* writs so as to deprive lords of their jurisdiction was understood to be aimed at deliberate poaching by the king's courts, part of the supposed royal policy of undermining feudal jurisdiction[2]. We now know that the matter was less simple. There were claims, even claims to hold in fee of a mesne lord, which would anyway come to the king's court. Suppose for example that the demandant claims to hold Blackacre in fee of Harry, and that the tenant who actually has Blackacre is doing service for it to Ralph: even if the demandant brings a writ patent to Harry, Harry's court cannot take jurisdiction over a tenant who does not acknowledge Harry as lord; it must refuse to act on the writ; the sheriff will carry out the order with which it ends and take the case away; and from his county court it will usually be removed again to the Bench at Westminster. In such a case time and trouble would be saved by issuing a *praecipe* writ in the first place; and from Glanvill's description it appears that before the Charter there was a discretion to issue it whenever appropriate[3]. But then suppose that

1. The 'writ of right of dower' is of course well known, and is contrasted with the *praecipe* writ of dower *unde nihil habet;* F. W. Maitland, *The Forms of Action at Common Law*, p. 36; but they are not discussed in the *History of English Law*. Registers place their writs of right of dower among the other writs of right patent: E. de Haas and G. D. G. Hall, *Early Registers of Writs* (Selden Society, vol. 87), CA 2, CC 6, CC 6a, R 16–18; *Registrum Omnium Brevium*, f. 3. On the phrase '*breve de recto*' see S. F. C. Milsom, *Legal Framework of English Feudalism* (1976), p. 67.
2. *Magna Carta* (1215), c. 34; (1225), c. 24. See N. D. Hurnard, 'Magna Carta, Clause 34', *Studies in Medieval History presented to F. M. Powicke* (1948) p. 157; M. T. Clanchy, 'Magna Carta, Clause Thirty-Four' (1964) 79 English Historical Review, p. 542.
3. *Glanvill*, I, 5 (ed. G. D. G. Hall, 1965, p. 5).

in the same case the demandant was mistaken and that the tenant is after all doing service for Blackacre to Harry, the lord of whom the demandant claims to hold. We now know that there was a mechanism by which Harry could reclaim his jurisdiction; but this placed upon him the onus of continual vigilance. Inconvenience to somebody was inevitable. Discretionary issue of the *praecipe* cast it upon lords; and what *Magna Carta* did was to shift it to demandants. The demandant must always begin with a writ to the lord of whom he claimed to hold, even when he knew that the lord's court would not act so that he would have to go through the cumbersome processes of removal. After the Charter, indeed, Glanvill's undifferentiated *praecipe* writ disappeared; and *praecipe* writs always contained explanatory clauses, specifying for example that the claim was to hold in chief of the king or that the lord had expressly waived his jurisdiction.

Another kind of *praecipe* writ with an explanatory clause which became common after the Charter were the writs of entry, to be dicussed later in this chapter. They are mentioned now to emphasise that we have no reason for regarding the *praecipe* as a 'writ of right', and indeed no reason for associating *praecipe* and writ patent with any conceptual entity. All we know is that the writ patent was described as a *breve de recto* because it directed a lord to do right to a demandant, and that the demandant might be a widow claiming her dower as well as a would-be-tenant claiming fee. Something within the addressee's control is wrong and he is to put it right: there is no evidence of more to it than that.

What happens in court upon such a writ? On the writ patent in a lord's court, the most significant thing that may happen is nothing: the lord's court declines to act. The demandant then shows his writ to the sheriff who, upon proof of this 'default of right', removes the case to the county court. This removal, known as *tolt,* is authorised by the concluding sentence of the writ patent itself and requires no further writ; but a second removal from the county to the Bench at Westminster, which was usual, did require a further writ of *pone*. In the thirteenth century this double removal was usual; and there is the seeming paradox that lords rarely exercised the jurisdiction they were so concerned in *Magna Carta* to protect. But this is only one aspect of the indifference with which, on the traditional view, they treated the whole process of jurisdictional transfer, including the rise of the writs of entry: presumably the profits of justice were not worth the trouble.

But there is a simpler explanation of an order which in terms expects disobedience and is commonly disobeyed. The lord and his court are not just apathetic: they could not or would not act for an expected reason. One such has been mentioned: if the tenant does not acknowledge this lord, his court cannot summon him to answer. Another was more common: this tenant is indeed tenant of this lord, having done homage to him and taken livery of seisin from him, both normally in the presence and with the assent of the lord's court. That court has taken its decision about the tenement: the tenant has freehold, has done no wrong for which he can be deprived, and has the only title there can be. And so long as the decisions of that court were final, that was the end of the matter: however strong the demandant's claim had been, for example as undoubted heir mistakenly supposed to be dead, he has come too late.

But the decision of the lord's court is no longer the end of the matter: 'do full right, and if you do not the sheriff will'. Now the claim can proceed in the county or the king's court, and the tenant must answer. He can answer in either of two ways. Although his title is no longer conclusive against the demandant, it is still good against the lord: if he did homage, became the lord's man, he is still entitled to his 'pay'; and if he cannot keep this tenement, the lord must find him another. One thing he can do, therefore, is to 'vouch to warranty', a process long known to historians though it has not been appreciated that the vouchee was indeed the tenant's lord. If the duty to warrant is admitted or proved, then the vouchee must either admit the demandant's claim or defend as himself tenant to the action. If he wins, his original tenant keeps the tenement undisturbed. But if the vouchee yields or loses, the demandant gets this tenement, and in exchange the vouchee must find another of equal value for his original tenant. The 'title' which a lord can confer is no longer absolute; but it is still guaranteed.

If the tenant has not done homage or has, for example, a charter in which the warranty is expressly limited, or for any reason does not wish to vouch the lord, he can forego any reliance upon the warranty and take it upon himself to deny the demandant's claim. And if he chooses he can no doubt do that in the lord's court before the case is removed; but once accepted as tenant he can never be made to answer by the lord's court. It is only the king's writ which can make him liable to answer at all; and this factual proposition is the likely origin of the maxim that no one could be made to answer for his free tenement without the king's writ[1].

But even if the tenant took it upon himself to deny the demandant's claim to the tenement, that claim was still a claim against the lord and not the tenant. The tenant was of course interested: but the juridical dispute was between demandant and lord, not demandant and tenant. To the demandant, it does not matter whether the lord still has the tenement in his own hand or has given it to a new tenant: the claim is that he was under an obligation to give it to the demandant.

Apart from the widow's dower, the only such obligation was the hereditary one. If a demandant claims fee, his count, the formal statement in court of his claim, begins by asserting the seisin of a named ancestor in the reign of a named king; and it elaborates this assertion by setting out the nature of the profits taken by that ancestor from each of the parcels claimed, 'as in rent, in grain, in sale of wood, in pasturing his cattle, in toll of the mill' and so on. This is, as it were, the root of the demandant's title. He then traces the pedigree, the descent of the right, from that ancestor to himself; and apart from a formal offer of 'proof' that is the end of his count[2].

A possible interpretation of the order to the lord in the writ followed by the hereditary claim in the count is that the writ manifests a royal policy of enforcing the customs of inheritance. It has been suggested that such a policy was prompted by events during the Anarchy after the death of Henry I, in which there were briefly re-created in England conditions such as those which had so long before brought about the process of feudalisation in Europe. On each side the lands of enemies were 'escheated' and granted to supporters, for whom in turn surrender became as unthinkable as defeat. On this view the desire for political stability caused regularity of inheritance to be perceived as itself a desirable goal. But the perception of the time was probably less ample and less

1. See p. 134, n. 1, below.
2. See the formularies: *Brevia Placitata* (Selden Society, vol. 66), pp. 1–3, translated at pp. 224–26; *Novae Narrationes* (Selden Society, vol. 80), pp. 2–3, 25–37, 144–58.

abstract; and in ordinary times, even in lords' courts and without any coercion from the king, inheritance was already the regular thing. The immediate trouble was that for two decades the times had not been ordinary. One of the provisions of the settlement by which order was restored required that those dispossessed by the fortunes of war should also be restored. Just forty years later, when the surviving series of plea rolls begins, claims in the right appear to be based upon that provision. In a substantial proportion the king in whose reign the demandant's ancestor is said to have been seised is Henry I, and with him, though not with later kings, the assertion is more specific: the ancestor was seised 'in the reign of king Henry I, namely on the day that he died'. That was the last moment of peace and legitimate title; and although Henry I himself recedes into the past, another reminder lasts as long as actions in the right. The ancestor's seisin is always alleged to have been 'in time of peace'[1].

The process which survives as 'the writ of right' seems therefore to have begun as the implementation of a particular provision concerned with particular events; and the apparent association with inheritance is equally accidental, a consequence of those events lying in the past. Many of the dispossessed who had been seised at the death of Henry I must themselves have been dead by the time the settlement was made some twenty years later, let alone at the time of the earliest plea rolls some forty years after that. It had to be heirs who were restored, but the original concern was with the restoration rather than with inheritance. And the important juridical consequence of this accident is not even the external enforcement of the rules of inheritance: it is precisely that the action reaches back to undo things done in the past. Within lords' courts inheritance, however regular and predictable, was a matter for decision on every death. If Harry's court decides in favour of Dick rather than Tom, Tom becomes irrelevant: Dick does homage to Harry, and when Dick dies it will be Dick's heir who has a claim to be admitted. But when some descendant of Tom can undo the consequences of that original decision in favour of Dick, the matter ceases to be thought of as one for the decision of Harry and his court. An abstract ownership devolves according to rules fixed in the sky, and it is Harry and his court that become irrelevant.

1. S. F. C. Milsom, *The Legal Framework of English Feudalism* (1976), pp. 177 ff. Cf. R. H. C. Davis, *King Stephen* (1967), pp. 121 ff.

The consequences of reaching into the past are further illustrated by the mode of proof. The demandant's count always ended with an offer of proof by one prepared to do battle; and it has already been mentioned that what battle tested was the affirmative oath of a witness. The demandant's champion was in principle one of his free tenants who would swear that he had seen that seisin of the demandant's ancestor upon which the claim was founded. Although based upon an irrational premise, this was therefore a logical verification of the claim; and for the hard-headed Glanvill an advantage of the grand assize, a jury process to be discussed shortly, was that twelve witnesses are better than one. But even for Glanvill, writing shortly before the death of Henry II and more than half a century after the death of Henry I, the underlying fact might lie too far in the past to be attested by a living witness; and the champion might have to swear that his ancestor had seen the fact, and had on his death-bed laid upon the champion the duty of proof. Later even this logic was lost. Battle became rare but was not abolished with the ordeals after the Lateran Council's decree of 1215 because that decree operated by prohibiting the participation of priests. In the ordeal by water, for example, the water had to be conjured by a divine agent so that it should not accept a liar. But in battle there was only the champion's oath, and though there is reason to think that this had once been addressed to a priest, it was later addressed to the court. Since professional champions came to be employed, it was, of course, hardly ever true; and in 1275, to avoid perjury, statute excised the words which made the champion out to be a hereditary witness: '. . . but let the oath be kept in all other points'. The trial was now entirely mystical. But so, by that time, was the right itself[1].

Although the demandant had always to offer proof by battle, a provision attributed to 1179 allowed the tenant to choose instead the grand assize. Four knights of the county would elect twelve others who were to declare which party had the greater right to the land. The demandant was bound by the tenant's choice; but if he could show that they were both of the same stock, the question

1. Champion as single witness, against twelve of the grand assize: *Glanvill*, II, 7 (ed. G. D. G. Hall, 1965, p. 28). Oaths of champions in later form: *Brevia Placitata* (Selden Society, vol. 66), p. 127; *Novae Narrationes* (Selden Society, vol. 80), pp. 28, 150. Change made in 1275: Stat. 3 Ed. I (Statute of Westminster I), c. 41.

which was nearer heir would not go to the grand assize but be decided by the court[1]. This looks like an early example of the process by which questions of law were forced into the open by the introduction of rational trial. Glanvill's praise does not tell us why the grand assize was introduced. Perhaps rational doubt about battle was intensified as champions increasingly had to swear to what their ancestors rather than they themselves had seen. But there is a different possibility. The relationship between lord and man was sacrosanct; and battle between them may have been objectionable for its implications of perjury even though they would not fight in person[2]. And the most important fact that we learn from plea roll entries of cases going to the grand assize is that the issue was often whether or not the parties were lord and man.

This is another example of questions being brought within our vision by rational trial. The tenant who chose to take up the demandant's offer of battle seems never to have departed from a single formula denying the count in general terms. But the tenant choosing the grand assize often discloses a new fact, namely the tenurial orientation of the dispute. The 'mise', the question which the grand assize is to answer, may be general: whether the demandant has greater right than the tenant or vice versa. But in about half the cases in the early rolls, the mise is 'special', and there are two forms of special mise: one asks whether the demandant has greater right to hold the land of the tenant or the tenant to hold it in demesne; and the other asks whether the tenant has greater right to hold the land of the demandant or the demandant to hold it in demesne. In both cases the dispute is vertical, between a would-be tenant and a 'lord' who is denying the relationship and claiming to hold the land for himself. In the first it is the 'lord' who actually has the land and is therefore tenant to the action, and the demandant is making the 'upward' claim to be his tenant. In the second it is the 'tenant' who actually has the land, and the 'lord' is making the 'downward' claim to get him out[3].

1. *Glanvill,* II, 6 (ed. G. D. G. Hall, 1965, p. 26). For discussion see S. F. C. Milsom, 'Law and Fact in Legal Development' (1967) 17 Toronto Law Journal, p. 1 at p. 16.
2. References in S. F. C. Milsom, *The Legal Framework of English Feudalism* (1976), p. 84, n. 7.
3. Despite their early frequency, there has been little discussion. See S. F. C. Milsom, ibid., p. 7, n. 4 and *passim*; *Novae Narrationes* (Selden Society, vol. 80), p. xxxvi.

Special mises are mainly important as showing how far we have overlooked the tenurial element in our traditional view of the writ of right as a proprietary remedy; but they throw light also on other actions. The 'upward' claim represents the simplest that an heir can make. When his ancestor died, the lord took the tenement into his own hand and kept it, perhaps as an escheat on the supposition that there was no heir. We know that the appropriate writ was the writ patent: 'do full right to the demandant concerning such-and-such land of which you yourself deforce him; and if you do not the sheriff will'[1]. We do not know whether the addressee would often entertain the claim in his own court; but if he wished to have the grand assize it would anyway be removed to the king's court. And we know that direct royal remedies were later provided for this situation. The earliest was the assize of mort d'ancestor, to be discussed later in this chapter. But that was available only when the dead ancestor was closely related to the demandant. One claiming as heir of a more remote ancestor had to sue by writ patent until about 1237, when new actions called aiel and cosinage were created. These were begun by *praecipe* writs; and the magnates sought to confine them to cases in which the claim was indeed against the alleged lord or against one who could vouch the lord[2].

The possibility of voucher is relevant also to our understanding of mort d'ancestor, as will appear later, and of the 'upward' special mise itself. The lord who took an escheat would usually grant the land to a new tenant rather than keep it in his own hand. This would make no difference to the nature of the demandant's claim, which is based upon the lord's obligation to himself. But it does mean that his action might begin as a 'horizontal' one against the new tenant. The new tenant could choose to take upon himself the burden of denial, and of course would do so if there was any doubt about his warranty; and that denial could go to battle or to the grand assize with 'general' mise. But if he vouched and the lord warranted him, the lord would become tenant to the action. And if the lord chose to go to the grand assize, it would be on the 'upward' special mise just as if the action had begun against the lord himself.

1. See e.g. *Early Registers of Writs* (Selden Society, vol. 87), Hib. 1; *Pleas before the King or his Justices*, vol. I (Selden Society, vol. 67), nos. 3551–2. Discussion in S. F. C. Milsom, *The Legal Framework of English Feudalism* (1976), pp. 80 ff.
2. *Bracton's Note Book*, no. 1215.

The 'downward' claim will be discussed later in this chapter in connection with the writs of entry; and that reflects something more than just convenience of exposition. The situation is that Tom is in, asserting that he is Harry's tenant; and Harry is denying the relationship and seeking to get him out. Tom wants recognition and Harry wants the land; and it may be Tom who takes the initiative by bringing an action *de homagio capiendo* against Harry in the king's court. Harry's answer is then to claim the land just as if it was he who had sued; and in either case the issue may go to the grand assize with 'downward' special mise. But what writ and what court are appropriate if it is Harry who takes the initiative? The writ patent would take it to the court of Harry's lord; and since Tom does not claim to be that lord's tenant, his court could not act and the case would have to be removed. Before the Charter, convenience would obviously be served by bringing it directly to the king's court with a *praecipe;* and there was no possible harm to Harry's lord in doing so. Not only did his court have no jurisdiction over Tom, it had no interest in the dispute: Harry's upward right to be his lord's tenant was in no way in question in his downward claim to get Tom out. The effect of the Charter was to require that any *praecipe* should contain a clause showing that the demandant's lord was not being deprived of jurisdiction, for example because he had waived it or because the claim was to hold of the king in chief. It will appear later that this was one function of the entry clause in a *praecipe* writ of entry.

The difficulty over writs reflects an underlying incongruity in the situation. Consider Harry's claim. Not only is the 'right' which in other circumstances a writ patent would enjoin upon his lord not in question, so that the customary count upon the seisin of an ancestor and the hereditary descent could only be a formal recitation irrelevant to the case against Tom: he has no positive case at all against Tom. As the later writ of entry makes clear, he is simply denying whatever 'right' Tom is setting up against him. Then consider again the question of jurisdiction. On feudal principle, Harry's own is the proper court to decide whether or not Tom is entitled to be his tenant. On feudal principle, indeed, the situation is itself anomalous: there could be no tenant whom the lord did not accept, and anybody not accepted as tenant would be put out of the tenement. What Harry would once have done was to summon Tom to his own court, to answer *quo warranto* he held his tenement; and if Tom could not show proper warrant, he would indeed have been put out. What has stopped that is royal interference of another kind, namely the assize of novel disseisin. As will shortly appear, this was not meant to inhibit proper seignorial action. But this once proper action of Harry's has been made to look improper by an accident. The maxim that no one can be made to answer for his free tenement without the king's writ seems to have begun as a statement of fact: a lord could not question, or allow others to question, the 'title' of his accepted tenant. But the assize has turned the maxim into a rule of law, and one that protects Tom who is physically in possession although not accepted as tenant by Harry. It is one of many situations in which a lord is driven to ask the king's court to do what once he would have done for himself[1].

THE ASSIZE OF MORT D'ANCESTOR

'The king to the sheriff: summon twelve lawful men to say on oath whether Geoffrey the father of Tom was seised in demesne as of fee of such-and-such land on the day that he died, whether he died since my coronation' (or some other arbitrary limitation period) 'and whether Tom is his next heir; and summon Dick who holds that land to hear the recognition'. Such is the essence of the writ of mort d'ancestor; and if the recognitors answer its three questions, known as 'the points of the assize', in Tom's favour then Tom recovers the land without more. It is a summary and simple remedy. What is not simple is to make out the precise need which it filled. Are heirs commonly being kept out of their inheritances, and if so why? Who is Dick? Is he a mere opportunist wrongdoer who has forestalled the heir and annexed a tenement vacant by death? That is the assumption which has generally been made; but these assizes were so common that it postulates an unthinkable degree of disorder. If Dick has some claim of right, what can it be? What it

1. Discussion has assumed that the maxim began as a rule, and has asked whether it was customary or legislative in origin; R. C. Van Caenegem, *Royal Writs in England from the Conquest to Glanvill* (Selden Society, vol. 77), pp. 223 ff; D. M. Stenton, *English Justice between the Norman Conquest and the Great Charter* (1965), pp. 26 ff. For a lord's *quo warranto* and fuller discussion, see S. F. C. Milsom, *The Legal Framework of English Feudalism* (1976), pp. 45 ff, 57 ff.

cannot be is a rival claim to be the dead man's heir: if the parties are of the same stock, the assize is stayed and Tom must bring his action in the right[1]. So what is left?

At least we know something about the mischief originally aimed at. 'On the death of a free tenant, his heirs shall remain in such seisin of his fee as their father had on the day he died; and they must later seek out the lord and discharge their obligations concerning relief and the like. And if the heir is under age, the lord shall take his homage and keep him in wardship. And if the lord of the fee denies seisin to the heirs, the king's justices shall inquire by twelve lawful men what seisin the dead man had on the day he died, and in accordance with the finding shall restore it to his heir.' That is the essence of a provision in the Assize of Northampton enacted in 1176, and the enforcement procedure which it established is indeed the assize of mort d'ancestor[2]. The mischief originally aimed at was therefore not a disorder of which wrongdoers might take advantage, but an order in which lords might abuse their customary powers of control. If, as is suggested by the references to homage and wardship, the enactment was concerned with military tenures, probably few lords would be so hardy as simply to repudiate their obligations to heirs; and the common abuse may have been in demanding more for livery of the land than the customary relief. In the case of the adult heir, the remedy was to prevent the lord from taking the land into his own hand in any real sense; and though that could not be prevented in the case of the infant, the taking of homage would be a public and inviolable acknowledgment of the capacity in which the lord was holding.

In practice even before the enactment an adult heir living in the tenement may not have been disturbed on the death; but formally to prohibit the lord from taking an actual possession, even for the purpose of making a routine livery to the heir, was to alter the look of inheritance[3]. The heir who enters in his own right will not think

1. *Glanvill*, XIII, 11 (ed. G. D. G. Hall, 1965, p. 155).
2. Assize of Northampton, 1176, c. 4. The text is printed in *Stubbs' Select Charters* (9th edn., reprinted 1946), p. 179. See F. Pollock and F. W. Maitland, *History of English Law* (2nd edn., 1898; reissued 1968), vol. I, p. 148, and vol. II, p. 57, n. 1.
3. S. E. Thorne, 'English Feudalism and Estates in Land' [1959] Cambridge Law Journal, p. 193; S. F. C. Milsom, *The Legal Framework of English Feudalism* (1976), pp. 170 ff.

of himself as in by the lord's grant, not even by a grant that the lord was obliged to make. Homage continues, but as an incident to a state of affairs which has an independent existence. Having dropped out of the process, with not even a ceremonial part to play in investing the heir with the land, the lord drops out of the idea. Inheritance becomes the automatic devolution of an abstract right, a magical event transacting itself without human intervention until 1897, when land like other property was made to pass through the hands of the personal representatives[1]. Nor was it just inheritance itself of which the appearance was altered. 'Fee', which had denoted the lord's obligation, became an idea of the same nature as the 'freehold' which he had been obliged to confer; and new magic was in the making, the common law's doctrine of estates.

The original aim of the assize is therefore clear enough; and its effect on legal ideas is as inevitable to hindsight as it was unimaginable to those responsible for the legislation. But a mystery remains, perhaps two mysteries: how quickly did the assize lose its original orientation? And to what use was it being put in the late twelfth and thirteenth centuries? The plea rolls alone will not answer. Even if Dick is the lord of whom Tom claims to hold, the enrolment itself never says so and rarely shows it indirectly. The ordinary 'general verdict' on the points of the assize tells only of Tom and does not even mention Dick. But his identity may emerge more or less clearly if he pleads an exception; and other sources may show at least that Dick is a lord in the place concerned, even if there is no other trace of Tom.

This, however, is the easy part of our difficulty. Suppose now that Harry and not Dick is the lord of whom Tom claims to hold, and that Dick is in because Harry put him in: it is Dick whom the writ requires to be summoned; and Harry, although the central figure in the story, will normally not even be mentioned in the enrolment. Harry's control is effective within his lordship and simply irrelevant in the king's court; and that is why in records of the king's court Dick can be mistaken for a mere wrongdoer. The impression of disorder so given is doubly misleading. Very few of the innumerable assizes of the late twelfth and early thirteenth centuries concern the military holdings to which the original legislation seems to have been directed. Nearly all concern small

1. Land Transfer Act 1897: 60 & 61 Vict., c. 65.

peasant tenements, and come from a level of society at which daily life was indeed still controlled by the lord's court. What had happened in the lord's court is something we cannot often learn. But one mistake may have been common: sometimes it appears that the tenement concerned, and no doubt its peer holdings within that manor, had been assumed to be unfree and therefore at the lord's disposal. Nor was this necessarily in the ordinary sense a mistake by the lord and his court: in some of these cases it is clear that the question of the freedom of the tenement is being asked for the first time, precisely because it is only mort d'ancestor and novel disseisin that have made it a meaningful question[1].

For social historians of the thirteenth century, the important conclusion is that assizes may more often than appears reflect a background not of disorder but of seignorial order. And in the case of mort d'ancestor there is other and more direct evidence. About 1237 the actions of aiel and cosinage extended the principle of the assize, giving protection to the heirs of ancestors not close enough to be within the assize itself. But it has already been noted that the magnates were willing to sanction these *praecipe* writs only for use against the lord himself or against one who could vouch the lord to warrant him, who would of course be the lord's new grantee[2]. Again, a provision in the statute of Marlborough of 1267 harked back directly to the Assize of Northampton, which had provided only that offenders should be amerced: but now damages were to be given in mort d'ancestor or in cosinage, as though for a disseisin, against the lord who put an undoubted adult heir out of his inheritance, or who held over after an infant heir came of age[3]. The assize has not yet become a merely possessory remedy for use only between equals.

THE ASSIZE OF NOVEL DISSEISIN

'The king to the sheriff: Tom has complained to us that Dick unjustly and without a judgment has disseised him of his free tenement in such-and-such a place since my last voyage to

1. S. F. C. Milsom, *The Legal Framework of English Feudalism* (1976), pp. 22–3, 167.
2. *Bracton's Note Book*, no. 1215; S. F. C. Milsom, op. cit., p. 84.
3. Stat. 52 Hy. III (Statute of Marlborough), c. 16; Provisions of Westminster, cc. 9, 10.

Normandy' (or some other arbitrary limitation period). 'So you are to have the chattels which were taken returned to the tenement, and to have it viewed by twelve lawful men who are to come on such-and-such a day to make the recognition; and summon Dick, or his bailiff if he himself cannot be found, to hear it.' Such is the essence of the writ of novel disseisin; and if the recognitors find that Tom's complaint is true, then he is put back without more. It is an even more summary remedy than mort d'ancestor and similarly common; and as with mort d'ancestor the difficulties arise in making out why it was created and how it was used.

To both questions the received answer has been given in the terms of a possessory remedy, perhaps based upon a Roman model: the original aim and use of the assize was protection against wrongdoers, thieves of land; and then in the fourteenth century play was made with the words of the writ so as to allow the originally possessory remedy to perform a proprietary function. By this later development, to be discussed in the following chapter, the assize became for a time the main vehicle for litigation about title to freehold land; and its theoretical availability was the question upon which most such litigation turned for centuries.

As in the case of mort d'ancestor, the assumed possessory nature of the legal remedy requires further assumptions about the state of society in the late twelfth and thirteenth centuries. One is quantitative: the frequency with which the possessory remedy was needed – and novel disseisin is very common on the rolls – can only reflect disorder; and the growing proprietary use of the assize presumably reflects a growing stability in which its police function is less needed. Another assumption is qualitative: the disorder is taking place in an essentially flat world. Lords are neither suppressing it nor playing any other part, and the assize can be discussed as though lordship did not exist.

That mort d'ancestor was devised to protect the heirs of tenants against their lords is something that is conclusively shown only by the Assize of Northampton which created it. The provision which created novel disseisin does not survive. It is supposed to have been part of the Assize of Clarendon in 1166; but there is some reason to think that what that established was what we should call a 'criminal' offence, casting upon local people a duty to present recent disseisins to the justices in eyre. If so the regular 'civil' remedy was a later development, victims being permitted to procure individual inquiries at their own suit. This would explain the verbose form of the writ, beginning with a redundant recital of the plaintiff's complaint; it would explain also Glanvill's choice of language to describe the parties, *appellans* and *appellatus*; and it would explain the odd fact that he discusses it last of all the assizes. When he wrote it may have been relatively recent as an ordinary civil process[1].

The suggestion that the assize grew from 'criminal' presentments was of course made on the assumption that it was directed against mere wrongdoers. But if the mischief was abuse by lords of their control, such a beginning would help explain what is on any view a remarkable fact, namely that small tenants found the courage to bring the assize against great lords. It began as another assertion of that control over those with local power which was the essence of the eyre. But though the text of the legislation, if it survived, would tell us whether the original machinery depended upon collective presentment or direct individual complaint, it would not necessarily show us the nature of the original mischief. The Assize of Northampton had to describe what must and must not happen because no one word denoted the various steps that a lord could or should take when his tenant died. But a legislator could well have drafted a provision about disseisin on the basis that seising and disseising were acts by definition done by or on the authority of a lord, and we could still read it as aimed at dispossession by wrongdoers.

Although we do not have the legislation we do have writs; and we have indeed assumed that early writs giving ad hoc orders, for example that individuals should be 're-seised' of their lands, were about the abstract possession by a tenant of his land[2]. It has not occurred to us to ask whether the order is made by or to the tenant's lord or implies that he is to be constrained. But once one has questioned the assumption, it is hard to read the writ of novel disseisin itself as about an abstract possession without reference to the lord. Consider the condensed rendering given at the beginning

1. *Glanvill*, XIII, 32–9; the use of *appellans, appellatus* is in XIII, 38 (ed. G. D. G. Hall, 1965, p. 170). For the suggested 'criminal' nature of the assize, see R. C. Van Caenegem, *Royal Writs in England from the Conquest to Glanvill* (Selden Society, vol. 77), pp. 261 ff.
2. R. C. Van Caenegem, ibid., pp. 261 ff, 444 ff.

of this section. Dick has not just disseised Tom: he has done so unjustly and without judgment. The chattels are to be put back. If Dick cannot be found his bailiff is to be summoned. Who is Dick? It is not much of a riddle if one remembers the tenurial situation. The tenant's obligations were enforced by the lord's court, which went through process of summons, the taking of chattels, and then a taking of the land itself. Dick is Tom's lord, and has deprived him without proper observance of that due process. As the writ comes to be used otherwise than by tenant against lord, of course, the tell-tale phrases lose their sense[1]. 'Unjustly and without judgment' merely anticipates possible though improbable justifications. The order for chattels to be restored, realistic only in the context of distress, becomes dead verbiage; and damages are given for simple misappropriations. Oddest of all is the future of the bailiff whom Dick is assumed to have: the clause becomes a warrant for representation by any friend having no lasting relationship with the defendant and no formal appointment to act in the particular case.

Novel disseisin was not aimed at simple disorder any more than mort d'ancestor was. Both were intended as additional sanctions for feudal custom at the two points, considered in the preceding chapter, at which tenants were vulnerable to seignorial abuse. Mort d'ancestor was concerned with fee, with a lord's obligation towards the heir of his dying tenant. Novel disseisin was concerned with freehold, with the living tenant's tenure, his right not to be put out except for cause and after due process. But there is only the writ itself to show us this so clearly. Less than twenty years after the Assize of Northampton the earliest rolls hardly ever disclose the use to which mort d'ancestor is being put, and they are no less reticent with novel disseisin. Sometimes an exception made by the defendant reveals the facts, and sometimes those facts are exactly what the writ suggests: Dick says that the assize should not proceed because Tom was in default, and he took the tenement into hand by judgment of his court. But then it is up to him to prove his exception by producing the men of his court to say what they did; and it seems that the royal judges would seize upon any small

1. Another tell-tale feature is the nature of the nuisances complained of in assizes also first regarded as novel disseisin: S. F. C. Milsom, in new Introduction to the reissue in 1968 of 'Pollock and Maitland', vol. I, p. xlii; and for discussion generally see his *Legal Framework of English Feudalism* (1976), pp. 8 ff.

irregularity to give judgment for Tom. It was probably safer and certainly less trouble for Dick to allow the assize to proceed; but then the enrolment will show nothing of the facts. In the usual general verdict, 'he did' or 'he did not disseise him thus', there is only the 'thus' to make us wonder[1].

But, again as with mort d'ancestor, the detection of Dick as lord when that is the case is the easy part of our difficulty. Suppose that Harry is the lord of whom Tom claims to hold, but he brings novel disseisin against Dick: if Dick is not a mere wrongdoer caring as little for Harry as for Tom, who can he be? An obvious possibility, especially if Harry is a great lord, is that Dick is his bailiff or other local agent. Persons named as bailiff, reeve or the like are common defendants, especially in assizes brought against groups; and these surely reflect not riotous disorder but community action directed by the ordinary management. Nor was that management necessarily defying the customs. Sometimes in such cases it is suggested that Tom or his tenement are unfree, and as in mort d'ancestor that question may be arising for the first time precisely because Tom has dared to bring the assize[2].

Another possibility, and one less likely to leave any trace on the record, is that Dick is a beneficiary rather than just an agent of Harry's order. Mort d'ancestor required the present tenant to be summoned; and he could obviously be the new grantee of a lord who would not himself be named. But novel disseisin required the disseisor himself to be summoned; and if Harry disseised Tom and then gave the tenement to Dick, Tom could bring the assize only by charging both Dick and Harry as disseisors. Harry would then at least be named in the enrolment, though of course not identified as lord. But a lord can exercise control by leaving his beneficiary to help himself, and then he will not feature in the enrolment at all. Suppose that Dick's father died seised, but Tom for some reason took possession of the tenement: it sounds like a case for mort d'ancestor; and if it is Tom who has Harry's authority as lord, then that indeed is Dick's proper remedy. But if Harry acknowledges Dick as heir then Dick may simply enter; and if Tom brings novel disseisin against him the verdict should be for Dick. Seisin was still not just a possession which Tom could gain by his own wrongful

1. Ibid., p. 15.
2. See p. 137, n. 1, above.

act. He had not the lord's authority, and could not be seised of the tenement as against one who had; and so when Dick entered he did not disseise Tom but did himself become seised. That this was an ordinary case appears from an unusual text of about 1240 which describes the working of various simple kinds of legal proceeding, ecclesiastical and criminal as well as this example of a lay civil action[1]. But we can never detect it in the plea rolls: a general verdict would say that Dick did not thus disseise Tom, and Harry would not even be mentioned.

Even when lords ceased to play a real part in the facts behind assizes, their ghosts continued to haunt not only novel disseisin but the idea of seisin itself. Suppose that in the case just considered the story had taken a further turn, namely that Tom instead of suing Dick had simply put him out again. By entering with Harry's authority, Dick had himself become seised of his tenement and could now bring novel disseisin against Tom; but a general verdict in his favour would mention neither Harry nor Dick's dead father, nor anything else to show that Tom had been the man in possession and that Dick had entered in assertion of some right. It is to such a use, far from that of a possessory remedy in the ordinary sense, that the next chapter will show novel disseisin being put in the fourteenth century; and the 'rights of entry' on which it turned are as arcane as seisin itself, and probably from the same cause.

Although in the great majority of novel disseisin cases we cannot tell whether the lord played a central part, a vestigial part, or no part at all, we can see structural changes which seem to have been caused, or at least precipitated, by the existence of the assize. Consider again a lord's enforcement of his services. Avowed disseisin as an ultimate sanction quickly disappears, and process stops short at some formal sequestration of the tenement which itself becomes rare as the thirteenth century proceeds; and near the end of the century statute has to provide a new royal action by which a lord can enforce a forfeiture against a persistent defaulter[2]. Distress itself, effectively confined to chattels, then loses its identity as the process of a lord's court; and the replevin of chattels taken

1. *Consuetudines Diuersarum Curiarum* printed in H. G. Richardson and G. O. Sayles, *Select Cases of Procedure without Writ under Henry III* (Selden Society, vol. 60), p. cxcv, at p. cc. Cf. *Bracton's Note Book*, no. 1976.
2. *Cessavit:* Stats. 6 Ed. I (Statute of Gloucester), c. 4; 13 Ed. I (Statute of Westminster II), c. 21.

becomes matter for county courts, with further consequent artificialities[1]. Nor is it only this 'disciplinary' jurisdiction of a lord that is emasculated. One aspect of his 'proprietary' jurisdiction also disappears, namely his power to challenge in his own court one holding a tenement by some title which the lord does not accept as binding upon him. If Tom was in under a death-bed grant from Harry's father who was out of his mind at the time, Harry would once have put him out by *quo warranto* challenge in his own court. But now Tom could recover in novel disseisin because Harry had no writ; and the end of it will be that Harry has a *praecipe* 'writ of entry' in the king's court[2]. But before turning to these writs, the significance of their name may be brought out by mentioning another effect of novel disseisin, namely its effect upon a lord's control of alienations by his tenant. If he cannot put his tenant's grantee out because of the assize, and cannot demand service from him without accepting his homage or the like, there is de facto a power of substitution without the lord's consent[3]. For reasons considered in the preceding chapter, this result was finally accepted by the statute *Quia Emptores*. That statute and other provisions concerning alienation describe the mischief in terms of the grantee 'entering' the lord's fee. Like 'seisin', 'entry' was a word with seignorial connotations[4]. What one entered was a lordship, not just the property of an equal.

WRITS OF ENTRY

'The king to the sheriff: order Dick to yield up such-and-such land to Tom which he claims as his right and inheritance and into which Dick had no entry save through (*per*) Hugh, his father, to whom (*cui*) William, Tom's father whose heir Tom is, granted it while he was out of his mind; and if he will not, then summon him to answer

1. Stat. 13 Ed. I (Statute of Westminster II), c. 2; T. F. T. Plucknett, *Legislation of Edward I*, pp. 61 ff. The tenant could in the county court with impunity deny holding of his lord. The statute provided for a transfer to the king's court where the disclaimer would be of record. Even then, the lord would have to bring proceedings by royal writ to recover the land. In his own court the disclaimer would have led to immediate forfeiture.
2. See p. 133, above; p. 146, below.
3. See p. 115, above.
4. S. F. C. Milsom, *The Legal Framework of English Feudalism* (1976), pp. 92 ff.

before the king's justices.' That is an example of a writ of entry, and such writs became common in the thirteenth century. Why? Does their proliferation represent only a technical change in the law, so that old kinds of dispute came to be handled in a new way, or were the disputes somehow new, growing from a deeper change in society?

Both answers have been proposed, and their divergence begins from a simple question of fact: in the example given, was the grant which Tom's father made to Dick's father a grant by substitution or by subinfeudation? On the traditional view, cast in the terms of property in land, the question was never asked. If it had been, those terms would have dictated the answer: the idea that land can be owned and alienated without reference to lordship assumes grants by substitution. The 'entry' given by such a grant was into the land of an equal; and the dispute is seen as one between equals. There must of course be a lord of whom Dick is now holding, and of whom Tom will hold if his claim succeeds: but he played no part in the grant and plays no part in the dispute. His only relevance is negative: because writs of entry go to the king's court, he must be losing jurisdiction.

That loss of jurisdiction by some Harry of whom the land is held is central to the traditional view of the writs of entry. So long as Tom was driven to proceeding by writ of right (understood as the original 'proprietary' remedy) the case must at least begin in Harry's court. But novel disseisin and mort d'ancestor had established a principle that 'possessory' claims could go directly to the king's court. The writs of entry began as possessory claims because based upon recent and easily ascertainable facts. But the further back in time you can reach, the more 'proprietary' does the question become. A seemingly arbitrary limit to the reach of the writs of entry has therefore been seen as protecting the proprietary jurisdiction of lords' courts, and perhaps as established for that purpose. It is sometimes expressed in terms of 'degrees', but can be put more simply. It was necessary to trace the land back from the present tenant to the person from whom it had been wrongfully obtained (and it did not matter whether that person was the demandant himself or some ancestor) by using no more than the two connecting words, *per* and *cui*. The imaginary writ at the beginning of this section is just within the limit: but if another hand had intervened between Dick and William, Tom would before 1267 have been driven to his writ of right and therefore, on the received view, to Harry's court. An enactment of that year allowed a new kind of writ of entry to transcend the limit: Dick would be said to have no entry save after (*post*) the defective grant, and the intervening links would then not even be stated. The result of the whole development, intended or not, has been seen as bringing virtually all litigation about freehold land into the king's courts. A possessory remedy has been allowed or encouraged to reach upwards until it leaves no work for the proprietary writ of right to do[1].

This view depends partly upon the range of mishaps covered by the developed writs of entry. If one is thinking in terms of ownership, they seem to cover almost every event which might divert land from its rightful owner: grants by persons without capacity or having only limited titles; grants of limited titles now spent; and disseisins seen as mere takings. These last are critical. The classical account of the writs of entry begins with the situation arising when one of the parties to a disseisin dies before the matter can be put right by assize; and if novel disseisin was indeed the first and most elementary 'possessory' remedy, then this case would be a likely first extension. Of course this was only a matter of exposition[2]. The writer knew that spent and defective grants appeared earlier, and that writs based upon a disseisin were somehow special; though he could not know how limited their use long was, or that the entry formulation was not always used[3]. The case was not organic to the development of the writs of entry, which revolved around grants. But this only accentuates a larger

1. Stat. 52 Hy. III (Statute of Marlborough), c. 29. For its background see: *Bracton*, f. 219b (ed. Woodbine-Thorne, vol. III, pp. 159–60); E. F. Jacob, *Studies in the Period of Baronial Reform* (1925), pp. 81, 88, 124, 142–3, 368–9, 376; T. F. T. Plucknett, *Legislation of Edward I* (1949), p. 27, n. 1. For the working of the degrees see S. F. C. Milsom, *Novae Narrationes* (Selden Society, vol. 80), pp. cxxxiv ff. For the received view of the development, see F. Pollock and F. W. Maitland, *History of English Law* (2nd edn., 1898; reissued 1968), vol. II, pp. 62 ff; F. W. Maitland, *The Forms of Action at Common Law* (edn. of 1936), pp. 39, 42 ff; F. W. Maitland, *Select Pleas in Manorial Courts* (Selden Society, vol. 2), pp. lv–lvi.
2. F. Pollock and F. W. Maitland, op. cit., p. 64.
3. G. D. G. Hall, 'The Early History of Entry sur Disseisin' (1968) 42 Tulane Law Review, p. 584.

incongruity in the received picture. Even assuming an accepted contrast between possessory and proprietary protection, the lack of any seignorial protest at the writs of entry is hard to square with the attitude taken in *Magna Carta* to *praecipe*, and with the difficulty encountered twenty years later in extending the principle of mort d'ancestor.

Another incongruity brings us back to the underlying assumption that the defective grant was a substitution, that land was property which could be passed from hand to equal hand without reference to lordship. Whether or not, and in whatever sense, substitution without the lord's consent was possible before *Quia Emptores*, it was certainly not common a century earlier when the development of the writs of entry was beginning. Both the grant in question and the dispute questioning it were in the vertical dimension; and all the details fit together differently if we turn the picture right side up. Jurisdiction still plays a central but a different part. Tenure was a relationship, and a lord was interested in any transaction or dispute affecting the identity of his tenant. If the dispute between Tom and Dick can be envisaged as a triangle, with Harry at the apex, then it should go to Harry's court. But Harry is here at the top of a dangling chain. Tom's position as Harry's tenant is not in question. And Dick's position as Tom's tenant is no concern of Harry's: indeed, since Dick is a stranger, Harry's court has no power even to summon him. The writs of entry do not represent cases diverted from Harry's court, but cases over which he never had any jurisdictional claim[1].

But they were the product of evolution rather than invention. In principle the question whether Dick is entitled to be Tom's tenant is one for Tom's court; and the earliest plea rolls contain a clear example of Tom summoning Dick to his own court to answer *quo warranto* he held the tenement. But we know about it only because Dick challenged the result by bringing novel disseisin; and he won on the ground that Tom was not entitled to make him answer without writ[2]. This royal interference produces artificiality. There is no writ which will bring the case to Tom's court, and Tom must get either a *praecipe* writ to the king's court or a writ patent to Harry's. Since Harry's court cannot act for reasons already noticed,

1. S. F. C. Milsom, *The Legal Framework of English Feudalism* (1976), pp. 88 ff.
2. Op. cit., pp. 93 ff, referring to *quo warranto* case discussed at pp. 45 ff.

the case will anyway end in the king's court; and before *Magna Carta* a *praecipe* would therefore seem sensible.

The resolution of this difficulty about the writ developed from a deeper artificiality. The claim itself is transformed when removed from its natural habitat in Tom's own court. Although there are early traces of lords making the *quo warranto* challenge in the king's court, seeking to make the tenant set up his 'right', they are soon obliged to set up their own 'right' like any other demandant. But the only right they can set up is irrelevant to this dispute: Tom's hereditary claim to be Harry's tenant has nothing to do with Dick's claim to be Tom's tenant. And if Dick puts himself on the grand assize with special mise, as he often does, it will of course be Dick's right against Tom and not Tom's against Harry that the knights consider. All this is slow and roundabout as well as artificial; and what begins to happen in such cases is that after counting on his irrelevant right, Tom seeks to go straight to the real issue: he proffers payment to have put to a jury the question whether Dick had entry into the land otherwise (to return to the imaginary case) than through Hugh, his father, to whom William, Tom's father, granted it while out of his mind. Unable to make Dick set up his title, he takes the initiative by asserting the defect in the title upon which he knows Dick must rely. It is the frequent association of such proffers on the plea rolls with eventual issues to the grand assize with 'downward' special mise that shows us most clearly what is happening[1].

The first appearance of 'entry' clauses, then, is not in original writs of entry. It is in requests by demandants in 'writs of right' for a special issue to be put to a jury; and if the clause found its way into any writ, it would be a judicial writ summoning the jury. The writs of entry proper reflect a further development: instead of waiting until the case has come into court, the demandant makes his request for a special issue when buying his original writ. Enrolments of the two things are often indistinguishable, but there is reason to think that importation of the entry clause into the original writ became common only after *Magna Carta* and as a result of its provision about the *praecipe*. Although the lord was not in fact losing jurisdiction, a *praecipe* could now be issued only if it contained a

1. Op. cit., pp. 88 ff.

clause making that clear on the face of the writ. The entry clause served this purpose just as did a clause stating that the claim was to hold of the king in chief or that a mesne lord had waived his jurisdiction: it signalled a case in which the demandant's lord had no interest[1].

The seignorial orientation of the writs of entry suggests further questions which are probably answerable from the plea rolls; but it will be with difficulty because the rolls so rarely make tenurial relationships explicit. This difficulty affects all the actions discussed in this chapter, including novel disseisin; and because of the part played by writs based upon a disseisin, that will multiply complexity in unravelling the writs of entry. One question looks backwards: can the 'downward' nature of the writs of entry throw light on the mysterious 'degrees'? The elementary facts are in doubt. Some writers have thought that the relaxation of 1267 was primarily directed to writs based upon a disseisin, others that these writs were not even subject to the restriction and that the statute was concerned only with writs based upon grants[2]. If it turns out that the restriction grew up in claims based upon grants, and also that in early cases any change of hand after the questioned grant was by inheritance rather than by a further alienation, then the downward nature of the claim and of the grant is indeed suggestive. Instead of thinking in terms of an abstract ownership which was or was not transferred by a once-for-all grant, we must think in terms of a renewable relationship. The lord granted freehold to this tenant, and undertook that after this tenant's death he would make a new grant to his heir. Insanity at the time of the original grant might in some sense invalidate that undertaking: but if a new grant was then in fact made to the heir, the circumstances of the original grant ceased to be decisive. Devolutions by inheritance would raise at least what we might express as a presumption that fee had been validly granted; and there may be some connection between these

1. Op. cit., pp. 69, 101 ff.
2. Stat. 52 Hy. III (Statute of Marlborough), c. 29. References are given in G. D. G. Hall, *Early Registers of Writs* (Selden Society, vol. 87), p. xlvi, n. 4. See also F. W. Maitland, *Select Pleas in Manorial Courts* (Selden Society, vol. 2), p. lv, n. 5; G. Booth, *The Nature and Practice of Real Actions* (1701), p. 173. The documents printed in E.F. Jacob, *Studies in the Period of Baronial Reform* (1925), at pp. 369, 376, give specimen writs *ad terminum qui preteriit*.

degrees and those in *maritagium*, to be discussed later, in which they mark the transition from a precarious to an ordinary tenure[1].

Another and more practical question looks forwards: how long did the first orientation of the writs of entry, as of the other actions, remain important or real? Are we to suppose that as substitutions became common the writs of entry turned obediently on their side, so that the received picture came true? One detail is hard to square with that, as with the received picture itself: the relaxation of the degrees in 1267, so long seen as the final blow to seignorial jurisdiction, was certainly approved and probably promoted by the baronage[2]. Perhaps the writs of entry were still thought of in 1267 as essentially remedies for lords. It is even possible to wonder whether their relative decline in the fourteenth century may not be associated with the disappearance after *Quia Emptores* of grants by subinfeudation in fee simple.

THE NATURE OF THE CHANGE

The received picture of the developments discussed in this chapter has been of an essentially unchanging society throwing up essentially unchanging disputes: the changes are in legal mechanisms. The only new idea is that of possessory protection; and what has seemed worth discussing about that is whether the idea was borrowed from Roman law or invented all over again. About the use made of the idea there has been no question: it was exploited and expanded, more or less consciously, so as to provide the king's court with a range of remedies so superior that they drew business away from lords' courts by a process analogous to market competition.

It is a compelling picture, perhaps because it envisages no change in a world always juristically like ours. Tenants were never less than

1. See p. 172, below. The parage relationship established when land was inherited by daughters also ends after the third degree; *Glanvill*, VII, 3 (ed. G. D. G. Hall, 1965, p. 76). Consider also the case discussed in S. F. C. Milsom, *The Legal Framework of English Feudalism* (1976), p. 170, at n. 3.
2. E. F. Jacob, *Studies in the Period of Baronial Reform* (1925), p. 145, n. 1, above; the text printed at p. 376 gives fraud as the reason for the change. For similar pressure for another writ of entry, see Petition of the Barons, c. 27 (*Stubbs' Select Charters*, 9th edn., 1946, p. 377).

owners and lords never more. What lords had were fixed economic rights arising in fixed events, and these included jurisdiction over essentially modern disputes about title. As with a franchise jurisdiction, encroachment might be resented; but it made no difference to the terms of the dispute or to its outcome. No substantial control was at stake. Externally fixed rules could be applied in this court as well as in that; and in those rules there existed the uncouth versions of ownership and possession that tenants had.

This rather static picture has resulted from carrying back our own two-dimensional model, and we have been able to do that because all the seignorial words survived to serve a two-dimensional world. Freehold and seisin, fee and the right, entry and warranty all lost their seignorial connotations; and today we use 'tenure' itself in a non-tenurial sense. Profound changes can lie hidden behind the changing content of legal words[1]; and in the case of seisin and the right, concealment was perfected by the Roman analogies of possession and property. But these analogies were not drawn by legal historians: they can be seen in the pages of *Bracton*, and they may have played a part in bringing about the juristic transformation.

That transformation now seems to have been slower than was suggested in the first edition of this book. It is not only lawyers and legal historians who work to models: how people think and act depends partly upon their vision of their own society. Just as it has been natural for us, looking backwards, to carry back our two-dimensional model, so was it natural for lordship as an organising idea to outlast all the individual powers which made it a reality. The assumptions of society change with passing lifetimes, not with passing years. All the legal phenomena of the thirteenth century begin to look different and less comfortable. Legislation, even that of Edward I, was still mostly in response to the disappearance of seignorial powers. And the copious litigation, which we have seen as reflecting the good order of the king's courts, reflects also the uncertainty brought to ordinary people as their lords' order disappeared.

How far lordship was a reality in the late twelfth century is a question which cannot be answered shortly, if at all. But it certainly

1. Cf. 'trespass', pp. 285 ff, below.

arises, as it did not on the traditional view of novel disseisin and mort d'ancestor. They were directed to the powers of lords, not of course in the sense that the king was confronting feudalism, but as additional safeguards for a framework in which all parties believed. That they were largely instrumental in destroying the framework seems clear: but of course that is not to say that they were the prime cause of its destruction. It seems equally clear that the reality of a lord's powers outlasted the reality which they were understood to serve, namely the balance between land and service. The law does not passively follow social change any more than it can actively cause it. There is an interaction in detail, and the largest changes are the hardest to see.

7 *Later Actions*

We know even less about the later actions for the recovery of land than about the earlier, and have tried less to find out. The enigmatic plea rolls are now supplemented by year books and then reports, but we have not learned to decode the technicalities in which they are expressed. Even more discouraging is the assumption that there is nothing behind worth knowing. For the early actions we imagined procedural improvement and jurisdictional transfer proceeding more or less painlessly in an unchanging world. The development was completed when the relaxation of the degrees enabled the writs of entry to take in the remaining territory of the writ of right; and the common law of property in land, with its hierarchy of better titles on a possessory basis, was at that point fully established. For the later actions our assumptions have continued in the same vein. Nothing important was left to happen; and from the fourteenth century to the nineteenth all changes were lawyers' devices to reach the result of a writ of entry, but with some mechanical advantage in speed, cost or security against an opponent's own devices. There must be more to it than that. But this chapter can do no more than suggest what was happening behind the earlier changes, and barely record the later. And since the later changes depend upon an independent development not yet discussed, which reaches back into the period and the conceptual framework of the earlier actions, it is necessary to begin with what may seem a digression.

PROTECTION OF THE TERM OF YEARS

In our language, the lease for years was not at first a property right but a contract; and the only tenure to survive in England today did not begin as a tenure at all. There was no relationship of lord and man between the parties and no homage was done. Indeed, in comparison with an ideal feudal grant, the parties are reversed. There the grantor was at first the buyer, the services the thing bought, and the land the price paid. But in the case of a term of years the grantor was clearly in the position of seller, and the termor was an investor and sometimes a money-lender. The arrangement was about the profits rather than the land itself. The feudal tenant might seek to secure the actual profits by entrusting the land to a bailiff who would account to him, or he might sell them to a farmer for a fixed annual return or anticipate them for a capital sum. They were modes of exploitation, not grants; and they did not affect the feudal tenant's lord. Suppose, for example, the lessor died leaving an infant heir: his lord took the land itself in wardship free of any rights in the lessee; and the lessee's rights were just interrupted and began to run again when the heir came of age.

We have bewildered ourselves about the legal protection of the tenant for years by placing him in the company not of the bailiff but of the tenant for life, who was of course a tenant in the feudal sense, and by overlooking the feudal dimension in the early actions. If novel disseisin was a possessory remedy, why could he not use it? We have resorted to Roman theories about possession and to economic theories about the nature of seisin: but at the time the question did not arise[1]. The termor had no tenure, no freehold, no tenement even; and he was not seised. He was simply not within the contemplation of those feudal customs for which novel disseisin was meant to provide a further sanction. Like the bailiff he was no more than the hand of his lessor, and it was the lessor who would be disseised if the lessee was ejected. The lessee had no remedy of his own against anyone except his lessor, and that was a remedy in contract on the writ of covenant. Ejection by the lessor himself was clearly a breach. Ejection by a stranger might or might not be, depending on the terms of the agreement: but if the lessor retrieved the land, in novel disseisin or otherwise, he had to restore it to the lessee and allow him such possession as he needed to take the benefit of his bargain.

1. F. Pollock and F. W. Maitland, *History of English Law* (2nd edn., 1898; reissued 1968), vol. II, pp. 110 ff, esp. pp. 114–5; F. W. Maitland, 'The Seisin of Chattels', *Collected Papers*, vol. I, p. 329, esp. at p. 349; F. Joüon des Longrais, *La conception anglaise de la saisine* (1924), esp. at pp. 139 ff.

The first extension from covenant appears to have been a definite event about 1235, when a writ was invented for use against the lessor's grantee. The lessee ejected by him would have a remedy in covenant against his lessor, but could not get the land back because the lessor no longer had it; and against the grantee there would be no action at all. The writ *quare ejecit infra terminum* allowed direct recovery of the land from the grantee; and the lease, like the equity of redemption and the restrictive covenant in later centuries, had taken the first seductive step on the path from contract to property. But it is clear that this first step was confined to the case of a grant made by the lessor; and the writ was sometimes known as the *occasione cujus venditionis* from words reciting that grant.

This needs to be emphasised because Bracton, although he twice recites the writ with its reference to a grant by the lessor, says that it lies against any ejectors[1]. On the face of it, this is a mistake. But a little later actions were being brought which did not recite a grant and appear to have been indeed available against any ejectors. These were the actions *de ejectione firmae*, and they alleged that the ejection had been done *vi et armis* and *contra pacem regis*. These writs have been supposed to originate later and to belong to a definite and different entity, 'trespass'. But there was no such entity in the thirteenth century. The two characteristics now relevant which have been attributed to it are the restriction of the remedy to damages and the allegation of *vi et armis*. But it was only in the fourteenth century that the common law courts refused specific orders in certain actions begun by writs alleging *vi et armis*. And as for the allegation of *vi et armis* itself, there was a general rule that it could never be alleged against one acting within his fee[2]. In *quare ejecit* the defendant, as grantee from the lessor, had necessarily

1. *Bracton*, ff. 220–220b (ed. Woodbine-Thorne, vol. III, pp. 161–2). For covenant by the termor, see S. F. C. Milsom, *Novae Narrationes* (Selden Society, vol. 80), pp. clxxxvi ff. For *quare ejecit* and *ejectio firmae*, see ibid., pp. clxxxviii ff; and see his 'Trespass from Henry III to Edward III' (1958) 74 LQR, pp. 195, 407, 561, at pp. 198 ff.
2. For the fourteenth-century view that *quare ejecit* could not have *vi et armis* and *contra pacem* because the defendant was the freeholder, see YBB Mich. 38 Ed. III, f. 33v; Hil. 48 Ed. III, pl. 12, f. 6v; Pasch. 1 Hy. V, pl. 3, f. 3v. The rule that one could not act *vi et armis* or *contra pacem* within his fee is commonly referred to Stat. 52 Hy. III (Statute of Marlborough), c. 3 about distraint: '*non ideo puniatur dominus per redemptionem*'. For an example of *quare ejecit* being called a writ of 'trespass', see YB 6 Ed. II (Selden Society, vol. 34) p. 222.

acted within his fee; so that *vi et armis* could not have been alleged against him. There is in short little evidence of any original difference in nature between *quare ejecit* and *ejectio firmae*. *Quare ejecit,* which dealt with the more blatant and more frequent case, certainly appeared earlier. But we must not assume that it was instantly labelled as an entity, a form of action with a definite boundary. Those who sanctioned writs against strangers may have seen themselves as covering an a fortiori case, and the different wording of the writ as a formality consequent upon the defendant having no right in the fee.

If so, they were perhaps the first common lawyers who got into difficulty by giving proprietary effect to a personal obligation; but at the time the difficulty probably appeared as procedural. What was a court to do if the question turned out to be one of title as between the lessor, not even a party to this action, and the defendant? In the sixteenth century this possibility was to be exploited, and nominal leases made to enable that very question to be settled in this action. At the close of the thirteenth century the courts seem to have taken fright, mistrusting any action against third parties. One writer apparently thought that the lessee was left with no remedy except covenant against his lessor; and although there is no other evidence that even the *quare ejecit* form against the lessor's grantee fell temporarily out of use, there is evidence of doubt about awarding recovery of the term itself upon that writ[1].

This confusion between property and wrong arose also in the analogous context of wardship. The action of *ejectio custodiae,* for one ejected from his wardship, began as a trespass writ alleging *vi et armis* and *contra pacem,* and having the stringent process appropriate for those allegations. In that case the preponderance of the proprietary element was recognised in the early decades of the fourteenth century, the allegations ceased to be made, and the process was correspondingly relaxed[2]. Only the plea rolls will tell us for certain what happened with the term of years, but it looks as

1. See *Britton,* II, xxxiii, 3 (ed. F. M. Nichols, 1865, vol. 1, p. 417). The passage seems in particular to deny the existence of *quare ejecit.* On recovery of the term see *Casus Placitorum* (Selden Society, vol. 69), p. 42; YB 4 Ed. II (Selden Society, vol. 42), p. 181, where the reporter had thought it worth collecting opinions.
2. S. F. C. Milsom, *Novae Narrationes* (Selden Society, vol. 80), pp. cxlviii ff, and 'Trespass from Henry III to Edward III', (1958) 74 LQR, at p. 408.

though the two actions fell apart. *Quare ejecit* lay on the proprietary side of the line, being available only against the lessor's grantee and perhaps only while the term was still current; and it apparently gave recovery of the term. *Ejectio firmae* retained its allegations of breach of the king's peace and its concomitant stringent process, was available against strangers, and gave only damages.

For the restriction to damages only one reason is stated in the sources: the action is one of trespass, and it is unheard of for such actions to give redress for the future[1]. If the word trespass is taken to mean wrong, this proposition may reflect a juridical assumption of wider importance. It was advanced in the late fourteenth century, when actions for wrongs were breaking new ground in the king's courts. Hitherto only wrongs in which there was a supposed royal interest, such as breach of the king's peace, could be brought there instead of to local courts; and the removal of this jurisdictional boundary raised conceptual boundary disputes. What could be sued on as a wrong? The boundary which gave most trouble was that between wrong and what we call contract, between trespass and covenant. In that dispute we shall again discern the idea that wrongs are by nature in the past, and that actions about wrongs are essentially different from actions claiming rights.

In the case of contract that difference was slurred over at the turn of the fifteenth century; and in the sixteenth, plaintiffs whose grievance was the mere failure to carry out a promise were allowed to get their remedy in actions which formally complained of wrongs. The remedy in that case was only damages, which is all they would then have got in covenant itself. But it may be no coincidence that at the same time the lessee was given specific recovery of his term in *ejectio firmae*. What was abandoned in both cases was a dogma that actions for wrongs could deal only with the past, with harm actually done, and that they could not provide sanctions for rights, for what ought to be done. In neither case are the legal arguments for this abandonment known, if indeed there were any. Decisions of great consequence for the future are

1. See *Vieux Natura Brevium* (ed. c. 1518), f. 49v; (ed. 1584), f. 123; Fitzherbert, *Abridgment*, Eiectione firme 2. For the withdrawal of specific relief in trespass writs, see S. F. C. Milsom, 'Trespass from Henry III to Edward III' (1958) 74 LQR, esp. at p. 409.

recorded only in exiguous notes. The contractual story will be taken up in a later chapter. *Ejectio firmae* has been discussed here because it was to begin a new life as a remedy for freeholders. But that was in the sixteenth century, and the real actions were left in the thirteenth. The present chapter must therefore return to make a second start.

NOVEL DISSEISIN AND THE TRIAL OF TITLE

The writs of entry did not fall out of use. But there was a relative decline in the fourteenth century, and instead the assize of novel disseisin was increasingly used for the trial of title[1]. Instead of beginning with a writ, the claimant was advised simply to go into the land he was claiming. One might suppose that this amounted to a disseisin of the tenant. But no: if the claimant had something called a 'right of entry', he became seised when he actually entered, so that when the tenant put him out, it was the claimant who would recover in novel disseisin. Great artificiality resulted. In 1334 a claimant was hauled out by his heels when half-way through a window, and an assize on this determined the validity of a grant. Thirty years later another claimant was held to have been disseised although he had not dared to enter at all; and curious learning about 'continual claim' preserving rights of entry seems to have followed[2].

Novel disseisin therefore became a principal vehicle for litigation about the title to land, with striking institutional effects. Serious difficulties could be adjourned by the justices of assize and raised before the common pleas at Westminster; and it was in such cases that special verdicts were first frequently taken. But usually there was no such adjournment, so that questions which would have been raised and decided in the common pleas were now emerging outside the purview of that court and of the serjeants. And the *Liber Assisarum*, the one year book not devoted to their doings, probably came into being to meet the need so created; but the collection covers only the reign of Edward III, the heyday of this mode of proceeding.

1. D. W. Sutherland, *The Assize of Novel Disseisin* (1973), pp. 153 ff; F. W. Maitland, 'The Beatitude of Seisin', *Collected Papers*, vol. I, p. 407.
2. YB 8 Lib. Ass., pl. 25, f. 17; YB 38 Lib. Ass., pl. 23, f. 228v.

It follows that much of this development is also outside the purview of historians. The earlier year books show us little of what was happening; and for the thirteenth century we have only the plea rolls, and the likelihood that most relevant cases are hidden behind general verdicts in assizes. Our assumption has been that the writs of entry had come to cover almost all possible claims to land, that they proved too slow, too expensive, or perhaps too precise, calling for more exact information than a demandant might commonly have when purchasing his writ, and that practical advantages of novel disseisin were consciously exploited at the expense of its supposed character as a possessory remedy.

There may turn out to be more than that to both elements in the development. Take first the decline of the writs of entry. We may be wrong in assuming that after the relaxation of the degrees in 1267 they could comprehend almost any imaginable claim to land. As was explained in the preceding chapter, the writs of entry came into being for 'downward' claims arising out of grants, at a time when almost all grants were by subinfeudation; and the entry claim was inserted into the *praecipe* writ to make this orientation explicit, and so to demonstrate that the demandant's lord was not being deprived of jurisdiction. The question is when this orientation came to be forgotten: had it happened before the provision about the degrees in 1267 which, it will be remembered, must have been desired by lords? This question merges into larger ones. When did it become common for grants in fee simple to be made by substitution? How far had that happened by 1290? Did substitution become universal immediately upon the enactment of *Quia Emptores*? And how quickly was the change assimilated into law-suits? The writ of warranty of charter, for example, continued to allege tenure between the parties, and that became a fiction which could not be questioned[1]. With the writs of entry the only change needed was invisible, in the understanding given in that context to the word 'entry'. But it is possible that this did not happen all at once, and that their relative decline in the fourteenth century was associated with *Quia Emptores*, which itself uses 'entry' in the seignorial sense in its preamble.

Related doubts affect the proprietary use to which novel disseisin was put. Is it a verbal coincidence that we turn from writs of entry

1. S. F. C. Milsom, *Novae Narrationes* (Selden Society, vol. 80), p. clix.

to rights of entry? What was a right of entry? We have supposed that the possessory novel disseisin was transformed by the piecemeal admission of matters going to title. A right of entry must therefore be a proprietary defence to the assize; and a beginning has been seen in a passage in Bracton allowing the victim of a disseisin a period for self-help[1]. Within that period the disseisor himself does not acquire such a seisin as brings him the protection of the assize, at any rate against his victim; and the victim's self-help is the prototype of the rights of entry. The idea was then extended to persons wrongfully deprived of their lands by means other than a simple taking. But because the process was piecemeal it remained incomplete in untidy ways; and this explains the anomalous situations in which a claimant might have no right of entry although he had a good title which could be vindicated by action. These exceptional cases, of which the most notorious was the 'descent cast', the magical rule that you could not enter upon one who had come to the land by inheritance, survived into the nineteenth century, preserving a capricious use for the real actions, as well as bewildering generations of young lawyers and enriching their elders.

This again is a purely 'possessory' explanation, and it may reach further when the seignorial dimension is introduced. If at first it was only a lord who could, as a matter of language, seise or disseise a tenant, the process by which seisin became an abstract concept like possession cannot have been either simple or quick. It was historians of our own age rather than lawyers in the thirteenth century, for example, who had to ask why the leaseholder was not seised. Contrary to our traditional view, it seems that lords still had some say in who was seised even after their courts had lost any effective jurisdiction over 'the right'. Consider again a situation discussed in the preceding chapter. It comes from an essentially non-professional account of simple law-suits about 1240, and puts into the mouth of an imaginary defendant in novel disseisin a story which we should not otherwise hear. A tenant dies leaving a son, but a stranger has somehow obtained possession. The son enters, the stranger brings novel disseisin, and the son explains that as heir

1. F. W. Maitland, 'The Beatitude of Seisin', *Collected Papers,* vol. I, p. 407, esp. at pp. 415 ff; D. W. Sutherland, *The Assize of Novel Disseisin* (1973), pp. 97 ff, disagreeing in detail but seeing a beginning similar in principle.

he was put in by the lord[1]. As between rival possessors, it may still be the lord's authority that determines which is seised. Stray reflections have been observed in the plea rolls[2]; but normally a blank general verdict would give no hint of such facts.

Perhaps then the 'entry' of a right of entry also had seignorial connotations, in this case comparable with the sense of the word in the 'entry fine' paid by unfree tenants; and if so, the rights of entry are the last vestige in the land law of an older order of things. Even their oddities may fall into place, as the 'descent cast' certainly would. The putting of an heir into seisin of his inheritance had been a central act of lordship; and although this was obscured by the provision of the Assize of Northampton that the undoubted heir of full age could go in by himself, it was not yet forgotten a century later. Even in that clearest case, a statute of 1267 allowed the lord 'a simple seisin in recognition of his lordship'[3]. The adult heir formally had seisin by the lord, as the infant had in a real sense; and the lord could not later lend his authority to a rival claimant. However good his claim the rival must proceed by action because even as against him the tenant is clearly seised. But of course the process which the Assize of Northampton had helped to start worked its way through the whole field of land law: lordship lost even its conceptual part. Just as inheritance became an abstract devolution of title, and seisin an abstract possession, so did the allocation of seisin as between rival possessors come to depend exclusively upon abstract rules rather than any actual authority of a flesh-and-blood lord. The reality must have died in the thirteenth century; and perhaps that was a condition precedent to what looks like a deliberate expansion of rights of entry in the fourteenth. But it is another question when the terms of thought were forgotten.

If a right of entry had indeed begun as a manifestation of a lord's remaining authority, its exercise would have been protected by the local forces of order. Pure self-help by a private individual in assertion of some abstract right not necessarily even known to the neighbours is socially a far more hazardous process; and in the fourteenth century the resulting disorder must have become a problem, because in 1381 there was passed the first of a series of

1. *Consuetudines Diuersarum Curiarum*, printed in H. G. Richardson and G. O. Sayles, *Select Cases of Procedure without Writ under Henry III* (Selden Society, vol. 60), p. cxcv at p. cc.
2. D. W. Sutherland, *The Assize of Novel Disseisin* (1973), p. 108.
3. Stat. 52 Hy. III (Statute of Marlborough), c. 16; Provisions of Westminster, c. 9.

statutes prohibiting forcible entries[1]. In terms this subjected to imprisonment and ransom at the king's pleasure, the old penalty for a disseisin committed *vi et armis*, two classes of person: those entering even peaceably, without any right of entry; and those having a right of entry but using violence or '*multitude des gentz*' in its exercise. The intention, presumably, was to permit peaceable entry by those entitled; but the claimant choosing to proceed in this way must have been very confident of his right. The effect still lies hidden in the plea rolls; but it may not be coincidence that from about this time the use of novel disseisin for trying title to land begins to decline. Title increasingly comes into issue in all kinds of action, including actions based on the statutes of forcible entry themselves; but that may sometimes reflect not a deliberate choice of this action as a vehicle to try title, but a claimant who has miscalculated. Trespass actions of various kinds are pretty clearly being manipulated for the purpose; but there seems to be no common form. In particular there was no general resort to writs of entry, although curiously a new writ of entry was invented to do exactly the work of novel disseisin, enabling disseisee to recover from disseisor. Many explanations are possible. Perhaps the shift reflects a desire to escape the uncertainties resulting from the laxity of pleading in the assize[2]. Or perhaps, since justices of assize were also a part of the criminal administration, it may have been dangerous to rely before them on the exercise of rights of entry, although relatively safe in Westminster Hall. Most of these remedies, including one now to be discussed which became a new common form, still depended upon rights of entry. But it is possible that the growing artificiality was partly intended to keep the claimant out of range of criminal sanctions.

USE OF EJECTMENT BY FREEHOLDERS

We come now to the confluence of the two stories outlined in this chapter, namely the use of the leaseholder's *ejectio firmae* as a new and final common form for the trial of freehold titles. The claimant made a formal entry as before. But instead of being put out himself, so that his right of entry would be tested in novel disseisin, he arranged for a lessee to be put out. The lessee brought *ejectio*

1. Stats. 5 Ric. II, stat. 1, c. 7; 15 Ric. II, c. 2; 4 Hy. IV, c. 8; 8 Hy. VI, c. 9.
2. D. W. Sutherland, op. cit. (p. 160, n. 2, above), pp. 186 ff.

firmae, which he was entitled to win if the true claimant indeed had a right of entry. The action therefore raised the same issue as the assize which the claimant could have brought if he had chosen to treat the ejection of his lessee as a disseisin of himself. An element of pantomime was involved, and the advantages of *ejectio firmae* over novel disseisin must have been considerable. But we do not know what they were. It is possible that there was less danger under the statutes of forcible entry, and probable that there were procedural advantages.

By the start of the seventeenth century this action of ejectment had become the usual mechanism for claiming land. The claimant or his attorney entered, made a lease to his accomplice, and left the accomplice to be turned out. The turning out might be done by the true tenant or someone on his behalf, or by anybody else including a second accomplice. This last possibility shows how far the court had to take over control if justice was to be done. Judgment for the lessee would be followed, not just by execution against the defendant, but by a writ ordering the sheriff to put the lessee in possession of the land. If therefore the claimant had arranged for one accomplice to be ejected by another, the arrival of the sheriff's men might be the first that the actual tenant had heard of the matter. The steps by which the action was moulded to its task are of little interest, except as an illustration of what Maitland called the 'Englishry of English law': but from a live performance in which real people acted, being made to take such elementary steps as giving notice to the true tenant, it was slowly turned into a recital of the fictitious doings of fictitious people; and the faithful John Doo and Richard Roo, after years of apprenticeship as pledges to prosecute, were promoted to a more exciting role. The true tenant was permitted to defend the action instead of Roo, on terms that he admitted that Roo had ejected Doo, and that Doo had gone in under a lease from the true claimant; and all that was left in dispute was the true claimant's right to enter and make a lease[1].

1. For the change whereby the termor might get specific recovery in *ejectio firmae*, and its small effect until the second half of the sixteenth century, see J. H. Baker, *Spelman's Reports*, vol. II (Selden Society, vol. 94), pp. *179* ff. For the use of the action by freeholders, see A. W. B. Simpson, *An Introduction to the History of the Land Law* (1961), p. 135; W. S. Holdsworth, *History of English Law*, vol. VII (2nd edn.), p. 4. See too Blackstone, *Commentaries* (5th edn.), vol. III, p. 198. There is a useful short account in R. Sutton, *Personal Actions at Common Law* (1929), p. 52.

In the nineteenth century the fictions were got rid of; and ejectment was made universally applicable by the abolition of the few cases it could not reach, in particular the cases in which a right of entry was tolled so that a real action was still needed. These convolutions were therefore the immediate source of the modern action for the recovery of land; and it is the more remarkable that we do not really know why they were gone through. The story will later be matched by others. In the sixteenth century almost all the old actions were replaced by varieties of trespass and case; and for replacing the older personal actions we shall at least think that we can see good reasons. Certainly large substantive effects followed from the procedural changes. The use of ejectment, however, appears to have had no effect on the substantive law regarding freehold land. All kinds of oddity followed, most notably that a judgment was no bar to another action: it formally concluded nothing beyond the particular trespass supposed to be in issue. This inconvenience had to be dealt with first by chancery injunctions and then by rules of court preventing successive actions on the same real claim[1]. But the nature of that claim, the right of entry which was the true issue in the action, was unchanged[2].

COPYHOLD

One substantial change was connected with the use of ejectment, however, and that was the assimilation of copyhold land with freehold. Little has been said of villein land; and its story, although of the first importance as a matter of social and economic history, had no major effect on the intellectual development of the common law as a whole. The realities of the medieval situation are obscure, both as to the personal status of villeins and as to their rights in their

1. See W. S. Holdsworth, op. cit. in the preceding note, p. 17. In *Earl of Bath v Sherwin* (1709) 4 Bro. Parl. Cas. 373, the House of Lords held that after five trials a perpetual injunction should be granted. But Cowper LC, 10 Mod. Rep. 1, refused it even in that case, largely because of the capricious strictness of the common law rules.
2. W. S. Holdsworth, *History of English Law*, vol. VII (2nd edn.), p. 62 and (1940) 56 LQR, p. 479; refuted by A. D. Hargreaves, 'Terminology and Title in Ejectment', ibid., p. 376.

land; and although these two things became distinct because a free man, an adventive, might take a villein holding, each darkens the other.

In the broadest outline, the development of unfree holdings reproduces after an interval that of the superior tenures. Both begin with the land playing the part of the payment for services actually desired; and to the extent that the lord had what we should identify as managerial control of some sort, the ownership of the land must remain in him. The passing of what we can only call ownership from lord to tenant reflects the ending of such control. Both kinds of tenure go through a phase in which control sinks to a mere jurisdiction to apply rules having external force; and both end with the tenant being the effective owner, protected directly by the king's courts, and the lord having only economic rights over the land in the nature of servitudes.

But whereas in the case of the superior tenures, the law of the king's courts kept pace with events, and perhaps partly caused them, in the case of villein land it never caught up. The starting-point, a difficult one to move away from, was that all rights in villein land were in the lord and that the tenant was merely a tenant at will. Within the manor he might be protected both against his neighbours and against arbitrary action of the lord by the customs of the manor, a local law; but this was enforced in the lord's court and not the king's. The point may best be seen by considering the death of a tenant. There were customs of inheritance, perhaps at this level more ancient than the law governing the lord's own inheritance. But the custom was for the lord to admit the heir: the heir's title was an entry on the court roll recording his admission, and his document of title, so long as copyhold lasted, a copy of that entry. To the lord's court, and this is a point we should remember in considering the heritability of freehold land, it may long have been a meaningless question whether this admission was a declaration of existing rights or a fresh grant by the lord. To the king's court, and this is what matters in the present context, it neither declared nor created any right: the tenant was in at the lord's will.

The logic of this dictated what appears to be the earliest royal remedy of the copyhold tenant. Only the lord's court could give him justice; and all the king's court could do was to act upon the lord. This was done by the chancellor, and the copyholder appears to have gained a measure of equitable protection late in the fifteenth century. But such indirect means as this can have been of little use; and in that most obscure period of freehold actions before the use of ejectment, it seems that the copyholder, like the freeholder, was raising questions of title by various actions of trespass. Ejectment brought these questions in directly, so that by the early seventeenth century the copyholder was protected in the same way as the freeholder – namely by the abuse of an action properly belonging to the leaseholder[1].

Although copyhold now had equal protection, it retained its separate identity for three useless centuries, providing a measure of economic obstruction, traps for conveyancers, and puzzles for the courts. These puzzles concerned such matters as the entailing of copyholds, and they were of absorbing legal interest. Today their only value is as an object lesson in the great intellectual difficulty a legal system can encounter when it seeks to rejoin matters which became separated for reasons which are extinct. Of this the law of torts will provide another example.

1. See A. W. B. Simpson, *An Introduction to the History of the Land Law* (1961), p. 145; C. M. Gray, *Copyhold, Equity, and the Common Law* (1963); J. H. Baker, *Spelman's Reports*, vol. II (Selden Society, vol. 94), pp. *184* ff.

8 *Settlement of Land at Law*

The settlement, by which an owner of property can divide the ownership in time between beneficiaries who will take one after another, is the most distinctive juristic creation of the common law, and perhaps the most unfortunate. There is something blasphemous in a power of today's owner to reach indefinitely into the future, and something prodigal in the need for a separate rule against perpetuities to prevent its exercise too far beyond the point of absurdity. For the historian the special interest of the development is its repeated demonstration of the strength of purely legal phenomena. Results were reached which, although absorbed and exploited, cannot have been desired. The most important of these phenomena was the transfer of jurisdiction from feudal to royal courts. There is no magic about an arrangement reaching into the future made by one whose own control, or that of his heir, will similarly reach into the future. He now states or promises that he will give the land first to this person and then to that person; and as events unfold he will make his gifts accordingly. But if the arrangement is to be moved into the king's court, it has to subsist without him. It becomes a package of property interests which, once launched, must make its own way and distribute its cargo without further human intervention.

ESTATES IN LAND

The first and largest casualty of the jurisdictional transfer was the difference in nature between the two original entities of freehold and fee. Freehold was in some sense a proprietary idea. Once the lord had made his gift and delivered seisin, the tenant was entitled to stay in as long as he lived, subject only to a power of removal by due process of the lord's court for some failure on the tenant's side. Fee was a matter of obligation. By accepting the tenant's homage, the lord undertook that after the tenant's death he would make a fresh gift to the tenant's heir, who would then have a new freehold. At first this obligation probably bridged only one lifetime and promised only one gift; but of course the heir would himself do homage when accepting livery of seisin, so that the obligation was indefinitely renewable.

So long as the matter remained within lords' courts, these two entities were distinct in nature. The obligation imposed by homage was sacred and expectations were confident; but you had no property right until you had the land; and that you could get only by livery from the lord, and necessarily relinquished to him when you died. It was royal control, and especially mort d'ancestor, that began to change the pattern of thought: the lord was dissolved out, inheritance became automatic, and in their new and flat world freehold and fee seemed to be creatures of the same kind. The common law was acquiring estates in land differing only in duration.

DOWER AND CURTESY

We have confused ourselves by reading the idea of estates back into times to which it does not belong. Because dower and curtesy both became 'life estates', for example, we have persisted in supposing that they were always of the same nature. At the humblest levels of society they may have been, but not at the level of feudal custom from which the common law was derived. Dower was the right of the widow to hold a proportion of her dead husband's land, generally a third, as long as she lived. She would hold it of her husband's heir, not of his lord; and unless the heir was an infant, the lord was not concerned. If the widow had to sue, for example, she would bring her writ of right to the heir's court, not the lord's; though if the heir was denying her right altogether, she could go directly to the king's court with a *praecipe* writ *unde nihil habet*. But even then, if the land was in the hands of a third party, she could not sue him in her own name without joining the heir[1]. In

1. *Glanvill*, VI, 8–11 (ed. G. D. G. Hall, 1965, pp. 62–4). The tenant could refuse to answer without her 'warrant'; and there are many examples on the early plea rolls.

principle there were two distinct disputes: whether or not the heir owed this land in dower to the widow; and whether or not he was bound to honour the grant which the dead husband or he himself must have made to the third party. And often he had to admit both obligations, and find an extra tenement for the life of the widow[1]. Dower in short was an internal arrangement within the inheritance, a tenure of which the husband's heir was lord. The widow often had to sue to get her dower; but once she had it, she was protected like any other tenant, at first by the customs of the heir's court, and then by novel disseisin in the king's court. Of course she had no fee and no homage was done. But she had freehold.

The widower also had freehold in his dead wife's land, the whole of which he held in curtesy for life provided only that issue capable of inheriting had been born of the marriage. The land might have come to the wife either by inheritance, for example because she was her dead father's only child, or as the portion almost invariably given by a living father when his daughter married[2]. The marriage-portion will be considered later in this chapter; and the nature of curtesy can more easily be explained in terms of the wife's inheritance. Suppose that she was an only daughter, and that her father died before she was married: she and her inheritance would both fall into the wardship of her father's lord, and would remain in his hands until he arranged a suitable marriage. But it was not only for the daughter that the husband had to be suitable: he would become also the lord's man and do homage for this land. From the lord's point of view, the son-in-law was a substitute son of the dead tenant. But like the lord he held in a kind of wardship: the homage that he did was in the wife's name, and the heirs who took the fee created by that homage were the wife's heirs and not his. The husband himself never had more than his freehold, his position as the lord's tenant so long as he lived. But he was the lord's tenant like any other tenant, holding for the services normally done from the land. Curtesy was not, like dower, itself a tenure, and was not held of the heir as an internal arrangement within the wife's inheritance.

1. S. F. C. Milsom, *The Legal Framework of English Feudalism* (1976), p. 43.
2. *Glanvill,* VII, 18 (ed. G. D. G. Hall, 1965, pp. 92–3) mentions curtesy only in connection with *maritagium*, but it no doubt extended also to inheritance at that time; F. Pollock and F. W. Maitland, *History of English Law* (2nd edn., 1898; reissued 1968), vol. II, pp. 414 ff, esp. p. 420, n. 1.

Indeed it was not really a separate entity, and was slow to acquire even a name. Nor was it a frequent object of litigation because the husband never had to sue for the land: he had held it since the day of his marriage. He needed only the protection of any tenant, first within the lord's court and then by the assize of novel disseisin. The only question is why his right was dependent upon issue having been born alive; and since the role of the wife was to transmit her father's rights rather than hold herself, it is likely that the whole arrangement was seen as conditional upon the birth of a new heir.

FAMILY GIFTS

If we ask whether in the twelfth century there were life estates other than dower and curtesy, we ask a question which is real but would have made no sense at the time. Even the tenant who had done homage could not hold longer than for his life. What we need to know is when at the superior level grants were made without homage sc that no fee was created. The military tenure, the equivalent of our 'commercial interests', of course always carried homage; but it was otherwise with benefactions, gifts to churches or members of the donor's family. Homage was not done for land given to a religious house in free alms, but of course there was no question of inheritance for a perpetual corporation. In England, so far as the lay customs were concerned, such a gift seems to have begun as in principle precarious, an allocation of land by way of charitable subscription, but with a spiritual obligation on the donor and his heirs to maintain it[1].

For gifts within the family, the modern terms in which we should think are those of the father's allowance to his children or the voluntary pension paid to an old retainer. Land might be allocated by way of maintenance, to be held of the donor or his heir; but it was not meant to be a permanent arrangement, and homage would not be taken. When the gift was made, the donee would be in much the position of a widow with her dower. But there was no obligation, or at any rate no obligation in the lay law, to make such gifts; and with one exception they gave rise to few law-suits and therefore left little trace on the plea rolls. The one exception was the

1. F. Pollock and F. W. Maitland, op. cit., vol. I, pp. 240 ff.

daughter's marriage-portion; and its original bearings can be understood only if we bring in an element for which our modern analogy has no place. The 'allowance' was not just a matter between father and daughter. If the gift was to endure beyond the father's life-time, it would be a charge on the inheritance in the hands of his heir, and therefore a subtraction from the resources available for the lord's services. There had to be customary rules about the size of the gifts which it was permissible for a man to make and which, if made, his heir would be obliged to maintain. He might give reasonable amounts to a religious house in free alms and to a daughter by way of marriage-portion, which might also be free in the sense that no service would be received from the beneficiary; and these two were particularly troublesome because they might last beyond a single life-time although no homage was done. He might also give reasonable amounts, though here only the lives of the donees might be involved, to his bastard children and to old retainers. But, perhaps to safeguard heirs from the emotional pressures arising from second marriages, which were frequent, a father could impose no obligation at all on his heir to maintain any similar provision for a legitimate younger son[1].

Since these rules were really about what gifts the donor's heir was bound to maintain, they were at home in the heir's own court; and as all questions about freehold land moved to the king's courts they disappeared. But the difficulties did not disappear; and they had to be solved in terms of 'ownership'. The spiritual obligation to maintain a gift in free alms did for religious houses what homage did for laymen, and created a perpetual property. The only control then available in the king's courts was on the making of such gifts in the first place; and hence the treatment of grants in mortmain[2]. Gifts within the family proved more intractable; and for the sake of such clarity as can be had, they will be discussed in relation to an imaginary father having two sons and a daughter. He would give *maritagium* to the daughter; and the provision which he tried to devise for his younger son was to give rise to the entail.

1. These rules are stated in *Glanvill*, VII, 1 (ed. G. D. G. Hall, 1965, pp. 69 ff). They are discussed in S. F. C. Milsom, *The Legal Framework of English Feudalism* (1976), pp. 121 ff; S. E. Thorne, 'English Feudalism and Estates in Land' [1959] Cambridge Law Journal, p. 193 at pp. 204 ff.
2. See p. 113, n. 1, above.

MARITAGIUM

Custom allowed the father to make reasonable provision for the daughter and her issue; and obliged the eldest son as heir to maintain it[1]. Like dower it was a provisional tenure, an internal arrangement within the inheritance; but it was expected to last longer than dower. The land would normally be given with the woman to her husband on the marriage; and at the least it was a provision for the woman for her life, to be actually held by this or a later husband or by herself if she was left a widow. If no children were born, the tenure ended and the land reverted to the donor or his heir when the woman died. The mere birth of a child entitled the surviving husband to curtesy, as with the woman's own inheritance. If children survived they took after the death of the woman (or of their father or other surviving husband entitled to curtesy). They and their issue took by inheritance; but of course the woman's heirs were not confined to her issue, but included brothers and sisters and so on. That is why the father could not make a simple gift in fee. The land was to go only to the woman's issue; and if and when her issue failed, it was not to go to her collateral heirs but to come back to the donor's eldest son or whoever was then the donor's heir. It was a limited allocation intended in that event, like dower, to reunite with the central inheritance.

It followed that, again as with dower, no homage must be taken, whether from the original husband or from succeeding issue. To take homage would create fee, so that when the woman's issue failed the land would not revert to the central inheritance but pass to heirs found among or through her brothers and the like. And since the homage itself would be within the family, curious consequences would follow. Suppose for example that the woman's husband had done homage in her name to her father when he made the gift, and that all her children died before she did. Suppose too that her father has also died, so that the central inheritance has passed to her elder brother. The elder brother is lord of the tenure by which the woman held, and so cannot be her heir in respect of this land (as of course he would be in respect of any land she held of a stranger).

1. F. Pollock and F. W. Maitland, *History of English Law* (2nd edn., 1898; reissued 1968), vol. II, pp. 15 ff; S. F. C. Milsom, *Legal Framework of English Feudalism* (1976), pp. 142 ff.

Nor can he take it back as lord if the younger brother or his issue survives, because in that case the woman has not died without heirs. The land would therefore go to the younger brother, and could not revert to the central inheritance as desired[1].

The special characteristic of the *maritagium* was therefore that it was heritable, and the donor's heir was obliged to maintain it, although no homage was taken. But it was unstable: without homage there was only the customary obligation to prevent the heir from taking the land back; and women were sometimes driven to seek spiritual sanction from the church against their brothers. Donees would therefore from the beginning be anxious that homage should be taken; and by custom the third heir from the donee could insist on doing homage. If the woman's issue had not by that time failed, it would normally have multiplied so that there was anyway little chance that the land would revert to the central inheritance; and the arrangement was therefore stabilized. A subsidiary effect was that the donees would now owe to the donor's heir whatever services were customarily due from that land, even if the original gift had been free of service. The tenure had ceased to be a provisional arrangement within the inheritance and became a normal holding as between strangers.

BEGINNINGS OF THE ENTAIL

Custom allowed no comparable provision for the younger son. The father could make him a gift of land, and hope that the elder son as heir would maintain it. But he could impose no obligation upon an unwilling heir short of taking the younger son's homage; and that would have the capricious effect of homage within the family already explained. Even if the younger son's issue failed, the land could not revert to the central inheritance so long as heirs could be found among or through other brothers or the like. It would be held as a satellite to the inheritance; and in some societies this was

1. For the rule that one could not be lord and heir, see *Glanvill*, VII, 1 (ed. G. D. G. Hall, 1965, p. 69, at pp. 72 ff.); S. F. C. Milsom, op. cit. (in the preceding note), pp. 138 ff; F. Pollock and F. W. Maitland, op. cit. (in the preceding note), pp. 289 ff.

institutionalized as the *appanage*, an accepted mitigation of the family inequity of primogeniture[1].

The common law's fee tail seems to have originated in gifts intended to avoid this result, but still to be secure in the hands of the donee and his issue. The donor apparently took homage, and certainly conferred fee. But he sought to limit the obligation to heirs issuing from the body of the donee, so that the fee would not enure to collateral heirs but be cut down, *taillé*. When heirs of the body failed the tenure would be at an end: nobody else could take as heir, and the land would come back to the donor or his heir by what would in principle be an escheat.

These explicit arrangements evidently seemed attractive. A gift to a husband and wife and the heirs of the wife's body might seem safer than the inexplicit *maritagium*, and might have advantages for the surviving husband. A gift might be limited further still, for example to husband and wife and the heirs proceeding from their two bodies; and the idea seems to have gained ground that a donor could form his gift as he pleased[2]. That such gifts seemed to be getting out of hand is a possible explanation of what happened to them during the thirteenth century.

Unfortunately we do not know exactly what did happen to them, mainly because we do not yet know enough about the framework within which it must have happened. All these gifts were treated as in some sense conditional; and that has something to do with a mischief arising from alienations by donees. In 1258 a baronial complaint says only that alienations are preventing the land from reverting to donors, but in 1285 they are said also to be disinheriting issue entitled under the gift[3]. One difficulty is over the nature of the alienations. Most modern discussion has thought in modern terms and apparently assumed substitution. To the donor at any rate the end result would be much the same; but it seems more

1. That the 'lord and heir' problem arose from gifts to younger sons is made clear by the passage in *Glanvill* cited in the preceding note. For the acceptance of the result as a mitigation of primogeniture see F. Pollock and F. W. Maitland, op. cit. (p. 171, n. 1, above), pp. 292–3; P. R. Hyams, a book review in (1978) 93 English Historical Review, p. 856 at p. 859.
2. *Bracton*, ff. 17 ff (ed. Woodbine-Thorne, vol. II, pp. 66 ff); F. Pollock and F. W. Maitland, op. cit., pp. 11 ff, 25 ff.
3. Petition of the Barons, c. 27 (*Stubbs' Select Charters*, edn. 1946, pp. 377–8); Stat. 13 Ed. I (Statute of Westminster II), c. 1 (*De Donis Conditionalibus*).

likely that the donee would make a subinfeudation, annexing some of the true value in a capital payment, and imposing on donor or issue a tenant they could not get out. The difference would be relevant to the ways in which they might try to get him out; but the donor would anyway be making a 'downward' claim, so the suggestion of the barons in 1258 that he should have a writ of entry is consonant with either view.

This difficulty joins with a larger uncertainty about the precise sense in which these gifts were thought to be conditional. Should we think in terms of a condition subsequent, going to the nature and duration of the interest which passes, or just of a condition precedent, going to whether any interest at all passes? The fee which is *taillé*, cut down to benefit only heirs of the body, is obviously different from the simple fee which may benefit also collateral heirs. But we must not identify that difference with the difference between the fee tail and the classical fee simple, as left by *Quia Emptores*, fully alienable even by substitution. The difference betwen a *taillé* and a simple fee was probably not at first thought to touch alienability at all. In either case the tenant could make a grant by subinfeudation which his heirs would be bound to warrant; and the heirs in tail might not see themselves as more aggrieved than the heirs of a simple fee who inherit only a seignory. The person who might feel aggrieved was the person who first expresses grievance, the donor who does not get the land back in demesne although the grant which he made is now spent.

But even he seems first to confine himself to the obvious case, that of an alienation by the donee to whom he actually made the gift. And in this context, it is clear that the condition referred to is a condition precedent. Many variations are found, some depending upon the difference between an express condition and that inherent in any gift in *maritagium;* and probably there were various views. But the conclusion generally reached was that these gifts were immediate gifts of freehold only, to end with the life of the donee; but they were also conditional gifts of a fee, the condition being the birth of issue. This dealt satisfactorily with the most obvious case: before a child was born the donee had no more, in our language, than a life estate, and could not harm the donor's reversion. But of course it left room for argument if a child was born but died. The result might then seem as odd as the husband's curtesy in the same case; and taken together they suggest that the idea of the birth as satisfying a condition was not invented as a solution to the present problem. It may go back to a state of things in which a woman could not herself be a tenant but only transmit the right of inheritance.

The condition precedent could prevent only the most immediate wrong to the donor. Any claim which he might make after issue had been born would have to be in the nature of an escheat, depending upon the limited range of heirs to whom the *taillé* fee could pass. And of course not even this approach could avail issue deprived of the land in demesne by a grant made by the donee. They would have to argue that the heirs of a *taillé* fee were not obliged to warrant grants made by their ancestors as were the heirs of a simple fee. That might seem an extreme argument to make before *Quia Emptores:* only then would the deprivation be total, leaving not even a seignory for later heirs.

DE DONIS CONDITIONALIBUS

A comprehensive remedy was attempted in 1285 by the statute known as *De Donis.* There is room for doubt about its exact intention, and many of the problems can hardly have been envisaged: but it probably did not intend much of what followed. It orders that the will of the donor shall be observed, and that the donee shall have no power to alienate to the prejudice of his issue or of the donor. Protection of the issue is new; and the statute provides the writ known as formedon in the descender by which the donee's heir could recover from the grantee[1]. For the donor, it says that a writ is already available in the chancery; and this writ, known as formedon in the reverter, had indeed evolved in conjunction with the writ of escheat. A third possibility does not appear in the statute, but should be mentioned: instead of the implied reversion,

1. Stat. 13 Ed. I (Statute of Westminster II), c. 1. Such a writ is found before the statute, but not to recall a grant: if the gift was to donee and the heirs of his body by a second marriage, and he died seised leaving a son by the first, the latter would take as heir general and mort d'ancestor would not avail against him: S. F. C. Milsom, 'Formedon before *De Donis*' (1956) 72 LQR, p. 391.

the grant might have expressly given the residuary interest by way of remainder. A writ of formedon in the remainder came into being shortly before the statute, and seems to have been the only remedy for remaindermen whether following after an entail or otherwise. Since remainders had been limited from an early date, the apparent absence of an early remedy must reflect their original nature as agreements sanctioned and enforced in lords' courts[1]. This is also reflected in a difficulty which even the formedon remedy posed: the remainderman could not in his count rely, like the demandants in all other real actions, on the seisin of an ancestor. In formedon in the descender, for example, the heir in tail reclaiming land from the donee's grantee relied upon the seisin of the donee and claimed as his heir.

This form of count was to become relevant to the construction placed upon *De Donis*. The draftsman may have intended no more far-reaching change than a variation on the idea of the conditional gift. Whereas earlier construction had, in our language, given a life estate to the donee at once and passed the fee to him if and when issue was born, the statute can be read as giving a life estate to the donee at once, and as passing the fee upon the birth of issue to the issue. The earliest year books show that some lawyers believed this to be the effect of the statute[2]. It would restrain alienation only by the original donee. It would also make the issue of the donee into a sort of remainderman: he would be entitled to the fee at birth as purchaser, that is to say as grantee. All sorts of difficulties would follow about his right during the lifetime of the donee, about his death before the donee and so on. And he would also face the remainderman's difficulty: upon whose seisin should he rely when suing for the land? In fact he relied in his action of formedon in the descender upon the seisin of the donee, and gave himself title not by purchase from the donor but by descent from the donee. He claimed as heir and not as grantee or remainderman. Perhaps more than anything else it was the need to fit into the pattern of the real

1. See p. 192, below. For the earlier existence of formedon in the remainder itself, see now P. A. Brand, 'Formedon in the Remainder before *De Donis*' (1975) 10 Irish Jurist, New Series, p. 318, and references there given.
2. See e.g. YBB 20 & 21 Ed. I (Rolls Series), p. 59; 21 & 22 Ed. I (Rolls Series), p. 321; 33–35 Ed. I (Rolls Series), p. 497; 1 & 2 Ed. II (Selden Society, vol. 17), pp. 70, 115; 5 Ed. II (Selden Society, vol. 31), p. 159.

actions, fixed when there was only heritability, that established the entail as a thing in itself, a fee altogether different from the fee simple.

The process by which this happened is obscure, as well it might be. But if the issue of the first donee took by descent and not by purchase, must he not take something limited as it had been in the first donee's hands? Why should he, any more than the first donee, be free to alienate? The decisive step seems to have been taken in 1312[1]. In formedon in the descender by the grandson of the first donees, it was argued that he was beyond the help of *De Donis:* he admitted that his father, the donees' son, had gained seisin, and so, argued his opponent, the gift had been fulfilled in the father's person (*comply en sa persone*). But the most masterful of English judges had a masterful answer: the draftsman meant the statute to apply to the issue as well as to the donee and to bind them until the fetter was dissolved in the fourth degree; and it was only by oversight that he did not say so. Bereford's speech is famous as showing that legislation was still seen as internal amendment to the body of custom in the king's courts, and not as something outside and above it. It may also have been the beginning of the classical entail. The first was the step that mattered. If the issue was restrained as well as the donee, and the grandson's rights of the same nature as the son's, there was no reason why the descent of this sort of fee should not be limited for ever. It would have been possible, and Bereford had this in mind, to say that the entry of the third heir satisfied some condition and freed or purified the fee; but still it was necessary in the meantime to accommodate fees of two very different kinds. The degrees were sometimes mentioned, with increasing bafflement, into the fifteenth century; but there is no evidence that they ever limited the duration of an entail.

It is hard to say which story is the more extraordinary: the evolution of the fee simple as ownership, with only its name and its necessary words of limitation to remind us of its tenurial beginnings; or the series of seeming accidents which produced the fee tail. But this juridical monster, beyond the desires of donors seven hundred years ago, beyond the intention of the legislator and far beyond reason, is with us yet.

1. YB 5 Ed. II (Selden Society, vol. 31), p. 176 and (vol. 33), p. 225.

LATER HISTORY OF ENTAILS

Tentative as any account of the beginnings of the entail must be, we know more about that than about its history between the fourteenth century and the seventeenth. We do not know how secure it was, or was thought to be; nor do we know exactly what use was made of it in family arrangements. Nor do we truly understand the legal technicalities by which entails came to be barred; and therefore we cannot tell whether those technicalities were master or servant, whether the courts were driven by logic or led by ideas of policy. But we are too simple-minded if we view the matter as just a struggle between the living and the dead. If the entail had first been clearly established, and if after that lawyers had begun to seek ways of breaking it, then indeed we could attribute to those involved through a century and more the states of mind of some family at the end of the story, grandfather seeking to tie up, and father seeking to untie to the disappointment of son. But the question of barring comes up before the fee tail has established its separate nature. It comes up not directly between the generations but between son and father's grantee: and it is with the grantee that the merits rest. In the end the grantee will be an accomplice in a scheme to defeat the settlement; but he begins as an innocent purchaser from one with no power to pass title.

ENTAILS AND WARRANTIES

In principle any grant carried a warranty, and this had two effects[1]. First, it barred any claim which the grantor's heirs might later make to the land. And secondly, it provided the grantee with a means of meeting any claim which a third party might make against him. He could vouch the grantor to warrant or bring an independent action against him called *warrantia cartae*. If the vouchee accepted the duty to warrant, or if it was proved against him, then he took over

1. For warranty as a bar to claims by the warrantor or his heirs, see S. J. Bailey, 'Warranties of Land in the Thirteenth Century' (1944) 8 Cambridge Law Journal, p. 274, and (1945) 9, op. cit., p. 82. For voucher to warranty in response to a third party's claim, see p. 127, above. For *warrantia cartae*, see S. F. C. Milsom, *Novae Narrationes* (Selden Society, vol. 80), pp. clix ff.

the defence of the principal action. If he won it, no land changed hands. If he lost it, the demandant was awarded the land he claimed in the principal action, and the tenant got a simultaneous judgment against his warrantor for land of equal value. This was known as the *escambium*, the land taken in exchange. But if the vouchee was not the original warrantor but his heir, then although his duty to warrant was as full as his ancestor's, his liability to provide *escambium* was limited to lands which he had by inheritance from the warrantor. He was liable if he had *assetz* by descent, and it is from the French word for 'enough' that the English language derived its singular noun 'an asset'.

Our present concern is with the barring effect upon any claim by the grantor's heirs. It was this which before *De Donis* had prevented the heir in tail from recovering the land if the donee had granted it away, just as it barred the heir of a tenant in fee simple who had made a similar grant. In providing formedon in the descender, *De Donis* tacitly annulled the warranty; and its framers may not have realized how much the protection given to the heir would be at the expense of an equally innocent purchaser. Within a generation of the statute, a compromise had been settled: the heir was after all to be barred, but only to the extent that he had assets by descent, other land having come to him in fee from his father. The case that tells us this shows clearly how the grantee could appear as a victim. Father, having alienated with warranty the land given to him in tail, later made an *inter vivos* grant of his other lands to his son: the idea was that the son should have nothing by descent, and so should not be barred from his formedon[1]. This was a dishonest attempt to evade what was then a clear rule, but we do not know how the rule was reached. Assets by descent were at home in the liability to give *escambium*, and at common law there had been no limit on the barring effect of a warranty. Seven years before *De Donis*, however, another statute had dealt with the husband alienating his wife's land with warranty, whether during her lifetime or as tenant by the

1. YB 33–35 Ed. I (Rolls Series), p. 387. The jury expressly found that the father had within a few days of his death enfeoffed his son of lands which would have come to him by descent, and that this was by fraud and collusion to exclude the warranty. The rule which this case evidences was in 1365 enacted in general terms for the city of London; see *Calendar of Letter Books of the City of London, Letter Book G*, p. 190; *Liber Albus* (Rolls Series), vol. I, p. 495, vol. II, p. 196.

curtesy after her death: their son was to be barred only to the extent that he had assets by descent from his father[1]. The *maritagium* would be common ground between the two statutes, and it is possible that the general rule was derived from this earlier statute. There is, however, another possibility. In an obscure case of 1292 the father's grantee, instead of claiming that the son is barred by his father's warranty, seeks to vouch him[2]. On the face of it voucher of a demandant is absurd; but if it was generally thought that *De Donis* overrode any bar, then this tenant was conceding the land demanded, and preparing to make an independent claim for *escambium* based upon the warranty. This claim might have been less confusingly made in an independent action of *warrantia cartae;* but it was not without logic. And since the right to *escambium* did depend upon assets by descent, the rule actually reached, holding the son barred to that extent, would prevent circuity of action.

This compromise has some general interest. The system of *escambium* shows a grant of land as essentially a grant of wealth; and what the compromise ensured was that the heir in tail would get the value of the land entailed. The overreaching policy of the Settled Land Acts restored an old view of a settlement. Another point looks back to *De Donis.* The assets which descended to the heir and barred him had to be land of which the father could have disposed, held in fee simple. They could equally be disposed of by the heir, so that only he was protected and not his issue. It again suggests that the statute itself at first reached no further.

Although this learning was relevant to the effectiveness of a grant of entailed lands, it was not in itself a basis for machinations to bar an entail and make the land freely disposable. But the learning was confined to 'lineal' warranties, and a magical distinction arose. 'Collateral' warranties, in which a demandant claimed the land under one title and was heir to the warrantor under another title, after doubts retained the barring effect of warranties at common law[3]. Again the result was no doubt reached in terms of genuine conflicts; but it became a trick which, if members of the family

1. Stat. 6 Ed. I (Statute of Gloucester), c. 3.
2. YB 20 & 21 Ed. I (Rolls Series), p. 303. The report is not ideally clear, but there is no doubt about what happened.
3. Until Stat. 4 & 5 Anne, c. 3, s. 21. See F. Hargrave and C. Butler, *Coke upon Littleton* (1832), note 2 to f. 373b.

signed up and then died in the right order, enabled warranties to be given for the express purpose of freeing the land from claims under the settlement. But it was never as reliable or as frequently used as the common recovery, in which warranties also played a part.

FINES AND RECOVERIES

The barring effect of warranties, therefore, was not invented. A solution had to be found for genuine disputes between two interests, and that solution could be abused. That this equally happened with the barring of entails by collusive litigation is almost the only proposition which can confidently be made about that obscure subject. Fines and recoveries became more important than barring by warranties, and there is much learning. But some of their development is obscure, and only a tentative outline can be given.

Although fines and recoveries both used the mechanics of litigation, and although the text-books on property have taught us to think of them as a pair, they were of different ages and different natures. The fine that survived into the nineteenth century was a conveyancing mechanism that had worked in much the same way at the end of the twelfth. It took the form of a compromised law-suit, generally an action of covenant or *warrantia cartae*. The terms of the agreement were written out three times on a single piece of parchment which was then cut into three, one part remaining with each party and one, across the bottom and known as the 'foot', with the court. Livery of seisin was as necessary as if a private charter had been drawn up, but the fine had three advantages. There was first the evidential security of the arrangement; and the faith of conveyancers has been justified by the use which historians today can make of the accumulated feet of fines. Secondly, because there were no difficulties of proof, fines were easy to enforce; and at the end of the thirteenth century the action *de fine facto* was replaced by a yet simpler process of *scire facias*[1]. Thirdly, the dispositive as well as the evidential authority of a fine was greater than that of a private grant. For example a married woman could not convey her own land away; and although her husband could do so, she or her

1. For the action *de fine facto*, see S. F. C. Milsom, *Novae Narrationes* (Selden Society, vol. 80), p. clxxxii. *Scire facias* was provided instead by Stat. 13 Ed. I (Statute of Westminster II), c. 45.

heir – though the latter might be barred by his father's warranty – could recall the conveyance after the husband's death. But her land could be alienated by fine, upon which she would be separately examined by the court.

This power to do more than the parties could do by their own act is not a trick harnessing the force of a judicial decision, and it comes from a time when judicial decision was not the only business of courts. In the king's courts of the late twelfth century, the fine looks so much an established routine that it is possible to suspect the writ and compromised action of being drill added to an older custom of seeking royal authority for private arrangements. And in the days of true feudal control, arrangements concerning land would call for feudal authority. A final concord made in the court of an honour should not be assumed to show just a lord copying the king. It equally shows a lord and his court giving the authority needed, the only authority there could be, for dealings with the lands held of him[1].

The fine may thus have had diverse origins. But however large a part the genuine compromise of a genuine action had once played, the litigious form played no part from the time the evidence becomes considerable in the late twelfth century. There was no need, and this is the essential point of difference from recoveries, for courts or legislature to deal with fines on the footing that what they did might affect actual disputes. *De Donis* could and did provide that a fine levied by the donee in tail should be void. It could not have provided that a judgment against him should similarly be void without enabling a wrongful possessor of land to defeat the rightful owner by settling it.

The effect to be given to a fine was thus a matter for direct decision, and was mainly regulated by legislation. The preclusive effect against third parties was at first considerable, but the express provision in *De Donis* ensured that the heirs in tail and their reversioner could not be barred, though there was room for argument about the remainderman[2]. The court would not accept a

1. See F. M. Stenton, *The First Century of English Feudalism* (2nd edn., 1961), ch. II, esp. at pp. 47–54.
2. Remainderman: see the discussion in YB 11 Ed. II (Selden Society, vol. 61), p. 12. Court refusing to pass fine dealing with entailed land: W. C. Bolland, *Eyre of Kent*, vol. II (Selden Society, vol. 27), p. 201.

fine if it transpired that the land was held in tail; and if a fine of such land did get through, it was no answer to a subsequent formedon. The security of the entail was thus not threatened, and was not affected when in 1361, because of the mischiefs to third parties, statute provided that strangers to fines were not to be barred at all. But the uncertainty so introduced proved more harmful than the possibility of fraud, and statutes of 1484 and 1490 went to the other extreme, establishing an even greater preclusive effect subject to safeguards of publicity and lapse of time; and this time entails were affected. After some uncertainty, a statute of 1540 declared that a fine was to bar the heirs in tail. Nothing was said about reversioners and remaindermen, but their position was clear under the earlier acts: they were barred, but only in the unlikely event of their making no claim within five years of the accrual of their rights. But it is to be emphasised that these results did not follow from the litigious form of a fine, or from any legal logic. They were chosen, though not very coherently[1].

This is not so in the case of the recovery which, certainly until the fifteenth century, perhaps until the sixteenth, was indeed seen as a law-suit, its efficacy depending upon the force of a judgment. It was of course a collusive law-suit and often fraudulent; and legislature and courts could and did intervene to protect the victims of fraud. But they could not, as they did with the fine, regulate its effects as an identifiable act in law, because it was not an entity distinct from genuine actions. The known formality for passing a clear title was built up from many individual decisions, no doubt traceable but not yet traced, about the preclusive effect of a judgment. A third party brings a real action demanding the land from tenant in tail: what can heir in tail, reversioner or remainderman do about it?

1. Stat. 34 Ed. III, c. 16, removed the barring effect against strangers to a fine. Stats. 1 Ric. III, c. 7 (1484), and 4 Hy. VII, c. 24 (1490), provided that a fine with proclamations, would bar strangers with immediate claims after five years, and reversioners and remaindermen five years after their interests accrued. Nothing was said about heirs in tail, who had always hitherto been protected by *De Donis*. But since entails were now barrable by recovery, it perhaps seemed pointless to preserve immunity against the fine. So far as reversioners and remaindermen were concerned, this made little difference: they had their five years after the accrual of their interests. But the heirs in tail succeeded to the estate of their ancestor, and that was now destroyed by the fine. They were held to be barred in *Anon* (1527), Dyer 2b; reaffirmed by Stat. 32 Hy. VIII, c. 36. See generally C. A. F. Meekings, *Surrey Feet of Fines* (Surrey Record Society, vol. 19).

The first question is whether they can intervene in this action. In the thirteenth century a coherent scheme had been built up. A tenant for life ought not to defend an action alone, but should bring in the person entitled to the fee by voucher to warranty or in some cases by a process known as aid-prayer[1]. But of course if the tenant for life had instigated collusive proceedings against himself, he would not vouch or pray aid; and to deal with this, statute in 1285 allowed heir or reversioner – there was no mention of remaindermen – to take the initiative and 'pray to be received to defend their right'. This statute, however, is a nice example of the main point underlying the story of recoveries: fraudulent abuse of judicial process is difficult to deal with. The legislator thought of the obvious cases of the tenant for life confessing the demandant's title or losing by default: but he did not foresee the tenant who would put up a sham fight by pleading faintly. That tenant had to be thwarted by a second statute in 1390[2].

But by the time of this second statute, something else has happened. Entails were not mentioned in 1285: they are mentioned in 1390, but the only kind of tenant in tail against whom receipt can be demanded is the one who is in effect a life tenant, namely the tenant in tail after possibility of issue extinct. The gift was entailed to the heirs of a particular marriage, and one of the spouses has died without issue. There is and can be no heir able to inherit, and the reversion must take effect upon the present tenant's death. If he puts up an accomplice to demand the land from him, the reversioner can demand to be received and prevent the recovery. And under an act of 1572 the recovery, even if it goes through, is void against

1. See T. F. T. Plucknett, *Concise History of the Common Law* (5th edn., 1956), p. 411. The two processes are discussed, none too clearly, in YB 21 & 22 Ed. I (Rolls Series), p. 469.
2. See T. F. T. Plucknett, op. cit., and *Legislation of Edward I* (1949), p. 123; S. F. C. Milsom, *Novae Narrationes* (Selden Society, vol. 80), p. cxxxi. Receipt was not unknown at common law: T. F. T. Plucknett, *Statutes and their Interpretation in the First Half of the Fourteenth Century* (1922), p. 131; *Bracton*, f. 393b (ed. Woodbine-Thorne, vol. IV, pp. 228–9); YB 33–35 Ed. I (Rolls Series), p. 399. But it was regularised in 1285 by Stat. 13 Ed. I (Statute of Westminster II), c. 3. This was open to abuse, and in 1292 Stat. 20 Ed. I, stat. 3 (*De Defensione Juris*) provided that one received who then lost should compensate the demandant for the delay, and should also be amerced or imprisoned. In 1390 Stat. 13 Ric. II, stat. 1, c. 17, allowed receipt with the same safeguard, when the tenant was pleading so as to lose the tenements.

reversioner or remainderman. In the terms of later substantive law, tenant in tail after possibility cannot bar the entail[1].

The chance of intervening in the law-suit, of preventing the recovery from being made, thus became limited to this case: and since it was a case in which there could be no heir, it follows that the heir could never intervene. But this had not always been so. In the early fourteenth century heirs in tail prayed to be received, and were received, in actions against their parents, the donees[2]. This seems to reflect the early analysis of *De Donis* as passing the fee to the issue upon the birth of issue; and it is likely that the rights of both heir and reversioner to be received in the ordinary case were casualties of the changing concept of the entail. The thirteenth-century scheme of voucher, aid-prayer and receipt had envisaged the simple situation of one entitled for life, another in fee. But now there were two fees in every entail: one in the reversioner, another in tenant in tail. And if tenant in tail had a fee which was going to pass by descent to his heir, the heir could have no fee now. It was in this confusion, it seems, that both heir and reversioner lost their right to be received. They could not prevent the tenant in tail from losing the land by judgment.

The second and less tractable question then arose. Tenant in tail has lost the land by judgment: can the others later get it back again in spite of this recovery? For the heir there were possibilities of direct attack on the judgment by error or attaint, but these would not normally arise unless the action had been genuine. Our concern is with later assertions of title under the entail against the tenants now in possession under the recovery. The demandant might proceed indirectly; but it is easiest to imagine him bringing a formedon against the tenant who would plead the recovery in bar.

The historian who tackles this subject will have to trace the three kinds of formedon separately. One would expect that the heir would be barred more easily than the reversioner or remainderman,

1. Stat. 13 Ric. II, stat. 1, c. 17; Stat. 14 Eliz., c. 8.
2. YBB 33–35 Ed. I (Rolls Series), p. 497; 1 & 2 Ed. II (Selden Society, vol. 17), p. 70; 5 Ed. II (Selden Society, vol. 31), p. 159. In 1292, Stat. 20 Ed. I, stat. 3 (*De Defensione Juris*) assumed that receipt was available on a claim against tenant in tail. Cf. T. F. T. Plucknett, *Statutes and their Interpretation in the First Half of the Fourteenth Century* (1922), pp. 45 ff; S. F. C. Milsom, *Novae Narrationes* (Selden Society, vol. 80), p. cxxiii, n. 2. In 1346 an heir was denied receipt on the ground that tenant in tail had a fee: YB 20 Ed. III (Rolls Series), vol. 1, p. 137.

but again the conceptual obscurity of the entail no doubt played its part: the vulnerability of the heir's title would depend upon the extent to which it was seen as deriving from the ancestor rather than from the original grantor. But the subject has not yet been examined in this way, and must be approached, probably anachronistically, in terms of barring the entail instead of barring this claim or that.

Suppose the simplest case of tenant in tail putting up an accomplice to claim the land from him and losing. Whether or not he should, if the action was genuine, have taken steps to bring in his heir-apparent or any remaindermen, he should certainly have vouched his grantor, normally the reversioner. Suppose now that he had done so, and that the reversioner had warranted and lost: if justice has been done, it follows that the land had never been the settlor's to settle, the demandant is entitled to the land he claims, and tenant in tail has his rights against the grantor on the warranty. Suppose further that the grantor provides *escambium:* tenant in tail will hold it on the same terms as the land he has lost, and the rights of his heirs, remaindermen and reversioners, will have been overreached in the modern sense, detached from the land originally settled and attached to the *escambium*. But suppose no *escambium* is forthcoming: tenant and all others entitled under the entail have lost; they never had any right to the land, and their right on the warranty proves valueless. They are disappointed but not wronged.

If therefore a recovery was pleaded as a bar to a formedon, it was inevitable that the courts would accept it as good if tenant in tail had vouched the grantor, irrespective of any actual loss to those entitled under the entail, and equally inevitable that they would reject it as fraudulent if he had vouched nobody. But suppose he vouched somebody else? It had become common for warranties to be given *in vacuo*, and this was in itself a device for barring entails. But it was not necessarily fraudulent. Suppose an honest but unlucky tenant in tail who first finds that his grantor had no title and who secures from the person he believes to be truly entitled a release of his rights with warranty. He is then confronted by a second claimant, who sues for the land. Tenant in tail knows that his grantor was not entitled, so he relies upon the warranty of the first claimant and vouches him. This is sensible, not fraudulent.

But there will be nothing on the record to distinguish this case from that in which tenant in tail, with intent to defeat others entitled under the settlement, takes or affects to have taken a release with warranty from another accomplice, a landless man against whom a judgment for *escambium* will be ineffective. Neither the voucher of one other than the grantor, nor the absence of genuine compensation, conclusively indicates the cheat. Frauds and fictions do not appear on the record, and much common law development has depended upon this. In the case of recoveries only readiness to make individual investigations could have prevented what happened. And the courts, perhaps not unwillingly, were driven to the result that entails could be barred by collusive recoveries in which warranty was given and the action lost by the 'common vouchee', a court crier whose only care was to invest the money he thereby earned in something other than land[1].

The developed trick was in fact more complicated than this, beginning with a conveyance by tenant in tail to another accomplice called the 'tenant to the *praecipe*'. It was against him that the collusive action was first brought, he vouched tenant in tail, and tenant in tail vouched the common vouchee; and when the dust had settled the entail had vanished more surely than with the simpler form. The point of this double voucher was technical: a recovery would destroy any right of a vouchee, but would destroy only that estate of the tenant for which he was actually seised at the time of the recovery. If therefore tenant in tail had entered into earlier transactions with the land, he might not be seised under the entail; and if so the recovery would not bar others entitled under it. But, there seems to be no lasting interest to this, except that it may indicate the extent to which the courts abandoned themselves to logic. It is when wider issues are clouded, as with revenue law in more recent times, that judges seem most content to leave parties to the rigour of the game.

1. See A. W. B. Simpson, *An Introduction to the History of the Land Law* (1961), p. 121; T. F. T. Plucknett, *Concise History of the Common Law* (5th edn., 1956), p. 620; J. H. Baker, *Spelman's Reports*, vol. II (Selden Society, vol. 94), p. *204*. The debate about who had to be vouched, and whether it was enough that judgment went against the vouchee without *escambium* being forthcoming, appears in *Taltarum's Case*, YBB Mich. 12 Ed. IV, pl. 16, f. 14v and pl. 25, f. 19; and perhaps Mich. 13 Ed. IV, pl. 1, f. 1. 'Under the common law system, everything ought to have a history, and so a singularly obscure case came to be conventionally regarded as the historical foundation for common recoveries': T. F. T. Plucknett, op. cit., p. 621.

CONTEMPORARY ATTITUDES TO ENTAILS AND THEIR BARRING

Logic did odd things in the fifteenth and sixteenth centuries; and for most of them we have no evidence about contemporary moral attitudes. But there is some evidence about entails and their barring. Early in the fifteenth century a London merchant, perhaps more scrupulous than most landowners, was so remorseful at having bought land which he knew to be entailed that he directed his successors to make some restitution to his vendor's heirs in tail[1]. Early in the sixteenth century St Germain devoted some of the most telling discussion in his *Doctor and Student* to the matter[2]. The debate is opened by the Doctor, who recites with affected incredulity ('I have heard say', 'I have been credibly informed') what was then no doubt the usual procedure, the recovery with single voucher. How, he asks, can this stand with conscience? The Student in his turn professes not to understand the doubt: how can it be wrong to do what is necessary 'for the [safety] of the buyer that hath truly paid his money for the same'. Then they are off. It is a long argument, including some theology from the Doctor and an artfully arranged series of examples from the Student in which natural justice more or less obviously requires that the recovery should be upheld. For the Student, *De Donis* was a bad law 'made of a singularity and presumption of many that were at the said parliament, for exalting and magnifying of their own blood'. For the Doctor it may have been 'made of charity, to the intent that he, nor the heirs of him to whom the land was given, should not fall into extreme poverty'; and anyway a positive law must be obeyed if it is not against the law of reason or of God. For the Student it is equally positive law that a recovery bars the entail. For the Doctor 'the judgment is derived and grounded of the untrue supposal and covin of the parties, whereby the law of the realm . . . is defrauded, the court is deceived, the heir is disinherited'. This drives the Student to desperate speculation about the vouchee acquiring lands; but after a while he rallies and observes that these strictures may have been true of the earliest collusive recoveries, but do not apply to a known common form. In the end they reach agreement. It

1. *Calendar of Plea and Memoranda Rolls of the City of London, 1413–1437*, pp. 291, 298.
2. *Doctor and Student*, Dialogue I, cc. 26–32 (Selden Society, vol. 91, pp. 156 ff).

would be wrong to require those who held under past recoveries, 'so many and so notable men' as the Student laments, to yield up what they held. But those who went through recoveries perhaps imperilled their souls, and the responsibility was upon those who allowed the law to remain in such a state. 'And . . . it were therefore right expedient, that tailed lands should from henceforth either be made so strong in the law that the tail should not be broken by recovery, fine with proclamation, collateral warranty, nor otherwise; or else that all tails should be made fee-simple, so that every man that list to sell his land, may sell it by his bare feoffment, and without any scruple or grudge of conscience'. This is the Doctor's conclusion, and the Student can only agree 'that the rulers be bound in conscience to look well upon it, to see it reformed and brought into good order'; though he meanly adds 'that there be divers like snares concerning spiritual matters suffered among the people, whereby I doubt that many spiritual rulers be in great offence against God'.

But if the Student was ungenerous, at least he conceded defeat in an indefensible position. The remarkable part of the story, however, both the particular story of entails and their barring and the wider story of the devices which were transforming the law in the sixteenth century, is that the position did not need defending. There was no attack. The Doctor and his successors did not seek to change the common law: they concentrated upon the reform of substantial injustice in the chancery. Formal dishonesty was left unchecked, and by these means the medieval law was made over for use in a modern world.

The recovery itself became what it already was to the Student, a common assurance upon which, for example, uses could be declared, its solemnity proof against intellectual doubts and against the grumbles of the disinherited, the Athanasian creed of the common law. And although Blackstone considered the automatic enlargement of every entail into a fee simple, he favoured a less radical solution. This, warranted 'by the usage of our American colonies', was to allow their barring by deed enrolled: it was adopted in 1833 and, unbelievably, the structure of entails and their barring is with us yet[1].

1. Blackstone, *Commentaries on the Laws of England* (5th edn., 1773), vol. II, pp. 357 ff; Stat. 3 & 4 Wm. IV, c. 74 (Fines and Recoveries Act).

SETTLEMENT AND RESETTLEMENT

The logic of lawyers is not merely wanton: their astonishing structures reflect actual desires. The Doctor's prescription of abolishing entails was indeed proposed, and was thwarted by much that 'singularity and presumption' that the Student attributed to those who had passed *De Donis*. One of the legislative projects that preceded the Statute of Uses sought to turn every commoner's entail into a fee simple[1]. This came to grief on many grounds; but dynastic sentiment and wishes 'for exalting and magnifying of their own blood' were more real, and not only among the nobility, in the sixteenth century than in the thirteenth or fourteenth. The thrust of conveyancers, as never before, was toward the creation of enduring settlements.

Outside the sphere of uses, the entail was the most promising method; and various attempts were made to provide that any move to suffer a recovery or to bar in any other way should work an immediate forfeiture. Logically these were as acceptable as the recovery itself or as the entail. But logic was given its head no longer. The matter is now indeed seen as a struggle between the generations, and the position reached by logic is regarded as a reasonable compromise in life. The entail is accepted on terms that it can be barred[2].

But it is only tenant in tail who can suffer a recovery, and all that the settlor can do to postpone the time at which his settlement will be destructible is to keep tenant in tail at bay. Sometimes in the late sixteenth century, often in the seventeenth, he makes his first

1. Printed in W. S. Holdsworth, *History of English Law*, vol. IV (3rd edn.), p. 572. For the place of this project see T. F. T. Plucknett, 'Some Proposed Legislation of Henry VIII' (1936) 19 Transactions of the Royal Historical Society, 4th series, p. 119; E. W. Ives, 'The Genesis of the Statute of Uses' (1967) 82 English Historical Review, p. 673; J. M. W. Bean, *The Decline of English Feudalism* (1968), p. 258.
2. For early devices to prevent barring see J. H. Baker, *Spelman's Reports*, vol. II (Selden Society, vol. 94), pp. *206–7*. Those used later were of two kinds. One would extrude only the tenant in tail himself 'as if he were naturally dead', and so pass the land on to the heir in tail; see *Corbet's Case* (1599–1600), 1 Co. Rep., 77b; Moore K.B. 601; 2 Anderson 134; see also *Mildmay's Case* (1605), 6 Co. Rep. 40a; Moore K.B. 632. The second device would destroy the fee tail 'as if they were dead without heirs of their bodies', and so pass the land on to remaindermen etc.; *Scholastica's Case* (1572), Plowden, 403; rejected in *Mary Portington's Case* (1613), 10 Co. Rep. 35b. For a statement that an entail is by nature barrable, see Co. Litt. 223b-24a.

beneficiary tenant for life only, and the first tenant in tail will be that beneficiary's son. The result resembles that reached by the earliest interpretation of *De Donis*. Then the issue in tail was thought to be the first to get a fee, and the fee was thought to be alienable. Now again the issue will be the first to get a fee, and this fee is known to be barrable. Logic has led the law to the limits of unreason, and brought it back to its starting-point.

Even tenant in tail cannot suffer a recovery until he is in possession or has the co-operation of the tenant for life, because a real action lies only against a tenant actually seised. If therefore there is a tenant for life who will not assist in the recovery, the most tenant in tail can do is to levy a fine, for which a personal action is the vehicle and to which seisin is therefore irrelevant. But a fine bars only the issue in tail and not the reversioner or remainderman, and therefore produces in the hands of the purchaser a 'base fee', a fee simple determinable upon the failure of the vendor's lineal heirs, surely the most absurd imprint ever left by logic on human affairs.

These things were the legal bases of the classical strict settlement, which did not endure but reproduced itself in each generation. Father settles on himself for life with a rent-charge for father's life in favour of son, then upon son for life, then upon son's first and other sons successively in tail. Grandson is born, father dies, and grandson comes of age and marries. Son and grandson now collaborate in a recovery, destroying the first settlement, and resettle as before, with son getting the first life interest, grandson the rent-charge and the second life interest, and with no prospect of a tenant in tail able to do anything until great-grandson is born and comes of age. Historians have attributed the regularity of the cycle to the legal leverage exerted each time by the older generation on the younger: an immediate rent-charge was obviously more desirable than the wasteful sale of the base fee, which was all that the younger generation could produce unless the older as tenant in possession would co-operate. Settlors no doubt had this leverage in mind, and they could do no more. But we now know that in fact the older generation would commonly die too soon, so that the regularity of resettlement which kept so much of the English countryside so long in the same families must have been due as much to the force of tradition and sentiment as to the law[1]. But those forces had to

1. Unpublished thesis by Dr. L. Bonfield.

work only once in each life-time to lock ownership up against whatever pressures that life might bring.

So odd a story as that of the entail deserves a backward look. What began as a temporary provision for dependants, to be borne by the inheritance, came to be used as a means of safeguarding the inheritance itself. The change in economic function reflects a change in conceptualisation: the arrangements of one in control become the means by which an owner can divide the economic content of his ownership between persons in the future, and so deprive them of control in their turn. In the case of the entail itself, the apparatus of barring reduced the reach of the settlor to a reasonable limit. At the end of the story he can in effect limit an alienable fee after a life interest, exactly the result reached by the first interpretation of *De Donis* and probably the intention of its draftsman. But other means of settling wealth were not so limited, and are not; and probably none of them would have come into being unless the entail had shown the way.

REMAINDERS

For the sake of continuity in discussing the entail, another feature of settlements at law has been assumed, namely the validity of remainders. These present a problem already noticed. The remainderman was nobody's heir, and until he had himself gained seisin he could not assert his rights in any of the normal real actions. This is a problem to which there is no clear answer for most of the thirteenth century. For the twelfth – and remainders seem to be as old as grants of land – the answer must lie in seignorial control: the grantor is the lord and is in a sense the law that controls his grant, and the remainderman like the heir is relying upon what we should analyse as a promise. The word *conventio* is actually used to describe a remainder in a case of 1220[1]. But the writ of right and other royal remedies provided only for heirs. Bracton, perhaps significantly, speaks of remaindermen as 'quasi-heirs', and says he will give a writ suitable for them: perhaps more significantly, this promise is not kept[2]. He may have been unable to find a specimen.

1. *Bracton's Note Book*, no. 86; *Curia Regis Rolls*, vol. VIII, p. 213.
2. *Bracton*, ff. 68b, 69 (ed. Woodbine-Thorne, vol. II, pp. 200–1).

Later it seems that the remedy for all remaindermen, and not just those after entails, was formedon in the remainder. In that action the remainderman is presented as a quasi-heir, though nobody could decide whether to father him on grantor or first grantee; and he ended by relying upon the seisin of both[1].

Even when the remainderman was secured by an action, he was constantly overlooked or rebuffed. If for example a tenant for life alienated, the heir or reversioner had a writ of entry to retrieve the land from the grantee, but only on the death of the tenant for life. In 1278 statute provided an immediate writ of entry for the heir if doweress alienated, and this was soon extended to other tenancies for life by analogy. But the remainderman, to whom the mischief was the same, was held not to be within the scope of the analogy[2]. He was similarly left out of the statute of 1285 which allowed reversioners to 'be received' when tenant for life was about to lose a real action by confession or by default; and in the first half of the fourteenth century there was doubt about allowing him receipt, although this was in fact done[3].

The reasons for this seem essentially conceptual. The reversioner, or the heir in the case of dower and curtesy, clearly had the fee now. But had the remainderman anything during the prior estate? If not, it was inappropriate to allow him receipt or an immediate remedy if tenant for life alienated. And if he had the fee now, how had he got it? There had been no livery of seisin to him, not even such attornment by the tenant for life as would have been necessary to complete a grant of the reversion. It could be said that the livery to the particular tenant carried the fee to the remainderman; but then there is a difficulty about what the later law will call contingent

1. For the writ, see p. 176, above. For the difficulty about counting on the writ, see S. F. C. Milsom, *Novae Narrationes* (Selden Society, vol. 80), p. cxxvi.
2. S. F. C. Milsom, op. cit., pp. cxxxvii–cxl. Stat. 6 Ed. I (Statute of Gloucester), c. 7, provided an immediate writ of entry for the heir upon an alienation by doweress. The remedy was extended to alienations by other kinds of tenant for life by applying the spirit, though not at first the letter, of Stat. 13 Ed. I (Statute of Westminster II), c. 24, the famous *in consimili casu* clause. But it was not extended from heirs and reversioners to remaindermen: YBB 33–35 Ed. I (Rolls Series), p. 427; 3 Ed. II (Selden Society, vol. 20), p. 16; 12 Ed. II (Selden Society, vol. 70), pp. 18, 90; Pasch. 7 Ed. III, pl. 19, f. 17; *Registrum Omnium Brevium*, f. 237r, *Nota*; Fitzherbert, *Natura Brevium*, f. 207B.
3. Omitted from Stat. 13 Ed. I (Statute of Westminster II), c. 3, giving receipt to heirs and reversioners. Allowed receipt: YBB 5 Ed. II (Selden Society, vol. 63), p. 98; 18 & 19 Ed. III (Rolls Series), p. 375.

remainders, in which at the time of the grant the remainderman does not exist, is not ascertained, or has to satisfy some condition such as the attainment of a specified age. Here, if all rights leave the grantor when he makes his grant, the fee can only go, as the year books put it, into the clouds.

CONTINGENT REMAINDERS

We cannot be sure what happened in such cases, and even less why. It seems that the first reaction was to hold the remainder bad. But the difficulty seems to have arisen only in one kind of case, namely where the remainder was to the heirs of a living person, and to have emerged with the dogma that a living person can have no heir. This dogma was associated with another, inevitable in a system which had done what the common law did with a grant to A and his heirs: this was that heirs took by inheritance and that if one was named as heir he could not claim as purchaser. This in turn coincided with, though we do not know how far it flowed from, an elementary policy interest which may have had a tacit influence on the whole subject of remainders. Now that lordship had become an economic relationship, much of the value of which lay in the incidents due to the lord when the heir of a dead tenant entered, any arrangement by which the new tenant would come in as purchaser would deprive the lord of wardships and the like.

The cases in which a remainder is limited to the heirs of a living person can, as has been pointed out, be divided into two kinds[1]. If the living person is himself granted an interest, we are in the realm of the notorious rule in *Shelley's Case*. This was a reaffirmation late in the sixteenth century of a result reached in the fourteenth; and that was to give the fee to the living person[2]. For example a grant to

1. See A. W. B. Simpson, *An Introduction to the History of the Land Law* (1961), pp. 90 ff.
2. *Shelley's Case* (1581), 1 Co. Rep. 88b; 1 Anderson, 69; Moore K.B. 136; 3 Dyer 373b; Jenkins' *Centuries*, p. 249. See T. F. T. Plucknett, *Concise History of the Common Law* (5th edn., 1956), p. 564; A. D. Hargreaves, 'Shelley's Ghost' (1938) 54 LQR, p. 70. Relevant fourteenth-century cases are YBB 32 & 33 Ed. I (Rolls Series), p. 329; 2 & 3 Ed. II (Selden Society, vol. 19), p. 4; Mich. 18 Ed. II, p. 577; Mich. 24 Ed. III, pl. 17, f. 32v, pl. 79, f. 70; Mich. 38 Ed. III, f. 26; Hil. 40 Ed. III, pl. 18, f. 9; Trin. 41 Ed. III, pl. 10, f. 16v; Pasch. 42 Ed. III, pl. 4, f. 8v.

A for life remainder to B for life remainder to the heirs of A gave A the fee simple which, subject to B's life interest, he could alienate at once. If A's heirs ever came to the land it was by inheritance. The feudal result was that the lord got his incidents. The conceptual result was that the difficulty of the contingent remainder was avoided. The fee did not have to float among the clouds, unable to come to earth until the death of A ascertained his heir: it went at once to A.

But a remainder to the heirs of a living person who was not given an interest raised insoluble problems[1]. In a grant to A for life remainder to the heirs of B, it was intended that B's heir should come in as purchaser: there were evident possibilities of evading the incidents; and, if the arrangement was to be held good, the fee was back in the clouds. Its validity was doubtful in the late fourteenth century, and seems to have been accepted with reluctance in the fifteenth. The reasons for the change are not known. There may have been specially hard cases or it may have been a concession to an increasing practice of conveyancers. We lack any systematic study of the forms or the terms of actual conveyances, although materials are abundant.

One of the important cases in which such a remainder was accepted is known only from the abridgments, which differ[2]. One version says that the remainder to the heirs of a living person will be good if that person dies in the lifetime of the grantor. If this is other than a misunderstanding, it may reflect an idea that the fee does not after all leave the grantor when he makes his grant. But there seems to be no other suggestion that a remainder is a grant of delayed action, the grantor's rights leaving him by instalments; and the later

1. In YB 11 Ric. II (Ames Foundation), p. 283 such a remainderman succeeded in an action of detinue for the charter. Discussion includes the following from the bench: 'Then you think that although he was alive when the remainder was limited, it is enough that he was dead and had an heir by the time that it fell in'. In YB Trin. 11 Hy. IV, pl. 14, f. 74 the ancestor was in fact dead at the time of the grant. But the question was whether the heir took as heir or as purchaser (heir, but not purchaser, could have advantage of infancy on aid-prayer by tenant for life), and this provokes speculation about the operation of such a grant when the ancestor is alive: is it void, does it have delayed action, does the fee exist *in nubibus*, etc.? There is puzzled discussion in court, and evidence of more in moots, in YB Trin. 9 Hy. VI, pl. 19, f. 23 at bottom of f. 24.
2. It is attributed to Hil. 32 Hy. VI (1454): Statham, *Abridgment*, Done 7; Fitzherbert, *Abridgment*, Feffements & faits 99; Brooke, *Abridgment*, Done & remainder 37. Cf. Littleton, s. 721.

theory is clear that the grant is complete when made, and the livery of seisin to the first grantee somehow carries the right of the remainderman. The other versions of the case speak of a grant in tail with remainder to the heirs of the living person; and they say that the remainder will take effect only if that person has died in the lifetime of the tenant in tail. Since tenant in tail must have died without issue for the remainder to take effect at all, this would represent the rule later governing all contingent remainders, namely that they must vest before the ending of the prior estate. Modern books have sometimes treated this as needing explanation, and suggested feudal objections to an abeyance of seisin. But it was probably inevitable on conceptual grounds. If the grant operated at once, and the livery of seisin to the first grantee carried the right of the remainderman, the remainderman must at least be able to take seisin when the prior estate ends. The remainder supported by its prior estate was not so far from Bracton's picture of the remainderman as quasi-heir.

But the remainder to the heirs of a living person was no more than a well-known anomaly, an exception to the general picture of remainders taking effect at the moment of the original grant. There was no category of contingent remainders, of which this happened to be the only permissible kind. The source of such a recognised category seems to have been in attempts by conveyancers to do something quite different, namely to cut short estates by gifts over. The remainder subject to a condition precedent arose from provisions intended mainly to take the land away from the holder of some prior interest. Such provisions may first have been put in when devices to bar entails were commonplace but still resistible, the aim of the settlor being that any attempt by tenant in tail to bar should operate as a forfeiture, passing the land to another[1]. This met a special difficulty about persons other than a grantor taking advantage of conditions; and as barring became an accepted routine, such conditions were struck down as seeking to deprive entails of their inherent characteristic. But they seem to have started a fashion among conveyancers of experimenting with conditions, and a period of confusion followed.

1. See p. 190, n. 2, above; p. 230, below. For the proposition that only the grantor or his heirs can re-enter for breach of condition, see p. 206, below.

An accommodation between conditions and remainders was reached in the middle of the sixteenth century[1]. The notion that a remainder must vest at the moment of the grant was abandoned, and the case of the heir of a living person was generalized. A remainder could be subjected to a condition precedent; and since the right could not vest in the remainderman until the condition was satisfied, it must be carried by the preceding estate, and must fail if it does not vest before that estate comes to an end. But it is only the metaphysical right that can and must so vest: the satisfaction of the condition cannot operate to cut short the preceding estate and give an immediate right to possession of the land.

This added to the range of what conveyancers could do for their clients, but its limits were predictable at the outset. On the negative side, there was nothing here that provided for estates to be cut short, and the rules about forfeiture and the protection of entails could be handled on their own merits. On the positive side there was obvious danger that settlors would seek to build up perpetuities by indefinite series of contingent remainders. Special rules thwarted the more blatant attempts[2]. But the lasting safeguard, and the lasting trap for settlors, was that contingent remainders were destructible by the termination of the precedent estate before the remainder had vested[3]. The safeguard against perpetuities depends upon the proposition that any gift to an unborn person was contingent, and would fail if the precedent estate ended before the remainderman was born. Settlors could not confidently reach further into the future than the ending of lives in being. The trap was in the working of this. If land was granted to A for life, remainder to his grandsons equally, the remainder would fail altogether if no grandson had been born when A died; and if only the first of a final total of ten grandsons had been born, that one took all to the exclusion of the others. The metaphysical support of the precedent estate had consequences not in themselves desired.

1. *Colthirst v Bejushin* (1550), Plowden 21. For earlier confusion see: Littleton, s. 723; YB Mich. 18 Hy. VIII, pl. 17, f. 3; YB Mich. 27 Hy. VIII, pl. 2, f. 24 (Brooke, *Abridgment,* Done & remainder 3, Fines levies de terres 5).
2. See e.g. *Perrot's Case* (1594), Moore K.B. 368; *Rector of Chedington's Case* (1598), 1 Co. Rep. 148b.
3. For a very clear statement of the settled rules see R. E. Megarry and H. W. R. Wade, *The Law of Real Property* (4th edn., 1975), pp. 183 ff.

It was, moreover, the precedent estate that provided the support, and not the life of its owner. If in the example A had forfeited his life estate, and if his ten grandsons were born after that forfeiture and before his death, their remainder failed just the same. This let logic loose again. Suppose a settlement upon A for life, remainder to his first and other sons successively in tail, remainder to B in fee simple. This was the heart of the strict settlement already discussed, and the machinations now to be described imperilled it. If before he had any sons, so that the remainders in tail were still contingent, A granted his life interest to B, or if B granted his fee simple to A, A's estate 'merged' in the fee: it ceased to have a separate existence, the contingent remainders failed for lack of support, and no entail came into existence. In the seventeenth century this was countered by the extraordinary device, which became common form, of 'trustees to preserve contingent remainders'. In the example the conveyancer would, after the life interest to A, insert a remainder to trustees for the life of A; and then he would grant the remainders over as before. If A destroyed his estate there was another and exactly equivalent prop to support the remainders. After beautiful argument not to be followed here, it was agreed that this remainder was itself vested and so immune from destruction; and conveyancers could plan their settlements on the basis of natural lives and deaths[1].

In the nineteenth century, statute made contingent remainders immune first from artificial and then from natural destruction[2]. By reason of the developments to be discussed in the next chapter, this learning was all becoming unreal. Settlors had more effective ways of tying up land, and other limits had been set to what they could do. Moreover, with the growth of other forms of capital, the tying

1. See W. S. Holdsworth, *History of English Law*, vol. VII (2nd edn.), p. 112. The conceptual basis of the device was pointed out as early as 1597; *Cholmley's Case*, 2 Co. Rep. 50a at 51a. Its exploitation by conveyancers appears to date from the mid-seventeenth century. That the remainder of the trustees was itself vested, and therefore not subject to artificial destruction, was finally decided in *Smith d. Dormer v Packhurst* (1740), 3 Atkyns 135.
2. Stat. 3 & 4 Wm. IV, c. 27 (Real Property Limitation Act 1833); 8 & 9 Vict., c. 106 (Real Property Act 1845); 40 & 41 Vict., c. 33 (Contingent Remainders Act 1877). See R. E. Megarry and H. W. R. Wade, *The Law of Real Property* (4th edn., 1975), pp. 192 ff. All this learning was rendered obsolete by the Settled Land Acts 1882 and 1925: the idea derived from special powers in settlements and from the distinct institution of the trust for sale; and the economic need is well stated in *Bruce v Marquess of Ailesbury*, [1892] A.C. 356 at 364.

up of physical land was causing economic distortion; and the Settled Land Acts were to take settlements back in spirit to their starting-point[1]. Land was to be treated only as a form of wealth, and overreaching powers were to ensure that only the wealth could be settled. But it is necessary to remember that these things did not begin to seem unreal until the nineteenth century was well advanced. The rules under which so much of the wealth of England was held for so much of its history were made and unmade by these processes, so extraordinary when looked at as a whole and backwards, so reasonable step by forward step.

1. See p. 180, above.

9 *Uses and Trusts of Land*

THE PROBLEM OF ORIGINS

The noun use, in the sense under discussion, has in principle nothing to do with the modern verb to use. Property held by one person to the use of another was held for that other's benefit, *al oeps* in Norman French, *ad opus* in Latin. To begin with the term most often describes an agent acting on behalf of his principal: a bailiff may collect tolls *ad opus communitatis villae* or *domini regis* or of the franchise owner; and conversely the owner may complain that a wrongdoer has taken the tolls *ad opus suum*. Such events may or may not give rise to legal proceedings, but those proceedings will not revolve around a legal concept for which there is a term of art. In Plucknett's phrase, the use began as 'a situation rather than an institution'[1].

The question of origins can be divided into two. From what situation or situations did the institution develop? And were those situations themselves derived from an older institution or idea? To take the second question first, Germanic law had an institution not altogether unlike the later use, that of the *salman*[2]. But there is no evidence that he ever came to these shores, let alone survived to play any part in the rise of the use. And even if custom had known this or some similar arrangement with land of which the mode of protection had been obliterated by feudal theory, it would have perished. Traditions do not survive unsupported; and the realistic question is whether there was something in the immediate and not the remote background, whether analogous relationships were

1. T. F. T. Plucknett, *Concise History of the Common Law* (5th edn., 1956), p. 579.
2. W. S. Holdsworth, *History of English Law*, vol. IV (3rd edn.), p. 410. J. L. Barton, 'The Medieval Use' (1965) 81 LQR, p. 562.

being made and protected somewhere out of our sight. The chief possibilities are in local and in ecclesiastical jurisdictions.

As for local jurisdictions, fiduciary relationships were not unknown in towns, where ancient ideas may have been protected from feudal disturbance. These relationships look as though they were connected with the customary power to devise; and it is impossible to read the early wills enrolled in the London husting without supposing a mode of enforcement much like the chancery jurisdiction over trusts centuries later. In 1259, for example, one ordered 'his houses to be sold and provision made thereout for some honest chaplain, a scholar studying in a university, to celebrate for the good of his soul and the souls of others, and on his ceasing so to study, then for some other student, at the hands of his executors, and so in perpetuity'[1]. Such arrangements must be the subject of a rule found in a custumal of 1324 from Godmanchester: if any one receives lands or other property in perpetuity and fails to maintain the perpetuity, he shall lose the property and it shall at the community's order be assigned to persons 'in order to keep up and carry out the said perpetuity'[2]. Again, although the London orphans' court, whose name survives only on the western shore of the Atlantic, acquired a separate existence after the equitable jurisdiction of the chancery was established, it got it by delegation from a much older body; and the city's system of fiduciary wardship appears to be older than that established for guardians in socage in the mid-thirteenth century[3].

If, as some have supposed, the key to the matter is the power of a court to order personal conduct, then here too the London courts never abandoned this as the king's courts did. Their orders for specific performance and restitution may, as will appear in a later chapter, have played some part in the development of the common law of contract. But it was the courts of the church that above all others proceeded in this way; and this necessarily led to some blurring of the jurisdictional limits which the lay power sought to impose upon them. They had, for example, no jurisdiction over lay debts. But that could not prevent them, when a transaction had

1. *Calendar of Wills Proved and Enrolled in the Court of Husting, London* (1889), vol. I, p. 5.
2. *Borough Customs*, vol. II (Selden Society, vol. 21), p. 163.
3. See *Calendar of Plea and Memoranda Rolls of the City of London, 1323–1364* (1926), p. 123, n. 1, p. 205, n. 1.

been accompanied by pledge of faith, from offering to mitigate penalties for the breach of faith if lay restitution were made. Similarly they had no jurisdiction over freehold land; but here, at any rate after early struggles, there were few situations in which interference would be proper even on their own principles. An early one is mentioned by Glanvill: because faith was pledged on marriage contracts, the church courts would protect a woman's *maritagium* against the donor or his heir. A later one is probably connected with the testamentary jurisdiction. So long as the feudal structure was a reality, the only kind of freehold to be devisable was the urban tenement. And an early annotator of the late thirteenth-century book known as *Britton* explains why such devises were enforced by lay courts in the towns rather than by the church: although 'will and intention not carried into act are spiritual matters', yet spiritual judges could not enforce any judgment about freehold. But what was to happen when the structure had so changed that freehold tenants saw their land as just wealth but, unable to make a formal devise, made *inter vivos* grants to friends to whom they would then give what were really testamentary instructions? On the view taken in this chapter that was the important situation in which land came commonly to be held by one person for the benefit of another; but until the chancellor intervened there was no lay court able to enforce the arrangement. When souls might be imperilled, could the church refuse to give instructions to the friends to whom the land had been entrusted? We now know that in some dioceses at least the church courts did so act; and it may turn out that it was the impropriety of any such interference with freehold land that prompted the chancellor to take jurisdiction himself[1].

SITUATIONS IN WHICH ONE HELD LAND FOR ANOTHER

Of the situations in which land was held by one for the benefit of another, those concerning the church will be considered first. An

1. Enforcement of *maritagium*: *Glanvill*, VII, 18 (ed. G. D. G. Hall, 1965, p. 93); no longer true in *Bracton*, f. 407b (ed. Woodbine-Thorne, vol. IV, p. 267). 'Will and intention not carried into act': F. M. Nichols, *Britton*, vol. I, p. 174 n.f. and, on the annotator, op. cit. Introduction, pp. lx ff. Early enforcement of uses in church courts: R. H. Helmholz, 'The Early Enforcement of Uses', (1979) 79 Columbia Law Review, p. 1505.

ecclesiastical body might figure, in modern language, as trustee or beneficiary or both. If it was trustee, then the enforcement problem would not arise. Indeed, the church would have said, though in other language, that all its property was held upon charitable trusts; and as between one charity and another, the reality of the question lay in the internal accounting of individual religious houses: this income for the poor, that for the soul of the founder, and so on.

More relevant is the situation in which laymen hold for the benefit of a church. Two situations are discussed. The Franciscan friars were forbidden to own property; and difficulties arose over their houses. At the end of the thirteenth century attempts were being made in Rome to resolve these, naturally based upon civilian concepts. The friars might not have *dominium*, but they might have *usufructus*. This was the background to a remarkable case in the plea rolls of 1308, in which the Friars Minor of Oxford, in answer to a claim for certain houses in St. Ebbes, say that they claim nothing *nisi tantum usum et aisiamentum*. They produce a grant which indeed purported to give them *usum plenarium et aisiamentum*, and claim that they are only tenants at will of the grantor's heir[1]. The case never reappears, perhaps because the heir happened to be the king. But it is doubtful how far this situation was in the main stream of development of uses. The Franciscans' problem was soon solved by allowing them to own their houses, and confining the prohibition to capital wealth; and they seem to play no later part in the story. But the 1308 case remains of interest. The grant of *usus* had surely been inspired by the Franciscans themselves, and if the matter was analysed at all it must have been in civilian terms. *Usus* here was not translating *oeps*, and the grantor probably did not see himself as, in our language, declaring a trust: he saw himself as giving a Roman right to use and enjoy. English law could accommodate this in only one way. The grantee had to say that he was tenant at will, just as a villein must say of his holding; but he did not necessarily think himself rightless.

1. YB 2 & 3 Ed. II (Selden Society, vol. 19), p. 75. See F. Pollock and F. W. Maitland, *History of English Law* (2nd edn., 1898; reissued 1968), vol. II, pp. 231, 238; T. F. T. Plucknett, *Concise History of the Common Law* (5th edn., 1956), p. 577, n. 3; J. L. Barton, 'The Medieval Use' (1965) 81 LQR, p. 562 at p. 564.

The other situation in which laymen might find themselves holding land for the benefit of a church may be in the main stream of uses. It arose out of the statutes of mortmain[1]. This legislation was inspired by the same motives as *Quia Emptores*. Religious houses did not die leaving heirs, so that when land got into their hands, incidents were permanently lost. If we look solely at grantor and ecclesiastical grantee by subinfeudation, of course, the only loser seems to be the grantor; and why not? But there was a loss to his lord, whose wardship of the grantor's infant heir, for example, would bring no services and no chance even of a 'wardship by reason of wardship' and so on; and if the grant was by substitution, as it would have to be after *Quia Emptores*, the loss is even more obvious. But as things turned out, it was the king rather than lords in general who gained by the legislation. While providing that land granted to religious houses should be forfeited to the grantor's lord, or if he did not act, to his lord and so up the tenurial chain, it also provided that any such grant might be made with royal licence. The result was not to prevent religious houses from acquiring land, but to make them pay money to the king every time they did so. And the further result was that land was often held by laymen to the use of religious houses. This was not at first an evasion. The price of a licence might be fixed after bargaining with the king, and the money might take years to raise. Religious houses buying or being given land were therefore forced to arrange for it to be held in the meantime by lay nominees, and there was no fraud about this. But it became common to leave things as they were indefinitely, not bothering about the licence; and a statute of 1391, enacting that lands held to the use of religious houses were caught by the mortmain legislation, was inspired by this revenue interest. The provision about uses comes second in the act, which deals first with the unlicensed enlargement of parish graveyards; and the numerous early licences in respect of small plots of land suggest that graveyards had indeed brought in a steady income[2].

1. Stat. 7 Ed. I (*De Viris Religiosis*). For earlier provisions and for discussions see p. 113, n. 1 above. For the relevance of mortmain to uses see J. L. Barton, op. cit. (in the preceding note), at p. 565.
2. Stat. 15 Ric. II, c. 5. For licences concerning small plots of land under Edward I see J. M. W. Bean, *The Decline of English Feudalism* (1968), p. 54.

GRANT AND REGRANT

This situation, although it might last many years, was probably always thought of as a temporary arrangement rather than an enduring relationship; and there is no difficulty in understanding how it became common although there was no means of enforcement. Few men in the fourteenth century would have dared to cheat the church. Even more obviously temporary, at first, was the next situation to be considered, and much the most important. This had nothing to do with the church and arose out of settlements. The preceding chapter described how the idea of ownership divided in time separated from the tenurial background in which it had begun, so that the various estates in land acquired an independent conceptual existence. This created a wish among settlors so commonplace to us that we can hardly imagine it as a novelty: they wished to include themselves in their own settlements. The principal motive for this will be explained later: it is of central importance. But perhaps first came the tenant who saw that his lord's right of wardship would be diminished or circumvented if his land were held by himself and his wife jointly for their lives, to go to his heir only after the death of the survivor. Then perhaps there came the tenant who could recognise his fee as a fee simple and could know that a more limited kind of fee existed, the fee tail, and who wished to make himself tenant in tail or tenant for life with remainder over in tail. Many problems grew out of this, one already noted. This kind of settlor would normally start with a fee simple, and would wish it ultimately to remain with his own heirs general; and he would thereby raise the question later associated with *Shelley's Case*[1].

But a more practical and immediate difficulty confronted him: the law did not cater for a grant to oneself. Even if livery of seisin is seen as just a required formality, a man could not deliver to himself. But of course the incongruity was deeper than that; livery of seisin survived from a world which did not have to accommodate so metaphysical an operation as changing one's estate. The tenant in fee simple who wished to settle upon himself and others had therefore to begin by granting his fee simple to a third party; and the third party would actually make the settlement. For the sake of

1. See p. 194, above.

what simplicity could be had, this was ignored in the chapter on settlements; but it was common, and the artificiality thereby introduced into the warranties surrounding many settlements may have played a part in the devices by which they came to be broken. That, however, is by the way. Our interest is in the third party to whom the land was granted for the purpose of his granting it back again. While he had it, he was clearly holding for the benefit of others[1].

In itself this situation was within the reach of the common law. If the grant to the third party was made conditional upon his carrying out the regrant, and he did not do so, then the grantor could re-enter and take back his original estate[2]. He would have failed of his purpose, but he would not have lost his land. This was established by the middle of the fourteenth century, but we do not know how old it then was; and as time went on, limitations appeared upon its usefulness. The first is obvious. A grant could not be conditional unless the condition was known when the grant was made. The settlor must declare the terms of his settlement when conveying to the third party; and any change of mind might imperil titles under the settlement. The second limitation has already been mentioned. Only the grantor or his heirs could re-enter for breach of condition; and they could apparently always do so if the condition had not been satisfied even though the third party intended to do what he could to satisfy it. Suppose that a grantor conveyed to a third party intending that the land should be reconveyed to the grantor for life with remainder to his younger son; and suppose the grantor died before this reconveyance was made: the elder son could re-enter as heir and so defeat the younger. The condition was not satisfactory even for the protection of the simple grant and regrant, being at once too limited and within its scope too strict. Grantors seem to have relied rather upon the good faith of their grantees.

RELATIONSHIP WITH DEVISE

Of all the situations considered, this is most likely to be the origin of the use. The connection will be traced only by the accumulation

1. See T. F. T. Plucknett, *Concise History of the Common Law* (5th edn., 1956), p. 577; J. L. Barton, 'The Medieval Use' (1965) 81 LQR, p. 562 at pp. 565–6.
2. See *Littleton*, ss. 352 ff; J. L. Barton, op. cit. (in the preceding note), pp. 566–8 ff.

of evidence about actual dispositions. It may turn out that the landowner who desired to change his estate was not a rare but a frequent figure, and that he merged imperceptibly into the testator. Consider again the grantor who desired a reconveyance to himself for life with remainder to his younger son. Since freehold land could not be devised by will, this was the only way short of an out-and-out gift in his lifetime by which a landowner could provide for his younger son, or for anybody except his heir. But if he made the grant to the third party conditional upon the regrant being made, his heir might be able to re-enter for a breach in various events including his own premature death. He might therefore expressly make his grant to the third party unconditional, and simply trust him. But if he was willing to do that, he might go a step further. Instead of deciding now what to give to his younger son and what to his daughter, he could postpone the choice, could indeed make a will. He would have to grant now to the third party, taking back the land for the rest of his life under some nominal transaction; and the heart of the arrangement would be that the third party would ultimately convey according to directions to be declared in his will[1].

Before turning to the implications of this, we must be clear about what we know and what we can only conjecture. We know that, when uses were an established institution, a main motive for putting land into uses was to secure a power to devise. We can only conjecture that this was neither a new employment of something which had come into existence independently, nor a sudden invention which was itself the origin of uses, but a development from the grant and regrant. When capital wealth was entirely in land, primogeniture and the absence of any power to devise meant that most rich men could not provide after their death for younger or illegitimate children, for their souls, or even for their creditors. Their chattel wealth was divided equitably; but it would be relatively tiny. Even the dynast dying with all his wealth in fee simple may have felt the position to be unsatisfactory, since he

1. *Calendar of Wills Proved and Enrolled in the Court of Husting, London 1258–1688* (ed. R. R. Sharpe, 1889–1890), 2 vols., is revealing. Citizens mainly dispose of city tenements; but leaseholds outside the city also appear; and towards the end of the fourteenth century, directions to feoffees of ordinary freehold lands are found. For a complement in the wills of outsiders see next note.

could not protect his grandson against alienation by his son. In these circumstances the pressure would be for means of diverting property or its control from the heir after the father's death. Some magnates may have bought customarily devisable tenements precisely in order to have an investment at their free disposal[1]. But normally the only advice conveyancers could give would be to make an *inter vivos* grant: and since most people desire to enjoy their property during their own lifetimes, this grant would normally be a settlement upon the settlor himself with remainders over.

If this is right, the rule that one could not change one's estate without the interposition of a third party is not just one of a series of small matters from which uses developed. It was a small thing in itself, but it affected an operation which many people desired to carry out. By a further accident, the only protection which the common law could give against the third party was the condition, and this could benefit only the heir, so that the arrangement could be upset by the very man it was meant to exclude. The third party had therefore to be trusted, but if he was to be trusted, why not trust him to convey after the settlor's death rather than now? And so the institution of the use and the will of land grew together, and essentially by accident.

THE FEUDAL INCIDENTS

If this was the plot, one would expect a sub-plot. Behind the heir there was always the anxious figure of the lord: what would not descend to the heir on his ancestor's death would equally not come by wardship or escheat to the lord on his tenant's death. *Quia Emptores* and the statutes of mortmain had protected the lord against grants by his tenant which permanently impaired the incidents arising from the tenure. But as to ordinary individual grants, the lord had to take his chance. If a dying tenant with an infant heir conveyed to a healthy young man, the lord lost that

1. J. M. W. Bean, *The Decline of English Feudalism* (1968), p. 31, draws attention to wills of magnates disposing of city properties. In 1310–11 the earl of Lincoln directed that city land should 'be sold by order of my executors to assist in fulfilling my testament'; in 1324 the earl of Pembroke left houses in London to his wife; in 1348 the earl of Pembroke left city rents for the maintenance of two chantries; *Calendar of Wills* cited in the preceding note, vol. I, pp. 218, 310, 507.

particular wardship; but his right to incidents continued in respect of his new tenant, and he could not object to the conveyance. Only the king retained the old power of all lords to insist that grants by their tenants needed their licence[1].

But suppose that the dying tenant with an infant heir conveyed to that heir. This was an ordinary individual grant and also an ordinary individual cheat. The heir was to be smuggled in duty-free as purchaser; and in 1267 statute provided that the lord should none the less have his wardship. The same statute discloses also a more sophisticated device. The tenant would convey his land by subinfeudation to third parties, reserving a rent service at least as great as the annual value of the land, and falsely acknowledging that this was paid up to a certain future date. This date was that at which the infant heir would come of age. The third parties were accomplices always intended to surrender to the heir at that time, and any temptation to keep the land was repressed by the large rent-service that became payable. The statute provided that the lord could bring the ordinary writ claiming wardship against the third parties; and if the arrangement was found by inquest to be collusive, it was treated as a lease for years over which the right of wardship took precedence[2].

Quia Emptores, by prohibiting subinfeudation in fee simple, would on the face of it have put paid to that device, though at least one conservative estate planner seems to have tried to do it with an entail[3]. But the growth of the conditional grant, which worked independently of tenure between the parties, enabled the same thing to be done more simply. The tenant would make his grant to the third party conditional upon his regranting to the heir when he came of age: if he did not, the heir could simply enter. In the middle of the fourteenth century the courts were apparently prepared to apply the 1267 statute to this, making inquiry into collusion. But of course the terms of the problem were rarely so straightforward, the grant to the heir often being one of several possibilities in alternative

1. See generally J. M. W. Bean, op. cit. (in the preceding note).
2. Stat. 52 Hy. III (Statute of Marlborough), c. 6. See T. F. T. Plucknett, *Legislation of Edward I* (1949), p. 79. On the former device see Fitzherbert, *Abridgment*, Garde 155 (Pasch. 31 Ed. I); YB 17 & 18 Ed. III (Rolls Series), p. 321.
3. See Fitzherbert, *Abridgment*, Garde 119 (Trin. 4 Ed. II); YB Pasch. 18 Ed. II, p. 602; S. F. C. Milsom, *Novae Narrationes* (Selden Society, vol. 80), p. clxxxv.

events; and the year books echo predictable arguments. Was the arrangement immune if the grant to the third party was not conditional but absolute, so that there was no legal protection for the heir? Was it necessary to defeat wardship that the heir should in fact be intended to take nothing?[1]

The upshot seems to have been that only blatant transactions were in danger, in which the land was to come back to the heir, perhaps by a condition which he could enforce. This was in the spirit of the 1267 act; indeed it was as close as could be to the letter. It was also in accord with current notions of a lord's rights. The lord could not object to any grant that his tenant might make, except one designed to circumvent his wardship but still carry the land directly or indirectly to the heir. He could not attack a grant to a younger son, nor one to third parties to convey to a younger son, nor any other that disinherited the heir.

The question of the lord's rights was thus asked and answered in terms of grants: what mattered was whether the ultimate grantee was to be the heir or another. But as the grant for an immediate regrant slowly turned into a grant for regrant according to the grantor's will, as a transaction turned into a relationship, these ceased to be the terms of the problem. It would then often happen that the death of the true tenant was bridged by third parties holding the legal title; and it might seem that the third parties were the lord's tenants and that it was to their deaths that he should look. There is little reason to suppose that anyone would have thought this a proper approach, just as today nobody would wish to levy estate duty on trust property when a trustee dies. But it would anyway have been unthinkable for a reason best understood in terms of the grant and regrant. It was usual to interpose not a single third party but several, and this was not just to guard against betrayal. If the land was held by a single third party who died, it would pass to his heir, his widow in dower, the lord in wardship or

1. *Vieux Natura Brevium* (ed. c. 1518), f. 39; Fitzherbert, *Abridgment*, Collusion 29 (Pasch. 31 Ed. III); ibid., Garde 33 (Trin. 32 Ed. III); YBB 42 Lib. Ass., pl. 6, f. 258v; Trin. 45 Ed. III, pl. 25, f. 22; Fitzherbert, op. cit., Garde 102 (Trin. 47 Ed. III); ibid., Collusion 47 (Mich. 8 Ric. II), also Bellewe 99; YBB Mich. 9 Hy. IV, pl. 20, f. 6; Mich. 10 Hy. IV, pl. 3, f. 2v, and pl. 11, f. 4; Trin. 11 Hy. IV, pl. 23(1), f. 80v; Hil. 12 Hy. IV, pl. 5, f. 13v; Hil. 12 Hy. IV, pl. 11, f. 16; Hil. 3 Hy. VI, pl. 23, f. 32; Pasch. 33 Hy VI, pl. 6, f. 14v. See also J. M. W. Bean, *The Decline of English Feudalism* (1968), pp. 183 ff.

escheat and so on; and these might seek to keep it. By granting to a plurality of third parties in joint tenancy, the grantor ensured that the land would stay in the hands he had chosen, because on the death of one his title would accrue to the others. This was in a sense a conscious safeguard against claims by the lord or others; but it was not a cheat to which lords would object. The grant and regrant was a proper transaction which they themselves employed, and the need to interpose a third party at all probably seemed a technicality which must not be allowed to have undesired effects.

As the title of the third parties ceased to be a merely temporary thing, it developed into an unassailable mortmain to which lords could not have looked for their incidents. But there is little reason to think that they would have looked in that direction anyway, would for example have thought it right to take incidents if by accident there was a single feoffee who died[1]. Their attention was always concentrated upon the realities of the situation not its technicalities, and their concern continued to be with the death of their original tenant, the feoffor, and the succession of his heir. But because their defences were against the heir coming in by grant, they were still defeated when the matter ceased to be seen in terms of grants and regrants, when a transaction lengthened out into a lasting relationship.

USES AS AN INSTITUTION

That defeat provoked counter-measures which were to transform the common law of property. But before turning to them, or to the way in which the defeat itself came about, we must face a question so far evaded. When and how did a situation become an institution? But events evaded that question too. The meaningful questions are two. The first is about the factual situations, and it will be answerable, if at all, only by assembling the evidence about actual dispositions in the fourteenth and fifteenth centuries. Even if this account is right in outline, we do not know when it became common for grants to be made with the intention that the land

1. See YB Mich. 7 Ed. IV, pl. 11, f. 16v at f. 17v *per* Markham; J. L. Barton, 'The Medieval Use' (1965) 81 LQR, p. 562 at p. 574.

should remain in the hands of the third parties for some time[1]. The landowner who wished to provide for persons other than his heir, and who began by intending an immediate regrant to himself with remainders over, did not become a testator in one imaginative leap. In between he probably went to the wars, and his feoffees were to regrant to him if he came back, to others if not.

The second question is when and how this situation or these situations generated a distinct legal concept. Both answers are to be sought in legal and official treatment, but the evidence is slippery. Statutes about situations, for example, tell us no more than the situations themselves. The earliest commonly cited is one of 1376, the first of a line about debtors who grant their property to others for their own benefit and then take refuge from personal process in certain liberties[2]. Then comes the act of 1391, already mentioned, which subjected land held for the benefit of religious houses to the mortmain law[3]. But there is no reason to think that the two draftsmen saw themselves as dealing with the same problem. A general act of 1398 about forfeiture for treason and a series of later acts about particular traitors show that the factual situation was becoming increasingly common among great landowners[4], but only a contemporary index listing these acts under 'uses' as well as under 'forfeiture' and 'treason' would tell us what we want to know. Indeed if we accept such a linguistic test as valid, seeking the word 'use' as a noun capable of going into the plural as in our modern 'law of trusts', we may have to postpone the emergence of a clear concept until the sixteenth century.

But that test might well not be satisfied until there was a substantial body of learning to which lawyers would wish to make compendious reference; and that learning must largely have grown up around the doings of the chancellor. About these we still know little. We do not know at what date, or at what stage in the

1. '. . . about the middle of the fourteenth century it becomes noticeable that feoffors in general do not seem in any great hurry to take a reconveyance' J. L. Barton, op. cit. (in the preceding note), p. 566. Cf. the observation about London wills p. 207, n. 1, above.
2. Stats. 50 Ed. III, c. 6; 2 Ric. II, stat. 2, c. 3; 3 Hy. VII, c. 4, concerning chattels only; 13 Eliz., c.5.
3. Stat. 15 Ric. II, c. 5.
4. Stat. 21 Ric. II, c. 3. For the lands of particular traitors see Stats. 5 Hy. IV, c. 1; 7 Hy. IV, c. 5; T. F. T. Plucknett, *Concise History of the Common Law* (5th edn., 1956), p. 581. Cf. J. M. W. Bean, *The Decline of English Feudalism* (1968), p. 139.

evolution of situations, he first intervened at all[1]. Probably it was near the end of the fourteenth century, and when lawyers were still thinking in terms of grant and regrant. Certainly one must not imagine any chancellor ever able to ask himself, 'Shall I protect uses?' The earliest intervention may not at the time have seemed important. For feoffees to concur in dishonesty would be rare, and so outrageous that its prevention would not be striking. The first initiative may even have come from feoffees themselves, perplexed when their instructions were frustrated by a death.

The decisive happening would not be intervention in blatant cases but the formulation of rules in cases in which the result required by justice was not obvious. And here the present difficulty merges into an earlier one. When can we think of the chancellor as formulating rules at all? The rise of the equitable jurisdiction and the rise of uses have been considered separately by historians, who have assumed the former as a necessary condition of the latter. But it is likely that uses were as much a cause as a product of regular chancery intervention, of an equitable jurisdiction which would evolve into a secondary system of law. Most other kinds of early case came to the chancellor because the normal legal machinery had given or would give an unacceptable answer. If the parties had behaved on the basis of any legal assumptions, it was the normal machinery that they had assumed. But it was otherwise with the kind of situation now being considered. Landowners were being advised to entrust their wealth to arrangements which, as their advisers knew and intended, were outside the reach of the common law courts. The chancellor's must soon have been thought of as the ordinary jurisdiction for such matters; and, if it is too much to say that he must have come under pressure to declare principles, lawyers must at least have wanted to know what he was likely to do in various circumstances.

All this is reflected in the year books[2]. They tell us nothing of the earliest stages of chancery intervention. Their first notice, in the

1. See J. L. Barton, 'The Medieval Use' (1965) 81 LQR, p. 562 at pp. 568–9.
2. See the notes attributed to Mich. 5 Ed. IV, but perhaps earlier; J. L. Barton, op. cit. (in the preceding note), at p. 570. On feoffor dying without declaring his will see YBB Mich. 5 Ed. IV, pl. 16, f. 7v; pl. 18, f. 7v. On his declaring his will twice see YB Mich. 5 Ed. IV, pl. 20, f. 8; Fitzherbert, *Abridgment*, Sub pena 23 (Mich. 31 Hy. VI); YB Mich. 20 Hy. VII, pl. 20, f. 10v; Keilwey 120–1. On the effect of a declaration in favour of a third party at the time of the feoffment or after, see J. L. Barton, op. cit., p. 571; *Doctor and Student*, Dialogue II, c. 22 (Selden Society, vol. 91, at p. 224).

second half of the fifteenth century, is of morally neutral questions to which the chancellor is having to give 'legal' answers. At first these questions seem almost always to arise out of a grant to feoffees to perform the feoffor's will. Instead of declaring his will and dying in an orderly manner, the feoffor has either died without declaring his will at all, or he has declared it twice. In either case the question is not whether the feoffees are bound, but to whom. When the feoffor had not declared his will at all it was easy to say that his heir should have the subpoena, but further sophistication was inevitably required: should it be the heir general or, which might not be the same, whoever would have inherited that particular piece of land? And suppose the feoffor had been hanged for felony so that at law the land would have escheated?

More fundamental to our eyes would be the problem raised by the feoffor who had declared his will twice, and in favour of different people. If the first beneficiary had acquired an interest, the second declaration must be ineffective; and if the question had been asked in those terms, a definite answer could hardly have been avoided. But it arose not in terms of present interests or subsisting relationships, but in the less exacting terms of conveyances. The intended function of the feoffees, and what the chancellor would compel them to do, was at first simply to make a conveyance as required by the feoffor. They were his agents for that purpose and any instructions he gave were revocable by him until they had been acted upon or until his death had made further change impossible. The expression of his will that came normally to matter was thus his last will. But to this there was from the beginning an exception, deriving no doubt from the common law condition in a grant and regrant: if at the time of the feoffment the feoffor gave directions to his feoffees, for example to regrant in tail, he could not change them. But not until well into the sixteenth century does it seem that any instruction given after the feoffment could without more confer an immediate irrevocable right upon the beneficiary: not until then, perhaps, is anybody thinking primarily in terms of a subsisting relationship between feoffees and beneficiary.

If therefore the use seems to have come into being by stealth, this is probably because what was happening did not attract attention. Landowners and lords, lawyers and even chancellors were all thinking mainly in terms of conveyances. There was nothing occult about what was going on, but it was not seen as involving legal apparatus beyond the familiar learning of the conveyancer. The limited decisions of a legal nature that the chancellor was being compelled to make, so important to hindsight, probably seemed peripheral. In one sense the origin of the use was not a change in the world of fact but a shift of attention: men began to think in terms of a present relationship rather than a future transfer. To Littleton the whole practice deserved only one sustained mention. That was about a relationship, but a strictly legal one: what was the technical position of a feoffor who had conveyed to feoffees to perform his last will? Was he their tenant-at-will or what? And even this question arose out of an academic problem in conveyancing: could the feoffees pass the legal title back to their feoffor by a simple release? Yet Littleton, when he died in 1481, like all his substantial contemporaries left a will disposing of lands held by feoffees[1].

For Littleton as a lawyer, in short, there was nothing much to discuss; even had he been a commentator on social habits, there was nothing new about what landowners were doing. What seems to us his blindness – his inability to see with hindsight – is shown by his having missed what a little later would have been almost the point of his own discussion. The man who enfeoffed others to perform his last will remained on the land, looking and behaving as though the legal title were still his. And if, without doing anything to get it back from his feoffees, he proceeded to make new dispositions, he was laying up trouble for his purchasers and their successors, 'insomuch that no man that buyeth lands . . . be in perfect [safety], nor without great trouble and doubt of the same'. The words come from the preamble of a statute passed in 1484, and described by modern writers as having conferred upon *cestui qe use* the power to convey a legal estate[2]. That was the effect; but the spirit was rather that which today protects the second buyer of a chattel against the first when the vendor has stayed in possession after the first sale. The intention was not to help *cestui qe use* do as he pleased, but to safeguard those who dealt with him in the belief that he still owned the lands he still occupied.

1. *Tenures*, ss. 462–4. For his will see the edition by E. Wambaugh (1903), p. xlvii.
2. Stat. 1 Ric. III, c. 1. For this statute and its effects see J. L. Barton, 'The Medieval Use' (1965) 81 LQR, at p. 574; J. H. Baker, *Spelman's Reports*, vol. II (Selden Society, vol. 94), pp. *195–6*.

This statute was important at the time for what it did, and is now important for what it shows us. As to what it did, the feoffees were overridden only if at the time of the dealing in question they held solely to their feoffor's use. Over and above the factual disputes this was likely to generate, it gave new weight to the problems about the effect of a declaration of his will by the feoffor. If he gave his feoffees a general direction in favour of one person, and then sold part of the land to a second, the second would be protected under the statute only if the direction to the feoffees had given no right to the first. The question which could hitherto arise only before the chancellor, and only in the terms of his choosing whether to decree a conveyance in accord with an earlier or a later declaration of will, would now arise in a common law court in an action to try title. The rapid crystallisation of rules was inevitable. The evolution of the use as an entity with known properties may well, therefore, owe as much to the common law courts as to the chancery; and it is even possible that it was the shared jurisdiction over uses that truly started the process by which equity was to harden into a new system of law.

THE MISCHIEFS OF USES

What the statute of 1484 did, therefore, was to compel decisions which would settle the properties of the use as a relationship between feoffees and beneficiary. But its mere enactment shows how and why attention was beginning to focus on that relationship, on the existing state of affairs, instead of on the conveyance by the feoffees which would bring it to an end. The technical position as between *cestui qe use* and the land, as between feoffor and feoffees, had attracted the passing curiosity of Littleton. But the factual position was now producing the mischiefs inevitable whenever a legal title can be locked away, however innocently, without any visible change.

But purchasers and creditors were not the only victims: loss was suffered also by feudal lords. Their rights had been carefully defined: the lord was entitled to incidents out of what descended to the heir on the death of his tenant. The tenant could grant away what he liked in his lifetime, and equally grant it to feoffees to dispose of according to his will after his death; and the lord, though he might suffer a loss, had no complaint. When everybody was thinking of such arrangements in terms of conveyances, the only discernible mischief was the grant to feoffees to regrant to the heir; and if the grant to the feoffees was conditional upon their making such a regrant, the lord could attack it as collusive and get his wardship.

From the lord's point of view this scheme, measuring his allocation by the heir's, was broken down when a feoffment to uses became an object in itself. There was no mischief so long as the tenant conveyed to his feoffees only such land as he actually left away from his heir. But if for example he conveyed all his land to feoffees to perform his will and died without declaring any will, the lord got nothing although the heir got all. The heir was as well protected by the chancellor as he would have been by any common law condition, would succeed to the land as certainly as if the feoffment had never been made; but the lord's incidents were lost between the two.

Once again we cannot be sure what happened until we know more about actual dispositions. But it is likely that this situation first arose by accident, the feoffor having conveyed to feoffees only such of his land as he intended to leave away from the heir, and having died before he could declare his will. The chancellor had no difficulty in deciding that the heir must have the land; and a year book note about the possibility of an escheat for felony is so emphatic in tone as to suggest that no claim by the lord would have been entertained[1]. Conscience required that the feoffees should convey to the heir, and if the lord thought he had a claim he could pursue his legal remedy: it was nothing to the chancellor that, since the conveyance had not been collusive, there was no legal remedy.

What the chancellor's attitude would have been to a feoffment made for the purpose of evading incidents we do not know. Nor do we know when or how far feoffments came to be made with that as the primary purpose, and good evidence will be hard to come by. A statute of 1490 deals with the feoffor who 'dieth his heir being within age, no will by him declared nor made in his life', and though it speaks of fraud, this seems to describe the effect rather

1. YB Mich. 5 Ed. IV, pl. 18, f. 7v. On the date of these reports see p. 213, n. 2, above.

than the intention[1]. As with the Statute of Marlborough more than two centuries earlier, the remedy is to give the lord a writ of wardship. But this time his entitlement is automatic, and there is no inquiry into the state of mind of individual feoffors. In 1504 the principle was extended to socage tenure: 'after the death of him to whose use any person or persons . . . be seised, and no will thereof declared', lords were to have their reliefs, heriots and other dues as if he had died seised[2]. These statutes subject the new situation created by the chancellor's decisions to the traditional rights of lords: equitable inheritance was equated with legal.

Like that of 1484, these statutes are important both for what they show us and for what they did, or, in this case, did not do. Although by this time other duties to convey, such as that arising from a bargain and sale, were also regarded as creating the immediate proprietary relationship of a use, the statutes suggest that *cestui qe use* was still typically the man who had made a feoffment for the purpose of declaring his will. But what they did was not an attack on that practice. They accepted the feudal loss caused whenever land was left away from the heir, and sought to secure the most important feudal rights – wardship in chivalry and relief in socage – only in respect of what actually descended to him. Nor, although that of 1490 made special mention of the king, do the statutes protect only the royal interest. Feoffments for the purpose of making wills were causing genuine mischiefs, feudal and other, to subjects as well as to the crown. Those mischiefs were countered piecemeal, and the counter-move in each case inevitably took the form of allowing victims to proceed as though *cestui qe use* had been himself seised. But there was no attack on the situation as a whole.

THE STATUTE OF USES

Such an attack was made in 1536 by the great Statute of Uses, or, to give it its more significant title 'An Act concerning Uses and Wills'; and the solution adopted was precisely to enact that *cestui qe use* 'shall from henceforth stand and be seised, deemed and adjudged in

1. Stat. 4 Hy. VII, c. 17. See J. M. W. Bean, *The Decline of English Feudalism* (1968), p. 242.
2. Stat. 19 Hy. VII, c. 15.

lawful seisin, estate and possession . . . to all intents constructions and purposes in the law'[1]. Before turning to the nightmare results elicited from this, something must be said of its aims. The preamble begins by recalling that at common law land was neither devisable nor transferable *inter vivos* without livery of seisin or the like, and then proceeds to catalogue the mischiefs resulting from the circumvention of this principle. Three deserve attention, two because they are familiar, the objects of the acts just considered: titles have been made insecure, and lords have lost their incidents. But the third is new. From the evils which could flow from the means by which wills of land had to be made, the attack is extended to the making of such wills as a thing in itself: the dying are influenced by those who scheme to gain by the unjust disherison of heirs[2].

This last probably reflects nothing but the financial aims of the crown. The special concern of the king with the evasion of incidents is obvious. What a lay subject lost from his tenants would be balanced by what he saved from his lord on his own death. But there was no compensation for the king who was never tenant, and to whom more than to other lords, wardship was of particular value. On the death of a tenant-in-chief his prerogative brought him the wardship even of lands not held of him. It also brought him the wardship of the heir, the ordinary rule allotting the person of the heir to the lord of the oldest feoffment being displaced by the liege rights of the crown. For a long time the crown was content to secure these, by refusing to license an alienation by which the tenant parted with all the lands that he held in chief[3].

But the value of wardship and marriage was diminished by a will which left land away from the heir; and the crown had been attacking devises even before the Statute of Uses. The act of 1490 applied only when *cestui qe use* died without leaving a will: it did not even contemplate a devise to the heir. But a landowner might require his feoffees to raise money out of certain lands for the

1. Stat. 27 Hy. VIII, c. 10.
2. Cf. *Glanvill*, VII, 1 (ed. G. D. G. Hall, 1965, p. 70).
3. See J. M. W. Bean, *The Decline of English Feudalism* (1968), esp. at pp. 197 ff. On prerogative wardship, see also S. E. Thorne, *Prerogativa Regis* (1949), pp. xv ff. On the ordinary rule as between two mesne lords, see Stat. 13 Ed. I (Statute of Westminster II), c. 16; S. F. C. Milsom, *Novae Narrationes* (Selden Society, vol. 80), p. cxlix and references there given.

payment of debts or like purposes, and when it was raised to convey to the heir. Just before the Statute of Uses, a tenant-in-chief was found to have put lands into uses, and by his will to have devised in tail to a third party, remainder in tail to his heir, with remainders over. The heir was an infant, and an escheator's inquest surprisingly found this collusive. But when the feoffees questioned the finding, the judges were even more surprisingly induced to hold, apparently independently of any collusion, that uses of land could not in principle be the subject of devises. It may have been the consequent threat to existing titles that forced acceptance of the statute[1].

To the political and institutional historian, therefore, the financial motive of the Statute of Uses seems uppermost. It is part of the fiscal feudalism of the Tudors, soon to be embodied in that most effective of anachronisms, the court of wards[2]. But the legal historian, contemplating the consequences of the statute, will do injustice to the royal advisers if he takes the whole affair as an accident in which the law happened to be involved. Whatever the special loss caused to the crown by devises, the general mischiefs of the machinery by which they were made are beyond doubt. The purchaser of any land had to reckon that his vendor might have conveyed it to feoffees; and if the statute of 1484 had given him a chance of winning the resulting law-suit, it had not reduced the chance that a law-suit would result. Legislation suggested in 1529 would have disposed also of other sources of uncertainty: uses would have been made void unless registered; conveyances would have required both registration and public proclamation; and entails, except for those of the nobility, would have been abolished and turned into fee simple[3]. Neither in this nor in any other branch of the law was reform so radical seriously considered again until the nineteenth century.

1. YB Pasch. 27 Hy. VIII, pl. 22, f. 7v; *Spelman's Reports*, Uses, pl. 4 (Selden Society, vol. 93, p. 228). Discussed: J. H. Baker, *Spelman's Reports*, vol. II (Selden Society, vol. 94), pp. *200* ff; J. M. W. Bean, op. cit. (in the preceding note), pp. 275 ff; E. W. Ives, 'The Genesis of the Statute of Uses' (1967) 82 English Historical Review, p. 673.
2. See H. E. Bell, *The Court of Wards and Liveries* (1953); J. Hurstfield, *The Queen's Wards* (1958).
3. See the references p. 190, n. 1, above.

THE STATUTE OF WILLS

The Statute of Uses attempted less, and within its narrower ambit proved to be too radical. One cannot take legal problems out by the root, when the root is so reasonable and so universal a wish as to be able to provide for persons other than the heir. The statute allowed a short period of grace during which the wills of those dying would continue to be effective; but thereafter the landowner could provide for his creditors, younger children and so on only by *inter vivos* grant. This was intolerable, and in 1540 there was passed the Statute of Wills restoring a power of devise[1]. The preamble, dwelling mainly on the king's benevolence, explains the mischief in terms of a conflict between social obligations and capital structure: subjects who maintain their fitting standard of living and bring up their children properly are unable also 'of their proper goods, chattels and other moveable substance, to discharge their debts, and after their degrees set forth and advance their children and posterities'.

The statute is long and complicated, and three years later required long and complicated adjustment[2]. The provisions came to this. Socage land was made freely devisable with no general saving of lords' rights; but the king's rights as lord were fully safeguarded, mainly by treating the devisee as though he were heir. Of land held in knight service only two-thirds could be devised. The king and all other lords would have their wardships of the remaining third part, and lords other than the king would have to be content with that; but the king, who could exact a payment when his tenant-in-chief alienated *inter vivos*, could do so equally upon a devise. The opportunity was also taken to exact this payment when a tenant-in-chief suffered a recovery, now seen as just a conveyance.

That a devise should operate as a direct conveyance, its validity questionable like that of any other conveyance only by a common law action to try title, was inevitable when testaments of personalty remained under ecclesiastical supervision. Not until the Land Transfer Act of 1897 did land pass through the hands of executors

1. Stat. 32 Hy. VIII, c. 1. For discussion see J. M. W. Bean, *The Decline of English Feudalism* (1968), pp. 293 ff; J. L. Barton, 'The Statute of Uses and the Trust of Freeholds' (1966) 82 LQR, p. 215, esp. at pp. 222 ff; J. H. Baker, *Spelman's Reports*, vol. II (Selden Society, vol. 94), pp. *202–3*.
2. Stat. 34 & 35 Hy. VIII, c. 5.

or other representatives[1]. Not until the Wills Act of 1837 were wills of land and testaments of personalty subjected to the same formal requirements, though the Statute of Frauds in 1677 had imposed an unfortunately worded need for witnesses to wills of land[2]. The Statute of Wills itself had required only writing. More striking still was what happened to land not devised. Not until 1925 was the heir put down, so that land and personal wealth were shared out similarly on the death of an owner intestate. But since 1660, with the abolition of the military tenures and therefore of any restriction on the power to devise, the heir had been no more than the person who succeeded to land when there was no will[3].

To Henry VIII and his advisers in 1540 it probably seemed that the Statute of Wills was the end of a story. St Germain, writing his second Dialogue between Doctor and Student a few years before the Statute of Uses, makes his Doctor ask why people put their land into uses[4]. The Student, ante-dating the institution as lawyers and historians have done ever since, first runs through the statute book: lands were put into uses to avoid mortmain, to defraud creditors and so on. But then he gives two principal reasons: for the making of wills, and for the safety 'of divers covenants in indentures of marriage and other bargains'. To the second of these we shall come back: the royal lawyers were conscious of it, though perhaps not conscious enough. But as to the first, even if they could not look back as we can and see that uses and devises had probably grown together, even if they thought that the devise was only one application of the use seen as a distinct entity, still they saw it as by far the most important application. Their 'Act concerning Uses and Wills', had abolished both together. The Statute of Wills had revived the devise, but made it operate directly at law and not through the old mechanism. The use probably seemed dead. But it was only cut in two, and it had two lives ahead of it.

USES AT LAW

One of these lives was a brilliant and disreputable career at common law. The Statute of Uses worked by 'executing the use', transferring

1. Stat. 60 & 61 Vict., c. 65.
2. Stats. 29 Car. II, c. 3 (Statute of Frauds); 7 Wm. IV & 1 Vict., c. 26 (Wills Act).
3. Stat. 12 Car. II, c. 24 (Tenures Abolition Act).
4. *Doctor and Student*, Dialogue II, c. 22 (Selden Society, vol. 91, pp. 222 ff).

the legal title to *cestui qe use*. When persons were seised, 'or at any time hereafter shall happen to be seised' to the use of others, those others were to 'stand and be seised, deemed and adjudged in lawful seisin, estate and possession . . . of and in such like estates as they had or shall have in use, trust or confidence . . .'. If we think in terms of an intending testator holding in fee simple and about to make the kind of arrangement the statute was aimed at, this execution of the use seems complicated: why not somehow annul his arrangements? But our assumption is not realistic. For one thing, persons purchasing lands had commonly taken conveyances to themselves with others so that they could declare their wills to their co-feoffees: and there would be no justice in leaving title with the vendor. More fundamentally, there would be no justice in leaving title with all the existing feoffees. The device adopted, only an extension of the way in which the statute of 1484 had worked, was a neat solution of the draftsman's problem. But despite his future tense he cannot have expected that his device would have much work to do except in the immediate aftermath of the statute. Events and lawyers proved more imaginative. The execution of uses, so far from being merely a way of invalidating undesirable transactions, became a desirable end in itself. Conveyancers made grants to uses knowing that they could not have their expressed effect, but intending that the Statute of Uses should play upon them and produce results otherwise unattainable.

USES AND CONVEYANCING

These results still exist in many common law jurisdictions; and in England they existed recently enough still to need explanation in books on real property[1]. They will therefore be discussed only in outline. But first must come the least spectacular, because it is one that the draftsman probably did foresee; and it might have put him on his guard. This was the bargain and sale. The chancellor had long since decided that the duty to convey arising out of a contract to sell land was one that he should enforce; and from this it was deduced, when the proposition became meaningful, that the vendor held to

1. See e.g. the very clear accounts in R. E. Megarry and H. W. R. Wade, *The Law of Real Property* (4th edn., 1975), esp. pp. 160 ff.

the use of the purchaser. St Germain, a year or two before the Statute of Uses, had mentioned bargains and agreements together with the making of wills as circumstances bringing uses into being[1]. The draftsman evidently anticipated the effect of the Statute of Uses on this, namely that the mere contract would convey a legal title without livery or the like, and so would work one of the very mischiefs the statute was designed to frustrate.

This was prevented by the Statute of Enrolments of the same year[2]. It provided that no land 'shall pass, alter or change from one to another, whereby any estate of inheritance or freehold shall be made or take effect in any person or persons, or any use thereof to be made, by reason only of any bargain and sale thereof' unless the bargain and sale was embodied in an indenture and registered. Registration schemes had been independently considered in the years before the Statute of Uses; but as a safeguard for the public, this registration eventually proved almost as useless as livery of seisin. It did not cover all uses raised by promises to convey. To return once more to St Germain, writing before the statute, he had coupled with bargains 'divers covenants in indentures of marriage'[3]. In later language, a covenant to stand seised in consideration of marriage or of natural love and affection also raised a use; and this was executed by the Statute of Uses but not caught by the Statute of Enrolments[4]. Family settlements could thus be made to take effect at law, passing legal estates to the beneficiaries, although there was no means by which the world at large could know about them. Ingenuity later found a way of doing the same upon ordinary sales. The vendor bargained and sold not his freehold but a term of years. He thereby became seised to the buyer's use for the term, and this use was executed by the Statute of Uses to pass a legal term of years to the purchaser without his actually entering upon the land. But although within the Statute of Uses, the transaction was not caught by the Statute of Enrolments, which spoke only of 'any estate of inheritance or freehold', so that

1. *Doctor and Student*, Dialogue II, c. 22 (Selden Society, vol. 91, at p. 224).
2. Stat. 27 Hy. VIII, c. 16. See Bacon's 'Reading on the Statute of Uses', *The Works of Francis Bacon* (ed. J. Spedding), vol. VII (1861), p. 432; quoted by W. S. Holdsworth, *History of English Law*, vol. IV (3rd edn.), p. 455, n. 4.
3. *Doctor and Student*, Dialogue II, c. 22 (Selden Society, vol. 91, at p. 224).
4. *Sharington v Strotton* (1565), Plowden 298. Cf. *Callard v Callard* (1594), Cro. Eliz. 344; Popham 47; 2 Anderson 64.

no registration was necessary. Having got his purchaser metaphysically in as lessee, but without any change of possession, the vendor would then release his freehold reversion, which could be done by a deed at common law[1].

This was clearly established by 1620. But not until 1841 did the Conveyance by Release Act allow the magic of the bargain and sale of a lease to be omitted; not until 1845 did the Real Property Act recognise that land could be transferred by a deed of grant; and not until 1925 was the possibility of livery of seisin finally abolished[2]. Livery of seisin had of course begun as something more fundamental than a formality designed to signal the invisible passage of an invisible title. But in this respect Henry VIII's advisers lived in our world: they rationalised the matter in this way, and suggested the better signal of registration. We have hardly caught up with them yet.

LEGAL EXECUTORY INTERESTS

The story of the bargain and sale may thus point a dismal moral. But its present interest is in the fact that the draftsman of the Statute of Uses perhaps ought to have foreseen that he was supplying lawyers with a magical force which they could harness. The matter is usually put in this way. At common law settlements of land had to obey certain rules, especially those governing contingent remainders. A remainder had always to be supported by a prior estate, and had to take effect as soon as that prior estate came to an end; this was because there had always to be somebody seised. But equally a remainder could not intervene and cut short the prior estate; and this was to prevent conditions being used to create indestructible settlements. Then it is said that in equity before the Statute of Uses, with a fee simple continuously in the hands of the feoffees and continuously obeying the law, interests could be made to spring, that is to break the first of these rules, or to shift, to break

1. See A. W. B. Simpson, *An Introduction to the History of the Land Law* (1961), pp. 177 ff; W. S. Holdsworth, *History of English Law*, vol. IV (3rd edn.), p. 460, n. 1; op. cit., vol. VII (2nd edn.), pp. 360 ff. The result was recognised in *Lutwich v Mitton* (1620), Cro. Jac. 604.
2. Stats. 4 & 5 Vict., c. 21 (Conveyance by Release Act); 8 & 9 Vict., c. 106 (Real Property Act).

the second. Then lastly it is said that when the Statute of Uses brought such interests into the law, it was decided after hesitation that they should retain the plastic quality they had enjoyed in equity and not in general be subjected to the legal rules. The undoubted result was a new and distinct class of legal future interests, shifting and springing uses[1]. They were brought into being by a conveyance expressed as granting the land to feoffees to uses; and the uses, being at once exposed like magic ink to the rays of the statute, were transmuted into legal interests. The feoffees were real people, but in the nature of a fiction: no real title ever lodged in them, although in order to explain events after the first vesting it became necessary to postulate a *scintilla juris* always existing in their persons[2]. In the case of devises even this measure of intellectual satisfaction was withheld. The Statute of Wills was understood by its language to have enabled testators to produce these results even though the devise was expressed as conveying the land directly to the beneficiaries and not nominally to others to their use. Springing and shifting uses and executory devises, collectively known as legal executory interests, thus took their place beside entails and remainders to make the common law of future interests the most elaborate folly ever built by logic.

But it did not happen – one likes to believe that it could not have happened – quite in the simple stages represented. That representation assumes a starting-point at which there were visibly two sets of rules governing settlements, the legal and the equitable. But even the legal rules were by no means in their final form at the date of the Statute of Uses; and it is doubtful how far at that date equitable rules were seen to exist, how far it is real to imagine a settlor deciding to make a settlement in equity because he could not achieve what he wanted at law. St. Germain's Student mentions no such reason why land should be put into use[3]. Indeed, with the exception of bargains and agreements, his long enumeration considers only the case of one conveying to feoffees to his own use, including of course the one wishing to make a will; and his Doctor

1. See Brooke, *Abridgment*, Feffements al uses 50 (30 Hy. VIII, springing use); Feffements al uses 30 (6 Ed. VI, shifting use). Cf. *Brent's Case* (1575), 2 Leonard 14, esp. *per* Manwood, J. at p. 16.
2. See W. S. Holdsworth, *History of English Law*, vol. VII (2nd edn.), p. 138.
3. *Doctor and Student*, Dialogue II, c. 22 (Selden Society, vol. 91, p. 222). The Doctor's question is at p. 224.

actually asks, 'May not an use be assigned to a stranger as well as to be reserved to the feoffor, if the feoffor so appoint it upon his feoffment?' In that climate the only common approach to what we should call an equitable settlement *inter vivos* would raise no questions: it would be a grant for the purpose of resettling, when some accident intervened before the feoffees had made the intended conveyances.

The important case, here as elsewhere, was that of the testator; and it is uncertain how long or how often even he had intended what we should call an equitable settlement. It is possible that before the statute some advantage was seen in entails intended to take effect behind a continuing use rather than under a conveyance to be made by the feoffees. But his will normally directed his feoffees to convey legal estates to his beneficiaries, and that in itself would raise no new questions. He might, however, and often did, require that the conveyance be postponed until the beneficiary reached a certain age, until money had been raised out of the land for another beneficiary, or until some other condition had been fulfilled or purpose achieved. To him, thinking in terms of conveyances, these directions would have no relation to the rules about future interests. They were purely ministerial. There is a curious analogy with what had happened so long before when arrangements for the future made in feudal courts had to be accommodated in the king's courts as grants of property rights. That had created remainders as future interests which somehow did not fit. So now it was arrangements for the future, directions to the feoffees telling them what to do, that created legal executory interests. In both cases hindsight can look back and assert that the new creations had some prior existence. But all that anybody could see at the time was not a 'legal' entity at all but a commonplace arrangement that somebody should do something.

Can the draftsmen of the Statutes of Uses and of Wills reasonably be charged with lack of foresight? The former did its damage by giving to beneficiaries 'such like estates as they had or shall have in use'. If wills were to be abolished, the only directions to feoffees that the draftsman may have contemplated were those in wills saved by his transitional provisions[1]. And even for these, for example a direction to use income for a period and then convey the legal

1. Stat. 27 Hy. VIII, c. 10, s. 9.

estate, he may have intended simply that the direction should be carried out: the exception of truly 'active' uses is a matter to which we shall return. If so, as his language suggests, the only entities he contemplated were the legal estates. The Statute of Wills did its damage by allowing the testator to make such devises as the statute permitted 'at his will and pleasure'[1]. And again the conclusions reached were probably compelled by features of earlier wills about which the draftsman, mainly remembering wills before the Statute of Uses as directions to convey, was just not thinking. He saw himself as simply giving to the testator a power to do for himself what before he had to get others to do for him, and did not consider that one can tell others to do things in the future that cannot be done now.

No attempt will be made to trace the relationship between executory interests, once it was accepted that they were distinct, and legal remainders[2]. Just as it looks as though testators before the statute were giving directions to their feoffees without much consciousness that they were controlling the devolution of their lands in a way that they could been not have done by a settlement at law, so it looks as though the Statutes of Uses and Wills were allowed to operate on such directions still without regard to what could have been done by a direct legal settlement. The question whether the legal rules were applicable had thus been answered before being asked; and conveyancers were no doubt quick to take advantage of the freedom thus offered. As the sixteenth century advances it becomes clear that the struggle is between conveyancers seeking to tie up land and courts allowing one expedient after another to defeat such arrangements. The final settlement of the rules concerning remainders themselves is part of this struggle; and so was an attempt at the end of the century to apply these rules to executory interests and thereby to make them destructible[3].

Dismal results followed. The danger of perpetuities was not removed, and great uncertainty was introduced. Bacon, lecturing on the Statute of Uses in 1600, described it as 'a law whereupon the

1. Stat. 32 Hy. VIII, c. 1. This phrase, or 'at his free will and pleasure', appears in all the powers of devise.
2. See generally A. W. B. Simpson, *An Introduction to the History of the Land Law* (1961), p. 204; R. E. Megarry and H. W. R. Wade, *The Law of Real Property* (4th edn., 1975), pp. 190 ff.
3. *Chudleigh's Case* (1595), 1 Co. Rep. 113b; Popham 70; 1 Anderson 309.

inheritances of this realm are tossed at this day, as upon a sea'; and though he favoured the attempt to subject executory interests to the legal rules, he saw that it was adding to the uncertainty[1]. The result of that attempt would have appalled him. This was the rule known by the name of *Purefoy v Rogers*, a case of 1671[2]. Expressed as a rule of construction, which might, especially in the case of devises, have made sense, it was an inexorable rule of law which for over two hundred years ordained a caprice. If the beneficial limitation could have existed as a legal remainder, it was to be treated as though it was one and therefore to fail if it had not vested when the prior estate fell in. In a gift to one for life, remainder to the first of his sons to marry, the remainder would fail if no son had married when the father died; and under the rule in *Purefoy v Rogers* it was not saved by the whole settlement being made by devise or behind a grant to uses. But if the limitation would be simply void as a remainder, because incapable of obeying the rules, it was, if made by devise or behind a grant to uses, immune from them. A gift by will to one for life, and then to the first of his sons to marry after his death would be good; and so would a gift by will in fee simple, to shift to the first son to marry at the time of his marriage. Results of some intellectual beauty and also of some hardship were produced, being mitigated only by statutes which in the nineteenth century made contingent remainders themselves indestructible[3]. The process was all but completed by the Contingent Remainders Act in 1877, which in effect restored for the last half-century of the life of the Statute of Uses the freedom apparently enjoyed in its first half-century.

PERPETUITIES

But it was a freedom constrained by other rules, one of which still exists; that is the modern rule against perpetuities. For a long time the most likely means of tying up wealth indefinitely seemed to be the entail; and this was curbed by barring. Then there were attempts

1. Bacon's 'Reading on the Statute of Uses', in *The Works of Francis Bacon* (ed. J. Spedding), vol. VII (1861), p. 395.
2. *Purefoy v Rogers* (1671), 2 Wms. Saunders 380.
3. See p. 198, above.

to set up entails which could not be barred, by providing that the interest of one trying to bar should go over to another; and these played their part in the establishment of the rule that a remainder could not operate to cut short the prior estate, the rule against shifting. The rule preventing remainders from springing also had perpetuity implications. Not only was a settlor unable to limit an estate to arise in the future: he had also to reckon that unless his contingencies were satisfied and his remainders vested by the time the prior estate fell in, they would fail. It followed that limitations to unborn persons, necessarily contingent, were necessarily destructible. By the beginning of the seventeenth century there was no serious perpetuity danger in settlements at common law. A settlor who wished to reach beyond living persons had to use either an entail, which could be brought down by a recovery, or contingent remainders, which could fail naturally or be brought down by the holder of the prior estate destroying it artificially.

The belated attempt at the end of the sixteenth century to subject executory interests to the legal rules, in effect to abolish springing and shifting interests, was motivated by the perpetuity danger which they presented; and its failure, except to the half-hearted extent of *Purefoy v Rogers*, left the danger standing. There then arose the connected question whether springing and shifting uses, admitting that they could be created, could not somehow be destroyed. There were three possibilities. Destructibility by artificial destruction of a prior interest was ruled out by immunity from the remainder rules. If an interest could spring up independently of any prior interest, it did not need the support of any prior interest; and it would not fail if a prior interest was destroyed. The analogy of contingent remainders was therefore no help.

A more likely possibility flowed from the logic of executory interests themselves or at least of some varieties. It was worked out with executory devises of terms. The most remarkable effect of the wording of the Statute of Wills was to allow something like estates to be created in terms of years. At common law a term could not be granted to one for life, remainder to another; and the result could not even be achieved under the Statute of Uses because uses of personalty were not executed. But it could be achieved by devise. There was, however, a difference from freehold estates, because true estates in a chattel seemed to the lawyers against nature. The term was not thought of as divided between the holder for life and his successor: the whole term went to the holder for life, and after his death passed intact to the successor. The arrangement was seen not as a remainder but as a shifting interest. But if the holder for life had the whole term, and the successor a mere possibility of getting it later, could not the holder for life destroy that possibility by disposing of the term in his lifetime? It appears that in the late sixteenth century the lawyers had accepted this outcome, presumably feeling compelled to it by logic, and that the chancellor had intervened to prevent it: he had compelled tenant for life to give security not to destroy the subsequent interest. In two cases early in the seventeenth century, perhaps following the chancellor's lead, such executory devises of terms were declared by common law courts to be indestructible. The earlier logic was simply stood on its head: 'it lies not in the power of the first devisee to bar him who has the future devise, for he cannot transfer more to another than he has himself'. Stout assertion by Coke worked many wonders[1].

The third possible means of destroying executory interests may be approached through these executory devises of terms. There was no perpetuity danger in a gift over after a life interest, and the courts refused to go further. If the devise of a term was expressed to be in tail, it operated as a devise of the whole term absolutely, and subsequent interests were simply void[2]. This was indeed for fear of perpetuities. If there could be tenant in tail of a term he could not suffer a recovery: he could not be seised of the freehold estate necessary to a real action. The ability to entail personalty was a treat reserved for the twentieth century. Within the sphere of executory devises of terms, therefore, the perpetuity danger was checked by the restriction to a life. But what about executory limitations of freehold? If under a devise the whole term shifted from the holder for life to his successor, and still the latter's interest was

1. *Matthew Manning's Case* (1609), 8 Co. Rep. 94b at 96a. Cf. *Lampet's Case* (1612), 10 Co. Rep. 46b. For earlier doubts about the validity and destructibility at law of executory devises of terms, see: *Anon* (1552), Dyer 74a; *Anon* (1568), Dyer 277b; *Anon* (1573), Dyer 328b; *Welcden v Elkington* (1578), Dyer 358b and Plowden 516. For particular tenants compelled in chancery 'to let it go according to the devise', see: *Price v Jones* (1584), Tothill 122; *Cole v Moore* (1607), Moore K.B. 806.
2. See *Leonard Lovies's Case* (1613), 10 Co. Rep. 78a; *Child v Baylie* (1623), Cro. Jac. 459; W. Jones 15; Palmer 48, 333; *Leventhorpe v Ashbie* (1635), 1 Rolle, *Abridgment*, 831.

indestructible by the former, what about a shifting fee? It necessarily followed that a mere alienation by the first holder would not destroy the executory interest; but since this was freehold could he not conjure up the magic of a recovery? He could, but the spell proved not powerful enough. In *Pells v Brown* in 1620 a father had devised freehold land to one son 'and his heirs for ever', providing that if that son should die without issue in the lifetime of his brother it should go over to the brother. The first devisee, probably supposing his estate to be an entail though it was held to be fee simple, suffered a common recovery and died without issue devising the land elsewhere. His brother was nevertheless held entitled[1].

This was a momentous decision. Not only did it finally reject the argument that the legal remainder rules would apply to prevent the existence of executory interests. It also finally held such interests to be indestructible by any means except by the act of their owners. There was of course no perpetuity danger in the case itself, because the gift over was to operate if at all upon the dropping of an existing life; but the mischief was pressed in argument, and subordinated to the hardship of allowing destructibility.

Perhaps this was the better choice. There had been much perversity in the results reached over the entail and over contingent remainders, allowing the extravagant creation of settlements and countering the mischief by allowing their capricious destruction. The alternative mode of control, to which the courts were now driven, was to impose some external limit upon the reach of settlors beyond which their dispositions would be ineffective. Although undertaken by judges, this was an essentially legislative process motivated by policy. But since courts cannot easily be explicit about such operations, individual decisions in the seventeenth century were justified by whatever line of argument lay nearest to hand. The result was that the nature of each limitation still seemed to matter, for example whether the executory interests were in freehold or leasehold, whether the preceding interest was for life or something more. In the learned confusion only common factors could be discerned. Of these the most important came immediately from the executory devise of a term: if the fetter ended during the lifetime of a living person, there was a growing idea that this was innocuous.

1. *Pells v Brown* (1620), Cro. Jac. 590.

Out of the welter the vision and strength of Lord Nottingham was able to extract a general rule[1]. In the *Duke of Norfolk's Case* in 1681 he enunciated the basis of the modern rule against perpetuities. This took no account of the nature of the limitation as a whole, nor of the extent of the prior estate; nor did it concentrate, as some earlier decisions had done, on the moment of time at which the fee would become fully alienable. A contingent interest was good if the contingency had to be resolved within a certain period, so that the interest was incapable of vesting outside that period. The period that he set as clearly acceptable was that of a life in being, though he thought extension possible until experience disclosed some new mischief[2]. The extension later permitted was that of a minority, a throw-back to the idea that what mattered was the time at which the fee became alienable; and this in turn became the modern period of twenty-one years in gross[3].

Although the rule against perpetuities has produced its own complexities, Lord Nottingham's achievement slowly reversed the process by which the law relating to settlements had been growing more complicated. The entail and its barring had worked itself too deeply into society to be removed; and to our shame it survives in ghostly form today. But there was no reason to preserve contingent remainders and their complex destructibility; and they were by degrees equated with executory interests. The process was completed in 1925 when the varieties of future interests were reduced to one, controlled only by the rule against perpetuities.

RISE OF THE TRUST

That one was the future trust; and this chapter must end by returning to the Statute of Uses and asking how it is that we nevertheless have a law of trusts.

1. See D. E. C. Yale, *Nottingham's Chancery Cases*, vol. I (Selden Society, vol. 73), pp. lxxiii ff.
2. *Duke of Norfolk's Case* (1681–1685), 2 Swanston 454; 3 Chan. Cas. 1; D. E. C. Yale, *Nottingham's Chancery Cases*, vol. II (Selden Society, vol. 79), pp. 904, 922, 999.
3. *Stephens v Stephens* (1736), Cases temp. Talbot, 228 (minority); *Cadell v Palmer* (1833), 1 Clark & Finnelly 372 (21 years in gross). Cf. *Thellusson v Woodford* (1805), 11 Vesey Jun. 112 (lives need have no connection with property). The Perpetuities and Accumulations Act 1964, by introducing 'wait and see' has further increased the practical reach of settlors as well as the complication of the law.

The traditional starting-point is the proposition that there were three kinds of use which the statute did not execute: the use of property other than freehold; the active use, in which the feoffees had positive duties to perform; and the use upon a use. The last of these is a great mystery, and will be deferred. The first is said to flow from the word 'seised' in the statute; and the second, most obviously justified as a necessary exception, can be referred to the passive mood of the same phrase: 'when any person or persons stand or be seised . . . to the use, confidence or trust of any other . . .'.

For these two, however, it will be convenient to begin before the statute. Personal property, including leases, might be devoted to charitable purposes or the like; but this would usually be by will and the relevant jurisdiction would be that over executors. Since such property could be freely disposed of by will, moreover, there was no need for a testator to grant it away in his lifetime, as he had to do to make a will of freehold. If the statute was really about wills of freehold, other property was outside its contemplation; and this is confirmed by the preamble to the Statute of Wills which says that the power of devise is being restored because a man's 'proper goods, chattels and other movable substance' is normally insufficient to provide for his creditors, younger children and so on. Nor is it just that uses of personal property were not intended to be executed by the statute. The phrase itself would probably have seemed a contradiction in terms. Almost the only motive for an *inter vivos* arrangement which could be so described would be to defraud creditors; and an act of 1487, the latest of a series dealing with this, instead of speaking in terms of collusion as the others had, declared deeds of gift of chattels 'of trust, to the use of' the makers of those deeds to be simply void. Not until the middle of the sixteenth century does it seem to have been settled that this applied only to dispositions in fraud of creditors[1]. And although it became clear that the Statute of Uses did not execute uses of leasehold[2], it appears that chancellors were reluctant to intervene on the ground that long terms could be employed to defraud the revenue. It is

1. Stat. 3 Hy. VII, c. 4. For the restriction to dispositions in fraud of creditors, though the statute is wrongly attributed to Ric. III, see Brooke, *Abridgment*, Feffements al uses 60 (3 Mary): '*sic est le preamble & intent del cest estatut.*'
2. *Question by the Lord Chancellor* (1580), Dyer 369a.

therefore possible that there was no continuity of equitable interests in personalty before and after the statute in the sense usually understood, and that the true trust of personalty began later. In the case of leaseholds a desire to evade the feudal dues of the crown may have played a part in this[1], and another part may have been played by the movement into chancery of testamentary trusts. What again seems clear is that the draftsman of the Statute of Uses was not addressing himself to equitable interests as such: he was dealing with wills of land. To think of trusts of personalty as evidence that he did not intend to abolish uses, or as evidence that he did intend it but was incompetent, is to think in unreal terms.

Active uses of freehold, however, must have been within the contemplation of the draftsman. The commonest provisions by testators were those directing their feoffees to raise money out of their lands for the payment of debts, for marriage portions and the like, and for religious or other charitable works for the donor's soul. These last, not within even the extended ambit of mortmain because not for the benefit of religious corporations, had indeed attracted legislative attention just three years before the statute; and such arrangements had been made void if to last more than twenty years. Although that Act had contemplated *inter vivos* creation, its main concern was with such gifts made by will: it had, for example, expressly saved local customs permitting devises into mortmain[2].

The draftsman of the Statute of Uses, therefore, who supposed himself to be abolishing wills of land, may have thought that for the future such uses would just not arise. What may be surprising is that he was not explicit about provisions in the wills he was expressly saving by his transitional provisions. What was to happen, for example, about a direction that the feoffees should raise money out of land for the payment of debts or the like? Such provisions were of the essence of wills before the statute, and of those permitted four years later by the Statute of Wills; and the only possible

1. *Risden v Tuffin* (1597), Tothill, 122: 'No relief in equity touching leases of one thousand years, because they tend to defraud the crown.' *Anon* (1599), Cary 8: '. . . the Lord Egerton pronounced openly, that he would give none aid in Chancery for the maintenance of any perpetuities, nor of any lease for hundreds or thousands of years, made of lands holden *in capite;* because the latter be grounded upon fraud, and the former be fights against God.'
2. Stat. 23 Hy. VIII, c. 10. It would be interesting to know how this statute, with its miscellaneous saving clauses, came into being.

conclusion seems to be that both draftsmen intended what happened, and perhaps supposed themselves to be saying as much in allowing the wills to have any force at all, namely that the trustees should retain the legal title for the purpose of carrying out their directions. If so, the truly unexpected consequences were in provisions which could be 'executed'; and there may never have been any doubt about the propriety of a truly active use[1]. Since all modern trusts are active, though passive trusts of freehold seem sometimes to have been created in the eighteenth and nineteenth centuries, the substantive mystery is on this view at least much reduced. And the double use becomes largely a conveyancing mystery. Why did conveyancers creating an active trust come regularly to express a first use in favour of the trustees?

The form which they employed was 'unto and to the use of' the trustee 'upon trust for' the beneficiary, and it must be asked whether there was any difference between 'use' and 'trust'. Lord Nottingham said that they were and always had been different things; and he worked out a theory, intended to explain the rise of trusts, which would have equated uses with those arrangements caught by the statute of 1484. That was the statute protecting purchasers from feoffors against claims by or through feoffees holding only to their use. Nottingham's theory looks like *ex post facto* logic, but it is interesting that the greatest of all chancellors thought it reasonable to suppose that uses and trusts had always been different. It is in fact possible to suspect some association between 'trust' and active arrangements. But the Statute of Uses itself spoke of 'use, confidence or trust'; and the likeliest view is that 'trust' came to be employed for clarity to describe an arrangement not caught by the statute[2].

1. On directions to feoffees to raise money for a purpose, see Brooke, *Abridgment*, Feffements al uses 52 (36 Hy. VIII): direction that J. N. shall take profits raises use in J. N.; direction that feoffees shall take profits and deliver them to J. N. does not raise use in J. N. On directions to convey, see *Humphreston's Case* (*Lane v Cowper*) (1575), and *Bettuan's Case* (1576), p. 238, n. 1, below.
2. For Lord Nottingham's theory, see D. E. C. Yale, 'The Revival of Equitable Estates in the Seventeenth Century: an Explanation by Lord Nottingham' [1957] Cambridge Law Journal, p. 72. For the 1484 statute, see p. 215, above. For the 'active' connotation of 'trust' see J. L. Barton 'The Statute of Uses and the Trust of Freeholds' (1966) 82 LQR, p. 215, disagreeing with the categorical assertion in J. B. Ames, 'The Origin of Trusts', *Lectures on Legal History* (1913), p. 243 at p. 245, also printed in *Select Essays in Anglo-American Legal History*, vol. II, p. 747 at p. 750. As a matter of usage there seems to be a correlation.

Was it by design or by accident that grants came to be made 'unto and to the use of' one in trust for another? The oldest view was that it was by design, a deliberate attempt to evade the Statute of Uses. This has generally been rejected on the ground that the statute was central to the revenue, and that no chancellor would connive in its evasion. The case for accident rested largely upon the existence of a trap which made accident likely; and it certainly caught the settlor in the earliest clear case of a double use. The bargain and sale enrolled had come to be regarded as the equivalent of a feoffment, and it was easy to forget that it worked only because the bargain and sale raised an implied use. If then a grant to uses was intended, and the land was conveyed to the feoffee by this method instead of by feoffment, a use upon a use necessarily resulted[1]. In *Tyrrel's Case* in 1557 a tenant in fee simple desired to settle land upon herself for life, remainder to her son in tail, remainder to her own right heirs. She bargained and sold to the son to those uses, presumably intending that the statute should execute them. But they were held void as repugnant to the implied use[2]. It has been suggested that the accident repeated itself, that chancellors were asked to intervene against the party unconscientiously seeking to retain the benefit for himself, that the redress he came to give was to decree a conveyance or put that party on terms, and finally that after the abolition of the feudal incidents this decree could be for a subsisting relationship, a trust. But it now seems clear that intervention came in cases in which the first use was not implied but express: if conveyancers had made a mistake, it was not that mistake[3].

The evidence suggests that there was no mistake, that the first use was inserted for a reason, and that the reason was indeed to avoid

1. This accident was emphasised by T. F. T. Plucknett, *Concise History of the Common Law* (5th edn., 1956), pp. 599 ff; but see K. E. Digby, *An Introduction to the History of the Law of Real Property* (5th edn., 1897), pp. 368 ff esp. at pp. 371–2.
2. *Tyrrel's Case* (1557), Dyer 155a; Benloe 28; 1 Anderson 37; Benloe with Dalison 61.
3. The haphazard reporting of cases (and the haphazard reading by historians of even the printed reports) long gave prominence to *Sambach v Dalston* (1635), Tothill 188; Nelson 30. The decree was for a conveyance on terms, to resolve a contradiction between uses. But the report in Nelson, for which see J. E. Strathdene, '*Sambach v Dalston*: an Unnoticed Report' (1958) 74 LQR, p. 550, shows that the contradiction did not arise from a bargain and sale or, probably, any other accident. Nor, as will appear below, was interference by the chancellor then a novelty.

any operation of the Statute of Uses, but not in ways which might defraud the revenue. In at least one situation it seems to have been inserted to make it clear that an active use was what was intended. Consider again a settlor who has played a larger part earlier in the story, the tenant in fee simple who wishes to settle upon himself in tail with remainders over. He must still employ a third party. When the potency of the Statute of Uses is understood the third party can be a passive conjuror's assistant, holding the property only for a moment while the spell is cast and uses executed in favour of the settlor and remaindermen. But the settlor who is scared of magic and desires an old-fashioned grant and regrant must give his third party a firmer grasp of the legal title. It must not flash through him to the beneficiaries, and equally it must not rebound intact upon the settlor by the instant execution of a resulting use. There was some discussion of this situation about 1575; and the conclusion reached was that the third party must hold to his own use[1]. A conveyance 'unto and to the use of' the third party upon trust to execute the settlement would be the natural result. It therefore looks as though the first use may have come to be regularly inserted in active trusts as a charm to ward off the Statute of Uses even when it did not threaten to strike. And that is a sufficient explanation not only of the regular conveyancing oddity but also of the substantive problem, the present existence of trusts despite the statute. But it is not the whole story, and it would not of course explain passive trusts of freehold to the extent that truly passive trusts came to be created.

Whether or not, as has been suggested, the revenue interest was guarded by the Stature of Wills rather than by the Statute of Uses[2],

1. In *Humphreston's Case* (*Lane v Cowper*) (1575), Moore K.B. 103; 2 Leonard 216; note to Dyer 166a (also reported, without discussion of the present point, in Dyer 337a; Owen 64; Benloe 29; Benloe with Dalison 195) the settlor had suffered a recovery so as to resettle. All agreed that the recoverors must hold to their own use, otherwise they could not make the required estates by livery as was intended; but if they did not make the estates within a reasonable time, some thought that a use would be raised in the settlor. In *Bettuan's Case* (1576), 4 Leonard 22, grantees by fine were to make an estate to whomever the grantor should name; and it was said that they must be seised to their own use until the grantor made nomination, but if he died without nominating they would be seised to the use of his heir.
2. See J. L. Barton, 'The Statute of Uses and the Trust of Freeholds' (1966) 82 LQR, p. 215. The article suggested also that passive trusts of freehold might be recognised before the end of the sixteenth century.

it is now clear that the chancellor would sometimes interfere even in what seem to have been created as passive trusts long before abolition of the feudal incidents made a possible revenue interest irrelevant. Indeed he did so within a year or two of *Tyrrel's Case*, though in that early case it may have been only because of politically special circumstances. A lady obliged to flee the country under Queen Mary granted certain lands to a lawyer expressly to the lawyer's own use, but subject to a secret trust in favour of herself. Under Queen Elizabeth she returned, and secured a chancery decree that the lands should be returned to her[1]. We do not know how common cases were, how often the chancellor was willing to interfere at all, or how far he might be willing to enforce a continuing relationship instead of decreeing a conveyance. But we can be sure that he would not feel himself automatically unable to prevent unconscientious conduct just because of the Statute of Uses. Our difficulty has partly been created by our own vision of the statute as a categorical prohibition of equitable interests seen as an entity.

1. J. H. Baker, 'The Use upon a Use in Equity 1558–1625' (1977) 93 LQR, p. 33.

III

OBLIGATIONS

10 *Old Personal Actions*

To turn from property to obligations is to turn from one modern concept to another. The modern law of obligations, roughly that concerning contract, tort and personal chattels, is the result of a continuing interplay between two simple ideas from which the common law started. It, and the earlier jurisdictions from which it sprang, knew two kinds of legal claim: the demand for a right and the complaint of a wrong. The complaint of a wrong split into two, the criminal law resulting from administrative changes in the handling of cases begun by public authority rather than by the victims. Proceedings begun by the victims became preoccupied with compensation rather than punishment, and hence the law of tort. The beginnings of this are traced in the next chapter; and it will be seen that when the king's courts begin to concern themselves with essentially private wrongs, they issue writs of appropriate form: the sheriff is to summon the defendant *ostensurus quare* (prepared to show why) he did whatever he did.

But these writs are relatively late comers. The king's courts first interested themselves in the other kind of claim, the demand for a right. For this writs were in the *praecipe* form. The sheriff was first to order the defendant to satisfy the plaintiff's claim; and only in default was the defendant to be summoned to court. One writer sees the formal change as reflecting only a process of judicialisation: the king begins by issuing executive orders on behalf of claimants whom he believes without inquiry, then orders inquiry if the claim is contested (*praecipe*), then orders it anyway (*ostensurus quare*)[1]. But there is an underlying juridical difference: in *praecipe* situations the defendant can put matters right by a definite render, whereas in

1. R. C. Van Caenegem, *Royal Writs in England from the Conquest to Glanvill* (Selden Society, vol. 77).

most *ostensurus quare* situations he has done an irreparable wrong for which compensation must be assessed.

It was by argument based upon this elementary difference between the kinds of possible claim, rather than by unreasoned interplay between 'forms of action' seen as primeval entities, that the common law of obligations was hammered out. We have already seen that the *praecipe* writs for land were replaced by *ostensurus quare* actions: the point about ejectment was that even property in land came to be decided by an action of trespass, an action formally in tort[1]. But property in land had already become a system set into rules and concepts; and the change of remedy appears to have been a technical development, securing procedural advantage at the cost of obvious artifice, but producing no change in either substantive rights or in proprietary concepts. This is not true of the corresponding changes in the field of obligations. The motives of individual plaintiffs were equally practical; and they are easier for historians to understand. But the steps which their lawyers took did more than introduce artificiality into law-suits: it broke down the original categories, and introduced artificiality into the law itself. The old *praecipe* claims known as debt, detinue, covenant and account are important dead as well as alive. Their lives were in the middle ages, and are our immediate concern. But the ways in which they were circumvented by *ostensurus quare* actions left traces in the law which are with us yet.

The pressures which produced these results built up largely at the jurisdictional boundaries, especially those between local courts and the king's courts. For wrongs, the original principle was that only wrongs breaking the king's peace, his own special law, would be dealt with in the king's courts; and the disintegration of that will be traced in the following chapter. But an early stage produced a subsidiary rule. Because the king's peace was personal, there was some confusion about the principle after the death of king Henry III, whose peace had been decisive for more than half a century. In 1278 the Statute of Gloucester, seeking to re-affirm the principle and keep out cases which should not come to the king's court, added a new requirement: for goods taken you could anyway not get to the king's court unless you swore that the goods were worth

1. See pp. 161 ff, above.

at least forty shillings[1]. In itself this set only a threshold for royal courts, not a ceiling for local courts. But it became confused with a different and older rule concerned with claims of the *praecipe* type, and especially claims for debts. These were no concern of the king, and he would lend his aid to their recovery only in return for a share which was taken by way of payment for the writ; and since the share was worth bothering about only for large sums, claims for amounts below forty shillings could, and could only, be made by plaint in local courts. But for forty shillings or more the king came to insist upon helping you with a writ for which you had to pay, though it might, presumably at your option, be a *justicies* writ ordering the sheriff to deal with your case in the county or a *praecipe* writ returnable in a royal court. The effect was to establish for debt a clear jurisdictional boundary between local and royal courts, with *justicies* writs seen as referring to county courts cases not within their inherent competence. In records of local courts, the boundary line is emphasised by numerous claims for a half-penny less than forty shillings, in records of the king's courts by claims for exactly forty shillings reached by an addition of items one of which is visibly fictitious[2]. In the fifteenth century it becomes clear that these separate considerations have merged into a single rule; and forty shillings is seen as in principle a ceiling for local and a threshold for royal jurisdiction in both *praecipe* and *ostensurus quare* claims.

To claims of the *praecipe* type, which are our immediate concern, this matters in two ways. Since their primary home was in local jurisdictions, they started with modes of proof suitable for local jurisdictions. Wager of law, for example, made sense in the court of a community in which the standing of all concerned was at stake; and it still made sense in the eyre, where the neighbours as well as the parties were present before the king's justices. It did not make much sense in Westminster, where your lawyer probably hired

1. Stat. 6 Ed. I, c. 8. On the effect of this provision, and the confusion with the originally separate rule about writs of debt, see J. S. Beckerman, 'The Forty-Shilling Jurisdictional Limit in Medieval English Personal Actions', *Legal History Studies 1972*, p. 110.
2. H. M. Cam, *The Hundred and the Hundred Rolls* (1930), p. 182; S. F. C. Milsom, 'Sale of Goods in the Fifteenth Century' (1961) 77 LQR, p. 257 at pp. 258 ff. In 1601 statute attempted to prevent evasion in the superior courts: Stat. 43 Eliz., c. 6.

oath-helpers; but, for reasons to be discussed later, it had to be retained. And this was one cause which led to the eventual replacement of these actions by *ostensurus quare* actions which had always had jury trial. Another cause is related. The parties could exclude difficulties of proof by providing the incontrovertible evidence of a document under seal. But in certain situations the king's courts came to insist upon this, notably in covenant. There was no harm so long as only large transactions were affected, so long as forty shillings was a large sum; and in the thirteenth century it was of the order of a year's pay. But the figure was never altered; and as it sank to a level which daily transactions might reach, daily transactions were brought not only into the king's courts but into the ambit of unsuitable rules of proof. Individual lawyers could not do much about forty shillings; and that is why the pressure which was built up by the jurisdictional boundary was brought to bear along the conceptual boundary. Whenever there was ambiguity or doubt, a claim would be expressed as the complaint of a wrong rather than the demand for a right; and little by little the boundary was pushed back.

COVENANT

The action of covenant will be considered first, not because it is the oldest in the king's courts or probably in local courts, but because it represents an elementary legal idea which is familiar to the modern mind. The word covenant, Latin *conventio,* means just agreement; and we are wrong to use the definite article and write of 'the' action of covenant. Actions of covenant were simply actions to enforce agreements; and when in the year books we find counsel arguing whether an action should be in 'trespass' or in 'covenant', they are not pitting rival 'forms of action' against each other, but rival analyses of their facts in terms like our 'tort' and 'contract'.

Because of its history, however, our 'contract' embraces a wide range of separable kinds of liability, whereas 'covenant' seems to have been narrower and simpler. Its essence is expressed in the *praecipe* writ: tell the defendant to keep to his agreement concerning the building of a house (or the leasing of so much land or whatever the agreement did concern). It was an action to compel performance; and although, except in the case of the lease, the common law for reasons of convenience ceased to make orders for specific performance and contented itself with damages, the damages were understood to be for the non-performance. When in 1284 instructions were sent to guide the application of English law in Wales, for example, the case was considered of an agreement for the sale of land which the seller breaks: ordinarily the appropriate remedy will be an order that the feoffment should be made and seisin delivered in accordance with the agreement; but if the seller has since enfeoffed a third party, the only possible redress is compensation[1]. It is a case to which we shall return in another context; and in that context we shall misunderstand the interplay between *ostensurus quare* claims and the *praecipe* covenant unless we remember to take the *praecipe* writ to that extent literally[2].

Covenant, then, was essentially about compelling performance or compensating for the value of performance. Could one demand the performance of any agreement, even for example a gratuitous promise? Customs may have varied, but in any community the answer would no doubt have been obvious; and its likely nature would align the liability with that to be discussed in connection with debt and detinue. Suppose an agreement between a builder and his customer: the builder can sue for his money when he has built; and probably the customer can sue for performance only when he has paid, at least in part. But the answer would have been more obvious than the question. Contemporaries were concerned not with substantive law but with proof. One would ask not: 'When is an agreement legally enforceable?', but 'What kind of proof must the plaintiff tender in order to put the defendant to his answer?'. His own bare word was not enough. He must produce at least good suit, that is persons prepared to support his claim somehow, even if only as witnesses to his credibility; or he might do better and tender witnesses to the transaction itself, or even some writing. And upon the nature of his tender would depend the proof by which the defendant's denial would be tested and the case decided. To take as an example the commonest case, it seems to have been invariably accepted that a claim supported only by good suit could be denied

1. Stat. 12 Ed. I, c. 10.
2. See pp. 328 ff, below.

by wager of law. Both turned upon standing with one's fellows. And in the community situation, whether a community of neighbours who lived with each other or of merchants who dealt with each other, such guarantees of good faith probably ensured that only honest claims were pressed as well as that only honest denials were carried to wager of law and the like[1].

But neither side could bring the neighbours across England; and in the king's courts these proofs to be tendered by the plaintiff lost their bite as much as wager itself. The plaintiff's *secta* remained, but as an empty formality. 'And thereof he produces suit' says the plea roll, and goes on saying it through the centuries. But the defendant could not in fact demand that the suit should be examined, could not therefore require the plaintiff to produce any real guarantee of good faith. One solution was to impose jury trial, so that the issue between the parties was put to neighbours; and this was indeed proposed for Wales in the instructions of 1284[2]. But in any action on an agreement there are always two possible questions. Was the agreement made in the terms alleged by the plaintiff? And then was it carried out or broken or what? And the two are connected: the defendant says he has built the promised twenty feet of wall; the plaintiff says the agreement was for thirty. The general question between the parties must not therefore be put to a jury unless the jurors know about both ends of the story; and since agreements are often publicly made and privately discharged, and are sometimes made in one county and discharged in another, jury trial would often be unworkable. The initial stand of the king's courts that private agreements were not for them depended upon a view of what was the king's business: but it proved to be justified by practical considerations also. There could be no turning back now, but questions of proof had as far as possible to be excluded. Early in the fourteenth century the king's courts finally decided that they could not entertain any ordinary action of covenant unless the plaintiff produced a document in which the defendant had acknowledged the terms of the agreement by affixing his seal, the equivalent in a largely illiterate age of our signature. At least there could be no dispute over what was agreed, so that only performance could be in issue.

1. See generally R. L. Henry, *Contracts in the Local Courts of Medieval England* (1926).
2. Stat. 12 Ed. I, c. 10.

This was to have large consequences, and it is important not to be deceived by them. Centuries later covenant lost its original sense altogether. It became the name of a 'form of action', and the underlying concept was supposed to be that of a formal contract analogous to the Roman *stipulatio:* you go through ritual steps and you are magically bound. This was seen as something archaic, from which the shining *assumpsit* rescued us; and the idea of agreement being a cause of action in its own right is attributed to the seventeenth century[1]. The linguistic reflection of all this, since the word 'covenant' was disabled from its original function, was that 'contract' was eventually recruited in its place; and since that word also had its own different sense in the middle ages, confusion for historians grew. Nor, of course, was there a moment of time at which lawyers changed from the one word to the other to express the same idea. The idea itself became lost, and there was an interregnum in which the best that legal vocabulary could do was to use the name of another 'form of action', *assumpsit.* And since that was formally an action in what we call tort, the development would have been impossible if lawyers had thought consistently in terms of principle[2]. The way in which it came about will be explained later. What matters now is that the medieval covenant did reflect principle, an elementary legal idea; and there was nothing magical about it.

It is this idea of covenant, common coin in the year books, that is important for understanding what later happened. The action of covenant itself was never very important in the king's courts, because never very common. Plaintiffs probably preferred to go to local courts; and the only early restriction of which there is evidence would exclude agreements concerning land worth more than forty shillings a year[3]. In the nature of things the obligation left outstanding by most transactions is to pay money or to deliver goods; and for that, even if the obligation was what we should call contractual, the appropriate writ was not covenant but debt or detinue: the sheriff was to tell the defendant to pay the money or

1. Notice the sense of discovery felt even by Maitland on finding informal covenants enforced in local courts, *The Court Baron* (Selden Society, vol. 4), at pp. 115 ff.
2. S. F. C. Milsom, 'Reason in the Development of the Common Law' (1965) 81 LQR, p.496 at pp. 500 ff.
3. *Early Registers of Writs* (Selden Society, vol. 87), note preceding Hib. 49.

deliver the goods, or to answer before the king's justices. Such actions were always common in the king's courts. And when other kinds of agreement came to be brought there, they were artificially made in such a way that the law-suit would be in debt rather than in covenant.

DEBT ON AN OBLIGATION

A claim in debt for money (or, as we shall see, for goods) never required a document under seal in the king's courts as did a claim in covenant. But if the plaintiff had one it was even more effective. What the defendant acknowledged under seal was not just the terms of an agreement: he acknowledged that he owed the money. Effectively, therefore, there was no law-suit. Against his own deed he could not deny that he owed, could not plead *non debet*. The only thing he could deny was the genuineness of the plaintiff's otherwise conclusive proof, *non est factum suum;* and this plea was extended from simple forgery to cover certain kinds of duress, and also to the case of the illiterate to whom the deed had been read wrongly. It was put to a jury; but if they found that the deed was in fact the defendant's, he was sent to prison for making the plea. For the same reason, the convenience of avoiding litigation altogether, the defendant could not plead that he had paid the amount due, unless he could produce an acquittance under seal. If he had paid without either getting an acquittance or having his bond returned to him, he would have to pay again, not, as the Student explained to the Doctor because this result was in itself desired, but because 'the general grounds of the law of England heed more what is good for many than what is good for one singular person only'[1]. This singular person naturally became a common supplicant to the chancellor.

The straightforward use of the simple bond was to secure the payment of debts. The borrower of money or the buyer of land or goods would often give a bond for the amount due. But bonds could also be used to secure obligations different in kind, so that any litigation would be in debt rather than in covenant. The buyer and seller of land for example might execute bonds, the former for the price, the latter for some appropriate penal sum, and deposit

1. *Doctor and Student*, Dialogue I, c.12 (Selden Society, vol. 91, pp. 77–9).

them with a stakeholder. If the conveyance was made as agreed, the bonds would both be delivered to the seller, if not, to the buyer. But the same result could be achieved without the intervention of a third party by making bonds not simple but conditional[1]. The seller of land would execute a deed binding himself to his buyer in a large sum unless the condition written on the back of the bond was satisfied; and the bond would be endorsed with some such words as these: 'The condition of this obligation is that the seller will by such a date make estates good and acceptable in the law in such and such lands'[2].

If the conveyance was not made, the buyer would not sue the seller in covenant for failing to convey: he would sue him in debt for the penalty. Since the bond was conditional, it was of course open to the defendant to plead satisfaction of the condition, and that would be the normal issue for the jury. This was the form in which most important transactions were made and sued upon until the sixteenth century, and it accounts for a considerable proportion of the business of the court of common pleas. Since the records of this court have not been much used by economic historians, it may be added that the conditions were pleaded and enrolled verbatim: the exact terms of every kind of dealing are therefore preserved in the rolls.

COVENANT AND CONDITIONAL BONDS

Why were agreements regularly made in this form, and not by direct promises under seal of the performance desired? Why did the man who wanted a house built, instead of getting the builder to execute a deed promising to do it, get him to execute a deed securing a penal sum if he did not do it? It is not just a matter of preference showing up in statistics. The action of covenant as a genuine remedy is almost unknown in the king's courts after the middle of the fourteenth century; and the rare examples mostly arise out of

1. S. E. Thorne, 'Tudor Social Transformation and Legal Change' (1951) 26 New York University Law Review, p. 10 at p. 19; A. W. B. Simpson, 'The Penal Bond with Conditional Defeasance' (1966) 82 LQR, p. 392; *A History of the Common Law of Contract* (1975), pp. 90 ff.
2. The buyer's bond would commonly fix a penalty of twice the agreed price.

apprenticeship articles. The formalities of apprenticeship were entrenched in civic customs, and change was no doubt unthinkable. But it is evident that whenever they could lawyers were advising their clients to set up their dealings in a way which would bring up any litigation in debt rather than in covenant.

After 1352 there is a simple explanation. In that year a statute extended to other personal actions the rigorous process associated with trespass *vi et armis*[1]. In that action, as will be seen later, the king's interest had carried with it the possibility of *capias*, of arresting or outlawing the defendant; and the statute made this available in debt and other personal actions. There was the obvious convenience of being able to reach more quickly a defendant who could anyway be reached ultimately, and the less obvious advantage that defendants who could not be reached at all could be outlawed and treated as dead; and in the case of joint obligations this enabled proceedings to continue against their co-defendants. But this statute did not extend to the action of covenant, which was left slower and less convenient than debt. The omission may be explained by the use of the writ of covenant as a vehicle for the levying of fines. Conveyancers have always liked to take their time, and would not wish impatient clients to hurry things along by having each other arrested.

But the contractual use of covenant was already rare before the statute, so there must be some older reason for the preference. Human nature may be a sufficient explanation. Most people are optimistic about the performance of their own obligations under an agreement, pessimistic about that of the other side; and until the chancery began to interfere with the enforcement of penalties, the conditional bond both provided an effective sanction and prevented argument about damages. But there may be a more fundamental reason for the disuse of covenant.

In other *praecipe* writs, since performance was primarily commanded, the defendant could end the action and avoid damages by tendering performance. In debt, for example, he could tender payment. But in the case of covenant, this might be no remedy for the plaintiff. Suppose he had low-lying land, and had got the defendant to promise under seal to strengthen the river wall; and suppose that the defendant had not done it so that the land was

1. Stat. 25 Ed. III, stat. 5, c. 17.

flooded and a harvest lost. The plaintiff does not want just the failure made good: he wants compensation for the consequential damage. His lawyer may have advised him to take a conditional bond in the first place, rather than a direct promise of the desired performance, precisely so that he could provide against any likely damage in fixing the penal sum.

If so, then what is emphasised once again is the need to take forms literally, this time the *praecipe* form of the writs we are now considering. They were about a performance or a render and no more. Looking back from a law of contract which provides compensation for almost any harm arising in the context of a transaction between the parties, we misunderstand a simpler and clearer system of ideas. In detinue, for example, we shall be tempted to describe the action as somehow defective because it did not provide compensation if the chattel was returned in bad condition. In debt, we forget altogether the possibility that non-payment may cause independent damage. And in covenant, we suspect lawyers' trickery whenever we see an *ostensurus quare* action brought by one party to an agreement against the other. We forget that the comprehensiveness of our own law of contract represents a confusion of juridically distinct claims; and as we shall see, that came about because *ostensurus quare* actions for wrongs done in a contractual context swallowed up the *praecipe* demands for simple performance.

DEBT ON A CONTRACT

An agreement to do something other than to pay money or deliver goods could not be enforced in the king's courts without a document under seal, whether the direct undertaking to do the act which would be enforceable by writ of covenant or the conditional bond which would be enforceable by the writ of debt. But this was not the case with obligations to pay money or to deliver goods: the king's courts did not apply to actions of debt and detinue the requirement which they imposed in covenant, and for these the plaintiff could proffer some lesser proof.

But the range of possible proofs which a plaintiff might proffer in local and mercantile courts was not practicable in Westminster. Some early year book cases turn on the status of the mercantile tally, the stick recording the amount of a debt by notches of varying width and split so that the creditor retained the 'stock' and the debtor the 'foil'[1]. And some attempts were made to give witnesses to the transaction some effect, namely in excluding wager of law. Wager was universally accepted as sufficient proof of a defendant's denial against a plaintiff who produced only good suit. The law-suit was then one man's word against another; and when that was not so, because the plaintiff's suit could testify to the actual facts, some local jurisdictions regarded wager as inappropriate. But, perhaps because of the practical difficulties, the king's court allowed other logic to prevail. Even if the transaction was made before witnesses, the debt so created might have been privately paid; and then it would still be one man's word against another[2].

With few exceptions, therefore, actions of debt in the king's courts in which the plaintiff has no document under seal assume a remarkable uniformity. The count recites, with more or less precision as we shall see, some transaction such as a loan of money or a sale of goods, asserts that the debt is unpaid, and makes formal tender of good suit. The defendant then makes his general denial: its early form denies that he is bound, *non tenetur*; but as the fourteenth century proceeds this gives way to *non debet*. On this he either wages his law or chooses to put himself on a jury, and in the late fifteenth and sixteenth centuries jury trial becomes about as common as wager[3]. But even then the verdict entered on the plea roll is a blank *debet* or *non debet*, so that we know no more than when law was waged.

This blankness is important. First, it conceals the facts of disputes from us. Was the defendant always denying that he had ever entered into the transaction? From the plea rolls one might suppose this,

1. E.g. YBB 3 Ed. II (Selden Society, vol. 20), p. 46; 4 Ed. II (Selden Society, vol. 26), p. 153; 8 Ed. II (Selden Society, vol. 41), p. 179.
2. The decisive step in the king's courts was the general abandonment of any possibility of examining the plaintiff's suit: YBB 2 & 3 Ed. II (Selden Society, vol. 19), p. 195; 17 & 18 Ed. III (Rolls Series), p. 73. For early attempts to rely on witnesses to the bailment of charters, see YBB 4 Ed. II (Selden Society, vol. 26), p. 15; 5 Ed. II (Selden Society, vol. 31), p.148 (wager came any way to be excluded from detinue of charters). For a vigorous attempt to exclude wager when the countryside had knowledge see YB 2 & 3 Ed. II (Selden Society, vol. 19), pp. 195–6. For late statements of the general principle, see YBB Hil. 33 Hy. VI, pl. 23, f.7v, at f.8v; Mich. 18 Hy. VIII, pl. 15, f. 3.
3. S. F. C. Milsom, 'Sale of Goods in the Fifteenth Century' (1961) 77 LQR, p. 257 at p. 266.

and conclude that in all actions one side or the other was merely dishonest. But the year books indicate a more life-like picture. Genuine disputes arose out of all sorts of facts, but they were nearly all forced into the mould of the old denial. Argument is about a special plea that the defendant wishes to make; but eventually he is forced to *non debet*, and this is generally all that will appear on the plea roll.

The rule that the general issue must be pleaded unless there is a clear possibility of injustice was pushed to surprising lengths. Suppose that the defendant had indeed incurred the debt, but had paid it. He could not plead the payment specially: it was subsumed within *non debet*. The nearest he could sometimes get was a plea 'paid and so *non debet*'; but this 'conclusion to the *debet*' made it a plea of the general issue, and the concession was in letting him draw the jury's attention to the possibility of payment. Now suppose that the defendant had incurred the debt in Kent and paid it in Essex. Either a plain '*non debet*' or a 'paid and so *non debet*' would go to a Kentish jury, who could have no means of knowing about the payment. Surely, therefore, the defendant could make a true special plea, confessing the transaction in Kent and saying just 'paid in Essex' to an Essex jury? But no: if he chose he could wage his law and avoid any jury; there was therefore no hardship in keeping him to the general rule. There were, however, a few ways in which debts could be incurred without any deed but upon which wager was not permissible. Most prominent were the lease of land and the taking of an account before auditors: if the action was for the rent, or for the balance found due on the account, the defendant could not wage his law. He could, however, unlike the defendant in debt on an obligation, plead the general issue; and normally he put just '*non debet*' to a jury. But here we have at last found a situation in which he could sometimes insist upon a true special plea. Suppose that the action was for rent upon a lease of land in Kent, and that the defendant had paid in Essex. He had to have a jury, and it was clearly unjust to force him to a Kentish jury. But that would inevitably happen if he pleaded the general issue or 'concluded to the *debet*', because the transaction itself was put in question. He must, in this extremely special case, be allowed to confess the lease and simply plead his 'paid in Essex'[1].

1. S. F. C. Milsom, 'Law and Fact in Legal Development' (1967) 17 University of Toronto Law Journal, p. 1, at pp. 4, 16.

What matters about this is its consequence in inhibiting legal development. Term after term and century after century disputes of every kind were hidden under *non debet*. And it is not only that the facts are hidden from us today. The legal questions that they might have raised were hidden from legal examination at the time. Take the rule in *Pinnel's Case,* that acceptance of a smaller sum in full satisfaction does not discharge the balance of a debt[1]. We may think the answer given unfortunate: but the question is an obvious one and some answer is necessary. And yet the rule is not much older than the case, decided in 1602, because the question was not asked. How could it be, if the defendant is just to plead *non debet*? A jury might possibly have asked for directions, but nobody at *nisi prius* would have been much interested if they had. A particularly scrupulous litigant might have asked whether he would perjure his soul in waging his law. Or a court might have elicited the facts in examining him before admitting him to make his oath; and this in fact happened, but only some fifteen years earlier than *Pinnel's Case* itself.[2] In debt on a contract, the matter could have been raised formally by plea only in some such case as that just considered, namely a lease in one county and an acceptance of part of the rent in another. In *Pinnel's Case* itself the action was for the penalty in a conditional bond, and the question was whether a condition to pay so much could be satisfied by the acceptance of less. The question – not quite the same question, perhaps, but taken to be so – was at last raised squarely, because raised in a context in which the general issue was excluded.

If therefore somebody had sat down about 1500 to write an account of 'the law' behind the action of debt, there would not have been a great deal to write about. There would not have been much more than could be found in the early books of entries: a series of standard counts. Wager of law, usually taken as a symptom of backwardness in contractual matters, was really a cause. It was the availability of wager that enabled the courts to insist upon the general issue in such situations as the payment in another county; and without it special pleas and new legal questions would have been more frequent, and substantive law would have been generated more quickly. Of course at the time nobody saw the matter in this

1. 5 Co. Rep. 117a.
2. *Anon* (1588), 4 Leonard 81.

way, and if they had they would have thought it a merit in wager rather than the reverse: lawyers have never welcomed new problems.

Nor was wager itself regarded with contempt as a mode of proof. Although separated from its community sanctions, the defendant himself still had to swear his oath; and few would lightly perjure themselves. Perhaps the one feature that might have seemed wrong was the consequential immunity of executors. They could be sued on their testator's bond, because a jury could still compare seals. But they could not know what simple contractual debts he had incurred, still less whether he had paid them, and so could not swear. The conclusion that they could not be sued had been avoided in London by an ordinance allowing them to swear to the best of their knowledge; and it seems to have been avoided in the exchequer in *quo minus* on the ground that the testator himself could not have waged his law against the king[1]. But it remained in other royal courts to cause some injustice, and so to lend force to later moves to replace the action of debt itself.

THE BASIS OF OBLIGATION IN DEBT

Wager affects the historian's understanding as well as the actual development of the law. We can identify the underlying idea of covenant: it was that of agreement. What is the idea underlying debt? It is a harder question, because probably unreal. In the network of assumptions we make when we think in terms of 'the forms of action', the most insidious is the assumption that writs must represent juridical entities. In terms, the writ of debt is just a practical instrument: the sheriff is to tell the defendant to pay the money claimed, or if not to answer in court. It would be an appropriate start to the resolution of diverse legal claims; and in the case of detinue, which itself will turn out to be not wholly distinct from debt, we shall see that claims fundamentally different in legal nature might be made on the same common form of writ. We must not assume that there was some single idea behind debt as there was

1. Executors' oath in London: *Borough Customs*, vol. I (Selden Society, vol. 18), pp. 210 ff. Suing in exchequer: YBB 20 Ed. III (Rolls Series), vol. I, p. 17; Trin. 11 Hy. VII, pl. 9, f. 26v.; Trin. 27 Hy. VIII, pl. 21, f. 23.

behind covenant, or even that there was some single list of ways of becoming indebted. One can imagine a claim made on a *justicies* writ which would be regarded as showing a debt by the customs of Berkshire but not by those of Devon. And when we see the action begun by returnable writ in Westminster, we cannot exclude the possibility that the differing customs are still operating inside that blank denial. In the year books, general statements about the basis of liability are not early but late. Perhaps even that most elementary of questions is only then coming to the surface.

If so, it is not only general denials that have kept it under. There are also general admissions. Consider first debt on an obligation: it was, as we have seen, so effective that there was neither need nor room for discussion of its basis. Was the document dispositive or evidentiary: did it create the debt or just prove it? If proof is conclusive, the question never matters in practice. Here it is even in theory unreal. What the bond conclusively proved was not that there had been some transaction, such as a loan, which as a matter of independent substantive law would have created a debt: it proved indebtedness itself. Suppose an action by a lender who has no bond. We have seen that the defendant's denial does not go to the past facts of the case, the loan or its repayment: he denies that he is liable now, *non tenetur* or *non debet*. The function of a bond was precisely to preclude that denial: it witnesses that the maker is bound. Just as one might make a debt enforceable by entering into a recognizance, in effect losing an action of debt in advance so that the creditor had only to levy execution, so by giving him a bond one provided him with proof which would automatically win the action.

When the bond is seen in these almost procedural terms, another kind of claim falls into place. Although examples in the year books are rare, and easy to mistake as concerning bonds, the plea rolls of the fourteenth century show that it was not rare for a plaintiff to rely in his count upon some lesser formality of acknowledgement. He says that the defendant *concessit se teneri* to the plaintiff, to which the defendant commonly answers *non tenetur* and wages his law[1]. There seems to be no direct evidence of the nature of this

1. Such cases are not uncommon on 14th century plea rolls. See S. F. C. Milsom, 'Account Stated in the Action of Debt' (1966) 82 LQR, p. 534 at p. 539. See also YB 3 Ed. II (Selden Society, vol. 20), p. 191.

'grant that he is bound'; but the picture it conjures up is of some more or less formal acknowledgement originally at home in local courts, and there probably having some probative effect if an action had to be brought. It is something like a local recognizance or an oral bond. But in the king's courts, although long accepted as a sufficient basis of action, it fell into the common run of debt claims unsupported by the conclusive document under seal; and it was open to wager.

For this reason these *concessit se teneri* cases always look anomalous in the king's courts. Sometimes what seems anomalous to modern eyes is that the case proceeds at all without a written bond. The *concessit se teneri* may appear alone, without reference to any underlying transaction. Or, perhaps even more striking, it may be expressed as conditional upon something being done or not done. It is an oral bond; but whatever its effect in a local court, here it is just the basis of a claim and is always answerable by wager. Sometimes, on the other hand, the claim looks anomalous in another way: the *concessit se teneri* seems at first sight to add nothing to a claim no worse without it. Consider the defendant who *concessit se teneri* in so much money for each week that his family boarded with the plaintiff, and whose family boarded for so many weeks. Whatever formality was involved in the acknowledgement made no difference to the proof, because the defendant waged his law just as if the rate had been fixed without it. Did it make any difference to the intrinsic validity of the claim? Compare one last such case: a defendant *concessit se teneri* for the price of goods sold to a third party[1]. Such cases were later to give rise to much discussion. It would be said that the first defendant had *quid pro quo* because he was bound to provide for his family, but that the second defendant had no *quid pro quo* and was therefore not liable in debt; and in a later chapter we shall see the beginning of an important development when the seller sues the guarantor instead by *ostensurus quare* writ.

No doubt because of their anomalous appearance when seen exclusively in the context of the king's courts, these *concessit se teneri* claims die out in the later fourteenth century; and the plaintiff who has no written bond must rely in all cases, as he had always

1. Both cases are in the common pleas roll for Trinity term, 1358; CP. 40/395, mm. 226d, 162d respectively.

relied in most cases, directly upon the underlying transaction. It may be no coincidence that at about the same time we find increasing talk of the *quid pro quo* as being the basis of liability in debt. What seems to have been tantamount to an easy formal contract may both have obviated need for discussion and made workable a basis of liability which, when articulated in terms of the *quid pro quo* was to seem restrictive. It has been generally supposed that the 'contract' of debt on a contract referred not to an obligation arising directly out of an agreement but to an obligation contracted *re* in the Roman sense. The idea is no doubt ancient, and difficult for us only because it cuts across the later ideas of property and obligation. The borrower of money or the buyer of goods is liable not because he agreed but because he received the money or the goods: this raised a plus in him and left a minus in the lender or seller; and the resulting charge must be discharged by the return.

Although this idea is never made explicit, except in so far as it lies behind the relatively late talk of *quid pro quo*, it accommodates virtually all early claims in which liability is rested directly upon the transaction rather than upon some formal acknowledgement. Counts are for money lent or for the price of goods sold or services rendered and so on. And it shows up in odd points of detail. A religious house, for example, could of course buy goods only through the agency of one of its members; and the house itself was liable for the price only if the goods had come to its use. Another example arises out of a series of transactions between the same parties. In London and some other places they could reckon the balance due before witnesses, and the debtor's undertaking to pay that amount was then itself a cause of action, and one which precluded wager of law[1]. But this was never permitted in the king's courts. Although a single writ could claim a sum total, as we have seen in connection with the forty-shilling threshold, there were in effect separate counts. Each transaction raised its own separate debt, had to be separately set out, and could be separately answered. Not until developments to be discussed in a later chapter could a subsequent undertaking to pay itself ground an action; and

1. Known as *concessit solvere*. See G. D. G. Hall 'An Assize Book of the Seventeenth Century' (1963) 7 American Journal of Legal History, p. 228 at pp. 236–8; S. F. C. Milsom, 'Account Stated in the Action of Debt' (1966) 82 LQR, p. 534.

then, as we shall see, the action was again not in debt but on an *ostensurus quare* writ.

Questions will be resolved, if at all, only by further work on the records of both the king's and of local courts. But it looks as though the rejection by the king's courts of varying local customs about proof, which had produced workable results in practice, left as the only general basis of liability the narrow 'real' doctrine enshrined in the *quid pro quo;* and that, in turn, was to play its part in the supersession of debt by other writs. But within debt itself, there seems to have been some movement from the truly 'real' liability. What seems to be one symptom, in itself small, is of some juridical interest and perhaps of some practical importance. About 1300 there are signs that the writ could be used to recover money paid or goods delivered for a purpose which has failed: a lady gave goods to a man who was to marry her but did not, and she sues him in debt[1]. So long as one thinks in terms of a 'real' obligation, a plus in the defendant corresponding to a minus in the plaintiff, such a claim is entirely congruous. But it is a claim for restitution rather than performance, and ceases to fit when debt comes to be regarded as enforcing one side of a transaction. Whether or not for that reason, the claim seems to disappear after the early fourteenth century; and that fact may assume practical importance when considered together with the requirement of a seal in covenant. Suppose a building contract. If the builder builds and the customer does not pay, the builder can sue in debt. But if the customer pays and the builder does not build, the customer can sue neither in covenant for the building nor in debt for his money back; and it is against that background that we shall later have to consider the *ostensurus quare* actions which the customer comes to bring against the builder.

The other symptom of movement towards a more modern idea of 'contract' in debt on a contract is a seeming change in the sale of goods. This undoubtedly became in effect a consensual contract, in that the seller could recover not only if he had actually delivered the goods but also if he was willing to deliver them. This has been seen as an exception growing up to what was otherwise a general rule that the *quid pro quo* must have been actually received. But we

1. YBB 20 & 21 Ed. I (Rolls Series), p. 367; 2 & 3 Ed. II (Selden Society, vol. 19), p. 194; *Novae Narrationes* (Selden Society, vol. 80), B220, C261. A similar claim could be made for land by the writ of entry *causa matrimonii praelocuti*.

cannot be sure of the rule any more than we can trace the steps by which the apparent exception developed, and for the same reason. The facts are commonly hidden from us behind the general denial of a count which is always specific about the bargain, but not always about the plaintiff's performance. We are asking a more precise question than could normally arise[1].

DEBT AND DETINUE

We now turn to an even larger question which could not at first arise. To us the loan of money is obviously different from the loan of a book. There is the factual difference that the money is not specific and the book is, the difference in legal consequence that accidental loss can matter in the case of the book but not in the case of the money, and the difference in legal analysis that property in the money passes to the borrower while property in the book remains with the lender.

But even the factual difference did not at first much matter. In a society in which the main chattels were beasts and grain, the distinction between specific and unascertained goods, though not unintelligible, would not be important. The earliest form of the writ was the same whatever was claimed, and it was not unlike a *praecipe* for land. The sheriff was to tell the defendant to hand over the fifty shillings, the five quarters of barley, or the horse of which he 'deforced' the plaintiff, and if not, to come to court. In court the plaintiff would recite the transaction on which he relied; the defendant, unless he conceded the claim, would deny that he was bound, *non tenetur*; and this denial would be tested, usually by wager of law.

The first sign of differentiation comes in the writ, in which *deforciat* is replaced by *debet* and *detinet*. It became settled that *debet et detinet* was the appropriate phrase when money was demanded and when the law-suit was between the parties to the original transaction. In all other cases, *detinet* alone was appropriate. The difference later spread to the denial: *non tenetur* was replaced by *non debet* if the writ had *debet*, *non detinet* if not. We

1. See generally S. F. C. Milsom, 'Sale of Goods in the Fifteenth Century' (1961) 77 LQR, p. 257.

do not know what provoked this change, and therefore cannot claim to understand the meaning of the new words. *Debet* suggests obligation, but it was confined to a money obligation: the seller of unascertained barley, even the man who executed a deed obliging himself to a payment in barley, would not owe but only detain. And *detinet* suggests property, but could apply to money: one who executed a bond obliging himself to pay money would himself owe; but if he died, his executor would only detain. This last case, discussed in terms of a bond because that is the simplest case in which the executor could be sued, is worth carrying one step further. Although money is demanded, the executor's liability is normally confined to his testator's assets; and the use of *detinet* and not *debet* must here exclude the truly personal obligation. But the promisor of barley was under a personal and unlimited liability, so that no single principle seems to explain all cases. *Debet* does not exactly reflect obligation, even the personal obligation of one who has bound himself; and *detinet* does not exactly reflect property, let alone a claim for specific objects.

This differentiation was merely in the words of the writ. Later there was a further development: the action of detinue came to be seen as something different from the action of debt. But this was a less distinct development than has been supposed because it happened only in lawyers' heads and they were never obliged to formalise it or to define the result. So far as the formalities of the action went, there was no further development beyond the usage of *debet* and *detinet* that we have just discussed. The buyer of barley would have to claim it by a writ in the *detinet*. Later analysis would call his action detinue if what he had bought was a specific parcel of barley, 'debt in the *detinet*' if it was so much of such a quality. But there is no sign of a distinction in the records; and although actions with *debet* can always confidently be called 'debt', there is no necessary correlation between *detinet* and 'detinue'.

Even the difference in the name of the action was confined to lawyers arguing in court, and to literature produced for them. Glanvill had used the word debt for all these actions, and so far as the formalities of litigation went this remained the name for the whole range[1]. To our loss enrolling clerks did not often have

1. *Glanvill*, X, 3 and 13 (ed. G. D. G. Hall, pp. 117, 128). For discussion generally, see S. F. C. Milsom, 'Law and Fact in Legal Development' (1967) 17 University of Toronto Law Journal, p. 1, at p.6.

occasion to give an action a name: they recited the writ. But they identified the action less cumbrously when recording such formal steps as a respite or the appointment of an attorney, and it is usually possible though laborious to match entries and find the name by which they identified any particular action. In this case the result is interestingly negative. *De placito detencionis* normally identifies replevin actions: debt and detinue appear alike as *de placito debiti*, and the year books twice show clerks telling the court that this is so[1].

The printed *Register of Writs* tells the same story. Except for detinue of charters there is no heading of detinue. The writs are all *de debito* as they were for Glanvill. But the greatest of commentaries on the *Register*, Fitzherbert's *Natura Brevium*, has two headings as though there were two separate actions[2]. A distinction evidently grew in the minds of lawyers after the formalities had become settled, so that for them there were two actions although for the clerks in court and the clerks in chancery there was still only one.

This development is a striking example of law being generated by the introduction of rational trial and the concomitant possibility of some answer other than the ancient general denial. Early law classifies claims only; and its classification does not go beyond what is necessary. It was not necessary to distinguish between the loan of money and the loan of a book so long as there was only the general denial and wager. But when the defendant could put forward his own facts, all sorts of matters would be forced upon the attention of lawyers. It had happened centuries earlier in Rome, where a tidier rationalisation had produced the series of contracts *re:* and the great difference between the loan for consumption and the loan for use was crystallised in the borrower's plea of accidental destruction. This Roman conclusion was reproduced in the thirteenth-century book known by Bracton's name; and the author perhaps found it so compelling that it was obviously 'law'. But it made little sense to at least one English lawyer without much Roman learning. Britton, seeking to make Bracton's work accessible in a shortened French

1. YBB 17 Ed. III (Rolls Series), p. 141; Hil. 14 Hy. IV, pl. 37, f. 27v, at f. 28v.
2. *Registrum Omnium Brevium* (ed. 1634), f. 139 (*De debito*) and f. 159v (*De cartis reddendis*). Fitzherbert, *Natura Brevium* (ed. 1588), f. 119 (*Dette*) and f. 138 (*Detinue*; placing apparently dictated by detinue of charters). Notice the definitive effect of the headings in *Vieux Natura Brevium* (ed. 1584), ff. 60v, 63 compared with the same work (ed. c. 1518), ff. 25 ff.

version, followed a correct rendering of this passage with a comment totally misunderstanding it: he supposed that accidental loss could in suitable circumstances excuse the money debtor[1]. Book learning had run ahead of life. English law-suits were only just reaching the stage when such questions could be discussed. Whether Roman influence played any part over this point we shall probably never know. Nor does it much matter. Once there is some rational being to whom the borrower can explain about the accidental loss, he is likely to try it, whether or not he knows that other borrowers in another civilisation had done the same.

The novelty of course was not in the facts. It was in their being forced on the attention of lawyers because they were raised in a law-suit and must somehow be dealt with. From this and other pleas, there began a new process of rationalisation beyond that which had produced the claim; and in this case the result was to divide the claim into two. Lawyers arguing in court had to separate detinue from debt, although the clerks' formalities preserved the old unity. But we must not forget that the starting-point had been a unitary concept or, worse, suppose that lawyers were stupid because they did not separate what we separate. For them the borrower of a book owed the book as much as the borrower of money owed the money; and this had consequences which are still reflected in our law. But we must not deduce that for them the borrower of the book owned the book as, for us, the borrower of the money owns the money. Legal questions have to be asked before they are answered. The borrower had the book and had the money, and the lender wanted them, and lawyers had to deal with the situation. They did not have to ask what abstract word to apply to the relationship between the borrower and what he had borrowed: he had neither ownership nor possession, only the money and the book.

DETINUE FOR GOODS BOUGHT

The original unity is illustrated by the buyer's claim against his seller even more strikingly than by the bailor's claim against his bailee; and for that reason, although less important, it will be taken

1. *Bracton*, ff. 99–99b (ed. Woodbine-Thorne, vol. II, p. 284); *Britton*, I, xxix, 3 (ed. Nichols, vol. I, p. 157).

first. Glanvill draws no distinctions: the thing bought is always owed to the buyer in the same way as the price is owed to the seller[1]. To later learning, which knows that debt is a matter of pure obligation whereas detinue has some element of property, the buyer's action for unascertained goods can only be debt; but since, as we have seen, *debet* can be used only of money, it must be 'debt in the *detinet*'. But for specific goods it can be 'detinue', and should be when once the common law has come by its rule that on such a sale the property may pass at once without delivery. An attempt by a simple-minded historian to find the beginning of this remarkable rule by looking for a change from the one action to the other came predictably to grief[2]. On the plea rolls there is no way of telling whether an action is 'detinue' or 'debt in the *detinet*', or even, normally, whether the goods were specific or unascertained. The idea that property passes is probably to be attributed to a period at the end of the fifteenth century in which buyers allege a kind of constructive delivery, asserting that they had left the goods with the seller for safe keeping. And just as in the case of the true bailment the development was first started by cases of accidental destruction, so here it was probably started by fluctuations in the market price. In England the artificiality is still with us today. Although the law is stated in terms of property passing from seller to buyer, all that really passes on the mere contract is the risk of loss and the chance of gain. Other possible consequences are cancelled out by special provisions like the seller's lien and the right of a second buyer from the seller still in possession. Common law jurisdictions elsewhere have found it simpler to turn history back, and state the law in terms which give remedies according to the facts without reference to this 'passing of property'.

DETINUE ON A BAILMENT

Detinue by a bailor against his bailee of course always claimed specific goods, and goods which the bailor had necessarily had. Does it follow that the claim was a matter of property rather than of

1. *Glanvill*, X, 14 (ed. G. D. G. Hall, p. 129).
2. S. F. C. Milsom, 'Sale of Goods in the Fifteenth Century' (1961) 77 LQR, p. 257. See generally also A. W. B. Simpson, *A History of the Common Law of Contract* (1975), pp. 164 ff.

contractual obligation? The point of that question is that it is ours: it did not arise at the time. We can ask only to which of our modern ideas the original claim was closer, and note that the lender of specific goods, like the buyer of goods or the lender of money, had an action which was first called debt. The question was brought to the surface through the making of pleas other than the old general denial. Suppose the borrower of specific goods pleads contractual incapacity[1]. The borrowing did not bind him, but what of the proprietary claim: is he not keeping the plaintiff's goods from him? Suppose he pleads that the goods have accidentally perished. He is not keeping the goods, so this answers the proprietary claim; but what of the contractual?

Only the accidental destruction will be considered, because this was the practically important situation. The earliest form of the general denial, *non tenetur,* is even less definite than the later *non detinet;* but it suggests obligation and fits with the original classification of the action as debt. The first indication of any question about liability comes in Glanvill, who knew the Roman difference between *mutuum* and *commodatum.* But, perhaps because there was only one writ, he gave the answer that the bailee was strictly liable as a money debtor[2]. Bracton gave the opposite Roman answer, that accident might excuse; and Britton, knowing no Roman law and misunderstanding Bracton's point, sought to apply the excuse to a money debtor. The question could not be avoided by anyone knowing the language of Roman law. But in England it had not arisen, unless it was in the consciences of defendants who pleaded *non tenetur* and waged their law.

Not long after Britton, in the last years of the thirteenth century, we first find a defendant putting forward the special plea. Cases are rare in both year books and plea rolls, probably because defendants in fact continued to plead the general issue and wage their law. But the cases that do occur in the fourteenth century suggest that the question, once asked, was given a liberal answer[3]. Any loss

1. YB 20 & 21 Ed. I (Rolls Series), p. 189.
2. *Glanvill,* X, 13 (ed. G. D. G. Hall, p. 128); *Bracton,* ff.99–99b (ed. Woodbine-Thorne, vol. II, p. 284); *Britton,* I, xxix, 3 (ed. Nichols, vol. I, p. 157).
3. *Brinkburn Cartulary* (Surtees Society), p. 105; YBB 8 Ed. II (Selden Society, vol. 41), p. 136; 12 & 13 Ed. III (Rolls Series), p. 245; 29 Lib. Ass., pl. 28, f. 163.

genuinely without fault, including theft, appears to be an acceptable plea. In the fifteenth century, however, liability was tightened up. The main evidence for this is the year book discussion in a case which was not one of detinue at all. If a debtor was committed to prison in execution of a judgment, the jailer was responsible for his safe keeping to the judgment creditor, and was himself obliged to meet the debt if the prisoner escaped. Doubts have been raised, but it seems that the jailer was indeed thought of as bailee of the prisoner, and that his liability was thought to be the same as that of any other bailee. There was, however, a relevant procedural difference. The jailer, whose receipt of the prisoner was a matter of record, could not wage his law, or indeed plead the general issue at all. Although there is no reason to think that his liability was theoretically different from that of the bailee, therefore, there was the practical difference that the bailee could and the jailer could not dodge. This question was inexorably raised, as a different question was inexorably raised for a different reason in *Pinnel's Case*.

The jailer had lost the prisoner because the prison was broken open by a mob. The analogy with an ordinary bailment would be loss by robbery, and in the fourteenth century mere theft seems to have been sufficient. But now superior force was rejected, unless it was by the king's enemies; and the point appears to be that the bailee is to be excused only if he has, even in theory, no remedy over because there is no party responsible within the jurisdiction[1]. This linkage between the bailee's liability and his rights against a third party wrongdoer eventually became a kind of chicken-and-egg problem: was the liability deduced from the right of action, or the converse? It was settled in the early years of this century as a matter of law – and, in so far as a court has jurisdiction over the past, also as a matter of history – that the bailee's right of action was the primary thing[2]. It is true that he could always sue the third party

1. YB Hil. 33 Hy. VI, pl. 3, f. 1; E. G. M. Fletcher, *Carrier's Liability* (1932), p. 253.
2. *The Winkfield*, [1902] P. 42; F. Pollock and F. W. Maitland, *History of English Law* (2nd edn.), vol. II, pp. 170 ff; O. W. Holmes, *The Common Law*, Lecture V. The idea that the rights against third parties of a possessor depend upon his liability to the 'owner' is elegant, and had been widely accepted before *The Winkfield*. It was expressly applied to the bailee in *Claridge v South Staffordshire Tramway Co*, [1892] 1 Q.B. 422; and it provides the easiest explanation of the much-discussed judgment of Patteson, J. in *Bridges v Hawkesworth* (1851), 21 L.J.Q.B.(N.S.) 75; 15 Jurist (Part I) 1079.

and that the bailor himself could not until the fourteenth century was nearly over. But to ask whether this or the liability was primary is to think in terms of our analysis of a bailment; it is to assume 'ownership' in the bailor. A bailment began, not as a delivery of possession without ownership, but as a delivery of the thing. The bailee had the thing and could sue third parties, and the bailor had not and could not. The bailee owed the thing as he might have owed money, and his liability was therefore in principle unaffected by the fate of the thing.

The stiffening of liability in the fifteenth century was consolidated in *Southcote's Case* in 1601[1]. Robbery was no plea because the bailee could in theory sue the robber. The only mitigation of this strictness was that the bailee could accept the goods in the first place on special conditions, and these could then be pleaded in detinue. This remained the position as ordered by detinue, but it became unimportant because detinue fell out of use. Bailees came to be sued in actions on the case, and their liability came to be rested either upon what we should call contract or upon what we should call the tort of negligence[2]. There was therefore a break with the past and a fresh beginning; and the later history of the bailee's liability involves different ideas. What matters here is the nature of the break. In negligence the bailee's fault was a necessary part of the bailor's case: the bailee was charged as a wrongdoer. In detinue his innocence was a matter of defence: he was under a prima facie liability arising from the transaction by which he got the object. As against him, detinue was still close kin of debt, and the nature of the liability had not changed much from that implied by his earliest denial: *non tenetur*.

DETINUE NOT BASED UPON TRANSACTIONS

Detinue provides the clearest warning against the assumption that writs represent juridical entities. The claims of buyer against seller and bailor against bailee are as clearly related with debt on a

1. Cro. Eliz. 815; 4 Co. Rep. 83b.
2. *Coggs v Bernard* (1703), 2 Ld. Raymond 909.

contract as they are unrelated with the claims now to be discussed, in which detinue enforces liabilities which are in no way contractual.

The first is of some social importance but not central to our present concern. By custom, surviving to quite modern times in parts of England, the widow and children of a dead man were entitled to a share of his chattels, a half if there were only widow or only children and a third each if there were both; and it was only the remainder that he could dispose of by his will. But all chattel wealth went to the personal representatives, so that widows and children might have to sue for their rightful shares. Their action *de rationabili parte bonorum* was known by the name of detinue, and discussion in an early year book case turns upon the propriety of the writ, which was in common form. That the plaintiff 'does not say that he bought them of us, nor that he bailed them to us, and by no contract are we obliged to him' is the first objection of the defendant executors. But the conceptual argument is overruled by the practical: 'the cause of his writ is a detinue'; and the case goes off on a different point[1]. Reflection suggests that the *praecipe* form would not be appropriate in practice: the render ordered would be definite in form, so much worth of chattels, but reached by calculation itself based upon an estimate. For one or both reasons a special writ was developed almost immediately after this case; and although the substantive complaint was always of detention, it was in *ostensurus quare* form so that there was no formal possibility of forestalling the action by a render[2].

For the principal use of detinue not arising out of a transaction, there was even more obviously nothing like a contractual obligation. But the *praecipe* form of the writ was plainly appropriate in practice, ordering exactly what the plaintiff required; and once adopted it seems never to have been questioned. An ear-marked chattel belonging to the plaintiff has come, no matter how, into the possession of the defendant. The claim rests not upon any transaction but upon the ear-mark. In modern or Roman terms this is the elementary proprietary claim, the claim of owner against possessor.

1. YB 1 & 2 Ed. II (Selden Society, vol. 17), p. 39.
2. The writ in YB 6 & 7 Ed. II (Selden Society, vol. 36), p. 30 bases the claim upon *Magna Carta* (1215), c. 26, (1225), c. 18. The later form bases it upon the custom of the county; *Registrum Omnium Brevium* (1634), f. 142v.

But it first came into being in a world which, as we have sought to emphasise in connection with the bailment, did not work with ideas of ownership and possession. It was also a world which did not separate criminal from civil justice; and the original place of this claim seems to be in the outworks of protection against theft. The loser of a chattel should proclaim his loss in the neighbourhood, particularly in the fairs and markets where honest buying and selling will be done; and if eventually he finds it in the hands of a third party, he will make a claim which may be or become an appeal of felony. The defendant may show that he is honest because he bought it in market overt, or may vouch a private seller against whom, if he warrants, the claim will proceed; and so one may get back to a thief. But the commonest of chattels are beasts, which can go away of their own accord whether from owner or from thief; and what is more, they often look alike. It was therefore too rigorous to force every loser to choose in the end between abandoning his chattel or appealing somebody as a thief; and there was a local process *de re adirata* by which apparently he could just claim the chattel itself[1].

Few chattels would be worth enough to claim in central courts; and appeals and even more their preliminaries were clearly local matters. But at the end of the thirteenth century some such claims seem to have been made by bill before justices in eyre[2]; and this may be why compilers of formularies of counts for royal courts thought it worthwhile to include precedents captioned *De beste adire* or the like[3]. But as a regular institution the eyre was at an end, and with it its humdrum business by bill. If such claims were now to be made in the royal courts, it would have to be in the common pleas and by writ. That the writ issued should be the common form of detinue writ has confused legal historians, and may have done something to confuse the law itself: it brought two distinct kinds of liability under the same 'form of action'. But those were not the terms of thought. The writ ordered the remedy desired, and it may not have occurred to anyone at the time that other than practical considerations were relevant, that a form of

1. See e.g. *Selected Rolls of the Chester City Courts* (Chetham Society, 3rd series, vol. 2), pp. 50, 60.
2. J. M. Kaye, '*Res addiratae* and Recovery of Stolen Goods' (1970) 86 LQR, p. 379; YB 21 & 22 Ed. I (Rolls Series), p. 467.
3. *Novae Narrationes* (Selden Society, vol. 80), B233–4, C337.

writ was to be associated with a particular kind of liability. If there was any discussion in the chancery, the matter would have seemed to be settled by a precedent. The same writ had long been used for the recovery of charters; and charters were the one kind of chattel to which there was plainly a kind of 'title' independent of possession of the document, namely the title to the land itself. The working of this action cannot be discussed here. But, at any rate to one who believes that legal history is largely about the classification of claims, the placing of the writ in registers is interesting. At first it is included with all the other debt-detinue writs; but later it is removed and becomes the only 'detinue' writ to be clearly separated from debt[1].

With ordinary chattels there was no independent title; and extensions from the elementary protection against theft raised difficulties of proof. How can the plaintiff establish that this horse is indeed the one that he somehow lost? A year book note of 1294 says that if the claim is denied the plaintiff must wage his law that the thing had gone from his possession. In pleading terms, the plaintiff was probably denying an assertion by the defendant that the thing found in his possession is another one and his own. But in substance his wager plainly went to identity[2]. In a situation like that of the strayed beast, there was nothing for it but assertion. But often the plaintiff would be able to make a better prima facie case. Although he could not rely on a bailment to the defendant, he could still relate a series of events by which the thing had gone from his hand and come to the defendant's: a bailment to one who had bailed to another who had died leaving the defendant his executor, and so on. And it was probably because such a narrative disposed of the question of identity that the plaintiff would normally count in this way. It is known as the *devenit ad manus,* which was not at first a bald assertion that the thing had come to the defendant's hands but an explanation of how it had so come.

Inherent in this, however, there was a new difficulty. Was it open to the defendant to take up some detail of that narrative? Suppose the plaintiff counted that he had lent to one who had died and whose executor had given the object to the defendant: could the

1. *Early Registers of Writs* (Selden Society, vol. 87), CC 147, 147a, R 485, R 515–7; *Registrum Omnium Brevium* (1634), f. 159v.
2. YB 21 & 22 Ed. I (Rolls Series), p. 467.

defendant escape liability because he had got it from the borrower's widow rather than from his executor? This would be absurd; and the main year book discussion was in a case of 1355 in which the defendant was a woman of the name of Halyday[1]. Almost exactly a century later a new form of count was under discussion in the common pleas. The plaintiff makes no attempt to trace the actual steps by which the thing went from himself to the defendant: he says that he lost it and the defendant found it. This is the famous count in trover, which became standard for plaintiffs in detinue who could not rely upon bailment. And this early appearance was greeted by a whisper which unluckily reached the ears of the reporter and has been a mystery ever since: it was described as a 'new found haliday'[2].

It is not improbable that the speaker was referring to the earlier case. There is much citation in the year books, not of course for the sake of authority in our sense but because cases became known as illustrating a particular line of thought. The 1355 report is the principal discussion of the proposition, apparently decided earlier, that the defendant to a *devenit ad manus* count could not go off on the details: he had to answer the allegation that he detained the plaintiff's property. The point of any narrative in the count, that it established the identity of the thing, was therefore lost, and some pleaders seem indeed to have used *devenit ad manus* as a bare assertion on its own. But most continued to tell a story, and the count in trover was a convenient standard story and proof against legal objection. If, for example, the defendant had actually come to the thing as executor of a former possessor, and the plaintiff said this in his count, it might be objected that the defendant should have been named as executor in the writ. There was no such trap in the story of a loss and finding. But the count in trover may not have been just a happy invention; and if it was, coincidence led the inventor to think of something curiously like the starting-point in *de re adirata*. Establishing identity by following foot-prints, as it were, had quickly proved unworkable, and there was only assertion to fall back on. In 1294, if the year book is to be believed, the effective assertion had to come from the plaintiff[3]. The end of the

1. YB Trin. 29 Ed. III, f. 38v.
2. YB Trin. 33 Hy. VI, pl. 12, f. 26v.
3. YB 21 & 22 Ed. I (Rolls Series), p. 467.

matter was to cast the burden, or the benefit, where it usually fell, upon the defendant's denial. He says that he does not detain the plaintiff's thing.

Among the things which that *non detinet* has concealed from us is the point of this particular story. Thinking of detinue as a form of action representing some single elusive idea, we have imagined *non detinet* as always making essentially the same denial. But the denial is of the liability asserted in the count, and the count on a *devenit ad manus* or a trover asserted a liability entirely distinct from that of the bailee. The difference emerges in the case in which the defendant no longer has the goods by the time the action is brought and the order for their return is formally made. The liability of the bailee arose out of the 'contract' by which he received the goods; and it came to be distinguished from that of the money debtor only by the case of accidental loss, which was thought to excuse him from his prima facie liability. But of course he was still liable if he had deliberately parted with the goods or was to blame for their loss. Merely being out of possession made no difference to his essentially contractual liability; and it would never have occurred to anyone that he could wage his law on *non detinet*, and save his soul by explaining in his prayers that he was not in a literal sense detaining the goods. For him, indeed, the earlier formulation was more appropriate: there would not be even a verbal excuse for *non tenetur*. But for the mere possessor of the ear-marked chattel, the newer form was exactly appropriate, and he may have played a part in the change. He had never been 'held' by an obligation, and *non detinet* could be understood in its most literal sense. If he no longer had the goods when he received the *praecipe* order for their return, he could conscientiously deny detaining them. He might of course be liable to some separate legal claim based upon wrongdoing; and we shall come later to the tort of conversion in which that liability was eventually given expression. But if before the detinue writ was issued he had sold the goods to a third party, even knowingly and dishonestly, he can honestly wage his law without any artifice over the sense of *non detinet*. It is against the third party to whom the goods were sold that the detinue action now lies, if he still has them. The contractual liability of the bailee or vendor is independent of possession; but the proprietary claim lies against only one person at a time, the person who has the goods. It is a self-evident truth which had later to be denied because of the way in which the *praecipe* claims in detinue came to be replaced by the *ostensurus quare* action for conversion. But it seems to have been clear enough to lawyers so long as the two claims were made on the detinue writ[1]. It is only legal historians who failed to see that *non detinet* meant different things because the two claims were different in kind.

ACCOUNT

The last of the old personal actions to be discussed is the action of account. It was of great practical importance in the middle ages, and the idea behind it deserved a better future than it had. The loss, however, is ours, and has been more nearly made good in other common law jurisdictions than in England. Our shifts have not done much to get round the dogma that a monetary relationship between two people must be that of creditor and debtor. The hypothesis behind account was that one could have something like a property right in money in another's hands.

The ordinary form of the writ was a *praecipe* ordering the sheriff to tell the defendant to render rightful account of the plaintiff's money that he had had in a certain capacity. The plaintiff's count set out the relationship upon which he relied, and then followed the writ in demanding just an account. The defendant would generally either deny the relationship or assert that he had already accounted; and if the defendant then failed in his proof, judgment for the plaintiff would order the account.

The judgment thus ordered the performance that the defendant should have rendered willingly, just as a judgment in debt ordered the payment of the debt. The process of accounting was gone through before two auditors. These were appointed by the court if the account had to be ordered by judgment, but were appointed by the claimant himself if the accountant was accounting willingly. It follows that the relationships themselves and the process of accounting were established social institutions; and an account before auditors appointed by the claimant was no less 'official' than

1. YB Pasch. 27 Hy. VIII, pl. 35, f. 13; Brooke, *Abridgment*, Detinue de biens 1; *Anon* (1577), 4 Leonard 189; *Vandrink v Archer* (1590), 1 Leonard 221 at 222.

one taken before auditors appointed by the court. Nor was the process a mere authentication of arithmetic. Factual disputes might have to be settled, for example by ordering wager of law on a disputed payment. And the auditors had powers of allowance and disallowance analogous to those of a district auditor today, or of the tax inspector with a claim for expenses; but their discretion was even wider, and in the fourteenth century the word 'equity' was used to describe it[1].

But it was only the actual process of accounting which could be so described. Whether or not an accountable relationship existed was a question of strict law; and the result of the accounting was equally strict. The balance found due by the auditors was a debt. Although the underlying idea was that the accountant had been handling money 'belonging' to the claimant, there were of course no actual coins that he owned, so that this was the only possible outcome. The account raised a debt, and was itself a sufficient foundation for an action of debt. But at first the claimant hardly ever had to bring one. In 1285 statute conferred upon auditors appointed by the claimant a power which was no doubt inherent in auditors appointed by the court. They could commit the accountant to the king's prison until the amount found due was paid[2]. An accountant so committed could appeal to the court of exchequer by a process called *ex parte talis*; but the power of committal shows the accepted status of accounting and of auditors.

The loss of this status in the course of the fourteenth century is reflected in actions of debt based upon accounts. The only early examples are in the rare situation in which the auditors have found the accountant to be in credit with the claimant. They could not commit the claimant to prison, and so the accountant was obliged to sue for the balance owing to him. But in the later fourteenth century actions begin to appear in which the claimant sues the accountant in debt; and this must mean that the process of committal was failing[3]. The accountable relationships were becoming less clear-cut at this time; and this dilution was evidently accompanied by a loss of status in auditors. The 1285 statute assumed that they would

1. YBB 12 Ed. II (Selden Society, vol. 70), p. 146 at p. 147; Hil. 19 Ed. II, p. 655 at p. 656.
2. Stat. 13 Ed. I (Statute of Westminster II), c. 11.
3. S. F. C. Milsom, 'Account Stated in the Action of Debt' (1966) 82 LQR, p. 534.

be persons of such standing that royal jailers could identify them and know that they had to accept prisoners at their hands. The resort to actions of debt shows that this had ceased to be true: anybody might be an auditor and almost anybody might appoint him.

This is strikingly confirmed by a statute of 1404. We have seen that the action of debt based upon an account was one of the exceptional cases in which wager of law was not available. The accounting before auditors was a matter of record. From the statute, it is clear that tradesmen wishing to claim the amount of their bills were going or affecting to go through some reckoning process, naming their servants or apprentices as 'auditors', and then suing upon this so-called account instead of on the individual items in their bills[1]. By custom in London and elsewhere an acknowledgement before two witnesses of the sum due on a series of transactions was actionable of its own force, and not answerable by wager[2]. And what the tradesman were trying to do was to reach the same result in the king's courts by elevating the witnesses into auditors of an account, and so to oust the defendant from the wager of law with which he was entitled to answer an action on the original debts themselves.

From all this two things emerge. The first is that auditors of a true account lost their status as 'judges of record' in the sense that their power to commit the accountant to prison was more or less lost. The claimant had to sue in debt to get his money. But they retained that status to the extent that when so sued in debt the accountant could not wage his law. This disability, however, was confined to the accountant. If the auditors found him in credit, he could sue the original claimant in debt. But the auditors were not judges of record over the claimant because they could not commit him to prison; and he could therefore wage his law. Another argument sometimes raised in that situation, although deservedly unsuccessful, illuminates the nature of accountability. If the accountant was in credit, it was argued, he must have spent his own money; and since the accounting was concerned only with the claimant's money, this

1. Stat. 5 Hy. IV, c. 8, providing for examination of plaintiffs' attorneys.
2. S. F. C. Milsom, 'Account Stated in the Action of Debt' (1966) 82 LQR, p. 534 at p. 537 and references there cited.

surplus did not lie in account at all[1]. The common law has never had anything like an *actio negotiorum gestorum*, so that if the claimant in such a case had not insisted on an account, the accountant would have been remediless unless he could call it a loan. The argument shows that even an account was not a truly bilateral affair: credits and debits might be made both ways in the actual accounting; but the relationship of accountability was that between an 'owner' of money and one handling it.

That an account was not just a matter of dealings between the parties is the second point illustrated by the 1404 statute. The tradesmen were not conjuring up merely an account and auditors: they were supposing a situation to which an account and auditors would be relevant. Their customers had not been handling their money and were not accountable to them. The relationship was not one of accountability but of debtor and creditor, and the two things were mutually exclusive. An accountant became debtor, or sometimes creditor, when the account was taken; but he was not so before. The money he was handling was in some sense not his, and there was no contract between the parties in the medieval sense of that word.

The earliest accountable relationship was that of lord and bailiff, and it is difficult for us today to understand how important the bailiff was. He might be a man of various social levels and of various areas of responsibility, depending upon the wealth of his master, the administrative methods chosen, and the agrarian structure of the district. But his were the hands in which most of the annual surplus of England first materialised, and his the mind that took many of the decisions producing it. Just as the ultimate control of government as well as revenue was at first in the exchequer, so the bailiff's account checked on more than arithmetic: it controlled the proper and honest use of managerial discretion. The difficulty of ensuring that the equity of an undertaking is enjoyed by its owners rather than by its managers is notorious in any age, and no doubt reflects economic artificiality. In the middle ages, it may have been one cause of the rise of the husbandry lease. Bailiffs tended to be replaced by farmers, or to become farmers in fact if not in name, rendering a fixed sum whether as rent or as conventional 'balance'.

1. YBB Hil. 19 Ed. II, p. 655; Pasch. 29 Ed. III, f.25v; Mich. 10 Hy. VI, pl. 84, f. 24v; 14 Hy. VI, pl. 71, f. 24v; Mich. 38 Hy. VI, pl. 14, f. 5v.

But the bailiff's account remained an important institution, and it was around this that the legal ideas of account first grew[1].

The status and functions of the auditors are wholly intelligible in this context. The identity of a lord's auditors would be as well known as the identity of his bailiff for this manor or that group of manors. And the element of 'equity' lay in their power of judging the bailiff's decisions. Should he have sown corn of his own growing, instead of paying so much to get seed from elsewhere as was normally the best practice? Should he have insisted upon the customary dues when the men were so desperate that they fled? Equally intelligible is the underlying assumption that the money and property handled by the bailiff were not his own. He was not the lord's debtor for the price of the corn he had sold: it was the lord's money, out of which the bailiff had authority to pay for mending the mill. Of course he did not keep two purses. If therefore we argue that the money cannot have been the lord's unless specific coins were, we are pushing the logic that argued against the bailiff found in credit: he must have spent his own money, so his credit balance could not lie in account. Ideas like that of property in a fund are not without difficulty when analysed, but they are a practical need.

The second relationship to be considered, perhaps out of place but characterised by an equal conceptual clarity, is the case of the guardian in socage. The property of infants was dealt with by various kinds of fiduciary arrangement. The testamentary jurisdiction of the church might supervise their personal wealth. Many towns had special arrangements for urban land. Land held by military tenure went beneficially to the lord, subject to an obligation of maintenance and to liability for waste impairing the capital value of the inheritance. And socage land went usually to relations unable to inherit, but not beneficially: they were to administer it on behalf of the infant. In 1267 statute provided a special writ of account to enforce this duty[2]. It was in form unlike the writ against the bailiff or against the receiver to which we shall next turn: instead of being in *praecipe* form it was an *ostensurus*

1. See generally T. F. T. Plucknett, *Legislation of Edward I* (1949), p. 151; *The Medieval Bailiff* (1954), p. 22; N. Denholm-Young, *Seignorial Administration in England* (1937), pp. 120 ff, esp. p. 154.
2. Stat. 52 Hy. III, c. 17.

quare. But the action appears to have worked in much the same way as that against a bailiff except, of course, that the doings of many years might come under scrutiny. In particular, it covered all aspects of the relationship. Unlike the guardian in chivalry, for example, the guardian in socage could not be sued in waste. Nor could the bailiff. In both cases the liability was enforced in the account. Their powers of management were wide; but it was not their property that they were managing and not their money that they were handling.

The third kind of person who was accountable was the 'receiver of the plaintiff's money'; and it was he, less clear even to start with, who was mainly responsible for the loss of distinctness in account. After the early fourteenth century the bailiff was never charged just as bailiff but always as bailiff and receiver. We do not know whether this was to cater for payments made to the bailiff which might be outside his capacity as such, or whether any receipt of money, even for example of manorial rents, made one a receiver. Nor, to look at the converse question, did lawyers know for certain what made a bailiff. Any management of land did, even of a town house. Some thought that any agricultural dealing was enough: the seller of cows would be a bailiff, of silks a receiver. Others thought that any dealing was enough: the seller of silks would be a bailiff; the man sent to collect the price due on a sale by the master would be a receiver. But the early actions against a bailiff do charge him as bailiff only, and it looks as though the receiver is of independent origin and that confusion arose because the two things grew together rather than because they failed to separate[1].

If so, the origin of the receiver is probably, though not certainly, mercantile. The other possibility is the mere collector of money rents, ecclesiastical dues and so on. But the mercantile receiver seems to come first, mere agents being quickly followed by partners. In the early cases these arrangements look like relationships lasting for some time. But, as with mercantile agents in more modern times, the difficulty of drawing a line led to the result that a status might have to be postulated for a single transaction. And this in turn led to an artificiality in the use to which account was put. If a hundred payments to a merchant's agent lie in account,

1. S. F. C. Milsom, *Novae Narrationes* (Selden Society, vol. 80), p.clxxx; T. F. T. Plucknett, *The Medieval Bailiff* (1954), p. 24, n. 2.

why not a single payment to one to pay over to another? That other did not of course authorise the receipt, but nor did the merchant authorise any particular receipt. In so far as such situations were not easily accessible in debt, the result was also convenient, utilising the idea of property to give a remedy where there was no contract between the parties. But it had nothing to do with accounting; and yet presumably, against an obdurate defendant, the action establishing the receipt, the relationship, had to be followed by a formal accounting to establish that the money had not already been paid over to the plaintiff or the like[1].

This leads to the last aspect of account to be considered, more for the light it throws on the other actions than for its own sake. The defendant could not plead 'Not accountable', a general denial like *non debet*, perhaps because the duty to account was distinct from the duty to pay the balance. Suppose that a receiver had received the plaintiff's money, and had in fact paid it to the plaintiff. His receipt raised a duty to account which had not been discharged, even though when auditors heard the account they would find that there was no balance due to the plaintiff. But in such a case the accountant would, if the possibility was open to him, inevitably and understandably plead a general 'Not accountable', and so by-pass the accounting which, especially in the case of the bailiff, was the necessary aim of the action.

There was in short no general issue in account. Unless there were special circumstances such as a deed saying that he was not to be accountable, the defendant had either to deny that an accountable relationship had existed, or to admit that it had and plead that he had accounted. The latter plea had always to go to a jury, and the same seems to have become true of a denial by one charged as bailiff that he had been so. There was reluctance to allow any rights over land to be subjected to wager: one example already noted was in the action of debt brought for rent, and another was the action of detinue for charters. In principle, however, one charged as receiver could wage his law upon his denial that he had been receiver. The receipt might have been in private, and so not within a jury's knowledge. But if it had not been in private he could be ousted from his wager; and it became settled that if the plaintiff alleged receipt

1. See generally S. J. Stoljar, 'The Transformations of Account' (1964) 80 LQR, p. 203.

by the hand of somebody other than himself – and this became a conventional form – he could insist that a denial should be tried by jury[1].

This reasoning, however, depended upon the absence of a general issue which would comprehend both a denial that liability had been created and an assertion that it had been discharged. It was not applicable to debt on a contract or to detinue: however publicly a loan had been made, it might have been discharged by private payment. These actions were therefore poised upon one horn of the dilemma of proof: the availability of wager and the generality of the general issue probably caused injustice, and certainly retarded legal development. Debt on an obligation and covenant were caught on the other horn: the general issue was excluded and precision ensured at the cost of the opposite injustice, too much strictness, and at the cost of a formality which became increasingly oppressive as forty thirteenth-century shillings dwindled to their sixteenth-century value.

By the early seventeenth century the old personal actions were for better or worse effectively dead. Covenant and debt still had to be used if the action was based upon a document under seal; and incorporated companies, which had to contract under seal, found themselves at a curious disadvantage against their unincorporated rivals. The old actions had to be brought against them, and the old rules prevented them from pleading the general issue; and they had to procure legislation allowing them to do this. But the survival of the contract under seal, still a force in England, has provided a way of making gratuitous promises enforceable without artificiality. This may be partly why the full-blooded law of promissory estoppel which developed in the United States has not been found necessary in England. That development, by which reliance upon another's promise can be the basis of a remedy even if the promise would not in itself be otherwise enforceable, is curiously parallel to the way in which the old single duties of the *praecipe* writs became submerged under a welter of *ostensurus quare* claims for harms suffered in the context of a transaction between the parties. But before turning to that process, the rise of the *ostensurus quare* writs themselves must be explained.

1. S. F. C. Milsom, 'Sale of Goods in the Fifteenth Century' (1961) 77 LQR, p. 257 at p. 261, and references there cited.

11 *The Rise of Trespass and Case*

By the eighteenth century almost all litigation at common law was being conducted in *ostensurus quare* actions of trespass and case. Trespass was now a term of art referring to *ostensurus quare* writs alleging a breach of the king's peace, which had become common during the thirteenth century. Although these writs covered various harms to persons, goods and land, they were understood as representing a single entity: the essence of trespass was direct forcible injury. It was for the origins of trespass so understood that historians looked, seeking earlier entities from which it might have developed. One suggestion looked to the assize of novel disseisin, itself of course seen as simple protection against wrongdoers: suppose an invader to have beaten the tenant and his household, reaped crops, taken chattels, and then left the land so that the assize was not needed[1]. Another suggestion looked to the appeal of felony, envisaging some truncation whereby the gravest criminal charge and penalty were foregone and just compensation sought[2]. Both suggestions saw procedural and conceptual developments occurring essentially within the law of the king's courts.

Actions on the case by the eighteenth century covered the remainder of our law of torts and almost the whole of our law of contract; and by contast with the direct forcible injury of trespass they were identified with consequential harm. They were begun by *ostensurus quare* writs which did not allege a breach of the king's peace, but did describe the factual background more fully in a

1. G. E. Woodbine, 'The Origins of the Action of Trespass' (1924) 33 Yale Law Journal, p. 799; (1925) 34, p. 343.
2. F. W. Maitland, *The Forms of Action at Common Law*, (separate edn., 1936), pp. 48 ff; F. Pollock and F. W. Maitland, *History of English Law* (2nd edn.), vol. II, p. 526. See also H. G. Richardson and G. O. Sayles, *Select Cases of Procedure without Writ* (Selden Society, vol. 60), pp. cviii ff.

preamble introduced by the word *cum* (whereas). These actions began to appear in the king's courts about 1370; and historians did not have to look far for their origin. Their full name 'trespass on the case' seemed to show that they were a development from trespass, a conscious reaching out from the central idea of direct forcible injury; and tradition attributed the extension to a statutory provision of 1285 giving the chancery clerks power to frame new writs *in consimili casu* with existing remedies[1]. The tradition is old, and may have influenced legal development in the sixteenth century. But it turned out that the statutory clause, itself an afterthought to the filling of certain small gaps, had only minor and more or less immediate effects, all in the land law. Other suggestions were therefore made, but still assuming that actions on the case were an extension from the central entity of trespass[2].

That assumption underlay the classical account of the growth of the modern law of contract and tort; and elementary legal argument was in consequence represented as the almost unreasoned interplay of forms. More fundamental was the tacit inference that the extension of remedies to other than direct forcible injuries had to do with the onset of civilisation. The story does not begin in a world in which the law can understand only violent wrongs, and there was no central entity. There were only limits upon the kinds of wrong with which the king's courts would deal[3].

1. Stat. 13 Ed. I (Statute of Westminster II), c. 24.
2. The traditional view was guardedly accepted by F. W. Maitland, *The Forms of Action* (1936), p. 51. It was destroyed by T. F. T Plucknett, 'Case and the Statute of Westminster II' (1931) 31 Columbia Law Review, p. 778. This article was attacked by W. S. Holdsworth in a note in (1931) 47 LQR, p. 334; and by P. A. Landon, 'The Action on the Case and the Statute of Westminster II' (1936) 52 LQR, p. 68. See Plucknett's answer to this last, 'Case and Westminster II', op. cit., p. 220. It was then suggested that although statute had played no part, case was derived from trespass by a common law development. See E. J. Dix, 'The Origins of the Action of Trespass on the Case' (1937) 46 Yale Law Journal, p. 1142; and this view was adopted in C. H. S. Fifoot, *History and Sources of the Common Law* (1949), pp. 66 ff.
3. The view set out in this chapter was stated at documented length in S. F. C. Milsom, 'Trespass from Henry III to Edward III' (1958) 74 LQR, pp. 195, 407, 561; and references in this chapter to (1958) 74 LQR, are to that series of articles. See also G. D. G. Hall, 'Some Early Writs of "Trespass"' (1957) 73 LQR, p. 65. Further light will be shed by a forthcoming Selden Society volume of fourteenth century trespass cases edited by Professor Morris S. Arnold.

THE EARLY TREATMENT OF WRONGS

In the middle ages the word trespass, Latin *transgressio*, means just wrong. We have misunderstood the early development by reading back a later and narrower meaning, and by imagining substantive ideas where contemporaries were concerned only with jurisdiction and proof.

Glanvill in the late twelfth century describes pleas as either civil or criminal; but his distinction is not ours[1]. Civil pleas are those concerning land and the old personal actions; and all wrongs are criminal, presumably because there is offence to the community as well as to the victim so that penal consequences may follow. But of course penal consequences did not exclude redress for the victim; and if he himself brought the charge home to the wrongdoer, then he might recover goods taken or obtain other compensation, and the wrongdoer would still be punished. Early law-suits revolved around proof; and the essence of the victim's role in such proceedings lay not in their initiation, as has been supposed, but in his making the proof. He was a witness; and if the charge was one of those grave wrongs known as felonies, his proof would be by his body, by battle. Battle had been introduced by the Conqueror for Normans only; and its appropriation to the writ of right and the appeal of felony, irrespective of national origin, is probably connected with the appropriation of the word felony, originally the breach of a man's homage obligations to his lord, to those grave wrongs involving escheat of lands. Trespass was then left to denote the whole range of lesser wrongs; and for these, lesser proofs presumably continued undisturbed by the Conqueror's innovation. They were of the nature of those already considered. If the victim could produce other witnesses to the fact, for example, there might be some inquest procedure. But if he tendered only the usual good suit, the defendant could traditionally prove his denial by wager of law.

But even for a felony there might be nobody who could swear as witness. There might be a wrong without a victim. And sometimes, perhaps, the community interest would require that somebody be charged as a wrongdoer, a common night-walker, for example, or even a common thief, without reference to any specific misdeed. In

1. *Glanvill*, I, 1 (ed. G. D. G. Hall, p. 3).

all such cases the initiative could be taken only by some official such as a bailiff. But even he, as the Great Charter had to re-emphasise, could not put a man to answer by his own bare word[1]. He had to bring witnesses, but not of course necessarily witnesses to the fact. Their testimony was like that of good suit, enough to put the defendant to his denial: and those who testified to the suspicion of the countryside were to become, in the king's courts, the indicting jury of the classical common law.

JURISDICTION OVER TRESPASS

The line between felonies on the one hand and trespasses on the other did not correspond with a jurisdictional boundary. If Glanvill could have written down a list of felonies, which is far from certain, he would probably have included theft. It carried forfeiture of chattels and escheat of land, though the lord's escheat was not subject to the prior right of stripping the land which the king had after other felonies[2]. But for Glanvill theft was not a plea of the crown: it was indeed the only kind of wrong which he assigns directly to the sheriff in his county[3]. Many trespasses, on the other hand, were matters for the king's own courts. Whether suit is made by a private accuser or on behalf of authority, the appropriate court to hear a trespass is that of the authority whose 'peace' has been broken. We should not think of peace in our sense, an antonym of violence, but of protection, law. It was not a mere abstraction but belonged to a person, usually the king or the lord. Glanvill makes it clear, in three words which have been overlooked, that for him the primary jurisdiction over trespass was that of lords. Beatings and such come to the sheriff only *per defectum dominorum*, and not even then if a breach of the king's peace is alleged[4]. A hundred years later, although manorial courts are certainly hearing trespasses, not all merely petty, we shall see that the king's courts regard the sheriff's as the primary forum for cases in which the king's own

1. *Magna Carta* (1215), c. 38; (1225), c. 28.
2. *Glanvill*, VII, 17 (ed. G. D. G. Hall, p. 91).
3. *Glanvill*, I, 2 and XIV, 8 (ed. G. D. G. Hall, pp. 4, 177).
4. *Glanvill*, I, 2 (ed. G. D. G. Hall, p. 4). See also *Bracton*, f. 154b (ed. Woodbine-Thorne, vol. II, p. 436).

peace is not said to have been broken. It is not only land law that was affected by the central shift in the structure of society.

Glanvill lists the king's peace broken among the pleas of the crown; and in his time it was a serious matter[1]. He might give his peace to his servants, his favourites, those who might pay for the privilege. It might be widened at the great feasts of the church, or extended to all persons in certain places, wherever the king was, the king's highway. It was in short a personal thing and not a governmental abstraction; and for example, it died with the king. It follows that what made a breach of the king's peace was not the intrinsic quality of the act, but the person, the place, even the season. The same act, or one more outrageous, might in other circumstances be a breach only of a lesser lord's peace or the sheriff's; and proceedings would then be in the lord's or the county court.

The change by which breach of the king's peace was supposed to depend only upon the intrinsic quality of the act cannot be followed from the records: we have only the allegation and no way of relating it to the facts. In the 'criminal' context of trespasses presented on the king's behalf, it was no doubt a matter of policy. And as the word trespass began to acquire a distinct 'civil' sense, these criminal trespasses, offences less than felony, came to be known by the alternative name of misdemeanours. Our concern is with 'civil' trespasses, in which the initiative is taken by the victim. The allegation of breach of the king's peace makes it a plea of the crown, and as such, as the Great Charter reaffirmed, outside the sheriff's competence[2]. But about the middle of the thirteenth century such cases begin to appear on the common pleas section of an eyre roll. And by about the end of the century it is reasonably clear that the allegation is being inserted not because of any element in the facts but because the plaintiff desires some consequence, presumably that of royal jurisdiction. He can, as it were, choose his court. In the printed *Register of Writs* there are two kinds of trespass writ. The first set of precedents is captioned *De transgressione in comitatu*; and the first writ is a writ of battery not alleging breach of the king's peace, and followed by a warning that neither *vi et armis* nor *contra pacem nostram* must be mentioned 'because the sheriff cannot deal

1. *Glanvill*, I, 2 (ed. G. D. G. Hall, p. 3).
2. *Magna Carta* (1215), c. 24; (1225), c. 17.

with those'. The second set of precedents is captioned *De transgressione in banco*; and the first writ is another writ of battery, this time alleging that the act was done *vi et armis* and *contra pacem nostram*. And this arrangement in registers, dividing viscontiel from returnable writs, goes back at least to the early fourteenth century[1].

We do not know how this situation had come about, and the viscontiel writs of trespass are part of the puzzle. What was their purpose? The sheriff cannot in principle have needed royal authorisation to hear an ordinary trespass in the county court; and it seems that even the forty-shilling ceiling on local jurisdictions was not applied to trespass until much later. So long as trespasses were primarily for lords' courts, it is possible that sheriffs might sometimes refuse to act without a direct order. If so, the viscontiel writs may be old. But they do not appear in manuscript registers until near the end of the thirteenth century; and if they were first formulated so late, they were probably part of an attempt to return to county courts cases which plaintiffs were for one reason or another trying to bring to the king's court. That attempt was embodied in a provision in the Statute of Gloucester in 1278: sheriffs were to hear pleas of trespass in their counties as the custom was[2].

Six years earlier Henry III had died after more than half a century as king; and it was only during the last half of his reign that 'civil' trespass actions had become common in royal courts. It is not impossible that artifice had been common from the beginning in allegations that the king's peace had been broken, another consequence of the decline of seignorial jurisdiction. It is reasonably certain that the ending of Henry's peace upon his death caused jurisdictional confusion. Even if it had been broken by a wrong done in his lifetime, an action brought after his death could not refer to it. And as a not unnatural consequence, there was a freshet of actions in which no breach of the king's peace could have been alleged even if that king had still been alive[3]. The statute sought to

1. *Registrum Omnium Brevium* (ed. 1634), f. 92; *Early Registers of Writs* (Selden Society, vol. 87), R283 ff and R299 ff.
2. Stat. 6 Ed. I, c. 8. See G. D. G. Hall, *Early Registers of Writs* (Selden Society, vol. 87), p. cxxxii, and J. S. Beckerman, 'The Forty-Shilling Jurisdictional Limit', *Legal History Studies 1972*, p. 110.
3. (1958) 74 LQR, pp. 576 ff.

restore a jurisdictional principle that was being forgotten or ignored; and formally it succeeded. Almost all trespass actions in the king's courts were soon alleging breach of the king's peace again. They were even emphasising it with a further allegation that the wrong had been done with force and arms. Previously this had been common only in cases involving some invasion of land; but by the end of the century it is almost invariable in trespass writs[1]. But *vi et armis* seems to have been no less artificial than *contra pacem regis* itself.

This artificiality shows itself in various ways. In 1304 a jury found a defendant 'Guilty' but tried to add, for a reason to be mentioned shortly, 'but it was not done *vi et armis*[2]. Unreality is also implicit in the conventional expansion of that phrase in trespass counts. Although knives and sticks and stones sometimes feature in the king's bench, almost all trespasses in the more conventional common pleas turn out to have been committed 'with force and arms, to wit with swords and bows and arrows'[3]. Sometimes, moreover, it is obvious not only that weapons played no part but also that the wrong complained of did not accord with later notions of trespass *vi et armis*. In 1317 a plaintiff counted that he had bought a tun of wine from the defendants, and had left it with them until he could arrange for its transportation; the defendants however, with force and arms to wit with swords and bows and arrows, drew off much of the wine and replaced it with salt water, so that the wine was wholly spoilt, to the plaintiff's great damage and against the king's peace[4]. Those defendants had committed a wrong, a trespass, for which the plaintiff could certainly have got a local remedy. But Glanvill's breach of the peace has sunk to a pair of incantations put in to get the dispute into a royal court.

Blatant cases like that are rare for the next half century, not, it seems, because plaintiffs were not bringing such actions in royal courts but because their lawyers were being discreet. As with the universal adoption of the *vi et armis* allegation, moreover, it seems that their discretion was in the interest of propriety rather than because the actions were objectionable. The evidence comes from

1. Op. cit.(in the preceding note).
2. YB 32 & 33 Ed. I (Rolls Series), p. 259.
3. (1958) 74 LQR, p. 222.
4. YB 10 Ed. II (Selden Society, vol. 54), p. 140. Was it just a sale of adulterated wine? Cf. YB 7 Ed. II (Selden Society, vol. 39), p. 14.

cases of varying facts, but the point can most easily be made in terms of an action against a smith for professional negligence: he injured the plaintiff's horse in shoeing it, and the horse died. In a local court the plaintiff would have a straightforward remedy. But he could not be straightforward if he wanted to come to a royal court, because he had to allege breach of the king's peace. If he simply added the allegations to the plaint he would make in a local court, his writ would run something like this: why with force and arms the defendant in shoeing the horse drove his nails into the quick of its hoof so that it died, to the plaintiff's damage and against the king's peace. This is the equivalent of the writ obtained by the buyer of the tun of wine; and an objection actually made in that case but not pressed came to be fatal. The complaint was in the technical sense repugnant within itself. It showed that the horse was lawfully handed to the defendant, or the wine lawfully left in his possession; and whatever he then did to it, however wrongful, could not be in breach of the king's peace. If a document is bad because self-contradictory, it can be cured only by excising one allegation or the other. To excise the *vi et armis* and *contra pacem* left the good complaint from which the plaintiff had started: but it was not a plea of the crown, and so not within the jurisdiction of a royal court. To bring the matter to a royal court, therefore, he had to excise the other allegation, that which showed that the object was lawfully in the defendant's possession. Instead of complaining that the smith did his work so badly that the horse died, his writ would run something like this: why with force and arms the defendant killed the plaintiff's horse, to his damage and against the king's peace. The count would follow the writ, the defendant would plead Not guilty, the jury would find him Guilty or Not guilty, and the record would look like that of an action for malicious injury by a stranger. Knowledge of what happened in later times might make us suspect that it was really a road accident or the like. But were it not for the chinks of a few unusual cases, there would be nothing to make us suspect the truth, except this: the defendants in many such actions for killing horses are named or described as smiths[1].

About 1370 the story of the smith's liability reached its happy ending. The chancery sealed and the court upheld a writ in the form of the old local court plaint, without any allegation of breach of the

1. (1958) 74 LQR, pp. 220–1, 562–7, 585–7.

peace: why the smith drove his nails into the quick of the horse's hoof so that it died, or so that it was injured and unable to work[1]. Other writs appear at about the same time complaining of wrongs but with no allegation that they had been done *vi et armis* or *contra pacem regis*. A decision had evidently been taken that the king's courts would hear wrongs, trespasses, even though they were not pleas of the crown. This decision was the 'origin' of actions on the case in the king's courts. But the history behind the smith shows that in some situations at any rate the change was a formal one. Neither the liability nor its substantive enforcement in royal courts was new.

Since the facts are nearly always hidden behind formal pleadings and a blank general verdict, we cannot be sure what liabilities had come to be so enforced behind a fictitious *contra pacem regis*. Considering what happened to the smith, for example, it would not be surprising if some actions for battery turned out to be against surgeons, for whose professional negligence an action on the case quickly appeared. But there is a range of situations in which some accident disarranged the formalities enough for us to catch a glimpse of the underlying facts. The *vi et armis* writ for cattle trespass was first used for acts which were deliberate and perhaps violent: animals were driven into the plaintiff's land by way of asserting a right of common. But it had been extended to the case of straying animals when wrongs could still not come into royal courts unless *contra pacem* was alleged; and in this case the writ was never modified as was the smith's to make an honest action on the case. Nor was this a curiosity without consequence: in the twentieth century the defendant owner would still be liable without the affirmative showing of fault which became necessary in an action on the case. For another wrong concerning animals, a modified and straightforward writ was promptly devised: the *scienter* action, which will be examined in another context, appears as one of the earliest actions on the case. But the same liability had at least once been earlier imposed under cover of a *vi et armis* writ alleging that the defendant had set his dogs on to do the damage[2]. Equally illuminating are writs concerning abductions. The husband's action

1. *The Farrier's Case*, 1372: YB Trin. 46 Ed. III, pl. 19, f. 19.
2. Cattle trespass: Glanville Williams, *Liability for Animals* (1939), p. 127; (1958) 74 LQR, p. 202. *Scienter*: pp. 310 ff, below.

on the case for enticement of his wife appears as a new tort in 1745[1]. Before that date, so far as the legal records go, Englishmen had kept austerely to kidnapping. The Statute of Labourers provided an action for the master whose servant was enticed away, but it covered only servants. In the printed *Register of Writs* there is a precedent about an apprentice abducted *vi et armis*, and an apologetic note explains that it is necessary because the statute does not cover apprentices[2]. Another special situation is that of fire. An early action on the case was that for the careless keeping of a fire in the defendant's house, so that the neighbouring house of the plaintiff was burnt; but a case of 1368, also to be mentioned later for another reason, suggests that the same liability had been enforced in the king's courts by the writ appropriate to arson[3]. This writ was used also in another misleading situation, a pair to that of the kidnapped apprentice. If tenant for life or for years burned a house down, he was made liable by action of waste. But there was no writ of waste for use against tenant at will, and resort was had to the writ of trespass *vi et armis*[4].

We know what had been happening. But we cannot be sure why, or exactly what change was intended about 1370. Was it just to obviate existing fictions, or positively to admit trespass in general? The latter is more likely, because there seems to have been a short-lived school of thought which would achieve the result by ignoring repugnancy and putting *contra pacem* into every returnable trespass writ. About 1370 the allegation appears briefly and incongruously in the writs for certain exceptional wrongs which had long been coming in without it[5]. Other wrongs, in which the allegation could never colourably have been made, soon came to be admitted for the first time. The customary liability of the innkeeper, for example, was for the acts of other people, and he could not sensibly have been charged with a breach of the king's peace. But it is interesting that the earliest action, in 1368, was brought by a royal officer on the king's behalf as well as his own, and alleged contempt of the king[6]. Or consider the sale of a diseased horse deceitfully

1. *Winsmore v Greenbank*, Willes 577.
2. *Registrum Omnium Brevium* (ed. 1634), f. 109.
3. YB 42 Lib. Ass., pl. 9, f. 259v.
4. YB Mich. 48 Ed. III, pl. 8, f. 25.
5. See p. 302, below.
6. YB Pasch. 42 Ed. III, pl. 13, f. 11; 42 Lib. Ass., pl. 17, f. 260v.

warranted sound. As early as 1307 a buyer had sued in the king's court, but again only because he was on the king's service[1]. The ordinary plaintiff could hardly represent the wrong as *contra pacem*: but it might seem capricious that he could not get to the king's court when the smith's ill-used customer could.

But if the decision about 1370 was directly to accommodate such plaintiffs, we must not misunderstand its scale. Not all kinds of wrong could now come in. Defamation, a familiar local trespass, was not to appear in the king's courts until about 1500. And of those wrongs that could come in, not many did. Whatever the pressure for change, it was not that of a numerically large demand. Until the sixteenth century there was only a small though steady flow of actions on the case. Most plaintiffs must have been content to stay in their local courts; and the real question may be why these exceptional ones wanted royal justice, and had earlier been making such flights of fiction to obtain it. Local bias is one possibility. Growing confusion about the forty-shilling limit is another. Speed and, as we shall see, perhaps also spite may have played a part. And another possibility would make the jurisdictional consequence secondary. An allegation of breach of the king's peace precluded a defendant from waging his law. Some plaintiffs may possibly have inserted it primarily to secure this result. And hindsight can see that a consequential decision of the royal courts was almost as important as their decision to admit cases without the allegation. Despite an unambiguous statement of the logic[2], they did not allow wager of law in actions upon the case, any more than they allowed related logic to confine such actions to the court of common pleas. They just accepted the reality which fiction had produced.

The fiction was not without harm to defendants; and their grievance may have played some part in the relaxation of 1370. Because breach of the king's peace had been a serious offence against the king, *capias* had always been available to make the defendant answer; and if he was convicted it would issue again to secure his imprisonment until he both made fine with the king and satisfied the plaintiff for his damages. The fine to the king became standardised and unimportant; but we do not yet know when that

1. *Select Cases in the Court of King's Bench*, vol. III (Selden Society, vol. 58), p. 179.
2. YB Hil. 48 Ed. III, pl. 11, f. 6.

happened, and so do not know how long the *contra pacem* allegation carried a real penalty. The *capias* itself came to be seen as process in the interest of the plaintiff, as appears from events following the deposition and death of Edward II. There could be no arrest for breach of the peace of a former king, and an outcry about the hardship to plaintiffs thereby deprived of effective process for the damages they had been awarded led in 1328 to a statute: process for trespasses committed under Edward II was to be the same as for those committed under the new king[1]. But ordinarily the *capias* still followed formally from the *contra pacem*; and it seems for example that a royal pardon of the fine would lift it[2]. In 1352 statute extended *capias*, of course just as process and with no fine to the king, to most other personal actions[3]. Trespass was not mentioned because only *contra pacem* trespasses were then ordinarily coming to the king's court; and the *capias* consequence of a 'fictitious' *contra pacem* would thereafter seem less of a hardship. But it remained an anomaly, aggravated by even a standard fine; and the anomaly survived the relaxation of 1370. Although trespass writs could now come to royal courts without the allegation, there was nothing except the repugnancy danger to stop a plaintiff inserting it; and when it was colourable he generally did.

Defendants can be heard grumbling about this, though surprisingly rarely, throughout the fourteenth century. As early as 1304 a jury found defendants guilty of cutting trees, but tried to add that it was not done *vi et armis*: *capias* was ordered notwithstanding their rider[4]. In 1320, after an unusual special verdict, a court actually declined to order *capias*: but the writ itself showed that the *contra pacem* was fictitious because the goods had been delivered to the defendant, and a little later it would have been quashed as internally repugnant[5]. The grievance was ventilated without avail in 1378. In a *vi et armis* action for damaging the plaintiff's house and removing

1. Stat. 2 Ed. III, c. 13; petitions described in G. O. Sayles, *Select Cases in the Court of King's Bench*, vol. IV (Selden Society, vol. 74), p. xv; YB Hil. 1 Ed. III, pl. 10, f. 2. Cf. YBB 3 Ed. II (Selden Society, vol. 20), p. 104; 10 Ed. II (Selden Society, vol. 52), p. 159. Other references in (1958) 74 LQR, p. 574.
2. YB 11 & 12 Ed. III (Rolls Series), p. 609.
3. Stat. 25 Ed. III, stat. 5, c. 17.
4. YB 32 & 33 Ed. I (Rolls Series), p. 259.
5. Morris S. Arnold, 'Accident, Mistake, and Rules of Liability in the Fourteenth-Century Law of Torts' (1979) 128 University of Pennsylvania Law Review, p. 361 at p. 371.

tiles, the defendant pleaded that trivial damage was done by building materials which accidentally fell when his own abutting house was being repaired. We shall return to the form of his plea in connection with liability for accident. But unless the fall had been caused by something like a thunderbolt, he was clearly liable; and his real concern was the unfairness of a *contra pacem* action, with its fine to the king, for damage both trivial and unintentional. One judge sympathised, suggesting that the plea would have been good if it had alleged a tender of amends[1]. That was a well-meaning muddle. Even in cattle-trespass, where the damage was often trivial and unintentional, the defendant could not by tender stop the action of a persistent plaintiff, and so could not avoid the *capias* and fine[2]. So long as the formalities were in order, it seems that even a 'fictitious' *contra pacem* had its inexorable consequences. The defendant could only plead Not guilty; no jury would deprive the plaintiff of redress for a genuine wrong on the ground that it was not genuinely *contra pacem*; and their verdict of Guilty would attract the *capias* and whatever was involved in the fine to the king[3].

LIABILITY IN TRESPASS *VI ET ARMIS*

The special pleas found in actions of trespass *vi et armis* seem to follow the usual principle: they are permitted when the blank denial would be in some way misleading. The statements in the plaintiff's count were true; the general issue might seem to deny them; the defendant may therefore plead in confession and avoidance. Pleadings designed to raise proprietary questions became complex and disingenuous; but the ordinary pleas in justification are much

1. YB 2 Ric. II (Ames Foundation), p. 69.
2. YB Mich. 21 Hy. VII, pl. 9, f. 30; *Kent v Wichall* (1590), Owen 48; *Cubit v Harrison* (1601), Cro. Eliz. 820. Tender permitted under Stat. 21 Jac. I, c. 16, s. 5. The confusion arose because tender was relevant if the animals were distrained *damage feasant* and the owner had to bring replevin.
3. Professor Morris S. Arnold has made the interesting suggestion that there were in effect two liabilities: a strict liability to the plaintiff for damages, and a distinct 'criminal' liability to the king: 'Accident, Mistake, and Rules of Liability in the Fourteenth-Century Law of Torts' (1979) 128 University of Pennsylvania Law Review, p. 361 at pp. 370 ff. But it is hard to imagine how this could work in practice.

what one would expect. Jailers and peace officers plead that they were acting in the course of their duty. Defendants who say they are the plaintiff's kin admit that they shut him up and beat him: he was having a fit, and this was the treatment[1]. One sued for knocking the plaintiff's house down had knocked it down: fire had engulfed neighbouring houses, and he and others were trying to make a fire-break to stop it spreading[2]. Such pleas in justification normally ended with words like 'as well he might', an assertion that the act done was lawful. Similar, but not quite a plea of justification, was *son assault demesne*: the defendant in battery could say that the plaintiff had started the trouble and he had only defended himself, so that any harm that came to the plaintiff was his own doing. Any such plea could be answered in one of two ways. If the plaintiff denied the defendant's facts, he made the replication *de injuria*. If for example the alleged epileptic was not having a fit, he would say that the defendant had acted of his own wrong and without any such cause. If he admitted the facts but thought that they did not constitute a valid excuse in law, he would demur. The epileptic who was having a fit, but thought it wrong to drive out the devils by beating him, would say that the plea was insufficient in law to disable him from his action. This last, however, is rarely found, because discussion before the plea was formally made and entered would indicate the general opinion of its legal validity. If a defendant thought his proposed plea might fail on demurrer, he would not risk making it; and the case would then go off on the general issue.

We may never know what could lie behind the general issue in the middle ages, or for long after. Sometimes, perhaps generally as in criminal trials today, the defendant who pleaded Not guilty really meant 'It was not me'. But the important question is whether and when and in what sense he might mean 'It was not my fault'. If he could not put that to the jury on the general issue, he could not put it at all. In the whole of the year books there is no special plea of accident in trespass, and this led most historians to think that liability was strict or absolute, that if the defendant had in any sense done the harm he was liable. And some conjectured that the automatic liability came to be questioned only after the invention of

1. YB 22 Lib. Ass., pl. 56, f. 98.
2. KB 26/201, m.7d. Cf. Dyer 36b; *Mouse's Case* (1608), 12 Co. Rep. 63.

gunpowder and other forms of stored power, which enabled harm to be done out of all proportion to what ordinary people would regard as the fault involved. Medieval man could more easily foresee what his own strength might do, or that of his horse. But speculation must be based upon the procedural possibilities. The defendant did knock the plaintiff down, and the plaintiff is suing him for battery; how, if at all, can the defendant say that his horse bolted or that the plaintiff suddenly ran across the road?

The plea rolls bear out the year books: there was no special plea. To this there is an interesting early exception. In 1290 a *contra pacem* writ is brought against two defendants for burning the plaintiff's house down. But, as in the case of the tun of wine a quarter of a century later, the count does not show a genuinely *contra pacem* wrong. The plaintiff says that the defendants were guests in his house, and caused the harm by foolishness with an unwatched candle. The defendants expressly plead accident, and that special plea is put to a jury. The jury find that when the second of the two defendants went to bed on the night in question, a third guest would not let him put the candle out and then himself went away leaving it burning. They also assessed damages in case the defendants should be held liable on these facts, but no judgment is recorded[1]. Not until modern times could one find a pair to that modern-looking entry; but this is probably because such cases are hidden behind forms rather than because civilisation went backwards.

To take first the matter of the count, it has been noted in connection with the smith that writ and count came to be adjusted so that *contra pacem* looked sensible, and was not repugnant to the facts as stated. In the case of the smith the facts as stated then looked like malicious injury by a stranger. And in the case of the 1290 fire, if the facts repeated themselves half a century later, the writ and the count would look like simple arson. There would be no mention that the defendants were guests, and no allegation that they were foolish. Nor would there be any special plea denying fault, or probably any account of what really happened in a special verdict. The plaintiff's facts would have been hidden under standard formal allegations. Are we to suppose that this pleading change made the defendant's facts simply irrelevant, imposing upon him an absolute

1. *Select Cases in the Court of King's Bench*, vol. I (Selden Society, vol. 55), p. 181.

liability? Or is there just a pleading change on his side too? Why do we find no special pleas of accident after 1290? There is year book evidence that at about that time teachers were saying in connection with waste and replevin – there is no direct evidence about trespass *contra pacem* – that accident should not be raised specially: the general issue should be pleaded and the matter left to the jury[1]. We do not know the reason for this advice. It may have been human rather than technical, and based on the hope that a jury would be lenient. Or it may have sprung from perception of a point to be made explicit centuries later: 'Not my fault' is in the end indistinguishable from 'not me'. It was indeed made explicit in the words of the general issue itself: *In nullo est inde culpabilis*, in no way is he to blame. The defendant's case is that he did not cause the harm and therefore he should not confess the fact at all, as he would if pleading a justification.

The clearest statement of the proposition was as late as 1695; but law-suits arising out of accidents must always be frequent, and it was no doubt common knowledge. In an action for battery the defendant pleaded specially that he was riding on his horse, the horse bolted, he shouted a warning but the plaintiff failed to jump clear, and so he ran him down by accident. He was held liable, not because the liability was absolute but because he had pleaded wrongly. He had confessed the fact, and sought to avoid liability by alleging further facts which did not constitute a lawful justification such as that of the constable making an arrest. What he should have done, as the court remarked, was to plead the general issue and give these facts in evidence[2]. The pleading propriety was equally obvious in the 1378 case of the falling building materials already mentioned. The defendant pleaded that the fall was accidental and the damage trivial, because he vainly thought that in these circumstances the consequences of the fictitious *contra pacem* were unfair. Had he pleaded Not guilty, no jury would have freed him of liability for the damage actually done. But the plaintiff did not even allude to the substance and went straight to the pleading point: the defendant had not admitted the wrong nor denied it nor justified it[3]. It went without saying that accident was not a justification and could not be specially pleaded.

1. *Brevia Placitata* (Selden Society, vol. 66), p. 207; YB 21 & 22 Ed. I (Rolls Series), p. 29.
2. *Gibbons v Pepper*, 1 Ld. Raymond 38; 2 Salkeld 637; 4 Mod. 405.
3. YB 2 Ric. II (Ames Foundation), p. 69.

It follows that whatever discussion there was of fault would be before the jury at *nisi prius*, and of no interest to pleaders or to year book reporters concerned with pleading. Formal special verdicts are rare in the year book period. But if a reporter happened to be at a *nisi prius* hearing, he might note some statement by the jury which the clerk would probably enrol, after the judge had given his opinion on its effect, as a general verdict. The only early collection of reports from the country is the *Liber Assisarum*. And in 1368 there was indeed such a case. The plaintiff was seeking to enforce the customary liability for fire between neighbours, soon to be enforced openly in an action on the case, by a *vi et armis* bill for arson. The defendant pleaded Not guilty, and judgment was given in his favour when the jury found that the fire had started in his house by accident and had spread to the plaintiff's house[1]. Such indications would inevitably be rare until mechanisms developed by which facts found at *nisi prius* might be reported to the court *in banc*. When those mechanisms do develop, discussions of fault indeed begin to appear in the reports; and that probably reflects the procedural change rather than a coincidental advance of civilisation.

It further follows that we can never hope to know what standards were in fact applied, at first by juries bringing to bear their own perceptions of right or wrong, then by judges seeking to focus those perceptions; and it is only when judges begin regularly to give directions relating to the evidence in each case that the question becomes in any real sense a question of law. Absence of fault would naturally lead a jury to absolve a criminal defendant from punishment more readily than to deprive a civil plaintiff of compensation for his injury. All civil liability was in that sense strict. But we must not think of a mechanical general rule. Trespass *vi et armis* was not a juridical entity for which a separate or a single rule could have existed. A collection of separate substantive wrongs had been given a terminological unity for procedural reaons. For some there was evidently a known customary standard. Straying cattle, for example, were one thing; and biting dogs, which as we shall see might or might not wear a *contra pacem* collar to court, were another. For accidents not involving such things as animals or fire, later discussions show an assumption of strictness which was no doubt old. The man holding the weapon when it went off would

1. YB 42 Lib. Ass., pl. 9, f. 259v.

not easily make good his *in nullo est inde culpabilis*: 'Not my fault' had to amount to something like 'Not me because a stranger took my hand'. But the man on the horse could say that it bolted because of a stranger's act or a clap of thunder or even its own fancy.

The bolting horse is the most telling cause of accidents. It was said in 1695 that the rider sued for battery should plead Not guilty; and this came to be stated, as we have seen, only because a defendant made the elementary mistake of pleading specially[1]. Later in this chapter, in another context, that case will be set beside another of 1676. This time it was the plaintiff who introduced special matter. Instead of bringing a simple *contra pacem* writ for battery, he brings an 'action on the case' which bases his claim on the rashness of breaking in untamed horses in a public place[2]. We now know that another plaintiff had proceeded similarly nearly three centuries earlier. A writ of 1398 expressly rests the claim on riding carelessly and without foresight; and the real issue turned out to be whether or not the defendant knew that the horse, which was not his own, was a bolter[3]. When it bolted, he had done all he could to pull it up and avert harm; and if sued as usual in battery, there was every chance that a jury would find him Not guilty. That is why this plaintiff, like the plaintiff of 1676, sought to rely not just on the actual collision but on pre-existing circumstances showing independent fault in the defendant. In an action based on the mere impact, a jury would not automatically find a defendant Guilty just because he was there; and there is no more to it than that.

ACTIONS ON THE CASE

If a trespass, a wrong, was not a plea of the crown, proceedings against the wrongdoer, whether undertaken by public authority or by a victim, were matter for a local court. The formal relaxation of this principle in the third quarter of the fourteenth century is the 'origin' of the action on the case; and the immediate source of that action is therefore trespass in local courts. But an enumeration of

1. *Gibbons v Pepper*, 1 Ld. Raymond 38; 2 Salkeld 637; 4 Mod. 405.
2. *Mitchil v Alestree* (1676), 1 Ventris 295; 2 Lev. 172; 3 Keb. 650.
3. Morris S. Arnold, 'Accident, Mistake, and Rules of Liability in the Fourteenth-Century Law of Torts' (1979) 128 University of Pennsylvania Law Review, p. 361 at pp. 366 ff.

the kinds of act remedied as trespasses in local courts would of course include acts which, if breach of the king's peace was alleged, would also be remediable in royal courts. It has already been noted, for example, that the printed *Register* has two writs of battery, one *vi et armis* and *contra pacem* and returnable in the common pleas, the other omitting these allegations so that, as the *Register* says, the sheriff can hear the case in the county court[1]. But even after the jurisdictional principle was relaxed, batteries and the like never appeared in the king's courts unless they were properly clothed in their *vi et armis* and *contra pacem*, possibly because the king wanted his fine, however formal, possibly because the plaintiff would never forgo the process by *capias* which *contra pacem* entailed.

Our concern therefore is with those trespasses which had been in principle remediable only in local courts, because *contra pacem* could not colourably be alleged. That there was no conceptual unity among them is even more obvious than in the case of the trespasses *vi et armis*: they were a miscellaneous residue, whatever local custom classed as a wrong but could not be brought or smuggled into a royal court. And so long as the jurisdictional frontier mattered, wrongs as peaceful as that of the smith could be smuggled in as *contra pacem regis*.

But even at that time occasional trespass actions came to the king's courts in which *contra pacem* was not and could not sensibly be alleged. In so far as there was a formal frontier, it limited the jurisdiction of local courts: they could not hear pleas of the crown. The king's own jurisdiction was not formally limited; and his courts did not hear ordinary trespass actions only because, as a matter of policy, the chancery would not normally seal trespass writs returnable there. Sometimes, however, they did so; and the two most striking examples will be mentioned for the light they throw on trespass litigation generally.

The repair of river or sea walls was a duty commonly cast upon the riparian owners. It was enforced in various ways, sometimes by indictment; and this may explain why a royal interest was seen. In several cases, the earliest known dating from the early years of Edward I, actions were brought against such riparian owners by neighbours whose land had been flooded in consequence of their failure to repair. These actions are called trespass, though of course

1. See pp. 287–8, above.

there was no question of a breach of the king's peace; and they seem to have been well established, if not common, throughout the century preceding the relaxation of the jurisdictional principle. At the time of that relaxation, however, an odd thing happened. For a year or so about 1370 these and some other writs were issued with an incongruous *contra pacem* although they had never had it before. It is this that suggests a school of thought which proposed to achieve the relaxation by putting *contra pacem* into any trespass writ to be made returnable in a royal court. The result would have looked funny, as did the case of the tun of wine in 1317; but it was probably rejected not on aesthetic grounds, but because it would generalise the grievance about *capias* and inappropriate fines to the king. We may, however, regret either that this was not done or that the more radical step was not taken of excising *contra pacem* from its established place in writs of battery and the like. Its survival was responsible for the damaging distinction between trespass and case; but that is to look ahead. Writs against riparian owners soon lost their *contra pacem* again, looking much as they had in their earliest days; and they came to be classified as actions on the case[1].

Also known as actions on the case in later times, as trespass in their early appearances, are actions by the owners of fairs and markets against persons defrauding them of their tolls by selling secretly in their own houses, instead of in the market. The earliest example known was in 1241[2]. It seems likely that the king's courts heard such cases because the plaintiff's franchise was at least in theory his by royal grant; and actions for nuisance by operating a rival market also had special treatment in the matter of jurisdiction. The offence and the damage were purely economic, and perhaps even more remote from later ideas of trespass than the mere nonfeasance of the riparian owner with his wall, where at least the resulting damage was physical. To those brought up in the old belief that trespass in the king's courts had always had its eighteenth-century meaning, this was the remarkable feature of these cases; but they probably did not seem remarkable in their own day.

1. (1958) 74 LQR, pp. 430 ff. The earliest entry found is in 1273; CP 40/2A, m. 23d.
2. (1958) 74 LQR, pp. 421 ff. The 1241 case is now printed in *Curia Regis Rolls*, vol. XVI, nos. 1727, 1764. The best known example is YB 2 & 3 Ed. II (Selden Society, vol. 19), p. 71.

Trespasses no less sophisticated, though with less at stake, were of daily occurrence in local courts.

They will, however, serve to introduce the subject of the forms taken by trespass writs. They were all *ostensurus quare*, and so congruous with the complaint of a wrong. The simplest physical wrongs do not take much explaining; and standard phrases soon emerge for assault and battery, false imprisonment, the taking of goods and so on. But these phrases are ingredients rather than writs in themselves, appearing in any particular writ singly or in the relevant combinations: the defendant invaded the plaintiff's land, took his cattle, beat his servant, and usually committed *alia enormia* for good measure. The actual facts covered by any formula, moreover, were very various, so that the composition of even a simple writ required skill: only a lawyer could appreciate that 'with force and arm assaulted, beat and ill-used' was a suitable account of a road accident. But a lawyer could point to the phrases he needed, so that the writ was, if not common form, at least made of prefabricated parts.

Outside the area of the simplest physical wrongs, of those wrongs which could be described as *contra pacem* and so easily come into the king's courts in the thirteenth and early fourteenth centuries, the writ had to be drafted. There were no precedents except, perhaps, common forms of plaints in local courts. And the drafting problem might be real because the wrong needed explanation. Consider the case of the market. In the earliest example in 1241 the complaint is put in terms like these: why the defendants sold their wares in their own houses during the plaintiff's fair contrary to the liberties granted him by such-and-such kings. This would have been unwieldy if the franchise had been described in any detail; and in later examples it is more elegantly recited in a preamble: why, whereas the plaintiff has such a right under such a title, so that no sales during the market should take place outside its precinct, the defendants sold their wares in their own houses.

The device of the preamble came into general use. In the case of the river walls, for example, the writ might run: why, whereas by the custom of the district each man who has land on the banks of the Ouse should keep such banks as lie within his land in proper repair so that his neighbours come to no harm by his default, this defendant failed to repair his stretch of bank in due season so that the plaintiff's land was flooded and his crops lost. This was the form usually, though not always, adopted for the trespass writs which had to be composed when the jurisdictional barrier was relaxed. Most actions on the case have writs in the form *ostensurus quare cum*; and the *cum* clause, the preamble, sets out the source of the duty where that is not obvious, such as the custom of the realm in the case of the innkeeper or fire, the transaction in the case of the bailee or the buyer of defective goods warranted sound.

But there was no magic about this formulation. The preamble was no more than a convenient device when a good deal of matter had to be set out; and the salient feature of those trespass actions which first came, or first came openly, to the king's courts in the third quarter of the fourteenth century, was indeed that writs had to be composed specially setting out the circumstances. And this is how actions on the case came by their name. Phrases like 'on the case' are found in the thirteenth century, generally making the obvious point that a writ must be appropriate to the facts. By a natural shift they came more and more to be used of writs which had to recite special matter as opposed to the 'general' form, or which had altogether to be specially drafted as opposed to the 'common' writs in the formularies. And although many writs 'on the case' became standard, they preserved as their generic name the description of their earliest striking feature.

This then is how actions on the case began. Hindsight knows that their beginning is important because they were to be the vehicle of great developments; and our understanding of those developments has been affected by a mistaken view of their beginning. But it is necessary to emphasise again that a lawyer in the fourteenth or fifteenth century would not have thought the matter important. A jurisdictional adjustment had allowed some wrongs which had long come to the king's courts to come there without fictitious allegations, and other wrongs to come there for the first time. But in many kinds of case the allegations were still inappropriately made, causing a measure of hardship over process. And the number of plaintiffs taking advantage of the relaxation, suing in the king's court without alleging a breach of the king's peace, was to remain small for a century and a half. Most plaintiffs must still have preferred to take most wrongs to their local courts. Not until the sixteenth century, when forty shillings had become an upper limit there for all kinds of claim and had also shrunk to a relatively small sum, was there a substantial shift of legal business. And even then it was not the removal of actions concerning wrongs that mattered most: it was the removal of small contract litigation for which the king's courts had adopted inappropriate rules of proof. The important boundaries which actions on the case were to break down were not jurisdictional but conceptual.

THE RELATIONSHIP BETWEEN TRESPASS AND CASE

Had some lawyer in the late fourteenth century undertaken to write a book about what we should call tort, about actions brought by the victims of wrongs, he would have called his book 'Trespass'. Of actions for trespass in the king's court, he would have said that most were started by writ, and perhaps that writs could be classified in two different ways. Either they had *contra pacem* or not. And either they were 'general', 'common', or they were 'special', 'on the case'. Both classifications were formal. They did not reflect substantive concepts. There was no equation of trespass with *contra pacem* and no contrast between trespass and case. Indeed, there was no entity of 'case' or 'trespass on the case' or 'special trespass' as opposed to 'common trespass'. The only substantive concept was 'trespass' as 'wrong'. There were general or special writs of trespass, and writs with and without *contra pacem*; but that is all. Moreover, the two classifications of writs were not coincident or even parallel: they cut across each other.

Consider the various wrongs that might be done to a market. At one extreme is the case already mentioned: against the secret seller defrauding the franchise-owner of his tolls, the writ must obviously have special matter setting out the franchise, and must equally obviously not allege breach of the king's peace. At the other extreme is the defendant breaking up such fixtures as the toll-booth. Here the plaintiff could use an ordinary general *vi et armis* writ: his franchise was not relevant to the physical damage. But usually he would get a special writ reciting his franchise, perhaps because the likely defendant was a rival franchise-owner, perhaps because he wanted to recover consequential damages in lost tolls and so on. But this special writ would still be *vi et armis* and *contra pacem*.

Intermediate between these two is the defendant, again probably a rival franchise-owner, who pickets the market, preventing merchants from coming so that their tolls and other dues were lost. The writ would be *vi et armis* and *contra pacem*, and these phrases would be as truthful as they ever were in describing what had happened to the diverted merchants. But unless the writ was special, reciting the plaintiff's franchise in a preamble, it would disclose no wrong to him. And even with the preamble, of course, the wrong that it did disclose was the causing of damage which was both economic and indirect so far as the plaintiff was concerned, though it might have been assault and battery to the merchants[1].

A last example may be taken from another kind of franchise. The franchises of estray and wreck of the sea gave to a landowner, under the appropriate conditions, beasts found straying within his lordship or goods washed up there. Suppose that one with a franchise of estray took possession of a straying horse, and the defendant took it from him: he could have either a general writ *de bonis asportatis* or a special writ reciting his franchise. But suppose the defendant had got to the horse first: without his franchise the plaintiff would have no right, so he must have a special writ. That writ, however, still said *vi et armis* and *contra pacem* although the horse had not in any ordinary sense been taken from the plaintiff[2].

This last was among the cases which were to pose a problem to writers in the sixteenth century. Then there were two categories of 'trespass' and 'case', and they could not tell which was appropriate. Did the *contra pacem*, unreal as it was, make the action trespass? Or did the special matter make it case? But our hypothetical writer in the fourteenth century, to whom such writs were very familiar, would have had no difficulty. The categories had not come into existence. If he had discussed the significance of the two ways of classifying writs, he would not have attached much importance to the distinction between common writs and writs on the case. Little followed from it. But he would have stressed the consequences of *contra pacem*. Artificial as it was in substance, *contra pacem* carried *capias* and outlawry, and these were not available in trespass writs without it. This was an accident of chronology. In 1352 statute had extended *capias* to the important personal actions like debt[3]; but it

1. For market wrongs, see (1958) 74 LQR, pp. 418 ff.
2. Op. cit., p. 417.
3. Stat. 25 Ed. III, stat. 5, c. 17.

would have been otiose to mention trespass, since at that date only *contra pacem* trespasses came to royal courts regularly. When other trespasses began to come in some twenty years later, therefore, they were encumbered with dilatory process; and that was not put right until 1504[1]. This accident was probably responsible for the lasting division of trespass actions into two categories.

We do not know in detail how these categories took shape in lawyers' minds, but the outline seems clear. All 'common' writs had *contra pacem*, being the core of trespass actions in royal courts when in general only *contra pacem* actions could come there. Equally, all actions admitted only after the relaxation of that principle had writs that were 'special' or 'on the case'. Although the converse of neither proposition was true, and although special writs having *contra pacem* would come to look particularly anomalous, it was natural that the two ways of classifying writs should be aligned. Writs 'on the case' contributed their name to a category of which the important characteristic, because of process, was the absence of *contra pacem*. The name slowly became a term of art, so that by the sixteenth century even plea roll clerks, anxious not to recite a lengthy writ for the sake of recording a jury respite or the like, began to use *transgressio super casum*. The separation from plain trespass is reflected in the books of entries and in works like Fitzherbert's *Natura Brevium*[2]. But it does not reach, as the separation of detinue from debt did not reach, to the printed *Register of Writs*: many writs on the case, including even some in *assumpsit* for the mere failure to carry out a promise, are mixed up with battery and the like under *De transgressione*[3].

The separation is recorded with ironical clarity in the statute of 1504 which removed the last reason for it. This provided 'that like process be had hereafter in actions upon the case . . . as is in actions of trespass or debt'[4]. But although 'trespass on the case' and the like becomes unambiguous, it is still important to keep an open mind on the sense of 'trespass' except when the contrast is being expressly made. For Coke 'trespasser' means just wrongdoer, and

1. Stat. 19 Hy. VII, c. 9.
2. Ff. 85, 92. Note the difficulty in accommodating both viscontiel and returnable writs, and trespass and case; f. 86H.
3. *Registrum Omnium Brevium* (ed. 1634), ff. 92–112. For the *assumpsit* precedents complaining of nonfeasance, see p. 324, n. 3, below.
4. Stat. 19 Hy. VII, c. 9.

'trespass' itself, sometimes explicitly equated with trespass *vi et armis*, can sometimes still have what he knew to be its old sense of just 'wrong'. Consider for example the way in which he wrestles with the nature of *assumpsit*, the subject-matter of the next chapter: 'it is termed *trespass*, in respect that the breach of promise is alleged to be mixed with fraud and deceit to the special prejudice of the plaintiff, and for that reason it is called trespass on the case . . .'. The argument hinges upon the relationship between concepts like our tort and contract, and cannot be expressed without using some general word for wrong. Coke is conscious of the difficulty over using his italicised *trespass*, as the awkward reference to trespass on the case shows[1]. But there was no other word available to him. Only at the end of the seventeenth century does our sense of tort begin to appear[2]; and it was not a commonplace until much later. Coke's italics for 'trespass' are matched by Blackstone's for 'tort', which he feels he has to explain: '*torts* or wrongs'[3]. In 1720 there was published a book called *The Law of Actions on the Case for Torts and Wrongs*; and the two earliest treatises on tort as a whole have similar titles: Hilliard's *Law of Torts or Private Wrongs* published in 1859 in the United States was followed a year later in England by Addison's *Wrongs and their Remedies, being the Law of Torts*. As late as 1873 Underhill still thought some explanation desirable: his title was *Law of Torts, or Wrongs independent of Contract*. Pollock in 1887 seems to have been the earliest to use *Law of Torts* as simply as our hypothetical fourteenth-century writer, most nearly incarnate in those who compiled registers of writs, would have used 'trespass'.

Trespass, then, lost its original sense by being identified with trespass *vi et armis* and distinguished from case. It was from that distinction that the modern sense of trespass grew; and to hindsight the process seems perverse. When *contra pacem* lost its jurisdictional importance about 1370, its importance in the matter of process unhappily survived; and a chance of reuniting the law of wrongs was missed. A second chance came in 1504, when the same

1. *Pinchon's Case* (1611), 9 Co. Rep. 86b at 89a. For other examples of Coke's usage, see 10 Co. Rep. 76a; 2 Inst. 170.
2. M. J. Prichard, *Scott v Shepherd (1773) and the Emergence of the Tort of Negligence* (Selden Society lecture, 1976), pp. 24, 39.
3. *Commentaries* (5th edn., 1773), III, p. 117.

process was extended to all trespass actions. *Contra pacem* was thereafter without consequence in the real world except for a nominal fine to the king. But it was too late. The two categories existed in lawyers' heads, as the statute itself shows. It was certain that there was a distinction even if nobody knew what it was; and a distinction is never without consequence in a law court.

Its nature can best be seen by considering the effect on legal argument of the loss by 'trespass' of its original meaning. In the middle ages a discussion about the classification of a case as trespass or covenant was about the analysis of its facts. As those two words slowly became the names of actions, the question came to look like one merely between two actions. Lawyers began to think in terms of 'the forms of action'. The law itself was seen as based, not upon elementary ideas, but upon the common law writs, as consisting in a range of remedies which had as it were come down from the skies. If a case fell within the scope of no writ, then in general there was no law. If it fell within the scope of one writ, then in general no other writ could be proper. A defendant could therefore argue that on the facts put by the plaintiff there was a good case against him, but on some writ other than that chosen by the plaintiff. That argument was at the heart of great legal changes; and it continued to be made even when most litigation was started without writ. The form of action was still identifiable, and its identity was that of the notional writ upon which it was supposed to rest. 'We must keep up the boundaries of actions', said Chief Justice Raymond in a case of 1725, 'otherwise we shall introduce the utmost confusion[1].

That was in the course of argument about the distinction between trespass and case. There must, in that climate of thought, be something in the facts signalling which category was appropriate. The only factor ever truly common to actions on the case was formal, the 'special' nature of the writs. Legal mythology had endowed them with a common origin, but even that did not suggest any factual unity. It made them the creatures of a supposed statutory power to frame new writs by analogy to established remedies; and the whole development was seen as a series of extensions from the central analogy of trespass. Trespass was the entity with identifiable factual properties. And it was natural to assume that those properties must somehow depend upon *contra pacem*, the only common factor.

1. *Reynolds v Clarke* (1725), 1 Strange 634 at 635.

On facts outside the usual run, therefore, the plaintiff's lawyer was confronted with a problem in these terms. From the situations in which *contra pacem* had in the past been alleged he must deduce the principle determining whether or not his client should allege it now; and if he got it wrong the form of action would be wrong. But, though he could not know it, there was no principle. In the formative period *contra pacem* had been alleged not to reflect the facts but to secure a result, generally to sue in a royal court. The facts had played a part only at the limits of absurdity, when *contra pacem* would make visible nonsense; and the resulting artificiality had by no means disappeared when the jurisdictional principle was relaxed.

An instructive example is the *scienter* action. This ended up as an undoubted action on the case. The writ called upon the defendant to answer 'why he knowingly kept a dog in the habit of biting sheep, which dog bit sheep of the plaintiff's so badly that they died, to his damage of so much'. The vice and the animal might of course be different, for example a horse kicking people. Writs in that form, without *contra pacem*, appeared at least as early as 1373; but the liability seems earlier to have been capable of enforcement in a royal court under cover of a *vi et armis* writ for setting dogs on to bite the plaintiff's sheep. This writ for incitement sounds artificial, and the incitement to bite can hardly ever have been genuine. But the action had a more or less genuine use: the right to have the sheep of others folded on one's land for their manure was not uncommon, and in disputes about this it would often happen that one man was using his sheep-dogs to handle somebody else's sheep[1].

That is the background to *scienter*. But there was a persistent puzzle about its classification. That the earliest known example, in 1367, had *contra pacem* is not surprising. Some clerks may have thought an indiscriminate use of *contra pacem* the easiest way of bringing about the jurisdictional relaxation. The writ of 1373 does not have the phrase. But in the sixteenth century a leading formulary classifies the action as trespass rather than case, and it seems as often as not to have *vi et armis* as well as *contra pacem*, a form which appears in at least one formulary of the seventeenth century[2].

1. (1958) 74 LQR, pp. 215–18.
2. Rastell, *Entrees* (ed. 1574), f. 558: *Trespas per misfesans de chien*, with cross-reference at f. 3 under *Accion sur le case*. H. Winch, *Le Beau-Pledeur: A Book of Entries* (1680), p. 1118.

This looks odd to hindsight. But seen through the eyes of the plaintiff's lawyer there was a genuine difficulty. The dog had bitten the sheep. Of course the defendant had not intended this, but nor had he intended it in the usual incitement situation where his intention was only to use sheep-dogs as such, and the biting was outside the course of their employment. Nor had the defendant intended anything at all in cattle trespass; but again his beasts had done the damage. If the mere quality of the event determined whether a wrong was *contra pacem*, was trespass rather than case, and if the necessary quality was to be deduced from the precedents, the final answer for *scienter* was by no means obvious.

The incongruity that we see in a *scienter* writ formulated with *vi et armis* and *contra pacem* is reminiscent of fourteenth-century incongruities. The allegations do not go with the 'knowingly kept'. Why not then adopt a fourteenth-century solution and cut out the '*scienter*' allegation itself, producing a general writ strictly analogous to that for cattle trespass? The substantive answer, of course, is that *scienter* was relevant: the owner was liable for every foray made by his cow, but not prima facie for his dog's first bite. But it is the procedural reflection of that substantive answer that may throw light where we need it. The defendant would plead Not guilty: and he had not done the harm in the case of the dog's twentieth bite any more than in the case of the first. The wrong did not lie in the bite alone but also in the previous circumstances.

Similar considerations might affect the runaway horse. Ordinarily the rider would be sued in battery, and might be found Not guilty if the animal had bolted through no fault of his and he had done what he could to avoid the injury. This was foreseen by the plaintiff of 1676, also run down by a horse out of control, who chose to rely, as in a *scienter* action, upon a state of affairs which the defendant knew or ought to have known was dangerous. Instead of suing in simple battery and relying just upon the impact, he introduced special matter setting out the defendant's lack of foresight in breaking in untrained horses in a busy public place[1].

1. *Mitchil v Alestree* (1676), 1 Ventris 295; 2 Lev. 172; 3 Keb., 650. The count is given in R. Brownlow, *Latine Redivivus. A Book of Entries* (1693), p. 484; it is interestingly placed under 'Trespass' rather than 'Action sur le Case', but of course there is no *vi et armis* or *contra pacem*. The accident happened in Little Lincoln's Inn Fields, now New Square, where the defendant was training '*duas equas feroces & minime domitas in trahendo currum . . . improvide incaute & absque debita consideratione ineptitudinis loci illius . . .*'.

This was the fault from which the harm followed. The modern tort of negligence was in the making, and so was the conceptual distinction eventually drawn between trespass and case.

Considered in isolation the bite of the dog or the impact of the horse was as much *contra pacem* as many of the events remedied by *contra pacem* writs. But if the plaintiff put his case that way, the defendant might persuade a jury on Not guilty that he did not do the harm; and in a sense he did not. His responsibility rested, not just upon the physical event, but upon the state of affairs preceding it. The distinction between trespass and case was to be that between the bare event and the state of affairs from which damage flows, between direct and consequential injury. This test, and therefore the modern sense of trespass, were finally settled in 1773 in the great case of *Scott v Shepherd*, though even then the court differed about its application to the facts. The defendant had thrown a firework into a crowded place. It was twice picked up and thrown on, while still smouldering, by persons acting more or less instinctively in self-protection; and on the second occasion it hit the plaintiff and exploded in his face. The plaintiff passed over the intermediate hands and sued the defendant in battery. A majority of the court held that this was the proper form of action[1].

The test was no more than a rationalisation of jurisdictional artificialities which in the middle ages had been more or less harmless; though its settlement, as we shall see, did grave damage. Why had it taken so long? How could it be that the legal profession knew that there was a distinction, but did not know what it was? Once again, what matters is the way in which legal questions present themselves. This question had presented itself in the not very exigent terms considered in this chapter: plaintiffs' lawyers had asked themselves how to frame their writs and bills. And partly, at least, their choice had been governed by considerations of factual advantage. The plaintiff run down by the unbroken horse had better sue in case, because in trespass he may be defeated on the facts by a simple Not guilty. But he can be defeated on the point of law only when the defendant can bring the facts to the attention of the court and argue that the form of action is inappropriate. The early artificial use of trespass *vi et armis* depended, like so much else, upon the blank finality of the general issue. Only when the facts

1. *Scott v Shepherd* (1773), 2 W. Blackstone 892.

emerging at the trial could be brought back for legal discussion could the defendant contemplate such an argument. In *Scott v Shepherd* itself, the defendant had pleaded Not guilty to battery, and a verdict had been found for the plaintiff. In the middle ages that would have been the end of the matter. There was no mechanism by which the defendant could have made the point that on the facts that had emerged the form of action was wrong; and that is why he could not know that there was a point to make, why the distinction had not emerged. But now there were several mechanisms. The verdict in *Scott v Shepherd* was taken subject to a special case, the facts being put to the court *in banc* for them to decide whether the form of action was appropriate. Substantive law was not just being altered, nor just being refined: it was being made.

12 *Growth of the Modern Law of Contract*

Hindsight would find the changes now to be described beyond belief if they had not happened; and that is because hindsight has the eye of a law professor who assumes that life must always conform at least to his syllabus. The contractual claims made by the old *praecipe* personal actions came instead to be made in *ostensurus quare* actions formally complaining of wrongs. The old law governing transactions was not changed but abandoned; and what we should call tortious remedies came to create different contractual rules. But, at least until a late stage, there was no professional or legislative mind to see the matter in that way. Such changes are brought about by plaintiffs and their lawyers, who address themselves not to the system but to individual predicaments. The system sets boundaries between elementary categories like trespass and covenant which at any one time are clear. But there is always marginal injustice. A claim sounds in covenant and under the rules of covenant it will fail: but the plaintiff has suffered a loss which seems unjust. The sense of injustice suggests a legal wrong, and a complaint is formulated in trespass, based not upon the transaction but directly upon the loss. And so there grows up an alternative law about agreements springing from ideas of wrongdoing, detrimental reliance. Modern developments in the United States provide an instructive parallel.

The pressure on the conceptual boundary must depend upon the frequency with which it produces hard cases; and the hard cases were caused by changes in jurisdiction. So far as wrongs were concerned, plaintiffs were given a choice by the decision about 1370 to admit to the king's courts wrongs with no royal interest. But they took little advantage of it then, and only later were they forced from local into royal courts by a larger change which was not deliberate. Confusion made forty shillings a general boundary in all kinds of case, and inflation reduced it from a large to a small sum. For simple wrongs the principal effect upon litigants, apart from costs, was in the matter of proof. Wager of law which had commonly been available in local courts was illogically excluded. But even if they felt aggrieved, there was no initiative defendants could take to avoid this result.

It was otherwise with what we should call contract litigation diverted by the forty-shilling barrier, because the hardship of changes in proof fell upon plaintiffs, for whom the initiative of a differently formulated claim is always possible. The first hard cases were in situations remediable in local courts without special formalities of proof by actions called covenant; though in royal courts, if formalities of any kind had been satisfied, they would normally have been those of a conditional bond so that the proper action would have been in debt. Without a sealed document of the one kind or the other, contractual claims for services (indeed for anything except the payment of money or the delivery of goods) could not be made at all in the king's courts. And it is in such cases that we first see plaintiffs reaching for a trespassory remedy. For money or goods there was no bar to making the traditional claim, because a sealed document was never required in debt or detinue; and the hardship faced by the plaintiff was that wager of law was then too easy. He could not, as he could in local courts, exclude it by tendering such lesser proofs as witnesses to the transaction; and he knew that his defendant's oath would not be subject to the social pressures of its original community setting. And so plaintiffs who ought to be suing in debt or detinue also begin, though much later than in the case of covenant, to reach for a remedy based upon reliance.

But in both cases it is important not to antedate the reaching process, as we shall inevitably do if we carry back to the old personal actions a modern idea of contract in which almost any harm connected with the transaction is recoverable in an action based upon it. The *praecipe* writs were about enforcing the primary obligation and no more. Any harm other than mere non-performance of a covenant or non-payment of a debt was outside the ambit of those writs, and therefore properly remediable, if at all, in a trespassory action.

ASSUMPSIT FOR MISFEASANCE

The earliest *assumpsit* actions were indeed naturally trespassory, based upon what we should call professional negligence; and it was only hindsight that could see their sudden appearance about 1370 just as a new departure in contract. It was no more than the first coming to royal courts of wrongs which were not done in breach of the king's peace. The first and most instructive such case was indeed earlier. In 1348 a ferryman on the river Humber accepted a mare for carriage, but overloaded his boat with other animals so that the mare was lost. Such mishaps were no doubt frequent causes of litigation in county and other local courts, but this one is known to us because the king's bench happened to be in York and the owner of the mare brought a bill against the ferryman there. The argument as reported in the year books, obscured in the black-letter text by a small but damaging error, is one that was to be repeated in various forms for more than two hundred years. In our language it comes to this: tort or contract? The bill was a bill of trespass, and defendant's counsel argued that this was misconceived: the plaintiff's proper remedy was by writ of covenant. 'It seems', said the judge, 'that you did him a trespass when you overloaded the boat so that his mare perished'. The defendant pleaded Not guilty, and the verdict went against him[1].

Why was the year book reporter interested in this argument? If the only unusual thing about the case was that it happened to be brought before a royal court, so that we know about it, are we to suppose that such arguments were of everyday occurrence in local courts? Surely not. In a local court the classification of the dispute as trespass or covenant would be without consequence. If the facts were as stated by the plaintiff, he was entitled to a remedy; and it would be as unimportant as it is today whether the remedy was regarded as sounding in tort or contract, because in local courts, as in today's law, contract was not encumbered with any formality. But in the king's bench the ferryman's lawyer was bound to take the point. First, the king's bench could hear a trespass by bill, but a

1. YB 22 Lib. Ass., pl. 41, f. 94; (1936) 13 Bulletin of Institute of Historical Research, p. 35. A translation of the report is in T.F.T. Plucknett, *Concise History of the Common Law* (5th edn., 1956), p. 470; the variant readings there given in n. 1 reflect the true sense of the report.

covenant had to go by writ to the common pleas. Secondly – and this was the point of general application – if the case was one of covenant, the plaintiff could not in any common law court get his action on its feet without a document under seal. Truly elementary questions like this do not often arise in court, and when they do it is usually through some jurisdictional change. In modern times the same question was raised by a statute fixing the proper jurisdiction of inferior courts in terms of a monetary limit, and then fixing different limits for contract and tort[1].

Do such questions have a 'right' answer? If they did, legal development would come to a stop. But the judge who said that the ferryman had committed a trespass was clearer in his mind than any judge would be if asked today whether the action rested upon the tort of negligence or upon breach of contract. Covenant was about the enforcement of promises in an almost literal sense: it was aimed at people who did not do what they had promised to do. The ferryman had of course failed to carry the mare over the river. But he was sued, not because it was left behind, but because it was dead. He was not naturally liable in covenant, any more than the borrower who damaged what he had borrowed was liable in detinue. The complaint was not of failure to carry out the 'contractual' obligation, but of damage actually caused.

For the positive classification of the case as trespass, wrong, there may have been another reason. Ferrymen were under a public duty to provide a reasonable service at fixed rates[2]. Even a failure to act might be an offence, a trespass, punishable on presentment; and improper action, even if proceedings were taken by the injured party, would naturally appear in the same light. Nor were such reasons for the classification exceptional. Consider again the smith, whose fortunes were traced in the last chapter. He was reached by a straightforward writ on the case as soon as trespass actions could come in without *contra pacem*. But he had before that been reached by an ordinary *contra pacem* writ. He had 'done' the harm in a more obvious sense than the ferryman; and if the action against the ferryman had been: why with force and arms and against the king's peace did he kill my mare, the jury would perhaps have said Not guilty. But so far as the dilemma between tort and contract is

1. Stat. 9 & 10 Vict., c. 95, s. 129.
2. *Public Works in Medieval Law*, vol. II (Selden Society, vol. 40), pp. 306 ff.

concerned, there is little to choose between the two situations. Yet the ill performance by the smith was so obviously a trespass that the covenant objection was not even raised.

A later time might describe both the smith and the ferryman as belonging to 'common callings'. But in the middle ages, and particularly in towns where life so largely revolved around the crafts, bad workmanship and false dealing at every level were commonly regarded as offences against public authority as well as private wrongs to those damaged. Authority might initiate what we should call prosecutions; and if proceedings were taken by a private victim, they were still proceedings for a wrong, a trespass, and could still lead to the punishment of the wrongdoer as well as to compensation for the victim himself. In London, for example, the surgical profession was controlled. Master surgeons were publicly admitted and swore an oath to do their work well, to charge reasonably, and to present to the authorities the defaults of others who undertook cures[1]. Our earliest evidence of this is from 1369; but consider an episode as early as 1300. A surgeon entered into a recognisance in a city court with a patient, cryptically said to 'arise' out of a covenant between them for the effecting of a cure. The cure must have gone wrong, and the sum in the recognisance must have been compensation offered by the surgeon for liability he admitted. But the interesting thing is the attitude of the city: both parties were amerced for settling the matter privately; and all the city surgeons were summoned to say whether this one was fit to practise[2]. Although the affair had started with a 'covenant' between the parties, there would against that background be no reason for surprise if any action had been classified as 'trespass'. In 1377 one who botched a cure, and who may have been an unlicensed practitioner, was sued in a city court by his victim, who was awarded damages. But in addition the defendant's handiwork was viewed by master surgeons, and he was imprisoned for it[3].

In the king's courts the ferryman had been an early harbinger of such litigation. But it forms a substantial proportion of actions on the case, of trespass actions admitted without *contra pacem*, when

1. H. T. Riley, *Memorials of London and London Life* (1868), p. 337; *Calendar of Letter Books, Letter Book G*, p. 236.
2. *Calendar of Early Mayor's Court Rolls, 1298–1307*, p. 81.
3. *Calendar of Plea and Memoranda Rolls, 1364–81*, p. 236.

the flow begins about twenty years later. The surgeon himself first appears in the plea rolls in 1364, in year books in 1374; and we cannot exclude the possibility that he had earlier been sued in an ordinary writ of battery. The earliest year book report notes that the writ was not *vi et armis* or *contra pacem* in terms which suggest that it might have been. And yet the contractual bearings of the case are understood: issue is tendered on the undertaking to cure; and one judge even refers to the action as 'covenant'[1]. The ferryman's argument had been neither obviously absurd nor obviously right. When a horse doctor was sued in 1369 for a negligent cure so that the horse had died, his counsel argued first that the action should have been in covenant, and then that it should have been by a general writ of trespass *vi et armis*[2]. Neither argument was successful. That the two could be advanced together illustrates both the artificiality from which trespass litigation was emerging and the real doubt which the classification of such actions caused when once the question arose.

It repeatedly arose in royal courts because of their special rule about covenant; but they never wavered from the answer first given to the ferryman. Convenience may have played some part in this, but they were following what seems to have been a majority opinion in local courts. Although nothing there turned upon the classification, the question could still arise for the enrolling clerk, who might have to give the action a name. Sometimes he called it covenant, more often trespass. Probably this was due to what we can only call the criminal element common in such cases in local jurisdictions. But that element remained in those jurisdictions and ultimately perished, perhaps to our loss. The city of London might punish the surgeon for his wrong, but in the king's court there was only the injured plaintiff and the purely civil action. In the common law, therefore, the classification of such cases as trespass would come to seem anomalous and perhaps impracticable: the harmful cure would merge into the merely ineffectual cure, and the surgeon who had tried and failed into the surgeon who had not tried at all. Lawyers, like legal historians centuries later, would begin to think

1. YB Hil. 48 Ed. III, pl. 11, f. 6; record in A. K. R. Kiralfy, *The Action on the Case* (1951), p. 225. On actions against surgeons generally, see S. F. C. Milsom, 'Trespass from Henry III to Edward III' (1958) 74 LQR, pp. 571–2.
2. YB Mich. 43 Ed. III, pl. 38, f. 33.

of *assumpsit* exclusively in contractual terms, and to see it as subject to an irrational limit. Misfeasance, the ill performance of an undertaking, was remediable: nonfeasance was not.

ACTIONS ON WARRANTIES

But before turning to nonfeasance, to attempts to get a remedy in *assumpsit* for the mere failure to perform a promise, it will be useful to mention another situation which belongs with ill performance. That is the action on a warranty. The buyer who bought in reliance upon a false statement about the quality of his purchase, or more rarely about its size or value or the state of the title, was as clearly entitled to a remedy as the owner of the mare lost from the ferry. But again the remedy could be rested upon various juridical bases; and this should be no surprise to a modern lawyer used to the range of ways in which such statements can operate inside or outside the contract[1].

A similar range can be found from early times in local jurisdictions. The earliest remedy of which we know, stated in Glanvill, was rescission[2]; and although the common law eventually restricted itself to damages in the personal actions, apparently for practical reasons of enforcement, it may turn out that the equitable remedy of rescission was directly taken from local courts. In local courts the buyer's action was sometimes called covenant, but more often trespass; and not infrequently the word deceit is used. The background to this classification is the same as that for the misfeasance actions. The false seller was not seen just as the breaker of a private contract: he was a malefactor liable to punishment at the instance of authority as well as to a suit for compensation. Consumer protection is neither a modern invention nor an exclusively modern need. It was a part of the 'criminal' law of local jurisdictions, offences being seen as wrongs, trespasses, to the city or other community as well as to the party. But these local criminal laws perished, and with them the criminal sanctions against

1. See generally S. F. C. Milsom, 'Sale of Goods in the Fifteenth Century' (1961) 77 LQR, p. 257 at pp. 278 ff; A. W. B. Simpson, *History of the Common Law of Contract* (1975), pp. 240 ff, 535 ff.
2. *Glanvill*, X, 14 (ed. G. D. G. Hall, p. 129).

dishonest dealing. The false seller was a trespasser, a wrongdoer, to the city of London, but not to the king. And that is why the private victim, unless he was on the king's business which suffered in consequence[1], could not bring his action in a royal court until the requirement of a royal interest was abandoned.

In the king's courts, however, there was no hesitation about classifying the action of the party as 'trespass' rather than 'covenant'. In each of the earliest reported actions in common form alleging a breach of warranty the defendant naturally tried the objection that it sounded in covenant, but he was unsuccessful[2]; and the printed *Register* puts its precedents under *De transgressione*[3]. The nature of the *transgressio* appears from an alternative label that came into use among plea roll clerks, *De deceptione*. It appears also from the writ: the defendant is alleged to have sold the goods *falso et fraudulenter*, knowing them to be defective and warranting them to be sound. But the fate of these allegations is important. Deceit on the part of the seller was invariably alleged. In the case of food sold by retail to the actual consumer it may have lost all significance very early: an express warranty did not have to be alleged, and the seller's knowledge soon became immaterial. In the case of other commodities, an express warranty had to be alleged and the allegation could be put in issue. But is seems that the seller's knowledge again ceased to matter, so that while the buyer had to be deceived in one sense of that word, the allegation that the seller had acted deceitfully in the other sense became immaterial. If the seller had given the warranty and if the goods fell short he was liable.

That liability, however, is effectively a liability in contract. In the king's courts there was no 'criminal' element to anchor the action to its analysis as an offence, a wrong; and although in form it continued to be an action for a wrong done to the buyer by the seller, in substance the element of wrong, of fault, became irrelevant and the liability became absolute. Two things followed. The truly fraudulent seller was no more liable than the one who was mistaken;

1. See *Select Cases in the Court of King's Bench*, vol. III (Selden Society, vol. 58), p. 179 (1307).
2. YB 11 Ric. II (Ames Foundation), p. 4. For cases of 6 and 7 Ric. II, see Morris S. Arnold, 'Fourteenth-Century Promises' [1976] Cambridge Law Journal, p. 321 at pp. 331–2.
3. *Registrum Omnium Brevium* (ed. 1634), ff. 108, 111.

and deceit was for a time left without specific effect at common law. And the warranty itself, which had started on the basis of the modern tort of deceit, as a representation inducing the contract but operating outside it, had begun to move in as a term of the contract itself. The statement became a promise when belief in its truth ceased to matter.

In the fifteenth-century common law, then, trespass actions, actions for wrongs, were doing a range of work which we should call contractual and which lawyers at the time recognised as having affinities with covenant. The ill performance of a promise was remedied, not as a breach of it but as a negligent wrong. The false warranty, eventually to be treated as a promise in itself, was remedied as a deceit inducing the purchase. But there was nothing artificial about either. In local jurisdictions the analysis as between the parties did not matter; and it was the public interest that made it more natural to treat cases as trespass. In the king's courts this was inevitably followed, because otherwise they would be caught by the rule requiring a seal in covenant. But, since in the king's courts there was no public interest but only that of the parties to consider, the contractual element began to come uppermost in lawyers' minds; and the relationship of these actions with covenant became a question.

ASSUMPSIT FOR NONFEASANCE

The most important development, and the least clear, is the process by which an action based upon trespass, an action for a wrong, came to be available to a plaintiff whose case was only that the defendant had not kept his covenant, his agreement. But the importance is visible only in retrospect. To lawyers at the time, the dominant thing was not the cases now to be considered: they could not know, as we do, that a new law of contract was in the making for new worlds. They saw them against the background of an established law of contract ordered in the king's courts by covenant and the conditional bond. In these courts, therefore, we are to think of occasional plaintiffs who have neglected to comply with the formalities, and who are seeking some legal back door. But their apparent foolishness must be assessed against another background, a law of contract in local courts which was not encumbered with formalities. The hardship arises because agreements made with local courts in mind are brought into the king's court.

The facts are these. Such actions begin to appear on the records of royal courts as soon as trespass actions are regularly admitted without *contra pacem*. *Assumpsit* for nonfeasance, like *assumpsit* for misfeasance, is found in the plea rolls among the earliest actions on the case. There are entries in 1370[1], though no case is reported in the year books until 1400[2]. After some hesitation in the first decades of the fifteenth century, it seems to have been settled that the action did not lie. Towards the middle of the century, however, a remedy was given when the defendant had not only failed to keep his promise but had also put it out of his power to do so, for example by granting to another the land promised to the plaintiff. This added element was required until about 1500, when it was held that the action would after all lie for a mere failure to perform, but only when the plaintiff had himself carried out his side of the bargain. Not until some time in the sixteenth century did merely mutual promises become actionable. *Assumpsit*, which had started as an action in trespass, tort, was on its way to supporting a law of consensual contract; and our task is to interpret this series of events in terms of lawyers' thinking. But we must not imagine a single prolonged struggle with an identified and unchanging problem. What we need to identify are the various questions which presented themselves to lawyers.

THE EARLY NONFEASANCE CASES

The earliest cases are the hardest to understand. In local courts there were good reasons for the classification of many misfeasances as trespass, and there is no difficulty in understanding their appearance in royal courts. But the appearance of nonfeasance claims at the same time is a puzzle. Consider the writ in the earliest reported case: the defendant is to answer why, whereas he had undertaken to construct certain houses for the plaintiff well and truly and within a

1. CP 40/440, mm. 407d, 630d.
2. YB Mich. 2 Hy. IV, pl. 9, f. 3v. Cf. YBB Mich. 11 Hy. IV, pl. 60, f. 33; Hil. 3 Hy. VI, pl. 33, f. 36v.

certain time, he failed to do it within that time to the plaintiff's damage of so much. The defendant at once succeeded in the obvious objection: this is a case of covenant[1]. How could the plaintiff ever have thought otherwise?

A fair number did think otherwise. The year books report only a few cases, the earliest in 1400. But the plea rolls show a handful of such actions commenced each year from about 1370 onwards, though few go beyond the formal opening stages so that we rarely learn more than the formulation of the writ. The early claims seem all to be for failures to perform services such as to build, repair or roof houses or mills, or to sow, mow or carry; and from about the turn of the century there appear also writs complaining of failures to complete conveyances by making livery or the like[2]. Payment is sometimes but not always said to have been made in advance; the language of deceit is not used; and although the damage is always specified in amount, it is never itemised in kind – for the historian a more important lack than it sounds. All these points are illustrated in two precedents about the non-performance of promises in the printed *Register of Writs,* which seem to date from this period. One is against a mason who had been paid in advance for making a stone cross within a certain time. The other is against the seller of a house, for a price to be paid on an agreed future date, who undertook to deliver seisin within a certain time. Both are placed under *De transgressione,* though the second comes just before the transition to a new heading *De deceptione*[3].

How are these trespassory claims to be explained? Of course such agreements as these were unevenly treated in the king's court. If the defendant had performed his part, he could have sued for his money in debt: but his own liability would *prima facie* be in covenant, and even if he had been paid in advance he would be sheltered by the requirement of a sealed document. But hardship is a motive rather than an argument: it explains why plaintiffs in these situations may have been driven to try a trespass action, but it does not make that action appropriate.

1. YB Mich. 2 Hy. IV, pl. 9, f. 3v.
2. This observation is based upon the following rolls: CP 40/440; CP 40/488; CP 40/521; KB 27/533; KB 27/572; CP 40/574; CP 40/632.
3. *Registrum Omnium Brevium* (ed. 1634), ff. 109v (*De cruce lapidea facienda*), 112 (*De transgressione quia non posuit in seisinam*).

In the case of services, though not of sales of land, it is possible that the Statutes of Labourers had created confusion. They made it an actionable offence for an employee in certain circumstances to leave his employment or, a constructive departure, to refuse to act[1]. This is mentioned in both the earliest year book cases, where it is suggested that the action could have been based on the statutes[2]. Perhaps the plaintiffs' lawyers meant the action to be so based, but drew the writs wrongly, or thought that their cases though not within the letter were within the equity of the statutes.

Another approach goes deeper, looking to a feature of medieval jurisprudence which lies behind the statutes themselves. The narrow concept of covenant was the product of a society in which most obligations were seen as flowing from tenure or status. This was obviously the case with agricultural services. The ploughman who did not plough would be summoned to his lord's court as a wrongdoer long before anyone would think of suing him as an equal in contract. Even the obverse of that proposition may be relevant in a negative way: the contract between equals for the sale of land was also a relative novelty. Grants had been made precisely to create obligations for service, to plough or to fight; and the only common arrangement concerning land which had sounded in covenant was the term of years. This cannot explain why defaulting vendors came to be sued as wrongdoers: but such treatment for persons failing to perform services was not confined to the manor court. Duties to act might be imposed by communities independently of the tenurial relationship, for example on the ferryman and the innkeeper. But it is hard to believe that any of these matters are more than sources of confusion. They cannot by themselves satisfyingly explain the early nonfeasance cases, though they may have added force to some more basic difficulty.

If we think away our own ideas, and remember that much of the mist surrounding the year books is a morning mist, that lawyers were seeing problems for the first time, then we can discern a real difficulty about the juridical nature of actions of covenant. In the

1. Stats. 23 Ed. III; 25 Ed. III, stat. 2.
2. YBB Mich. 2 Hy. IV, pl. 9, f. 3v; Mich. 11 Hy. IV, pl. 60, f. 33. See also references in S. F. C. Milsom, 'Reason in the Development of the Common Law' (1965) 81 LQR, p. 496 at p. 508, n. 25. For a 'plea of trespass' for refusal to work contrary to a city ordinance see *Calendar of Early Mayor's Court Rolls of the City of London, 1298–1307*, p. 106 (1301).

king's court, the *praecipe* writ unambiguously represented the action as a claim for performance; and to the extent that a defendant could presumably always stop the action by performing in obedience to the writ, it remained so. But the king's court unlike some local courts, as we shall see, ceased to make specific orders by way of judgment except in actions concerning terms of years. If the action proceeded, therefore, the plaintiff would recover damages. What should the damages be for? They were in fact fixed by jurors who no doubt acted on their own notions of fairness. And in local courts, when actions of covenant ended in orders for damages rather than for specific performance, those notions were no doubt proper. But in the king's court the logic of the writ would formally limit damages to the value of the promised performance, taking no account of consequential or other losses. It may be that the *praecipe* form, no doubt first chosen in the context of terms of years and the like, actually imposed on the king's courts a narrower concept of covenant than was general in local courts. It has already been suggested that this constriction may explain the disuse in the king's courts of actions of covenant, and the habit of protecting agreements by conditional bonds in which the penalty could take account of all foreseeable losses.

This is the likely background to the puzzling early nonfeasance claims. All allege damage without specifying what it was; but grammatically it is always made to flow not from the mere failure to perform but from the failure to perform within the time promised[1]. Even if the plaintiff had a sealed document, a *praecipe* writ of covenant could not be obeyed; and, formally at any rate, the damages claimed are presumably not the value of performance, but the distinct loss suffered because performance was not in time, which may be less or more. Perhaps the plaintiff had not paid the defendant, has now engaged another builder, and has suffered only the expenses of delay. Or perhaps he has suffered large consequential damage. There is no evidence that in local courts such claims were ever classified, like misfeasance claims, as trespass rather than as covenant. But in the king's court a plaintiff might well feel that he had suffered a wrong for which the royal writ of covenant could any way provide no remedy.

1. For the earliest such cases, see Morris S. Arnold, 'Fourteenth Century Promises' [1976] Cambridge Law Journal, p. 321 at pp. 332–3.

Consider a year book case of 1425. The defendant undertook to build a mill by a certain date and did not do so. The plaintiff brings a writ of trespass, and the defendant's counsel does not even object to this. His argument, itself contractual in bearing, is that the plaintiff had failed to say what the defendant was to be paid. The cause of action, he says, is the covenant; and if a covenant does not settle what the employee is to be paid, it is void. It is one of the judges who raises the point that an action of trespass does not lie when the sole complaint is of failure to carry out a covenant. He is doubted by his brethren and by the reporter; and counsel for the defendant refuses to demur to the claim, and takes issue on a point of fact[1]. The majority opinion, therefore, seems to be in favour of the action; and since it was not followed for many decades, we can only suppose that an observation by the dissentient was taken to heart. 'If this action can be upheld on these facts, then for every broken covenant in the world one shall have an action of trespass.' Later events were to prove him a prophet; but immediately he may have missed the argument against him. Two cases are put; one about a roofing contract, the other about an agreement for the repair of ditches. The damage suffered in the first is the rotting of the timbers of the house; in the second it is a flood which destroys a harvest. In neither case would covenant be an adequate remedy if it was indeed confined to securing the promised performance or its value. That damages in covenant were in fact awarded on this basis is unlikely: juries would not be so mean. That there was a theoretical restriction to the performance or its value is suggested by the argument itself; and the want of mutuality in the king's courts between the remedies of employer and employee may have disposed lawyers and judges alike to seize upon it. But it is still remarkable that the argument came so close to succeeding. The action for the flooded land and the lost harvest would have to be expressed as a wrong like the action for failure to repair a river wall mentioned in the last chapter. But there the duty on the riparian owner was of independent origin, sometimes at least enforced by indictment. If the only source of the duty is an agreement, it is hard to deny that any action for damages caused by failure to carry out the duty must be governed by the law about agreements. Some of the participants in these early cases, indeed, seem to have been willing to accept the trespassory form of

1. YB Hil. 3 Hy. VI, pl. 33, f. 36v.

action if only the plaintiff had had a document under seal to witness the covenant[1]: perhaps they thought that consequential damage sounded in trespass, but still saw that the covenant was the basis of the action and so needed the normal proof.

DISABLEMENT AND DECEIT

The second phase of the development is more intelligible for the same reason that it was more fruitful: the case was rested upon a wrong which was clearly distinct from the mere failure to perform what had been promised. It will be convenient to begin with the most famous example, *Doige's Case* in 1442; and it is famous for the best of reasons. The defendant, sued in what we should call tort, raised the point of principle squarely: she demurred to the claim on the ground that the plaintiff's action, if any, ought to be in covenant. The dispute arose, not out of an agreement for services but out of the second kind of case causing hardship, an agreement to convey; and the want of mutuality in the common law courts between a buyer and a seller of land is emphasised in the argument. The action was commenced by bill of Middlesex in the king's bench, the bill being described by the reporter as a bill of deceit. It may be paraphrased as follows: that, whereas the plaintiff had agreed to buy certain land from the defendant for a certain sum paid in advance, and the defendant had agreed to enfeoff the plaintiff within a certain time, she had not done so but instead, *callide machinans defraudare* the plaintiff, had sold the land to a third party and *falso et fraudulenter* enfeoffed him. The defendant's demurrer was adjourned for argument in the exchequer chamber, and judgment was eventually given for the plaintiff[2]. From then on it seems that such actions were assured of success when the land had indeed been conveyed to a third party; but if the defendant simply kept the land, refusing to convey to the plaintiff, although the

1. In both the two earliest reported cases, the defendant objects that the action is based on a covenant for which the plaintiff shows nothing, not that because it is based on a covenant the action is misconceived: YBB Mich. 2 Hy. IV, pl. 9, f. 3v; Mich. 11 Hy. IV, pl. 60, f. 33.
2. YB Trin. 20 Hy. VI, pl. 4, f. 34; A. K. R. Kiralfy, *The Action on the Case* (1951), p. 227.

plaintiff could hope for a remedy in chancery, he had none at common law without a document under seal.

Historians looking backwards have taken this as a conscious step forward on the path leading to a general contractual remedy in *assumpsit*. But lawyers at the time could not see the path they were treading, and the novelty may have been not in the way in which the plaintiff's case was put but in the determination with which the defendant pressed the objection that it sounded in covenant. In 1401 a steward agreed to arrange a customary tenancy of certain land for the plaintiff, and took money from him; and then he caused the lord to convey the land to a third party. He was sued in deceit, and objected only that the action should be laid, not in the place where he had made the arrangement with the plaintiff, but in the place where he had procured the conveyance to the third party[1]. The report does not even hint at an objection that covenant was appropriate. Twenty years earlier in the city of London, on facts like those in *Doige's Case*, the seller who conveyed to another was sued in an action called deceit. Since the city of London did not require an action in covenant to be supported by a document under seal, the plaintiff had not been driven to the back door of deceit because the front door of covenant was barred against him; and deceit must have been the natural analysis. The reason is suggested by the remedy: the defendant was imprisoned until he should repay the money he had been paid on the sale[2]. The case is to be compared with another in the same city court just ten years earlier. A defendant was sued in deceit for having sold as fee simple land that was in truth entailed: rescission was ordered, and the defendant was imprisoned until he restored the cash and a bond he had taken by way of price[3].

The background to *Doige's Case*, in which the agreement was actually made in the city of London, seems therefore to be a well established idea of deceit in the city and probably in other local jurisdictions. The facts giving rise to such a claim generally involved a covenant, an agreement; and in the nature of things deceit is most common in a contractual context. But in London, at any rate, the

1. YB Mich. 3 Hy. IV, pl. 12, f. 3.
2. *Calendar of Select Pleas and Memoranda of the city of London, 1381–1412*, p. 23.
3. *Calendar of Plea and Memoranda Rolls, 1364–1381*, p. 126.

two claims were distinct. Covenant was directed at completion of the agreement; and for an agreement to sell land the normal city remedy would indeed be an order for specific performance. But if the seller had conveyed the land to a third party, he had made performance impossible and so made covenant inappropriate. The remedy in deceit, in this kind of case as in earlier claims based on warranty of goods and in later equity jurisdiction generally, was to undo the transaction and restore the parties to their original position. The seller was therefore imprisoned until he repaid the money. We do not know exactly what constituted deceit in London or other local jurisdictions, what facts added to a covenant allowed the plaintiff to seek to undo the transaction on this ground. It looks as though two conditions had to be satisfied: that the plaintiff had done his part or made a substantial payment, and not merely given earnest; and that the defendant had disabled himself from doing his part, as by granting the land away. But the distinction between the two kinds of proceeding is clear: covenant claimed performance of the defendant's undertaking, and deceit claimed rescission and restitution of the plaintiff's payment.

Doige's Case, therefore, does not reflect some inspiration by a lawyer trying to get a remedy in tort for the failure to perform a promise. It should be seen rather as analogous to the misfeasance cases. A claim familiar in local courts, where its validity as between the parties in no way turned on its treatment as a wrong rather than as a matter of covenant, is brought into a jurisdiction in which covenant is subject to the requirement of a deed. Its classification now becomes decisive, and the defendant inevitably argues that it sounds in covenant. The question debated was not whether to take a conscious step in a liberalisation of contract law. It was whether the deceit claim was sufficiently independent of the covenant to proceed although the covenant claim itself would be barred by the requirement of a sealed document. Consider an argument for the deceit action put by one of the judges: 'To what purpose would he have a writ of covenant, even if he had a sealed document, when the defendant cannot carry out his covenant? (as if to say, to no purpose)'[1]. But that is not in itself enough: it could equally have been said in the earlier actions for failure to convey or perform services within a promised time. Even if those earlier actions sought

1. YB Trin. 20 Hy. VI, pl. 4, f. 34 at f. 34v, *per* Newton.

not the value of the performance (the true demand of the writ of covenant), but whatever loss was caused by the failure to perform in time, still the claim was for damage flowing entirely from the breach of the agreement.

In London, the action in deceit was distinct from the action in covenant precisely because it did not claim damage which flowed from the breach of the agreement: it claimed restitution of what had been paid on the faith of the agreement. The report of *Doige's Case* ends in an adjournment, so we do not have all the argument; and of course we can never be sure whether year book reporters caught the point of arguments which we do have. But this elementary point is not made in the year book. Indeed, except to the extent that it is implicit in repeated references to the unequal treatment in the common law of the parties to a sale of land, even the fact that the plaintiff had paid in advance is not expressly relied upon in the reported argument. But in the king's courts the distinction was necessarily less sharp than it was in London, because there were no specific remedies. In covenant there could be no order for specific performance, and in deceit no imprisonment of the defendant to compel restitution of the payment. Both actions would lead to damages. And since damages were always a matter for the jury, the awards in both would no doubt be based upon the whole sequence of events, taking account both of the payment made and of any loss flowing from the breach. Even lawyers, accustomed to think of damages as essentially inscrutable, would therefore have to distinguish between the actions in the king's courts with no reminder of the point upon which in London the distinction turned. The difference between rescinding an agreement and enforcing it was blurred out of existence.

This blurring may largely explain the further step by which *assumpsit* became available for a nonfeasance even though there had been no disablement. Even in London the facts of a situation like that in *Doige's Case* could not be analysed as a deceit in modern terms. The plaintiff had paid over his money on the faith of a promise which at that time was presumably intended to be kept. The defendant's conveyance to a third party turned the transaction into a deceit in some wider sense of sharp practice; and the consequence of calling it a deceit was precisely to make available the remedy of restitution appropriate to deceit. When the action was transplanted into the royal courts therefore, where the distinct nature of the remedy was lost, there was no distinction left. There was just a rule of thumb that conveyance to a third party enabled the plaintiff to recover. Considering the legal situation of the parties as a whole, this happened to make sense: so long as the seller still had the land, the buyer might reach him in equity. But considering the common law as a self-contained system, it looked merely capricious. The buyer had paid his money and not got his land; and to him it made no difference whether the seller still had the land or had granted it away. Common sense would be on the side of the plaintiff who wanted a remedy even though the defendant had not disabled himself from performance. Legal principle, resisting the extension on the ground that the facts sounded in covenant, could not convincingly deny that they equally sounded in covenant when the defendant had disabled himself. Deceit was distinct in nothing but its name.

PURE NONFEASANCE

The third phase in the rise of *assumpsit* for nonfeasance is the victory of common sense. A remedy came to be given, apparently about 1500, even when there had been no disablement. But facts and reasoning are both obscure. The year books tell us the result, but casually and indirectly[1]. Whatever was going on, no reporter thought it of much moment. And the reason is clear from the plea rolls: cases are hardly more frequent than they had been a century earlier. The rolls of the common pleas for two Trinity terms, in 1404 and 1501, each contain nearly five hundred membranes of pleas. The total entries of *assumpsit* for nonfeasance, including formal entries of appearance, number five in the former, six in the latter. For debt the comparable entries would run into four figures in each case, and actions of debt actually pleaded run into three figures. Indeed, in that same Trinity term of 1501, nearly a hundred actions of debt are entered in which the pleadings proceed far enough to show that the plaintiff is relying on a conditional bond.

1. YBB Mich. 20 Hy. VII, pl. 18, f. 8v (also Keilwey 69, 77); Mich. 21 Hy. VII, pl. 66, f. 41 (also Fitzherbert's *Abridgment*, Accion sur le Case 45, dated 14 Hy. VII).

There is no threat to the traditional ways of making agreements enforceable; and *assumpsit* is still a back-door remedy for plaintiffs who would otherwise suffer hardship. Not until after the middle of the sixteenth century do actions for nonfeasance begin to become numerous in either of the two main courts; and it is the king's bench that leads the way. In one term of 1564 a common pleas roll of nearly a thousand membranes has nearly a thousand actions of debt of which the entries are not merely formal, and the total of nonfeasance entries, formal and other, is a little over twenty. A king's bench roll of 1557, with just over two hundred membranes has forty-five nonfeasance entries[1]. Only at about that time, and perhaps in that court, should we think in terms of an alternative law of contract visibly emerging. And it was not the result of puzzling, like this chapter, over the earlier cases. The falling value of forty shillings was now bringing in more cases of hardship than could be tolerated as anomalies. Rationalisation had to construct a new framework: and the framework had to accommodate the contractual realities from which the cases grew.

We may never know for certain how the small flow of cases in the early decades of the century was accommodated intellectually, and perhaps there was no single idea. In particular, we cannot tell what part was played by the idea of deceit. The plea rolls show that express allegations of an intent to deceive such as were made in *Doige's Case* are in the first quarter of the sixteenth century infrequent outside the disablement situation, but not unknown. After the middle of the century they are made more often than not, and eventually they become common form. The increasing use of the remedy is therefore matched by an increase in the proportion of cases in which there is mention of deceit. But neither its absence nor its presence tells us much.

Even on facts like those in *Doige's Case*, although their classification as deceit in London was intelligible, it could be little more than a name in a royal court. The distinct remedy of restitution was there lost in general damages; and the facts themselves showed a disregard of the plaintiff's contractual right rather than fraud in our sense. Whether or not he could be said to

1. Common pleas rolls for Trinity terms, 1404 and 1501: CP 40/574 and CP 40/957. Common pleas roll for Hilary term, 1564: CP 40/1215 and CP 40/1216. King's bench roll for Trinity term, 1557: KB 27/1183.

have been tricked out of his money, the plaintiff had in fact parted with it on the faith of the undertaking. He was deceived in one sense even if nobody deceived him in another; and to that extent the word would have been equally appropriate when the remedy was extended to cases in which there had been no disablement. But at first it was not generally used outside the disablement situation. Except that they almost always allege payment in advance, writs and bills in cases of nonfeasance without disablement might have been based upon their unsuccessful predecessors a century earlier. Two precedents in the printed *Register* seem to date from that period, one alleging payment in advance while the other speaks of an agreed future date[1]. In Fitzherbert's *Natura Brevium*, presumably written about 1530, only the disablement situation is classified under *Disceit*[2]. A case of pure nonfeasance is placed under *Action sur le case*, and is significantly mentioned also under *Covenant*[3]; and it alleges that part of the agreed price has been paid in advance. Even if the payment was not the cause of the action, as it were the damage flowing from the deceit, it was clearly a necessary condition when remedies were first given without disablement. 'If I covenant with a carpenter to make me a house', said a judge in 1505, 'and pay him £20 to make it by a certain day, and he does not make it by that day, now I have a good action on my case because of the payment of my money, and yet it sounds only in covenant; and without payment of money in this case, no remedy.'[4]

But as the allegations of deceit become relatively more frequent, and as the absolute number of actions begins to rise so that *assumpsit*, if not relied upon when contracts were made, must have established itself as a way of getting a remedy if need be, it becomes increasingly clear that the deceit alleged generally cannot be that the plaintiff was tricked out of his money. The action is not, even formally, one for restitution. Had it been so, of course, the plaintiff could never have got a remedy when he had not paid, and mutual promises would never have become actionable. Sometimes he is indeed said to have been tricked out of his payment, more often he is said to have been tricked out of what he should have had from the

1. *Registrum Omnium Brevium* (ed. 1634), ff. 109v, 112.
2. f. 98F.
3. ff. 94A, 145G.
4. Keilwey 77 at 78.

defendant, or out of his bargain, or he is said just to have been tricked. The more regularly deceit is alleged, in short, the more various do its particular manifestations become, and the more vague. Perhaps the common law lacks an argument and is beginning to shout.

The increase in allegations of deceit is preceded by an increase in the varieties of special damage alleged, and often alleged in great detail. Legal costs appear from time to time, and the loss of profit which the plaintiff would have made had the agreement been kept is common. But the most interesting is a variety of defamation. An action for breach of promise of marriage in 1549 is reminiscent of slander as much as of contract. The defendant is said to have acted at the instigation of the devil, scheming craftily to deceive and defraud the plaintiff. The plaintiff is said to have suffered not only in her goods by reason of the gifts she had made him, but also in the good name, fame and opinion she had previously enjoyed among her neighbours and others, by reason of the long familiarity between herself and the defendant[1]. More unexpected are allegations of analogous harm in actions arising out of market dealings. A decade and more earlier a plaintiff may sometimes say that he has suffered in his credit towards third parties, sometimes named, to whom he owed money or had made some promise on the strength of that made and broken by the defendant[2]. Later in the century such allegations become disingenuous, as we shall see. But when they first appear they should be taken at their face value; and they may help us to get our bearings in the sixteenth-century development of *assumpsit*.

If one stands back from these events, one can see two separate strands of reason merging into a pattern which at first lacks its own unifying idea: and perhaps it takes that from a quite different source. There is first the unsuccessful logic of the earliest *assumpsit* actions for nonfeasance, the notion that consequential damage was distinct from the performance or its value which the *praecipe* writ of covenant secured. The cost of the rotted timbers was indeed something different from the cost of the agreed re-tiling: but the claim still rested upon the agreement, and there was no independent trespassory basis upon which the plaintiff could rely. Nor, though

1. CP 40/1140, m. 85d.
2. J. H. Baker, *Spelman's Reports*, vol. II (Selden Society, vol. 94), p. *280*.

it added to his hardship, would it make any difference to the logic that the plaintiff had paid in advance.

Payment in advance was the essence of the London process lying behind *Doige's Case*. Various formulations are possible for the claim to recover what a plaintiff has paid for something he is not going to get. Early debt actions had been on a quasi-contractual basis, and their disappearance had left hardship in all cases in which performance of the defendant's side of the bargain could not be compelled. When it could not be compelled because the defendant had himself put it out of his power, the city of London called it a deceit, and provided a penal consequence which enabled the plaintiff to secure restitution. It may have been the borrowing of that trespassory basis from the city that enabled the common law to move forward. But in Westminster Hall the wrong could be only a civil one and the remedy only damages: and even if jurors and parties realized that the damage suffered lay properly in the payment which the plaintiff had made, still it followed not specifically from a disablement, but from having entered into the transaction at all. And it was therefore applicable to any transaction in which the defendant's performance could not be compelled.

What seems to have happened after about 1500 was an unreasoned merger of these distinct approaches. Only if the plaintiff had paid in advance, at least in part, could he sue: but what he claimed, at any rate formally, was neither the value of the defendant's promised performance nor generally the amount of his own payment but some separate consequential damage. The precedent in Fitzherbert's *Natura Brevium*, for example, alleges part payment in advance for an undertaking to make some carts; but the damage complained of is the loss of the goods which were to have been carried[1]. The result is almost a rule of thumb dealing with the cases of greatest hardship, and perhaps consciously accepted without examination. Anomalies clearly making for justice are tolerable so long as numbers remain small: but then a coherent principle must be found.

The only factor common to the two approaches had been the element of reliance. Whether in paying over his money or in not making other arrangements to avoid the consequential damage, the plaintiff had trusted the defendant; and it is this that is particularly

1. Fitzherbert, *Natura Brevium*, f. 94A.

emphasised as the language of deceit becomes more general. Perhaps that language was not just taken from the disablement cases and put in elsewhere to lend trespassory colour: perhaps it represents this idea of reliance. But there may be more to it than internal rationalisation of the two original strands. The promise in which the plaintiff had placed his trust is commonly said to have been made *fideliter;* and it is possible that the common law language of deceit has become the delictual expression of a punishable wrong familiar to everybody at the time, the ecclesiastical breach of faith[1].

In the age which produced and read *Doctor and Student,* law and justice had not quite parted company. Some have seen the rise of *assumpsit* as spurred by competition from the chancellor. But the chancellor was not just competing for business: he was righting injustices caused by the common law modes of proof, and especially by the document under seal. In lesser matters, the frequent proceedings in spiritual courts for *fidei laesio* had probably been serving the same purpose, though indirectly. The proceedings were penal, for the good of the defendant's soul; and though the spiritual court could bring pressure on him to put things right, it could not formally order civil compensation for the injured party. Nor could it in cases of defamation: and it was precisely for that reason that actions on the case for slander claiming temporal loss are from the early sixteenth century brought in the king's courts. We shall later see a London merchant bringing such an action in 1513 because it had been said that he was excommunicated for heresy. His complaint of defamation was in principle as much a spiritual matter as the heresy charge against him, and only the damage could possibly have made it proper in a royal court: believing him to be excommunicated, other merchants had refused to deal with him[2]. What then about merchants refusing to trust a plaintiff because he had been forced to let them down by a defendant's breach of faith?

We cannot be more confident or more precise until further work has been done, and work which does not consider the common law courts in isolation. It is clear that the common law bench and bar thought it unjust that so many transactions were enforceable on one side only for want of a sealed document, and that they would not

1. See the important and suggestive article by R. H. Helmholz, 'Assumpsit and Fidei Laesio' (1975) 91 LQR, p. 406.
2. See p. 383, below.

look too closely at the exact formulation of cases of hardship. But they could not from their own resources supply a general trespassory basis; and it is possible that the spreading language of deceit was not just a disingenuous verbal cover, but a specific resort to the idea of breach of faith in cases in which the defendant had suffered actual damage by relying on the promise.

That reliance in a general sense was the original basis of *assumpsit* is almost certain; and it follows that something more had to happen before it became a regular contractual remedy. It had to provide redress not just for consequential damage and the like, but for the central contractual loss remedied by covenant, the value of the promised performance. This mostly happened out of our sight: we cannot tell how juries arrived at their awards of damages, but probably they always did a sum which took the whole sequence of events into account, subtracting any payment from the value of the performance and adding consequential damage and the like. But reliance damage was formally the cause of action, and without it a claim could not reach a jury. What we can see, therefore, as part of the formal claim on the record, is that plaintiffs are sometimes driven to make it up. We have already mentioned as a not uncommon item the loss of credit with third parties whom the plaintiff had let down because of the defendant's failure. In the 1530's these allegations are probably genuine and the third parties real. In the 1590's they are evidently conjured up by the plaintiff's attorney. Plaintiffs employing John Williams of London, for example, had made many kinds of agreement with many different people, but the various breaches of their various defendants had compelled them all to dishonour some obligation towards John Denne and Richard Fenne; and it was of the injury to their credit with this indignant pair that they all particularly complained[1].

Only important facts live on as fictions. These particular allegations did not live on for long, but the allegations of deceit did. What they show is that the genuine juridical claim based upon reliance has been stretched to do the work of enforcing agreements, covenants, for which the action of covenant was in principle proper,

1. See e.g. KB 27/1329 (king's bench, Easter term, 1594), mm. 305d, 306, 310. Like Doo and Roo they were familiar figures in the city courts: *London Possessory Assizes* (London Record Society, vol. I), pp. 133, n. 2; 134, n. 4; 135, n. 3; 137, n. 4.

and also that this result is part of the accepted order of things. The phenomena of the reliance claim still appear among the formalities in the plea rolls, and in one sense form the intellectual basis of the action. But they are not what the action is now really about, and are not discussed in court. What is being discussed in court in the later sixteenth century is the alternative law about agreements which these actions are now visibly providing; and the key word in these discussions is 'consideration'. As a contractual phenomenon it has been a mystery from that age to this, and something will be said about it later. But probably it had become important when actions were still thought to be about reliance, and in that context it would be less mysterious: the question would always be, was the plaintiff entitled to rely upon this promise.

In the end the argument that 'this sounds in covenant' had been neutralised quite rapidly. But incremental change should be measured not against the years but against the flow of business. The falling value of money was bringing in many local covenants for which the royal rules of proof would leave obviously injured plaintiffs altogether without remedy; and since much of the change had happened invisibly, within unanalysed awards of damages, there was no point at which even pedantry could make a stand even when the end was in sight. The change just happened. A similar change with actions of debt caused more of a stir, partly because plaintiffs were not formally without remedy in the king's courts so that the hardship was less, and partly perhaps because the debt claim was quantified, so that the figures in an unanalysed damage award still spoke for themselves. But the mechanics of the change were the same, as appears from a report of 1574: 'For here no debt is to be recovered but only damages for the debt; and this default of payment is a wrong . . .'[1].

ASSUMPSIT FOR MONEY: THE BACKGROUND

In the nature of things, most contracts leave outstanding an obligation to pay money. The bill is presented after the goods have been supplied, the services rendered or whatever it may be; and at

1. *Anon* (1574), 2 Leonard 221.

any period the commonest breach is default in payment. Most contractual actions diverted from local to royal courts by the falling value of forty shillings were therefore claims for money, which sounded naturally in debt; and plaintiffs were never deprived of all remedy, as they were by the arbitrary requirement of a sealed document for claims sounding in covenant. That is why there were no early attempts to use *assumpsit* instead, and why there was more genuine argument about the merits of the change eventually made.

The most obvious hardship for the plaintiff was procedural. In the common pleas, wager of law was nearly always open to the defendant in debt, and his oath-helpers came either from the streets or from the menial staff of the courts. His own conscience was the only safeguard, and the court may have taken new steps to work upon it: not until the last quarter of the century do we know that a defendant proposing to wage his law was somehow examined and admonished[1]. In local courts the community situation allowed two important differences. The defendant who was not believed would not so easily get his oath-helpers. And the *secta* or witnesses tendered by the plaintiff could be real; so that local rules could and did allow a range of situations, less exigent than having a document under seal, in which the plaintiff's case was at the outset well enough supported to exclude wager. In the king's courts the only important situations were the action for rent on a lease and that for the sum found due by auditors on an account.

There was also what appears to modern eyes as a substantive hardship, though contemporaries would probably have identified it as another manifestation of the point just made. Debt in the king's courts was more restricted than its counterpart in local jurisdictions, essentially because there was less flexibility over proof. We have seen for example that until the late fourteenth century the king's courts allowed claims based upon a *concessit se teneri*. This was a kind of oral bond, a formal admission of indebtedness which in local courts was perhaps made in the court itself; and in that court

1. Coke's mention in *Slade's Case*, 4 Co. Rep. 91a at 95a suggests that it may be recent. Early cases found are: *Anon* (1588), 3 Leonard 212; *Sanderson v Ekins* (1590), ibid., 258; and *Anon* (1588), 4 Leonard 81. The first two are *insimul computaverunt* situations. The third disclosed a *Pinnel's Case* question: cf. S. F. C. Milsom, 'Law and Fact in Legal Development' (1967) 17 University of Toronto Law Journal, p. 1 at p. 4 (written in ignorance of this case).

it probably worked like a bond, precluding the denial of indebtedness, *non tenetur*. But the king's court could accept it only as a cause of action, itself requiring support by good suit, and answerable by wager. In that form, it made no real sense; and plaintiffs were eventually driven to rely directly upon the underlying cause of the indebtedness[1]. Another customary claim was that based upon a *concessit solvere*. In London and elsewhere, persons who had dealt with each other could reckon up the state of the account between them and agree upon the balance due. The mere acknowledgment of this, not made in court, was itself a cause of action; and if made before witnesses, it might preclude the defendant from waging his law. Nor was it necessary that there should have been a series of dealings: an acknowledgment of indebtedness on a single transaction could similarly ground an action. But this custom seems never to have been accepted in the king's courts[2]. A series of dealings raised a series of claims; and though they might be claimed in one writ, each transaction had to be set out in what was in effect a series of counts. An acknowledgment was ineffective, though it might be smuggled in by stretching the distinct *insimul computassent*, in which the relationship between the parties was properly one of accountability rather than of indebtedness. If lord and bailiff or the like wished to account privately without auditors, they could do so, and the agreed balance was recoverable in debt; though since there was no element of 'record' the debtor could wage his law. But however close this came in practice to the London custom, the theory was distinct. The acknowledgment or promise in London created the debt: in the common law, apart from the magical document under seal, a claim must always be based upon the actual underlying transaction. The effect was to restore the ancient idea of 'real' obligation, or at least to give greater prominence to the manifestation of that idea in the *quid pro quo*.

The same difference in basis excluded other kinds of claim from the scope of debt at common law. Even when a promise of money was clearly not gratuitous, the *quid pro quo* might cause trouble if it consisted in the payment of a smaller sum or in a mere promise. The winner of a bet may not have seemed particularly meritorious, but

1. See pp. 258 ff, above.
2. See p. 260, above.

he carried with him the merchant who had insured his lost cargo[1]. And many entirely meritorious claims involving third-party transactions came to grief because no *quid pro quo* had come to the defendant. Prominent among these were the creditor's claim against an informal surety, and the same surety's claim to be reimbursed by his principal.

Nor was the *quid pro quo* the only cause of constriction. A promise in the alternative, for example to pay money or provide a benefice, even if not conceived in penalty terms, raised an obvious difficulty. And the need to claim a fixed sum excluded any *quantum meruit*. Consider the various obstacles in the way of the plaintiff who gave board and lodging to a third party at the request of the defendant, and who did not stipulate a rate but was to send in his bill at the end. If the third party had been the defendant's wife or child, and if a rate had been fixed, the claim would be one in debt which is not uncommon on the rolls. Even if a rate had been fixed, the *quid pro quo* would raise difficulty if the third party was a mere stranger. Even if the third party was one for whom the defendant was bound to provide, the absence of a fixed rate would be fatal to a claim based upon the original agreement. And at common law this could not be cured by the defendant making a subsequent promise, unless under seal, to pay the amount of the bill. The situation is then back to the *concessit solvere*: in London and elsewhere the promise to pay would itself be enforceable. But promise was not the basis of debt on a contract at common law.

Realisation of these constrictions by lawyers and hardship to their clients had both been minimised by the general use of conditional bonds for large transactions and by the fact that small transactions did not come to the common law at all. The fall in the value of forty shillings, therefore, did more than bring smaller and therefore more numerous transactions within the ambit of rules of proof which were either cumbrous or ineffective. It exposed substantive gaps. Just claims became increasingly frequent for which there was no remedy, because somewhere between the

1. For *assumpsit* in such cases between 1538 and 1543 see J. H. Baker, *Spelman's Reports*, vol. II (Selden Society, vol. 94), p. *286*. Later examples of what seem to be bets: CP 40/1353, m. 627d (1578); KB 27/1329, mm. 444, 476 (1594). Later examples of marine insurance: KB 27/1252, mm. 27, 158 (1575); KB 27/1329, m. 503 (1594).

formal covenant and the real *quid pro quo* the common law had lost the simple enforceable promise to pay money.

As a matter of social history, therefore, the rise of *assumpsit* is another transfer from local jurisdictions, and the transfer is of cases there often remedied directly on the basis of promise. Even some of the formulae of *assumpsit* actions seem to echo earlier claims in London and elsewhere. Conceptually, it is not as was once thought the dawn of the idea of enforcing promises: it is the difficulty of accommodating that idea within the framework already established. How was it done?

Essentially it was brought about by the same process as that which made *assumpsit* actions available for nonfeasance generally. Indeed the development now to be discussed lies at the heart of that process. Claims are first made in situations in which money has been promised but debt is not available to the plaintiff, and in which his reliance upon the promise has caused obvious hardship. Then they are made in situations in which debt is available, but in which the plaintiff's claim is not for the debt but for distinct damage flowing from his reliance upon a promise about its payment; and loss of credit with third parties consequentially let down is a telling example. Then lastly this remedy, formally about such consequential damage, is allowed to do exactly the work of the action of debt and recover the debt itself: the damage becomes fictitious, and the hard-working Denne and Fenne, who often feature in such cases, are playing an accepted if improbable part as law reformers.

For reasons that will appear, the matter was seen in terms of conscious change for some decades at the end of the sixteenth century. But here, as in covenant situations, there is no reason to doubt that the start was in genuine cases of hardship caused by reliance; and the language of deceit, expressing this in rather extravagant terms, may also have been the lay expression of the idea of breach of faith causing temporal harm. If the main body of actual litigation came from local courts, some seems to have come from church courts[1]; and church courts were very likely the source of the trespassory idea by which the king's courts were able to accommodate it all.

But the process of accommodation was complicated by a difference in approach between the king's two principal courts. It

1. R. H. Helmholz, 'Assumpsit and Fidei Laesio' (1975) 91 LQR, p. 406.

sprang ultimately from jurisdiction, but a theory was generated which may be relevant to what happened. Until the bill of Middlesex became common form, the king's bench could entertain a personal action only on the basis that it was a trespass, a wrong. Formally, indeed, it should have been confined to wrongs in which the king was interested; but we have seen that when about 1370 wrongs were admitted to royal courts without a *contra pacem* allegation, they were not treated as common pleas for the purpose of excluding king's bench jurisdiction. In the sixteenth century, although it does not seem to have had much practical effect, the suggestion that they should be so treated was made again, but seemingly on a new basis. The true 'origin' of actions on the case was now forgotten, and the myth grew up that they were based upon a statute of 1285 allowing the chancery clerks to issue writs for facts like those covered by existing writs, but not actually within their scope. Such a principle would have allowed development by analogy from any existing writ, of which trespass (now seen as an entity) was only one[1]. On this basis there could be actions on the case which were not trespass on the case, and the elementary nature of all actions on the case as actions for wrongs was obscured. Particularly in the case of *assumpsit* actions for misfeasance, the trespassory nature had already been obscured by removal of actions from their local setting, where bad craftsmanship and the like led naturally to penal consequences; and all this may have added to confusion over nonfeasance generally.

This misunderstanding led to two relevant conclusions. A jurisdictional conclusion, forgetting the part once played by the king's peace, was that what could properly come to the king's bench were actions for wrongs, including deceit but excluding many other kinds of action on the case. This may partly explain why the king's bench led the way in formulating *assumpsit* actions in terms of deceit. But, since other kinds of action on the case were not in fact excluded, the emphasis on deceit in *assumpsit* may equally reflect the historically true jurisdictional position: *assumpsit* had anyway to be treated as a wrong, and of all wrongs in the contractual context, deceit lies nearest to hand.

1. For the theory, see p. 284, above. A particular deduction long bedevilled discussions of *assumpsit:* deceit on the case was seen not as a species of trespass on the case but as a distinct genus.

Another conclusion from this mistaken history went to substance, and played its part in the common pleas. If actions on the case had indeed come into being as supposed, they must constitute a general remedy having only one limitation: it was residuary in nature. If your facts were within an existing writ, you could not seek the same remedy by an action on the case. This principle, whether deduced specifically from the myth or just from ideas of juridical propriety and due process, played a part in common law development until the nineteenth century; and in particular it determined the attitudes of the court of common pleas to the use of actions on the case where debt (or, as we shall see, detinue) might be appropriate.

For the common pleas, then, the main concern was not the trespassory nature of *assumpsit* for its own sake, but the problem of accommodating it together with all the other remedies over which the court had jurisdiction, including covenant and in particular debt. This could be done in either of two ways. One was to say simply that *assumpsit* would never lie where debt was available, to allow it to fill only the substantive gaps. This may have been the first attitude of the common pleas, but then they adopted a less radical position: the mere availability of debt was not in itself a bar to *assumpsit*, so long as there was some basis for the *assumpsit* action apart from the debt itself. The one impermissible result was that *assumpsit* should perform exactly the function of debt. Not only could there be no question of alleviating the procedural hardship of wager: wager was positively a reason for resisting any encroachment on debt. It was the subject's birthright; and to force him to a jury for a debt which he might have paid in private was a denial of due process[1].

The king's bench, hearing debt actions only by bill of Middlesex and anyway less hampered by considerations of propriety, were not under the same compulsion to accommodate the two remedies within a coherent framework. Beginning from a genuine trespassory basis, they simply ignored debt. Artificiality was at first more or less hidden behind inscrutable damage awards; but it came into the open when juries were directed that all the plaintiff need prove

1. See e.g. *Slade's Case*, 4 Co. Rep. 91a at 92b–93a; for other references see J. H. Baker, 'New Light on *Slade's Case*' [1971] Cambridge Law Journal, pp. 51, 213 at p. 219, n. 25.

was the debt itself, so that the action was visibly just about non-payment.

The *assumpsit* action was then doing exactly what the common pleas would not countenance. And whereas the arguments about *assumpsit* and covenant had an almost academic air, because of the obvious injustice of covenant and because its disuse blurred vested interests as well as legal principle, debt was still staple business in the common pleas. An alternative precluding wager might seduce even more plaintiffs than the bill of Middlesex. Nor must we assume that the arguments in favour of the *status quo* were merely obscurantist or selfish. Logic, as it always is in legal matters, was clearly against the change. There was a real question of due process. In contemporary conditions of jury trial and evidence, wager of law had genuine merits. A whole profession was divided about the question, and on each side protagonists were divided about their reasons. The historian cannot, as it were, reduce the development to a dialogue, or even be confident about the factual stages through which it passed.

ASSUMPSIT FOR MONEY: THE KINDS OF CLAIM

First will be considered the cases of substantive hardship, the claims for which debt might not be available. These were probably the earliest in both courts, and for some time remained the only kind of *assumpsit* for money clearly acceptable to the common pleas. Only claims against sureties and the like will be discussed. If the plaintiff claims that he supplied the third party in the first place on the strength of the defendant's promise, there seems in general to be no artificiality beyond the talk of deceit. In contractual terms there could hardly be a more obviously just claim. In trespassory terms there could hardly be a more obviously detrimental reliance. And since no *quid pro quo* had come to the defendant, there was no need to introduce an artificial difference from debt.

But if the plaintiff claims to have supplied the third party before the defendant made his promise, although debt is even more clearly not available, the promise is not obviously deserving of enforcement. One or more of the following allegations is then generally added: that the supplying had been at the defendant's special request; that the plaintiff had paid twelve pence or the like for the promise; or that the plaintiff had released some security from the third party, forborne to sue him, or discontinued an action actually started. As a matter of language, these cases of a past supply to the third party may be expressed in any one of three ways. The transaction with him may be recited in the pluperfect tense: whereas the plaintiff had sold, lent or whatever it is to the third party. Or it may be recited behind an *indebitatus*: whereas the third party was *indebitatus* to the plaintiff for a loan; or whereas the third party was *obligatus* to the plaintiff on a bond. Or the transaction may be left unexplained behind a blank *indebitatus*: whereas the third party was *indebitatus* to the plaintiff in so much, for which the plaintiff was proposing to sue, the defendant, in consideration that the plaintiff would forbear, promised to pay.

If the original transaction was not with a third party but with the defendant himself, if for example the plaintiff had sold the defendant goods, there was a difficulty about a claim that the plaintiff had supplied the defendant on the strength of his promise to pay. Justice required enforcement as clearly as in the case of a similar supply to a third party: but this obligation was precisely the one enforceable in debt. Some separate element of reliance damage was needed; and it may turn out that in both courts *assumpsit* actions were first used in cases in which the debt was not of money but of unascertained goods, when such damage was often natural. In 1532 a brewer, paying part of the price in advance, agreed to buy a quantity of malt to be delivered on a fixed future date; and he suffered both because his business was delayed and because he had then been obliged to buy elsewhere at a higher price. The objection that he could have sued in debt was expressly raised by motion in arrest of judgment; but the king's bench ruled that although this was true, his complaint of damage caused by reliance on the defendant's faithful promise was something different, and therefore that the action was proper[1].

With the king's bench leading the way, both courts then began to entertain *assumpsit* claims for money on facts in which debt was also available to the plaintiff; but some care was taken so to formulate the claim that it was not just for the debt. This is increasingly done

1. *Spelman's Reports*, vol. I (Selden Society, vol. 93), p. 4; vol. II (Selden Society, vol. 94), p. 247.

by emphasising a chronclogical separation between the transaction creating the debt and the subsequent promise to pay upon which the plaintiff relied to his damage. Consider a claim made in the common pleas in 1549:

> 'Whereas the plaintiff at such a date and place at the instance and special request of the defendant had delivered such and such cloth to the defendant, and upon that delivery the defendant afterwards, namely on the same date, faithfully promised the plaintiff and took it upon himself that he would well and truly pay the plaintiff such a sum at such a feast next following, and the plaintiff on the faith of this promise and undertaking entered into various other promises and writings for the payment of money to certain other persons at the same feast, but the said defendant, not heeding his promise and undertaking and scheming artfully, falsely and craftily to deceive the defraud the plaintiff of that sum, and that he should be harmed by the promises and writings he had made to others in the hope of that payment, has not paid it, whereby the plaintiff is hurt and damaged in his credit towards various subjects of the king, to his damage of so much.'

There are various points worth noting. The sale of cloth is recited in the pluperfect tense, and the promise was made *postea, scilicet eisdem die et anno*. This formulation is not uncommon. But even when the point is not emphasised in words the sequence of tenses always makes it clear; though the caution which here delayed any mention of the price of the cloth until the promise was less common. This matter of chronology goes to taking the matter outside the scope of debt. Other points go to the trespassory nature of the claim. The whole transaction is said to have been at the defendant's special request, and this became common. Later, when such actions are overtly contractual, it will be seen as having to do with some difference between 'executed' and 'past' consideration. But to begin with the defendant's initiative was no doubt asserted to emphasise his 'deceit' and to explain the plaintiff's reliance upon his subsequent faithful promise. And the trespassory nature of the consequential damage, resulting from the plaintiff's own undertakings to third parties, is brought out by the figures: the sum promised was a little over £8, and the damages claimed were £20[1].

Claims like this, based upon a past sale and delivery, a past bargain and sale, a past loan and the like, are common in the king's bench and not unknown in the common pleas for the remainder of

1. CP 40/1140, m. 535d.

the century. There are of course many variations. Sometimes the damage alleged is loss of profit that could have been made with the money, instead of or as well as the lost credit. Sometimes a nominal consideration is alleged to have been given for the promise; and sometimes the plaintiff is said to have forborne action on the strength of the promise.

This allegation of forbearance seems particularly common when the transaction was recited behind an *indebitatus*. This was done with growing frequency, but seems to be a mere alternative mode of expression. The plaintiff instead of saying just that he had sold, may say instead that the defendant was *indebitatus* in respect of goods previously sold to him by the plaintiff. Probably this made no difference: the *indebitatus* served no purpose beyond emphasising the chronology; and in both courts and beyond the end of the century, the plaintiff who was going to recite the original transaction generally did so directly. Indeed he did so in the great *Slade's Case* itself, in some sense the climax of this whole development; and to that extent it is wrong to describe it as the rise of *indebitatus assumpsit*. But no harm comes of this if one remembers that what was in issue was not a form but a proposition about the relationship between the debt and the *assumpsit*.

However it was formulated in detail, the *assumpsit* claim based upon reliance was juridically different from the claim to the debt itself. The defendant is indebted and, say, asks for time: the plaintiff accedes to this, and trusting that he will be paid on the day faithfully promised, he enters into further transactions with third parties, from which damage flows when the defendant lets him down. To his claim for that damage, the debt is relevant only as part of the story. It does not matter how it was incurred, and in the second half of the century he often does not recite the original transaction at all. He asserts blankly that the defendant was *indebitatus* to him in so much, and then passes directly to the promise to pay, perhaps given for some nominal consideration or the like, upon which he relied. This formulation was obviously unfair to the defendant when the action was in fact being used to recover the debt; and in the early seventeenth century, when the action was admittedly doing that, it was disapproved[1]. But it is perhaps the clearest demonstration of the difference in basis between the two actions.

1. See p. 354, below.

What made development possible was that the difference was not necessarily so clear in practice. All that had to happen to make the *assumpsit* action do the work of the debt action was that the jury should award the debt by way of damages. This was what the king's bench exploited; and by 1573 they were overtly allowing the action to be used simply for the recovery of the debt, and had probably been doing so for some time. A report of that year explains that on a plea of *non assumpsit* in the king's bench the jury would be directed that they should find for the plaintiff if the debt itself was proved without more[1]. He need not prove the separate promise which he had of course alleged; and slogans like 'Every contract executory is an *assumpsit* in itself' meant indeed that the mere fact of indebtedness imported a promise to pay[2]. Still less, of course, need he prove actual damage flowing from reliance on that promise: if he thought it wise to allege damage, he would enlist Denne and Fenne or their like.

The same report tells us that in the common pleas an actual *assumpsit* had to be proved; and there it seems that the *assumpsit* action was accepted, but only on the basis that it remedied a distinct wrong leading to some damage over and above the mere non-payment of the debt. But if, as is probably though not certainly the case, the common pleas thought it proper for a jury to include the amount of the debt in the damages, the difference in practice would be much smaller than that in principle; and this may be partly why the principle eventually proved indefensible.

Until nearly the end of the century the two courts went their parallel ways without particular friction. Then came the statute of 1585 establishing the Elizabethan court of exchequer chamber, a legislative quirk which left the judges of each court with effective jurisdiction in error over the other[3]. Plaintiffs losing because of the common pleas requirements seem never to have brought error to the king's bench, no doubt because their likely complaint would be about the direction to the jury and that would not be on the record. Nor could a defendant losing in the king's bench bring error to the

1. *Edwards v Burre*, Dalison 104.
2. The phrase has nothing to do with executory contracts in the modern sense, but there has been much misunderstanding over this. See now J. H. Baker, 'New Light on *Slade's Case*' [1971] Cambridge Law Journal, pp. 51, 213 at p. 226.
3. Stats. 27 Eliz., c. 8 (1585); 31 Eliz., c. 1 (1589).

new exchequer chamber with much hope of success if his plaintiff had in his claim deployed Denne and Fenne or such other assertions as would, if true, have satisfied the common pleas. But if the plaintiff relied to the full on the king's bench practice and asserted nothing beyond the debt and a notional *assumpsit* to pay it, there was a good chance that a judgment in his favour would be reversed. It is curious that this did not in fact happen until the new exchequer chamber had been in existence for a decade, and there is some reason to think that the king's bench itself retreated for a time and did not allow actions in which there was obviously no claim distinct from the debt. But they resumed their old ways on a change of chief justice in 1592, and writs of error were promptly brought. The first were by executors, who as we have seen were protected by the logic of wager from liability in debt on simple contracts made by their testators, and who therefore had a particular grievance at this use of *assumpsit*. But in 1596 the new exchequer chamber reversed a judgment against a living buyer himself, and the issue between the courts seemed to be squarely joined. But *Slade's Case* had then already been begun, and the matter was to be settled by other means[1].

The unseemliness struck at a more humdrum level than that of reversal in error. A case might be started in the king's bench, and yet be effectively decided by the direction given to the jury at *nisi prius* by a judge from the common pleas. *Slade's Case* was indeed started in the king's bench, and came up for trial before a *nisi prius* commission consisting of one judge from each court; and it may have been they who decided to handle it in a way which would make some definitive resolution possible. A general verdict would decide nothing, a king's bench judgment in the plaintiff's favour could at most lead to another challenge in error before the statutory exchequer chamber. What in fact happened was that all concerned agreed on a special verdict; and instead of giving judgment on this, the king's bench 'for the honour of the law, and for the quiet of the subject' (the words come from Coke's report), adjourned the case for argument before all the judges and the barons of the exchequer in the old informal exchequer chamber. This was not a court of error, or indeed a court at all: but it had great authority, and by

1. J. H. Baker, 'New Light on *Slade's Case*' [1971] Cambridge Law Journal, pp. 51, 213 at pp. 222 ff.

custom the court which had referred a case to it would give judgment in accordance with its conclusions.

The claim which that body debated was as follows. In consideration that the plaintiff had at the special instance and request of the defendant bargained and sold to the defendant certain growing crops, the defendant faithfully promised to pay the plaintiff £16 on a certain date; but scheming to defraud the plaintiff of the said £16 he did not do so, to the plaintiff's damage of £40. To this the defendant pleaded *non assumpsit modo et forma*. The special verdict was that the defendant had indeed bought the crop for £16, but 'there was no [other] promise or taking upon him, besides the bargain aforesaid'; and if upon the whole matter the court decides that the defendant did take upon himself in the manner and form alleged, then the jurors find for the plaintiff, with damages of £16 and 20s. for costs; if not, they find for the defendant[1]. There was in short no actual separate promise; and apart from the language of deceit and an inflated claim for damages, the nature of which was not specified, there was nothing except the debt.

Slade's Case has been the most discussed law-suit in the history of the common law; and that much new material should have been found within the last decade, in places where one might have thought to look for it[2], shows what small progress has yet been made in the scientific study of the subject. But it still does not answer all our questions about the case itself. There were at least three discussions before the exchequer chamber between 1597 and 1602, and other conferences between the judges without argument by counsel. The arguments on each side seem evenly balanced and evenly supported, and we have no report of a conclusion by the exchequer chamber. All we know is that in 1602 the king's bench gave judgment for the plaintiff and therefore in favour of its former practice. Its own resolutions, which may or may not reflect an eventual consensus of all the judges, were that a separate promise or *assumpsit* was to be implied from the transaction raising the debt, and that the availability of an action of debt was no bar to an action

1. The record is set out at the beginning of Coke's report, 4 Co. Rep. 91a.
2. J. H. Baker, 'New Light on *Slade's Case*' [1971] Cambridge Law Journal, pp. 51, 213. There are major additions to Coke's report of the exchequer chamber proceedings, and to the reports of the eventual judgment of the king's bench in Yelverton 21, and Moore K.B. 667 (cf. ibid., 433).

on the case on the *assumpsit*. They expressly reserved the question whether the *assumpsit* action could be brought against executors.

The main reported arguments revolved around the two points already considered: wager of law and due process, and the propriety of allowing an action on the case to do exactly the work of another action. The part played by the promise is naturally discussed for the most part in contractual terms; and the case is indeed the climax of the process by which a new law of contract was derived from trespassory remedies. But the original trespassory logic is not forgotten. Coke reports as resolutions of the exchequer chamber what may be just the propositions for which he himself had been arguing. But one of them still makes his own analysis clear: 'It was resolved, that the plaintiff in this action on the case on *assumpsit* should not recover only damages for the special loss (if any be) which he had, but also for the whole debt, so that' – and the conclusion shows that there is no mistake in the order of the words – 'a recovery or bar in this action would be a good bar in an action of debt brought upon the same contract; so *vice versa* . . .'[1]. The *assumpsit* action, then, is not theoretically an action to recover the debt at all. It is an action for consequential damage; and that the debt itself is recoverable, so that one action bars the other, is something that needs to be said. Coke, allowing *assumpsit* to perform the central function of contemporary contract, still looks down from that level of thought to the older level of the pleadings, the habitat of the wickedly scheming defendant and of Denne and Fenne. In the sixteenth and seventeenth centuries, as in the twentieth, contract was extricated from its own rules by resort to the essentially trespassory idea of detrimental reliance.

CONSEQUENCES OF *SLADE'S CASE*

However qualified and reluctant the acquiescence of some members of the exchequer chamber must have been, the law as stated in the judgment of the king's bench in *Slade's Case* was soon taken as having been definitively settled; and it was Coke's report that came to matter. Now the law of contract had to settle down on its accepted new basis, and it is a process about which we yet know little.

1. 4 Co. Rep. 91a at 94b.

Of the immediate and practical consequences, the most obvious was the effective ending of wager of law. That so many modern writers should treat wager as absurd will tell historians more about the legal climate of the twentieth century than that of the seventeenth. Although it is clear that there were then two views, it is equally clear that there was not just one; and it was the conservative view that events largely vindicated. The practical working of jury trial, especially the exclusion of evidence from the parties themselves, produced injustices comparable only to those added by the remedy attempted in the Statute of Frauds[1].

A consequential change was of great practical importance but needs no discussion. Executors had not been liable in debt on simple contract debts because of the logic of wager: the testator knew and could have sworn, but they could not know[2]. But in *assumpsit* the testator himself could not have sworn, and it could be argued that the executors were no worse off than he in answering before a jury. The king's bench had long been prepared to hold them liable; and although it expressly reserved the question in *Slade's Case*, that result was generalised within the following decade.

If the action was to perform exactly the function which had been performed by debt, two pleading questions arose, one about the facts and the other about the fictions. On the old trespassory basis, as we have seen, the transaction creating the debt was not relevant to the claim notionally being made. If the action had really been about damage suffered by reliance on a separate promise to pay, all that would have mattered was that at the beginning of the story the defendant was *indebitatus* to the plaintiff; and often that was all that was alleged. How the debt had arisen would not emerge until evidence was given at the trial; and when the action was really about the debt itself, that was obviously unjust. Soon after *Slade's Case* the general *indebitatus* allegation was held insufficient[3]. But instead of the transaction being recited in full, the practice slowly grew up of asserting that the defendant was *indebitatus* in the amount demanded for money lent, for the price of work and

1. Stat. 29 Car. II, c. 3 (1677).
2. See p. 257, above.
3. J. H. Baker, 'New Light on *Slade's Case*' [1971] Cambridge Law Journal, pp. 51, 213 at p. 214.

materials or of goods sold and delivered or the like; and these became the 'common counts' which told the defendant what kind of claim he was to answer without tying the plaintiff to more particularity than was often practicable when action was being initiated[1].

The fictions which had seemed necessary on the old trespassory basis mostly went out of use; but until the nineteenth century there were two substantial survivors. One was the allegation of deceit, which apparently did no harm in *assumpsit*, but perhaps made it harder for the common law to regenerate a genuine tort of deceit. The other was the allegation of a separate promise, which played some part in various extensions of the range of *assumpsit* remedies. The issues in the enforcement of customary dues and the like, which were debts not arising out of voluntary transactions, and in the enforcement of claims in *quantum meruit* and quasi-contract, which were never within the scope of debt at all, were in various ways confused by this allegation of a promise. But it is only by confusing the issues that legal development becomes possible; and the most fruitful of these were changes by which *assumpsit* was able to reach beyond debt into the ambit of the old action of account, and to recover for the common law some of its lost conceptual potentialities in quasi-contract and restitution.

These developments will not be traced here, nor will the development of contract law itself since the seventeenth century. Important work is now being done; but we still know too little to make the kind of statement appropriate to such a book as this. To derive a law of 'contract' from remedies in 'tort' involved more than the change of remedy. Tort actions look backwards from damage to its causation. A contract is an event in itself, happening at a particular moment and altering rights from that moment onwards; and that idea probably did not arise until the nineteenth century. Nor can such operations be done without anaesthetic: you had to argue about 'forms of action' because the wound to principle was too large to bear. And since in the end the law is a matter of words, it is important to remember the point of nomenclature. 'Covenant' lost its original sense as the name of the elementary idea long before 'contract' (which had first to lose its own original sense) was ready

1. H. K. Lücke, '*Slade's Case* and the Origin of the Common Counts' (1965) 81 LQR, pp. 422, 539; (1966) 82, p. 81.

to take its place. In between there was nothing but the name of the action: '*assumpsit*' had to serve as a legal category[1].

But until the nineteenth century that category did not include all questions about agreements. *Assumpsit* was never available when the plaintiff had a document under seal. He still had to bring covenant or debt as appropriate, and there are various possible reasons. To the extent that the development of *assumpsit* was consciously in response to such hardships over proof as wager, there were none. Obligations under seal were also seen as of a 'higher' nature, and may have been thought out of reach. And in the case of the bond for money, its point was to prove indebtedness and so exclude the general issue in debt: but it could not exclude *non assumpsit*, and then there would be no way of stopping the jury from going behind the document. A consequence in detail has already been noticed. Corporations had to contract under seal and so were necessarily sued in actions in which there was no general issue; and statute had to rescue incorporated insurance companies from what proved a serious disadvantage for them, as against their unincorporated rivals, in fighting claims. It is a curious illustration of the artificial division imposed upon contractual liability by 'the forms of action'[2].

In an English text-book of contract law about 1900, the most elementary statement would be about the formation of a contract: besides offer and acceptance, it was necessary that there should be either consideration or a document under seal. It is hard to realise how recent was that grouping of ideas, and indeed how recent was the idea of 'formation of a contract', or even of a law of contract as a body of doctrine which could be written out in a text-book.

CONSIDERATION

The essence of the common law of contract is the doctrine of consideration. In England it is supplemented by the contract under seal, a relic of the law before *assumpsit*, which enables a deliberate but gratuitous promise easily to be made binding. In the United States, partly perhaps because that facility does not generally exist,

1. See p. 249, above.
2. See p. 282, above.

there has grown up a new alternative law of contract based once again upon reliance; and some suggest that there the traditional consideration contract is dead or dying as covenant and debt died in England centuries earlier[1].

But consideration itself had its beginning in *assumpsit* conceived as a reliance remedy. The most typical sixteenth century *assumpsit* report will say that in consideration of something or other the defendant made the faithful promise for the breach of which the plaintiff is suing; the defendant will plead *non assumpsit;* the jury will find for the plaintiff; and then the defendant will move in arrest of judgment on the ground that the promise was not made for a sufficient consideration. What did that mean? What question was the court really being asked to decide? To begin with it was a trespassory question: were the circumstances such that the plaintiff was entitled to act on this promise? As *assumpsit* became an overtly contractual action, it became a contractual question: ought the court to hold that the promise made by the defendant in these circumstances was binding? But of course there was never a conscious transition from the earlier to the later context of the question; and so the rather miscellaneous answers given in the earlier context had later to be cobbled together into a more or less coherent set of rules.

That is the nature of the story; and, as with the 'origins' of trespass and case, it would not be right to look to single pre-existing entities like *quid pro quo* or the civilian and canonist idea of *causa.* But they are not necessarily irrelevant, and again the analogy with trespass is worth drawing. The appeal of felony is clearly not 'the origin of trespass' in the simple sense once thought: but equally clearly it is part of a story which cannot be understood without it[2]. So with consideration: when a court had to ask itself the earlier question, whether the plaintiff was entitled to rely on the promise, where did they look for an answer? Even introspection would not be merely uninformed. If the trespassory idea behind reliance was in part taken from the doings of church courts, then both the chancellor and the common law courts may have looked at these questions with ideas like *causa* in mind. There is more common ground than usual when the Doctor discusses these matters with the

1. Grant Gilmore, *The Death of Contract* (1974).
2. See p. 283, n. 2, p. 285, above.

Student[1]. But primarily, no doubt, common law judges would look to the circumstances in which agreements were enforceable in local courts; and to that extent the underlying reciprocity of the old actions, isolated and perhaps narrowed in debt under the name of *quid pro quo*, was a formative factor in the separate decisions later assembled and rationalised as the doctrine of consideration.

It follows that with this subject as with many others we have tried to be too precise, to trace the later meaning of a legal word back to some single source; and we have complicated the task by supposing that even in the later law the word had a meaning in the sense of representing an idea. What it represented was the equivalent of a substantial chapter in a modern text-book. The rationalisation which seeks to represent that body of rules as a single doctrine can be seen beginning in the reports of the later sixteenth century. But even then what we see is discussion of doubtful cases, and only the plea rolls will show us with certainty the regular and central allegations that seemed to plaintiffs sufficient. For the earlier period, when the question was asked in terms of reliance, reports are few: and the trespassory raw materials of the later contractual rationalisation will be recoverable only from the rolls, upon which work has only lately begun. We are hardly yet in a position to ask useful questions, let alone answer them.

'Legal principle avenges itself.' The comment is that of the greatest of historians upon the consequences of using an inappropriate remedy for practical reasons[2]. Our largest question is how far the contractual doctrine of consideration was deformed because it had to be assembled from trespassory materials. Consider the Student's formulation of the view of 'divers that be learned in the laws of the realm . . .: if he to whom the promise is made have a charge by reason of the promise, which he hath also performed, then in that case he shall have an action for that thing that was promised, though he that made the promise have no worldly profit by it.'[3] This is the reliance cause of action entitling the plaintiff to performance rather than to restitution. But the example which the Student gives is a three-party situation, in principle like the early

1. *Doctor and Student*, Dialogue II, c. 24 (Selden Society, vol. 91, p. 228).
2. F. W. Maitland, 'The Beatitude of Seisin', *Collected Papers* (1911), vol. I, pp. 407, 434 at p. 447.
3. *Doctor and Student*, Dialogue II, c. 24 (Selden Society, vol. 91, p. 228 at p. 230).

guarantee cases: the physician has treated the poor man at the instance of the good Samaritan, who now refuses to pay. There is no question of restitution, no *quid pro quo* coming to the Samaritan to ground debt, and an action to enforce the payment is the only just solution for the physician's reliance.

So far so good. But now turn the facts round. The Samaritan pays the physician who does not treat the poor man. Even if all three are together and the physician's promise is made to the poor man as well as to the Samaritan, still the poor man has no remedy against the physician. Later law will have a slogan that consideration must move from the plaintiff. It is not an obviously just or reasonable result, and it could be a legacy of the reliance approach: it was the Samaritan who had the charge by reason of the promise.

The slogan that past consideration is no consideration seems more clearly to follow from the logic. It is first stated in 1490: the buyer to whom a warranty is given after the sale cannot bring his action of deceit if the warranty proves false, presumably because it had not induced him to buy[1]. Nor is that result unreasonable. But suppose, as the Doctor asks the Student, that 'I promise thee £40, for that thou hast builded me such a house, lieth an action there?' The Student thinks not, but interestingly adds that such a promise would be binding in conscience[2]. A little later, he would probably have answered that he needed more facts. When such claims are made, it becomes common for the plaintiff to allege that he had done whatever it was at the special instance and request of the defendant. The original point of this was probably to bring the case back within range of the reliance approach, but the end of it was a lot of law about the difference between executed and past consideration.

A special case of the difficulty over past consideration arose when *assumpsit* was used to recover debt. If a seller of goods sues for the price, the goods themselves are the 'natural' consideration for the buyer's promise to pay for them. But he cannot put the case that way, because they are also the *quid pro quo* which shows that he ought to be suing in debt. After *Slade's Case*, of course, that natural consideration was the true issue: it was the *quid pro quo* which determined whether the defendant was indebted. But so long as the

1. YB Trin. 5 Hy. VII, pl. 7, f. 41v.
2. *Doctor and Student*, Dialogue II, c. 24 (Selden Society, vol. 91, at p. 231).

action lasts, the plaintiff has to allege both a separate promise to pay and consideration for that promise; and both are artificial. The consideration is said to be the sale itself or the indebtedness resulting from it, and two difficulties are discussed: the transaction was past and the promise was to do what the defendant was already bound to do[1]. Before *Slade's Case* there were various consequential artificialities, going to the plaintiff's entitlement to rely on the promise and to some charge he had by reason of it. The sale is said to have been at the special instance and request of the defendant; and some separate consideration for the promise is alleged, or a forbearance to sue on the faith of it. But when it is clear that the action is just for the debt, with no consequential damage or the like, neither reliance nor any other principle can really do the trick, and resort was had to simple assertion: an existing debt is itself consideration for a promise to pay it.

That development serves to remind us once again of the source of our own difficulty about consideration. Like the rational Lord Mansfield[2], we try to assign it some place as an element in a contract itself seen as an entity. But it has always been just the label on a package containing many of the separate rules about the liabilities which may arise in the context of a transaction. Separate questions were answered by assertion, and at first they were asked in terms of reliance. Perhaps some of the answers were not ideal when the questions come to be asked in contractual terms. But in this case it is largely upon legal historians that legal principle has avenged itself.

1. J. H. Baker, 'New Light on *Slade's Case*' [1971] Cambridge Law Journal, pp. 51, 213 at p. 218.
2. For Mansfield's attempt to present consideration as a matter of evidence, see *Pillans v Van Mierop* (1765), 3 Burrow 1663; overruled by *Rann v Hughes* (1778), 4 Brown P.C. 27; 7 T.R. 350n. For his attempt to make moral obligation sufficient see *Atkins v Hill* (1775), Cowper 284; *Trueman v Fenton* (1777), Cowper 544; *Hawkes v Saunders* (1782), Cowper 289.

13 Rise of Modern Law of Torts

The rise of *assumpsit* was not the dawning of an idea of contract. This was work that the common law had largely left to other courts, and so disabled itself from doing. Rules such as that requiring a deed in covenant had barred the natural approach to an everyday law of contract. What the common law had deviously achieved by about 1650 may be seen as a counterfeit, and in some respects an imperfect one, of the contractual system existing in say London three centuries earlier and more.

Similarly in the field of tort, it is important to remember that the sequence of events, the early appearance of trespass *vi et armis* and the later rise of actions on the case, was governed by jurisdiction. Local courts in the early fourteenth century had a law of wrongs which protected all the ordinary interests of life. In the common law, the initial unconcern with any wrongs except those affecting the king introduced an artificiality which, not unlike the seal in covenant, affected all later development. Again, the rise of the modern law of torts was not the creation of something new but the restoration of a lost simplicity.

DECEIT

Deceit is taken first because it illustrates this point, and because the subject is related with *assumpsit*. Nearly all the early cases about deceit in royal courts depend upon an allegation that the court itself has been deceived; and just as 'trespass' has been identified with *contra pacem regis* so deceit has been identified with abuse of legal procedure[1]. But the explanation is the same in both cases. Private

1. See e.g. W. S. Holdsworth, *History of English Law*, vol. II (4th edn.), p. 366; vol. III (5th edn.), p. 407.

cheating was clearly wrongful, but the king had no interest in the matter. The deceit of his courts was the only common kind of deceit in which there was an obvious royal interest; and of course the procedure was *ex officio* and almost summary. But just as stray trespasses came to the king's courts which were not *contra pacem*, so did stray complaints of private deceit by favoured persons and the like[1].

In local jurisdictions, moreover, it is clear that cheating, inducing others into actions detrimental to themselves, was a familiar idea. It was treated as a wrong because of what we should call the criminal element, because of the public interest in honest dealing. The seller of bad fish, or of caps made from reclaimed wool, wronged not only his buyer; and even if there was no private complainant, even if no sale had been made, merely to offer such things for sale was a wrong which the city authorities might punish[2].

Such a wrong, at any period of history, is most often done in a contractual context. The intention of the wrongdoer is not just to induce harm to his victim: it is to get a benefit for himself, commonly to sell something for more than it is worth. From the point of view of the victim, therefore, the background is in contract as much as in wrong; and in local jurisdictions the punitive element was sometimes harnessed to the victim's interest, being used to compel restitution, the undoing of the transaction, whenever that was possible[3].

1. For a case in 1280 of a woman induced to part with her land by a promise of marriage, see *Select Cases in the Court of King's Bench*, vol. I (Selden Society, vol. 55), p. 65; vol. II (Selden Society, vol. 57), p. 20; vol. III (Selden Society, vol. 58), p. xcix; vol. IV (Selden Society, vol. 74), p. lxx; H. G. Richardson and G. O. Sayles, *Select Cases of Procedure without Writ* (Selden Society, vol. 60), p. xlvii, n. 2; cf. *Brevia Placitata* (Selden Society, vol. 66), p. 122; *Casus Placitorum* (Selden Society, vol. 69), p. 30/3; S. F. C. Milsom, *Novae Narrationes* (Selden Society, vol. 80), p. cxxxii, n. 4. For a very early example of such inducement, see *Curia Regis Rolls*, vol. I, pp. 388–9. Because land was involved, it was inevitable that such cases came to royal courts; and a writ had to be devised, the writ of entry *causa matrimonii praelocuti*. For another kind of case see p. 321, n. 1, above.
2. E.g. *Calendar of Early Mayor's Court Rolls of the City of London, 1298–1307*, pp. 56 ('prosecution' for exposing for sale putrid veal, 1300); 258 (probably 'civil action' for selling putrid fish, 1307); 154 ('plea of trespass' for selling false and counterfeit lambskins 1304); 216 ('plea of trespass' for selling false ashes of woad, 1305).
3. E.g. *Calendar of Plea and Memoranda Rolls of the City of London, 1364–1381*, p. 126 (1371); ibid., *1381–1412*, p. 23 (1382).

In the royal courts deceit, like any other wrong, could come in after the requirement of a royal interest was abandoned; and the false statement made to induce a sale of goods, the false warranty, soon became familiar. But, as has been noted, the 'criminal' element was lost in royal courts, and this was the factor that had anchored deceit to wrong rather than to contract. The context in which cases came up for consideration was now exclusively that of the private dispute arising out of a contract, and the contractual merits of the matter could be weighed in isolation. If it seemed right to allow the buyer to recover against the merely mistaken seller who had given an untrue warranty in good faith, this could now be done: it would not mean that the seller would also be punished for dishonesty. Perhaps because this was the commercially convenient answer, perhaps because of the difficulty of proving actual dishonesty, that result followed; and warranties became in truth a matter of contract, though it would be long before they could be so in name[1].

Outside the field of warranty, deceit played the various parts discussed in the preceding chapter. And again the end of it was that the word lost its meaning. If promises are to be enforced on the basis that the promisor deceived the plaintiff, the promisor must not be allowed to say that he acted honestly: that is not what contract is about. Deceit became a series of meaningless allegations in the pleading of contract cases; and the idea itself virtually disappeared.

The consequence of these developments was that the common law hardly ever distinguished the true cheat from his innocent counterpart; and it was no doubt this that prompted star chamber and chancery to interest themselves particularly in fraud. They were indeed restoring different aspects of the old position in local jurisdictions. Chancery, in giving restitution to the victim, was knowingly or not reviving a civil remedy lost in the common law's concentration on damages. And star chamber, in punishing fraud, was knowingly or not making good a criminal sanction lost as the common law of crime became the only law of crime, as punishment was increasingly confined to the ancient pleas of the crown.

But even in the common law the realisation that deceit was itself a proper basis of liability probably never quite died. Cheating at dice or cards, for example, may have been actionable in the late fifteenth

1. See p. 321, above; and see S. F. C. Milsom, 'Sale of Goods in the Fifteenth Century' (1961) 77 LQR, p. 257 at p. 278.

century, though the matter was still not beyond argument in the early seventeenth century[1]. Late in the sixteenth century money had been paid to the plaintiff to pay over to a named third party; and the defendant, who got it by pretending to be that third party, was held liable in an action on the case for the deceit[2]. But claims of this nature were at least rare, perhaps because those who go in for such deceptions are not often worth suing.

It is in the contractual situation, especially the sale of goods, that deceit plays its largest part in real life; and it was here that the idea was now most beset by artificiality. If the defendant had given a warranty, it was immaterial whether he had in fact been deceitful; and if he had not given a warranty, there was an obvious difficulty no matter how deceitful he had been. The plaintiff would either have to use the warranty writ itself, and probably be met by a traverse of the warranty; or he would have to use what would look like a defective warranty writ, alleging deceit but omitting the warranty. The factual complaint was precisely that which the warranty writ had at first made.

Perhaps significantly, the one situation in which there does seem to be a continuous history of liability truly based on deceit is the one in which express warranties were not normally given, and in which therefore the ground was not taken up by a warranty action. This was the sale without title. Cases can be found from the fourteenth to the seventeenth centuries in which the defendant is sued for selling to the plaintiff something to which he knew he had no title[3]. But although his knowledge, *sciens*, is always alleged, we cannot be sure that it was material; and if and when it ceased to be so, the idea of deceit was again being abused to produce the essentially contractual result of an 'implied warranty'.

There was one situation in which a warranty of quality was 'implied', the sale of food by retail for immediate consumption. It is

1. Fitzherbert, *Natura Brevium*, f. 95D; *Baxter v Woodyard and Orbet* (1605), Moore K.B. 776; *Anon* (1633), Rolle's *Abridgment*, vol. I, p. 100, no. 9.
2. *Thomson v Gardner* (1597), Moore K.B. 538. Cf. *Bailey v Merrell* (1615), 3 Bulstrode 94 (harm to horses resulting from misstatement of load; opinion unfavourable to action).
3. YB 42 Lib. Ass., pl. 8, f. 259v; KB 27/731, m. 82 (1444; printed (1961) 77 LQR, p. 282); *Dale's Case* (1585), Cro. Eliz. 44; *Ruswell v Vaughan* (1601), Gouldsborough 123; *Roswel v Vaughan* (1607), Cro. Jac. 196. For London cases see *Calendar of Plea and Memoranda Rolls, 1323–1364*, p. 260; ibid., *1364–1381*, p. 126.

not clear whether this result was reached by using the warranty writ and not allowing the warranty to be traversed or by using a separate writ based directly on deceit, but probably it was the latter. In 1419, for example, an innkeeper was alleged deceitfully to have served cat to one who had ordered rabbit. There was no allegation of a warranty; and, in view of the possible importance of the matter in the history of contract, it is worth noting that the damage complained of was consequential, not the difference in value between roast rabbit and roast cat but the expense of an illness[1]. It is generally in the special context of sales of food that statements are found in the year books of a liability based simply on deceit. The seller who knows of a defect, it is said, will be liable even if he gave no warranty. But even in the case of food this ceased to be the true basis of the liability: the victualler was liable whether he knew or not and whether he warranted or not. And outside the cases of food and of defect of title, no examples have been found before the seventeenth century of claims based upon the knowledge of a defendant who had not given any warranty.

The question was raised in 1603 in the obscure case of *Chandelor v Lopus*[2]. The defendant was a goldsmith who knew about precious stones, and he sold the plaintiff what he affirmed, but did not warrant, was a stone of a particular kind; and it was not. Either the plaintiff brought two separate actions, or a single action was reported in very different ways. According to a reminiscence in the report of a later case, the plaintiff eventually won in an action which rested the defendant's liability purely on his making an affirmation which he knew to be untrue. But even if he did win, the reports agree at least over the unease felt about imposing liability on this basis in the absence of a warranty: 'for everyone in selling his wares will affirm that his wares are good . . . yet if he does not warrant them to be so, it is no cause of action'; and 'if it should be decided for the plaintiff it would trench on all the contracts in England, which would be dangerous . . . '; and since cases based only upon *sciens* do not seem to be reported thereafter, it is likely that *caveat emptor* continued to stand even against actual fraud.

1. CP 40/632, m. 476d (1419; printed (1961) 77 LQR, p. 279, where year book references are also given).
2. *Chandelor v Lopus* (1603), Cro. Jac., 4; (1894) 8 Harvard Law Review, pp. 282–4; A. K. R. Kiralfy, *The Action on the Case* (1951), p. 220. The later mention is in *Southern v How* (1618), Cro. Jac. 468 at 469.

The interest of this story, however, lies not in an answer reached at the time but in a question for us. Since fraud is always difficult to prove, it was no doubt desirable, when penal consequences ceased to be involved, to make the liability on a warranty independent of knowledge; and this in turn made it desirable to require express words for a warranty, so that it should be distinguishable from mere commendation by a seller. But was it really desirable to withhold a remedy for clearly dishonest commendation? Was this not truly a legalistic result, a consequence of abusing the idea of deceit? The common law had, as it were, used the cry of 'Wolf' as a summons to tea. Not until 1789 in *Pasley v Freeman* was a liability for deceit clearly established as an entity in its own right, neither necessarily associated with contract nor excluded by it; and this resurrection of an ancient and elementary liability has been treated by modern writers as an example of the rare 'invention' of a new tort[1]. In our own day history has repeated itself. Just as the difficulty in establishing this 'new' tort was the pre-emption of the ground by contractual actions, so has there been a difficulty over liability for misstatement that is merely negligent; and that has been because the ground was pre-empted by the tort of deceit.

CONVERSION

Just as the growth of *assumpsit* was chiefly conditioned by the older actions of debt and covenant, so the growth of trover was chiefly conditioned by detinue. But whereas *assumpsit* became a new mechanism for handling old ideas, the very definition of the developed tort of conversion shows it to be an artefact.

The word 'conversion', however, is old[2]. Its original sense was almost one of accounting: it denoted the application of assets to one purpose rather than to another, not necessarily wrongful. An abbot who borrowed money and 'converted it to the use of the house' was acting rightfully, and only an unfortunate constellation of circumstances brought this 'conversion' into court[3]. But the conversions

1. *Pasley v Freeman* (1789), 3 T.R. 51. See the treatment of this case in P. H. Winfield, *Text Book of the Law of Tort* (5th edn., 1950, the last by the author himself), pp. 15, 17, 379 n. (f.), 379–80.
2. E.g. *Bracton's Note Book*, no. 687; *Bracton*, f. 91b (ed. Woodbine-Thorne, vol. II, pp. 264–5).
3. YB Hil. 20 Hy. VI, pl. 19, f. 21, at f. 21v.

with which lawyers were concerned were usually wrongful; and the word is most often used of the executor who, while debts are still outstanding, treats the testator's goods as his own. His liability for specialty debts owed by his testator is normally limited to the testator's assets, but if it is found that those assets are exhausted because the executor converted some to his own use, then he is liable from his own goods[1]. The cause of action in that case is of course the debt: the conversion affects only the pocket which the judgment will reach. The conversion might be a cause of action for a legatee; but the legatee was protected by the church courts, not the king's. At common law much of the ground was covered by the action of account, and conversion was not an independent wrong for which action might be brought until the developments now to be considered.

These linguistic considerations have been put first at the expense of chronology in order to make the point that there was at the beginning a definite concept of conversion, although it was not in itself a cause of action and although it was not much concerned with specific goods. How did it come to be so?

It will be convenient to begin with the civil protection given by the common law to the owner of a chattel at about the middle of the fifteenth century. If the wrong is done while the chattel is in the plaintiff's hands, his remedy is trespass *vi et armis*; and this may extend to the case in which the defendant did the wrong after securing a delivery to himself for some temporary purpose such as to look at a deed[2]. So long as the plaintiff was at the time actually or constructively in possession of the thing, he has this remedy; and it will cover all possibilities, whether the thing was taken away or destroyed or merely damaged. But if the plaintiff was not at the time in possession, it is necessary to distinguish destruction or disposal from mere damage. If the thing was damaged in the hands of the defendant, the plaintiff's primary remedy is an action on the case. This may rest upon an *assumpsit* or negligence or, as in the

1. YBB Mich. 11 Hy. VI, pl. 12, f. 7v; Hil. 11 Hy. VI, pl. 9, f. 16; Pasch. 11 Hy. VI, pl. 30, f. 35v; Mich. 34 Hy. VI, pl. 42, f. 22v; Rastell, *Entrees* (ed. 1574), ff. 306–306v.
2. *Registrum Omnium Brevium* (ed. 1634), f. 92v; cf. f. 106v; YBB 1 & 2 Ed. II (Selden Society, vol. 17), p. 170; 5 Ed. II (Selden Society, vol. 31), p. 215; 11 Ed. II (Selden Society, vol. 61), p. 290. Cf. YB Hil. 39 Hy. VI, pl. 7, f. 44 (action on the case).

misfeasance cases, it may often rest upon both; but the defendant is even more obviously a wrongdoer if he did the damage deliberately.

He is of course equally a wrongdoer if he destroyed the chattel altogether or allowed it to perish or disposed of it. But in these cases the primary remedy of the plaintiff is detinue. Whatever the reason, the plaintiff is not going to get his chattel back: and even if the reason is a wrongful act by the defendant, his remedy upon the wrong is occluded by the older action. Once again, the point of growth is a boundary between an action on the case and an older remedy.

But boundaries can always be drawn more clearly on paper than in real life; and since detinue was subject to wager, it was inevitable that any uncertainty should be exploited. There might be uncertainty on the facts. If the owner brought detinue in respect of an extensively damaged chattel, the defendant could end the action by obeying the *praecipe* writ and returning the remains; and the plaintiff would still have to bring his action on the case for the damage. He would therefore prefer to write the chattel off as a total loss, and sue at once in case; but then the defendant would argue that since judgment in detinue would be for the object or its value, a claim for the full value must properly lie in detinue. In a case of 1472, indeed, a defendant said that he had in fact been sued in detinue in respect of the loss concerned, and had successfully made his law; and the question was whether the one action barred the other[1]. That was an action on the case against a bailee for negligent keeping so that the object perished; and it neatly illustrates both the uncertainty created by the two kinds of analysis and the temptation to exploit it.

This factual uncertainty is general, covering all kinds of harm and all kinds of possessor. And its most important outcome was in connection with the liability of bailees for accidental harm. In principle their liability for accidental damage would come up in actions on the case, and would rest either upon an *assumpsit* or upon an affirmative allegation of negligence. Their liability for accidental loss or destruction, however, would be in detinue; so that they were prima facie liable, and the burden of raising absence of fault would rest upon them. That is the true basis of the 'bailee's liability'. The dramatic change which came over that liability,

1. YB Mich. 12 Ed. IV, pl. 10, f. 13; A. W. B. Simpson, 'The Introduction of the Action on the Case for Conversion' (1959) 75 LQR, p. 364 at p. 369.

signalled in *Coggs v Bernard*[1], was due precisely to the final abandonment of detinue, so that even for a total loss or destruction the bailor would bring an action on the case based affirmatively upon wrongdoing, an action using the principle tried in 1472.

That development runs parallel to the rise of the tort of conversion, but is distinct and will not be traced here. A conversion was at least a positive act; and it was settled in the sixteenth century that an allegation of conversion could not be supported by evidence of negligent keeping no matter how destructive[2]. But the 1472 action against the bailee alleging loss by negligent keeping is matched by the earliest actions on the case alleging conversion by possessors. The first reported use of the word to denote a wrong was in the famous *Carrier's Case* in 1473 in which the question debated was whether a carrier who opened a package entrusted to him and converted the contents to his own use could be treated as a felon[3]. It may be significant that many of the earliest civil actions are cases of 'breaking bulk', opening containers of money or fungible goods and converting the contents[4]. Such situations, typified by the deposit of money in a bag, had always caused trouble on the borderline between debt and detinue[5]. The money could not be claimed in debt, and only the container as a whole could be claimed in detinue; and so neither action would provide a remedy if, say, half the contents had been taken. In the terms just considered, this was analogous to damaging a bailed object, rather than destroying or disposing of it. It was therefore arguably justifiable to use an action on the case in such circumstances, and natural to use the language of conversion; and though the argument seems not to appear it may have been obvious, and may explain many of the early cases. Sometimes, indeed, it was pressed further: the contents themselves had never passed into the defendant's possession before he 'broke bulk', and so a *vi et armis* action could be used[6].

1. *Coggs v Bernard* (1703), 2 Ld. Raymond 909.
2. *Walgrave v Ogden* (1590), 1 Leonard 224; cf. *Anon* (1584), Savile 74.
3. YB Pasch. 13 Ed. IV, pl. 5, f. 9.
4. J. H. Baker, *Spelman's Reports*, vol. II (Selden Society, vol. 94), p. *249*, at n. 3.
5. E.g. YBB 6 Ed. II (Selden Society, vol. 43), p. 65; 12 & 13 Ed. III (Rolls Series), p. 245.
6. J. H. Baker, *Spelman's Reports*, vol. II (Selden Society, vol. 94), p. *249*, n. 3. For early examples see *Eyre of London, 1321*, vol. II (Selden Society, vol. 86), pp. 149, 150; KB 27/201, m.22d, printed in (1958) 74 LQR, p. 565; see also cases discussed ibid., p. 566, suggesting fictional early development.

But it was a different matter if the object had not been packaged, so that it clearly had been in the defendant's possession and the detinue claim would be for the object itself and not for a container with contents. In 1479 a bailor of silver cups brought an action on the case against a sub-sub-bailee for breaking them up and converting them to his own use[1]. Two related arguments are made. One is practical, and reminiscent of the argument that covenant was inappropriate if the agreement could not in fact be performed. If the thing itself cannot in fact be recovered, so that the primary demand of the *praecipe* writ cannot be satisfied, then the plaintiff should not be driven to detinue. The other argument is metaphysical. The plaintiff must use detinue if the substance of his claim is to his property: and it does not matter that the object itself is in fact irrecoverable because detinue always claims the object or its value. The latter is the strict conservative position; and as with the use of *assumpsit* in place of debt, the argument of propriety is reinforced with that of due process. It is wrong to oust the defendant from his wager of law.

But even the conservatives perhaps accept that if the conversion deprives the plaintiff of his property, legally and not just factually, then the detinue action is gone and case is therefore available. Reference was made to a case of 1472 in which a bailor's executor sued a sub-sub-bailee in respect of cloth of gold and other valuable fabrics which the defendant had cut and made up into clothes. It was apparently argued, with rare reference to a Roman idea, that this amounted to what the Roman lawyers would have called a *specificatio*. The plaintiff's property in the cloth was gone, the clothes which had been made were a new thing belonging to the defendant; and by this alteration of property the plaintiff's action of detinue would be not merely unavailing in fact but unavailable in law. Nor was this an ingenious argument excogitated to counter the objection in an action on the case that the plaintiff ought to be bringing detinue. As in the case of careless custody in the same year, the plaintiff had in fact brought both actions: but in this case it seems that the court was no more able than the plaintiff to make up its mind which was proper[2].

1. YB Hil. 18 Ed. IV, pl. 5, f. 23. See A. W. B. Simpson, (1959) 75 LQR, at p. 372.
2. The action on the case: references in preceding note; A. K. R. Kiralfy, *The Action on the Case* (1951), p. 220; J. H. Baker, *An Introduction to English Legal History* (2nd edn., 1979), p. 331. The detinue action (not mentioning the action on the case): YB Mich. 12 Ed. IV, pl. 2, f. 11v; pl. 14, f. 14.

On the conservative view, then, detinue was generally appropriate; and the only real difficulty arose when the conversion had altered the property; and *specificatio*, which has been proposed as the very origin of conversion[1], seems just to have been a way in which that could happen, and was perhaps the first way to be discussed. What other ways could there be? Putting coin into circulation seems an obvious example, though in practice the case could arise only from a deposit of money in a bag. Later there is discussion about the sale of a specific object. That the sale was made to persons unknown goes to the factual unavailability of detinue. For legal unavailability the sale would have to be in market overt; and here we run into the familiar difficulty of not knowing what is being assumed. It may have been only in the sixteenth century that sales in market overt became so exceptional that they needed to be specified.

This goes to the nature of a conversion at this time: in modern language it involves a legal power to alter the property although of course it is a power that is here wrongfully exercised. But there is a prior question: what is this 'property' which detinue supposes? And before leaving the 1472 case of the fabrics and the 1479 case of the silver cups, it is worth observing that in both the defendant was a sub-sub-bailee. A detinue action would therefore have been, and in the earlier case it actually was, on a trover and not on a bailment. Detinue on a bailment, as we have seen, was next-of-kin to debt. The defendant's liability was contractual in nature; and although it comes to be said that the bailee is estopped from denying the bailor's title, that is only another way of saying that his contractual liability is independent of any question about whose the property is. It is in detinue on a trover that 'property' matters, because that is the sole basis of the plaintiff's claim. In strict propriety it would therefore follow that even if a conversion by a bailee altered the property, as by a sale in market overt, that would not affect his essentially contractual liability in detinue, and that the action on the case for conversion brought by a bailor against his bailee could never be justified on the basis that detinue was not available. How far this reasoning was accepted in the early sixteenth century is not clear. For reasons already explained it would not apply to cases in

1. A. W. B. Simpson, 'The Introduction of the Action on the Case for Conversion' (1959) 75 LQR, p. 364.

which the bailment was of container with contents, and the contents were converted; and this may account for many of the early actions against bailees. Some lawyers, perhaps specially those in the king's bench, were evidently prepared to meet the logic with bald assertion: the bailee's sale was a misdemeanour different from the mere detinue[1]. But even in the king's bench care was sometimes taken to present a more distinct wrong: in 1513, for example, a depositee for reward is said to have sold to persons unknown and converted the purchase money to his own use[2]. Later in the century that too becomes common: and perhaps the thought is that the bailor abandons his claim to the goods by adopting the sale, and then makes an independent complaint about the money.

In fact, however, conversion actions against bailees – or at least against persons who are identified as bailees – cease to be brought. Detinue is here formally invincible because of the contractual nature of the liability, and alteration of property is irrelevant to that. The way forward is in actions on the case against persons who are not bailees, or at any rate not said to be. They are persons against whom a detinue action would have to be brought on a trover or in the older *devenit ad manus* form. Here the plaintiff's case rests entirely upon his 'property'; but a simpler escape from detinue is found than by talk of the property being altered. It is reminiscent of the escape from covenant in nonfeasance cases on the basis that the *praecipe* covenant action became irrelevant once the stipulated time for performance had passed. And juridically it is impeccable. If detinue on a trover was essentially the proprietary claim, then it lay only against the possessor; and if the defendant had parted with the object before receiving the *praecipe* order, then he was no longer target of that action. It should be brought against his purchaser or whoever now had the goods. And it followed that if his parting had been wrongful, there was no objection to an action on the case for the wrong[3].

It is at this point that legal historians, and perhaps some fifteenth century lawyers, have most confused themselves by thinking of detinue as a conceptual entity instead of a single writ originating

1. Keilwey 160.
2. KB 27/1006, m. 27; it is a bill *de placito decepcionis in accione super casum*.
3. S. F. C. Milsom, 'Not Doing is no Trespass' [1954] Cambridge Law Journal, p. 105, at p. 113, a much over-simplified statement of this development as a whole but making the present point.

distinct claims. The contractual liability of the bailee was of course unaffected by his parting with the goods. But the difference would not be reflected in a special plea. It was hidden in the sense of the general issue, *non detinet*. The bailee and the non-bailee who had parted with the goods before the detinue action was brought could of course both wage their law: but the one perjured his soul and the other did not. It is even possible that this particular distinction between the claims had been forgotten, and was brought to light again by the probing of detinue which followed upon the use of actions on the case. It was clearly stated in 1535 and repeated from time to time throughout the sixteenth century[1].

To return now to actions on the case for conversion, it is easy to see why they ceased to be brought against bailees, or rather why they ceased to be brought against persons expressly said to be bailees. The bailee sells in market overt to a third party unknown to the plaintiff, so doing all he can to put the bailor's property out of his reach in law as well as in fact. His own liability to the bailor arises from the bailment itself, and is unaffected by his being out of possession, or by any alteration of the property; and the bailor can and therefore must sue him in detinue. Now suppose the finder or other neutral possessor to do the same. Detinue is no remedy against him: it would have to be detinue on a trover; and since he was out of possession when the writ was issued, he can honestly plead *non detinet*. Nor is detinue on a trover any remedy against his purchaser, the present possessor: even if the plaintiff knew who he was, the property was altered by the sale in market overt. The conversion has indeed deprived him of a detinue remedy against anyone.

It is also easy to see why these actions on the case for conversion came to be formulated as they were. Although at first some plaintiffs used a *devenit ad manus* count, as they once had in detinue, it had by the middle of the sixteenth century become

1. YB Pasch. 27 Hy. VIII, pl. 35, f. 13; Brooke, *Abridgment*, Detinue de biens 1. See *Anon* (1577), 4 Leonard 189: '. . . if one hath goods by trover, and bails them over before any action brought against him, detinue doth not lie against him . . ., but where such a person, who hath goods by trover, bails them *quibusdam ignotis*, such an action will lie against him.' Cf. *Vandrink v Archer* (1590), 1 Leonard 221 at 222: 'Where goods come to one by trover, he shall not be charged in an action, but for the time he hath the possession; but that is to be intended in an action of detinue, and not in an action upon the case . . .'.

common form to borrow from detinue the standard allegations of loss and finding, the count in trover. It is possible that this was to avoid the kind of pleading difficulty which had arisen in detinue from attempts to trace the real means by which the thing had come to the hands of the defendant[1]. But probably the general practice in detinue had made the trover count the simplest way of making the one assertion that mattered to the action on the case: the defendant had not come to the goods by bailment from the plaintiff. With the king's bench leading the way as usual, such actions so formulated became common; and the best known and earliest reported example was *Mounteagle v Worcester* heard in the common pleas in 1555[2]. The plaintiff alleges that he was possessed of the goods and lost them; they came to the possession of the defendant by finding; and the defendant, knowing they were the plaintiff's and scheming to defraud him, sold them to persons unknown and converted the proceeds to his own use. With one exception, every precaution has been taken against the objection that detinue is appropriate: the count in trover shows that it would be no remedy against the defendant himself; as against the defendant the plaintiff has any way waived his claim to the property and is complaining that the purchase money has been converted; the sale was to persons unknown, and so he cannot in fact bring detinue against the possessor. But still Dyer, reporting the case, seizes upon the one precaution missed: the sale is not said to have been in market overt, the plaintiff's property is not altered, and detinue is therefore in theory available to him. In the common pleas, at any rate, it was better to take no chances. But to many lawyers, and certainly in the king's bench, the circumvention of detinue was now the aim; and a decade later a precedent book actually has the caption 'Action on the case instead of action of detinue'[3].

Nor was this action being used instead of detinue only in the trover situation. Although detinue was always available against the bailee, so that the action on the case was never proper, all the plaintiff had to do was to suppress the bailment and count as usual on a trover. Even if anybody had wanted to prevent this, and the common pleas may have wanted to, it would have been practically

1. J. H. Baker, *Spelman's Reports*, vol. II (Selden Society, vol. 94), pp. *252–3*.
2. Dyer 121a.
3. Rastell, *Entrees* (ed 1566), f. 4.

impossible. The count in trover had established itself as a fiction in detinue, not true but having the conventional sense of possession otherwise than by bailment. In detinue there was no danger of abuse, because the bailor who counted in that way was only giving up advantages. In case, however, the advantage was reversed; his count hid the fact that he was using an inappropriate action. But to allow the bailee to take the point would be to allow a traverse of what everybody knew to be untrue; and the pleading convenience would be endangered even in the cases where it did no harm.

Since all actions for conversion used the trover fiction, and since most ended in the general issue, it is impossible to tell how often the parties were really bailor and bailee. An early reported case is in 1550, where the defendant turns out to be holding as pledgee in respect of an unpaid debt; and the question is whether this should be pleaded specially or whether he should say Not guilty and give it in evidence[1]. This particular plea is in fact found from time to time on the rolls in the second half of the century[2]. Again in 1557 a defendant pleads that he is a common carrier, that the plaintiff entrusted the goods to him for carriage, and that they were taken from him in an inn by the negligence of the innkeeper. The plaintiff demurs and there the entry unhappily ends[3].

So well accepted did the use of the action by bailors become that toward the end of the century they occasionally ventured out into the open. In 1594 a plaintiff who counted on a bailment secured a verdict and judgment apparently without objection being made[4]. But in 1600 the objection was made, though unsuccessfully[5]; and in 1615 the question was rationalised out of existence. In *Isaack v Clark* in that year a count in the common trover form was answered by the general issue, Not guilty; and the facts emerged on a special verdict[6]. In effect, the plaintiff had pledged his own property to the defendant on behalf of a third party, and later demanded it back before the third party's obligation was resolved. It was said that the fact that there was a bailment did not invalidate the action alleging a

1. Brooke, *Abridgment*, Action sur le case 113.
2. E.g. KB 27/1252, m. 366 (Hilary term, 1575); KB 27/1329, m. 328 (Easter term, 1594).
3. KB 27/1183, m. 193. Cf. *Owen v Lewyn* (1672), 1 Ventris 223.
4. KB 27/1329, m. 369d.
5. *Gumbleton v Grafton*, Cro. Eliz. 781.
6. 2 Bulstrode 306.

trover: if there had been a conversion, it terminated the bailment. A good slogan will work wonders. *Slade's Case* accepted that the separate promise upon which the *assumpsit* action rested could be conjured up by 'every contract executory imports in itself an *assumpsit*'; and by this magic the action of debt, the proper remedy upon a contract executory, was replaced. So here the bailment was disposed of, and with it the action of detinue which was its proper remedy, by mere words. The bailee ceased to be such by the act of conversion, and was thereby properly chargeable as a neutral possessor.

The result was that both the bailee and the neutral possessor who had sold or otherwise dealt with the goods could now be reached in this action instead of in detinue. But what about the bailee or other possessor who merely kept the plaintiff's property? On the face of it detinue must be the proper remedy, and fiction could not help. And this conclusion seems at first sight to be reinforced by a pleading decision. Between the finding and conversion, there was often inserted an allegation that the plaintiff had demanded his goods and been refused. But it was held, in connection with cases in which they had been sold, that such failure to redeliver was not necessary to the gist of the action, the conversion[1]. This, however, could be turned round. The pressure was to replace detinue, and even when the defendant still had the goods it could be argued that there was a difference between his detaining the plaintiff's property, and his 'converting' it by applying it to his own purposes. On this view an unqualified refusal to deliver in the absence of other circumstances, for example that the goods were pledged for a debt not yet paid, might amount to a conversion; and it seems that the king's bench dealt with conversion and detinue much as it had dealt with *assumpsit* and debt. Juries were directed that a mere refusal to deliver was sufficient evidence of a conversion, unless special circumstances were shown on the other side; and the result was that the action on the case provided a remedy in exactly the circumstances which properly grounded the action of detinue. A similar dispute between the courts seems to have followed; and at about the same time as in *Slade's Case* a special verdict was taken instead of the customary general verdict: the defendant gained possession by a trover, knew the goods to be the plaintiff's, and refused to give

1. See *La Countess de Rutland's Case* (1596), Moore K.B. 266; Owen 156.

them up; and the jury left it to the court to decide whether this was a conversion[1]. Again the hope was probably to secure a definitive settlement, but it seems to have been in vain. Three reporters fail to tell us much about the argument or its outcome, but there was evident perplexity. What was to happen, for example, if there was a conversion in this metaphysical sense, and then the goods were in fact returned?[2]. And what was to happen about the property, supposed by detinue to be in the plaintiff, if conversion was supposed to have altered it? These matters too were finally settled in *Isaack v Clark*, which in effect ratified the king's bench practice. The plaintiff who proved a mere refusal to deliver had proved a detinue but not a conversion: but if the refusal was absolute, such as to show that the defendant was indeed appropriating the goods to himself, that was a conversion. What the plaintiff could then recover was the value of the goods, the one action barred the other, and satisfaction of the judgment changed the property[3].

Detinue could now be avoided in every situation; but it was an end that had not been reached without cost. There was some damage to legal thinking and perhaps some to justice. The conceptual damage appears at a prosaic level in the definition of the tort of conversion. What is the essence of the 'denial of title'[4]? What, indeed, must be the nature of the title denied? Litigants at the end of the eighteenth century paid heavily to learn that ownership was neither necessary nor sufficient and that the title in question was once again a relative thing[5].

But there was perhaps a deeper wound, and it may be looked at from two angles. The concept of conversion would have been congruous with things as they were before the common law had committed itself to the basic idea of property in chattels, to the rule that *nemo dat quod non habet*. The defendant by converting has altered the property, and *mobilia non habent sequelam*. The plaintiff can look only to him for his remedy, and cannot follow the goods. All innocent purchasers would have been protected, and the

1. *Easton v Newman* (1596), Moore K.B. 460; Gouldsborough 152; Cro. Eliz. 495.
2. See the statement of Popham in Gouldsborough 155.
3. *Isaack v Clark* (1615), 2 Bulstrode 306; 1 Rolle, 59, 126. Again a special verdict had been taken.
4. See e.g. *Oakley v Lyster* [1931] 1 K.B. 148.
5. *Ward v Macauley* (1791), 4 T.R. 489; *Gordon v Harper* (1796), 7 T.R. 9.

'owner' left to recoup himself against the wrongdoer. But the common law has been kind to the owner. This concept of conversion has been utilised to give the owner full recovery against the wrongdoer. And yet, although he cannot recover more than once, he can still follow the goods and attack all into whose hands they come except through market overt; he can still reply upon *nemo dat*.

The same damage can be viewed from another angle. What was to be the position of the innocent purchaser of the plaintiff's goods? Once again it is worth observing that so long as his purchase was presumptively in market overt this question could not arise. Nor would it arise at all in detinue. *Ex hypothesi* the plaintiff would count on a trover. If the defendant had the goods, he would be liable, and nobody would wish him to be excused by his innocence: that is what is meant by property in chattels. If the defendant had not got the goods, he would not be liable in detinue at all. The plaintiff would then have to sue him as a wrongdoer; and in terms that is what he does in the action of trover. The defendant is said to have known that the goods belonged to the plaintiff, and to have acted dishonestly.

In 1590 a defendant pleads that he acted honestly: he supposed that his vendor had been entitled, and resold before he heard of the plaintiff's right[1]. Backward glances are cast at detinue, but the plea is held bad. It is by no means clear, however, that the defendant would have been held liable if he had pleaded the general issue and proved his lack of knowledge to the jury. The case is at least discussed in terms of what we should call tort; and when the alleged conversion was some positive disposition, these terms would have continued to be acceptable. But detinue was not just supplemented: it was replaced. What was to happen with the innocent buyer who did not resell the goods, but simply refused to give them up because he believed his vendor to have been entitled? If the action on the case was to do the work of detinue here, the purely proprietary work, his honest belief must be made irrelevant. And once it was made irrelevant in that case, it was inevitably made irrelevant when he had resold: the entity of 'conversion' had to be endowed with a general rule.

1. *Vandrink v Archer*, 1 Leonard 221.

The result was to allow the owner to fix the almost absolute liability appropriate to the proprietary claim not merely upon the present possessor, the proper target of that claim, but also upon past possessors. The innocent auctioneer who sells another's property may find himself liable for its full value to an owner of whom he could not have known, and although he got nothing out of the sale but his commission[1]. We tell ourselves that he is a victim of a policy discouraging theft; but in truth he is a victim of history.

DEFAMATION

Defamation, and indeed slander of goods and of title, were familiar in local jurisdictions in the fourteenth century; and there is some mystery about their late arrival in the common law. When the king's courts took in actions for wrongs in which the king had no interest, one would have expected to find actions on the case for words. But they do not appear until after 1500.

Various explanations suggest themselves. Until that time no actions on the case were common, presumably because litigants preferred the cheapness of local justice; and perhaps words never seemed to matter enough. Or perhaps it was the judges who feared the flood of difficult and pointless litigation that did indeed ensue when actions were accepted. Or again, like other wrongs, defamation had been treated in local courts from the two aspects that we should call criminal and civil: the victim might be compensated, and the wrongdoer might be punished[2]. For punishment two motives were at work: the general threat to good order inherent in insult, and the particular threat to authority inherent in sedition; and it

1. *Consolidated Co v Curtis*, [1892] 1 Q.B. 495. Cf. *Hollins v Fowler* (1875), L.R. 7 H.L. 757.
2. Defamation is of course a 'trespass' in local courts; see e.g. G. H. Fowler, *Rolls from the Office of the Sheriff of Beds. and Bucks., 1332–1334* (1929), p. 66. The London records show very clearly the various motives for repressing defamations. See e.g. *Calendar of Early Mayor's Court Rolls, 1298–1307*, p. 40 (1299, 'civil action' by employer against disaffected employee who told others he would not pay); *Calendar of Plea and Memoranda Rolls, 1323–1364*, p. 69 (1328, 'prosecution' for saying that the mayor was *pessimus vermis* that had come to London for twenty years); ibid., *1381–1412*, p. 40 (1383, tailor 'prosecuted' for speaking evil and shameful words of a tawyer, whence discord might have arisen between the two misteries of tailors and tawyers).

may be that these so overshadowed the 'civil' aspect, that the king's courts did not feel it appropriate to allow cases to be treated purely as private wrongs.

What was actually said by the king's courts on the eve of the change was that defamation was a spiritual offence and matter for the church[1]; and we are beginning to learn more about this jurisdiction[2]. It rests upon ecclesiastical legislation of the early thirteenth century, by which excommunication was ordained for those who maliciously impute crimes to persons who are of good fame, so that they have to clear themselves at least by compurgation or are otherwise harmed[3]. 'Fame' and its derivatives have a more or less technical sense, and must be understood against a background in which in both ecclesiastical and, as will appear in the following chapter, also in the lay law, ill fame among good people or the suspicion of the countryside was enough to put a man to answer a charge; but if there was nothing more, ancient principle in both jurisdictions allowed him to clear himself by compurgation. Whether the original constitution was intended to embrace allegations giving rise to lay as well as ecclesiastical proceedings is perhaps doubtful: the word *crimen* would have no distinct meaning in that context. But of course most serious temporal wrongs are also spiritual offences; and it is clear that the church courts did in fact deal indiscriminately with allegations of temporal and ecclesiastical crimes, and so covered almost the whole potential field of defamation. But they could not deal with allegations which did not relate to any kind of crime, such as professional incompetence; and if these were remediable at all it must have been in local courts.

As yet we know little of the relationship between local jurisdictions and this jurisdiction of the church in the middle ages. But we do know that the king's courts sought to impose limits on the church jurisdiction which, although largely ineffective in fact, were to be important for the future. One concerned allegations of temporal crime. The danger was that the church jurisdiction would interfere with indictment and similar procedures; and a statute of

1. YB Trin. 12 Hy. VII, pl. 2, f. 22, at f. 24v (1497).
2. R. H. Helmholz 'Canonical Defamation in Medieval England' (1971) 15 American Journal of Legal History, p. 255. Professor Helmholz is editing for the Selden Society a volume of ecclesiastical and lay materials on defamation.
3. Quoted op cit., p. 256. F. M. Powicke and C. R. Cheney, *Councils and Synods*, vol. II, A.D. 1205–1313 (1964), Part 1, p. 107.

1327 indeed forbade proceedings against indictors[1]. But the requirement of malice in the original constitution, always observed by the church courts, would anyway have excluded most such cases; and the two jurisdictions seem in fact to have ignored each other more or less amicably. The church dealt with allegations of temporal crime on its own principles. And the king's court, in principle always prepared to intervene with a prohibition, in fact rarely did so. Another limit which the king's court sought to impose concerned compensation for an injured party. Its own constitution confined the church to ecclesiastical penalties; and in 1286 the so-called statute *Circumspecte Agatis* (really a writ of instruction to justices), was intended to compel the observance of this[2]. And formally it was observed. But there was nothing to stop a church court from mitigating its penalty if the wrongdoer made restitution to his victim; and this is probably what often happened.

The ecclesiastical jurisdiction deserves, and is receiving, more investigation for its own sake. But from the view-point of this book, its main interest is in its influence on the common law. It played two parts, and the first is of the familiar negative kind. Just as the old personal actions and even, as we shall see, trespass *vi et armis* itself, formed a kind of mould into which the action on the case was poured, so was another part of the mould formed by this ecclesiastical jurisdiction over defamation. The king's courts here set out to do exactly what the church could not effectively or properly do. The other part which the ecclesiastical jurisdiction played cannot yet be assessed, but to an unknown degree it seems to have provided a model for what was done in the king's courts, or at least for plaintiffs in formulating their complaints.

The earliest actions which seem relevant in royal courts become regular in the second half of the fifteenth century. The plaintiff complains that the defendant claimed him as his villein. The preamble to the writ sets out the plaintiff's free condition much as later writs set out his good name and reputation; but the gist of the action is that the defendant so lay in wait for the plaintiff and threatened him that he dared not go about his business. The writ may have *vi et armis* and *contra pacem*, and so far as the nature of

1. Stat. 1 Ed. III, stat. 2, c. 11.
2. *Statutes of the Realm*, vol. 1, p. 101; E. B. Graves, '*Circumspecte Agatis*' (1928) 43 English Historical Review, p. 1.

the wrong goes its affinity is with assault. But the damage is consequential, the business injury to the plaintiff flowing from the constraint upon himself, not from the disinclination of others to deal with him[1]. In contrast, an entry of 1511 is truly one of slander:

> 'That whereas the plaintiff was of good and honourable name, fame and bearing, and was so held, spoken of and esteemed among good and grave men, the defendant, scheming wrongly to harm and take away his name and estate, called the plaintiff *nativus*, in English bondman, and at such a day and place he publicly said and pronounced these words in English "Thow knave, thow ar sir John Rysley bondman and somme of thes days he will seize thy body and thy goods" whereby the plaintiff is widely harmed and wronged in his estate and name and in his lawful business of buying selling and dealing with honourable persons, whereof he says that he is injured and suffered damage to the value of £20.'[2]

The complaint must have been drawn with the church jurisdiction in mind. The plaintiff's recital of his reputation 'among good and grave men' is a direct quotation from the constitution upon which it was based; and the allegation of wicked motive may have come from the same source. But equally this was not a case which could have come to a church court. It was no crime, temporal or ecclesiastical, to be a bondman; and the gist of the action was temporal damage for which, formally at any rate, the church could not have ordered compensation.

But whether or not the old action for claiming the plaintiff as a villein had somehow led the way, this was not the first action on the case for words in a royal court. In 1508 actions appear in which the plaintiff complains that the defendant called him a thief, though in these earliest cases the actual words are not recited in English as becomes general. There is the same reference to the plaintiff's standing among 'good and grave men', the same allegation of wicked motive, and the same emphasis on temporal loss following from the defamation because honest people would not deal with him[3]. Theft was of course a crime in either jurisdiction, and the

1. YBB Pasch. 2 Ed. IV, pl. 10, f. 5; Trin. 15 Ed. IV, pl. 15, f. 32; Trin. 17 Ed. IV, pl. 2, f. 3. The case in the last two references is discussed in J. H. Baker, *Spelman's Reports*, vol. II (Selden Society, vol. 94), p. *237*; other cases are listed ibid., p. *190*. See also CP 40/957, mm. 320d, 442 (Trinity term, 1501).
2. KB 27/999, m. 73d: defendant pleaded Not guilty.
3. KB 27/988, m. 42d; for other cases see now J. H. Baker, *Spelman's Reports*, vol. II (Selden Society, vol. 94), pp. *237–8*.

case was therefore one over which the church had jurisdiction according to its own lights, but one which in principle the king's court would prohibit it from hearing. So far as the king's court was concerned, therefore, the victim of such allegations could not even procure their punishment; and this must be why it was persuaded to entertain such cases itself. Allegations of theft are not only the earliest defamations to appear in the plea rolls: throughout the sixteenth century they are by far the commonest, though other temporal crimes follow in smaller numbers.

The other category of defamations in the ecclesiastical sense were allegations of purely spiritual offences; and these of course were in principle left to the church. To call a man adulterer or heretic is not actionable: only the church can investigate the charge, and a lay court would be powerless if a justification were pleaded[1]. Doubtful cases were possible, as is illustrated by 'witch'. This was for the church, unless it was alleged that the witchcraft had caused death or consisted in conference with the devil: these were felony by statute[2]. But the simplicity of the distinction was disturbed by the other great limitation on the church, namely that it might not order (though it could in fact induce) compensation in money. Suppose the allegation of a spiritual matter caused worldly loss? As early as 1513 a sad figure sought to raise this point and perhaps to give his name to a leading case. A London merchant embroiled with church authorities, he was charged with heresy. And when he tried to go to church, the parson declared before the congregation that he was 'accursed', that is excommunicated, and ordered him from the church, refusing to begin the service while he was there. For this the merchant sued the parson, saying that in fact he was not excommunicated, and that because of the statement that he was, other merchants dared not deal with him. To this claim the parson demurred; and after adjournments it ended without a decision, as did a *praemunire* also brought by the merchant. The cases ended because the plaintiff had died; and his death in a church prison gave his name, not to the leading case he had hoped for, but to one of the

1. YB Trin. 27 Hy. VIII, pl. 4, f. 14. Cf. *Anon* (1561), Moore K.B. 29; *Parret v Carpenter* (?1596), Noy 64.
2. *Morrice v Smith* (1587), Moore K.B. 906; *Clark and Green's Case* (1588), 2 Leonard 30; *Mutton's Case* (1609), 13 Co. Rep. 59; *Stone v Roberts* (1617), Noy 22; *Shuter v Emet* (1623), Benloe 127.

episodes leading up to the reformation. But, suspicious though the circumstances were, it is likely that the cases were going against him, and that he took his own life in disappointment[1].

Such cases occur from time to time throughout the sixteenth century and after. Incontinence, for example, was in itself a spiritual offence at any rate so far as the king's courts were concerned. To accuse a woman of having a bastard child might be actionable, because this was an offence by statute, though doubts arose: the statute punished only the having of bastards chargeable to the parish. But even an allegation of the purely spiritual offence would be actionable if it caused a temporal loss, as of a marriage; and a report in 1593 can be matched in the rolls nearly sixty years earlier[2]. Imputations of heresy and sorcery have long been unfashionable, and the narrow effect of this line of thought was upon allegations of sexual misconduct not amounting to a crime. It is a legacy of the church jurisdiction that men today cannot sue upon these unless they can prove actual damage; and women could not do so until 1891, although in the nineteenth century actual damage was as likely as it was hard to prove[3].

But temporal damage was to play a wider part than in bringing into the lay jurisdiction allegations of a purely ecclesiastical offence. This coalesced with a distinct notion that temporal damage might itself be a cause of action even if the words were not a 'defamation' in the ecclesiastical sense, because they did not import a spiritual or temporal offence. The earliest known example of this distinct notion was the case of 1511 in which the plaintiff had been called a bondman. This was neither a crime nor a sin, and its wrongful imputation should not lead people to think worse of him in the moral sense. But they might treat him differently, being unwilling to deal with him as in 1511 or unwilling to contemplate a marriage with him as in another case of 1530[4]. Similar considerations apply to

1. KB 27/1006, m. 36. See S. F. C. Milsom, 'Richard Hunne's Praemunire' (1961) 76 English Historical Review, p. 80. Cf. YB Trin. 27 Hy. VIII, pl. 4, f. 14; *Barnabas v Traunter* (1640), Rolle's *Abridgment*, vol. 1, p. 37, no. 15.
2. *Davis v Gardiner* (1593), 4 Co. Rep., 16b; cf. case of 1536 in J. H. Baker, *Spelman's Reports*, vol. II (Selden Society, vol. 94), p. *241*, n. 4. For 'whore' see *Anon*. (1586), Owen 34; *Pollard v Armshaw* (1601), Gouldsborough 173; *Elizabeth Tomson's Case* (1624), Benloe 148.
3. Slander of Women Act 1891, 54 & 55 Vict., c. 51.
4. CP 40/1064, m. 516d.

to 'alien' and 'Scot', and later to 'bankrupt' said of a merchant[1]. The affinities are with slander of title, which itself appears soon after the 1511 bondage case[2]. 'Bastard' was particularly confusing. Bastardy was in principle triable by the ecclesiastical courts; but equally it was not a crime, spiritual or temporal, and the imputation was therefore probably not an ecclesiastical defamation. The lay court would entertain an action if an inheritance was imperilled, but the results could be incongruous: if land is entailed, for example, suppose the plaintiff's father is called bastard, or his bastard elder brother said to be legitimate?[3]

From this mixture of scandal and monetary loss, two features of the modern law developed, though neither can be dated. One is the incoherence of the definition of the tort. The other is the division of slanders into those actionable *per se* and those requiring proof of special damage. The slanders actionable *per se* began as those categories of words which were accepted as actionable at all. They will be considered one by one. Allegations of temporal crime were by nature defamatory in the ecclesiastical sense; but the church could not hear them. Allegations of professional misconduct and of certain diseases similarly seem to have begun as allegations of wickedness; in both temporal loss gained the upper hand, but the question of proving it never arose. The rule about proving an actual loss first arose with allegations of purely ecclesiastical offences, where it was the temporal loss that gave the lay court jurisdiction. But this category became merged in the wider and woollier idea that temporal loss itself could be a cause of action, so that into the nineteenth century the law of slander would be stated, not in terms of actionability *per se*, but as a list: imputations of crime, professional incapacity, disease, and imputations causing loss[4].

1. 'Alien' (actually 'Knave mungerel half a Guysian, and no meer Englishman quia a cel temps le Duke de Guyse fuit reported Comon Enemy al Realme'): *Anon.* (1564), Dalison 63. 'Scot': CP 40/1064, m. 78d (1530). 'Bankrupt': *Anon.* (1586), Godbolt 40; *Anon.* (1588), Gouldsborough 84; *Dotting v Ford* (date unknown) Noy 33; *Courtney v Thompson* (date unknown), Noy 158.
2. J. H. Baker, *Spelman's Reports*, vol. II (Selden Society, vol. 94), p. *244*, n. 2. For later examples see *Booth v Trafford* (1573), Dalison 102; *Mildmay's Case* (1582–84), 1 Co. Rep. 175a; Moore K.B. 144; *Johnson v Smith* (1584), Moore K.B. 187; *Penniman v Rawbanks* (1595), Moore K.B. 410; *Williams and Linford's Case* (1588), 2 Leonard 111; *Gerard v Dickenson* (1590), 4 Co. Rep. 18a; KB 27/1329, m. 273 (1594).
3. 'Bastard': *Anon.* (1564), Dalison 63; *Anon.* (1598), Owen 32.
4. *Thorley v Lord Kerry* (1812), 4 Taunton 355; quoted at p. 391, below.

And the last, beginning from allegations that were merely disadvantageous, morally as neutral as a slander of title, could only be brought within a definition by having a definition that did not mean much.

In the sixteenth and seventeenth centuries, however, the question is why the common law stopped with its artificial categories, with its list of diseases that left out smallpox, its refusal to remedy general imputations of roguery unless aimed at professional men or, later, causing actual damage. And the answer lies in the flow of litigation. The extent of this can be seen only from the plea rolls, where a surprising proportion of the weary annual miles of parchment is taken up with actions for words. Most concerned imputations of crime; and it was particularly to these that another limit was applied. This was the *mitior sensus* rule, well known from the reports. Defendants would seek to construe the abuse which they had uttered so as to show that it did not necessarily impute a crime. Some absurd examples can be found. 'Thou art a thief and hast stolen my appletrees out of my orchard' is actionable, because the two propositions are separated and the first can stand though the second falls; but it would have been otherwise had the words been 'for thou hast stolen my appletrees'[1]. 'Thou has stolen by the high-way side' is not actionable 'for it may be taken, that he stole upon a man suddenly, as the common proverb is, that he stole upon me, innuendo, that he came to me unawares'; or 'it may be intended that he stole a stick under a hedge, and these words are not so slanderous, that they are actionable'[2]. 'If ever man was perjured, Wittam was' and 'Thou art as very a thief as any in Gloucester Gaol' are not actionable without averments, respectively, 'that any man was perjured' and 'that there was a thief in Gloucester Gaol'[3].

Similar arguments could be raised over imputations of disease. 'Leper' was unambiguous[4]. But 'pox' could be the French pox or smallpox[5]; and if the latter, the speaker may have been warning rather than defaming, an early indication of something like

1. *Ayres v Oswall* (?1609), Noy 135. Cf. *Norman's Case* (1587), Gouldsborough 56; *Colt and Gilbert's Case* (1613), Godbolt 241. Cf. also *Anon.* (1591), Savile 126.
2. *Brough v Dennyson* (1601), Gouldsborough 143.
3. *Wittam's Case* (date unknown), Noy 116.
4. *Taylor v Perkins* (date unknown), Noy 117.
5. *James v Rutlech* (1599), 4 Co. Rep. 17a; Moore K.B. 573.

privilege. Behind the seeming absurdity there lies a serious question. What was the basis of these actions for diseases? 'Pox' was the earliest and the commonest to come in issue; and it may at first have been because of the stigma of sin, temporal damage being mentioned only to take the case out of the jurisdiction of the church. Then the damage was made the basis of the action, so that imputations of past venereal disease were not actionable and imputations of disease not shameful by nature might be so[1]. The accidental end of it was the illogical list of ills, imputations of which were actionable *per se*.

This shift whereby temporal damage might be the ground of the action irrespective of any imputation of wickedness, irrespective of 'defamation' in the ecclesiastical sense, may also be reflected in imputations of professional unfitness. The early cases seem all to concern lawyers or public officers, and to involve allegations of dishonesty or other misconduct rather than mere incompetence. An early example is in 1513: the defendant had said of Richard Eliot, a king's serjeant, that he had advised clients against the crown; and this was to the prejudice of the plaintiff's good name as well as of his fees[2]. In 1557 Roger Manwood was not accused of stupidity: he was 'the craftiest and falsest man of law that ever was, and I would that all men should beware of him for he is so full of falsehood and deceit'; and what is more his defendant sought to justify it[3]. In 1564 an attorney recovered for 'He is the falsest knave in England, and by God's blood he will cut thy throat'; though at that time a mere layman could not have recovered for 'false knave', or for far more specific allegations of murderous intent[4]. Not until 1591, upon error to the exchequer chamber, does it seem that mere incompetence in a lawyer was held sufficient[5]. In the same year it was laid down in the case of a surgeon that professional disparagement was actionable by those who gain their living

1. *Anon.* (1586), Owen 34; *Smith's Case* (date unknown), Noy 151.
2. KB 27/1006, m. 62. Cf. KB 27/1183, m. 189 (1557): 'Denton is a false offycer to the Quene & hath deceaved the Quene and yf there were foure such as he is hanged in any quarter of Yngland one we should have a mery Yngland and I care not who tell hym.'
3. KB 27/1183, m. 190.
4. *Anon.* (1564), Moore K.B. 61; Dalison 63. For 'knave' said of a layman, see *Anon.* (1561), Moore K.B. 29. For allegations of murderous intent, see *Bray v Andrews* (1564), Moore K.B. 63; Dalison 66.
5. *Heale v Giddye* (1591), Moore K.B. 695; 2 Anderson 40.

through practice of a trade, an art or a science[1]. But in both cases there is some suggestion of deliberate misconduct, and there may still have been doubt about the nature of the allegation necessary. Mere unfitness had to be extreme; and there was ample scope for the *mitior sensus* rule. 'He hath as much law as a jack-an-apes, or my horse' is actionable 'because they are unreasonable creatures, but if he had said, that he hath no more law than I.S. that is not actionable, although I.S. be no lawyer'[2]. 'He is a blood-sucker and sucketh blood', or 'He is a blood-sucker and thirsteth after blood', spoken of a justice of the peace and of oyer and terminer was twice argued before all the judges, and eventually decided for the defendant, 'quia poit thirst after blood en care de Justice', or 'for it cannot be intended what blood he sucked'[3].

The internal mysteries of slander are therefore due to the boundary between the ecclesiastical and the lay jurisdictions. The greater mystery in the modern law, the distinction between slander and libel has traditionally been regarded as a legacy of defamation in yet another jurisdiction, that of the star chamber. The star chamber was seemingly prepared to entertain complaints of private defamation in the fifteenth century, before the common law courts had opened their doors to actions for words[4]. But its motives were not those of private law, of the compensation of injury, but of criminal law.The approach was much that of the local courts, seeking primarily to repress disorder and disaffection.

The earliest governmental dealing with subversive words not amounting to treason was a statute of 1275 creating an offence of *scandalum magnatum*, which punished the publication of discreditable matter about important people. This statute was several times re-enacted with changes, the last occasion being in 1559[5]. It was the occasional basis of proceedings at common law, though the only ones of sufficient interest to lawyers to be reported were civil in nature. The substantive effect was to allow 'magnates' to recover for words which their lesser neighbours would have to swallow,

1. *Anon.* (1591), 1 Anderson 268; Savile 126. Cf. 2 Anderson 40 (preceding note).
2. *Palmer's Case* (1594), Owen 17; Cro. Eliz. 342.
3. *Hilliard v Constable* (1593), Moore K.B. 418; Cro. Eliz. 306.
4. J. H. Baker, *Spelman's Reports*, vol. II (Selden Society, vol. 94) p.*236*, at n. 7 (1433); *Select Cases in Star Chamber*, vol. I (Selden Society, vol. 16), p. 38.
5. Stats. 3 Ed. I (Westminster I), c. 34 (1275); 2 Ric. II, stat. 1, c. 5 (1378); 12 Ric. II, c. 11 (1388); 1 & 2 P. & M., c. 3 (1554); 1 Eliz., c. 6 (1559).

though their advantage was not great: in 1562 for example 'un covetous & malicious Bishop' was sent empty away[1]. As to proceedings of a criminal nature, the statutes could cause jurisdictional problems; and what came in fact to happen was that cases were handled by the star chamber without reference to statutory authority.

In the early years of the seventeenth century the star chamber built up a body of law about words, stemming mainly from the criminal basis of its action. Although redress might be ordered for the victim, the chief concern was with the punishment of sedition on the one hand and of words likely to cause private disorder on the other. It did not matter that the victim was dead, or that what was said of him was true, or that it was 'published' only to him. 'Publication' was whatever fell within the mischief. Copying was not in itself a publication; but unless the copy were handed to a magistrate it was a suspicious act. Repetition was punishable, but mere listening was not. And it did not go without saying that 'cestuy que laugh quant il oye un auter a lier le libel n'est un publisher sil ne fait pluis'[2].

It will be noticed, however, that the laughing audience was listening to something being read, not just spoken. And it is curious how regularly the early discussions of libel assume writing or the like. The earliest major statement, Coke's report *De Libellis Famosis* in 1605, does indeed say that a libel '*aut est in scriptis, aut sine scriptis*'. But '*Famosus libellus sine scriptis* may be, 1. *Picturis*, as to paint the party in any shameful and ignominious manner. 2. *Signis*, as to fix a gallows, or other reproachful and ignominious signs at the party's door or elsewhere.' His only mention of words is in his account of how a libel *in scriptis* may be published: '1. *Verbis aut cantilenis*: as where it is maliciously repeated or sung in the presence of others. 2. *Traditione*,' when the libel or any copy of it is delivered over to scandalise the party.'[3] Since, as the star

1. *Archbishop of York v Markam* (1562) Dalison, 38. For other actions see *Beauchamp v Croft* (1497), Keilwey 26; *Abergavenny v Cartwright* (1572), Dalison, 80. For an example of criminal proceedings see *Oldnoll's Case* (1557), Dyer 155a.
2. *Lambe's Case de Libells* (1610), Moore K.B. 813; 9 Co. Rep. 59b. Cf. W. Hudson, 'A Treatise of the Court of Star Chamber', *Collectanea Juridica* (1791–2), II, p. 1, at p. 102. 'Therefore, to hear it sung or read, and to laugh at it, and to make merriment with it, hath ever been held a publication in law.'
3. *De Libellis Famosis* (1605) 5 Co. Rep. 125a.

chamber itself concluded, the mischiefs of the offence could lie as much in speech as in writing, the early preoccupation with writing must have had a deeper cause than the chronic governmental dislike of the printing press. The only trace of a reason given by Coke is an analogy with poisoning: harm easily done in secret must be severely punished when brought to light. Nor was this merely fanciful: another writer thought it necessary expressly to deny that the essence of a star chamber libel lay in anonymity, so that the author who signed his work was not punishable[1]. The peculiar malice inherent in writing may also lie behind a difference in legal consequence between writing and speech said to have emerged in the star chamber: spoken words could be justified, but truth was no defence if the libel was written[2].

There is no doubt that the common law of criminal libel largely derives from this work of the star chamber, being simply adopted by the common law courts after the Restoration; and it was not until the early eighteenth century that the crime was finally confined to written matter[3]. The question is how far the modern tort of libel, defamation in written or other durable form, similarly derives from the star chamber. The name does; and it is tempting to attribute its important characteristic, actionability without proof of actual damage, to the star chamber's criminal motivation. But the matter has been discussed in rather unrealistic terms. The traditional picture is that the common law found itself with a new weapon to set beside its own action on the case; and although the action on the case had covered written as well as spoken matter, its deficiencies led to the use of the new remedy whenever the defamation was written. An alternative picture is that the common law took nothing from the star chamber but the name, and that all development after the Restoration as before was internal to the action on the case[4]. But legal remedies are not identifiable objects, and may be identified differently by different lawyers. Nor was the star chamber jurisdiction seen as having been entirely distinct from the law of the

1. W. Hudson, 'A Treatise of the Court of Star Chamber', *Collectanea Juridica* (1791–2), II, p. 1, at p. 102.
2. Ibid.
3. *R v Langley* (1704), Holt K.B. 654; 2 Salkeld 697.
4. For the traditional view, see W. S. Holdsworth, *History of English Law*, vol. VIII (2nd edn., 1937), pp. 361 ff. For the contrary view, see J. M. Kaye, 'Libel and Slander – Two Torts or One?' (1975) 91 LQR, p. 524.

common law courts. The realistic questions are not about derivations but about the reasons for decisions.

What the common law courts first decided, in *King v Lake* in 1667, was to admit an action for defamation without proof of special damage because the fact of writing showed it to be specially malicious[1]. The emphasis was on the malice rather than on the writing; and there are earlier signs that malice might make a defamation outside the normal categories actionable, because it raised a presumption of harm or at least hurt. But the approach, and especially the association between malice and writing, was more familiar in the star chamber; and the criminal motive must have played a part.

What happened next was more unfortunate. The malice was forgotten, and the writing itself was held to justify an action with no proof of actual damage. Only in *Thorley v Lord Kerry* in 1812 was the position finally established, and then with regret. The defendant sought by writ of error to reverse a judgment against him for damages for mere abuse. His counsel 'contended that all actionable words were reducible to three classes: 1, where they impute a punishable crime; 2, where they impute an infectious disorder; 3, where they tend to injure a person in his office, trade, or profession, or tend to his disherison, or produce special pecuniary damages.' This argument reflects the old classification as clearly as the judgment shows how the modern tort acquired its definition. 'There is no doubt', said the court, 'that this was a libel, for which the Plaintiff in error might have been indicted and punished; because, though the words impute no punishable crimes, they contain that sort of imputation which is calculated to vilify a man, and bring him, as the books say, into hatred, contempt, and ridicule; for all words of that description an indictment lies; and I should have thought that the peace and good name of individuals was sufficiently guarded by the terror of this criminal proceeding in such cases. The words, if merely spoken, would not be of themselves sufficient to support an action . . . The purpose of this action is to recover a compensation for some damage supposed to be sustained by the Plaintiff by reason of the libel. The tendency of the libel to provoke a breach of the peace, or the degree of malignity which actuates the writer, has nothing to do with the question. If

1. Hardres 470.

the matter were for the first time to be decided at this day, I should have no hesitation in saying, that no action could be maintained for written scandal which could not be maintained for the words if they had been spoken'[1].

But the court allowed the clarity of its own thought to be overborne by authority, and gave the common law a tort with a function and a definition both partly appropriate to the criminal law. In our own day we have chosen to preserve it, and even to refine and extend the distinction between libel and slander[2]. The possibility of large damages for gossip and scandal is no doubt a deterrent. But inappropriate tools are always clumsy; and confused motive in the liability leads to confusion between the public and the private interest in matters of defence. The story may have a moral related to the last chapter of this book. The separation of crime and tort has mostly harmed crime; but there may also be harm to private law when compensation of the victim is left as the only effective protection of a general interest.

NEGLIGENCE

Negligence and deceit are the two moral ideas which the common law has used as a basis of liability; and in both cases the process may have been assisted by ambiguity. One can neglect to do something without being negligent, and one can be deceived although nobody intended deception. In the case of deceit, as appeared particularly in the rise of *assumpsit*, the moral idea performed a pioneering role: it opened up new territory for the common law, and itself died in the process. The liability which it had created was generalised, reaching defendants whom nobody thought fraudulent but who were called so, in a stylised way, for the purpose of fixing them with the liability. First the law ordains that the result should follow from the facts, then it ordains the facts because it desires the result. The fraudulent machinations of the eighteenth-century defendant in contract were as much a fiction as the force and arms attributed to the fourteenth-century defendant in tort.

1. 4 Taunton 355.
2. Defamation Act 1952, 15 & 16 Geo. VI and 1 Eliz. II, c. 66. See also the report upon which it was based, Cmd. 7536.

When the history of negligence in our own time comes to be written, and our own will be the important period in the story, it may seem that something similar has been happening. The incidence of loss is allocated by the use and abuse of a moral idea. But society is now so geared that the loss may be beyond the means of any individual, and out of all proportion to a fault itself impossible to locate; and growing artificiality may force us in England to follow other common law jurisdictions and seek another approach to the problem. How did the artificiality arise? How did it happen that this moral idea became accessible as the basis of a claim for plaintiffs in so wide a range of situations?

The modern tort of negligence resulted from the confluence of two streams which had been separated in the first instance only by the jurisdictional division that produced 'trespass' and 'case'. One stream was that of the accident between strangers, for example the road accident. From the fourteenth century to the seventeenth, this was almost always dealt with under the form of battery or other writ of trespass *vi et armis*; and until the seventeenth century the nature of the facts and the problem of fault are uniformly hidden behind a blank Not guilty.

The other stream was that of the harm arising out of a situation or a pre-existing relationship between the parties. These could not be brought within a *contra pacem* formula, and so were dealt with by actions on the case. But the owner of the house from which fire spread, the keeper of the inn from which goods were stolen, the riparian owner who did not mend his stretch of wall, the smith, the surgeon, the carrier, the bailee – these were not different in kind from the careless driver. They were first separated by jurisdiction and kept apart, as has been seen, by a mishap over process[1].

The chance nature of their separation is seen in the use of *contra pacem* to smuggle actions against smiths and the like into royal courts at a time when they would not accept cases without that

1. P. H. Winfield, 'The History of Negligence in the Law of Torts' (1926) 42 LQR, p. 184; *Select Legal Essays* (1952), p. 30; 'Duty in Tortious Negligence' (1934) 34 Columbia Law Review, p. 41; *Select Legal Essays*, p. 70; P. H. Winfield and A. L. Goodhart, 'Trespass and Negligence' (1933) 49 LQR, p. 359; *Select Legal Essays*, p. 49; M. J. Prichard, 'Trespass, Case and the Rule in *Williams v Holland*, [1964] Cambridge Law Journal, p. 234; *Scott v Shepherd (1773) and the Emergence of the Tort of Negligence* (Selden Society lecture, 1976).

passport[1]. 'Why with force and arms and against the king's peace did the defendant smith kill the plaintiff's horse' raised exactly the same question as was later raised by 'Why did the smith do the job of shoeing the horse so badly that the horse died'. But there was no less artificiality in reaching the careless driver in battery, asserting that he had broken the king's peace. And this artificiality was perpetuated, because there was no change in the form of the writ when the king's peace ceased to be necessary for jurisdiction.

Chance, however, has consequences; and this chance was to obscure until our own day the most elementary questions in the law of torts, namely questions about the principles of liability. There was no initial separation in this respect. The smith smuggled into the common pleas under a *contra pacem* writ was procedurally worse off than his colleague later brought in openly by a writ on the case, because *capias* went with *contra pacem*. But he cannot have been worse off as a matter of substantive law: the *contra pacem* would not harden a jury's attitude to the basis of his liability. The growth of a difference represents a movement of 'trespass' rather than of 'case'. Writs on the case commonly set out an element of fault in the writ, saying either that the defendant had failed to perform a distinct duty, or that he had acted *negligenter, incaute, improvide* and the like. Such an element was affirmatively a part of the plaintiff's case, and when jury trial so evolved that questions of 'burden of proof' could arise, the burden was on the plaintiff.

But it was otherwise with 'trespass'. The language of the writ and count against the careless driver suggested deliberate wickedness. But everybody knew it was nonsense, and there could be no holding the plaintiff to proof of his formal allegations. The pleadings therefore reduced themselves to the plaintiff's assertion that the defendant had done the harm, and the defendant's Not guilty. Almost inevitably that Not guilty came to mean 'I did not do it'; and if the defendant in some sense had done it, then it was for him to allege and prove, in the words of *Weaver v Ward* in 1616, that it was 'utterly without his fault', 'that it had been inevitable, and that the defendant had committed no negligence to give occasion to the hurt'[2]. The *contra pacem* fiction did its damage long after it had done its useful job: it excluded from the formalities of

1. P. 290, above.
2. Hobart 134.

the plaintiff's case any genuine statement of fault, so that fault ceased to be an ingredient of his case. In terms of jury trial, the burden of proving accident or the like was on the defendant. Not until 1959 was a statement of claim that 'the defendant shot the plaintiff' held to disclose no cause of action without an allegation that the shooting was intentional or negligent[1].

There is, of course, nothing absurd about fault playing a different part and being subject to different burdens of proof in different kinds of situation. The absurdity lay in the circumstance that the situations were not necessarily different. For well over a century the plaintiff of 1959 had been able to choose between 'trespass' with its laconic 'the defendant shot the plaintiff', and 'negligence' or 'case' in which he would have to state and prove the nature of the fault on which he relied. The same was true of the plaintiff run down by the careless driver; but in highway cases, inevitably the most common, the point was obscured by a premature attack of common sense which had required the plaintiff to prove fault even if he sued in trespass[2]. This was the exception, however: the rule allowed the plaintiff in such cases to choose the form of action and thereby to determine the burden of proof; and the choice was an important part of his lawyer's learning.

This had come about as a result of the process described in an earlier chapter, whereby trespass *vi et armis* became a legal concept. Lawyers did not know, as we do, that the division between 'trespass' and 'case' was juridically accidental: and since it had consequences, for a time over process, always in the form of the writ, they hunted its essence. The essence that they found was the test of directness. In terms of the plaintiff's writ and count, 'direct forcible injury' was the meaning that remained to *vi et armis* and *contra pacem* when all the more likely things they did not mean were set aside. In terms of the defendant's Not guilty, when in the seventeenth century the changing mechanics of trial brought the content of that denial to the surface of legal thinking, what it seemed to mean was that the defendant had not directly done the harm.

1. *Fowler v Lanning*, [1959] 1 Q.B. 426, Cf. *Letang v Cooper*, [1964] 2 Q.B. 53.
2. P. H. Winfield and A. L. Goodhart, 'Trespass and Negligence' (1933) 49 LQR, p. 359; *Select Legal Essays* (1952), p. 49.

Consider the defendant in 1695 whose horse had bolted and run down the plaintiff[1]. The plaintiff sued in battery; the defendant, if well advised, would have pleaded Not guilty; and the jury, if satisfied that the bolting was not his fault and that he had done all he could, would have given their verdict in his favour. Then consider the defendant of 1676 whose horse had also bolted and run down the plaintiff; but this was an unbroken horse being trained in a busy public place[2]. Its bolting was equally not the immediate doing of the defendant; and if sued in battery he might well be found Not guilty. The plaintiff therefore brought his action on the case setting out the circumstances; and it is an early example of what we should call an action for 'negligence' instead of the customary 'trespass' brought upon an accident between strangers.

The 1676 case has already been compared with the *scienter* action. In both, although the physical impact was by nature as much *vi et armis* and *contra pacem* as any other 'trespass', the pre-existing situation, keeping such a dog or breaking such a horse in such a place, was a necessary ingredient of the wrong. Nearly a century before *Scott v Shepherd*[3] the hazy outline can be seen of the test of directness, of the difference between the mere collision and the situation with its sequel, between the log that hit the plaintiff and the one lying in the road to trip him. But the test was not enunciated as a proposition of law until the late eighteenth century, and not until then was real harm done[4].

We do not know to what extent actions on the case were brought in the intervening period for road accidents and the like. Plaintiffs would no doubt prefer trespass except when there was apparent danger that upon Not guilty a jury would exonerate a culpable defendant on the ground that he had not 'done' it. This would most obviously arise when the harm had immediately been done by the defendant's servant. Unless the master had actually ordered it, his liability if any would have to be in case: he might be responsible for the situation, but no jury would say that he had done the harm. If no servant was involved, trespass would generally serve. The

1. *Gibbons v Pepper*, 1 Ld. Raymond 38; Salkeld 637; 4 Mod. 405.
2. *Mitchil v Alestree*, 1 Ventris 295; 2 Levinz 172; 3 Keble 650. For discussion, and the comparison with *scienter*, see p. 311 above.
3. *Scott v Shepherd* (1773), Wm. Blackstone 892.
4. For a full discussion of the harm, see M. J. Prichard, 'Trespass, Case and the Rule in *Williams v Holland*' [1964] Cambridge Law Journal, p. 234.

carelessness of a careless driver would not often need to be set out like the rashness of training an unbroken horse in a public place. But it might be. If there was a collision between two moving parties, the plaintiff might rest his case expressly on the improper speed of the defendant. Or if a boat had been blown against sluice-gates despite the proved efforts of the helmsman, the owner of the gates might wish to say that the helmsman should never have come so close. These were the kinds of case that were to raise difficulty. But they did not raise it until the last quarter of the eighteenth century, when the test of directness had become a rule of law, and when the facts which emerged at *nisi prius* could be brought back to the court at Westminster and subjected to the rule.

When that happened, there were distinct forms of action appropriate for identifiably distinct kinds of fact situation. The plaintiff would fail unless he chose the right one. He could not guard himself by using them in the alternative, because they could not be joined. He must therefore predict how the court would analyse the facts in rare cases like *Scott v Shepherd*. And he must also, and in cases not at all rare, predict what facts would emerge at the trial. The owner of the sluice-gates brings case against the owner of the barge that stove them in; and the owner says that he himself was at the helm, not his servant, so the action should be in trespass. The owner of the gates sues in trespass, and upon Not guilty is faced with evidence of the sudden gust of wind.

The ancient artificiality began to cause injustice as soon as it was formulated into a rule; and the rule in its full rigour lasted little more than half a century. The distinction between trespass and case of course survived the abolition of the forms of action, and continued to affect the proof of fault until our own day. But this was a distinction of forms. What was unworkable was the proposition that the forms corresponded to distinct kinds of fact and were mutually exclusive. It continued to be true that a plaintiff could not bring trespass unless the injury was 'direct'. But in *Williams v Holland* in 1833 it was held that he was not obliged to bring trespass for a 'direct' injury[1]. Except in the rare and unimportant event of wilful harm, he could if he chose bring case.

1. 2 L.J.C.P. (NS) 190; 10 Bingham 112; 6 Car. & P. 23 (at *nisi prius*); M. J. Prichard [1964] Cambridge Law Journal, esp. at pp. 241 ff.

Three consequences followed. Immediately, the plaintiff was freed from the necessity of deciding whether his injury had been 'direct' or 'consequential' before he knew the defendant's version of the facts. If he did not know who had been driving, or whether some external factor had at the last moment caused the driver to lose control, he would choose case rather than trespass. The carelessness of the driving would then be the basis of his claim and would have to be proved; but he could not be defeated on purely formal grounds.

The second consequence was the oddity already described. Until 1959 the plaintiff had a choice of forms of action. So long as the injury was 'direct' he could proceed by way of 'trespass' on the one hand, or 'case' or 'negligence' on the other; and the precise relevance of the defendant's fault depended openly upon the plaintiff's choice of form rather than upon the facts.

But this oddity was only the most recent example of a situation often reached by the common law. Much of its development has turned upon the question whether an action on the case should be allowed on facts covered by some other action. That 'trespass' and 'case' should ever have become so clearly distinct that the question could arise between them is extraordinary; but as soon as they did, the question was punctually asked. Its affirmative answer, which in 1833 seemed to break down some great barrier, did no more than correct an old oversight. About 1370, when *contra pacem* ceased to be necessary for jurisdiction, the writ against the careless driver could have become as truthful as the writ against the careless smith. Only conservatism and the advantage of *capias* kept the old form in use, and divided the law of torts into two. The beginning of its reunification may be seen as the last and greatest consequence of the process epitomised in *Williams v Holland*.

It may also be regarded as the 'origin' of the modern tort of negligence[1]. Only when the two streams had come together was it possible for negligence to be considered as an independent basis of liability. But there is still some mystery about the way in which it became 'a' tort. The writ system had the effect of organising the common law of wrongs by reference to the nature of the injury

1. M. J. Prichard, *Scott v. Shepherd (1773) and the Emergence of the Tort of Negligence* (Selden Society lecture, 1976); see also the other references on p. 393, above.

suffered by the plaintiff: defamation, conversion, deceit up to a point, even 'trespass' conceived as 'a' tort, were all distinguished by the nature of the wrong rather than the fault of the wrongdoer. Negligence is part of a different organisation, cutting across the others; and that is why today we can still have territorial disputes like those between the old forms of action. Difficulties arose over negligence in making statements because the liability for statements appeared to be fixed by the tort of deceit.

But of course any law of torts must take account of both elements, and the choice is between modes of statement: is the primary organisation to be in terms of kinds of harm or kinds of fault? But actions on the case, as it were the residuary wrongs, had always resisted any organisation, and had always allowed great freedom to the plaintiffs to formulate their complaints as seemed best; and in a new situation it often seemed best to put the case in moral terms like deceit or negligence. There built up a steadily increasing body of miscellaneous complaints, ranging from professional misfeasance to the training of unbroken horses in public places, all using the same language of negligence. There also built up in the legal profession a body of traditional learning about that language, arising from the need to direct juries at *nisi prius*. Negligence came to be seen as a legal idea, manifested in all the miscellaneous complaints which used the language. But probably it was legal writers, whose struggle through the centuries to classify actions on the case is in itself an interesting study in lawyers' thinking, who eventually made negligence into 'a' tort. In the eighteenth century one used negligence in its other sense of neglecting to act, and separated 'actions on the case for negligence' from 'actions on the case for misfeasance'[1]. Another used negligence as a heading for careless conduct causing personal injury; but for damage to property he was thrown back on 'case for consequential damages'[2]. In the nineteenth century negligence becomes a general heading, and the idea that it exists as an independent tort begins to form.

1. Comyns' *Digest of the Laws of England* (ed. 1762); J. H. Baker, *An Introduction to English Legal History* (1979), pp. 345 ff.
2. F. Buller, *An Introduction to the Law Relative to Trials at* Nisi Prius (ed. 1772), pp. 25, 73; J. H. Baker, op. cit. in last note.

More than language was involved. However freely new writs or bills on the case had been composed, there was always the possibility of objection to the complaint as such. Innovation is less obvious when new facts are brought within the ambit of an established wrong. But the two processes are really the same, differing only in apparent magnitude. Whether this accidental freedom has been well used is a question for the future. It may have been too much used. Many situations have been discussed in which liability was based upon a wrong, not because that was the natural analysis of the facts but because the natural analysis, in contract for example, could for some reason not be brought to bear. *Donoghue v Stevenson* ended a difficulty inherited by negligence from that strain in its ancestry which went back to *assumpsit* for misfeasance: if a contract was involved, privity came into play[1]. At the time it seemed a triumph to reach the manufacturer purely on the basis of wrong, and to exclude any trace of contractual analysis. But perhaps it was the contractual position that really needed reconsidering. Individual moral fault begins to seem as artificial a basis for reaching the manufacturer today as it was for reaching the ordinary contractor in the sixteenth century; and we may follow other common law jurisdictions in a new approach. But it was the moral idea that opened up the way.

1. [1932] A.C. 562. Cf. *Winterbottom v Wright* (1842), 10 M. & W. 109.

IV

CRIME

14 *Criminal Administration and Law*

The miserable history of crime in England can be shortly told. Nothing worth-while was created. There are only administrative achievements to trace. So far as justice was done throughout the centuries, it was done by jurors and in spite of savage laws[1]. The lawyers contributed humane but shabby expedients, which did not develop into new approaches. From the view-point of this book, indeed, the main interest of the subject is as a control against which to assess developments in other branches of the law. The various institutional changes which made those developments possible did not happen in the area of criminal administration. Perhaps they could not have. The kind of discussion by which law develops as an intellectual system is a luxury in the context of preserving elementary order. In murder and theft there are no competing general interests to accommodate. It is the constable and the hangman who can do something about them, not the lawyer. Until relatively modern times the lawyer was not even allowed to play any real part; and if he had been, few defendants could have paid him. The criminal law became segregated as one of the dirty jobs of society. It cannot even be called a failure of the common law because, until the age of reform, it was nobody's business to try.

PLEAS OF THE CROWN: FELONY AND MISDEMEANOUR

When Glanvill distinguished criminal pleas from civil, his civil pleas were the real and the old personal actions; and criminal pleas were those concerning wrongs[2]. Wrongs were not divided into two conceptual categories, offences against society to be punished, and

1. See pp. 421 ff, below.
2. *Glanvill*, I, 1–4 (ed. G. D. G. Hall, pp. 3–5).

injuries to victims who must be civilly compensated. But they might be brought to justice at the instance of either authority or the victim, and it is from these different procedures that the conceptual distinction grew. The justice to which they might be brought and the authority which might bring them to it were the same, the body controlling the law that had been broken; and for ordinary offences it was the immediate community, the manor, the city, the hundred.

But the ancestor of the modern criminal law is of course in those wrongs which were matters for royal justice, in pleas of the crown. Or rather, it is in the mechanism by which pleas of the crown were brought to justice at the instance of the crown. They might also be brought to justice at the instance of the party, by appeal of felony in the case of felonies, by action of trespass *contra pacem* in the case of those other wrongs which were in contravention of the king's special law, his peace.

There were, then, three distinctions to be made about wrongs. One was procedural: authority or the victim might take the initiative. The second was, or came to be, jurisdictional: the wrong might be a plea of the crown or a 'local' offence. And the third did in principle go to the nature of the wrong: it might be a felony or something less. The two last will be taken first.

Pleas of the crown were originally matters in which the crown had an interest, as opposed to common pleas; and they included 'civil' claims involving royal rights. But these dropped away, so that until the nineteenth century information about what we call the criminal law was to be sought in books entitled 'pleas of the crown'. Pleas of the crown were either felonies, in which the royal interest was in a forfeiture of property, or trespasses against the king's peace for which neither life nor property was forfeit; but the offender was imprisoned until he redeemed himself, made fine with the king. In the civil action of trespass, as was noted above, the king's fine became nominal, and the imprisonment became process for the benefit of the plaintiff. But when the trespass was prosecuted at the king's suit, the penal consequence was the object; and to avoid confusion trespasses so prosecuted came to be known instead as misdemeanours.

As in the context of the civil action, the king's peace lost its original sense and became stylised, though apparently never fictitious. These misdemeanours, criminal trespasses, became a broad miscellany of offences against good order[1]. But they were confined to purely physical wrongs; and this brings us to one of the casualties of the common law of crime. It grew from the methods evolved by the crown for prosecuting pleas of the crown at its own suit, and wrongs which did not involve a breach of the king's peace remained in local jurisdictions. In the civil sphere of actions by the victim for compensation, the common law allowed itself to come back to the local jurisdictions for a second helping and take in those wrongs which it had first left behind. At the instance of the victim, as on its own initiative, it would first accept only pleas of the crown, only trespasses *contra pacem*. But for reasons already described this became artificial; and in the years around 1370 plaintiffs were allowed to bring to royal courts trespasses which were not *contra pacem*. The 'origin' of the action on the case was this second reception of wrongs[2]. But it was confined to actions for redress by the victim. There was no corresponding change in the criminal sphere. The list of pleas of the crown was not reconsidered, and the catalogue of common law crimes remained as it had first been fixed. Local offences died with local justice, and were simply lost; and in particular offences of dishonesty not amounting to theft were left without penal consequences, and had later to be invented all over again. It is hard to say which did more damage, the correction of the jurisdictional accident in the civil sphere, or the failure to correct it in the criminal. But in both it is important to remember that the later law reflects an accident, and not a society so primitive that it could address itself only to physical wrongs.

The origin of the old common law misdemeanours, then, though unfortunate is at least straightforward. The felonies are more mysterious. Their ancestors were ancient lists of offences so grave as to forfeit the offender's life and property; and one mystery concerns the settlement of a final list and its relationship with pleas of the

1. B. H. Putnam, *Proceedings before the Justices of the Peace, in the Fourteenth and Fifteenth Centuries* (Ames Foundation), especially the Commentary on the Indictments by T. F. T. Plucknett.
2. See pp. 289 ff, above. In 1395 a Nottinghamshire jury was persuaded to indict before justices of the peace a physician for failing in a cure and extorting large sums by way of payment; *Proceedings before the Justices of the Peace in the Fourteenth and Fifteenth Centuries* (Ames Foundation), p. 130. But cf. Marowe (1503): 'transgression que est sur le cas ne serra enquire par force de le commission purceo que nest suppose encontre le peace'; B. H. Putnam, *Early Treatises on the Practice of the Justices of the Peace* (1924), p. 368.

crown. In Glanvill's time, as we shall see, theft was probably a felony or capable of being one, but he tells us expressly that it was not a plea of the crown[1]. A darker mystery concerns the name. 'Felony' has feudal connotations: it originally meant a breach of the faith owed by a man to his lord so fundamental as to end the relationship and so entitle the lord to retake the tenement and treat it as at his own free disposal[2]. And this effect remained associated with the word even when the word meant something quite different. Although the chattels of a felon were forfeited to the king, his land 'escheated' to his lord just as did the land of a tenant dying without heirs. The mystery is that the word altogether lost its original feudal sense. Except for this consequence of escheat, it became detached from the relationship between lord and man, and attached instead to the list of grave but in no way feudal offences. The only possible connecting link seems to be the forfeiture which those offences had entailed before there were lords to worry about it. If an offence had placed all a wrongdoer's property, land as well as goods, at the king's disposal, an obvious difficulty would arise when the land was no longer 'his' in the same sense. His lord would not see why part of his fee should be subtracted because of his tenant's wrong; and he might call the wrong a felony precisely because it made that result possible. To him it was a wrong of the same nature as that committed when his tenant did homage to some other lord for his tenement; and such a disclaimer was indeed the typical feudal felony. An accommodation between the conflicting interests of king and lord is suggested by the 'year, day and waste': the tenement would go first to the king to be stripped, so that only the bare land then came to the lord as his escheat. The king's right on this view would be to the ancient forfeiture, and the lord's to an escheat for the feudal felony of endangering the fee by attracting that forfeiture.

ACCUSATION AND PROOF

Just as the history of civil liabilities was traditionally seen in terms of the forms of action, with its emphasis on the original writs, so

1. *Glanvill*, I, 2; XIV, 8 (ed. G. D. G. Hall, pp. 4, 177).
2. F. Pollock and F. W. Maitland, *History of English Law* (2nd edn.), vol. I, pp. 303 ff; vol. II, pp. 464 ff.

was the early criminal law seen in terms of the initiation of proceedings. The ancient entity, it was thought, was the appeal of felony, by which the victim or his kin would bring the offender to justice and prove the accusation by battle[1]. In 1166, according to this account, an invention was given legislative effect; and a duty was cast upon local people to delate suspects to royal officers[2]. This was seen as intended to supplement the appeal of felony, and so to ensure that suspects were indeed brought to justice; and we saw in connection with the eyre system that the checking of presentments against the coroners' rolls indeed made negligence or concealment difficult. Although historians have long suspected that the legislation of 1166 did not introduce an entirely new institution, a central feature of this traditional picture has remained undisturbed: the appeal of felony and the presentment procedure are still generally taken to have been distinct.

But it is clear from Glanvill that the heart of the matter lay not in the initiation of a charge but in its proof. Either there was a witness to the fact or there was not[3]. If there was a witness, he could swear to what he saw and heard and the law-suit could be determined by testing his affirmative oath. If there was no witness, but yet there was enough to put the accused to answer, then the law-suit could be determined only by testing his oath of denial. The initial distinction, therefore, was about whose oath was to be tested, and how. Trial by battle tested the affirmative oath of a witness. As we have seen it was introduced at the Conquest but only for proof by Normans; and in the following century it had somehow become appropriated to certain very important kinds of claim, especially the writ of right and the appeal of felony, whether involving Normans or English. The appeal of felony and its battle remained a reality, partly because if goods had been taken they could be recovered by appeal but not on indictment, and partly because of the system of 'approvers' whereby a convicted person could win his own life by appealing other malefactors known to him[4]. And the very name

1. Op. cit., vol. II, pp. 605–6; J. M. Kaye, *Placita Corone* (Selden Society Supplementary Series, vol. IV); C. A. F. Meekings, *Crown Pleas of the Wiltshire Eyre, 1249* (Wiltshire Archaeological Society, vol. 16), pp. 69 ff.
2. Assize of Clarendon; N. D. Hurnard, 'The Jury of Presentment and the Assize of Clarendon' (1941) 56 English Historical Review, p. 374.
3. *Glanvill*, Book XIV, especially XIV, 1: *aut certus apparet accusator aut non;* and if not *fama solummodo eum publice accusat* (ed. G. D. G. Hall, p. 171).
4. R. F. Hunnisett, *The Medieval Coroner* (1961), pp. 68 ff.

reminds us what the appeal was all about: an approver was one who proved charges against others.

Proceedings with no specific witness to prove the charge are no less ancient. In any community and in any period suspicions may arise which cannot be ignored. Sheep disappear without explanation and Tom grows richer without explanation. Some process of public accusation organised by authority is inevitable: and a statement by local people of the suspicion of the countryside was enough to put Tom to answer. But by definition nobody in the countryside knew for certain. Only Tom knew whether he was guilty or not, so it was his oath of denial that had to be tested; and this was the province of wager of law. There were two levels at which law could be made. The lesser was the familiar compurgation, in which Tom would swear to his denial and would produce a set number of neighbours who had to swear to his law-worthiness, credibility; and here some slip in the formulae would disclose a lie. But there was also a greater or manifest law, by which Tom's oath would be tested by the elements of fire or water. In the ordeal of water, for example, the priest would conjure the water not to accept a liar, and Tom, having sworn to his innocence, would be lowered in. If he floated, the water was rejecting a liar as it had been told, and Tom was therefore guilty.

For lesser matters only the lesser law of compurgation was available. But for graver matters the choice between compurgation and the manifest law of the ordeal apparently depended by custom upon other circumstances over and above the suspicion of the countryside. Just as an appeal had to be supported by the material evidence of the corpse, the wound and the like, so here some material evidence at least that a definite wrong had been committed was necessary to put a man to the ordeal[1]. Without it, the suspicion of the countryside was enough to put him to answer: but he was entitled to answer with oath-helpers. And it was this that the legislation of 1166 seems to have altered. What was new was not the process of communal accusation based upon the suspicion of the countryside, but the large effect given to that suspicion without more.

1. Notice the unease in *Glanvill*, XIV, 2 (ed. G. D. G. Hall, p. 173) about a charge *ob infamiam* of concealing treasure trove, an offence which leaves no material trace like a wound. Cf. *Curia Regis Rolls*, vol. I, p. 91 (1199).

The original distinction between appeal and presentment procedures was therefore less fundamental than has been generally supposed; and thirteenth-century developments, especially the ease with which abandoned appeals are continued at the king's suit, may be less puzzling when seen in terms of alternative proofs rather than altogether separate procedures. But it was of course from the presentment process that the common law of crime was to grow; and we still know little of how it really worked, where from time to time the initiative lay. So long as royal justice was normally manifested at a meeting of the county court, the actual presentment of a suspect for trial would be by a presenting jury of truly local people, a jury of the hundred. But when royal justices came to hold sessions independently of the county court, the collection of juries from every hundred became impracticable. The 'grand jury' of the county was a body which made the final presentment after earlier processes; and the dignified body of later days with a partly judicial function was something very different from the humble hundred jury from which it had grown[1]. Of the nature of these earlier processes we know little. In the sixteenth century justices of the peace, as a by-product of their functions concerning bail, came to make and record preliminary examinations[2]. And after the organisation of police forces in the nineteenth century, this function of justices came to duplicate that of the grand jury; both decided whether there was a case for the accused to answer. In our own day the grand jury was abolished in England[3], though it survives in the United States.

What the social historian needs to know about these developments is how the police function actually worked before the organisation of police forces. For the legal historian, however, they have another significance; and there is a second casualty to be recorded. The indictment was the king's suit: and although actual initiative surely often lay with the victim, he played no formal part in the proceedings and had no interest in their outcome. This may even have been a matter of policy at first, to encourage immediate

1. F. Pollock and F. W. Maitland, *History of English Law* (2nd edn.), vol. II, pp. 645 ff.
2. Stats. 1 & 2 P. & M., c. 13 (1554) and 2 & 3 P. & M., c. 10 (1555).
3. 23 & 24 Geo. V, c. 36 (Administration of Justice (Miscellaneous Provisions) Act 1933); 11 & 12 Geo. VI, c. 58 (Criminal Justice Act 1948).

appeals. But the result was a segregation of crime from other aspects of the law which became too fundamental to reconsider. In practical terms it is not self-evident that a road accident, for example, should be followed by separate criminal and civil proceedings which can reach different conclusions about responsibility. And in social terms, it is not self-evident that the penal and civil disincentives should be separately considered, that offenders should see themselves and be seen as ranged against an impersonal society, or that their victims and other law-abiding persons should see the whole matter as somebody else's business.

TRIAL BY JURY

The suspicion of the countryside first put a man to his law: to the ordeal if there was some material proof beyond the suspicion, to compurgation if not. The Assize of Clarendon in 1166 seems to have provided that the mere suspicion should always be enough to put a suspect to the ordeal; and for half a century that was the routine. But the mechanism of the ordeal turned upon the invocation of the priest; and after anxious inquiry the church in 1215 decided that it was superstition and forbade priests to take part. The decree was promptly obeyed in England, and the mode of trial of centuries was brought to an end[1].

It is today impossible to imagine the practical and intellectual disarray caused by this decision. The responsibility for putting men to death could no longer be rested comfortably upon God, and the only known governmental decision did not seek to rest it anywhere. The justices going on eyre in 1219 were told to imprison those accused of grave crimes and thought dangerous, 'yet so that they do not incur danger of life or limb by reason of our prison'; to allow those accused of medium crimes to abjure the realm; and to take security for good behaviour from those accused of lesser offences[2]. No trials were contemplated because no trials were now possible.

1. T. F. T. Plucknett, *A Concise History of the Common Law* (5th edn., 1956), p. 118; J. W. Baldwin, 'The Intellectual Preparation for the Canon of 1215 against Ordeals' (1961) 36 Speculum, p. 613; H. C. Lea, *Superstition and Force* (ed. 1892), pp. 408 ff.
2. *Patent Rolls, 1216–1225*, p. 186.

But the issue could not be avoided. There had to be a method of trial, and in the decades that followed the justices seem to have solved the problem for themselves. The grand assize had familiarised them with the idea that even on matters of ultimate right a defendant might choose to abide by a human decision instead of divine judgment; and in the thirteenth century they embraced the proposition that he could offer a verdict of neighbours as his own proof of his denial. Their difficulty was with the indicted suspect who would not so choose, since the only alternative, the ordeal, was forbidden. At first they seem sometimes to have imposed the verdict of a specially large body of neighbours; but sometimes recalcitrance was rewarded by a bargain for abjuration of the realm or the like. Nothing illustrates the magnitude of the difficulty so clearly as the solution. By 1275 trial by the countryside, by a petty jury, was the normal thing: but it had to be chosen by the accused, and if he refused statute provided that he should be put into a *prison forte et dure*[1]. The hardness of the prison was slowly increased until the word itself was read as *peine*, torture; and under this some accused died: they were not convicted felons, their property was not forfeit, and their choice was between deaths. This choice was taken away in 1772, when a refusal to plead became a conviction[2]; and only in 1827 was a plea of Not guilty entered so that jury trial was imposed upon one who would not 'choose' it[3].

Because a jury was the defendant's own proof, chosen by himself, attaint was in principle not available in criminal cases[4]. This process, by which a verdict could be challenged before a larger jury, was appropriate to such procedures as the petty assizes, where the defendant had no choice either in the question or in the means by which it was to be answered. Although given wider scope by statute in civil cases[5], it was never extended to criminal; and it followed that criminal defendants could make no direct 'appellate' challenge on the facts. And for legal historians it also follows that in the

1. Stat. 3 Ed. I, (Westminster I), c. 12; J. B. Thayer, *A Preliminary Treatise on Evidence at the Common Law* (1898), p. 74.
2. Stat. 12 Geo. III, c. 20.
3. Stat. 7 & 8 Geo. IV, c. 28.
4. T. F. T. Plucknett, *A Concise History of the Common Law* (5th edn., 1956), pp. 131 ff; J. B. Thayer, *A Preliminary Treatise on Evidence at the Common Law* (1898), pp. 137 ff.
5. Culminating in Stat. 34 Ed. III, c. 7.

criminal context they must do without one measure of the changing nature of the jury from witnesses to judges of fact. Because attainted recognitors were punished as perjurers, attaint juries became unwilling to convict when they saw a wrong verdict as a mistaken judgment of facts rather than a lie; and the changing nature of jury trial is to that extent reflected in the decline of attaint. But in the criminal context there are other reflections. For example a trial jury would at first always include some members of the presenting jury; how else could the trial jury be informed? But in 1352 statute permitted the challenge of a trial juror on the ground that he had been a member of the presenting jury[1]. As late as 1670, on the other hand, a ground for preventing judges from punishing jurors who found a verdict contrary to the evidence was that the jurors might have other facts within their own knowledge[2].

Of the actual conduct of a trial we know almost nothing before the sixteenth century, not nearly enough until the eighteenth. How the jury informed itself or was informed, how rules of evidence emerged, when and in what detail directions were given by the justices, these are things we do not know. In the sixteenth century evidence was given under oath on behalf of the crown. But the prisoner, whether or not he could call willing witnesses, had no means of compelling them. Nor was he allowed counsel at the trial itself, and this rule lasted until 1696 in cases of treason, until 1836 in cases of felony[3]. He was allowed to argue for himself as best he might at the discretion of the judge; and in the sixteenth century as many cases would be heard as the jury felt they could remember before they gave their verdicts[4]. But the process was probably not quite so brutal and blank as is suggested by these facts and by the mere verdict which is all the plea rolls tell us. In the sixteenth century, at any rate, there is reason to think that judges sought to err in favour of life[5]. And throughout the middle ages, when the facts were largely within the control of presenting and other jurors, there is evidence that they manipulated them so that the outcome would reflect their own rather than the strictly legal view of right and wrong[6].

1. Stat. 25 Ed. III, stat. 5, c. 3.
2. *Bushell's Case*, Vaughan 135.
3. Stats. 7 & 8 Will. III, c. 3; 6 & 7 Will. IV, c. 114.
4. Sir Thomas Smith, *De Republica Anglorum* (ed. Alston, 1906), p. 100.
5. J. H. Baker, *Spelman's Reports*, vol. II (Selden Society, vol. 94), pp. 299 ff.
6. See pp. 421 ff, below.

The blankness of the general verdict reflects yet another casualty in the law itself. By the sixteenth century the common law had in civil matters created one intellectual system, that represented by the old actions, and was engaged in replacing it by another. In criminal matters there had been almost no substantive development. Why should there have been this difference? Largely the answer lies in the invariable plea of Not guilty. In civil matters, it was the possibility of some other answer, the growth of pleading, that forced questions to the surface and so made the common law. To this process the only equivalent in criminal cases was the possibility of objecting to the indictment; and in the fifteenth century counsel were apparently permitted for strictly legal argument[1]. But hardly ever would a prisoner know there was anything to say about that, such objections were probably rare, and argument as on demurrer in a civil case was effectively unknown. To this day, it is only in appellate proceedings that the law relating to a criminal case can be found in a judgment: at first instance, it appears only in a direction to the jury. The judgment is as automatic, except in the matter of sentence, as that which followed an ordeal. The mere form of a criminal trial is surely the most ancient relic in any modern legal system.

ORGANISATION OF CRIMINAL COURTS

The failure of development represented by the unalterable general issue is connected with another institutional point. Before whom were those indicted to be tried? Pleas of the crown were for royal justice, but obviously the eyre system could not handle such work. Eyres could check on a balance sheet of crimes and criminals, but could not come often enough actually to clear the lists. The citizens of London did indeed have the privilege to be tried only before the justices in eyre; and a scandal in the eyre of 1321 illustrates the point. Years earlier one suspected of grave crime had corruptly procured his registration as a citizen to be ante-dated so that he could have the privilege; and at the time, since eyres were now so infrequent, he must have thought he had bought effective immunity[2].

1. YB Pasch. 9 Ed. IV, pl. 4, f. 2.
2. H. M. Cam, *The Eyre of London, 1321*, vol. I (Selden Society, vol. 85), pp. cxx ff, 94 ff.

Something less high-powered and more frequent than the eyre was needed; and an early solution was to use the king's regular local agent, the sheriff. But this gave him too much power for anybody's comfort, and it was brought to an end in 1215 when *Magna Carta* provided that sheriffs were not to hear pleas of the crown[1]. This left as the only practical possibility the frequent issue of special commissions, known generally as *oyer* and *terminer* and jail delivery.

These commissions might be issued to two classes of people, professional justices from the central courts or other professional people, and to prominent laymen; and in both cases geography might play a part in their choice. Moreover there was an obvious convenience in combining judicial sessions, so that these criminal commissions might be combined with commissions to hear pending possessory assizes. And when in the fourteenth century the *nisi prius* system was put on a regular basis, the same commissioners would take verdicts in civil cases on issues which had been reached by the pleadings in Westminster. This was the origin of the assize system which ironically took its name from the first of these functions to die, and which itself lasted in England until 1971. After the Judicature Acts, the *nisi prius* function was converted into full jurisdiction over civil cases to be heard on circuit; and the civil jurisdiction of the commissioners then became a jurisdiction over the whole case from first to last. But their criminal jurisdiction had always been of that nature; and this must be emphasised now because it will prove important. The assize judge was never a delegate in criminal matters: he was the court before which the entire case from pleading to judgment was transacted.

But no great legal skill was needed to hear a man say Not guilty, to take the verdict of a jury, and to pronounce sentence. Although it became steadily less common for laymen to play much of a part in the commissions sent out from the central courts, the old practice of using local magnates in some matters continued. And it combined with a different institution. Besides the coroners, the crown in the thirteenth century took regularly to appointing 'keepers of the peace' in some parts, with a police and sometimes almost military function. They did much administrative work in connection with pleas of the crown, receiving indictments and arranging for suspects

1. *Magna Carta* (1215), c. 24; (1225), c. 17.

to be kept until the royal commissioners came. And in the fourteenth century they came to be used for trial. The quarter sessions of justices of the peace, which like the assizes lasted until 1971, were simply the result of issuing standing commissions to local persons, who were at regular intervals to meet and deal with indictments[1]. An attempt was made in the early days to ensure that these sessions would include justices with some technical knowledge; but this became ineffective and the result was secured in modern times only by the system of professionally qualified chairmen.

The division of functions between these two kinds of justice, the assizes and the justices of the peace in quarter sessions, was a matter which fluctuated. In the early days there was hesitation about leaving felonies to the justices of the peace, but they were within their commission after the late fourteenth century. It seems, however, to have been customary to reserve the most difficult and serious matters for the justices of assize; and by the eighteenth century this had become invariable with capital offences. The greatest part of the work of the quarter sessions was therefore always concerned with the indictable trespasses, the earliest common law misdemeanours.

The nature of the proceedings, however, was the same in quarter sessions and in assizes. The accused was indicted by a presenting or grand jury and pleaded his Not guilty; the issue was put to a petty jury, and judgment followed upon their verdict. The case began and ended before the justices in the country; and this may be seen as the cause of yet another casualty in the development of the criminal law.

In civil cases, it will be remembered, there were two sources of legal development. The earlier was the possibility of special pleading, the process represented by the year books; and it has already been noted that this was shut out by the invariable Not guilty of a criminal case. But in civil cases, even when the general issue was pleaded, a second means of development later came into play. The facts which emerged at the trial could be caught by various mechanisms, such as the special verdict; and they could then be returned to Westminster for legal discussion.

1. A. Harding, 'Origins and Early History of the Keeper of the Peace' (1960) 10 Transactions of the Royal Historical Society, 5th series, p. 85; B. H. Putnam, *Proceedings before the Justices of the Peace in the Fourteenth and Fifteenth Centuries* (Ames Foundation).

None of these mechanisms were available in criminal cases. It would have been technically possible, and no doubt in effect sometimes happened, that a jury would find a special verdict: but only the justices present could consider the legal effect of the facts so raised. The other ways in which in civil cases legal discussion was commonly started at Westminster all depended upon the *nisi prius* system. The motion for a new trial and the motion in arrest of judgment, for example, were mechanically possible precisely because judgment was not formally given by the trial judge, because the verdict had to be reported back to the court in Westminster. But in criminal cases, other than charges of misdemeanour first preferred in the king's bench and committed for trial at *nisi prius*, there was no opportunity for raising matters that had emerged at the trial. This mechanism of development was shut off as effectively as the earlier mechanism of special pleadings.

Both points are reflected in the dismal history of criminal appeals. The writ of error was always available, and almost always uselessly. The record that it evoked would contain the indictment, the invariable Not guilty, the verdict and the judgment. The trial, all rulings on the admissibility of evidence, the direction to the jury – all this was encapsulated in the recital of plea and verdict; and there was not even the chance, useless though it would have been to accused without counsel, of supplementing it with a bill of exceptions. The means of appeal open to the accused was of little value to him and, since only the formalities appeared on the record, of no value to legal development.

The judges, however, recognising this and accustomed in civil cases to motions for a new trial and the like, could and did reserve difficult questions for discussion in London. The discretion was theirs, but at the request of the accused or on their own initiative they could adjourn a case for discussion in Serjeants' Inn or the exchequer chamber; and these informal discussions no doubt played a larger part in such development as took place in the criminal law than with civil matters, where they were ancillary to the regular discussions *in banc*[1]. In 1848 they were formalised by statute, largely in the interest of chairmen of quarter sessions who would

1. J. H. Baker, *Spelman's Reports*, vol. II (Selden Society, vol. 94), p. *302*, where emphasis is laid also on the importance of readings and discussion in the inns.

otherwise have no access to the club; but it was not until 1907 that accused persons could appeal as of right even on a point of law[1].

But it is with legal development that this book is concerned. The medieval arrangements for the quick local trial of offenders were an administrative achievement and a legal disaster. Crime was cut off from the stream of discussion that shaped other branches of the common law; and though a defendant's facts might cause the jury to adjust its verdict in his own case, they could not lead to any adjustment in the law itself.

VEHICLES OF CHANGE IN CRIMINAL LAW

It follows from what has been said that there was little chance for development by the mechanisms which made the common law in Westminster; and such changes as came about in the criminal law were made from outside. The most important method was the direct one of legislation, which played a larger part here than in any branch of private law; and the patchwork result suggests some general reflections. The criminal law had by the eighteenth century attained an incoherence which seemed to defy even the modest order of the alphabet[2], and at its less serious levels was perhaps dependent for its workability on the ignorance of all concerned. However devious the conceptual manipulations by which change came about in civil matters, the result was more coherent and more practical: the solution of today's problem had to be squared with yesterday's and would play its part in tomorrow's.

But there may be another side to this. Legislation in the common law system may have suffered from its long association with crime. To lawyers in the fourteenth century a statute was not something external to the law: it was an internal alteration, and it lived in its context so that its application was neither mechanical nor unalterable. The disappearance of this organic view of a legislative act may have followed inevitably from the lawyer's instinct to play upon the words. But that instinct would be reinforced by the shadow of a gibbet; and the restrictive and wooden view of legislation traditional

1. Stats. 11 & 12 Vict., c. 78; 7 Ed. VII, c. 23.
2. See such manuals as R. Burn, *Justice of the Peace and Parish Officer* (1st edn., 1755). A random run of headings is: Game; Gaming; Gaol and gaoler; Gunpowder; Habeas corpus; Hackney coaches and chairs.

in the common law may owe something to the decent feeling which today requires penal statutes to be construed with exceptional strictness.

A second method of adjustment by which much was contributed to the criminal law was the creation by the star chamber of new offences which, after its fall, were absorbed as common law misdemeanours[1]. Some of these seem to have been true innovations. Perjury by witnesses, for example, could not be a common law offence because witnesses had no formal existence. The jurors themselves, although of course never witnesses in a real sense, were the persons responsible for telling the truth about the matter; and the medieval equivalent of perjury was the process of attaint against the jurors. As juries slowly became judges of fact, proceeding upon evidence, perjury by witnesses became a problem; and it was dealt with by the star chamber and also by statute.

Some star chamber offences, however, were not innovations at all. They were matters which had been familiar in local courts and had just not been pleas of the crown. The civil aspect of fraud, for example, had come to the common law courts when they took in trespasses with no royal interest; and, for reasons already considered, it there largely lost its identity. But the criminal aspect remained in local courts; and the star chamber was the first royal jurisdiction to undertake punishment for fraud, not because its wickedness had not previously been seen but because it had not been a plea of the crown. Libel provides another example. Denigration and insult had been a local wrong; but not even the civil aspect had come to royal courts with the early actions on the case[2]. This may have been due to the interest of the church or to simple unconcern; or it may have been because the criminal aspect bulked so large. And this introduces another aspect of the star chamber's work. Like local courts it treated wrongs as injuries to be compensated as well as offences to be punished, and a good deal of its work consisted in hearing essentially private disputes. Indeed, in the matter of establishing jurisdictional propriety, history may be

1. For the traditional view of the star chamber's contribution to the law, see W. S. Holdsworth, *History of English Law*, vol. V, pp. 155 ff. For the institution itself see G. R. Elton, *The Tudor Constitution* (1960) and *Star Chamber Stories* (1958); R. A. Guy, *The Cardinal's Court* (1977). For some materials see *Select Pleas in the Court of Star Chamber* (Selden Society, vols. 16, 25).
2. See p. 379, above.

heard to repeat itself, though indistinctly and in an undertone. To match the old mechanical *vi et armis* and *contra pacem regis*, star chamber wrongs are often equipped with flimsy allegations of riot and conspiracy, matters advertised as the special business of that body[1].

But this dual treatment in the star chamber could not survive its fall. The procedural segregation of the ancient pleas of the crown had divided the common law system too deeply: a wrong was either a crime or not. Even if a misdemeanour was brought before the king's bench, it was treated wholly as a crime, the injured party being left to bring separate proceedings for compensation if he would; and the main surviving legacy from the star chamber was the possibility of commencing a prosecution by information. Whether the substantive result was beneficial is a matter of opinion. But it is a fact, and possibly an important one, that the rigid separation of the civil from the criminal aspect of a wrong is not a course that was ever chosen: even upon this latest reception of work from an undifferentiated jurisdiction, the question did not arise.

The other two methods of adjustment were indirect. The law was not changed, but its application was made a little less insensitive by regularising special treatment. The pardon played a considerable part until the establishment of a proper appellate procedure in this century. In the middle ages it was at first a matter of purchase, but its availability prompted two connected developments: juries would seek to distinguish the gravity of crimes, so that the worst offenders would find it difficult to get their pardons; and statute sought to restrain the issue of pardons in various classes of case. And, although the process has been little traced, some legal differentiation was thereby brought about[2]. Later, of course, penal differentiation was similarly achieved: and in the eighteenth and nineteenth centuries only a fraction of the death sentences passed were executed, a growing proportion being commuted to transportation and the like.

1. G. R. Elton, *The Tudor Constitution* (1960), p. 170.
2. E. g. Stats. 2 Ed. III, c. 2 (1328); 13 Ric. II, stat. 2, c. 1 (1390). On the former see G. O. Sayles, *Select Cases in the Court of King's Bench*, vol. III (Selden Society, vol. 58), p. xli. On the latter see p. 423, below, and references there cited. On the early history of pardons see N. D. Hurnard, *The King's Pardon for Homicide* (1969).

Similar in its operation, though in the middle ages more capricious, was the benefit of clergy[1]. A great dispute in the late twelfth century established the principle that jurisdiction over ordained clergy belonged to the church. The procedure which eventually evolved was for the accused to be tried as though he were a layman, and then, if he satisfied the test of clergy, to be handed over to the church. The lay trial, however, was conclusive of nothing. His chattels were impounded to await the trial which would now take place in a church court; and if he was convicted there, the punishment was also for the church. Since the church's trial came to be by compurgation, and its punishment a commonly insecure prison, what really mattered was whether the accused could obtain this treatment. In the sixteenth century any pretence that the church played a real part was abandoned: the convicted accused was set free, though justices could imprison him for up to a year[2].

This irrelevant anomaly was harnessed in two ways. One was by rationalising the availability of the privilege. The first general test was ability to read, but even one who was literate might be disqualified. One might safely marry once but not twice; and it was important not to marry a widow. A woman, moreover, could not by any stretch be in orders; and in the seventeenth century parliament was obliged to prove that in this respect it could turn a woman into a man[3]. But the disqualification which became useful was that a clerk convicted would be degraded from his order, or at least that the lay courts could assume this to be so. One could therefore have the benefit only once, and in 1490 the branding-iron was brought into use to enforce this[4]. The benefit thus became a means of sparing first offenders. But we must not suppose that reason had entirely got the upper hand. The brand only raised a presumption that its bearer was not in orders, and it was still open to a second offender to show that he was in truth a clerk. And even a first offender still had to qualify himself by passing the reading test, which was not abolished until 1706[5].

1. L. C. Gabel, *Benefit of Clergy in England in the later Middle Ages* (1929); C. R. Cheney, 'The Punishment of Felonous Clerks' (1936) 51 English Historical Review, p. 215.
2. Stat. 18 Eliz., c. 7 (1576).
3. Stats. 21 Jac. I, c. 6 (1624); 3 Wm. & Mary, c. 9 (1691).
4. Stat. 4 Hy. VII, c. 13.
5. Stat. 6 Anne, c. 9 (sometimes identified as 5 & 6 Anne, c. 6).

The second means of harnessing the benefit was always more rational, but not the less remarkable. Just as statute might restrict the issue of pardons in specially bad kinds of case, so it might take away the benefit of clergy. This left the offence as punishable with death on first conviction, and so introduced some rough gradation into the list of felonies. But reasonable though this was, it made the development of the criminal law more oblique than anything that Westminster Hall had contrived. The common law would have sent all felons to the gallows; the benefit of clergy as it developed would have saved them all; and legislation sought to introduce order by deciding when the second anachronism should interfere with the first. This is not a matter for moral judgment; but it is a fact to be considered by those who feel surprised at the small part played by legislation in the development of the common law generally. What is a matter for moral judgment, by those who feel entitled to judge, is the use made of this mechanism in the age of reason: the list of felonies excluded from the benefit of clergy was steadily lengthened. Only in 1827 was the privilege abolished[1], and the process begun of adjusting punishments directly to offences.

SUBSTANTIVE DEVELOPMENT OF CRIMINAL LAW

There is either too much to say or too little. To describe the visible changes made by the methods just considered would be to compile a catalogue of facts. But there is no development to trace of the kind which has occupied the rest of this book. Our blank records, monotonously reciting indictment, general issue and verdict, conceal much that the social historian needs to know. They also conceal matters which would to us be matters of law, especially about mental elements. By bringing their own standards to bear, juries may have produced results more just and humane than we can see. But there could be no systematic development until those standards came to be articulated and their application to individual cases discussed; and that could not happen until the judge, himself having knowledge of the facts, could offer some direction on their legal effect.

1. Stat. 7 & 8 Geo. IV, c. 28.

If the facts cannot shape the law, the law will shape the facts; and the early history of crime may show almost a mirror image of the productive relationship which has been a theme of this book. Jurors made unacceptable rules produce acceptable results by adjusting the facts; and since it was the result that they desired to control, any facts that they stated would be those of a clear and predictable case. There is an analogy with more formal fictions. And a doubtful case that might have provoked discussion about the limits of a rule was edited so as to fall clearly on one side of the line or the other.

The only crime to have been investigated with such questions in mind is homicide[1]; and the background was an early stiffening of liability to ordain results which ordinary people, and therefore jurors, never accepted. In an age without police so that even the good citizen could hardly avoid participation in fights, and without much medical knowledge so that wounds were often fatal, killing was a hazard of the same order as today's involvement in a road accident. Only the worst kinds of homicide were felt to deserve the ultimate punishment; and in the old English law these were 'murders', killings by stealth, which probably included ambush, as opposed to open fight[2]. But a change came about, probably in the twelfth century though neither chronology nor mechanism is clear; and almost all killings became indiscriminately capital offences. 'Murder' ceased to be a legal term of art, except in what became the meaningless context of the murder fine: to protect his followers the Conqueror had imposed collective liability on any hundred in which a Norman was found killed; and failure to 'present Englishry' continued to bring in revenue long after it had lost any reason[3]. In popular usage 'murder' probably continued to mean those wicked homicides for which ordinary people felt the killer should forfeit his own life. But legally they were no longer distinguished from the much larger number of homicides which had

1. For the discussion which follows see T. A. Green, 'Societal Concepts of Criminal Liability for Homicide in Medieval England' (1972) 47 Speculum, p. 669; 'The Jury and the English Law of Homicide, 1200–1600' (1976) 74 Michigan Law Review, p. 413. See also N. D. Hurnard, *The King's Pardon for Homicide* (1969); J. M. Kaye, 'The Early History of Murder and Manslaughter' (1967) 83 LQR, pp. 365, 569.
2. Cf. *Glanvill*, XIV, 3 (ed. G. D. G. Hall, p. 174).
3. C. A. F. Meekings, *Crown Pleas of the Wiltshire Eyre, 1249* (Wiltshire Archaeological Society, vol. 16), p. 61. Abolished by Stat. 14 Ed. III, stat. 1, c. 4 (1340).

joined them as capital offences; and this was the change that jurors were for centuries to frustrate.

The simplest thing they could do for one who had killed, but not in a way they thought to deserve his own death, was to acquit him; and here there is nothing but statistics for the historian to catch hold of. But at the end of the fourteenth century statistics show something more telling than just a high rate of acquittal. Perhaps to emphasise concern with an increase in professional crime, justices' commissions began to make specific mention of 'murder'. It was still not different in legal consequence in the courts, but in 1390 statute sought to restrain pardons in such cases[1]. Probably for these reasons, though it still made no formal difference to what should happen at the trial, indictments themselves began to distinguish some homicides as 'murder'; and the acquittal rate in those cases turns out to be much lower than for other homicides[2].

If the defendant's involvement was notorious, and particularly if he had in court sought to exculpate himself by giving some account of his own, a simple acquittal would require great hardihood; and another way in which jurors might help a defendant was to find that his homicide was excusable. His chattels were still forfeit, but from an early date pardon was automatic. The categories were closely defined; and for self-defence, which was least incongruous with what had started as a quarrel, the rules were strict. There had to be no retreat or other recourse open to the defendant. Again the mere statistics are significant: surprisingly large numbers were said to have been cornered by their dead assailants in pedantic satisfaction of the rules. And again suspicion is confirmed when another source is brought to bear, this time the records of coroners' inquests into the same deaths; and the desperate attack can be seen as an edited version of the quarrel that got out of hand[3].

In such cases, even more than with mere acquittals, judges must have known what was happening. But without knowledge of the actual facts of individual cases, they were likely to think in terms of the law being cheated; and legislative amelioration was therefore made more unlikely, as well as common law development of such

1. Stat. 13 Ric. II, stat. 2, c. 1.
2. T. A. Green, 'The Jury and the English Law of Homicide' (1976) 74 Michigan Law Review, p. 413 at p. 432.
3. Op. cit. pp. 428 ff; T. A. Green, 'Societal Concepts of Criminal Liability for Homicide in Medieval England' (1972) 47 Speculum, p. 669 at pp. 675 ff.

matters as the proper limits of true self-defence. There was a kind of stalemate; and it was broken only by a change in the nature of jury trial itself.

As jurors lost their character as the witnesses who supplied the facts, and became persons to whom a case was presented and who had to decide on what they heard in court, they largely lost their control over the result. The judge had heard it all too. In the end, of course, jurors could still apply their own standards in a blank Not guilty; and questions were to arise over their liability to punishment for a perverse verdict. But while occasional juries showed the necessary hardihood, it became exceptional rather than regular. In general they lost control of the outcome, and shed the responsibility for it.

It is in the sixteenth century that judges can be seen to worry about pleas of the crown, and in particular about capital cases[1]. It was to them that the responsibility had passed. The judge is no longer presented by the jury with a story or a conclusion to which he must give unquestioning effect. He too now hears the case as it is presented and the unedited facts as they emerge in evidence; and it is he who must instruct the jury about their legal effect. The law is formulated in his direction, and his formulation may put the man in front of him to death. Perhaps he will wish to discuss it with other judges, and the familiar conditions for legal development are at last beginning to be satisfied. But the scale of the development which results is altogether different from that in other branches of the law. No doubt there was professional conversation in the inns, and more formal academic discussion at readings. But until the twentieth century a point arising in an actual trial would be formally discussed only if the judge himself decided to reserve the case[2]. Until modern times, indeed, few major changes were directly produced by this mechanism. It combined with the indirect mechanisms already considered. In the sixteenth century, for example, a lasting distinction between murder and manslaughter at last became established, but not in the common law itself. It operated not within the trial, but on such external matters as benefit of clergy. The lawyers could no more change the law than the jury could; but

1. J. H. Baker, *Spelman's Reports*, vol. II (Selden Society, vol. 94), pp. *299* ff.
2. Stat. 7 Ed. VII, c. 23 (1907).

they too could make slightly capricious arrangements to save the less culpable from hanging.

The shift in responsibility with the change in the nature of jury trial must of course have affected all crimes. But we do not know much about the ways in which medieval juries exercised their control over, say, theft; and homicide is the only common crime for which there is any chance of obtaining cross-bearings from the coroners' rolls. We do know, however, that indictments for theft were drawn with varying allegations of circumstantial wickedness; and since these could make no formal difference at the trial, it has been conjectured that they were put in to influence the granting of a pardon[1]. Perhaps they had a more direct but informal effect within the trial, as a message to the petty jury about the exercise of its own prerogative of mercy.

Apart from simple acquittal, the jury could also save a thief from the gallows by adjusting the value of the property he had stolen. In the thirteenth century the distinction had emerged between grand larceny which was punishable by death and petty larceny which was not; and it depended upon whether the goods stolen were worth more or less than twelve pence[2]. Juries seem to have been taking the obvious advantage of this by the early fourteenth century[3]; but of course the compulsion to do so increased as the value of money fell. Even the judges came to take a hand in a similar way. They could not undervalue things, but they could hold them to be without any value in law; and in the sixteenth century they tried this with jewels and later succeeded with bank-notes. However oddly they developed, judicial scruples seem to have begun in the fifteenth century over the theft of objects of luxury[4]. And although the ethical consideration probably first came up in connection with

1. T. F. T. Plucknett, 'Commentary on the Indictments' in B. H. Putnam, *Proceedings before the Justices of the Peace in the Fourteenth and Fifteenth Centuries* (Ames Foundation), p. cxxxiii, at pp. cxxxix ff.
2. F. Pollock and F. W. Maitland, *History of English Law* (2nd edn.) vol. II, pp. 495 ff; W. S. Holdsworth, *History of English Law*, vol. III (5th edn.), p. 366. The figure of 12d may be partly due to Stat. 3 Ed. I (Westminster I), c. 15, concerning bail.
3. *Eyre of London, 1321*, vol. I (Selden Society, vol. 85), p. 85; 18 Lib. Ass., pl. 14, f. 59.
4. W. S. Holdsworth, *History of English Law*, vol. III (5th edn.), p. 367; J. F. Stephen, *History of the Criminal Law* (1883), vol. III, pp. 142 ff; J. H. Baker, *Spelman's Reports*, vol. II (Selden Society, vol. 94), pp. *317–18*.

game-birds and the like, about which there were more mundane grounds for argument, its being raised is a revealing sidelight on the formal brutality of the law.

The principal factor in the development of theft, however, was a limitation which was all too clear. To be a plea of the crown there had at least to be an act that could be called *contra pacem*: there had to be a taking. This raised perennial difficulties over taking by servants and employees, which were put right mostly by piecemeal statutes. It meant that bailees could not steal, and even the fifteenth-century doctrine of 'breaking bulk' did not greatly help[1]. It meant that receivers were not thieves, and their position greatly improved as the old processes of appeal and *de re adirata* faded. Those actions had commenced against the possessor, innocent or not, and relied upon vouchers to warranty for producing the thief. For a time it seems that receivers were in fact indictable; but the logic of the king's peace left them immune, and they were eventually and hesitatingly reached by statute. A large part of the legislation concerning crime was indeed concerned to fill one gap after another in the punishment of dishonesty. It was the symptomatic treatment of a single ailment, the capricious scope of the king's peace.

The felonies should not be left without mention of two mysteries, probably unconnected. The first is an early mystery peculiar to theft, and specially relevant to the gaps caused by the need for a breach of the king's peace. Theft was not at first a plea of the crown, and the king's peace was then not relevant. Glanvill assigns jurisdiction to the sheriff[2], and mentions a consequential peculiarity: a thief's land escheated directly to his lord, with no royal right of year, day and waste[3]. These probably reflect the ancient realities of jurisdiction over the commonest of crimes. The escheat seems to show that theft was a felony; and there is probably no connection with a later mystery, which is anyway not exclusively confined to theft. Indictments in the fourteenth and fifteenth centuries sometimes charge what would otherwise be theft, or for example rape, but without alleging felony[4]. This is an ingredient of a different

1. See p. 369, above; *The Carrier's Case*, YB Pasch. 13 Ed. IV, pl. 5, f. 9.
2. *Glanvill*, I, 2; XIV, 8 (ed. G. D. G. Hall, pp. 4, 177).
3. *Glanvill*, VII, 17 (ed. G. D. G. Hall, p. 91).
4. T. F. T. Plucknett, 'Commentary on the Indictments' in B. H. Putnam, *Proceedings before Justices of the Peace in the Fourteenth and Fifteenth Centuries* (Ames Foundation), p. cxxxiii, especially at p. clix.

order of importance from other circumstances which may or may not be alleged. Without it, the charge was of a misdemeanour only, and of course not capital; and we cannot tell how far such cases reflect a discretion in the indictors or in the victim of the wrong.

There are other signs of elasticity in medieval indictments[1]. Besides a few charges of receiving stolen goods, for example, there are also found charges of attempt. But such offences seem to have been driven out by the king's peace; and they had later to be deviously resurrected. The crime of attempt is one of those reintroduced by the star chamber. And the list of misdemeanours attributable to that court reflects, as does the statute book, the way in which crime, like tort, was constricted by an anachronism. What had been the boundaries between royal and local justice became the boundaries of justice itself as local jurisdictions fell away.

But even in the fourteenth and fifteenth centuries justices of the peace dealt with some wrongs which were not offences against the king's peace, though they may have been rationalised in terms which recall the original sense of the king's peace as his special law: it was sometimes said that anything done against the king's command was done against his peace[2]. These were economic offences in breach of statute[3]. Much the most important were offences against the labour laws, the harbingers of a whole system of local government. Under judicial forms the justices came to exercise the administrative functions of the countryside, as well as to deal with statutory crimes which seemed to be new, but which must often have reproduced offences familiar in the truly local jurisdictions now dying.

It is not known how far this is true also of the last and largest growth to be mentioned, that of the summary offences[4]. From the sixteenth century on, statute took to the piecemeal creation of offences, conferring summary jurisdiction without jury upon one

1. Op. cit., esp. at pp. cxli (receiving), cliii (attempt).
2. YB 17 Ed. III (Rolls Series), p. 3, at p.5. Cf. *The Earl of Shrewsbury's Case*, 9 Co. Rep. 42a at 50b; *Shortridge and Hill's Case*, Godbolt 426
3. B. H. Putnam, *Proceedings before the Justices of the Peace in the Fourteenth and Fifteenth Centuries* (Ames Foundation), pp. cxxi ff.
4. F. W. Maitland, *Constitutional History* (1908), p. 231; W. S. Holdsworth, *History of English Law*, vol. IV (3rd edn.), pp. 134 ff. Their books have been long-lived. R. Burn, *Justice of the Peace and Parish Officer*, grew from two to six volumes in thirty editions between 1755 and 1869. W. Paley, *Law and Practice of Summary Convictions*, latest edition 1953, was first published in 1814.

justice or two, sitting in some special place or not, with some right of appeal or without, and all with little regard to the gravity of the offence or the severity of the penalty provided. The result was a patchwork, the capricious nature of which can be gathered only from the alphabetical manuals produced for justices. Not until the nineteenth century was any attempt made to systematise the result; and even then those parts of the law which most affected most people were among the most confusing. Only in very recent years has much effort been made in England to systematise the criminal law at all levels, and to state it in terms more appropriate than those left by medieval accident.

Tables of Cases

1—*Cases from Court Records*

Page

UNPRINTED PLEA ROLLS

KB 26/201, m. 7d (1271), trespass: justification 296
CP 40/2A, m. 23d (1273), trespass: repair of river wall 302
KB 27/201, m. 22d (1310), trespass: money in container .. 369
CP 40/395, m. 162d (1358), debt: *concessit se teneri* 259
CP 40/395, m. 226d (1358), debt: *concessit se teneri* 259
CP 40/440, m. 407d (1370), nonfeasance: service agreement .. 323
CP 40/440, m. 630d (1370), nonfeasance: agreement for carriage 323
CP 40/632, m. 476d (1419), deceit 365
KB 27/731, m. 82 (1444), deceit: sale without title 364
CP 40/957, m. 320d (1501), wrongful claiming as villein .. 382
CP 40/957, m. 442 (1501), wrongful claiming as villein 382
KB 27/988, m. 42d (1508), slander 382
KB 27/999, m. 73d (1511), slander 382
KB 27/1006, m. 27 (1513), conversion: bailee 370
KB 27/1006, m. 36 (1513), slander: Richard Hunne .. 383–84
KB 27/1006, m. 62 (1513), slander 387
CP 40/1064, m. 78d (1530), slander 385
CP 40/1064, m. 516d (1530), slander 384
CP 40/1140, m. 85d (1549), breach of promise 335
CP 40/1140, m. 535d (1549), *assumpsit* for money 348
KB 27/1183, m. 189 (1557), slander 387
KB 27/1183, m. 190 (1557), slander 387
KB 27/1183, m. 193 (1557), conversion: carrier 375
KB 27/1252, m. 27 (1575), *assumpsit*: insurance 342
KB 27/1252, m. 158 (1575), *assumpsit*: insurance 342
KB 27/1252, m. 366 (1575), conversion: pledgee 375
CP 40/1353, m. 627d (1578), *assumpsit*: bet 342
KB 27/1329, m. 273 (1594), slander of title 385
KB 27/1329, m. 305d (1594), *assumpsit*: damage to credit .. 338
KB 27/1329, m. 306 (1594), *assumpsit*: damage to credit .. 338
KB 27/1329, m. 310 (1594), *assumpsit*: damage to credit .. 338
KB 27/1329, m. 328 (1594), conversion: pledgee 375
KB 27/1329, m. 369d (1594), conversion: bailee 375

Page

UNPRINTED PLEA ROLLS (*continued*)
KB 27/1329, m. 444 (1594), *assumpsit*: bet 342
KB 27/1329, m. 476 (1594), *assumpsit*: bet 342
KB 27/1329, m. 503 (1594), *assumpsit*: insurance 342

PLEAS BEFORE THE KING OR HIS JUSTICES, vol. I (Selden Society vol. 67)
nos. 3551–2 (1206), writ patent against lord himself 132

CURIA REGIS ROLLS
vol. I, p. 91 (1199), proof: treasure trove 408
vol. I, pp. 388–9 (1201), deceit: inducing grant 362
vol. VIII, p. 213 (1220), remainder called *conventio* 192
vol. XVI, no. 1727 (1241): fraud of market 302
vol. XVI, no. 1764 (1241): fraud of market 302

BRACTON'S NOTE BOOK
no. 86 (1220), remainder called *conventio* 192
no. 687 (1232), 'conversion' by ward 366
no. 1215 (1237), aiel and cosinage 132, 137
no. 1976 (1221), inheritance: lord's control 142

LINCS. & WORCS. EYRE ROLLS (Selden Society vol. 53)
no. 1071 (1221), eyre system 28

PROCEDURE WITHOUT WRIT (Selden Society vol. 60)
pp. 87, 90 (1258), county courts 14

CASES IN KING'S BENCH (Selden Society)
I, vol. 55, p. 65 (1280), deceit: inducing grant 362
I, vol. 55, p. 181 (1290), trespass: accident 47, 297
II, vol. 57, p. 20 (1290), deceit: inducing grant 362
III, vol. 58, p. 179 (1307), deceit: warranty 293, 321
VI, vol. 82, p. 66 (1348), misfeasance: *Humber Ferry Case* .. 55

BRINKBURN CARTULARY (Surtees Society)
p. 105 (1299), detinue: bailee's liability 267

SEL. ROLLS CHESTER CITY COURTS (Chetham Society)
p. 50 (1317), *de re adirata* 271
p. 60 (1318), *de re adirata* 271

CAL. MAYOR'S COURT ROLLS, LONDON, 1298–1307
p. 40 (1299), slander 379
p. 56 (1300), deceit 362
p. 81 (1300), misfeasance: surgeon 318

Page

CAL. MAYOR'S COURT ROLLS, LONDON, 1298–1307 (*continued*)
p. 106 (1301), trespass: refusal to work 325
p. 154 (1304), deceit 362
p. 216 (1305), deceit 362
p. 258 (1307), deceit 362

CAL. PLEA AND MEMORANDA ROLLS, LONDON, 1323–64
p. 69 (1328), slander 379
p. 260 (1363), deceit: sale without title 364

CAL. PLEA AND MEMORANDA ROLLS, LONDON, 1364–81
p. 126 (1371), deceit: entail sold as fee simple 329, 362, 364
p. 236 (1377), misfeasance: surgeon 318

CAL. SELECT PLEAS AND MEMORANDA, LONDON, 1381–1412
p. 23 (1382), deceit: conveyance to third party 329, 362
p. 40 (1383), slander 379

CAL. PLEA AND MEMORANDA ROLLS, LONDON, 1413–37
pp. 291, 298 (1436–7), sale of entailed land 188

ROLLS FROM THE OFFICE OF THE SHERIFF OF BEDS. AND BUCKS.
p. 66 (1333), slander 379

PROCEEDINGS BEFORE JUSTICES OF THE PEACE (Ames Foundation)
p. 130 (1395), failed cure and extortion 405

CASES IN STAR CHAMBER (Selden Society vol. 16)
p. 38 (1493), defamation 388

2—*Year Book Cases*

This table is chronological except that (i) the *Eyre of Kent* is placed with the *Eyre of London* at the end of the Selden Society series of Edward II, (ii) the *Liber Assisarum* is placed at the end of Edward III, and (iii) the abridgments of Statham, Fitzherbert and Brooke are placed at the end of the table.

Page

ROLLS SERIES

20 & 21 Edward I, p. 59 (1292), effect of *de donis* 176
20 & 21 Edward I, p. 189 (1292), detinue 267
20 & 21 Edward I, p. 303 (1292), entail : warranty 180
20 & 21 Edward I, p. 367 (1292), debt-detinue: failure of consideration 261
21 & 22 Edward I, p. 29 (1293), waste: accident 298
21 & 22 Edward I, p. 321 (1294), effect of *de donis* 176
21 & 22 Edward I, p. 467 (1294), detinue: trover .. 271–73
21 & 22 Edward I, p. 469 (1294), voucher and aid-prayer .. 184
32 & 33 Edward I, p. 259 (1304), trespass: sense of *vi et armis* 289, 294
32 & 33 Edward I, p. 329 (1304), remainder: *heres viventis* .. 194
33–35 Edward I, p. 387 (1306), entail: warranty 179
33–35 Edward I, p. 399 (1307), receipt 184
33–35 Edward I, p. 427 (1307), remainder: writ of entry .. 193
33–35 Edward I, p. 497 (1307), entail: receipt 176, 185

SELDEN SOCIETY

1 & 2 Edward II, vol. 17, p. 39 (1308), detinue: *de rationabili parte* 270
1 & 2 Edward II, vol. 17, p. 70 (1308–9), entail: receipt 176, 185
1 & 2 Edward II, vol. 17, p. 115 (1308–9), effect of *de donis* .. 176
1 & 2 Edward II, vol. 17, p. 170 (1308–9), trespass: bailee .. 367
2 & 3 Edward II, vol. 19, p. 4 (1308–9), remainder: *heres viventis* 194
2 & 3 Edward II, vol. 19, p. 71 (1308–9), trespass: fraud of market 302
2 & 3 Edward II, vol. 19, p. 75 (1308–9), uses 203
2 & 3 Edward II, vol. 19, p. 194 (date unknown), debt-detinue: failure of consideration 261
2 & 3 Edward II, vol. 19, p. 195 (date unknown), examination of suit 254
2 & 3 Edward II, vol. 19, pp. 195–6 (date unknown), detinue, wager 254
3 Edward II, vol. 20, p. 16 (1310), remainder: writ of entry .. 193
3 Edward II, vol. 20, p. 46 (1310), debt: tally 254

Page

SELDEN SOCIETY (*continued*)

3 Edward II, vol. 20, p. 104 (1310), *capias*: demise of crown .. 294
3 Edward II, vol. 20, p. 191 (1310), debt: *concessit se teneri* .. 258
4 Edward II, vol. 26, p. 15 (1311), detinue of charters 254
4 Edward II, vol. 26, p. 153 (1311), debt: tally 254
4 Edward II, vol. 42, p. 181 (?1311), *quare ejecit* 155
5 Edward II, vol. 63, p. 98 (1311), remainder: receipt 193
5 Edward II, vol. 31, p. 148 (1311), detinue of charters 254
5 Edward II, vol. 31, p. 159 (1311), entail: receipt .. 176, 185
5 Edward II, vol. 31, p. 176 (1312), effect of *de donis* 177
5 Edward II, vol. 31, p. 215 (1312), trespass: bailee 367
5 Edward II, vol. 33, p. 225 (1312), effect of *de donis* 177
6 Edward II, vol. 34, p. 222 (1312–13), *quare ejecit* 154
6 Edward II, vol. 43, p. 65 (1313), detinue: money in container 369
6 & 7 Edward II, vol. 36, p. 30 (1313), detinue: *de rationabili parte* 270
7 Edward II, vol. 39, p. 14 (1313), trespass: seller in possession 289
8 Edward II, vol. 41, p. 136 (1315), detinue: bailee's liability .. 267
8 Edward II, vol. 41, p. 179 (1315), debt: tally 254
10 Edward II, vol. 52, p. 159 (date unknown), *capias*: demise of crown 294
10 Edward II, vol. 54, p. 140 (1317), trespass: seller in possession 289
11 Edward II, vol. 61, p. 12 (1317), remainder: fine 182
11 Edward II, vol. 61, p. 290 (1318), trespass: bailee 367
12 Edward II, vol. 70, pp. 18, 90 (1319), remainder: writ of entry 193
12 Edward II, vol. 70, p. 146 (1319), account: equity 276
Eyre of Kent (II), vol. 27, p. 201 (1313–14), entail: fine .. 182
Eyre of London (I), vol. 85, p. 85 (1321), petty larceny .. 425
Eyre of London (I), vol. 85, p. 94 (1321), indictment in eyre .. 413
Eyre of London (II), vol. 86, pp. 149, 150 (1321), trespass: bailee 369

BLACK LETTER

Mich. 18 Edward II, p. 577 (1324), remainder: *heres viventis* .. 194
Pasch. 18 Edward II, p. 602 (1325), evasion of incidents .. 209
Hil. 19 Edward II, p. 655 (1326), account: equity .. 276, 278
Hil. 1 Edward III, pl. 10, f. 2 (1327), *capias*: demise of crown .. 294
Pasch. 7 Edward III, pl. 19, f. 17 (1333), remainder: writ of entry 193

ROLLS SERIES

11 & 12 Edward III, p. 609 (1338), *capias*: pardon of fine .. 294
12 & 13 Edward III, p. 245 (1339), detinue: money in container 267, 369
17 Edward III, p. 3 (1343), trespass: sense of *contra pacem* .. 427
17 Edward III, p. 141 (1343), detinue: *de placito debiti* .. 264
17 & 18 Edward III, p. 73 (1343), examination of suit 254
17 & 18 Edward III, p. 321 (1343), evasion of incidents .. 209

Page

ROLLS SERIES (*continued*)

18 & 19 Edward III, p. 375 (1345), remainder: receipt 193
20 Edward III, vol. I, p. 17 (1346), wager of law: exchequer .. 257
20 Edward III, vol. I, p. 137 (1346), entail: receipt 185

BLACK LETTER

Mich. 24 Edward III, pl. 17, f. 32v & pl. 79, f. 70 (1350), remainder: *heres viventis* 194
Pasch. 29 Edward III, f. 25v (1355), account: credit balance .. 278
Trin. 29 Edward III, f. 38v (1355), detinue: *devenit* 273
Mich. 38 Edward III, f. 26 (1364), remainder: *heres viventis* .. 194
Mich. 38 Edward III, f. 33v (1364), *ejectio firmae* 154
Hil. 40 Edward III, pl. 18, f. 9 (1366), remainder: *heres viventis* 194
Trin. 41 Edward III, pl. 10, f. 16v (1367), remainder: *heres viventis* 194
Pasch. 42 Edward III, pl. 4, f. 8v (1368), remainder: *heres viventis* 194
Pasch. 42 Edward III, pl. 13, f. 11 (1368), innkeeper 292
Mich. 43 Edward III, pl. 38, f. 33 (1369), misfeasance: horse doctor 319
Trin. 45 Edward III, pl. 25, f. 22 (1371), evasion of incidents .. 210
Trin. 46 Edward III, pl. 19, f. 19 (1372), misfeasance: *Farrier's Case* 291
Hil. 48 Edward III, pl. 11, f. 6 (1374), misfeasance: surgeon 293, 319
Hil. 48 Edward III, pl. 12, f. 6v (1374), *ejectio firmae* 154
Mich. 48 Edward III, pl. 8, f. 25 (1374), trespass: accident .. 292
8 Lib. Ass., pl. 25, f. 17 (1334), novel disseisin: trial of title .. 157
18 Lib. Ass., pl. 14, f. 59 (1344), petty larceny 425
22 Lib. Ass., pl. 41, f. 94 (1348), misfeasance: *Humber Ferry Case* 55, 316–17
22 Lib. Ass., pl. 56, f. 98 (1348), trespass: justification .. 45, 296
29 Lib. Ass., pl. 28, f. 163 (1355), detinue: bailee's liability .. 267
38 Lib. Ass., pl. 23, f. 228v (1364), novel disseisin: trial of title 157
42 Lib. Ass., pl. 6, f. 258v (1368), evasion of incidents 210
42 Lib. Ass., pl. 8, f. 259v (1368), deceit: sale without title .. 364
42 Lib. Ass., pl. 9, f. 259v (1368), trespass: accident .. 292, 299
42 Lib. Ass., pl. 17, f. 260v (1368), innkeeper 292

AMES FOUNDATION

2 Richard II, p. 69 (1378), unintentional harm: fine to king 295, 298
11 Richard II, p. 4 (1387), deceit: warranty 321
11 Richard II, p. 283 (1388), remainder: *heres viventis* 195

BLACK LETTER

Mich. 2 Henry IV, pl. 9, f. 3v (1400), nonfeasance: building agreement 323, 324–25, 328

Page

BLACK LETTER (*continued*)

Mich. 3 Henry IV, pl. 12, f. 3 (1401), deceit: conveyance to third party 329

Mich. 9 Henry IV, pl. 20, f. 6 (1407), evasion of incidents .. 210

Mich. 10 Henry IV, pl. 3, f. 2v (1408), evasion of incidents .. 210

Mich. 10 Henry IV, pl. 11, f. 4 (1408), evasion of incidents .. 210

Mich. 11 Henry IV, pl. 60, f. 33 (1409), nonfeasance: building agreement 323, 325, 328

Trin. 11 Henry IV, pl. 14, f. 74 (1410), remainder: *heres viventis* 195

Trin. 11 Henry IV, pl. 23 (1), f. 80v (1410), evasion of incidents 210

Hil. 12 Henry IV, pl. 5, f. 13v (1411), evasion of incidents .. 210

Hil. 12 Henry IV, pl. 11, f. 16 (1411), evasion of incidents .. 210

Hil. 14 Henry IV, pl. 37, f. 27v, at 28v (1413), detinue: *breve de debito* 264

Pasch. 1 Henry V, pl. 3, f. 3v (1413), *ejectio firmae* 154

Hil. 3 Henry VI, pl. 23, f. 32 (1425), evasion of incidents .. 210

Hil. 3 Henry VI, pl. 33, f. 36v (1425), nonfeasance: building agreement 323, 327

Trin. 9 Henry VI, pl. 19, f. 23 (1431), remainder: *heres viventis* 195

Mich. 10 Henry VI, pl. 84, f. 24v (1431), account: credit balance 278

Mich. 11 Henry VI, pl. 12, f. 7v (1432), "conversion" by executor 367

Hil. 11 Henry VI, pl. 9, f. 16 (1433), "conversion" by executor 367

Pasch. 11 Henry VI, pl. 30, f. 35v (1433), "conversion" by executor 367

14 Henry VI, pl. 71, f. 24v (1435–6), account: credit balance .. 278

Hil. 20 Henry VI, pl. 19, f. 21 (1442), "conversion" by abbot .. 366

Trin. 20 Henry VI pl. 4, f. 34 (1442), deceit: *Doige's Case* 328–31

Hil. 33 Henry VI, pl. 3, f. 1 (1455), bailee's liability: *Marshal's Case* 268

Hil. 33 Henry VI, pl. 23, f. 7v (1455), wager of law 254

Pasch. 33 Henry VI, pl. 6, f. 14v (1455), evasion of incidents .. 210

Trin. 33 Henry VI, pl. 12, f. 26v (1455), detinue: trover .. 273

Mich. 34 Henry VI, pl. 42, f. 22v (1455), "conversion" by executor 367

Mich. 38 Henry VI, pl. 14, f. 5v (1459), account: credit balance 278

Hil. 39 Henry VI, pl. 7, f. 44 (1461), case: bailee 367

Pasch. 2 Edward IV, pl. 10, f. 5 (1462), wrongful claiming as villein 382

Mich. 5 Edward IV, pl. 16, f. 7v (1465), uses: will not declared 213

Mich. 5 Edward IV, pl. 18, f. 7v (1465), uses: escheat .. 213, 217

Mich. 5 Edward IV, pl. 20, f. 8 (1465), uses: will declared twice 213

Mich. 6 Edward IV, pl. 18, f. 7 (1466), trespass: accident .. 50

Mich. 7 Edward IV, pl. 11, f. 16v (1467), uses: incidents .. 211

Pasch. 9 Edward IV, pl. 4, f. 2 (1469), felony: counsel 413

Mich. 12 Edward IV, pl. 2, f. 11v (1472), detinue: *specificatio* .. 370

Page

BLACK LETTER (*continued*)

Mich. 12 Edward IV, pl. 10, f. 13 (1472), case: bailee 368
Mich. 12 Edward IV, pl. 14, f. 14 (1472), detinue: *specificatio* .. 370
Mich. 12 Edward IV, pl. 16, f. 14v (1472), entail: *Taltarum's Case* 187
Mich. 12 Edward IV, pl. 25, f. 19 (1472), entail: *Taltarum's Case* 187
Mich. 13 Edward IV, pl. 1, f. 1 (1473), entail: recovery 187
Pasch. 13 Edward IV, pl. 5, f. 9 (1473), conversion: *Carrier's Case* 369, 426
Trin. 15 Edward IV, pl. 15, f. 32 (1475), wrongful claiming as villein 382
Trin. 17 Edward IV, pl. 2, f. 3 (1477), wrongful claiming as villein 382
Hil. 18 Edward IV, pl. 5, f. 23 (1479), conversion: bailee .. 370
Trin. 5 Henry VII, pl. 7, f. 41v (1490), warranty: past consideration 359
Trin. 11 Henry VII, pl. 9, f. 26v (1496), debt against executors: exchequer 257
Trin. 12 Henry VII, pl. 2, f. 22 (1497), defamation a spiritual offence 380
Mich. 20 Henry VII, pl. 18, f. 8v (1504), pure nonfeasance .. 332
Mich. 20 Henry VII, pl. 20, f. 10v (1504), uses: will declared twice 213
Mich. 21 Henry VII, pl. 9, f. 30 (1505), tender of amends .. 295
Mich. 21 Henry VII, pl. 66, f. 41 (1505), pure nonfeasance .. 332
Trin. 21 Henry VII, pl. 5, f. 27 (1506), trespass: accident .. 50
Mich. 18 Henry VIII, pl. 15, f. 3 (1526), wager of law 254
Mich. 18 Henry VIII, pl. 17, f. 3 (1526), remainders and conditions 197
Pasch. 27 Henry VIII, pl. 22, f. 7v (1535), evasion of incidents: devise 220
Pasch. 27 Henry VIII, pl. 35, f. 13 (1535), detinue: bailment and trover 275, 373
Trin. 27 Henry VIII, pl. 4, f. 14 (1535), slander 383, 384
Trin. 27 Henry VIII, pl. 21, f. 23 (1535), debt against executors: exchequer 257
Mich. 27 Henry VIII, pl. 2, f. 24 (1535), remainders and conditions. 197

STATHAM'S ABRIDGMENT

Done 7 (1454), remainder: *heres viventis* 195

FITZHERBERT'S ABRIDGMENT

Action sur le case 45 (date unknown), pure nonfeasance .. 332
Collusion 29 (1357), evasion of incidents 210
Collusion 47 (1384), evasion of incidents 210
Eiectione firme 2 (1383), trespass: future damages 156
Feffements & faits 99 (1454), remainder: *heres viventis* .. 195

Page

FITZHERBERT'S ABRIDGMENT (*continued*)

Garde 33 (1358), evasion of incidents 210
Garde 102 (1373), evasion of incidents 210
Garde 119 (1311), evasion of incidents 209
Garde 155 (1303), evasion of incidents 209
Sub pena 23 (1452), uses: will declared twice 213

BROOKE'S ABRIDGMENT

Action sur le case 113 (1550), conversion: pledgee 375
Detinue de biens 1 (1535), detinue: bailment and trover 275, 373
Done & remainder 3 (1535), remainders and conditions .. 197
Done & remainder 37 (1454), remainder: *heres viventis* .. 195
Feffements al uses 30 (1552), shifting use 226
Feffements al uses 50 (1538), springing use 226
Feffements al uses 52 (1544), active use 236
Feffements al uses 60 (1555–6), trusts of chattels 234
Fines levies de terres 5 (1535), remainders and conditions .. 197

3—Cases from Reports

	Page
Anon (1591), 1 Anderson, 268; Savile, 126	386, 388
Anon (late 16th c.), Cary, 3–4	93
Anon (1599), Cary 8	235
Anon (1564), Dalison, 63 (22); Moore K.B., 61	387
Anon (1564), Dalison, 63 (23)	385
Anon (1527), Dyer 2b	183
Anon (1552), Dyer, 74a	231
Anon (1568), Dyer, 277b	231
Anon (1573), Dyer, 328b	231
Anon (1586), Godbolt, 40	385
Anon (1588), Gouldsborough, 84	385
Anon (1505), Keilwey, 69, 77	332, 334
Anon (undated), Keilwey, 120–21	213
Anon (1510), Keilwey, 160	372
Anon (1574), 2 Leonard, 221	339
Anon (1588), 3 Leonard, 212	340
Anon (1588), 4 Leonard, 81	256, 340
Anon (1577), 4 Leonard, 189	275, 373
Anon (1561), Moore K.B., 29	383, 387
Anon (1564), Moore K.B., 61; Dalison, 63	387
Anon (1598), Owen, 32	385
Anon (1586), Owen, 34	384, 387
Anon (1633), Roll. Abr. I, 100 (9)	364
Anon (1584), Savile, 74	369
Anon (1591), Savile, 126; 1 Anderson, 268	386, 388
Abergavenny v Cartwright (1572)	389
Atkins v Hill (1775)	360
Ayres v Oswall (?1609)	386
Bailey v Merrell (1615)	364
Barnabas v Traunter (1640)	384
Bath (Earl of) v Sherwin (1709)	163
Baxter v Woodyard and Orbet (1605)	364
Beauchamp v Croft (1497)	389

Page

Bettuan's Case (1576) 236, 238
Booth v Trafford (1573) 385
Bray v Andrews (1564) 387
Brent's Case (1575) 226
Bridges v Hawkesworth (1851) 268
Brough v Dennyson (1601) 386
Bruce v Marquess of Ailesbury (1892) 198
Bushell's Case (1670) 412

Cadell v Palmer (1833) 233
Callard v Callard (1594) 224
Chandelor v Lopus (1603) 365
Chedington's (Rector of) Case (1598) 197
Child v Baylie (1623) 231
Cholmley's Case (1597) 198
Chudleigh's Case (1595) 228
Claridge v South Staffordshire Tramway Co. (1892) 268
Clark and Green's Case (1588) 383
Coggs v Bernard (1703) 269, 369
Cole v Moore (1607) 231
Colt and Gilbert's Case (1613) 386
Colthirst v Bejushin (1550) 197
Consolidated Co v Curtis (1892) 379
Cook v Fountain (1676) 95
Corbet's Case (1599–1600) 190
Courtney v Thompson (date unknown) 385
Cubit v Harrison (1601) 295

Dacres, Re Lord (1535: *Spelman's Reports*, Uses 4) 220
Dale's Case (1585) 364
Davis v Gardiner (1593) 384
Donoghue v Stevenson (1932) 400
Dotting v Ford (date unknown) 385

Easton v Newman (1596) 377
Edwards v Burre (1573) 350

Fowler v Lanning (1959) 395

Gerard v Dickenson (1590) 385
Gibbons v Pepper (1695) 298, 300, 396
Gordon v Harper (1796) 377
Gumbleton v Grafton (1600) 375

Hawkes v Saunders (1782) 360
Heale v Giddye (1591) 387, 388

Page

Hilliard v Constable (1593) 388
Hollins v Fowler (1875) 379
Humphreston's Case (1575) 236, 238

Isaack v Clark (1615) 375–77

James v Rutlech (1599) 386
Johnson v Smith (1584) 385

Kent v Wichall (1590) 295
King v Lake (1667) 391

Lambe's Case de Libells (1610) 389
Lampet's Case (1612) 231
Lane v Cowper: see Humphreston's Case
Letang v Cooper (1964) 395
Leventhorpe v Ashbie (1635) 231
Libellis Famosis, De (1605) 389
Lovies's (Leonard) Case (1613) 231
Lutwich v Mitton (1620) 225

Manning's (Matthew) Case (1609) 231
Mildmay's Case (1582–4) 385
Mildmay's Case (1605) 190
Mitchil v Alestree (1676) 300, 311, 396
Morrice v Smith (1587) 383
Mounteagle v Countess of Worcester (1555) 374
Mouse's Case (1608) 296
Mutton's Case (1609) 383

Norfolk's (Duke of) Case (1681–5) 233
Norman's Case (1587) 386

Oakley v Lyster (1931) 377
Oldnoll's Case (1557) 389
Owen v Lewyn (1672) 375

Palmer's Case (1594) 388
Parret v Carpenter (?1596) 383
Pasley v Freeman (1789) 366
Pells v Brown (1620) 232
Penniman v Rawbanks (1595) 385
Perrot's Case (1594) 197
Pillans v Van Mierop (1765) 360
Pinchon's Case (1611) 308

Page

Pinnel's Case (1602) 256, 268, 340
Pollard v Armshaw (1601) 384
Portington's (Mary) Case (1613) 190
Price v Jones (1584) 231
Purefoy v Rogers (1671) 229–30
Pykeryng v. Thurgoode (1532: *Spelman's Reports*, Acion sur le case 5) 347

Question by the Lord Chancellor (1580) 234

R v Langley (1704) 390
Rann v Hughes (1778) 360
Reynolds v Clarke (1725) 309
Risden v Tuffin (1597) 235
Roswel v Vaughan (1607) 364
Ruswell v Vaughan (1601) 364
Rutland's (La Countess de) Case (1596) 376

Sambach v Dalston (1635) 237
Sanderson v Ekins (1590) 340
Scholastica's Case (1572) 190
Scott v Shepherd (1773) 312–13, 396–98
Sharington v Strotton (1565) 224
Shelley's Case (1581) 194, 205
Shortridge and Hill's Case (1623) 427
Shrewsbury's (The Earl of) Case (1610) 427
Shuter v Emet (1623) 383
Slade's Case (1602) 340, 345, 349–56, 376
Smith's Case (date unknown) 387
Smith d. Dormer v Packhurst (1740) 198
Southcote's Case (1601) 269
Southern v How (1618) 365
Stephens v Stephens (1736) 233
Stone v Roberts (1617) 383

Taylor v Perkins (date unknown) 386
Thellusson v Woodford (1805) 233
Thorley v Lord Kerry (1812) 385, 391–92
Thomson v Gardner (1597) 364
Tomson's (Elizabeth) Case (1624) 384
Trueman v Fenton (1777) 360
Tyrrel's Case (1557) 237, 239

Vandrink v Archer (1590) 275, 373, 378

Walgrave v Ogden (1590) 369

	Page
Ward v Macauley (1791)	377
Weaver v Ward (1616)	394
Welcden v Elkington (1578)	231
Williams and Linford's Case (1588)	385
Williams v Holland (1833)	397–98
Winkfield, The (1902)	268
Winsmore v Greenbank (1745)	292
Winterbottom v Wright (1842)	400
Wittam's Case (date unknown)	386
York (Archbishop of) v Markam (1562)	389

Table of Statutes and Documents

		Page
1100.	1 Henry I: Coronation Charter	
	c. 4 (wardship)	108
1166.	12 Henry II: Assize of Clarendon	138, 407
1176.	22 Henry II: Assize of Northampton, c. 4 (mort d' ancestor)	135, 137–40, 160
1215.	17 John: *Magna Carta*	
	c. 17 (common pleas)	32, 35, 52
	c. 18 (possessory assizes)	30, 32
	c. 24 (pleas of the crown)	287, 414
	c. 26 (*de rationabili parte bonorum*)	270
	c. 34 (writ *praecipe*)	125–26, 146–48
	c. 38 (bailiff's mere word)	286
1217.	1–2 Henry III: *Magna Carta*	
	c. 39 (lord's services)	113
1219.	Writ to Justices (abolition of ordeals)	410
1225.	9 Henry III: *Magna Carta*	
	c. 11 (common pleas)	32, 35, 52
	c. 12 (possessory assizes)	30, 32
	c. 17 (pleas of the crown)	287, 414
	c. 18 (*de rationabili parte bonorum*)	270
	c. 24 (writ *praecipe*)	125–26, 146–48
	c. 28 (bailiff's mere word)	286
	c. 32 (lord's services)	113
	c. 35 (county courts)	14
1258.	Petition of the Barons	
	c. 10 (mortmain)	113
	c. 27 (conditional fees)	149, 173
1259.	43 Henry III: Provisions of Westminster	
	cc. 9, 10 (lord's seisin on tenant's death)	137, 160
	c. 14 (mortmain)	113
1267.	52 Henry III: Statute of Marlborough	
	c. 3 (distraint)	154
	c. 6 (fraudulent feoffments)	209–10
	c. 16 (lord's seisin on tenant's death)	137, 160
	c. 17 (guardian in socage)	107, 279
	c. 20 (false judgment)	57
	c. 29 (entry in the *post*)	145, 148–49, 158

			Page
1275.	3	Edward I: Statute of Westminster I	
		c. 12 (*peine forte et dure*)	411
		c. 15 (bail)	425
		c. 34 (*scandalum magnatum*)	388
		c. 41 (oath of champion)	130
1278.	6	Edward I: Statute of Gloucester	
		c. 3 (alienation by husband)	180
		c. 4 (*cessavit*)	105, 142
		c. 7 (alienation by doweress)	193
		c. 8 (trespass and forty shilling limit)	245, 288
1279.	7	Edward I: *De Viris Religiosis*	113, 204
1284.	12	Edward I: Statute of Wales	
		c. 10 (covenant)	247–48
1285.	13	Edward I: Statute of Westminster II	
		c. 1 (*De Donis*)	173–77, 179–80, 182–83, 188
		c. 2 (disclaimer in replevin)	143
		c. 3 (receipt)	184, 193
		c. 11 (account)	276
		c. 16 (wardship and marriage)	219
		c. 21 (*cessavit*)	105, 142
		c. 24 (*in consimili casu*)	193, 284, 344
		c. 30 (*nisi prius*)	49, 76
		c. 31 (bill of exceptions)	57–8
		c. 45 (*scire facias*)	181
1286.	14	Edward I: *Circumspecte Agatis*	381
1290.	18	Edward I: *Quia Emptores*	113–18, 143, 146, 149, 158, 174, 204, 208–09
1292.	20	Edward I, st. 3: *De Defensione Juris*	184, 185
1299.	27	Edward I, st. 1: *De Finibus Levatis*, c. 4 (*nisi prius*)	49
1318.	12	Edward II, st. 1	
		c. 3 (*nisi prius*)	49
		c. 4 (*nisi prius*)	49
1327.	1	Edward III, st. 2, c. 11 (defamation: indictors)	381
1328.	2	Edward III: Statute of Northampton	
		c. 2 (pardons)	419
		c. 13 (trespass and demise of the crown)	294
		c. 16 (*nisi prius*)	49
1340.	14	Edward III, st. 1	
		c. 4 (Englishry)	422
		c. 16 (*nisi prius*)	49
1349.	23	Edward III: Statute of Labourers	325
1351.	25	Edward III, st. 2: Statute of Labourers	325
1352.	25	Edward III, st. 5	
		c. 3 (indictors on trial jury)	412
		c. 17 (*capias* in personal actions)	252, 294, 306

		Page
1357.	31 Edward III, st. 1, c. 12 (exchequer chamber)	56
1361.	34 Edward III	
	c. 7 (attaint)	411
	c. 16 (fines)	183
1365.	London ordinance (warranties)	179
1376.	50 Edward III, c. 6 (fraudulent debtors)	212
1378.	2 Richard II, st. 1, c. 5 (*scandalum magnatum*)	388
1379.	2 Richard II, st. 2, c. 3 (fraudulent debtors)	212
c. 1379.	London ordinance (debt against executors)	257
1381.	5 Richard II, st. 1, c. 7 (forcible entry)	161
1388.	12 Richard II, c. 11 (*scandalum magnatum*).	388
1390.	13 Richard II, st. 1, c. 17 (receipt)	184–85
1390.	13 Richard II, st. 2, c. 1 (pardons)	419, 423
1391.	15 Richard II	
	c. 2 (forcible entry)	161
	c. 5 (mortmain)	204, 212
1398.	21 Richard II, c. 3 (treason)	212
1402.	4 Henry IV	
	c. 8 (forcible entry)	161
	c. 23 (common law judgments: conciliar appeal)	92
1404.	5 Henry IV	
	c. 1. (treason and uses)	212
	c. 8 (wager of law and account)	277
1406.	7 Henry IV, c. 5 (treason and uses)	212
1429.	8 Henry VI, c. 9 (forcible entry)	161
1484.	1 Richard III	
	c. 1 (grant by *cestui qe use*)	215–16, 220, 236
	c. 7 (fines)	183
1487.	3 Henry VII, c. 4 (fraudulent debtors)	212, 234
1490.	4 Henry VII	
	c. 13 (benefit of clergy: branding)	420
	c. 17 (wardship and uses)	217–19
	c. 24 (fines)	183
1504.	19 Henry VII	
	c. 9 (*capias* in actions on the case)	307 (*twice*)
	c. 15 (socage incidents and uses)	218
1532.	23 Henry VIII c. 10 (pious uses)	235
1536.	27 Henry VIII, c. 10: Statute of Uses	218–30 *passim*, 234–39 *passim*
1536.	27 Henry VIII, c. 16: Statute of Enrolments	224–25
1540.	32 Henry VIII	
	c. 1: Statute of Wills	221–22, 227–30 *passim*, 234
	c. 30 (jeofails)	75
	c. 36 (fines)	183
1543.	34 & 35 Henry VIII, c. 5 (wills)	221

		Page
1554.	1 & 2 Philip & Mary	
	c. 3 (*scandalum magnatum*)	388
	c. 13 (justices of the peace: bail and examination)	409
1555.	2 & 3 Philip & Mary, c. 10 (justices of the peace: bail and examination)	409
1559.	1 Elizabeth, c. 6 (*scandalum magnatum*)	388
1571.	13 Elizabeth, c. 5 (fraudulent debtors)	212
1572.	14 Elizabeth, c. 8 (recoveries)	185
1576.	18 Elizabeth	
	c. 7 (benefit of clergy: purgation)	420
	c. 14 (jeofails)	75
1585.	27 Elizabeth	
	c. 5 (jeofails)	75
	c. 8 (exchequer chamber)	56, 66, 350
1589.	31 Elizabeth, c. 1 (exchequer chamber)	56, 350
1601.	43 Elizabeth, c. 6 (superior courts: small claims)	245
1624.	21 James I	
	c. 6 (benefit of clergy: women)	420
	c. 13 (jeofails)	75
	c. 16, s. 5 (tender of amends)	295
1660.	12 Charles II, c. 24: Tenures Abolition Act	222
1661.	13 Charles II, st. 2, c. 2 (bail)	64
1677.	29 Charles II, c. 3: Statute of Frauds	222, 354
1691.	3 William & Mary, c. 9 (benefit of clergy: women)	420
1696.	7 & 8 William III, c. 3 (treason: counsel)	412
1705.	4 & 5 Anne, c. 3, s. 21 (collateral warranties)	180
1706.	6 Anne, c. 9 (benefit of clergy: reading test)	420
1772.	12 George III, c. 20 (standing mute)	411
1813.	53 George III, c. 24 (vice-chancellor)	96
1827.	7 & 8 George IV, c. 28 (benefit of clergy; standing mute)	411, 421
1833.	3 & 4 William IV	
	c. 27: Real Property Limitation Act	198
	c. 42 (pleading)	80
	c. 74: Fines and Recoveries Act	189
1834.	Hilary Rules	80
1836.	6 & 7 William IV, c. 114 (felony: counsel)	412
1837.	7 William IV & 1 Victoria, c. 26: Wills Act	222
1841.	4 & 5 Victoria, c. 21: Conveyance by Release Act	225
1845.	8 & 9 Victoria, c. 106: Real Property Act	198, 225
1846.	9 & 10 Victoria, c. 95, s. 129: County Courts Act	317
1848.	11 & 12 Victoria c. 78 (crown cases reserved)	416–17
1873.	36 & 37 Victoria, c. 66: Supreme Court of Judicature Act	414
1875.	38 & 39 Victoria, c. 77: Supreme Court of Judicature Act	414
1877.	40 & 41 Victoria, c. 33: Contingent Remainders Act	198, 229
1880.	Order in Council, 16 Dec. (merger of common law divisions)	32

Page

1882. 45 & 46 Victoria, c. 38: Settled Land Act 198
1891. 54 & 55 Victoria, c. 51: Slander of Women Act 384
1897. 60 & 61 Victoria, c. 65: Land Transfer Act 136, 221–22
1907. 7 Edward VII, c. 23: Criminal Appeal Act 417, 424
1925. 15 & 16 George V, c. 18: Settled Land Act 198, 233
1933. 23 & 24 George V, c. 36: Administration of Justice (Miscellaneous Provisions) Act 409
1948. 11 & 12 George VI, c. 58: Criminal Justice Act 409
1952. 15 & 16 George VI and 1 Elizabeth II, c. 66: Defamation Act 392
1964. 12 & 13 Elizabeth II, c. 55: Perpetuities and Accumulations Act 233

Index

A

ACCIDENT
bailee's liability –
case, in, 269, 368–69
detinue, in, 264–265, 267–69, 274, 368
trespass, in, 47, 49–50, 79, 294–300, 394–95

ACCOUNT
accountable relationships, 278–81
accountant in credit, 277–78
auditors. *See* AUDITORS
bailiff, 278–79
committal of accountant to prison, 276
debt, action of, based on, 255, 277, 340, 341
equity in, 276, 279
ex parte talis, 276
fictitious, 277
general issue in, 281
guardian in socage, 107, 279–80
nature of, 275, 277–78, 279
pleas in, 281
receiver of plaintiff's money, 280–81
wager of law in, 281–82

ACTIONS ON THE CASE. *See* CASE

AIEL AND COSINAGE
damages in, 137
introduction, 132, 137
tenurial bearing, 132, 137

ANIMALS
liability for –
bolting horse, 298, 300, 311–12, 396
cattle trespass, 291, 295, 311
incitement, 291, 310
scienter, 291, 299, 310–11, 396
strayed, recovery of, 271–72

APPEAL OF FELONY
approvers, 407–08
battle, trial by, 285, 407
counsel allowed, 51
de re adirata and, 271
indictment and, 51, 404, 407–09
nature, original, 407–09
receivers of stolen goods and, 426
trespass and, 283, 285, 357, 404

APPELLATE PROCEEDINGS
attaint, 76, 411–12, 418
certiorari, 56–8
court *in banc*, 78, 416
Court of Appeal, origin, 78
Court of Criminal Appeal, 417
crown cases reserved, 416–17, 424
error, writ of. *See* ERROR
ex parte talis, 276
exceptions, bill of. *See* EXCEPTIONS
exchequer chamber. *See* EXCHEQUER CHAMBER

APPELLATE PROCEEDINGS
—*continued*
false judgment, 17–18, 57
house of lords, 55

APPRENTICE
articles of, covenant and, 252
legal practitioner, 45, 51, 52

ASSIZE. *See* CIRCUIT; GRAND ASSIZE; MORT D'ANCESTOR; NOVEL DISSEISIN

ASSUMPSIT
classification of, by Coke, 307–08
consideration. *See* CONSIDERATION
courts, differing treatment, 333, 344–45, 350–53
covenant and, 69, 249, 314–39
executors, liability in, 351, 353, 354
fidei laesio and, 337, 343, 357
indebitatus –
common counts, 354–55
entity, whether, 349
form reciting transaction, 349
form not reciting transaction, 349, 354
forms involving third party, 347
quasi-contract and, 355
Slade's Case, 351–53
misfeasance –
actions for, 316–20
classification as trespass, 317–20
covenant and, 317
money for –
background, 339–46
concessit se teneri, 340–41
concessit solvere, 341, 342
debt, as alternative to, 345–53
debt not avilable, 341–42, 343, 345, 346–47

ASSUMPSIT—*continued*
money for—
indebitatus. See that subheading
kinds of claim, 346–53
Slade's Case, 351–53
Slade's Case, consequences of, 353–56
trespassory basis, 343–53
wager of law and, 340, 353, 354
nonfeasance –
agreements for services, 323–24, 325, 327–28
agreements to convey, 324, 328–32
consequential damage and, 327–28, 335, 338, 343
deceit and, 324, 328–32, 333–39
disablement and, 323, 328–32
early cases, 323–28
failure to perform in time, 326
infrequency of cases, 332–33
labour legislation and, 325
mutual promises, 334
reliance, 282, 314, 315, 336–39, 343, 347–48, 349, 353

ATTAINT
assizes and juries, 76, 411
changing nature of jury trial, and, 412, 418
criminal cases, 411
perjury and, 418
special verdict and, 76

AUDITORS
accounting before, 275–77
appointment, 275, 277
fictitious, 277
functions, 276
power to commit accountant to prison, 276–77
status of, 276–77

B

BAILEE
conversion by, 371–72, 373–76
detinue against, 266–69, 274, 371
finder and, 274–75
jailer as, 268
liability of –
case, in, 269, 368–69
detinue, in, 264–65, 267–69, 274, 368
right to sue third parties, 268–69
trover, fiction of, 372–76

BAILIFF
hundred, 15–16
manorial –
account, 278–79
farmer, relationship with, 153, 278
novel disseisin, in, 140, 141
receiver, distinction from, 280
prosecuting claims, 285–6

BAILMENT
detinue on, 266–69
nature of, 7, 264–65, 266–67, 269

BANC. *See* COURT *IN BANC*

BATTLE
trial by –
approvers, 407–08
felony, in case of, 285, 407–08
grand assize and, 130–31
logic of, 39, 130, 285, 407
lord and man, between, 131
Normans, for, 285, 407
writ of right, 123, 130, 407

BENEFIT OF CLERGY
abolition, 421
branding, 420
origins, 420
tests of availability, 420
withdrawal of, from some offences, 421
women, 420

BILL PROCEDURE
enrolment of, 54
eyre, in, 29, 34, 82, 271
king's bench, in, 34–5, 54–5, 62–5

BLACKSTONE
entails, on, 189
provoking reform, 7

BOND
conditional –
general mode of contracting, 251–53, 315
Pinnel's Case and, 256
fraud, induced by, 88–9, 92
nature of, 258
non est factum, plea, 250
payment, effect of, 86, 250
simple, use of, 250

BOOKS OF ENTRIES
nature, 71
on –
debt, 256
trespass and case, 307

BRACTON
nature –
Roman learning, 41–2, 120, 150, 264–65, 267
substantive discussion, 41
Note Book, 41
on –
bailee's liability, 264, 267
debt and detinue, 264
disseisin and self-help, 159

BRACTON—*continued*
on—
forma doni, 173
quare ejecit, 154
remainders, 192, 196
seisin and right, 120, 150

BREACH OF PROMISE, action for, 335

BREVIA PLACITATA
nature and use, 40–1
year books and, 44, 47

C

CASE. *See also* NEGLIGENCE *and* TRESPASS
action on –
abduction, 291–92
assumpsit. *See ASSUMPSIT*
bailor, by, 367–69, 393
conversion. *See* CONVERSION
deceit. *See* DECEIT
defamation. *See* DEFAMATION
fair and market owners, by, 302–03, 305–06
fire, 292, 304, 393
frequency of, 304–05
innkeeper, 292, 304, 393
king's bench, in, 53–4, 293, 344
name, sense of, 304
negligence and, 300, 311–12, 392–400
riparian owners, against, 301–02, 393
origin, 284, 291, 300–01, 405
process in, 306–07
road accidents, etc., 290, 300, 303, 311–12, 396
scienter, 291, 299, 310–11, 396

CASE—*continued*
action on—
smith, against, 290–91, 317–18, 393–94
surgeon, against, 291, 318–19, 393
trespass and, 307–13, 396–98
wager of law, 293, 315
warranty, 292–93, 320–22, 363
writs, form of, 283–84, 303–04

CERTIORARI
nature, 56
writ of error and, 56–8

CESSAVIT, action, 105, 142

CHANCERY
equitable jurisdiction of. *See* EQUITY
inns of, 38
writs, 34, 36, 38, 82

CHURCH COURTS
jurisdiction –
contract, in, 23, 24, 90–1, 201–02, 337, 343, 357
defamation, in, 23–4, 380–88
freehold devise and, 88, 202
maritagium, 87, 172, 202
marriage, in, 23
scope, 23–5
testamentary uses, 88, 202
wills of personalty, 23, 87, 221
prohibitions, 23–4, 381
records, 25
working, 25

CIRCUIT. *See also* EYRE *and NISI PRIUS*
apprentices, 51
assizes, possessory, 30–1, 50–1, 414

CIRCUIT—*continued*
criminal work, 30–1, 51, 414
jail delivery, 31, 414
Judicature Acts, and, 78, 79, 414
Liber Assisarum, reported in, 51, 55, 157, 299
oyer and *terminer*, 414

CLERGY. *See* BENEFIT OF CLERGY

COMMON BENCH. *See* COMMON PLEAS

COMMON PLEAS
court of –
abolition, 32
Bill of Middlesex, effect of, 34–5, 62–5
counting, 39–42
false judgment, 57
jurisdiction, 35, 52, 60–5
origins, 32
pleading, 42–4, 60
private wrongs, actions for, 53–4, 293, 344
serjeants in, 40, 60–1, 63
trespass, fictitious action of, 64
volume of business, 60, 64–5, 69–70
writs in, 35–6
year books, work reflected in, 44–8
eyre, at, 28–30

COMPURGATION. *See* WAGER OF LAW

CONSCIENCE
Doctor and Student on, 89
entail, moral attitude to, 188–89
equity –
"Court of Conscience", 94

CONSCIENCE—*continued*
equity—
jurisdiction founded in, 86, 89–91
rise of, and, 86
Nottingham's distinction between natural and civil, 95
wager of law and, 86, 267

CONSIDERATION
causa and, 357–58
contracts under seal and, 356
indebitatus assumpsit and, 359–60
local rules and, 358
Mansfield and, 360
moving from plaintiff, 359
past, 348, 359–60
promissory estoppel and, 282
quid pro quo and, 357–60
reliance and, 282, 339, 348, 357–60

CONTRACT
account. *See* ACCOUNT
assumpsit. See *ASSUMPSIT*
bond. *See* BOND
breach of promise, action for, 335
centralisation, ill effect of, 29, 60, 67, 245–46, 247–48
church jurisdiction, 23, 90–1, 201–02, 337, 343, 357
city of London, in, 257, 260, 277, 318, 329–32, 343
consideration. *See* CONSIDERATION
corporation, by, under seal, 282, 356
covenant and trespass, relation with, 156, 246–47, 314–15
customs, nature of early, 12, 42
debt on. *See* DEBT
deceit. *See* DECEIT
disablement, 247, 323, 328–32

CONTRACT—*continued*
lessee's right, 152–53
local courts, in, 245, 247–48, 249, 258–59, 315, 322–23
misfeasance actions, 316–20
money, obligation to pay –
assumpsit for. *See* ASSUMPSIT
debt for. *See* DEBT
nonfeasance, 156, 322–39
proof, special problems of, 245–46, 247–48, 253–54, 255, 315
reliance, 282, 314, 315, 336–39, 343, 347–48, 349, 353, 357
sale of goods. *See* SALE OF GOODS
sale of land, 324, 328–32
seal, under. *See* BOND; *and* SEAL, DEED UNDER
services, 323–24, 325, 327–28
warranty. *See* DECEIT *and* WARRANTY
word, meaning of, 249, 260, 355

CONVERSION. *See also* TROVER
bailee, by, 371–72, 373–76
breaking bulk, 369, 426
courts, differing treatment, 376–77
detinue, relation with, 274, 275, 366, 368–79
innocent purchaser, position of, 378–79
market overt and, 371, 373, 374
meaning, 366–67
money in container, 369, 371, 372
negligent keeping, 369
proceeds of sale, 372
property, alteration of, 370–72, 373, 376–78
refusal to deliver, 376–77
specificatio, and, 370–71
title, denial of, 377
trover, significance of, 372–76

COPYHOLD. *See* VILLEIN

CORONER
eyre and, 26, 28, 407
inquest, origins of, 26, 28
rolls, evidence from, 425

CORPORATIONS, contract under seal by, 282, 356

COUNSEL, in criminal trials, 51, 412, 413

COUNTS AND COUNTING
Brevia Placitata, 40–1
count in year books, 45
counters, 40–2
counting, 38–42
formularies of counts, 18, 40
Novae Narrationes, 40
serjeants, 40–2, 71

COUNTY COURTS
early records, 17
jurisdiction, 16, 18
meetings of, 14
origins, 13
replevin in, 104–5
sheriff, 13–14
suitors, 14
viscontiel writ, 33, 84

COURTS. *See also* APPELLATE PROCEEDINGS; CHURCH COURTS; CIRCUIT; COUNTY COURTS; COURT *IN BANC*; EQUITY: ERROR; EXCHEQUER CHAMBER; EXCHEQUER OF PLEAS; EYRE; JUSTICES OF THE PEACE; KING'S BENCH; *NISI PRIUS*; STAR CHAMBER
baron, 22
central, rise of, 31–3
Crown Cases Reserved, 416–17, 424
customary, 22, 102

COURTS—*continued*
franchise courts, 15–16
honours, of, 20–1
hundred courts, 15–16, 17
local, records of, 17–18
manorial, 21–2, 101
merchant, 23
nature of early, 12
wards, court of, 220

COURT *IN BANC*. *See also* MOTIONS AFTER TRIAL
discussion in, 72–80, 312–13, 416
error and, 78, 416
no part in criminal cases, 415–16

COVENANT
action of –
apprenticeship articles, 252
assumpsit and, 69, 249, 314–39
concept underlying, 69, 246–47, 249, 252–53, 317, 325–26, 330
consequential damage and, 252–53
deed under seal, need for, 67–8, 248–49, 261, 315, 356
disablement, 247, 328–32
disuse of, 249, 251–53, 282
fines, to levy, 181, 252
king's courts, in, 248
lease, 153
local courts, in, 247, 249, 329
process in, 252
proof, difficulties of, 67–8, 247–48
word, meaning of, 246–47, 249, 309, 355

CRIME
civil and criminal pleas, early distinction, 285, 403

CRIME—*continued*
crime and tort, 53, 285–87, 392, 403–04, 410, 418–19
separate development of, 403–28

CURTESY
alienation by husband, 179–80
issue, birth of, 168, 174–75
maritagium, of, 168, 171
novel disseisin and, 169
tenurial bearing, 168–69
wife's inheritance, of, 168

CUSTOMARY LAW
legislation and, 1–2, 177, 417
nature, 1–3, 11–13

D

DAMAGES
award inscrutable, 69, 327, 331, 333, 338, 339, 345, 350
personal actions, in, 154, 156
specific remedies and, 154, 156–57, 252–53, 326, 327, 331–32

DE FINE FACTO, action, 181

DE RATIONABILI PARTE BONORUM
customary claims, 207, 270
detinue, 270

DE RE ADIRATA
appeal of felony and, 271
detinue and, 271, 273
receivers of stolen goods and, 426

DEBT. *See also* BOND; DETINUE; WAGER OF LAW
action of, based on account, 255, 277, 340, 341

DEBT—*continued*
assumpsit, as alternative to, 345–53
Slade's Case, 351–53
city of London, in, 257, 260, 277
common pleas interest, 346
concessit se teneri, 258–59, 340–41
concessit solvere, 260, 341
contract, on, 253–57
court christian and lay debts, 90–91, 201–02
detinet, in, 262–63, 266
detinue, distinguished from, 257, 262–65, 266–67
executors, liability in, 257, 263, 351
failure of consideration, 261, 336
general issue in, 250, 254, 258, 262–63
insimul computassent, 341
limitations of, 339–43
money in container, 369, 371
nature of, 257–62
obligation, on, 250–53, 258, 282
payment –
effect of, on action, 86, 250, 254, 255–56
Pinnel's Case, rule in, 256
pleading of, 250, 254, 255–56
process in, 64, 252
proof in, 250, 253–54, 261
quid pro quo, 259–62, 341–43
surety, against, 342
third parties, 259, 342, 346–47
wager of law, when excluded, 254, 255, 277, 281, 340

DECEIT
assumpsit and, 328–53
cheating at games, 363–64
city of London, in, 329–32, 336
contractual aspect, 321, 362

DECEIT—*continued*
criminal aspect, 321, 362–63, 366, 418
equity and, 88–9, 363
land, grant induced by, 362
land, sale of, 328–32
legal proceedings, in, 85, 361–62
local jurisdictions, 85, 320–21, 362
rescission, 320, 329–32, 362
royal courts, 85
sale without title, 364
tort of, modern, 85, 366
warranties and, 320–22, 363, 364–66

DEFAMATION
appearance of, first, 293, 379
church courts, defamation in, 23–4, 380–88
circumspecte agatis, 381
contract, defamation damage in, 335, 337, 338
criminal aspect, 379–80, 388–90, 418
definition, 385–6, 391–2
imputations –
alien, 385
bankrupt, 385
bastard, 385
crime generally, 380–81
diseases, 385, 386–87
excommunication, 337, 383
heresy, 337, 383–84
perjury, 386
professional incompetence, 385, 387–88
Scot, 385
sexual misconduct, 384
theft, 382–83, 386
villein, 381–82, 384
witch, 383
indictors, proceedings against, 380–81

DEFAMATION—*continued*
libel –
anonymity of, 390
criminal aspect, 390
slander and, distinction, 392
writing, association with, 389–92
local courts, in, 379–80
mitior sensus rule, 386, 388
publication, meaning of, 389
scandalum magnatum, 388–89
slander –
actionable *per se*, 385, 387
goods, 379
libel and, distinction, 392
spoken words, association with, 390
statement of law, 19th century, 385, 391
title, 379, 386
spiritual offence, 383–84, 385
spoken and written words, distinction, 389–92
star chamber, defamation in, 388–90, 418
temporal damage, 381, 382, 383–84, 384–85

DEMURRER
error and, 58
evidence, to, 58–9, 76
pleading, in, 46, 48, 72–3, 75, 413

DETINUE
bailee, liability in, 264–65, 267–69, 274, 368
bailment, on, 266–69, 274, 371
charters, of, 254, 272, 281
conversion, relation with, 274–75, 366, 368–79
de rationabili parte bonorum, 270
de re adirata, 271, 273

DETINUE—*continued*
debt, distinguished from, 257, 262–65, 266–67
devenit ad manus, 272–73, 372
distinct liabilities, 271–72, 274–75, 372–73
general issue in, 262–63, 267, 274–75, 373
goods bought, for, 265–66
goods damaged, 253
money in container, 369, 371
nature of action, 253, 262–65, 266–67
possessors other than bailees, 269–75
trover, count in, 273–75, 371, 373–76

DEVISE
customary, 88, 201, 202, 208
relationship of use with, 87, 118, 206–08, 211–12, 214, 218–20, 221–22, 226, 227, 234
terms, of, 230–31

DISTRESS
chattels, upon, 101, 104–05, 107, 112
lord's court and, 101, 104, 112, 114, 140, 142–43
nature, 101, 104
per feodum, 101, 104, 105, 140, 142

DOCTOR AND STUDENT
on –
bargains and agreements, 222, 224
barring of entails, 188–89
conscience, appeal to, 89
conscience of the party, 94
consideration, 357–59
covenant to stand seised, 222, 224

DOCTOR AND STUDENT
—*continued*
on–
paid bond, 94, 250
putting land into uses, 222, 226–27

DOWER
alienation by doweress, 193
curtesy and, 167–69
novel disseisin and, 168
tenurial bearing, 121, 167–68
unde nihil habet, 167
warranty of heir, 167–68
writ of right of, 121, 124–25, 126, 167

E

EJECTIO FIRMAE
advantages of, 162
claims in ejectment, successive, 163
copyhold and, 165
freehold and, 157, 161–63, 244
Quare ejecit and, 154–57
special verdict, 77
specific recovery in, 156, 162
use of, 154–57, 161–65

ENTAIL
abolition proposed, 189, 190, 220
alienability, 173–75
analysis of, early, 173
barring –
fines and recoveries, 181–87, 191
moral attitudes to, 188–89
warranties, 178–81
changing function, 172–73, 192
conditional gifts, as, 173–75, 176–77
De donis and, 175–77, 179–80, 185, 191
degrees in, 177
fee simple and, 174, 185

ENTAIL—*continued*
formedon –
descender, 175, 176–77, 179
remainder, 175–76, 193
reverter, 175
homage and, 172–73
maritagium and, 170, 173
personalty, of, 231
receipt and, 184–85
strict settlement and, 190–92, 198
tenant in tail after posibility, 185
term of years, 231
unbarrable, 190, 196–97
younger son and, 170, 172–73

ENTRY
feudal connotation of word, 143, 147, 148–49, 158, 160
forcible, 160–61
right of, 157, 158–60, 161–63
writ of. *See* WRIT OF ENTRY

EQUITY
acting *in personam*, 90–1, 92
as illegitimate appeal, 92–3
church courts and, 24–5, 87–8
common law judgment and, 92–3
conscience –
appeal to, 89–91, 93
civil and natural, 95
"Court of", 94
jurisdiction founded in, 86, 89–91
copyhold, protection of, 164–65
eyre, equity in, 29
law and –
conflict between, 91–3
early relationship, 5, 91–2
theoretical relationship, 88–91
procedural bearings of, 83–6, 87–8, 92

EQUITY—*continued*
regularisation of, 93–6, 213, 216
rise of, 5, 82–96
uses and, 86–8, 212–14

ERROR
certiorari, 56–8
criminal cases and, 416–17
demurrer and, 58
exceptions, bill of, 57–8, 416
exchequer chamber, to, 56, 65–6, 350–51
fictions and, 65
jurisdiction in, 55–8
king's bench, 55–8, 65–6, 350–51
writ, 58

ESCHEAT
double, 113
felony, 109, 406
heirs, failure of, 109, 116
Quia Emptores, effect of, 118
theft, for, 286, 426
uses and, 217

ESTATES IN LAND. *See also* CURTESY; DOWER; ENTAIL; FEE; FREEHOLD; REMAINDER
grant and regrant and, 205–06
life, for, 169–70
source of idea, 2, 136, 166–67

EXCEPTIONS
bill of, 57–8, 416
pleading, beginnings of, 50, 57, 140–41

EXCHEQUER CHAMBER
exchequer of pleas, from, 56
king's bench, from, 56, 65–6, 350–51
meeting for discussion, 56, 351–52, 416

EXCHEQUER OF PLEAS
jurisdiction, 32, 62
origin, 31–2
quo minus, 32, 62, 257

EXECUTOR
debt, liability in, 257, 263, 351
assumpsit, liability in, 351, 353, 354

EXECUTORY INTERESTS. *See* USES

EYRE
articles of, 28
business, 27–31
complaint to, direct, 29, 34, 82, 271
coroner, 26, 28, 407
common pleas, 28–30
equity, 29
nature of early, 26
novel disseisin and, 30, 139
pleas of the crown, 28, 413
sources, written, 27
year books reporting eyres, 27, 51

F

FALSE JUDGMENT
records of local courts, 17–18
writs of, 57

FAMILY PROVISION. *See also* CURTESY; DOWER; ENTAIL; *MARITAGIUM*; USES
bastard children, 170, 207
chattels, rightful shares, 207, 270
grants for maintenance, 169
old retainers, 169, 170
younger sons, 170, 172–73, 207

FEE. *See also* INHERITANCE
base, 191

FEE—*continued*
conditional, 174–75, 176
entail and, 174–75, 185
homage and, 106, 121, 167
nature, 105–07, 136, 166–67
simple, 106–07, 116, 174, 177

FELONY. *See also* APPEAL OF FELONY
assizes, tried by, 415
feudal concept, 285, 406
escheat for, 109, 406
justices of the peace, tried by, 415
theft as, 286, 406, 426
trespass and, 283, 285, 404–05

FEUDAL INCIDENTS. *See* ESCHEAT; MARRIAGE; TENURES; USES; WARDSHIP

FEUDAL JURISDICTION
aiel and cosinage and, 132, 137
honour courts, 20–1
inheritance and, 107, 128–29, 134–37
local, subjected to, 13, 19–20
manor courts, 21–2, 101–02
mort d'ancestor and, 134–37
nature, 99–100, 119–24
novel disseisin and, 137–43
right in, 120–22, 150
royal courts, relation with, 99–100, 119–34
seisin and, 120–21, 124, 139, 141–42, 159–60
services, enforcement of, 101, 102–03, 104–05, 139–43
writ patent, 124–34
writs of entry and, 133–34, 143–49

FICTIONS
barring entails, 186–87
Bill of Middlesex, 34–5, 62–5
contra pacem, 53, 289–95

FICTIONS—*continued*
credit, injury to in assumpsit, 335, 338, 343, 348, 353
deceit in contract, 338–39, 392
development of, 60–61, 63
ejectment, 161–63
quare clausum fregit, 64
quo minus, 32, 62, 257
riot in star chamber, 419
scintilla juris, 226
trover, 273–75, 373–76

FIDEI LAESIO, contract and, 23, 24, 90–1, 201–02, 337, 343, 357

FINDER. *See also* TROVER
bailee and, 274–75
Bridges v. Hawkesworth, rationale of, 268

FINE
alienation by, 181–82
barring of entail by, 181–83, 191
De Donis, provisions as to, 182
enforcement, 181
nature of early, 182

FITZHERBERT'S *NATURA BREVIUM*
nature and use, 38
on –
debt and detinue, 264
nonfeasance in contract, 334, 336
trespass and case, 307

FORMEDON. *See* ENTAIL

FRANCHISE COURTS. *See* COURTS

FRAUD. *See* DECEIT

FREE ALMS, FRANKALMOIN
mortmain and, 170
nature of early, 169, 170

FREEHOLD
actions concerning, fourteenth and fifteenth centuries, in, 157–61
copyhold, assimilation with, 163–65
devise of, 87, 118, 206–08, 211–12, 214, 218–20, 221–22, 226, 227, 234
nature, early, 103–06, 136, 166–67
passive trust of, 236, 238
trial of titles, *ejectio firmae*, 157, 161–63, 244
writ, need for, 29–30, 127–28, 133–34, 143, 146

G

GENERAL ISSUE
blankness of, 47–8, 51–2, 59, 75–9, 254–56, 258, 261–62, 281–82, 312–13, 412–13, 421–23
Hilary rules, 80
primacy of, 47–8, 59, 75–9

GLANVILL
nature, 18, 37
on –
bailee's liability, 267
criminal and civil pleas, 285, 403
curtesy, 168
death-bed gifts, 219
debt – detinue, 263, 266, 267
dower, 167
grand assize, 76, 130
king's peace, 287
lord and heir, 172, 173
maritagium, 202
mort d'ancestor, 135
novel disseisin, 139
parage, 149
praecipe, 125
prosecution and proof, 407

GLANVILL—continued
on—*continued*
theft, 286, 406, 426
treasure trove, 408
warranty of quality, 320
wrongs, jurisdiction over, 286

GRAND ASSIZE
battle and, 130–31
de homagio capiendo, in, 133
introduction of, 130, 131
same stock, 130–31
special mise, 131–33, 147
special verdict, 76

GRAND JURY. *See* INDICTMENT

GRANTS OF LAND. *See also* ENTAIL; *MARITAGIUM*; USES
conditional, 87, 196, 206, 207, 208, 209–10, 214
free alms, 169, 170
homage and, 111, 112, 169, 172–73
mortmain, 113, 170, 204, 208
subinfeudation –
artificiality, growing, 104, 114–15
gift, by way of, 111–12, 113–14, 169–70
lord's interest, 111–12, 113–14
nature, 110, 148, 153, 180
substitution –
lord's interest, 111, 114–16
nature, 110–11
Quia Emptores, 113–16, 146, 158
rarity, early, 114–15, 146
writs of entry and, 144–49

H

HOMAGE
de homagio capiendo, 133
family gifts, 112, 169–72

HOMAGE—*continued*
felony and, 285, 406
heir doing, 135, 136
inheritance and, 106, 121, 167
lord and heir, 171–72, 172–73
nature, 102
warranty and, 111, 122, 127

HOMICIDE
jury standards, 421–24
murder, 28, 422–23, 424
pardon, 423
self-defence, 423

HUNDRED COURTS. *See* COURTS

I

IN CONSIMILI CASU
deceit and, 344
exclusiveness of actions and, 345
king's bench jurisdiction and, 344
trespass and, 284, 309, 344
writs of entry and, 193

INDICTMENT
appeal of felony and, 51, 404, 407–09
circuit system and, 30, 51
counsel not permitted, 51, 412
defamation and, 380–81
good suit and, 286
grand jury and, 286, 409, 415
nature, original, 285–86, 408
ordeal and, 408
wager of law and, 408
working of, 409–10

INFANT. *See* WARDSHIP

INHERITANCE
aiel and cosinage, 132, 137
ancestor seised, 119
casus regis, 107

INHERITANCE—*continued*
descent cast, 159
homage and, 106, 121, 167
lord and heir, 171–72, 172–73
lord's control, 105–07, 119–22, 141–42, 159–60, 164
mort d'ancestor, 107, 132, 134–37, 160, 167
nature of early, 2, 3, 21, 105–06, 107, 119–22
partible, 11–12, 102
villein land, 102, 106, 164
women, by, 169, 175
writ of right, 107, 128–29

INNS
of chancery, 38
of court, 45, 424

J

JAIL DELIVERY, commission of, 31, 414

JAILER, bailee, as, 268

JURISDICTION
church and lay courts, 23–5, 87–8, 90–1, 201–02, 337, 343, 380–88
feudal and royal courts, 99–100, 103, 119–34
local and royal courts –
forty shilling limit, 33, 60, 67–8, 84, 91, 244–45, 282, 288, 293, 305, 315, 333, 339, 342–43
king's peace, 33, 53, 286–88, 404–05
royal courts *inter se* –
exchequer and common pleas, 32, 62
king's bench and common pleas, 34–5, 53–4, 60–1, 62–5, 69–70, 293, 344

JURY. *See also NISI PRIUS and* SPECIAL VERDICT
- attaint against jurors, 76, 411–12
- change in nature, 68, 412, 418, 424
- chosen by the defendant, 411
- direction of, 77–9, 299, 413, 421, 424
- geographical limitation, 44, 67–8, 248
- grand jury, 286, 409, 415
- indictors on, 412
- legal development, effect on, 42–8, 59, 79, 264–65, 413, 415, 421–22
- *peine forte et dure*, 411
- petty jury, 411, 415
- pleading and, 5, 42–4, 47–8, 83
- reports, absence of, 49, 51, 412
- rise of system, 5, 411
- standards applied –
  - in crime, 421–24
  - in tort, 296–300

JUSTICES OF THE PEACE
- governmental functions, 427
- origins, 31, 414–15
- preliminary inquiry, 409
- quarter sessions, 31, 415
- summary offences, 427–28

JUSTICIARS
- chief, 32
- local, 26

K

KING'S BENCH
- apprentices in, 52
- *assumpsit* in, 333, 344–45, 350–53
- bill, procedure by, 34–5, 54–5, 62–5
- business, volume of, 54–5, 62–7

KING'S BENCH—*continued*
- case in, 53–4, 293, 344
- chancery writs, 34, 54
- criminal jurisdiction, 53
- development of, 31–3
- error –
  - from, 55–6, 65–6, 350–51
  - to, 56–8
- jurisdiction, 52–4, 56, 62–5
- king's peace, jurisdictional effect, 53–4, 62–3, 293
- origin, 31–3
- writs in, 34

L

LEASE
- covenant, 153
- debt for rent, 255, 281, 340
- *ejectio firmae*, 154–57
- executory devise, 230–31
- lease and release, 224–25
- nature, 152–53
- novel disseisin, 153, 159
- *quare ejecit*, 154–56
- *Quia Emptores* and, 117
- use of, 234
- wardship and, 153, 209

LEGAL DEVELOPMENT
- jurisdiction, effects of –
  - centralisation, and proof, 29, 245–46, 314–15, 340
  - church, and defamation, 380–88
  - feudal, and property concepts, 2–3, 99–101, 119–24. 129, 136, 166–67
  - forty shilling limit, and contract, 60, 67–70, 244–46, 282, 315, 333, 339, 342–43
  - king's bench, and contract, 69–70, 344–45

LEGAL DEVELOPMENT
—*continued*
king's peace, and crime, 404–05, 418, 426
king's peace, and tort, 53–4, 85, 284, 286–88, 307–09, 393–95
local, and contract-tort boundary, 69, 245–46, 314–15
royal, and property concepts, 99–118, 119–51, 166–67, 227
writ system, and forms of action, 35–6
procedure, effects of –
ancient pattern of law-suit, 4–5, 38–9, 51–2
crime, 51–2, 79, 412–13, 415–16
demurrer, 46, 48, 72–3
facts emerging at trial, discussion of, 50, 75–9, 312–13
general issue, blankness of, 47–8, 51–2, 59, 75–9, 254–56, 258, 281–82, 312–13, 412–13
jury, direction of, 77–9, 81
jury, disuse of, 81
jury, introduction of, 5, 42–4, 47–8, 59, 79, 264–65, 413, 415, 421–22
nisi prius system, 72, 75–9, 299, 416
pleadings, oral, 42–8
pleadings, reconsideration after trial, 73–5, 416
pleadings, written, 72
special verdict, 50–1, 76–8, 351–52, 415–16
writ system, and forms of action, 35–6, 244, 249, 398–9

LEGISLATION
criminal law and, 417–18
nature of, early, 1–2, 177, 417
thirteenth-century, causes of, 150

LIBEL. *See* DEFAMATION

LIBER ASSISARUM, matters reported in, 51, 55, 157, 299

LITTLETON'S *TENURES*
early text-book, 3–4, 86
uses, on, 215

LOCAL COURTS. *See* COURTS

M

MANORIAL COURTS. *See* COURTS

MARITAGIUM
alienation by husband, 179–80
church courts and, 87, 172, 202
curtesy of, 168, 171
degrees, 149, 172
entail and, 170, 172–73
homage and, 112, 171–72
services from, 172
tenurial bearing, 170, 171–72

MARRIAGE
breach of promise, action for, 335
causa matrimonii praelocuti writ, 261, 362
church jurisdiction, 23
deceitful promise of, 362
gift in. See *MARITAGIUM*
heir, of –
right to, 108–09
value of, 109
loss of, by defamation, 384

MESNE, action, 105

MILITARY TENURES
abolition, 222
incidents, 107–10
origins, 20, 102–03

MISDEMEANOUR. *See also* FELONY *and* TRESPASS
classes of, 404–05, 418
creation of new, by star chamber, 85, 418–19, 427
early common law, 404–05
justices of the peace and, 415
origin, 287, 404–05
theft as, 426–27

MISFEASANCE. *See ASSUMPSIT*

MONEY
assumpsit for. *See ASSUMPSIT*
container, in, 369, 371
debt for. *See* DEBT
forty shilling barrier, 33, 60, 67–8, 84, 91, 244–45, 282, 288, 293, 305, 315, 333, 339, 342–43
theft, value in, 425–26

MORT D'ANCESTOR
conditional fee and, 175
damages in, 137
eyre and, 30
inheritance, effect on, 107, 132, 134–37, 160, 167
origin of, 135, 138, 140
possessory remedy, seen as, 123, 134, 144
principle extended, 132, 137, 146
same stock, 134–35
tenurial bearing, 30, 134–36, 151
unfree tenements and, 136–37
writ, form of, 134

MORTMAIN
grants in, 113, 170, 204, 208
uses and, 204, 212

MOTIONS AFTER TRIAL
arrest of judgment, 74–5
judgment *non obstante veredicto*, 73–4
new trial, 78–9
none in criminal cases, 416

MURDER. *See also* HOMICIDE
murder fine, 28, 422
secret killing, 422
separation of, 423, 424

N

NEGLIGENCE
assumpsit and, 400
direct injury and, 395
king's peace and, 394–95
master and servant, 396–97
relationship between parties, 393
road accidents, etc., 290, 300, 303, 311–12, 393, 395–96
tort, modern, 393, 398–400
trespass and, 300, 311–12, 392–400

NISI PRIUS
beginnings, 31, 49, 414
crime and, 79, 415–16
effects on law, 72, 77–9, 299, 416
Judicature Acts and, 70, 78, 79, 414
reports of, 51, 72, 299
Slade's Case and, 351

NONFEASANCE
assumpsit. *See ASSUMPSIT*
trespass, in, 301–02, 327

NOVAE NARRATIONES, nature and use, 40

NOVEL DISSEISIN
bailiff in, 140, 141
criminal bearing, 30, 138–39
damages, 140
exceptions, 50, 57, 140–41
eyre and, 30, 138–39
freehold, need for writ, and, 134, 143, 146
lessee and, 153, 159
nuisance, 140
origin of, 138–40
plaint in, 50
possessory remedy, seen as, 123, 138, 144, 153
proprietary use of, 138, 157–61
rights of entry and, 141–42, 157–61
special verdict, 50–1, 76, 157
tenurial bearing, 30, 139–43, 151
trespass and, 283
unfree tenements and, 141
writ, form of, 137–38, 139–40

O

ORDEAL
abolition, 4–5, 130, 410
good suit and, 39, 286
logic, 39, 407–08
wager of law and, 39, 408, 410

OWNERSHIP
goods of –
bailment and, 264–65, 266–67
conversion and, 376–78
detinue, in, 264–67, 270–75, 371
ear-marked chattel, 270–75
sale of goods and, 266

OWNERSHIP—*continued*
land, of –
concept, 99–100, 103–04, 106, 110, 114, 116, 119–24, 129, 136, 149–50, 166, 170
ejectment and, 163
lord and tenant, as between, 99–101, 103–04, 106, 114, 115–16
settlement of land and, 166–67, 192

OYER AND TERMINER, commission of, 414

P

PARDON
purchase of, 419
restriction on issue of, 419, 423

PASTURE RIGHTS, nature of early, 3, 21, 101

PEINE FORTE ET DURE. *See* JURY

PERJURY. *See also* ATTAINT
origin of offence, 418

PERPETUITIES
charities, 201
contingent remainders and, 196–97
rule against, 166, 232–33
unbarrable entails, 190, 196, 229–30

PLAINTS. *See also* BILL PROCEDURE
local courts, in, 33
novel disseisin, in, 50

PLEA, PLEADING. *See also* GENERAL ISSUE
books of entries, 71
crime, in, 51–2, 413, 415

PLEA, PLEADING—*continued*
demurrer, 46, 48, 72–3, 75, 413
exceptions, 50, 57, 140–41
jeofails, 75
justification and warranty, 42, 47
oral pleading, 42–8, 71–2
rolls, entries on, 46
written pleading, 70–2
year books, 44–8

PLEA ROLLS
beginning of, 5
error and, 56
historical evidence, as, 46, 54–5, 65–7, 251
year books and, 46

PLEAS OF THE CROWN
coroners, 26, 28, 407
criminal law, name of, 404
eyre, in, 28, 413
justices of the peace, 31, 414–15
king's bench, 53–4, 293
king's peace –
in crime, 405
in tort, 286–95, 405
Liber Assisarum, 51
process and, 293–95, 301, 306–07
sheriffs and, 287, 414
theft, 286, 406, 426
trespass and, 287, 404

POSSESSORY ASSIZES. *See* MORT D'ANCESTOR *and* NOVEL DISSEISIN

PROHIBITIONS, church courts, 23–4, 381

Q

QUARE EJECIT, action, 154–56

QUARTER SESSIONS, origins and functions, 31, 415

QUASI-CONTRACT, *indebitatus assumpsit* and, 355

QUIA EMPTORES
aims, 113–16, 208
consequences, 116–18

QUO MINUS, fiction in exchequer, 32, 62, 257

R

RECEIPT
entails and, 184–85
remainderman, of, 193
working of, 184

RECEIVER
account, in, 280–81
stolen goods, of, 426, 427

RECORDS
beginning of, 5
church courts, of, 25
error and, 56–8
eyres, of, 27
local courts, of, 17–18
plea rolls as evidence, 46, 54–5, 65–7, 251
year books and, 46

RECOVERY
barring of entail by, 181–87, 191
Doctor and Student on, 188–89
nature of, 183

REGISTER OF WRITS
nature and use, 37–8, 40
on –
assumpsit for nonfeasance, 307, 324
debt and detinue, 264, 272

REGISTER OF WRITS—*continued*
on—
trespass, 287–88
trespass and case, 307
warranty of goods, 321

REMAINDER
conceptual difficulties, 176, 192, 193–94, 195
contingent –
destruction of, 197–99
executory interest and, 225–29, 232
fee, whereabouts of, 193–94, 195
rules as to, 197–98, 225
safeguards against perpetuities, 197
trustees to preserve, 198
fines and, 182
formedon in, 176, 193
heir of living person, to, 194–96, 197
nature of early, 2
receipt and, 193
remainder as *conventio*, 192
remainderman as quasi-heir, 192, 193, 196

RENTS, *Quia Emptores* and, 116–17

REPLEVIN
disclaimer in, 142–43
nature, 104–05, 114
novel disseisin and, 142–43
vee de nam, 104

RESCISSION
deceit, 329–32, 362
warranty, 320

RIGHT
feudal connotation of, 120–22, 150
ownership and, 119–24

RIGHT—*continued*
seisin and, 119–22
writ. *See* WRIT OF RIGHT

RIGHT OF ENTRY
ejectment, in, 161–63
forcible entries and, 160–61
nature of early, 141–42, 159–60
novel disseisin, in, 141–42, 157–61

ROMAN LAW
comparison with English development, 1, 5
influence on English development –
clerical judges, 41–2
property concepts, 3, 43, 119–24, 138, 149–50, 153, 264–65, 267
reception, why no, 20, 40–1, 43–4

S

ST GERMAIN. *See DOCTOR AND STUDENT*

SALE OF GOODS
buyer's action for goods, 265–66
consensual contract, 261–62
property, passing of, 266
title without, 364
warranty –
action on, 320–22, 363
implied, 321, 364–65

SALE OF LAND
deceit and, 328–32
royal court, one-sided treatment in, 324, 328

SCANDALUM MAGNATUM. *See* DEFAMATION

SCIENTER
background to, 291, 310
classification, 310–11, 396
vi et armis and *contra pacem*, 299, 310–11

SCINTILLA JURIS, executory interests and, 226

SCIRE FACIAS, enforcing fines, 181

SEAL, DEED UNDER. *See also* BOND
corporation contracting by, 282, 356
covenant, in, 67–8, 248–49, 261, 315, 356
debt, in, 250–53, 258, 282, 356
non est factum plea, 250
payment, plea of, 86, 250
purpose of, 248, 250

SECTA
examination, 248, 254
nature, 39, 67, 247–48, 254, 286, 340

SEISIN. *See also* NOVEL DISSEISIN *and* OWNERSHIP
livery of, 104, 120, 225
nature, 119–22, 124, 139, 141–42, 150, 159–60
right and, 119–24
termor, 153, 159

SERJEANTS
common pleas, monopoly in, 40, 60–1, 63
counting, 40–1, 71
judges appointed from, 41
pleading, 42–8, 71–2
participating though not retained, 72

SHERIFF
office of, 13
peace of, 287

SHERIFF—*continued*
pleas of the crown and, 287, 414
viscontiel writs, 33, 84, 258

SLANDER. *See* DEFAMATION

SOCAGE
devise and, 218, 221
incidents, 107, 218
services, 107
uses and, 218
wardship in –
account, 107, 279–80
waste, 280

SPECIAL VERDICT
attaint and, 76
criminal cases, in, 415
discussion of facts on, 76–8, 351–52
ejectio firmae, in, 77
grand assize, in, 76
novel disseisin, in, 50–1, 76, 157
rise and decline, 76–7
trespass, in, 294
year books, in, 50, 76

STAR CHAMBER
criminal offences created by, 85, 418–19, 427
defamation in, 388–90, 418
prosecution by information, 419
riot and conspiracy allegations, 419

SUIT. *See SECTA*

SUMMARY OFFENCES. *See* JUSTICES OF THE PEACE

T

TALLY, mode of proof, 253–54

TENURES. *See also* HOMAGE
agricultural, 19, 101–02
alienability and, 100, 110–18, 144–46
heritability and, 2, 3, 21, 102, 105–07, 121, 164, 167
incidents –
consequences of, 118, 194, 208–11, 216–22
devise and, 118, 217–20, 221
escheat, 109, 406
evasion of, 115, 209–11, 216–22
marriage, 108–09
mortmain and, 113, 204, 208
Quia Emptores and, 113–15, 208
relief, 109
royal remedies, 109–10
socage, 107, 218
uses and, 208–11, 216–22
value of, changing, 107–10, 112, 122
wardship, 107–09, 115, 153, 209–11, 216–22
juristic nature, 100–01, 164
lord's court, place of, 101, 104–05, 107
military, 19, 20, 102–03, 222
ownership and. *See* OWNERSHIP
services –
acquittance by mesne, 105
certainty of amount, 101
cessavit, 105, 142
distress of chattels, 101, 104–05, 107, 112, 114, 140, 142–43
distress *per feodum*, 101, 104, 105, 140, 142
money, fall in value of, 109
Quia Emptores and, 116–18
replevin, 104–05, 114, 142–43
writ of right of customs and services, 105
socage, 107, 218, 221, 279–80

TENURES—*continued*
unfree, 22, 101–02, 117–18, 160, 163–65

TERM OF YEARS. *See* LEASE

TEXT BOOKS
contract, 5
land law, 4, 86
late appearance, 4, 5, 86, 308
tort, 5, 308

THEFT
escheat for, 286, 426
felony, whether, 406, 425–26
king's peace and, 426
plea of the crown, whether, 286, 406, 426
value of thing stolen, 425–26

TREASON
counsel allowed, 412
forfeiture for, and uses, 212

TRESPASS. *See also* CASE
appeal of felony and, 283, 285, 357, 404
case and, 307–13, 396–98
contra pacem –
abduction, 291–92
accident, 47, 49–50, 79, 294–300, 394–95
artificiality of, 53, 289–95
capias, 252, 293–95, 301, 306–07, 404
cattle trespass, 291, 295, 311
chattels temporarily delivered, 367
death of king, effect of, 288, 294
enticement, 291–92
fee, against lord acting within, 154
fire, 292, 297, 299
franchises, in case of, 302–03, 305–06

TRESPASS—*continued*
contra pacem—continued
jurisdiction and, 33, 53–4, 62–3, 85, 286–88, 293, 344
justification, 45–6, 73–4, 79, 295–96
liability, principles of, 47, 49–50, 79, 294–300, 394–95
plea of the crown, 287, 404
process and, 293–95, 301, 306–07, 404
road accidents, etc., 290, 300, 303, 311–12, 393, 395–96
scienter, 291, 299, 310–11, 396
smith, against, 290–91, 317–18, 393–94
son assault demesne, 47, 296
son tort demesne, 74, 296
wager of law and, 293, 315
waste by tenant at will, 292
ejectio custodiae, 155
ejectio firmae, 154–56
fair and market owners, actions by, 302–03, 305–06
fault, relevance of, 47, 49–50, 79, 294–300, 394–95
felony and, 283, 285, 404–05
justification, 45–6, 73–4, 79, 295–96
king's peace, original sense of, 286, 287
local and royal jurisdictions, 33, 54, 287–89, 300–01, 361
master and servant, 396–97
meaning of. *See* WORDS AND PHRASES
misdemeanour and, 287, 404–05
negligence and, 300, 311–12, 392–400
novel disseisin and, 283
origins, 283, 284, 285, 357

TRESPASS—*continued*
process in, 252, 293–95, 301, 306–07, 404
property and, confusion between, 154–56
redress for future, 156
riparian owners, actions against, 301–02, 393
scienter, 291, 299, 310–11, 396
vi et armis –
contra pacem and. *See that subheading*
regularity of phrase, 289
weapons specified, 53, 289
viscontiel writs, 287–88
writs, formulation of, 303, 305–06, 309–13

TRIAL
criminal, 412–13, 415–17
facts emerging at, 50, 75–9, 312–13, 415–17
modes of –
battle. *See* BATTLE
jury. *See* JURY
ordeal. *See* ORDEAL
wager of law. *See* WAGER OF LAW
new, 78–9
nisi prius, 31, 49, 51, 70, 72, 77–9, 299, 414, 415–16

TROVER. *See also* CONVERSION
conversion, in, 372–6
de re adirata and, 271–4
detinue, in, 272–75, 371, 373–6
finder and bailee contrasted, 274–75

TRUST. *See also* USES
active, 228, 234, 235–36, 237–38
form, 236, 237–38
passive, of freeholds, 236, 238
personalty, of, 234–35
use, distinguished from 236
use upon a use, 234, 236–38

U

USES
  active, 228, 234, 235–36, 237–38
  bargain and sale, 223–25, 237
  chancery intervention, 86–8, 212–14
  church courts enforcing, 88, 202
  church, for the benefit of, 203–04
  concept, emergence of, 211–16
  conditional grant and, 87, 206, 207–08, 209–10
  conveyance –
    cestui qe use, by, 215
    feoffees, by, 214
    requirements, proposed, 220
    Statute of Uses and, 223–25
  devise –
    power to, and, 87, 118, 206–08, 211–12, 214, 218–20, 221–22, 226, 227, 234
    terms, of, 230–31
  executory interests, 222–23, 225–29
  feoffees, multiple, 210–11
  feudal incidents and, 208–11, 216–22
  grant and regrant, 205–06, 207–08, 210, 238
  leaseholds, 234
  mischiefs of, 215–20
  mortmain and, 204, 212
  origins, 86–8, 200–08
  perpetuities and, 229–33
  purposes of, 222
  remainder rules and, 228–29
  Statute of, 218–20, 222–29, 233–39
  treason, forfeiture for, and, 212
  trusts distinguished from, 236
  use upon a use, 234, 236–38

USES—*continued*
  will of land, relation with, 87, 118, 206–08, 211–12, 214, 218–20, 226, 227, 234
  Wills, Statute of, 221–22
  year books, in, 213–14, 217

V

VILLEIN
  copyhold and freehold, 117–18
  ejectment and, 163–65
  entry fines from, 160
  inheritance of villein land, 101–02, 106, 164
  jurisdiction –
    common law courts, 22, 117–18, 164
    equitable, 117, 165
    manorial, 22, 101–02
  plaintiff called a villein, 381–82, 384
  plaintiff claimed as, 381–82

W

WAGER OF LAW
  account, in, when excluded, 281–82
  assumpsit and, 340, 353, 354
  case, in, 293, 315
  city of London, in, 257, 260, 277
  conscience and, 86, 267
  contra pacem and, 293, 315
  debt, in, when excluded, 254, 255, 277, 281, 340
  detinue of charters, 254, 281
  due process, as, 345, 346, 353, 370
  effectiveness of, 67–8, 245–46, 247–48, 257, 315, 340, 354
  examination in, 256, 340
  exchequer, in, 257
  executors, effect on liability, 257, 351, 354

WAGER OF LAW—*continued*
legal development, effect on, 254–56, 267
logic of, 39, 67, 247–48, 254, 285, 380, 408
ordeal and, 39, 408, 410
questions arising on, 49, 50, 256

WARDSHIP
by reason of wardship, 112, 113
competing claims, 108–09
ejectio custodiae, 155
evasion of, 115, 209–11, 216–22
heir's person, competing claims, 108–09
jointure and, 205
lease, effect of, 153, 209
right to, 107–09, 122
sale of, 108
socage tenures, of, 107, 201, 279–80
value of, 108–09, 112
  king, to, 219

WARRANTY
goods, sale of –
  contract and, 321, 364
  deceit and, 320–22, 364–66
  implied, 321, 364–65
  jurisdiction, 292–93, 320–22
  rescission for, 320
land –
  barring entail and, 178–81, 186–87
  collateral and lineal warranties, 180–81
  escambium, 111, 122, 127, 179, 180, 186–87
  homage and, 111, 122, 127
  voucher to, 127, 132, 178–79, 184
  warranty of charter, 158, 178–79, 181

WASTE
guardian in chivalry, by, 108, 280

WASTE—*continued*
guardian in socage, by, 280
tenant at will, by, 292

WILLS
land –
  customary devises, 87–8, 201, 202, 208
  uses and, 86–8, 118, 206–08, 211–12, 214, 218–20, 226, 227, 234
  Wills, Statute of, 221–22, 226, 234
personalty –
  church jurisdiction, 23, 87, 221
  uses and, 234

WITNESSES
battle as testing oaths of, 39, 130–31, 285, 407
grand assize as, 130–31
jurors as, 44, 67–8, 76, 412, 418, 424
perjury, 418
transactions, to, 254, 260, 315, 340, 341

WORDS AND PHRASES
case (action on), 304
concessit se teneri, 258–59
concessit solvere, 260
consideration, 358
contract, 249, 260, 355
contract executory, 350, 376
convert, 366–67
covenant, 246–47, 249, 309, 355
criminal plea, 285, 403
debet and *detinet*, 262–63
deceive, deceit, 321, 333–334, 392
defamation, 380, 384, 387
disseisin, 120, 139, 142, 159
entry, 143, 147, 148–49, 158, 160

WORDS AND PHRASES—*continued*
fee, 103, 106, 136, 150, 166–67
felony, 285, 406
freehold, 103, 136, 150, 166–67
livery of seisin, 104, 120, 225
misdemeanour, 287, 404
murder, 28, 422
neglect, negligence, 392, 399
peace (of king, lord, sheriff), 286, 287
right, 119–24, 150
seisin, 119–22, 124, 139, 141–42, 150, 159–60
tort, 308
trespass, 150, 154, 246, 283, 285, 305, 307–08, 309, 344
use, 200, 203, 212
writ of right, 124–25

WRIT
courts, part played in various –
common pleas, 35–6
county court, 33
eyre, 29
feudal courts, 33–4
king's bench, 34
forms –
ostensurus quare, 243–44, 247, 253, 282, 283
praecipe, 243–44, 246–47, 252–53, 282, 315
freehold land and, 29–30, 127–28, 133–34, 143, 146
functions, 33–5, 63, 243–44
juridical entities and, 124–26, 257–58, 269–70, 271–72, 274, 372–73
plaint or bill and, 29, 34–5, 54, 62–5
registers and commentaries, 37–8, 40
system, consequences of, 35–6, 64–5, 244, 398–99
viscontiel, 33, 84, 258

WRIT OF ENTRY
causa matrimonii praelocuti, 261, 362
decline of, 149, 152, 157, 158
degrees in, 144–45, 148–49, 158
disseisin and, 145, 148, 161
dum non compos, 143–44, 148
evolution of, 146–48
nature of claim, 133, 146–47
possessory remedy, seen as, 123, 144
praecipe form of, 126, 133, 146–48, 158
Quia Emptores and, 149
quo warranto and, 133–34, 143, 146–47
range of, 145
tenant for life, alienation by, 193
tenurial bearing, 126, 133, 144–49, 158, 174

WRIT OF RIGHT. *See also* RIGHT
battle, trial by, 123, 130, 407
count in, 128
customs and services, 105
dower, of, 121, 124–25, 126, 167
grand assize, 130–33
inheritance and, 107, 128–29
logic of, 127, 128
origin, 128–29
patent, 124–25, 132, 133
praecipe, 125–26, 132, 133, 137, 146, 147–48
proprietary remedy, seen as, 122–24
tenurial bearing, 120–34
tolt, 126
warranty, voucher and, 127, 132

Y

YEAR BOOKS
abridgments, 45

YEAR BOOKS—*continued*
authorship, 44–5
beginnings of, 44, 45
ending of, 71
eyres, reporting, 27, 51
legal process reported, 45–8

YEAR BOOKS—*continued*
Liber Assisarum, 51, 55, 157, 299
plea roll and, 46
precedent in, 273
uses in, 213–14, 217

Lightning Source UK Ltd.
Milton Keynes UK
UKOW06f1238130815

256875UK00013B/111/P

9 780406 625038